12/10

Apocalypse Dela'
The Story of Jehovah's
SECOND EDITION

Since 1876, Jehovah's Witnesses have believed that they are living in the last days of the present world. Charles T. Russell, their founder, advised his followers that members of Christ's church would be raptured in 1878, and by 1914 Christ would destroy the nations and establish his kingdom on earth. The first prophecy was not fulfilled, but the outbreak of the First World War lent some credibility to the second. Ever since that time, Jehovah's Witnesses have been predicting that the world would end 'shortly.' Their numbers have grown to many millions in over two hundred countries. They distribute a billion pieces of literature annually, and continue to anticipate the end of the world.

Apocalypticism is the key issue in this detailed history, but there are others. As a long-time member of the sect, now expelled, Penton offers a comprehensive overview of a remarkable religious movement. His book is divided into three parts, each presenting the Witnesses' story in a different context: historical, doctrinal, and sociological. Some of the issues he discusses are known to the general public, such as the sect's opposition to military service and blood transfusions. Others involve internal controversies, including political control of the organization and the handling of dissent within the ranks.

Penton has combined the special insight of an insider with the critical analysis of an observer now at a distance from his subject. From them he has created a penetrating study of a spreading world phenomenon.

In this second edition, an afterword by the author brings us up to date on events since *Apocalypse Delayed* was first published in 1985. Penton considers changes in doctrine, practice, and governance on issues such as medical treatment, higher education, apostates, and the apocalypse. This edition features a revised and expanded bibliography.

M. JAMES PENTON is a retired professor of history and religious studies, University of Lethbridge, Alberta.

APOCALYPSE DELAYED

The Story of Jehovah's Witnesses

SECOND EDITION

M. James Penton

UNIVERSITY OF TORONTO PRESS

Toronto Buffalo London

© University of Toronto Press Incorporated 1985, 1997
Published 1985. Reprinted 1986
Second edition 1997
Reprinted 1999, 2002, 2009
Toronto Buffalo London
Printed in Canada

ISBN 0-8020-7973-3

Printed on acid-free paper

Canadian Cataloguing in Publication Data

Penton, M. James, 1932–
Apocalypse delayed : the story of Jehovah's Witnesses

Rev. ed.
Includes bibliographical references and index.
ISBN 0-8020-7973-3

I. Jehovah's Witnesses.   I. Title.

BX8526.P45 1997   289.9'2   C97-930106-8

University of Toronto Press acknowledges the financial assistance to its publishing
program of the Canada Council and the Ontario Arts Council.

To Marilyn – friend, comrade,

wife, and sister in Christ –

without whom this book would

never have been written.

Eternity looks grander and
kinder if time grows meaner
and more hostile.

—THOMAS CARLYLE

Contents

Illustrations

Tables

Preface

Seldom should an author's preface be an *apologia pro vita sua*, but this one must be, at least in part. The reason is that some eight years ago I wrote the book *Jehovah's Witnesses in Canada: Champions of Freedom of Speech and Worship*, a work which is quite different in tone from the present volume. Consequently, some explanation is owed to those readers who may wonder why in that book I present a very favourable overview of the Witnesses and in this one a far more critical one.

The facts are as follows: My great-grandfather, Henry Penton, became a Bible Student, the name by which Jehovah's Witnesses were then known, around the turn of the last century. Shortly thereafter, my grandmother, Margaret Thomas Penton, became a convert as well; and, through her, eventually all the members of my immediate family became Jehovah's Witnesses. As a result, my grandparents and parents suffered greatly during both world wars as members of a religion which, in Canada, was under governmental restriction during the First and outright ban during the Second. Thus, I grew up in a Witness home and experienced personally many of the events which I describe in *Jehovah's Witnesses in Canada* and in the present study as well.

Over the years, I served in many capacities in Jehovah's Witness congregations in the United States, Puerto Rico, and Canada. During the years 1973 through 1979, I was a Witness elder in my present home community, Lethbridge, Alberta. So it was quite natural that I should have elected to write a book about the Witnesses in Canada and, in particular, their long struggle for religious freedom under Canadian law.

As I believe I demonstrate in *Jehovah's Witnesses in Canada,* the Witness community has had a major impact on Canadian law, a fact also recognized by such noted members of the Canadian bar as the late Jean-Charles Bonenfant, Walter Tarnopolsky, and Thomas Burger. In so far as the larger society was concerned, they were definitely 'champions of freedom of speech and worship.' Furthermore, as an oppressed minority, they were occasionally sincerely concerned about the civil liberties and rights of others. But in that earlier study, I did not discuss another side of Jehovah's Witnesses – the fact that in many ways they resemble those seventeenth-century English and New England Puritans who, while they were willing to fight against the tyrannies of an established church and a despotic king in the name of Christian freedom, were equally willing to be tyrannical to dissenters within their own ranks.

Following the publication of *Jehovah's Witnesses in Canada,* Professor Herbert Richardson of St Michael's College at the University of Toronto urged me to produce a study which would serve as an overview of Witness history, doctrine, and community. However, as I began to research the history of the movement in the United States in a way that I had not previously done, I became more and more doubtful of traditional Witness claims to spiritual authority. In addition, I became aware of the ongoing studies of a number of Witness scholars such as Richard Rawe of Soap Lake, Washington; Jerry Bergman of Bowling Green, Ohio; and Carl Olof Jonsson of Partille, Sweden, all of whom were uncovering data which made certain aspects of Witness doctrine incredible to many of us working in the field.

Nevertheless, like those men and many others – practically all of whom have since been excommunicated or have resigned from Jehovah's Witnesses – I was most reluctant to leave the community in which I had been raised. In the long run I was to have no alternative. As I travelled throughout Canada and the United States carrying on my research, I became more and more aware of the severe chastisement to which individual Witnesses everywhere were being subjected by their leaders when they dissented in any way from official organizational doctrines or policies, or even when they fell afoul personally of someone in a position of organizational authority. As a result, I journeyed to the world-wide headquarters of Jehovah's Witnesses at Brooklyn, New York, in the summer of 1979, both to carry on my research and to express a feeling of concern and frustration over what was occurring within the Witness community to Raymond Franz, then a member of the governing body of Jehovah's Witnesses and a man whom I had first come to know and respect while teaching at the University of Puerto Rico in 1959.

My trip to Brooklyn was quite distressing. Although everyone I encountered at the Brooklyn headquarters was fundamentally loyal to the movement, there were a great many who, like myself, believed that Jehovah's Witnesses must undergo a reformation or, at the very least, a spiritual renewal. Nevertheless, the governing body seemed unprepared to listen to any outside advice. Raymond Franz admitted that he was aware of many of the serious problems I described, but he urged me to be patient. Yet that was something which in all good conscience I could no longer do. Consequently, upon returning home, in August 1979, I determined to express my concerns and criticisms of what was transpiring within the larger Witness community to the Witness leadership as a whole in writing – a decision which, after over a year's great personal travail, led to my public disfellowshipment or excommunication from Jehovah's Witnesses on what amounted to charges of heresy.

These events caused me to curtail my research and writing for some time. Besides finding it necessary to continue my own developing spiritual reorientation and to give much time and attention to many others who were forced to leave the Witness community when they stood with me, I felt that I should allow some time to pass before I completed the present work. In that way I hoped that I would be able to regain some of the objectivity which one inevitably loses during a period of great spiritual crisis. Eventually, however, I took up my pen and completed *Apocalypse Delayed: The Story of Jehovah's Witnesses.*

Whether I have succeeded in being fair and reasonably objective in my presentation is a matter for my readers to decide. There are a few points I would like to make, however. In presenting data, I have attempted to document my statements scrupulously. Unless specific information given is adequately documented or is public knowledge, I have tried always to label it as hearsay or rumour. In so far as the treatment of Witness doctrines is concerned, I have avoided taking definite stands except where it can be demonstrated that these doctrines are right or wrong, historically, empirically, or logically. It is not the responsibility of an historian, which is primarily what I am, to argue from a particular doctrinal stance. Whether Witness doctrines are 'orthodox' or 'heterodox' from a religious point of view is hardly relevant to an historian as such. Yet at the same time I have no apology to give for making what I hope are learned evaluations derived from both my own experience and my research. That is not only my right; it is my duty.

A few words need to be said about the organization of *Apocalypse Delayed*. As may be noted, it is divided into three parts: the first, historical; the second, conceptual and doctrinal; the third, sociological and psychological. This structure, of course, has been adopted for a special purpose. Earlier studies of Jehovah's Witnesses have used the same academic genres, but they have generally mixed them in such a way that it is difficult to distinguish the approach at any given time. So, to avoid this problem, I have attempted to segregate discretely the various disciplinary genres that I have used in examining Jehovah's Witnesses.

Naturally, I am greatly indebted to those who have studied Jehovah's Witnesses before me. In particular, I have learned much from the insights of men such as William Cumberland, Joseph Zygmunt, Alan Rogerson, James Beckford, Melvin Curry, Gérard Hébert, Quirinus Munters, Bryan Wilson, and many others who have examined the Witnesses from a scholarly rather than an apologetic or polemic standpoint. Above and beyond these, however, I have relied most heavily on Timothy White's excellent study, *A People for His Name*.

Since all of the above except Cumberland, Hébert, and White are professional sociologists, I have relied heavily on their works, particularly in chapters 8 and 9 on organization and community. While I have tried to develop some new insights in those chapters based both on scholarly studies and on my own first-hand knowledge of Jehovah's Witnesses, I have not attempted to create any new or profound sociological theories in relation to them. That, I feel, should be done – if it is to be done – by someone with far more skills as a social scientist than I have or ever expect to have. Nevertheless, I hope that some of the information that I have provided in the third section of *Apocalypse Delayed* may be of use to professional social scientists as well as interested laypersons.

For help in obtaining new and significant data, I owe a great deal to Richard Rawe, Jerry Bergman, Heather and Gary Botting, Jacques Dupond, Edward Dunlap, Dwane Magnani, Carl Prosser, Willy Holiday, and James Parkinson. However, my deepest debt of appreciation in this respect must go to Carl Olof Jonsson and Raymond Franz, both of whom were most generous in providing information which they and they alone possessed. Raymond Franz was also most helpful in reading an earlier typescript of this work for accuracy, as were Peter Gregerson and John Poole. My colleagues James Tagg, Dean Frease, and Reginald Bibby examined it from a scholarly standpoint, and Professor Bibby in particular made a number of important suggestions to aid in improving it. Others who deserve mention for their help are Herbert Richardson, Moses Crouse, James Beverley, and Edward Orchard and Bahir Bilgin who gave important assistance by translating materials from languages of which I have no knowledge.

Much help in obtaining research materials was given to me by the University of Lethbridge. Some years ago the university provided me with a grant which permitted me to purchase some $1,800 worth of Adventist, Bible Student, and Jehovah's Witness primary sources. Since then, it has also provided other small, but very useful grants and recently it has aided me in obtaining one from the Social Sciences and Humanities Research Council of Canada for the final preparation of my manuscript. But it is not only to the university that I want to express my thanks; a number of persons there gave me especial help in preparing the text of *Apocalypse Delayed*. These include Owen Holmes, Lawrence Hoye, Phil Connolly, Ian Newbould, Ellie Boumans, Leanne Wehlage, Lana Cooke, Kerry Bullock, and Stan Devitt. Lisa Atkinson helped with editing, and the final typing of the manuscript was done by Charlene Sawatsky and Evelyn Harris.

At the University of Toronto Press, I want to thank Virgil Duff for his constant support and Beverley Beetham-Endersby for the many editorial improvements she made in this work. It has been a pleasure to work with both.

I owe appreciation, too, to both the Social Sciences and Humanities Research Council of Canada and the Canadian Federation for the Humanities. In particular, I am pleased to state that this book has been published with the help of a grant from the Canadian Federation for the Humanities, using funds provided by the Social Sciences and Humanities Research Council of Canada. Assistance also came from the Publications Fund of the University of Toronto Press.

Most of all, I am indebted to my son, David, who helped me with many suggestions regarding statistical matters covered in various parts of this book, and to my loving wife, Marilyn. Without her constant help, *Apocalypse Delayed* would never have seen the light of day.

M. JAMES PENTON
The University of Lethbridge
Lethbridge, Alberta
July 1984

Ink drawing of Nelson H. Barbour by Otto Rapp, based on a nineteenth-century original

Charles T. Russell, age 27
The Watch Tower Reprints, vol I (1919)

Charles and Maria Russell, c 1890
The Jerry Bergman collection

John Paton
The Jerry Bergman collection

J.F. Rutherford
The M. James Penton collection

(l. to r.) Leo Greenless, W. Glen How, Nathan H. Knorr,
Percy Chapman – Montreal 1947
The M. James Penton collection

Bethel, Brooklyn, NY
Watch Tower postcard (1958)

The Watch Tower Society's major printery or 'factory,' Brooklyn, NY
Watch Tower postcard (1958)

Frederick W. Franz
The Raymond V. Franz collection

Raymond V. Franz
The Raymond V. Franz collection

A dissident view of an attack on a major Watch Tower doctrine

APOCALYPSE DELAYED

Unless otherwise noted, all biblical quotations are from

The New World Translation of the Holy Scriptures

Introduction

The religious community now known as Jehovah's Witnesses originally developed into a separate sect in the 1870s and has remained one ever since. H. Richard Niebuhr assumed in 1929 that a sect, faced with increasing success, the upward social mobility of its members, and reconciliation with the world, would almost automatically become a denomination – a routinized and accommodated sect.[1] This has not happened with the Witnesses, however, as has been recognized by such noted sociologists of religion as Bryan Wilson and Thomas O'Dae. Rather, Jehovah's Witnesses have become an 'established sect,'[2] but one which, although routinized, is still hostile to society in general.

The motivating factor behind their development as a sect and their insistence on remaining one – that is, a religious movement alienated from the world which stresses that it alone is the bearer of 'the truth' – has been their peculiar millenarian eschatology. Melvin Curry has recently written: 'Indeed one may appropriately say that millenarianism has been the theological switchman for many doctrinal and organizational changes among Jehovah's Witnesses.'[3] Yet even in recognizing this fact, Curry has not gone far enough. It should be stated that except for their millenarian eschatology in its various forms, Jehovah's Witnesses would not have grown into the major, world-wide sectarian movement that they now are, nor would they manifest the particular organizational and sociological characteristics that they do today.

No major Christian sectarian movement has been so insistent on prophesying the end of the present world in such definite ways or on such specific dates as have Jehovah's Witnesses, at least since the Millerites and Second Adventists of the nineteenth century who were the Witnesses' direct millenarian forbears. During the early years of their history, they consistently looked to specific dates – 1874, 1878, 1881, 1910, 1914, 1918, 1920, 1925, and others – as having definite eschatological significance. Charles Taze Russell, their founder, organizer, and the first president of the Watch Tower Society (their primary legal society), originally believed that 1874 marked the beginning of Christ's 'invisible presence,' that 1878 and then 1881 would see the 'change' of members of the church from fleshly bodies to spiritual bodies, and that 1910 would witness the beginning of global troubles leading to the end of the world – an event which would occur in 1914. When these prophecies failed, they had to be reinterpreted, spiritualized, or, in some cases, ultimately abandoned.[4] This did not deter Russell or his followers from setting new dates, however, or from simply proclaiming that the end of this world or system of things was no more than a few years or perhaps even months away. As Melvin Curry has put it so nicely: 'Biblical chronology is the play dough of millenarians. It can be stretched to fit whatever timetable is needed, or it can be reduced to a meaningless mass of dates and figures so that future predictions can be molded out of the original lump.'[5] Thus, for well over a century, the constant theme of Bible Student–Jehovah's Witnesses has been: 'The end is near; Christ will reveal himself shortly to bring destruction upon the nations and all who oppose his messianic kingdom.'

That the apocalypse did not come when the Bible Student–Witnesses expected it is evident; in fact it has been delayed again and again. Yet, paradoxically, that fact has been as much an asset to the movement as a liability. True, at times when prophecies entailing specific dates failed to come true, there was great disappointment and some 'sifting' of membership. But like the Second Adventists before them, Bible Student–Witness leaders have always argued that the 'wrong thing [or things] had happened at the right time.' In spite of everything, they have held that their plan of salvation and timetables for the end of this world and the dawning of the next have been correct, or at least *nearly* so. So God has really given them 'new light,' 'present truth,' and has favoured them and those who have listened to them in a special way. If, therefore, one wants God's approval, one must stay in close association with those who truly know the significance of the divine plan – God's 'channel' or 'organization' – and by definition those who direct it.

Such an appeal to special knowledge, a kind of gnosticism, has been common to various groups within Judaism, Christendom, and Islam for centuries. One need only be reminded of the examples of Cabbalistic messiahs such as Abraham Abulafia, Solomon Molka, and Sabbatai Zevi within Judaism; the Montanists, the Anabaptists of Münster, the Fifth Monarchy Men, the Millerites, Adventists, Mormons, and others of Christianity; and the Mahdist tradition within Islam to see how this has been so. Furthermore, it is relatively easy to recognize that such movements have arisen out of the historic–prophetic traditions of the great monotheistic religions of the Middle East whose cosmologies are so different from those of the great oriental religions. For if, as those great monotheistic religions teach, history is really going somewhere and has some ultimate purpose, then it is important to know why, how, where, and when. Hence, if someone *knows* the answers to these questions, he can claim to have special knowledge and special authority.

Religious leaders and movements are not the only ones who have made claims to what amounts to 'prophetic' authority; some secular movements have as well. Marx and his followers certainly have with their doctrine of historical determinism and, to a lesser extent, so have various Fascist movements. Hegelian dialectic, which is basic to 'scientific socialism,' has its roots in the Judaeo-Christian concept of linear progression in history, and Hitler's dream of 'a thousand-year Reich' was plagiarized from Jewish apocalypticism, the book of Revelation, and the teachings of the early Fathers of the Christian church. Thus, in a real sense, both Marxism and Fascism are quasi-religious movements whose leaders have been able to make quasi-religious or 'prophetic' claims to authority.

The claims of such 'prophetic movements,' which all those discussed above were or are, often lead to totalitarianism of one sort or another. After all, to doubt those who claim to possess truth with a capital 'T' is to make oneself the enemy of 'God,' 'light,' 'revelation,' 'history,' 'the people,' 'the nation,' or whatever else is being used as the basis for the authority of the prophetic leader òr leaders. One must therefore take a stand: One must be *for* the leadership or *against* it; one must be a child of light or a child of darkness. So, as such prophetic movements have developed, they have become insistent on guiding, directing, and disciplining their own adherents and in maintaining an attitude of alienation towards the outside world.

This is exactly what has happened to Jehovah's Witnesses. In its formative years, the Bible Student movement, as the Witnesses were then called, was fairly 'liberal' in the sense that it believed that other Christians – in particular various Protestants – were part of the church of Christ and could gain salvation. Nevertheless, as time passed, Russell and his followers became persuaded that *he* had a special role: it was *he* who was 'that servant' mentioned at Matthew 24:45–7 who was to provide 'meat in due season' for the household of faith. Hence, by the first decade of the twentieth century, he began to encourage directed or Berean Bible Studies rather than free Bible study for his flock, and in 1910 he asserted that his *Studies in the Scriptures* was virtually the Bible in topical form.[6] Still, Russell always attempted to persuade his followers rather than to coerce them. Thus it was left to his successor, Judge Joseph F. Rutherford, to metamorphose the congregationally governed Bible Students into the highly structured, 'theocratically' ruled Jehovah's Witnesses during the years from 1917 to 1938. What Leon Trotsky stated about the Communist party under Lenin was virtually what happened to the Witnesses under Rutherford.[7] They evolved from a fairly broadly based, democratically governed movement into one ruled by a

single man, a dictator. It is not surprising, then, that at least one student of
Jehovah's Witnesses in the post-Rutherford era, Werner Cohn, has compared
them to various totalitarian movements.

Writing more than twenty-five years ago in *The American Scholar,* Cohn stated
that through a close study of Jehovah's Witnesses, he was able to place them in the
same 'proletarian' sociological category as various radical religious sects, the
traditional German youth movement (the Wandervögel), a number of Zionist
youth groups, and the Nazis and communists.[8] By so stating, he meant that they
are a socially estranged group which feels a sense of alienation from the larger
societies in which they live. In addition to classifying them, however, he went on
to examine and analyse the basic millenarian eschatology and utopian visions
underlying the nature of their community and, by such examination and analysis,
to explain the nature of their virtually totalitarian system of 'theocratic government.' Cohn says:

The onion form [of governance] of Jehovah's Witnesses is almost an exact duplicate of that
of the totalitarians. There are the leader and the elite that surround him; there are various
classes of field officials, and various classes of rank-and-file members. Some of these
classes are institutionally recognized – there are 'pioneers,' 'special pioneers' and
'company publishers' (the lowest grade) – though the stratification system as a whole is
neither institutionalized nor at all stable. It will be remembered that though there were
various official strata of Nazi members – the s.a., the s.s. and its various special
formations, among many others – the total stratification system of the Nazis depended on
the momentary relative standing of party, state police and army, as well as an identification
with a personal clique. The Witnesses' arrangement is similar.[9]

Cohn's analysis is no doubt valid although it may seem overly severe to the
reader who knows Jehovah's Witnesses as 'peaceful people and good neighbours.'
Had he painted his picture with somewhat broader strokes, however, perhaps his
analysis would not seem so harsh. For do not sectarianism, exclusivism, and
totalitarianism themselves often have their roots in the great monotheistic
traditions of the past and present? Is not the chosen-race concept of Judaism
basically sectarian? Was not early Christianity a *cult* until Christ's crucifixion and
a sect up to the time of the Emperor Constantine? Also, did not the church's early
collective leadership under the apostles and elders evolve rather quickly into the
role of monarchical bishops? At the time of the Reformation, were not Catholics,
Calvinists, Anglicans, and ultimately even the more benign Lutherans willing to
have heretics executed? And, often, has not the doctrine of *extra ecclesiam nulla
salus,* as stated in dozens of different forms, meant loyalty to the leadership,
clergy, hierarchy, or whatever, of a cult, sect, or even a great church such as that of

Rome? Thus, what Cohn says about Jehovah's Witnesses could be said about many organized western religious and political movements. But that does not take away from the rightness of his analysis; it only puts it into a broader historical framework.

In an important way, though, Jehovah's Witnesses are unique; they have preached millenarianism longer and more consistently than any major sectarian movement in the modern world. Millenarianism has been a phenomenon common to many movements over the centuries, but in its purely religious form at least, it has generally had to be played down, spiritualized, or abandoned within a relatively short time. By the second century of the Christian era, the church was already well on its way towards abandoning the millenarian excitement of the first century. Extreme millenarians such as Papias and the Montanists became an embarrassment to sober Christians,[10] and in the eastern part of the Roman Empire even the book of Revelation fell into disrepute among churchmen for a time. Again, when millenarianism became somewhat popular during the high Middle Ages, the Reformation, and the seventeenth century, seldom if ever did it become an important doctrinal concept which was held for much over a generation; and when it was, generally Christ's second coming and the millennium were forecast to occur at some time in the distant future.[11] Thus, the ordinary pattern has been for millenarian movements to surrender, ignore, or modify significantly their millenarian teachings – as has happened with the Seventh-Day Adventists, Latter-Day Saints, and many fundamentalists – or to become rather isolated within society – something which has taken place with the Christadelphians. Surprisingly, this has not happened to Jehovah's Witnesses who, in spite of many prophetic failures and vicissitudes for more than a century, have gone on preaching the nearness of the millennium and have grown to become a movement with nearly 2.7 million active members and several millions more adherents throughout the world.

The Witnesses have established a highly sophisticated printing and publishing empire, have developed a world-wide missionary program, and a highly structured hierarchical organization to govern their community, all of which has been done through their principal legal association, the Watch Tower Bible and Tract Society of Pennsylvania. In spite of their sectarian spirit, they have also had a profound impact on many of the societies in which they have lived, in particular those of the English-speaking world. In the United States and Canada above all, they have had a major influence on constitutional law and have done much to broaden civil liberties in such areas as freedom of speech, worship, and the press. They have done much, too, to force many countries to take conscientious objection more seriously than they had ever done before.[12] And, finally, they have served both as critics of medical practice and as medical guinea pigs as a result of their refusal to accept blood transfusions. So their history, doctrines, community, and their present problems have a significance which few similar sectarian movements have today.

The story of Jehovah's Witnesses is not entirely a success story. In recent years, time and history seem to have caught up with them. No longer can they boast as they did in both the 1950s and the 1970s that they are the fastest-growing Christian religion; and neither can they claim to be a united community. Today they are rent with small but significant schisms and are being analysed and criticized by former members as never before in their history.

In many ways the Witnesses have become ossified. For many decades now they have pursued the same missionary techniques with little adjustment for either societal or technological changes. More and more they have become hostile to new intellectual developments, the intellectual world, and to independent-minded intellectuals in their own ranks. And more significantly, their leadership has become a self-perpetuating caste which refuses to open itself to new and constructive criticism of almost any sort.

Just how serious this is is shown from the events which have overtaken the Witnesses since 1975. Prior to that date, for a period of nine years, Witness leaders, notably the present president of the Watch Tower Society, Frederick W. Franz, proclaimed that year as the *probable* date for the end of the world, and new millenarian excitement swept the Witness community. As a result, the number of new converts climbed significantly, particularly during the years 1968 through 1975. Yet, as had always happened in the past, the Witnesses were disappointed: again the apocalypse was delayed; again there was a 'sifting' of membership – this time in the hundreds of thousands. Furthermore, an aging leadership seemed incapable of developing anything like a satisfactory response to what *had not* happened in 1975. For several years after this latest prophetic failure, the only explanation given by the Watch Tower Society was one which it had abandoned prior to 1966.[13]

Gradually, however, Witness leaders attempted to divert their flock's attention by again stressing evangelism: More persons must be given a chance to hear the good news that the dawn of the millennium is about to break on an unsuspecting world, and only Jehovah's Witnesses will be saved from God's wrath at the battle of Armageddon. Curiously, though, the Witnesses' present governing body has made no serious attempt to revise its eschatological timetable, and as of now the Watch Tower Society still teaches, as it has for many decades, that the end must come prior to the passing away of the generation which was old enough to know what was happening in 1914, the year now marked as the beginning of Christ's invisible presence and the establishment of his kingdom rule in heaven. Although a few members of the governing body attempted recently to shift their latest 'anchor date' from 1914 to 1957,[14] a majority of the body refused to support that move. So as of now, Jehovah's Witnesses are still faced with the possibility of another major prophetic disconfirmation in the near future.[15]

The following pages are therefore an attempt to give a general overview of the history, doctrinal system, and community of Jehovah's Witnesses from their inception in the latter half of the nineteenth century and to demonstrate how, while their essentially Adventist millenarianism has long been the basis of their growth and success, it is also their greatest weakness. Since, for over a hundred years, the end of this world has been delayed for them – something which they never expected would happen – they have not been able to adjust satisfactorily to world events or to a world which, in their view, goes 'groaning on.'

Part One

History

CHAPTER ONE

The Beginning of a Movement

Jehovah's Witnesses have grown out of the religious environment of late nineteenth-century American Protestantism. Although they may seem remarkably different from mainline Protestants and reject certain central doctrines of the great churches, in a real sense they are the peculiarly American heirs of Adventism, the prophetic movements within nineteenth-century British and American Evangelicalism, Methodism, and the millenarianism of both seventeenth-century Anglicanism and English Protestant nonconformity. There is, in fact, very little about their doctrinal system which is outside the broad Anglo-American Protestant tradition, although there are certain concepts which they hold more in common with Catholicism than Protestantism. If they are unique in many ways – as they undoubtedly are – it is simply because of the particular theological combinations and permutations of their doctrines rather than because of their novelty. Then, too, it must be stressed that the thrust of both their ideas and practices has been developed quite largely, if not exclusively, in the United States during the late nineteenth and twentieth centuries. So unless one understands something of the broad themes of American history during this period, it is difficult to understand Jehovah's Witnesses. Nevertheless, after having said this, the best way to begin the study of the Witnesses is to examine the personal history of one man – Charles Taze Russell, the first president of what is now the Watch Tower Bible and Tract Society, the person most responsible for spreading the doctrines which served as the basis for the teachings of the International or Associated Bible Students, the names by which the Witnesses were known prior to 1931.

Charles Russell: The Early Years

Born in 1852 at Pittsburgh, Pennsylvania, Russell[1] was raised a Presbyterian by his deeply religious parents, Joseph L. and Eliza Birney Russell, both of Scottish-

Irish (Ulster Protestant) descent. When he was a child, his mother had encouraged him to consider the Christian ministry, but after she died, his father trained him to become his business partner. The young Russell was given a modest education in public schools, supplemented by study under private tutors. At the age of fourteen his father began to employ him in the management of his clothing store and by the next year was sending him several hundreds of miles away to Philadelphia as his purchasing agent. Shortly thereafter he became his father's full-fledged partner, and together they developed a major clothing-store business. By the late 1870s or the early years of the following decade he had amassed a sizeable fortune.[2]

In spite of his successes in the business world, Russell remained far more interested in religious matters. As a boy he was a devout Calvinist who would sometimes write dire warnings of hellfire in conspicuous public places to encourage working men to mend their wicked ways.[3] He was still only in his early teen years, however, when both he and his father began to become somewhat 'liberated' religiously. Charles joined the local Congregationalist church which was less austere than the Presbyterian, and Joseph began to show interest in Adventism.[4] Then, when he was only sixteen years of age, Charles Russell 'began to be shaken in faith regarding many long accepted doctrines.' In fact, like so many serious youths, he 'fell a ready prey to the logic of infidelity.' In trying to convert an 'infidel,' he was unable to defend his beliefs successfully and lost faith in the Bible. Nevertheless, he continued to pray to God and pursued his search for truth.

Just why the pious youth was shaken does not seem hard to understand. As his earliest writings show, he was influenced powerfully by the rationalistic spirit of his age and, from adolescence on, was never to stop asking how an all-loving God could punish sinners with the infinite torments of hellfire. But equally important, no doubt, was Russell's feeling towards the Almighty. To him God was his father in a pre-eminent sense, and because he had always had such a warm, loving relationship with his human father, Joseph Russell, it seems that he could never conceive of the Lord Jehovah as anything but a merciful diety.

Sometime in 1869 Jonas Wendell, an Advent Christian preacher, was holding a service in 'a dusty, dingy hall' in Allegheny, Pennsylvania. Russell stumbled onto the meeting and stayed and listened. As a result, his faith in the Bible was restored. Yet he did not become a 'Second Adventist' at that time or, from his own standpoint, ever after. Almost immediately he contacted several friends who began studying the Scriptures with him. Under his leadership, a Bible-study class was formed which was gradually to evolve into a separate movement.

Much attention has been devoted to Russell's concepts and teachings; surprisingly little has been paid to the sources thereof, either by his friends or by his enemies. The reasons are somewhat complex. It seems that because many of his followers long regarded him as the 'faithful and wise servant' of Matthew 24:45–7 and the 'Laodicean Messenger,'[5] they emphasized his personal role as a religious leader rather than his debt to his predecessors. Conversely, his critics have been anxious to picture his doctrines as having no respectable tradition behind them and, therefore, have also failed to examine in any depth the origins of his thinking. In addition, Jehovah's Witnesses themselves have been so engaged in proselytizing in expectation of the apocalypse that they have had little time or desire to study their own background. But Russell identified at least some of the men to whom, and the movement to which, he was indebted for aiding him in arriving at the doctrinal system which he developed over a span of forty-five years.

He frankly indicated his 'indebtedness to the Adventists as well as other denominations' and mentioned two persons, George Stetson and George Storrs, who had tendered spiritual assistance to him. Speaking about the period from 1869 to 1872, he said: 'The study of the Word of God with these dear brethren led, step by step, into greener and brighter hopes for the world, though it was not until 1872 that I gained a clear view of our Lord's work as our *ransom price,* that I found the strength and foundation of all hope of restitution to lie in that doctrine.'[6]

Who, then, were Stetson and Storrs, and what were their contributions to his thinking? The answer to the first part of this question is that both had long backgrounds in 'Second Adventism.' In fact, Stetson was an Advent Christian minister,[7] while Storrs[8] had been a major founder of the Life and Advent Union. Both were independent-minded, however, and shortly after Russell and his friends began their study of the Bible, Storrs broke all ties with the union.

George Storrs

Of these two men who influenced Russell, George Storrs was by far the more important. Born in 1796 in Lebanon, New Hampshire, he, like Russell, was raised in a stern Calvinist environment. But at the age of twenty-nine, he became a convert to Methodism and later was ordained as a minister of the Methodist Episcopal church. His position ultimately became untenable when in the 1830s he became an outspoken adversary of slavery in the United States. In 1840 he resigned from the church.

More important was the fact that in 1837 he read a tract by 'Deacon' Henry Grew,[9] an English-born, ex-Baptist pastor from Philadelphia. From that tract Storrs came to believe in what is called 'conditionalism':[10] the idea that man does not have an immortal soul but, rather, gains everlasting life *on the condition* that he receive such a gift from God through Christ. In consequence, Storrs became the foremost American proponent of conditionalism, or 'annihilationism'[11] as it was sometimes called, and of the teaching that the dead are unconscious or asleep until the resurrection. In 1841 he published *An Enquiry: Are the Souls of the Wicked Immortal? In Three Letters,* and in the following year an enlargement of the same theme in *An Enquiry: Are the Souls of the Wicked Immortal? In Six Sermons.* Significantly, nearly 200,000 copies of the *Six Sermons* were circulating in the United States and Great Britain by 1880.[12]

In 1842 Storrs also became involved with the movement led by William Miller, a New England Baptist, who was convinced on the basis of his computation of 'biblical chronology' that Christ's second advent would occur sometime between March 1843 and March 1844. Storrs then became a major supporter of Millerite eschatology and preached far and wide in 1842 and 1843 concerning the hoped-for advent. When Christ failed to appear as Miller had expected, a re-examination of his calculations by his followers brought forth the suggestion that the Lord Jesus would come on the clouds in October 1844. When that date did not bring the advent either, Storrs abandoned the Millerite movement. In fact, he had come to feel that he and others had been mesmerized by Millerite emotionalism. In addition, William Miller and certain prominent Millerite leaders rejected Storrs's doctrine of conditionalism. Nevertheless, Storrs's association with the Millerites and their successors, the various Second Adventists, led to the adoption of conditionalism by a number of nineteenth- and twentieth-century Adventist movements: the Advent Christian church, the Seventh-Day Adventists, the Life and Advent Union, the World-Wide Church of God, and perhaps the Christadelphians.[13] During his association with Millerism in 1843, Storrs founded a newspaper called the *Bible Examiner* which came to be published on a regular basis in 1847. Its object was expressed in its motto, 'No Immortality or Endless Life except through Jesus Christ alone.' By 1863 the *Bible Examiner* had become so influential that its supporters joined with Storrs in forming the Life and Advent Union. As a result, he was asked to edit a weekly paper called *The Herald of Life and the Coming Kingdom.* At that time, he suspended publication of the *Examiner.*

In 1871 he broke with the Life and Advent Union. He had formerly believed that the final destiny of all men would be fixed unchangeably at death, without regard to the unavoidable ignorance in which they had been placed in this life. That view he then abandoned, teaching that those who had died without knowledge of Christ would be given an opportunity to learn of his sacrifice for them after an earthly resurrection, and, if faithful, would receive the gift of everlasting life on a restored paradise earth. His associates in the Life and Advent Union rejected that position, and Storrs revived the *Bible Examiner.*

About that time Russell was becoming aware of Storrs, and it is quite obvious that Storrs contributed much to the young Pennsylvanian's thinking. An examination of the *Bible Examiner* indicates clearly that Russell learned the doctrines of the ransom atonement of Christ and the restitution of mankind to a paradise earth directly from Storrs and his associates[14] plus, of course, the doctrine of conditionalism. It is evident, too, that the practice of celebrating the Memorial of the Lord's Supper once a year on the supposed date of the Jewish Passover, 14 Nisan, as is done by Jehovah's Witnesses today, was learned by Russell from the editor of the *Bible Examiner*.[15] Then, finally, Russell's negative feelings towards churches and religious organizations may have come directly from Storrs. But he did not obtain his equally negative attitude towards secular authority, voting, or military service from him. Jonathan Butler is wrong in describing Storrs as an 'apolitical apocalyptic' Adventist.[16] In fact, in *The Herald of Life and the Coming Kingdom,* Storrs regularly opposed pacifism and supported the suppression of the Confederate States by the Union armies during the American Civil War because of his hatred of slavery.[17]

Russell and the Object and Manner of Christ's Return

It should not be assumed that Russell and his associates in the years 1869 to 1875 were simply taking their ideas from Storrs and Stetson. Russell was an avid student and began to develop his own doctrinal system based upon a close examination of the Scriptures, various Bible commentaries, and ideas common to much of nineteenth-century American Protestantism. For example, he followed Dr Joseph A. Seiss, a prominent Philadelphia Lutheran pastor and the editor of the *Prophetic Times* (1863–81), the foremost millenarian journal in the United States during the second half of the nineteenth century, in asserting that Christ had been resurrected in the spirit, not in the flesh.[18] Furthermore, upon an examination of the Emphatic Diaglott, an interlinear translation of Griesbach's recension of the New Testament by Benjamin Wilson, a member of the Church of God (Faith of Abraham), he noted that the Greek word *parousia,* translated 'coming' in the King James version, often more properly means 'presence.' Thus he came to hold that in the last days immediately before his revelation in wrath at the battle of Armageddon, Christ would be *invisibly* present. At that time, only his faithful followers would know that fact. So in the mid-1870s,[19] Russell had 50,000 copies of a small pamphlet entitled *The Object and Manner of Our Lord's Return* printed and published in order to make known his ideas.

Some of the ideas present in *The Object and Manner* were common to much of nineteenth-century Evangelical Protestantism. For example, Russell drew directly on the biblical commentaries of Adam Clarke and Sir Isaac Newton[20] from which he took a standard historicist interpretation[21] of the book of Revelation. Many more of his concepts, as stated in the pamphlet, appear to have been obtained directly from George Storrs and Adventism.

But the primary ideas in *The Object and Manner* did not come from the sources cited by Russell. In a three-part article recently published in *The Bible Examiner*,[22] Carl Olof Jonsson demonstrates clearly that there were many others in both Great Britain and America who believed in what is called 'the two-stage coming doctrine,' the idea of Christ's invisible presence prior to his revelation at the end of the present world and the teaching of an invisible rapture of the saints during his presence or *parousia* – all ideas presented in *The Object and Manner*. In fact, Jonsson shows quite conclusively that these concepts were originated in 1828 by Henry Drummond, a prominent British Evangelical who with Edward Irving was a co-founder of the Catholic Apostolic church or the Irvingites. Later, however, many of Drummond's ideas were popularized and spread throughout Great Britain and the United States by John Nelson Darby of the Plymouth Brethren (who had been in close association with Drummond and Irving), the Reverend Robert Govett, an Anglican divine, and in the 1860s and 1870s by the *Rainbow*, an important British millenarian journal which was edited in 1886 and 1887 by the well-known Bible translator Joseph B. Rotherham. In addition, Drummond's doctrines were taken up by Dr Joseph Seiss. So, Jonsson concludes, Russell most probably borrowed the central ideas which appear in *The Object and Manner of Our Lord's Return* from these millenarian predecessors and, in particular, from Seiss. Jonsson states: 'It is quite obvious that Russell did not originate his view of Christ's invisible coming and presence himself, but took it from others, and although it cannot be established with absolute certainty, the available evidence strongly indicates that he plagiarized the views of Dr Seiss on this matter.'[23]

Dr Nelson H. Barbour and the Three Worlds

In January 1876 Russell came in contact with the *Herald of the Morning* published in Rochester, New York, by Dr Nelson H. Barbour, an independent Adventist preacher who had also been a Millerite and an associate of George Storrs. Barbour had been connected with the circle of which Jonas Wendell had been a member. Like Wendell, he used a chronology which held that the year 1873 had marked 6,000 years from Adam's creation.

In the *Herald of the Morning* Barbour and a co-worker, John H. Paton, had gone far beyond Wendell and his associates, who had originally believed that 1873 would see the second advent and the consummation of the earth by fire. When nothing visible had happened in that year, they were at first quite perplexed until B.W. Keith,[24] a reader of the *Herald,* discovered Benjamin Wilson's translation of *parousia* as 'presence.' Then, like Russell, Barbour and Paton began to believe in the idea of an invisible presence of the Christ, which they felt had begun on schedule in 1874.

Russell, who had formerly rejected Adventist chronology and date-setting, as had George Storrs after 1844, now paid Barbour's expenses to come to Philadelphia to meet him and show 'fully and Scripturally, if he could, that the prophecies indicated 1874 as the date at which the Lord's *presence* and the "harvest" began.' As the young merchant, then only twenty-four, stated later: 'He came, and the evidence satisfied me.'[25] Once again Russell was impressed by rationalistic ideas.

Several important developments followed immediately. Russell threw his financial support behind the *Herald of the Morning,* gave Barbour money to prepare a book representing their beliefs respecting the end of the age, and curtailed certain business activities to engage in travelling and preaching while Barbour wrote and published. Shortly thereafter, according to Russell's account, he sent for Paton to join him in preaching and paid his expenses as well. Thus began a brief but important association.

The time features that Barbour explained to Russell were spelled out in the spring of 1877 in *Three Worlds and the Harvest of This World,* the book which Russell had encouraged him to write. Although it bore the names of both men as authors, it was composed entirely by Barbour.[26] Hence *Three Worlds,* with its elaborate chronology, prophetic speculation, and eschatology, contained some of his original thoughts, plus concepts drawn from a number of sources. Among other things, he continued to use the year-day system[27] of interpreting numerous prophecies; also, he accepted the idea of a 360-day 'prophetic year'[28] and a historicist interpretation of the book of Revelation. More significantly, he drew heavily on the millenarian studies of a number of nineteenth-century writers in formulating a system which demonstrated amazing, biblical-mathematical 'correspondencies,' a fact which impressed Russell greatly and has caused many thousands since to accept Barbour's system.

What, then, were the primary aspects of the 'plan of redemption' as outlined in *Three Worlds?* First, as the title of that work indicates, Barbour saw history divided into three major periods, or 'worlds,' plus a number of dispensations within those worlds. That, however, was not important in itself. Rather, what was significant was that he inferred that one could calculate the dates of the various ages from Bible chronology and prophecy and thereby determine God's timetable for Christ's second coming, the rapture of the saints, and the restoration of the earth to a paradise like Eden.

Barbour had no doubt that Bishop James Usher, whose chronology was then commonly printed in the margins of King James Version Bibles, had been off in his calculations of the age of mankind. He was 'one hundred and twenty-four years too short.'[29] Without blinking an eye before the difficulties of biblical chronology, Barbour wrote: 'one evening spent with the Bible, paper and pencil, added to a thorough determination to know just what it does teach, will enable you to master the whole subject, and measure for yourself.' Using this method, he simply calculated that six thousand years of human history had ended in the autumn of 1873 and stated that a 'morning of joy' was about to begin for mankind. Since a day with the Lord is a thousand years according to the Psalmist, six 'days' had passed. The seventh, the millennium, would be a great sabbath of restitution.[30] Equally important was the concept of the two covenants of the Jewish and gospel dispensations. With his *simple* arithmetic, Barbour reckoned the age of the Jewish dispensation which, he believed, had spanned a period of 1,845 years from the death of Jacob to the death of Christ in AD 33. Then, relying on his interpretation of Isaiah 40:2 in the King James Version, 'Comfort ye, comfort ye, my people saith your God; speak ye comfortably to Jerusalem, and cry unto her that her warfare [margin, appointed time] is accomplished, that her iniquity is pardoned, for she hath received at the Lord's hand, double, for all her sins,' he argued that the gospel dispensation must be a 'double' of the same length of time as the Jewish age. So, starting at the death of Christ, he held that the gospel age must end in 1878.[31]

Further, since the two dispensations were parallel in every way, and the last three and a half years of the Jewish age from Christ's baptism to his crucifixion had been a 'harvest time,' the same must hold true for the period from the autumn of 1874 to the spring of 1878. Barbour therefore looked for the saints to be taken away in the rapture in the latter year. So sure was he of that when he penned *Three Worlds* in 1877 that he wrote: 'If you have the spirit of a little child, you will please get a large piece of paper, your Bible and pencil, and begin with Gen.5:3. Let me urge you, a few months and "The Harvest will be passed, the summer ended."'[32]

To strengthen his arguments further, he used what was known as the jubilee cycle. Under Mosaic law, every fiftieth year was a year in which possessions, either personal or ancestral, were to revert to their owners or their owners' heirs. Slaves were also to be liberated. Hence, Barbour saw in the jubilee year a type of God's great day of restitution – the millennium. But he also saw it as having significance for the *beginning* of the millennial age. Had jubilees continued to be celebrated from the Jewish age to his own day, according to Barbour a jubilee year would have occurred in 1875, beginning (to be exact) on 6 April.[33]

In developing his system, Barbour was greatly influenced by his old mentor, William Miller, and he incorporated some of Miller's ideas in that system. He believed, for example, as did many others, that the 'time, times and a half a time' of Revelation 12:14 had ended in 1798 and that the 2,300 days (years) of Daniel 8:14 had ended in 1843. 'The mistake of [Miller and] the 1843 movement was not in the argument proving that the "days" ended there, but in assuming that they covered all the vision.'[34] Yet, as important as Millers's ideas were to Barbour, they were no more so than those of the Englishman John Aquila Brown.[35]

Perhaps the most important aspect of prophetic interpretation to be found in *Three Worlds* that is still largely adhered to by Jehovah's Witnesses involves the computation of the length of the 'times of the Gentiles' mentioned at Luke 21:24. That was something that intrigued Russell. Upon learning it from Barbour, he published an article in the *Bible Examiner* of October 1876 entitled 'Gentile Times: When Do They End?'[36] So Russell really made that interpretation his own even before publication of *Three Worlds*. Yet, in reality, the system of computing the times of the Gentiles originated neither with him, as is often believed, nor with Barbour.

In fact it was John A. Brown who first explained what he considered to be the key to the length of those times in a book called *Even-Tide*, published in London in 1823. What he posited was that the typical theocratic kingdom of Judah had fallen under Gentile rule in 604 BC. Thereafter, there would be no godly government on earth until four great empires – the Babylonian, Medo-Persian, Macedonian, and Roman – had had their sway. Then Christ, as David's heir, would rule in Jerusalem. But how long would it be before those empires expired? Brown found what was for him the answer in the fourth chapter of the book of Daniel.

In that chapter, Nebuchadnezzar, the king of Babylon, is recorded as having had a dream of a great tree. By divine command it was cut down, a band placed over its stump, and it was not to be allowed to grow again until 'seven times' had passed. When Daniel interpreted the dream, it was applied directly to Nebuchadnezzar who was to undergo seven times (years?) of madness before being restored to his throne. But Brown saw in Nebuchadnezzar a type of the human family. Prior to his madness he was seen as representative of the Jewish theocracy; during his madness he was regarded as a type of the 'beastly' Gentile nations; and after his recovery he was held to be a type of the messianic kingdom of Jesus Christ.

To calculate the 'seven times' Brown reasoned that they were seven years of 360 prophetic days each. By using the year-day principle, he simply multiplied 360 days by seven and arrived at a period of 2,520 years. Finally, by counting 2,520 years from 604 BC, he arrived at the year AD 1917, which he designated as the date for the end of those times.[37]

Barbour decided that Brown had marked the beginning of the seven times – which he regarded as the Gentile Times – two years too late. He held that they had begun with what he believed to have been the date of the destruction of Jerusalem by Nebuchadnezzar. So, instead of using 1917 as the terminus for those times, by calculating slightly differently he marked them as having their conclusion in the autumn of 1914.[38] In that year, Christ's kingdom would come to hold full sway over the earth, and the Jews, as a people, would be restored to God's favour.

During the interval between the time he wrote *Three Worlds* and 1914, Barbour expected many things to happen. Besides the rapture of the saints, he believed that the world would witness a time of trouble such as it had never seen before.[39]

Barbour was greatly impressed by his own system. He stated that he 'was not willing to admit that his calculation is even one year out.' To him there was 'such an array of evidence':

Many of the arguments, most of them, indeed, are not based on the year-day theory, and *some* of them, not based even on the *chronology;* and yet there is harmony existing, between them all. If you have solved a difficult problem in mathematics, you might very well doubt if you had not possibly made some error of calculation. But if you had solved that problem in seven different ways, all independent of one another, and in each and every case reached the same result, you would be a fool any longer to doubt the accuracy of that result.[40]

Even George Storrs, a man long hostile to such eschatological date-setting, regarded Barbour's chronology as 'the best I have ever seen.' Although he made it clear he could not assent to the conclusions that Barbour had reached, he indicated he had no disposition to oppose them.[41] And small wonder: Anyone living in late-nineteenth-century America and impressed by so-called mathematical 'proofs' might have regarded *Three Worlds* as an important prophetic study if he had the tenacity to read it. Referring to Barbour's system, as taken over by Russell virtually without change, Timothy White comments: 'Russell's chronological patterns, prophecies and parallels are enough to stagger the imagination. The dates 1799, 1874, and 1914 each are the result of several entirely independent methods of calculation. The whole system becomes very harmonious and balanced.'[42]

Three Worlds is therefore a very important work. In fact, it contains within it most of the ideas that Russell and those in association with him were to promulgate during the next nearly forty years. Even today many of the concepts within it – though frequently, but not always, changed in major ways – are still taught by Jehovah's Witnesses. Thus Barbour, who at best receives no more than a few, generally hostile paragraphs in standard Witness accounts of their history,[43] was and is a major contributor to their overall doctrinal system.

Early Schisms: 1878 and 1881

Barbour, Russell, and Paton were united briefly to preach and publicize the ideas outlined in *Three Worlds*. Russell quickly began to make converts, including A.D. Jones, one of his clerks, and A.P. Adams, a New England Methodist minister. But problems soon arose. The small band of unnamed Adventists expected, as *Three*

Worlds taught, that the spring of 1878 would see them, as Christ's chosen saints, carried away to heaven. When that did not happen, disillusion and division occurred.

Russell remained loyal to the teachings expressed in *Three Worlds* while Barbour set off on another course. Russell developed the explanation that those *dying in the Lord* from 1878 *forward* would have an immediate heavenly resurrection rather than having to sleep in their graves; so, he held, 1878 *was* a marked year. But Barbour refused to accept that solution and began a whole new exercise in date-setting.[44] In addition, he then took a position in conflict with that held by both Russell and Paton on the nature of the atonement. According to Russell: 'Mr. Barbour soon after wrote an article for the *Herald* denying the doctrine of the atonement – denying that the death of Christ was the ransom price of Adam and his race, saying that Christ's death was no more a settlement of the penalty of man's sins than would the sticking of a pin through the body of a fly and causing it suffering and death be considered by an earthly parent as a just settlement for misdemeanor in his child.'[45]

Russell disagreed with Barbour's new stance and a schism followed. Barbour was a particularly proud, severe man, and he had certainly been the most prominent member of the small association that had formed in 1876. But Russell was determined to differ from him on what he considered a fundamental doctrine. He took issue openly with Barbour's position on the atonement and obtained Paton's support in an article which was published in the December 1878 *Herald*. Early in 1878 the split between Barbour – with A.P. Adams in his camp – and Russell and Paton became complete. Russell accused Barbour of withdrawing money which he (Russell) had deposited and of treating it as his own. Then, when Russell founded a new magazine, *Zion's Watch Tower and Herald of Christ's Presence,* Barbour 'poured upon the Editor of the TOWER the vilest of personal abuse.'[46] What followed was a battle between the former associates to gain support from those who received the two journals, for the readers of them were the same persons.[47] At the time, Paton, as much as Russell, served as a leader of those who had broken with Barbour. Russell urged him to write a book called *Day Dawn* to replace *Three Worlds,* and A.D. Jones agreed to publish it. It was primarily Russell, however, who carried on the struggle with Barbour, and it was he who produced a small book called *Tabernacle Teachings* in answer to some of Barbour's criticisms of his doctrines.

Paton did not object openly to any of Russell's ideas; evidently he was a much more pacific man than Barbour. But he, too, soon began to produce articles which Russell regarded as a denial of the ransom doctrine of the atonement. Consequently, in 1881, he refused to publish any more of Paton's articles and the two separated with some bitterness.[48]

By 1881, of the five principal associates who had taken a stand on the doctrines outlined in *Three Worlds,* only A.D. Jones remained in fellowship with Russell; and even that relationship did not last. With Russell's blessings, Jones founded a journal named *Zion's Day Star* in New York City. Within a year he, too, denied Russell's theory of the ransom and eventually was to repudiate the Bible itself.[49]

Russell's Independent Ministry

It may well be said, then, that Russell, still a young man not yet thirty years of age, assumed leadership of those who supported his teachings not so much because he desired to do so, but, rather, because he felt compelled to maintain a defence of what he considered to be a basic Christian doctrine – the ransom theory of the atonement or, in fact, substitutionary atonement. Furthermore, he was determined to hold fast to Barbour's chronology even after Barbour had given up on certain aspects of it himself. So while he seems to have had no specific visions of grandeur at the time, he did feel that God was guiding and directing him in a very definite way.

That he had no long-range desire to establish himself as a new American prophet or the founder of a new religion, in the years 1879 through 1881 at least, is evident from his short-term eschatology. Again, basing his conclusion on Barbour's chronology, he assumed that the 'higher calling' or harvest of the supposedly 'elect 144,000 saints' of Revelation 7 and 14 would terminate in 1881. Writing in May 1881, he stated: 'the favor which ends this fall, is that of entering the *Bride* company [the 144,000]. We believe the *door of favor* is now open and any who consecrate *all* and give *all,* can come into the wedding and become members of the Bride, but that with this year the company will be reckoned *complete* and *the door to that high calling* (not the door of mercy) closed forever.'[50]

Melvin Curry writes: 'The effect of this short-term prediction was twofold: it served to turn the attention of the Bible Students away from the disappointment of 1878, and it provided an impetus for increased evangelistic activity';[51] however, Russell was no doubt serious in believing it. For he also predicted that with 1881 the churches (Babylon) would begin to fall apart and, more importantly, he expected that the rapture of the saints – of whom he considered himself to be a member – would take place in that year.[52] Rather than planning to carry on a major evangelical campaign beyond the next three and a half decades, he expected to be in heaven with his Lord.

In fact, in November 1880, he 'nearly created a crisis' among his followers by suggesting that the rapture or 'change' would 'be invisible to fleshly beings as He [Christ] is, and the Angels are.'[53] In the December issue of *Zion's Watch Tower,* he wrote concerning the change:

So now by *comparing* scripture with scripture, we shall endeavor to set forth the manner in which this will be fulfilled. First, we do not think that the scriptures teach that those who are taken will be taken to any locality (not Mt. Zion, or any definite point), neither do we think that those when taken, and for some time afterward, will be invisible to those around them. No, we believe, after they are taken that they will be *visible* and to all appearance just the same, but in reality, they will not be the same as before taken, for, if they were, then to be taken would not mean anything.[54]

In other words, as he went on to explain, they would be materialized spirit beings like the risen Christ who had appeared as a man.

Later, he again changed his position on both the nature and the timing of the rapture. Writing in May 1881, he stated: 'As to *when* our change is due we can only say: To our understanding it will be due at any time *after* October 2nd, 1881, but we know of no scriptural evidence as to *what* time we will be changed from natural to spiritual, from mortal to immortal.'[55] Sometimes he even made statements which on the surface seem to be bold-faced falsehoods. For example, in the May 1881 issue of *Zion's Watch Tower* (on page 224 of that journal as reprinted in volume form in 1919), he states: 'THE WATCH TOWER never claimed that the *body of Christ* will be changed to spiritual beings this year. There is *such a change* due sometime. We have not attempted to say when, but have repeatedly said that it could not take place *before* the fall of 1881.' Yet in the January 1881 issue of the same magazine, on reprints page 180, A.D. Jones, a 'regular contributor' to *Zion's Watch Tower,* had written: 'In the article concerning our change, in December paper [*Zion's Watch Tower* of December 1880], we expressed the opinion that it was nearer than many supposed, and while we would not attempt to prove our change at any particular time, yet we propose looking at some of the evidences which *seem* to show the translation or change from the natural to the spiritual condition, due this side or by the fall of our year 1881.' And there can be no doubt that Russell himself agreed with Jones. On reprints page 172 of the December 1880 issue, he states that 'the *"high calling"* – to be the bride – the temple[,] will end in the autumn of 1881' and then later, on the same page, says: 'When "the body," "the bride," *"the temple,"* is thus completed, all will have been thus changed.'

How can this be explained? Must we assume that Russell was thoroughly dishonest? Probably not. It seems, rather, that he was rationalizing as much to himself as to his readers and was practising self-deception on a grand scale. While his eschatological conjectures and later denials thereof may seem outrageous to the ordinary reader today, they are so startlingly contradictory that the most reasonable explanation of them is that Russell believed them himself.[56] He was evidently sincere in feeling that his ministry would not last beyond a few years at most.

Even earlier, in 1879, Russell's role, as a late-nineteenth and early-twentieth-century religious leader, had begun to unfold. In that year he married a very able and intelligent woman, Maria Frances Ackley. But he gave no thought to settling down to a quiet married life. Instead, he and his associates were busy organizing some thirty study groups or congregations in seven states between the eastern coast of the United States and Ohio. In the following year, he arranged to visit those congregations – known more commonly as *ecclesias,* classes, or churches – to spend six-hour study sessions with each one. In addition, he began to establish a set pattern of meetings based on the custom of his home Allegheny–Pittsburgh congregation.

In spite of his doctrinal vacillations, his tireless zeal and dynamic personality caught the attention of others to a much greater extent than did the activities or personalities of his early associates. He was also noted for his great speaking ability and for his warmth and personal kindness. It is therefore not surprising that he was soon generally recognized as the 'Pastor,' a position to which he was elected by his brethren in Allegheny–Pittsburgh in October 1876, and later in many other centres.[57]

His unbounded optimism and the faith that God was directing him caused him to advertise for 1,000 preachers as early as 1881.[58] Also, when one after another of his associates rejected the doctrine of the atonement as he understood the Scriptures to teach it, he began to write a stream of articles, books, pamphlets, and sermons, the number of which is enormous.

In all, his works totalled some 50,000 printed pages, and by the time of his death nearly 20 million copies of his books had been printed and distributed throughout the world.[59] While he had never had any formal university or seminary training – a fact his adversaries never allowed him to forget – his writing style was reasonably good. His works demonstrated that he had a broad knowledge of the world in which he lived and much of its current and historical literature.

Beginning in 1880, Pastor Russell and his associates began to publish and distribute tracts. In 1881 he produced two small books: *Tabernacle Teachings,* mentioned above, and *Food for Thinking Christians* which gave, among other things, an outline of his thinking on such subjects as the atonement, the resurrection, predestination and free will, the *parousia,* and God's 'plan of the ages.' Some 1.45 million copies of *Food for Thinking Christians* were distributed.[60] What was happening was that a new religious movement was beginning to develop.

Russell, following in George Storrs's footsteps, at first did not want to establish another denomination, nor did he consider himself as having any particular role beyond that of a preacher and brother in Christ. He refused to regard himself as a prophet or a divinely inspired person in any sense.[61] Furthermore, he long rejected any denominational name, saying that he and his brethren in faith would prefer to be known as members of the 'Church of Christ' had that name not already been taken by another group.[62] Yet Russell and his fellow believers were set apart in many ways, and therefore were being forced to become a separate and distinct religious organization.

They had already begun to develop their own congregational practices and forms of government. They had separated themselves from most churches by their acceptance of conditionalism, George Storrs's basic understanding of redemption, and by a pre-millennialist eschatology. Then, through Russell's breaks with Barbour and Paton, direct links with Adventism were weakened. But if all that were not enough, in 1882 Russell openly rejected the doctrine of the Trinity and adopted what is commonly regarded as an Arian theology.[63] Thus he broke quite definitely in another way from his former associates, Barbour and Paton, and even George Storrs who had been unclear on any doctrine of the nature of God.[64] Another way in which the congregations and isolated individuals associated with Russell soon were to become distinct was in their insistence on becoming a preaching brotherhood. In the July-August 1881 issue of *Zion's Watch Tower* on reprints page 241, Russell asked: 'WHO ARE TO PREACH? We answer,' said he, 'All who receive the anointing spirit and are thus recognized as members of the body of Christ.' Hence all those who regarded Russell as their Pastor were expected to preach to their neighbours in any reasonable way, a practice followed by Jehovah's Witnesses to this day. Yet, unlike the Witnesses, they did not regard preaching as their primary duty. Rather, they were interested in gathering a little flock of saints who through gradual sanctification and character development would become new creatures in Christ.[65] Russell and his associates believed that the vast majority of mankind would be given their opportunity to attain salvation during the millennium. There was, therefore, no need to preach to all. Conversion of heathens at the time was difficult, although not impossible, while conversion of the Jews, in most cases at least, would have to wait until after 1914.[66]

Over the next few years, Russell became well known throughout the western world. Using his personal wealth, in 1886 he published volume I of the *Millennial Dawn Series* or the *Studies in the Scriptures*. That book, which became known later as *The Divine Plan of the Ages,* came to be circulated far and wide; by the time of his death 4,817,000 copies had been distributed.[67] In 1889 he produced volume II, *The Time Is at Hand;* in 1891, volume III, *Thy Kingdom Come;* in 1897, volume IV, *The Battle of Armageddon;* in 1899, volume V, *At-one-ment between God and Man;* and in 1904, volume VI, *The New Creation.* Over the same period, *Zion's Watch Tower* was distributed ever more widely, and numerous colporteurs placed Watch Tower books, booklets, and tracts throughout America and in other lands. By 1881 two missionaries had already been sent to England,[68] and a few years

"Write Down the Vision and Make it Plain Upon Tables, That Everyone May Read it Fluently." — HABAKKUK 2:2

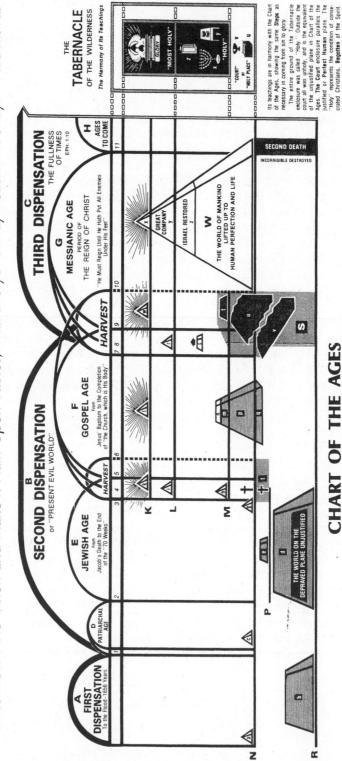

CHART OF THE AGES

ILLUSTRATING THE PLAN OF GOD FOR BRINGING MANY SONS TO GLORY, AND HIS PURPOSE—

Russell's Chart of the Ages (from *The Divine Plan of the Ages*)

later, Bible Students, as they were by then calling themselves, began to organize congregations in Canada.[69] By the time of the First World War they were to be found in many lands.

Greater organization became necessary throughout the years. To meet that need, in 1884 Russell incorporated the Zion's Watch Tower Tract Society, now known as the Watch Tower Bible and Tract Society of Pennsylvania. Years later, when he moved the headquarters of the society to Brooklyn, New York, another corporation, the Peoples' Pulpit Association, now the Watchtower Bible and Tract Society, of New York, Incorporated, was formed in 1909. In 1914 a British corporation known as the International Bible Students Association was established.

Russell did not only become known – and the Bible Students grow in numbers – as a result of the distribution of Watch Tower literature; he proved to be an amazingly active evangelist who made numerous trips throughout the United States, Canada, Britain, Europe, and around the world. He engaged in important debates with two prominent preachers, Dr E.L. Eaton of the Methodist Episcopal church and L.S. White of the Disciples of Christ.[70] Beginning in the first decade of the twentieth century, his sermons came to be printed in thousands of newspapers which were read by fifteen to twenty million persons weekly.[71] In addition, he spoke frequently at Bible Student conventions which, particularly from 1893 forward, became a regular feature of Bible Student life.

Finally, in the last years of his life, under his direction the Watch Tower Society produced the 'Photo-Drama of Creation,' a combined moving picture–hand-tinted slide program synchronized with phonograph records which carried recorded talks and music. The 'Photo-Drama' was seen by some ten million persons during the years of the First World War in the United States alone. By the time Russell died, he had become Pastor and prime spokesman for an international movement with thousands of members.

The Bible Students' Association

The movement that Russell organized at first had few of the *organizational* marks of a sect or denomination. Like George Storrs, Russell abhorred the churches of Christendom, seeing them as Babylon the Great. Nevertheless, he believed it possible to be a spirit-begotten member of the true church – Christ's church – while still a member of one of the churches of Christendom. However, upon recognizing that 'the greatest simplicity of Christ' was not generally observed except among the members of the Bible Students' Association, it behooved true Christians to leave nominal Christianity – particularly after 1881 – and associate primarily with other true Christians, members of the New Creation – the Bible Students. But such association was to be entirely free and voluntary. In describing the nature of Bible Student congregations as late as 1915, Russell stated:

On one occasion I was called upon by a minister of the Reformed church. He wanted to know how I managed my church. I said to him, 'Brother —, I have no church.' He said, 'You know what I mean.' I answered, 'I want you to know what I mean, too. We claim that there is only one church. If you belong to that church, you belong to our church.' He looked at me in surprise. Then he said. 'You have an organization; how many members are there?' I replied, 'I cannot tell; we do not keep membership rolls.' 'You do not keep any list of the membership?' 'No. We do not keep any list; their names are written in heaven.' He asked, 'How do you have your election?' I said, 'We announce an election; and any or all of God's people, who are consecrated and are accustomed to meet with this company, or congregation, may have the privilege of expressing their judgment of who would be the Lord's preference for elders and deacons of the congregation.' 'Well,' he said, 'that is simplicity itself.' I then added, 'We pay no salaries; there is nothing to make people quarrel. We never take up a collection.' 'How do you get the money?' he asked. I replied, 'Now, Dr. —, if I tell you what is the simplest truth you will hardly be able to believe it. When people get interested in this way, they find no basket placed under their nose. But they see there are expenses. They say to themselves, "This hall costs something, and I see that free lunch is served between meetings, for those living at some distance. How can I get a little money into this thing anyway"' He looked at me as if he thought 'What do you take me for – a greenhorn?' I said, 'Now, Dr. —, I am telling you the plain truth. They do ask me this very question. "How can I get a little money into this cause?" When one gets a blessing and has any means, he wants to use it for the Lord. If he has no means, why should we prod him for it?'

There would be nothing to come out of, as an organization, if one is an International Bible Student. You cannot get out of anything you have not gone into. If anyone can tell me how he got into Babylon by getting interested in the affairs of the Watch Tower Bible and Tract Society, let him show me how he will jump out, and I will jump with him.[72]

As Russell indicated, all Bible Student elders and deacons in their congregations were elected. If a majority of the congregation did not feel that they were teaching or behaving properly, they had the right not to elect them again to office in the following year.[73] But what if there was a schism? Those who disagreed with the majority could simply form another ecclesia and could remain in fellowship with the Bible Students so long as they did not deny fundamental beliefs. Of course, once they had left their former ecclesia, they were not to interfere with its activities.[74]

Church discipline was not the right or responsibility of any officers in local ecclesias or among the Bible Students, even including Russell himself. When asked if elders should sit as a court of inquiry, he was blunt: 'The Lord's word does not authorize any court of the Elders, or anyone else, to become busybodies. This would be going back to the practices of the Dark Ages during the inquisition; and we would be showing the same spirit as did the inquisitors.'[75] Over and over again Russell placed the highest value on Christian freedom and the right of everyone to be directed by his own conscience.[76]

What of difficulties in the various Bible Student congregations? Russell believed that most problems could be solved by love and should never become serious issues. If there was a grave matter, however, individuals should be guided by Jesus's counsel at Matthew 18:15–18. According to those verses, if a brother sinned against a member of the congregation, the latter could contact him personally to straighten out the matter. If that failed, he could take two or three others to ascertain the facts and again seek reconciliation. Only if that second step failed to work would he then take his case before the whole congregation for judgment. If the erring brother then did not repent his sin, the one sinned against and the ecclesia would legitimately treat him as a 'heathen man and a publican' – that is, as no Christian at all.[77]

What if one's sin were against the ecclesia as a whole? Following the steps just outlined, one could, if not repentant, be disfellowshipped from the congregation. But Russell recognized that majorities could be as wrong as individuals and stressed the need for almost complete congregational unanimity in depriving a person of Christian fellowship.[78] Even if one were disfellowshipped by a particular ecclesia, this did not mean that he was shunned in all social circumstances or by all other Bible Students. So, discipline was mild and was kept to no more than a bare minimum to preserve personal and congregational harmony. Beyond that Russell and the Bible Students refused to go, at least in theory.

Russell also believed in a great deal of tolerance and latitude in belief. Commenting in the *New Creation* on Romans 14:5, 'Let every man be fully persuaded in his own mind,' he recognized that while Christian unity was important, it was essential to note that doctrinal uniformity was not to be forced: 'The Lord's people do not only have differently developed heads, and differences in experience and education, but they are additionally of different ages as New Creatures – babes, youths, matured.' Of course, all had to recognize and assent to certain doctrines: 'They must grasp the *fundamentals* – that all were sinners; that Christ Jesus, our Leader, *redeemed* us by his sacrifice finished at Calvary that we are now in the School of Christ to be taught and fitted for the Kingdom and its service; and that none enter this School except upon full consecration of their all to the Lord.'[79] Beyond this there was to be great freedom. Even water baptism was not absolutely necessary,[80] and each was to have a right to express his feelings on all doctrinal questions in an orderly way.[81] No one was to fail to recognize him as a brother unless he refused to assent to the few *fundamentals*. Russell and the Bible Students therefore took as their unofficial motto: 'On essentials, unity; on non-essentials, charity.'[82]

In spite of his unwillingness to become a domineering religious leader, Russell became a dominant one. It was he, after all, who had taken the initiative to preach in the period from 1877 to 1881; and when he had broken with his former associates, Barbour, Paton, and the others, it was he alone who had the drive, the personal ability, and the *money* to develop a significant religious movement. Furthermore, since he continued to direct Zion's Watch Tower Society after its incorporation in 1884, it was he who was able to maintain control over what was published in Bible Student literature, over the activities of colporteurs who distributed that literature,[83] and over the activities of travelling preachers called 'pilgrims'[84] who, after 1894, regularly visited Bible Student congregations. While he did not intentionally use the society as a centralizing agency – he regarded it as no more than a business organization – it none the less did tend to become the vehicle through which the Bible Students came to be welded into a more cohesive religious community.

As time went by Russell also tended more and more to impose his own teachings upon the Bible Students. That was not because he was power hungry, but simply because he believed so firmly that he had discovered 'present truth' and wanted others to know it. In 1895 he suggested that the ecclesias study his then-published volumes of *Studies in the Scriptures* paragraph by paragraph.[85] In 1905 he established what were known as Berean Studies – directed studies on various topics set by Russell himself for the entire movement. As a result verse-by-verse Bible study was replaced in practically all congregations by the Berean Studies which, therefore, meant that Russell could exercise greater control over the beliefs of his followers.[86]

In 1910 Russell taught, and no doubt believed, that the six volumes of the *Studies in the Scriptures* 'were practically the Bible topically arranged.'[87] Although this was a gross overstatement, and one for which he has been severely censured,[88] two things should be recognized: 1 / Russell, although the author of the *six volumes,* was not the originator of most of the ideas in them, and 2 / even though he believed Berean Studies to be superior to 'free' Bible study, he left each and every ecclesia free to decide which system it would adopt.[89] His power was suasive rather than coercive, in sharp contrast to the present policy of the Watch Tower Society.

Nevertheless there was great danger in what Russell was doing. In *The Watch Tower* of January 1913 he wrote: 'We pause not to inquire what Brother Calvin or Brother Wesley taught, nor what others taught before them or since. We go back to the teachings of Christ and the apostles and prophets, and ignore every other teaching. True, all denominations claim more or less to do this, but they are more or less handicapped by their traditions and creeds. They look through colored spectacles. We ignore all those and strive to view the words of inspiration in the light of context only, or in the reflected light from other passages of Scripture.'[90] In fact, he was practising self-deception on a grand scale, and Bible Students, as much as anyone, were looking through 'colored spectacles.' As Timothy White says: 'His comments become for many like the creeds he so despised.'[91]

Russell as the Faithful and Wise Servant

A major reason that Russell was deceiving himself is that, in spite of his good intentions and unwillingness to assume the role of prophet, after 1895 he held a position among Bible Students which was more than just that of their Pastor. What happened is that Mrs Russell, at that time vigorously defending her husband against former associates, came up with a new doctrine respecting Matthew 24:45 –7. That text in the King James Version reads: 'Who then is a faithful and wise servant, whom his lord hath made ruler over his household, to give them meat in due season? Blessed *is* that servant, whom his lord when he cometh shall find so doing. Verily I say unto you, That he shall make him ruler over all his goods.' And Maria Russell chose to apply the term 'faithful and wise servant' from Jesus's illustration to her husband.

Earlier, Russell had held that 'that servant' was really an illustration of the church – the little flock of 144,000 mentioned at Revelation 7 and 14.[92] But his wife pointed to the fact that the 'servant' was singular while the church, the 'household' of faith, was plural. Furthermore, if the church were 'that servant' and also the 'household' it would end up serving itself. Writing in December 1895, Maria Russell stressed her point forcefully to George Woolsey, a New York Bible Student:

But when we come to Matt. 24:45–51 it appears to me to be a totally different case [from Revelation 16:15]. Here are brought to our attention – 'that servant,' 'his fellow servants' and the 'household.' Now, if the Lord wished to indicate a chief servant of the truth, and fellow servants assisting in serving the meat in due season to the household of faith, he could not have chosen more precise language to convey such a thought. And, on the contrary, to ignore such an order and reasonableness in the account, to my mind throws the entire narrative into confusion, making the 'servants' (plural) and 'that servant' interchangeable terms.[93]

She then went on to argue that since Christ was present and had assumed his office of king in 1878, the household of faith was being richly supplied with 'meat in due season' by one servant.[94] She did not have to say in so many words whom she meant.

Russell was somewhat cautious in adopting his wife's doctrine, probably because he had just been publicly accused of being authoritarian. Nevertheless, he was doubtlessly flattered by the new and enhanced role that she, by her exegesis, had created for him. Thus he accepted the logic of her interpretation, and his own writings began to make only slightly veiled statements to the effect that he was 'that servant.'[95] It is true that Russell never called himself the 'faithful and wise servant' publicly. Also, he was convinced that if 'that servant' became unfaithful and indiscreet, God would cast him off.[96] To him the role of the 'servant' was one of loving service, not arrogant oversight. Nevertheless, it is certain that he regarded himself as the 'faithful and wise servant' in spite of Watch Tower Society comments during the last several decades which state the contrary.[97] The Memorial Edition of *The Watch Tower* of 1 December 1916 made this explicit: 'Thousands of readers of Pastor Russell's writings believe that he filled the office of that "faithful and wise servant," and that his great work was giving to the household of faith meat in due season. His modesty and humility precluded him from openly claiming this title, but he admitted as much in private.'[98]

Another title given him by his followers was the 'Laodicean Messenger.' According to *Three Worlds,* the seven churches of Asia Minor mentioned in the first three chapters of Revelation pictured Christ's church as a whole during different ages. The Laodicean church was seen as a type of the 'last phase of the church.'[99] Consequently, since Bible Students believed that the last phase had begun in 1874, and Russell was being used as Jehovah's chosen spokesman for the exposition of 'new truths' to the church, he was, by definition, the 'Laodicean Messenger.'[100] A third title given Russell was 'the man with the inkhorn.' In Ezekiel 9, the prophet had a vision of six men with slaughter weapons in their hands and a seventh with a writer's inkhorn at his side. The seventh was to place a mark on the foreheads of the inhabitants of Jerusalem who were sighing and crying over the abominations committed in the city. Others not so marked were to be slain by the six men with weapons. Now the Bible Students believed that this vision would have an antitypical fulfilment during Christ's second presence, and Russell was therefore seen as the one marking those sighing and crying for the abominations committed in antitypical Jerusalem, or Christendom.[101]

In effect, to the Bible Students, Pastor Charles Taze Russell became God's spokesman, his channel, dispensing spiritual food in a way that no other could.[102] As noted, Russell always believed that the food had to be biblical, and in a real sense he always attempted to maintain the traditional *sola scriptura* – the Bible alone – doctrine of Protestantism. Yet, by granting him a special teaching role, the

Bible Students (and Russell himself) were beginning to adopt something like the Roman Catholic concept of the *magisterium* of the papacy.

Russell's Marital Tribulations

In spite of success and adulation, Russell did not escape problems or bitter criticism. During his lifetime, two sharp schisms occurred among the Bible Students: the first in 1894 which resulted from the feeling among some of his fellow workers that he was too domineering; the second in 1908 and 1909 over the doctrinal issue of the *New Covenant*. Much more painful, however, was his separation from his wife in 1897, the trial which legalized that separation in 1906, and the bitterness that followed. Russell's separation from his wife unfortunately occasioned and continues to occasion severe and largely unfair attacks on his reputation. A close examination of what took place from original documents[103] demonstrates that fact clearly.

For many years Maria Russell was a loyal supporter of her husband; she even served as secretary-treasurer of Zion's Watch Tower Society. When the 1894 schism occurred, she conducted a lecture tour of Bible Student congregations in Russell's defence. But shortly thereafter the two fell out. In the first place the relationship between them was a somewhat unhealthy one by most standards. When they were married they had entered into an agreement that their union should not be consummated at that time, nor would they cohabit in future.[104] Taken on the basis of their understanding of Matthew 19:12 and a Victorian attitude towards sex, it no doubt caused some strain between them. Russell seemed to have no problem, for he evidently had little interest in a physical relationship. He seems to have had little libido, perhaps owing to his constant concern with religious matters. He did state, however, that had his wife requested him, he would have fulfilled his obligations to her sexually.[105] He simply 'preferred to live a celibate life.' But the case must have been quite different with her. Although she 'agreed and expressed the same as her preference,' at their trial for divorce from bed and board, her 'attorney attempted to make out of this that she was deprived of one of the chief pleasures of life.'[106] From this statement and her outbursts of jealousy, it can be recognized that Maria Russell was, understandably, a sexually frustrated woman. Strangely, almost no one who has discussed the Russells' marital difficulties has dealt with any of these details, although Pastor Russell did so quite candidly.

But sexual difficulties were not the direct cause of their discord. Rather, the cause was Maria's desire for greater recognition and authority, coupled with a family quarrel over money matters. By 1894 at least, serious strain was beginning to develop between the Russells. Maria was becoming deeply jealous over any attention which her husband showed to other women including Rose Ball, a teenaged girl whom the Russells regarded almost as a foster daughter.[107] In addition, Maria resented what she considered to be Russell's lack of respect for her. She was a much better educated person than was he. Not only had she graduated from high school, but she had received teacher training at the Pittsburgh Curry Normal School. Hence she was able to help her husband with editing *Zion's Watch Tower*, wrote numerous articles for that journal, and co-authored the first four volumes of *Studies in the Scriptures*.[108] Nevertheless, probably because there was no intimate relationship between them, he showed little interest in her except as a writing and publishing assistant. She therefore came to feel that he had no more regard for her than for a serving woman.[109]

Some of those who became involved in the 1894 revolt against Russell's authority which resulted in schism sympathized with Maria and tried to recruit her to their cause. According to the Pastor these 'conspirators endeavored to sow discord in my wife's heart by flattery, women's rights arguments, etc.'[110] But in fact they probably simply felt that he was unnecessarily condescending towards her – a belief which seems to be justified. Nevertheless, when Russell's critics within the society attacked him openly and attempted to expose his marital problems, they went too far: Maria stood loyally, if not entirely honestly, beside her husband. 'Our home,' she said, 'so far from being a discordant one, is the very reverse, – most happy.'[111] She also defended the Pastor's moral character and took the trip mentioned above to speak on his behalf. And it was after her return in December 1895 that she openly indicated that she believed him to be the 'faithful and wise servant' of Matthew 24:45–7.[112]

Yet even while Maria was defending and promoting Russell publicly, the two were quarrelling bitterly. According to her sworn statement, in 1895 Russell proposed a separation: 'He proposed that on the ground of incompatibility that we agree to separate,' she affirmed, 'and if I would do so he would give me that house in which we were living, and when I broke down at the suggestion, he said if I did not agree to it, that I would not get anything.'[113]

No doubt Russell's behaviour towards his wife in this instance was cruel, and his own statements show that he had an exalted opinion of himself in his relations with her.[114] Yet she seems not to have been without serious fault during that time as well. He had reached a point of extreme exasperation, believing that she wanted to tell him what to do in his ministry. 'I was,' he stated, 'continually harassed with suggestions of alterations of my writings.'[115]

Part of the problem was, of course, that Russell and his wife had very different views on the nature of a woman's role in marriage. He was a traditionalist and, in keeping with attitudes common among American Christians in his day, believed that wives ought to be subordinate to their husbands. She, in contrast, was becoming somewhat of a feminist. Speaking about her in 1895 and shortly thereafter, he said later: 'the women's rights' ideas and personal ambition began to come to the top, and I perceived that Mrs Russell's active campaign in my defense, and the very cordial reception given her by the dear friends ... had done her injury by increasing her self-appreciation.'[116] From his point of view, then, his disapproval of her ideas and behaviour was not only proper but, as her Christian head, a duty. She, of course, did not see it that way. Writing in 1906 in a small *apologia* called *The Twain One,* she argued for the equality of the sexes and held that women should rightly serve as teachers in the church. Thinking most probably of her own marriage, she stated: 'If anyone in the church becomes heady, the church needs to beware. Or if the Christian husband, led away by the adversary by pride, or selfishness, or love of power, assumes thus to lord it over his wife and interfere with her supreme allegiance to God, then the Christian wife must beware, and not be beguiled into a "voluntary humility" which would bring under a yoke of bondage to sin a soul whom Christ has made free.'[117]

In 1896 Maria Russell faced another problem, one of her own making. If Russell was the 'faithful and wise servant' of Matthew 24:45–7 as she had postulated, how could she take such a negative attitude towards his authority? The answer is that she quickly came to the conclusion that he was becoming the 'evil servant' described in the next four verses of the same chapter. Russell's account reads:

Gradually her interpretation of 'that servant' worked upon her mind. First she suggested that as in the human body there are two eyes, two ears, two hands, two feet, etc., this might properly enough represent the twain one – she and I as necessarily one in marriage and in spirit and in the Lord. But the ambition did not stop here – (it is a plant of thrifty growth). Within a year Mrs Russell had concluded that the latter part of the statement (viz., Matt. 24:45–51) was not merely a warning, but that it would have actual fulfillment – that it meant that her husband would fulfill this description, and that she in consequence would take his place as 'that servant' in dispensing meat in due season.[118]

Whether Russell's statement is entirely true or not is impossible to say. It does, however, seem reasonable to believe that he was stating the facts. Maria was the originator of the 'faithful and wise servant' doctrine and later held that he had become unfaithful to that office. Also, she did think that she was capable of doing everything that he had done as 'that servant.' Still, there is no evidence that she ever openly applied the title to herself.

Early in 1897 the breach between the two widened, and Maria organized 'a [church] committee along the lines of Matt. 18:17' to hear charges against Russell. Besides raising the question of whether she had a right to publish uncensored articles in *Zion's Watch Tower* or not – a matter about which the two had been quarrelling – she brought up two additional issues. First, she and her sister, Emma Ackley Russell, charged the Pastor with having improperly influenced his father, Joseph Russell, in drawing up the latter's will. Joseph had married Emma some years before and had had a daughter by her in his old age. But when he wanted to prepare a will, he had turned to his son for advice – a fact which had angered Emma. She evidently believed that her stepson, who was also her brother-in-law, was trying to cheat her and her child, and Maria agreed. Second, Maria charged Russell with having failed to show her proper respect at a certain meeting.[119]

Russell replied that the offensive will had been destroyed some time earlier to placate Emma and was therefore a dead issue. As for his supposed rudeness to his wife at the meeting in question, he claimed he had begged forgiveness five times previously, and she had already forgiven him five times. Not surprisingly, the all-male committee came down on their Pastor's side. They must have been taken aback by Russell's answers to the charges against him, and one of them, W.E. Page of Milwaukee, Wisconsin, must have been more than a little disturbed to have been brought hundreds of miles to mediate in what was little more than a domestic dispute. As far as the question of Mrs Russell's demand that she be able to write what she saw fit in *Zion's Watch Tower,* they 'told her kindly but very plainly, that neither they not any other persons in the world had a right to interfer with Bro. Russell's Management of the WATCH TOWER: that it was his stewardship only, and that he alone was accountable for its management.'[120]

Although the Russells kissed and made up, the truce between them did not last. At her behest, he put her in charge of a weekly women's meeting of the Allegheny Bible Student church. Thus, she became the leader of a women's group which quickly became a centre of discontent against the Pastor. Evidently, too, Maria was supported by her sisters, Emma Russell, Lena Guibert, and Laura Raynor, in carrying on a whispering campaign against him and in declaring that they were no longer members of the Allegheny church.[121]

When Russell became aware of what was happening, he took drastic action. In clear violation of his own stated principles, he summoned some of his wife's women supporters before a meeting of the board of elders of the Allegheny church to charge them with slander. Using the argument that Maria and her sisters had withdrawn from the church, he had them excluded from the meeting. Next, he wrote angry letters to his father, Emma Russell, and Laura Raynor in which he called on them 'not to receive or harbor or entertain my wife under your roof under any pretext whatsoever.' Thus he attempted successfully to assert his authority in both the congregation and his own household; and again the Russells attempted another reconciliation. In September 1897, Russell, Maria, and her sisters signed a written agreement to forget past grievances and to treat one another with kindness. But on 9 November of the same year, Maria left her marital home, never to return.[122]

She immediately travelled to Chicago where again she attempted to bring charges against Russell before what was then the second largest Bible Student congregation in the world. When she was unable to accomplish anything there, she proposed to go back to her husband. But he refused to have her unless she agreed to his terms. In January 1899, she returned to Allegheny to live with the then widowed Emma Russell and to renew her public attacks on the Pastor. Fifteen months later the Russells again made peace and Maria moved into a rooming house next to her sister's which Russell owned. Although he refused to support her directly, he did provide her with furniture and allowed her to live on the income which she was able to obtain from a number of tenants.

Even though they were living apart, the truce between them did not last. Between April 1899 and the early months of 1903, Maria Russell laid aside enough money to prepare, print, and publish a tract which was an account of her relations with her husband over the years and another bitter attack on him. In it she published correspondence between them and attempted, with some success, to paint him as an arrogant tyrant. To make matters worse, she distributed tracts to all Bible Students she could reach and sent additional bundles of tracts to various clergymen with a note to the effect that they should circulate them to Bible Students wherever possible.

Russell was furious to say the least, and he decided to punish his wife for her action. Sometime in mid-March 1903 he and several associates from the Bible House, the Watch Tower headquarters, took possession of the boarding-house in which she and four or five tenants lived and removed all their personal possessions. Russell even went so far as to take his wife's purse with all of the rental money she still had in it and nearly got into a fistfight with one of the tenants when the latter discovered that his and his roommate's properties had been removed from their quarters. Not surprisingly, Russell soon found himself in court. Two angry tenants sued him for violating their terms of lease, one of them charged him with assault, and Maria sued him for divorce from bed and board. In all instances Russell lost, except that he was acquitted on the assault charge.[123]

Ultimately, Maria Russell became her husband's most bitter opponent. At their trial for separation, she tried to hurt him in a rather vicious way by stating that he had said that 'he was like a jellyfish floating around, embracing all who would respond.' Although that testimony was disallowed and she admitted under oath that she did not think him guilty of adultery, Mrs Russell succeeded in besmirching her husband's reputation.[124] Later, their battle continued over the question of his refusal to pay her court-awarded financial support, and again she did everything legally possible to make him look bad in the eyes of the world. He claimed he did not have the money and no doubt did not want to provide it to her anyway as she intended to use some of it to print and publish attacks on him.[125] Although she undoubtedly had some very justifiable complaints against him, it is difficult not to feel that, from 1903 on at least, her behaviour towards him was thoroughly vindictive. Yet, over the years, in assessing the bitter quarrels between Charles and Maria Russell, historians have failed to come even near to a consensus on the question of which of the two was more at fault.[126]

The New Covenant Schism

Following closely on the Russells' divorce case came the bitter and significant New Covenant schism. Basically, what happened is that during his quarrel with Nelson Barbour, Russell had developed what came to be known as 'the doctrine of the Mystery,' something which the youthful Pastor, his followers, and many since have conceived of as 'a new truth.' In fact, the Mystery, as understood by Russell, meant that not only had Jesus, the man, offered himself as a ransom sacrifice for mankind, but the body of Christ, the 144,000 members of his church, also participated in the ransoming and atoning work.[127] Russell, of course, did not realize that his 'new truth' had in a general way been part of Catholic doctrine for centuries.[128] That, however, did not matter. What did matter was that as a result of the Mystery doctrine, he also came to hold that members of the church of Christ were not under the New Covenant which the Scriptures spoke of as replacing the covenant that God had made with Israel through Moses. The reason was that the New Covenant could not apply to all mankind until *all* of the members of Christ's body had been sacrificed, had been resurrected, raptured, and joined together with their Lord in heaven. And after 1881, Russell did not expect that to happen until 1914.

In 1880 he was most explicit on the New Covenant. He stated emphatically: 'It should not be construed as being God's covenant with us – "the seed," no that was part of the Abrahamic covenant, and although in harmony with each other, they are not the same, nor is the "new covenant" made with the church at all.'[129] Yet, since as has been demonstrated, Russell was certainly not always a clear thinker, within a year, seemingly quite unconsciously, he reverted to the traditional Christian view that the church was under the New Covenant.[130] As Timothy White notes, he seems to have been thoroughly confused on the matter.[131] Nevertheless, since most of the Bible Students living in the first decade of the twentieth century had joined the movement after 1880, they knew nothing of his earlier thoughts. Consequently, when Russell reasserted his 1880 teaching with certain embellishments, many of the ablest Bible Students were shocked.

Russell would probably not have noted the discrepancy in his teachings had it not been for Paul S.L. Johnson, an able but eccentric colporteur who was to have a major effect on Bible Student history in later years. Johnson had been raised a Jew, was converted to Christianity, became a Lutheran pastor, and finally, a Bible Student. As perhaps Russell's best educated and most studious associate, through research he came upon Russell's 1880 view, pointed it out to him, and encouraged him to restate it.[132] Writing in the January 1907 issue of *Zion's Watch Tower*, Russell did.

Many close associates did their best to get Russell to relinquish this peculiar restated doctrine of the New Covenant. For not only did he hold that the church was not under or within that covenant, but even that the 144,000 did not need or have a mediator. The mediator for the rest of mankind, the *Christ*, was to be Jesus and the church together – the Head *and the body*.[133] But Russell would not be persuaded to give up this doctrine.

Russell's stubbornness made many of his Bible Student critics believe that he was becoming autocratic, and their feelings in this matter were strengthened by a secondary issue – the curious one of 'the vow.' The Russell divorce case brought attention to the matter of 'proper conduct between the sexes' among Bible Students. So, early in 1908, the Pastor developed and took a vow to the Lord which, among other things, stated: 'I further vow that, with the exception below, I will at all times and at all places, conduct myself toward those of the opposite sex in private exactly as I would do with them in public – in the presence of a congregation of the Lord's people, and so far as is reasonably possible I will avoid being in a room with any female alone, unless the door of the room stand wide open – wife, children, mother and sisters excepted.'[134]

No one, of course, objected to Russell's taking of such a vow. He did not, however, stop at that point; he began to promote it for others. In the first place, he suggested that all full- and part-time pilgrims working under the Watch Tower Society's auspices, plus all of 'the brethren of the Bible House family' at Pittsburgh, should take it as well. In a March 1908 general letter, he called on every pilgrim and member of the Bible House family to 'bind himself by a vow to the Lord' and to indicate to Russell in writing that he had done so.[135]

A storm followed. Most of those requested to take the vow did so, but some objected strongly to the whole idea. These latter quoted some of Russell's earlier teachings against vows and expressed resentment that their Pastor had felt free to publish the names of vow-takers in what they regarded as a less than subtle form of spiritual arm-twisting.[136] Russell responded with pique. Said he: 'It seems evident that a few ordinarily bright brethren have missed their education as respects the meaning of the word "vow"' and asserted that he had forced no one to take the vow.[137] While he agreed not to publish the names of vow-takers in the future, he wrote: 'continue to advise us, if you please, when you take the vow. We will preserve an alphabetical list which may be of use some time.'[138] Of course, his critics immediately came to regard this list as a *loyalty* list and were further alienated. Thus the vow became a secondary red flag to many of those concerned about the New Covenant issue.

The leading opponents of Russell's restated New Covenant doctrine and the vow were persons who were both prominent Bible Students and men and women who were among Russell's close and dear associates. They included A.E. Williamson (the Pastor's nephew-in-law); M.L. McPhail; E.C. Henninges, his wife, Rose; and Russell's own sister, Mae Land.[139] Among these, McPhail had served as the first full-time Watch Tower pilgrim in 1894.[140] Henninges had for a time served as secretary-treasurer of the Watch Tower Society, had promoted Bible Student activities in England, and had established a Watch Tower branch office in Melbourne, Australia.[141] In addition, he was married to Rose Ball, the Russells' foster daughter and the young woman to whom Maria Russell claimed her husband had told the infamous jellyfish story.[142]

In 1909 Henninges wrote a long letter of protest to Russell.[143] Shortly thereafter an 'open letter' was circulated 'to all [Bible Students] who realize the necessity for standing firm for the Lord and His Word in the midst of many subtle temptations and trials of this present time: to all who appreciate Jesus as their Mediator, and His blood of the New Covenant as their basis of favor during this Gospel Age.'[144] Following the publication of this letter, most of the Melbourne congregation, some Americans – including Williamson at Brooklyn – and other Bible Students throughout the world left to form the New Covenant Believers.[145]

Russell did not want the New Covenant Believers to leave and would have remained in fellowship with them. What he did not seem to realize was that his position as 'faithful and wise servant,' editor of *Zion's Watch Tower*, and elected Pastor of the Bible Student congregations gave him a pre-eminent role as their spiritual guide. Thus, to oppose his teachings while remaining within the Bible Student community was impossible, and the New Covenant Believers refused to remain silent. To them the traditional doctrine of the New Covenant was as important in 1909 as the doctrine of substitutionary atonement had been to Russell in 1878. Consequently, several hundreds out of a total of perhaps 10,000 Bible Students seceded.[146] Russell did not seem to realize that he had contributed greatly to the sectarianism which he hated so much.

Russell's External Adversaries

Problems caused by schisms among Bible Students and domestic quarrels were not the only tribulations which Russell suffered. Very early in his career he had come to look upon the majority of clergy as false shepherds: They were making no effort to preach Christ's kingdom, were frequently influenced by higher criticism, or were teaching the God-dishonouring doctrines of hellfire and the immortality of the soul. Furthermore, he regarded the passing of collection plates in church as a violation of the scriptural principle, 'Ye received free, give free.' So he adopted as a sort of trademark on his meeting announcements the words: 'Seats Free, No collection.'[147] Both Russell and the Bible Students aired their feelings respecting 'false shepherds' on the printed page and wherever they went. As a result they stirred up a hornet's nest.

Not surprisingly, Russell came under bitter personal attack. Newspapers and individual clergymen implied, after his legal separation in 1906, that he was an adulterer.[148] He was charged with financial chicanery, particularly in what came to be known as the Miracle Wheat episode. He was labelled a perjurer by a Canadian Baptist clergyman, the Reverend J.J. Ross, who asserted that he lied on the witness stand to the effect that he 'knew Greek' when he did not. Both the Miracle Wheat and Ross cases deserve some comment.

In 1904 a man by the name of Stoner, who knew nothing about Russell or the Bible Students, discovered in Fincastle, Virginia, an amazingly productive variety of wheat which he named 'Miracle Wheat.' Seven years later two Bible Students donated thirty bushels of it to the Watch Tower Society to be sold at a dollar per pound as seed grain. The proceeds – some $1,800 – were to be used by the society to carry on its activities. Russell gained nothing personally from the proceeds, but his enemies claimed that the sale was a religious fraud. A New York newspaper, the *Brooklyn Daily Eagle,* attacked him and lampooned both Russell and Miracle Wheat in a cartoon.

Russell sued the *Eagle* but lost. He was evidently quite sincere in selling the famous grain but was more positive about its qualities than he should have been. Miracle Wheat was apparently no more than a mutant strain, a 'sport.' It soon lost its outstanding vitality and was not, as he truly believed, a sign that the earth was soon to be restored to paradisaic conditions.[149]

J.J. Ross's charge that Russell perjured himself has been repeated and believed time and again. Yet it was Ross, not Russell, who bore false witness. In a pamphlet published after Russell's criminal action against him, Ross misquoted his lawyer as asking Russell if he 'knew the Greek.' Actually what the lawyer, George Lynch-Staunton, asked was: 'Do you know the Greek alphabet?' Russell simply answered, 'Oh, yes.' He made no claim whatsoever about knowing anything more of Greek or any other second language than that. Ross therefore distorted the truth.[150]

It is impossible to deal with all of Russell's trials and tribulations here, but a careful examination of each indicates that he was basically honest even when he was thoroughly misguided. In fact, his personal life was generally free from blemish. Furthermore, he was generally an attractive, kindly man, who was completely devoted to the stewardship which he believed to be his. But there can be no doubt that he had a streak of arrogant pride and that he was sometimes guileless to the point of naïveté. In one major relationship – his marriage – he lacked sensitivity and normal affection. Although he was no doubt blameless of fraud in the Miracle Wheat affair, he should have had better sense than to sell grain with that name to support evangelism. Had he used any forethought at all, he would have realized the bad odour that such a venture would cause. Also, had he taken time to think, he would have recognized his wife's sexual frustration and become a husband to her in more than name. But in spite of those real shortcomings, in comparing him with other nineteenth- and early-twentieth-century American religious leaders such as Joseph Smith, Ellen White, Mary Baker Eddy, and Amee Semple McPherson, Russell's character fares rather well.

Russell's Last Years and Death

During his last years Russell was lionized by the Bible Student community, and his sermons were published in both America and Europe while he travelled far and wide by train and steamship. In many ways, life must have been pleasant for him. On trips he spared no expense in making himself and his travelling companions, who included physicians, retired generals, professors, and judges, most comfortable. When he visited his widespread congregations, he was regularly surrounded by adoring men and women. After all, was he not their Pastor, 'that servant'? Still, his life was far from a bed of roses. He was almost constantly involved in litigation between 1903 and 1913, during which time he was sharply criticized by both the clergy and some segments of the press. Also he worked incredibly hard, driving himself as his health began to fail. Finally, as 1914 drew near, he began to become nervous about the possible disconfirmation of the Gentile Times prophecy that had been such a prominent part of his teachings since before his break with Nelson Barbour.

For years Russell and the Bible Students had expected that the Gentile nations of the world would go down in destruction during that year, or perhaps in 1915 if the 1914 date proved wrong. The saints were to be taken to heaven to be with Christ (since that had not happened in 1874, 1878, or 1881) and Christ's millennial rule over the earth was to begin. As the fateful year drew near, however, Russell had begun to hedge his ideas concerning it. Originally, he had been absolutely certain that it would bring the end. In *The Time Is at Hand* he had written that 1914 marked 'the farthest limit of the rule of imperfect man,'[151] but by the first decades of the twentieth century he was becoming more and more cautious. Melvin Curry states:

Russell used a number of devices to negate in advance the effect of prophetic failure. First, he denied that he was inspired and argued that his predictions were based on faith and were therefore not infallible, however, he still contended that the Biblical evidence is so strong 'that faith in the chronology almost becomes knowledge.' Second, he affirmed that his failure to predict accurately the events of 1914 'would merely prove that our chronology, our "alarm clock," went off a little before the time,' and that 'the error could not be very great.' For example, he conceded that the Gentile Times 'may end in October 1914, or in October 1915.' Third, he narrowed the predictions so that they were restricted to non-empirical supernatural events, such as, the expiration of 'the lease of power granted to the Gentile nations' and the end of 'the harvest period of the Gospel Age.' Fourth, in 1904 he reversed the sequence of events expected to occur and contended that 'world wide anarchy' would follow the ending of the Gentile Times in 1914 rather than proceed [*sic*] it. Fifth, he changed his prediction that the collapse of Christendom would be 'sudden and awful' to a denial that the nations 'will all fall to pieces in that year.' Instead, he claimed that the earthly phase of the kingdom will be established later than 1914; this left a period of time after the expiration of the Gentile lease for the fall of the nations and the 'gradual establishment of the kingdom on earth.' Finally, he likened his possible chronological error to other Biblical uncertainties.[152]

Russell nevertheless continued to believe what was now his own system, and by 1913 there was great millenarian excitement among the Bible Students. Thus, when the First World War broke out in 1914, Russell took *it* as a confirmation of his chronological, prophetic speculations. Unlike many of his followers, even at the Watch Tower Society's headquarters in Brooklyn, he was not discomfitted by the fact that he and they had not been taken away in the clouds. In his book *Faith on the March*, A.H. Macmillan recounts what happened in the autumn of 1914: 'Friday morning (October 2) we were all seated at the breakfast table when Russell came down. As he entered the room he hesitated a moment as was his custom and said cheerily, "Good morning, all." But this morning, instead of proceeding to his seat as usual, he briskly clapped his hands and happily announced: "The Gentile times have ended; the kings have had their day." We all applauded.'[153]

Bible Students throughout much of the world applauded. Although 1914 had not brought the end, like Jehovah's Witnesses today they were quite willing to accept the idea that the outbreak of the First World War in Europe had really proved that the Barbour–Russell chronology was basically sound.[154] Yet while the coming of the war saved their community from another major crisis of faith – at least immediately – it created other extremely grave problems. For one thing, since in their view the Gentile Times had ended, the Bible Students' 'apolitical apocalypticism' increased greatly. Russell took a stronger position in support of conscientious objection and condemned clergymen in Canada for acting as recruiting agents for the 'dragon's teeth of war.'[155] Of course, in taking this position in the United States from 1914 through 1916, he and his followers were not out of step with the majority of their countrymen. But the same was not true in other parts of the world; and in the summer of 1916, Russell was prohibited entry into Canada by Canadian immigration officers angered at him for 'interfering with recruiting' in the British Empire.[156]

Much more serious for the Bible Students was the fact that Russell died in great pain on a train in the southwestern United States on 31 October 1916.[157] He had been tired and ill for some time but insisted on carrying out his preaching and pastoral duties to his widespread flock to the very end. For in his last years of life he was convinced that the First World War would terminate in 1918 in the battle of Armageddon and the rapture of the church.[158] So, while his death saved him from the disillusionment that he might have felt had he lived to see the war end without the nations of the world passing into oblivion, it came at a most inopportune time for his followers. They had not expected to see their Pastor, 'that servant,' die before the end of the world and were not psychologically prepared to carry on his and their ministry into the future. More significantly, they were to be greatly disturbed by the fact that the church was again not 'taken home' to heaven, the Jews were not restored to Palestine, and the nations of the world were not broken in pieces as Russell had predicted when the war ended with the Treaty of Versailles rather than the apocalypse. In fact, the Bible Student movement nearly fell apart in 1917 and 1918 because of power struggles among Russell's successors and because of persecution from secular governments and mobs that came upon them after the United States entered the war in April 1917. Although Russell had made some plans for his death and the continuation of his work thereafter, he could have had no idea of what was soon to take place.

CHAPTER TWO

The Creation of
a Theocracy

On 6 January 1917, Judge Joseph Franklin Rutherford,[1] for some years Russell's personal lawyer, was chosen president of the Watch Tower Bible and Tract Society and its associate organizations to replace the late Pastor. With his election, a new era in the history of the Bible Student–Jehovah's Witnesses began.

Joseph Franklin Rutherford

Born on 8 November 1869 in Missouri and raised on the small farm of his Baptist parents, Rutherford was a very different man from Russell. Instead of growing up in a big-city atmosphere under the loving guidance of a prosperous and benevolent father, Rutherford had to work very hard in near poverty. By dint of great personal effort, he studied law under the old apprentice system then quite common in the United States and passed his bar examinations in 1892. On a few occasions he served as a substitute judge. Probably as a result of these early experiences and a commitment to the populist ideals of William Jennings Bryan,[2] he developed a strong personality, an outspoken although seldom-manifested sympathy for the downtrodden, and a thoroughgoing contempt for big business, politicians, and later, the clergy.

Like Russell, Rutherford was a big man, who, by his very presence, could demand respect. He had a loud, booming voice and looked every inch like a southern or border-state American senator. In relating to friends, he could be despotic; in dealing with enemies, ruthless. The Watch Tower Society's official history, *Jehovah's Witnesses in the Divine Purpose,* describes him as 'a brisk and direct type of person' with a 'directness in approach to problems in dealing with his brothers which caused some to take offense.'[3] In fact, he was moody and sometimes blunt to the point of rudeness with an explosive temper that could occasionally excite him to physical violence. He also had a streak of self-righteousness which caused him to regard anyone who opposed him as of the Devil. But most curious was the fact that while in some ways he was a Puritan of Puritans, in others he was thoroughly dissolute. He used vulgar language, suffered from alcoholism, and was once publicly accused by one of his closest associates of attending a nude burlesque show with two fellow elders and a young Bible Student woman on a Wednesday evening before the celebration of the Memorial of the Lord's Supper.[4]

However, there was much more to him than this terse, rather unflattering description would indicate. Rutherford first became acquainted with the Bible Students in 1894. In 1906 he was baptized and shortly thereafter became a pilgrim. After a time he became quite popular with his fellow believers because, as an attorney, he fought suits at law to clear Russell's name, debated publicly in defence of Bible Student doctrines, and, in 1915, penned an apology on behalf of Russell entitled *A Great Battle in the Ecclesiastical Heavens*.

It was, therefore, Rutherford's ability, his dynamic rhetoric, and his willingness to deal with Bible Student adversaries like a twentieth-century Jeremiah that made him a logical successor to Russell. Hence, in just over two months after the latter's death, he was unanimously elected president of the Watch Tower Society and its associate organs, although Russell had certainly not designated him as his spiritual heir.

In fact, Russell had hoped that his position as chief spokesman for the Bible Students would be taken over by a collective leadership. According to his will, *The Watch Tower* was to be under the superintendence of an editorial committee of five, and no article was to be published without the agreement of at least three members of that committee.[5] Interestingly, Rutherford was not named to the committee and was named only as one of five possible alternate members.[6] So, while Russell had had no intention of passing on his authority or role intact to any individual successor, Rutherford had other ideas.

Rutherford was an autocrat who obviously believed that for the good of the society – and all Bible Students – he should rule it with a rod of iron rather than simply administer the decisions of its board of directors. Although he refused to assume the title 'Pastor' in deference to Russell's memory,[7] he used Bible Student reverence for Russell as a prop for his his own authority. Furthermore, it is obvious that from before the time of his first election, he intended to wield as much if not more power than his predecessor.[8]

The Watch Tower Schism of 1917

Offical Witness history suggests that during the short period between Russell's death and Rutherford's election as Watch Tower president, others were scheming to attain that office also. Several figures are listed as among the 'schemers,' but the arch-villain, according to this account, was Paul S.L. Johnson. Accordingly, Johnson is described as the prime instigator of what was shortly to become a major schism in the Bible Student community during the summer of 1917. Briefly stated, the Watch Tower account goes as follows.

Before his death, Russell had instructed Alexander H. Macmillan, his personal, presidential assistant, to send Johnson to Great Britain to oversee the activities of the International Bible Students Association (IBSA) there. Consequently, as one of the triumvirate which administered the society's affairs from November 1917 through the first week of 1918, Rutherford dispatched him to London. When he arrived, he discovered the British organization in turmoil and dismissed two of the society's local officers, H.J. Shearn and William Crawford. According to Johnson, these men were plotting to create a separate organization independent from the Watch Tower Society in America. But Johnson himself then attempted to assume an independent role and claimed that he, personally, was Russell's successor and the steward of the penny mentioned in Jesus's parable at Matthew 20:1–16. Upon receiving word of what was transpiring, Rutherford cabled Johnson with the demand that he restore Shearn and Crawford.[9]

At that point Johnson began to send cables to Rutherford, certain that if he were 'enlightened,' he would support him. He believed that Rutherford was 'undoubtedly the victim of a cablegram campaign engineered by Shearn and Crawford.'[10] So he dispatched cablegrams of 85 to 115 words in which he identified himself and others with Ezra, Nehemiah, and Mordecai. Evidently he asked Rutherford to serve as his 'right-hand man.'[11]

Rutherford became convinced that Johnson was demented and cabled him to return to America. Thereupon Johnson sent a cablegram to Watch Tower Vice-President Alfred I. Ritchie and Secretary-Treasurer William E. Van Amburgh, the other two members of the triumvirate, repudiating Rutherford's authority. Using the statement of powers granted him when he had been sent to Britain, he tied up the International Bible Students' bank account and took over the London offices of the IBSA. He and another Bible Student named Housden seized all mails, opened the association's safe, and took all its on-hand funds. As a result, Rutherford, by then president, sent written cancellation of Johnson's appointment, and the latter's lawyer was forced to drop a suit to prohibit Rutherford loyalists from using £800 which had been temporarily tied up in the bank.[12]

Led by Rutherford loyalist Jesse Hemery, a group of Bible Students at the IBSA's London offices and residence eventually barricaded Johnson in his room. To escape, he was forced to leave by his window and climb down an outside drainpipe. Thereafter, he returned to New York where 'Rutherford established that Johnson was perfectly sane on every point but one, himself.'[13] Rutherford then reorganized the society's work in Britain under Hemery and brought peace. Johnson continued to demand to be sent back to that country, but Rutherford refused to send him.[14]

Then followed a bitter fight between Joseph F. Rutherford and four members of the Watch Tower Society's board of directors: Alfred I. Ritchie (who had been replaced in January as vice-president by Andrew N. Pierson), Robert H. Hirsh, Isaac F. Hoskins, and J. Dennis Wright. According to the Watch Tower version of events, these men were unhappy with Rutherford early in 1917 and 'ambitiously sought to gain administrative control of the Society.' As a result, when Johnson returned to Brooklyn he influenced the four members of the board of directors to work against Rutherford.[15]

The Watch Tower account then states that the board of directors determined to amend the society's bylaws in order to strip Rutherford of his legitimate authority and turn him into a figurehead. As a result, Rutherford was forced to remove them from office. He obtained the written opinion of a non-Bible Student Philadelphia lawyer to the effect that since the four directors had not been legally elected in January 1917, but were merely Russell's appointees, they had no legal right to remain in control of the Society. The *1975 Yearbook of Jehovah's Witnesses* states:

C.T. Russell had appointed those men as directors, but the Society's charter required that directors be elected by vote of the shareholders. Rutherford had told Russell that appointees had to be confirmed by vote at the following annual meeting, but Russell never took that step. So, only the officers who had been elected at the Pittsburgh annual meeting were duly constituted board members. The four appointees were not legal members of the board. Rutherford knew this throughout the period of trouble, but had not mentioned it, hoping that these board members would discontinue their opposition. However, their attitude showed they were not qualified to be directors. Rightly Rutherford dismissed them and appointed four new board members whose appointment could be confirmed at the next general corporation meeting, early in 1918.[16]

So, on 12 July 1917, Rutherford secretly declared the four removed and replaced them with A.H. Macmillan, W.E. Spill, J.A. Bohnet, and G.H. Fisher, all Rutherford supporters who were to be confirmed at the society's next annual general meeting.[17]

On 17 July, Rutherford released *The Finished Mystery* as a seventh volume to Russell's *Studies in the Scriptures*.[18] Russell had often spoken of writing the seventh volume[19] but had never found the 'key' or, more likely, the time and energy. Now, however, Rutherford released a book made up of various comments from Russell's works, plus numerous additions by the co-authors, Clayton J.

Woodworth and George H. Fisher, in a commentary on Revelation, Ezekiel, and the Song of Solomon. Styled the posthumous work of Pastor Russell, *The Finished Mystery* was an allegorical interpretation of the three books of Scripture and a panegyric to Russell.

The release of *The Finished Mystery* to the assembled Watch Tower Bethel family – the staff – at breakfast came as a 'bombshell' and, according to Watch Tower history, served to cause an open schism. Johnson, the deposed directors, and their supporters censured Rutherford in a long, bitter, breakfast-table debate.[20] On 27 July, to keep peace, Rutherford asked Johnson to leave Bethel, and, shortly thereafter, he did the same with the ex-directors.[21]

In all of this, Rutherford's supporters have pictured him as long-suffering and completely justified in his actions. Alexander H. Macmillan, writing many years later, remarked: 'He did everything that he could to help his opposers see their mistake, holding a number of meetings with them, trying to reason with them and trying to show them how contrary their course was to the Society's charter and the entire program Russell had followed since the organization was formed.'[22] But, in fact, the official Watch Tower account and Macmillan's picture of Rutherford are nothing more than thoroughgoing distortions of the truth.

Even the basic outline given in Watch Tower accounts is not accurate. It is quite true that several saw themselves as prospective successors to Russell in November and December of 1916. It is also quite true that Paul Johnson was a strange, erratic person who had caused Russell much trouble through his bad advice and who had visions of glory, to say the least.[23] Otherwise, the official version of the events of 1917 is false history.

In the first place, Rutherford and his supporters were playing hard-fisted church politics and were no angels. Although Rutherford had certainly been the most outstanding candidate for the presidency, his election had been engineered largely by two men – Alexander H. Macmillan and William E. Van Amburgh.[24] Second, at the time of his election he had insisted that the directors pass a series of bylaws which gave the society's officers greatly expanded authority.[25] Third, Rutherford's commissioning of the writing and publication of *The Finished Mystery* was a high-handed, unilateral action which certainly ignored the rights and prerogatives of the board and several members of the society's editorial committee.[26] Although Rutherford claimed he was exercising rights granted him under the People's Pulpit Association charter which gave the president 'the general supervision and control and management of the business and affairs of said corporation,' this did not give him plenipotentiary powers to formulate policy.[27] Furthermore, just as is the case today with the New York Watchtower Society, the People's Pulpit Association was, for all practical purposes, treated as subsidiary to the Watch Tower Bible and Tract Society and received all its operating funds from that corporation. Fourth, he and his 'kitchen cabinet' virtually ignored the supervisory rights, not only of the four directors, but of Vice-President Pierson as well.[28] Fifth, Rutherford, by trying to act as had Russell, in effect was ignoring Russell's expressed wishes as outlined in his will.[29] And, finally, had Rutherford ever been taken to court for dismissing the four directors, he might very well have lost. His contention that they were not legally elected does not bear up under close scrutiny, particularly in the case of Robert Hirsh who had never been appointed by Russell and had, for a time, been a Rutherford supporter. Then, too, as Vice-President Pierson, the ousted directors' lawyers, and Paul Johnson all pointed out, if the directors were not legally elected, neither were the society's three officers: Rutherford, Pierson, and Van Amburgh. In order to have been chosen officers in January 1917, they would have had to have been legally elected directors. Yet they had not been, and hence, by Rutherford's own logic, did not hold office legally.[30]

The suggestion that Rutherford and his supporters were reasonable, while their adversaries were not, hardly fits the facts either. Macmillan, who continued as presidential assistant under Rutherford, was an intelligent man with an open, pleasant personality. But he was also deeply disliked by the directors as a schemer and a religious politician of the first order.[31] Van Amburgh, a dapper, thin, white-haired man with rimless glasses and a goatee, detested democratic procedure and controlled Watch Tower accounts so that no one else but the society's president could see them.[32] During the Miracle Wheat trial he had hurt Pastor Russell as much as he had helped him by his unwillingness to give frank testimony.[33] But the least rational of all was Clayton J. Woodworth, one of the co-authors of *The Finished Mystery*. In later years he was to prove himself a thoroughgoing health faddist and hater of the medical profession, while in 1917 he was given to the sort of wild, allegorical interpretation that Paul Johnson engaged in.

With respect to that allegorical interpretation, Woodworth even outdid Johnson, a fact which has caused one historian to remark that 'in all probability, Johnson was as sane as his accusers.'[34] In fact, one is tempted to wonder if, in so far as the use of the Scriptures was concerned, they were not all equally mad. Woodworth used Matthew 20 to interpret Bible Student activities in 1917 just as Johnson had attempted to do earlier, and Rutherford and those around him evidently accepted Woodworth's ideas. In a five-page pamphlet called *The Parable of the Penny*, Woodworth claimed that the penny actually represented *The Finished Mystery*, Christ was the 'Lord of the vineyard,' and the 'steward' to whom Christ spoke in the illustration was none other than Judge Rutherford. The society's three hundred colporteurs were compared to the members of Gideon's band at Judges 7:3, 19–23. The dismissed directors were seen as the workers who wanted more than a penny in wages and complained against the 'goodman of the house.' In that instance, Rutherford was also held to be that 'goodman.'

No doubt it was Rutherford's personal behaviour, however, rather than that of his party which caused most of the problems. He was extremely secretive and refused to show any sense of responsibility to the board of directors. He not only kept the printing of *The Finished Mystery* a secret from the society's editorial board, but used donated money for its printing which was never placed in the society's accounts.[35] Equally seriously, he and Van Amburgh adamantly refused to allow anyone to inspect the society's books or to audit them. When Vice-President Andrew N. Pierson, the man who had originally nominated Rutherford for the office of president, asked to see them, he was told that he could only do so if he would agree to resign his office.[36] Pierson stated publicly in writing: 'We never had a satisfactory report from the treasurer since I have been a director. We do not know how the trust fund stands, nor how the Watch Tower Bible and Tract Society stands. What are the financial relations between the Watch Tower Bible and Tract Society and the People's Pulpit Association? How is the trust fund invested? What are the securities? What do they draw?'[37] Then, too, few others saw in Rutherford the kindness that Macmillan did. Johnson claimed that during the hearings which the Judge held with him after returning from Britain, Rutherford was both cruel and hateful.[38]

Just before Johnson was forced to leave Bethel on 27 July 1917, the deposed directors and Vice-President Pierson claimed that Rutherford rushed at him in a rage and attacked him physically. Their full account states:

At the noonday meal, Brother Rutherford reported to the Bethel Family that we would be compelled to leave the Bethel home by Monday noon. The brethren then considered it their duty to make some statement to the Family. Brother Rutherford wished the Family to hear only his statement; but we persisted, and one of our number said that he wished to read a letter from Brother Pierson stating that he 'would stand by the old Board.' Brother Rutherford refused to let the letter be read and shouted that Brother Johnson had been to see Brother Pierson and had misrepresented the matter to him. Upon Brother Johnson's firm denial of this, Brother Rutherford hastened to him and using physical force, which nearly pulled Brother Johnson off his feet, said in a fit of passion: 'You will leave this house before night; if you do not go, you will be put out.' Before night this threat was carried into effect. Brother Johnson's personal effects were literally set outside the Bethel Home and brethren, as watchmen, were placed at various doors to prevent him from entering the house again.[39]

In fact, in seizing complete control of the Watch Tower Society in 1917, Rutherford acted fully as though he was carrying out a Communist party purge rather than protecting the society from 'opposers.' He had seen nothing wrong with having Macmillan call on a policeman to have Wright, Hoskins, Ritchie, and Hirsh – then still fully recognized directors of the Watch Tower Society – ejected from the society's offices on Hicks Street,[40] even though he was still bound to regard them as brothers in Christ. And when the four were forced to leave the Brooklyn Bethel, they were treated with the greatest harshness that Rutherford and his supporters could manifest. Later Hirsh and Hoskins were removed as directors of the People's Pulpit Association, probably quite illegally, when on 31 July Rutherford and Macmillan used proxies from shareholders of that organization, which had been entrusted to them for the election of the previous January, to vote them out of office.[41]

It should not be inferred from this that the ousted directors were faultless; they were not. The New York ecclesia of Bible Students saw fault on both sides of the quarrels within the society.[42] Vice-President Pierson vacillated between Rutherford and his adversaries, but in the end he died in fellowship with the society's president.[43] Nevertheless, in retrospect, what Ritchie, Hirsh, Hoskins, and Wright demanded of Rutherford seems far more reasonable than the society would like to admit today. Perhaps even the society's officers know that. As recently as the late 1950s when William Cumberland, then working on a doctoral dissertation at the University of Iowa, sought to examine documents from the society relative to the 1917 schism, they refused to let him have them. He was forced to obtain them from the Dawn Bible Students, in many ways the heirs of Rutherford's adversaries.[44]

The expulsion of Johnson and the ex-directors from Bethel was followed by a pamphlet war, with the various parties presenting their sides of the issue. Rutherford's opponents hoped to unseat him at the upcoming annual meeting of the society's shareholders scheduled for January 1918. They suggested that Menta Sturgeon, Russell's private secretary and the man who was with him when he died, would make a good president.[45] But Rutherford completely outmanoeuvred them. The judge called for a democratic straw vote among the Bible Students in November 1917. While the vote was not binding, it laid the basis for his and his associates' re-election. No doubt the Bible Student community looked upon the society as a sacred institution because it had been so closely associated with Russell. Thus, since Rutherford controlled it during the autumn and winter, he obtained the support of most Bible Students, even though few knew what was going on.[46]

When the shareholders met, Rutherford was re-elected while his opponents received only a small percentage of the votes. Even Vice-President Pierson, who had wavered in his support of the judge, failed to maintain a position on the board of directors.[47] The four deposed directors and Johnson had, therefore, to submit to Rutherford and his associates or separate permanently. They chose the latter course.

By the spring of 1918 the dissidents determined to meet separately for the annual celebration of the Memorial of the Lord's Supper with those groups of Bible Students who supported them. Two new movements developed: one around three of the four former Watch Tower directors, and another around Paul Johnson. These were the Pastoral Bible Institute and the Layman's Home Missionary Society.[48] On the west coast of the United States and Canada a third group, calling themselves 'Standfasters,' also broke with the society. Although they were no doubt affected by events in New York, their primary concern was that the society had not firmly opposed involvement in patriotic endeavours during the First World War.[49]

The Bible Students and the First World War

As indicated earlier, Russell and the Bible Students were strongly opposed to participation in the war. Although they saw it as a fulfilment of prophecy, they regarded the nations involved as demonically controlled and outside God's favour. As a result, Bible Student men who refused to serve as combatants when conscripted for military service often underwent imprisonment and brutal treatment, and in a few cases were executed.[50]

When the Watch Tower Society launched a stinging campaign against clergy support for the war in the United States, Canada, and Great Britain during the summer of 1917, reaction was not long in coming. During the autumn of that year Canadian Bible Students distributed great numbers of *The Finished Mystery* and tracts entitled *The Bible Students Monthly,* both of which carried attacks on militarism and the clergy.[51] In January 1918, the Canadian government banned those publications and began an all-out campaign of persecution against the Bible Students.[52]

The clergy and others took up a cry against them in the United States. Bible Students began to be arrested, mobbed, tarred and feathered, and harassed throughout the country.[53] Warrants were issued for the arrest of eight directors of the Watch Tower Society: J.F. Rutherford, W.E. Van Amburgh, A.H. Macmillan, R.J. Martin, C.J. Woodworth, G.H. Fisher, F.H. Robinson, and Giovanni De Cecca. The charge against them was sedition under the terms of the American Espionage Act. On 21 June, seven of them were sentenced to twenty years each in the federal penitentiary at Atlanta, Georgia; De Cecca was given ten years. Thirteen days later, after they were refused bail pending appeal, the eight were taken to Atlanta where they were to be held for nine months. At that time, the remaining headquarters staff of the Watch Tower Society moved from Brooklyn back to Pittsburgh. Though they continued to publish *The Watch Tower* and *Herald of Christ's Presence,* in most other ways the Bible Students seemed nearly destroyed as a movement.[54]

Over the winter, Rutherford and his fellow directors were heartened by their re-election to office by members of the Watch Tower Society meeting in Pittsburgh in January 1919. Macmillan looked upon that election as a sign of Jehovah's favour. Unintentionally admitting that all previous elections of the society's officers had been predetermined – including the one held in 1917 – he stated to Judge Rutherford: 'This is the first time since the Society was incorporated that it can become clearly evident whom Jehovah would like to serve as president.'[55] Of course, the anti-Rutherford group had already been purged from the society's ranks and was no longer any threat. Second, the imprisoned directors were now seen as martyrs by Bible Students who were themselves experiencing persecution. All things being considered, it would have been surprising had Macmillan not received his sign of divine favour.

In March 1919, Justice Louis Brandeis of the u.s. Supreme Court ordered that Rutherford and his fellow directors be released on bail. In April, Judge Ward of the Federal Second Court of Appeal at New York declared: 'The defendants in this case did not have the temperate and impartial trial of which they were entitled, and for this reason judgement is reversed.' A year later the United States government dropped all charges against them.[56]

Post-war Reorganization

Upon release from Atlanta, Judge Rutherford began a major reorganization of Bible Student activities. On 4 May 1919, he addressed a convention at Los Angeles, and when his remarks were well received he determined to call a general convention of American and Canadian Bible Students at Cedar Point, Ohio.[57] At Cedar Point he declared that the Bible Students must 'bear the divine message of reconciliation to the world'; and to aid them, he announced the publication of a new magazine, *The Golden Age,*[58] in violation of a specific provision in Russell's will.[59]

In the autumn of 1919, the Bible Students began regular house-to-house distribution of *The Golden Age.*[60] More important, in 1920 'class workers,' that is individual Bible Students engaged in public evangelism, began to report their activities to the Watch Tower Society. *Jehovah's Witnesses in the Divine Purpose* indicates somewhat incorrectly what was then taking place under the new Watch Tower Society president: 'The tightening up of preaching responsibility began in 1920 when everyone in the congregation who participated in the witness work was required [sic] to turn in a weekly report. Before 1918 only colporteurs or pioneers [full-time evangelists] had reported their service activity. Definite territory assignments were being made to the congregations for their own field work. For the first year of reporting, 1920, there were 8,052 "class workers" and 350 pioneers.'[61] Thus began one of the greatest proselytizing campaigns in history – one which continues to this day.

Rutherford was anxious to extend preaching activities in lands outside the United States. So in 1920, at the same time that the public preaching work was being reorganized at congregational level, he made a number of important changes in Bible Student organization abroad. The Canadian branch office of the International Bible Students was moved from Winnipeg, Manitoba, to Toronto, Ontario.[62] On a trip to Britain, the European continent, Palestine, and Egypt, the judge provided for the establishment of a Central European Watch Tower branch office and printing plant at Zurich, Switzerland.[63] In addition, he created another branch at Ramallah, Palestine, within sight of Jerusalem.[64] In 1921 there was further expansion, and the Watch Tower counted eighteen foreign branches and twelve domestic American branch offices, formed to serve foreign-language groups in the United States.[65]

Millions Now Living Will Never Die

A major factor in Bible Student growth in numbers and activity during the early 1920s was something besides improved organization; it was the 'Millions Now Living Will Never Die' campaign. Shortly before his imprisonment in 1918 Judge Rutherford had delivered a talk with that title in California, but it was not until September 1920 that a book by the same name was published and heralded by a major speaking program and newspaper advertisements. The book was translated into eleven foreign languages – including Yiddish, Maylayalam, and Burmese – and became a best-seller. What evidently sparked so much interest besides the title of the new publication was the suggestion that the millennium would begin in 1925. That projection, based on Jubilee Year calculations found originally in *Three Worlds,* caused Rutherford to speculate that there would be a 'full restoration' of mankind at that time. Further, he stated: 'We may expect 1925 to witness the return of those faithful men of Israel [Abraham, Isaac, and Jacob] from the condition of death, being resurrected and fully restored to perfect humanity and made the visible, legal representatives of the new order of things on earth.'[66]

It is true that the judge, like Pastor Russell before him, claimed no inspiration for his ideas and in the next year took a more careful stance in *The Harp of God.* There he remarked: 'Chronology, to some extent at least, depends on accurate calculations and there is always some possibility of mistakes. Fulfilled prophecy is the record of physical facts which are actually existent and definitely fixed.'[67] Neither Rutherford nor his colleagues really paid much attention to this caveat, however, and continued to proclaim the forecasts published in *Millions Now Living Will Never Die.* For example, in *The Way to Paradise,* published in 1924,

William E. Van Amburgh prophesied in even greater detail all that was to transpire in the following year and immediately thereafter.[68] Consequently, as 1925 drew near, great excitment was generated among the Bible Students. According to reports still circulated by persons who were then members of the Bible Student community, many gave up their businesses, jobs, and even sold their homes in the expectation that they would soon be living in an earthly paradise. So when Judge Rutherford admitted in the 15 February 1925 *Watch Tower* that perhaps too much had been expected for that year,[69] it was too late. Numerous Bible Student farmers in both Canada and the United States refused to seed their spring crops and mocked their co-religionists who did. Thus, when 1926 came without the appearance of Abraham or the other 'ancient worthies,' and with no signs of paradise, there was great disappointment.

Although Rutherford failed to admit any real fault in the matter in the society's publications, he did give uncharacteristic apologies at IBSA conventions. Evidently, too, he was chagrined. In a public address given in Australia early in 1975, the present president of the Watch Tower Society, Frederick W. Franz, stated that the judge had admitted 'that he had made an ass of himself over 1925.' Yet this did not stop him from continuing to proclaim that the end of the world was 'near at hand' and might be expected within a few years or even a few months. Neither did the fact that he had prophesied falsely seem to give him second thoughts about the Bible Students' preaching campaign, his ministry, or his desire to maintain and increase his personal powers. But as events were to show, many Bible Students felt quite differently: the débâcle of 1925, coupled with a growing resentment against the Watch Tower's president, was to cause many thousands to leave the movement within the next few years.

Rutherford's Ministry

During the years following 1925, Rutherford poured forth a flood of new books and booklets including *Deliverance* in 1926, *Creation* in 1927, *Reconciliation, Government and Life* in 1929, and a number of others until the publication of *Children,* his last work, in 1941. In fact he produced an average of one book per year, and his publications reached a total of 36 million copies.[70] But he was not just a writer. He proved to be every bit as much a human dynamo as Pastor Russell had been. Again and again he spoke at Watch Tower conventions, over national and international radio between the mid-1920s and 1937, and on many phonograph recordings.

Conventions

Very important also was the fact that Rutherford made Bible Student–Jehovah's

Witness conventions into great publicity events. Although they had been important in Russell's lifetime, they had been little more than spiritual gatherings for the Bible Students themselves. Under Rutherford that changed dramatically.

Between 1922 and 1928 the Watch Tower Society held a series of conventions which Jehovah's Witnesses today believe were the seven angelic trumpet blasts mentioned at Revelation 8:1–9 and 11:15–19.[71] Accordingly, each convention condemned part of 'Satan's organization,' or Satan himself. In 1922 at Cedar Point, Ohio, the clergy's support for the League of Nations was condemned as disloyalty to Christ's kingdom. Immediately thereafter some 45 million copies of a resolution to that effect were distributed throughout the world. In the following year, at Los Angeles, attending Bible Students approved a resolution entitled 'A Warning' which again attacked the clergy and again was circulated throughout the globe. At Columbus, Ohio, in 1924, they adopted the 'Indictment' against men of the cloth and distributed even more copies of a leaflet entitled *Ecclesiastics Indicted* than they had done with former resolutions. Then, in 1925, at Indianapolis, Indiana, they proclaimed a 'Message of Hope' for humanity but continued to damn Christendom and its religious leaders. At London, England, in 1926, they shouted their approval of 'A Testimony to the Rulers of the Nations' which censured Great Britain and the world. The next year, at Toronto, Ontario, Judge Rutherford read a resolution to 15,000 assembled Bible Students entitled 'To the Peoples of Christendom.' A supporting talk, 'Freedom for the Peoples,' was broadcast over an international chain of fifty-three radio stations, an amazing number for that day. Finally, in 1928, at Detroit, Michigan, the Bible Students accepted a 'Declaration against Satan and for Jehovah.'[72]

In later years other conventions were also of prime importance, especially one held at Washington, DC, in 1935, and another held at St Louis, Missouri, in 1941. At the latter assembly, Judge Rutherford's last, some 115,000 persons were present,[73] and Jehovah's Witnesses were able to openly defy the terrible persecution that was then striking at them like a tidal wave as a result of the charge that they were unpatriotic enemies of the nations in which they lived.

Rutherford's Growing Power

While he was carrying on his writing and preaching activities, Rutherford gradually began to gain greater control over the Bible Student community. He had become absolute in so far as the society's business affairs were concerned in 1917. In 1925 he became equally absolute in the determination of what doctrines should be taught in Watch Tower publications. Over the objections of the society's editorial committee, he published an important and doctrinally revolutionary article entitled 'Birth of the Nation.'[74] As a result, he destroyed the committee.[75] But the ecclesias were still relatively independent under their own elected elders.

That was not to last, however. As Paul Johnson had suspected earlier,[76] Rutherford was determined to bring them under centralized Watch Tower control in the name of what he later chose to call 'Theocratic Government.'

According to Rutherford, the prime purpose of the Bible Student community was to preach. In order to fulfil that requirement, everything had to be done to promote evangelism – especially door-to-door evangelism with the society's publications. Thus, every convention from 1919 on stressed the importance of advertising the Watch Tower message.

Eventually, the constant barrage of propaganda convinced many Bible Students that, in a strange sense, they must 'publish or perish.' By the 1920s Rutherford had come to claim that *all* Christians must preach publicly in fulfilment of Matthew 24:14. Yet, in spite of such constant pressure, others – perhaps a majority – resisted being dragooned into the preaching work. Many still maintained the belief from Russell's day that character-building or Christian sanctification was more important than proselytizing. Many, also, could not accept the argument that all were required to witness from door to door. And, most important, numerous elected elders resented the society's growing authority over and manipulation of local congregations. Hence, to gain his end of complete domination of the Bible Student community, Rutherford had to take a number of steps. Among them, he had to destroy the concept of sanctification or character development, and also the idea that Russell had been the faithful and wise servant.

In order to accomplish the first step, he published an article in *The Watch Tower* of 1 May 1926, in which he completely discredited the term 'character development.' Interestingly, if one looks at that article and compares it with Russell's statements on the matter, he will see that Rutherford was attacking a straw man. Nevertheless, by discrediting the older Bible Student concept of sanctification as 'work righteousness,' he could, paradoxically, place greater stress on the *work* of evangelism.

It was obvious, however, that as long as the society distributed Russell's works and continued to regard him as the faithful and wise servant, Bible Students would be reluctant to adopt Rutherford's ideas without question. So, in the 1 January 1927 *Watch Tower* Rutherford published an article which was obviously produced to discredit Russell's reputation. Among other things that article stated: 'It is the enemy's scheme to turn man away from God, by inducing man to reverence some other man; and thereby many fall into the Devil's snare.'[77]

Shortly thereafter, in February of the same year, the society abandoned the idea that Russell had been the faithful and wise servant; henceforth 'that servant' was to be seen to be the remnant of the elect of God on earth – those of the 144,000 saints of Revelation 14:1 who had not yet been joined with Christ in heavenly glory.[78]

While Rutherford was discrediting Russell's memory and his teachings, he was

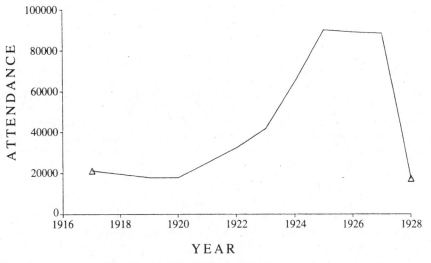

Bible Student memorial attendance, 1917–28

enhancing his own authority. As Timothy White so convincingly points out by quoting excerpts from *The Watch Tower,* what Rutherford did was to change the definition of the term 'Society' to mean the entire Bible Student community – in effect, the church. According to White, in 1919 and 1920 Paul Johnson circulated an article entitled 'The Church Organized in Relation to the Society.' In that article Johnson argued that the society should be the servant of the church (the Bible Students) rather than its master. In reply, Rutherford held: 'While the Society is a body corporate with required officers and servants, yet alone these do not constitute the Society. In the broader sense the Society is composed of the body of Christians organized in orderly manner under the Lord's direction for the carrying on of his work.' By this definition, as White asserts, Rutherford was claiming that by being the president of the society, he was also actually the 'president of the church.'[79] Although the judge did not dare to make such a claim in so many words, by 1940 the Watch Tower Society had come to recognize the fact openly. *Consolation (The Golden Age* under a new name) stated: 'The Theocracy is at present administered by the Watch Tower Bible and Tract Society, of which Judge Rutherford is the president and general manager.'[80]

The New Name

During the years following 1919, Rutherford and his associates labelled fellow Bible Students who no longer accepted the society's directions as 'evil servants,' the 'Judas class,' and the 'Delilah class.' Nevertheless many Watch Tower Bible Students still continued to regard such persons as brethren in Christ. Consequently, in order to differentiate more clearly his followers from the many independent Bible Students, on 26 July 1931 at 4:00 pm, he read a resolution before an assembled Watch Tower convention at Columbus, Ohio, which called on them to accept the new name: 'Jehovah's Witnesses.'[81]

The arguments which the judge used were a masterpiece of faulty logic and bad exegesis. For example, he used Isaiah 62:1, 2 from Rotherham's translation to show that God's people would ultimately be given 'a new name.' But as Timothy White notes, had he bothered to read on another two verses he would have discovered that the new name was to be 'Hephzi-bah,' not 'Jehovah's Witnesses.'[82] Nevertheless, the selection of the new name was a bold stroke of genius on Rutherford's part. For probably more than anything, it gave prominence and uniqueness to Watch Tower supporters that nothing else could have done. It served also as a major psychological break with Russell and the Bible Student past and was an important step in the creation of a highly centralized 'theocratic' arrangement under Rutherford and his hand-picked successors. Of course it offended some Bible Students who had formerly remained loyal to the society; it, in effect, meant the adoption of a sectarian name contrary to one of Russell's most heartfelt teachings. But Rutherford no doubt wanted such persons to submit or leave the movement anyway. To the judge, anyone who was not totally for him was against him – and Jehovah as well.

The Development of Theocratic Government

Changes in Bible Student doctrines with respect to eschatology, character development, and the faithful and wise servant caused many to leave the movement.[83] The article 'Birth of the Nation' in 1925 alone evidently caused many to do so.[84] Yet as long as local congregations or ecclesias were ruled by their own elders and organized their own affairs, they could, if they chose, ignore most of Rutherford's pronouncements and remain in fellowship with other Bible Students. Rutherford, therefore, decided to dominate the elders, or, if that did not work, to abolish them as a class.

As noted above, he used the argument that the society (the entire community of Bible Students) was consecrated to carry out a grand testimony or preaching work in the 'last days.' Consequently, anyone who opposed the work of *the society* (the

Watch Tower Bible and Tract Society) as directed by its president was opposing the will of God. Thus, he held that local elders who refused to go along with directives from Brooklyn were 'puffed-up,' 'self assuming,' and a host of other epithets by which Rutherford was wont to refer to them.[85]

The judge was too wise to simply attack the elders without having others to put in their place. During the years from 1919 to 1932, he gradually increased his control over local Bible Student congregations by developing new, society-directed preaching activities which were placed under the superintendence of the service directors who had first been appointed to distribute *The Golden Age* in 1919. These new activities included the circulation of various convention resolutions and, beginning in 1926, the house-to-house distribution of Watch Tower literature. Consequently, what Rutherford was doing was building up a corps of pro-society preaching directors in each congregation. While they were nominated locally by the ecclesias, they were *appointed* by the society, and they tended to be loyal to Rutherford and the society in every way.[86]

At the same time, Rutherford determined to weaken congregational autonomy by changing the nature of local meetings. He suggested that the traditional Bible Student prayer and testimony meetings be divided into two parts with one becoming a 'service meeting' – one devoted almost exclusively to promoting public preaching work. Public talks or sermons, delivered on various themes selected by the elders, were discouraged while question-and-answer studies in *The Watch Tower* were encouraged. Thus, gradually and subtly, the judge came to control more and more of the spiritual diet fed to Bible Student congregations.[87]

Rutherford and his supporters were still, as late as 1932, irritated by the independence of some elders and their unwillingness to accept without question the dictates of the Watch Tower Bible and Tract Society. After much discussion, the judge decided to solve the problem by eliminating the elders. So, there appeared in the 1 February 1932 *Watch Tower* a letter – obviously planted with an eye to coming events – from Charles Morrell, a long-time Bible Student and private secretary to Canadian Supreme Court Justice Sir Lyman Duff. The letter, which appeared on page 47, read:

The following question is submitted, as much for consideration as for answer, as I presume if the point involved is sound it will be dealt with by the *Watch Tower* in due course.

In substance, the apostle says that the holy spirit made the elders overseers of the flock of God. The Lord himself having taken oversight of Zion now, is there justification for the service of elders any longer?

Expressed differently, was it not the purpose of the Lord to limit the jurisdiction of the elders to the time of the absence from the earth of the Lord Jesus, commencing with his ascension, and the giving of the holy spirit as a guide or teacher, and the coming of Christ Jesus to the temple?

An extraneous evidence of this might lie in that there has been room for considerable criticism of the elders in recent years, particularly since 1922. Called to serve, many of them have been found to be a 'thorn in the side' of the Society, the directors, the service organization, and the faithful workers. Their election, presumed to express the 'Will of the Lord' by the holy spirit, has frequently been found to result in opposition to the 'mind of the Lord' as manifest through the Society.

Would not the withdrawal of the holy spirit imply the end of the church government from the 'ranks up,' and the coming of the King to his temple imply church government from the 'throne down'? And, if so, haven't we a dual organization, governed from the 'throne down' and from the 'ranks up'?

Answered in the affirmative would it not be in the interests of the kingdom, and Scripturally correct, to dispense with elders and deacons altogether, and substitute teachers in the same manner as are the directors appointed?

With warmest Christian love, by His grace, I am,

Your brother,

Charles Morrell, Ontario.

In direct 'reply' to Morrell's questions, *The Watch Tower* issues of 15 August and 1 September 1932 called for the abolition of the elective congregational elders, even going so far as to assert that the office of elder was clearly unscriptural. As a result, the system of democratically elected elders and deacons which had existed for more than fifty years was ended. Henceforth, the society's publications continued to pour scorn on the former elected elders. They were described as 'haughty' and 'lazy,' not willing, in most cases at least, to engage in the work of preaching the good news of Christ's kingdom.[88] In fact, their primary sin had been in refusing to buckle under willingly to Judge Joseph Franklin Rutherford.

For a time, the service committees which replaced the elders and deacons were elected by the local congregations. But in 1938 all their officers or 'servants,' as they were by then called, came to be appointed by the Watch Tower Society. Congregational democracy was superseded by theocratic government. The Bible Students, now Jehovah's Witnesses, had become an army of evangelizers. Even the names they used were military in nature. No longer were they to refer to their congregations as 'classes,' 'ecclesias,' or 'churches' as they had done for so long; they were 'companies' under 'company servants,' the successors of the service directors. Colporteurs were now full-time evangelizers known as 'pioneers,' many of whom had served as 'sharpshooters' in a spiritual war against the Devil and his system.

Growing Social Alienation

Other significant changes under Rutherford's presidency tended to make the Bible Student–Witnesses more sociologically sectarian or, as Werner Cohn has described them, more 'proletarian' in the original Marxian sense of that term.[89] In effect, they became more thoroughly isolated and alienated in a psychological sense from the rest of society, a community which lived and worked in, but did not partake of, larger societies.

Judge Rutherford came to feel, for example, that fewer persons would be resurrected than had Russell. The Pastor, a generally warm, kindly human being, had not believed in universal salvation, but had come close to it. But to the shock of many Bible Students, in 1923 *The Watch Tower* stated straightforwardly that there was no hope for the clergy of Christendom.[90] Later, dissenting Bible Students were classified as 'evil servants' and 'the man of perdition,' and therefore also condemned to everlasting destruction.[91] By the late 1930s, the society's literature was teaching, in stark contrast to Russell's views, that Adam and Eve, Cain, the inhabitants of Sodom and Gomorrah, Solomon, the scribes and Pharisees, and a host of others had perished eternally. Furthermore, it came to hold that anyone who rejected the message of Jehovah's Witnesses after 1918, plus all small children including babes in arms who might die at Armageddon, would have no hope of resurrection.[92] And while old-fashioned Bible Students who remained in association with the society often quietly refused to accept such teachings, new converts, who gradually replaced and soon outnumbered the handful of Watch Tower loyalists from Russell's day, did.

In *The Watch Tower* issues of 1 June and 15 June 1929, Rutherford also introduced a new exegesis of Romans 13:1–7 which caused Witnesses to regard the secular state as demonic and virtually without redeeming features. In 1932, he and the society abandoned a long tradition which had taught that natural Jews and Zionism had a special role in Jehovah's divine plan; thereafter, the Witnesses themselves were to be seen as the only Israel of God.[93] And in 1935 the Witnesses, encouraged by the actions of their brethren in Germany and a speech by Judge Rutherford, took a strong position against saluting national flags and standing for national anthems.[94]

Rutherford and those close to him had an ever-increasing influence on the Witnesses in other ways as well. The judge was a man with strong biases and deep prejudices. Thus, as an old-fashioned Populist, he had a loudly proclaimed sympathy for the poor and, following in Russell's footsteps, generally manifested a sense of racial tolerance. Yet, curiously, his outward sympathy towards Jews and blacks was often mixed with white, southern American bigotry towards those groups. For example, while giving a talk on the return of the Jews to Palestine in prophecy at a Bible Student convention in Winnipeg, Manitoba, in the early 1920s, he interjected: 'I'm speaking of the Palestine Jew, not the hooked-nosed, stooped-shouldered little individual who stands on the street corner trying to gyp you out of every nickel you've got.'[95] As far as women were concerned, he was a thoroughgoing misogynist. He lived apart from his wife for years and hated feminists. Thus, he even went so far as to suggest that it was morally wrong for Christian men to tip their hats to ladies, rise when they entered a room, or to show any particular deference to women. Mother's Day he regarded as a feminist plot. But perhaps most startlingly, he openly quoted Kipling's description of a woman as 'a hank of hair and a bag of bones.'[96] Not surprisingly, many Witnesses, particularly lower-class, blue-collar workers, took up the judge's values, either as explicitly stated or implied.

The judge was sometimes an austere person, too, and austerity became a rule of Witness life. Christmas, birthday parties, and other popular customs were described as of pagan origin, unchristian, and hence, not to be celebrated or practised.[97] For a time even congregational hymn singing was outlawed.[98] Beards, often worn by Bible Students in emulation of Pastor Russell, were prohibited at Watch Tower offices and printeries throughout the world.[99] A beard was regarded as a sign of vanity, though many older Witnesses ignored Rutherford on the matter and continued to wear one.

Rutherford was not the only influence on the Bible Student–Witness community in the 1920s and 1930s, although he was certainly the major one. Clayton Woodworth was a close second, and therefore deserves some description as well. As noted above, Woodworth was more than a little eccentric. In consequence, he was to impose some very unorthodox ideas on the Witnesses through the pages of *The Golden Age,* of which he was the editor. Among other things, he hated the American Medical Association, denied the germ theory of disease, constantly attacked smallpox vaccination as the filthy custom of injecting animal pus into the human system, and carried on a vendetta against the aluminum industry. Aluminum cookware, according to Woodworth, was poisonous.[100] Thus, from him the Witnesses were to pick up some additional strange attitudes and practices. Often, when they became nauseated after eating in a restaurant or cafe, Witness families would attribute their sickness to aluminum cookware rather than to food poisoning although the latter was more probably the cause.

Perhaps Woodworth's most extreme activity involved the creation of a new Jehovah's Witness calendar. In *The Golden Age* issues of 13 March, 27 March, and 10 April 1935, he published a three-part article entitled 'The Second Hand in the Timepiece of God.' With his usual zeal, he poured verbal vitriol on the clergy of the Church of Rome and went on to describe practically all calendars in current use as of the Devil. After a long-winded discussion of various Bible texts and

CALENDAR

Jehovah's Year of Ransom 1903

Redemption — First Month (Exodus 12:2) — No. 73740

Lightday	Heavenday	Earthday	Starday	Lifeday	Mansday	Godsday
•	•	•	*	•	1†	2
3	4	5	6	7	8	9
10	11	12	13	14	15	16
17	18	19	20	21	22	23
24	25	26	27	28	29	

Life — Second Month — No. 73741

Lightday	Heavenday	Earthday	Starday	Lifeday	Mansday	Godsday
						1
2	3	4	5	6	7	8
9	10	11	12	13	14	15
16	17	18	19	20	21	22
23	24	25	26	27	28	29
30						

Visitment — Third Month — No. 73742

Lightday	Heavenday	Earthday	Starday	Lifeday	Mansday	Godsday
1	2	3	4	5	6	
7	8	9	10	11	12	13
14	15	16	17	18	19	20
21	22	23	24	25	26	27
28	29					

Freedom — Fourth Month — No. 73743

Lightday	Heavenday	Earthday	Starday	Lifeday	Mansday	Godsday
		1	2	3	4	5
6	7	8	9	10	11	12
13	14	15	16	17	18	19
20	21	22	23	24	25	26
27	28	29	30			

Vindication — Fifth Month — No. 73744

Lightday	Heavenday	Earthday	Starday	Lifeday	Mansday	Godsday
				1	2	3
4	5	6	7	8	9	10
11	12	13	14	15	16	17
18	19	20	21	22	23	24
25	26	27	28	29		

Hope — Sixth Month — No. 73745

Lightday	Heavenday	Earthday	Starday	Lifeday	Mansday	Godsday
					1	2
3	4	5	6	7	8	9
10	11	12	13	14	15	16
17	18	19	20	21	22	23
24	25	26	27	28	29	30

King — Seventh Month — No. 73746

Lightday	Heavenday	Earthday	Starday	Lifeday	Mansday	Godsday
1	2	3	4	5	6	7
8	9	10	11	12	13	14
15	16	17	18	19	20	21
22	23	24	25	26	27	28
29	30					

Peace — Eighth Month — No. 73747

Lightday	Heavenday	Earthday	Starday	Lifeday	Mansday	Godsday
		1	2	3	4	5
6	7	8	9	10	11	12
13	14	15	16	17	18	19
20	21	22	23	24	25	26
27	28	29	30			

Order — Ninth Month — No. 73748

Lightday	Heavenday	Earthday	Starday	Lifeday	Mansday	Godsday
				1	2	3
4	5	6	7	8	9	10
11	12	13	14	15	16	17
18	19	20	21	22	23	24
25	26	27	28	29		

Logos — Tenth Month — No. 73749

Lightday	Heavenday	Earthday	Starday	Lifeday	Mansday	Godsday
					1	2
3	4	5	6	7	8	9
10	11	12	13	14	15	16
17	18	19	20	21	22	23
24	25	26	27	28	29	30

Jehovah — Eleventh Month — No. 73750

Lightday	Heavenday	Earthday	Starday	Lifeday	Mansday	Godsday
1	2	3	4	5	6	7
8	9	10	11	12	13	14
15	16	17	18	19	20	21
22	23	24	25	26	27	28
29						

Temple — Twelfth Month — No. 73751

Lightday	Heavenday	Earthday	Starday	Lifeday	Mansday	Godsday
1	2	3	4	5	6	
7	8	9	10	11	12	13
14	15	16	17	18	19	20
21	22	23	24	25	26	27*
28‡	29	30				

† This day, corresponding to Friday, April 5, 1935, is Edenic day No. 2177588, completing 311,084 weeks from the creation of Adam.

* Vernal equinox No. 5963, which is the last day of Jehovah's Year of Ransom 1903, occurs on this day.

‡ Jehovah's Year of Ransom 1904 begins with this day, corresponding to Sunday, March 22, 1936. It is Edenic day No. 2177940.

NOTE: *Lifeday, Redemption 14, 1903 Y.R.*, really begins at 6:00 p.m. of Wednesday, April 17, 1935 A.D., and was so shown in the calendar as originally published in the 1935 *Year Book*.

Jehovah's Year of Ransom (from *The Golden Age*, 13 March 1935, 381) astronomical calculations, he presented his new 'theocratic' calendar on page 381 of *The Golden Age* of 13 March. All the names of the months and the days of the week were changed from those in popular use. Additionally, the new calendar was to start with the crucifixion rather than the birth of Christ, and new years were to begin in the spring. Finally, the number of days in the new months was changed somewhat. Fortunately, Judge Rutherford had the good sense never to allow Woodworth's theocratic calendar to be used.

The Growth of the Bible Student–Witness Community

During most of Rutherford's administration, the growth in the number of Bible Student–Witnesses was surprisingly slow, particularly in view of the vast quantities of Watch Tower literature distributed, the number of Rutherford's sermons preached over radio, and the number of hours spent in making house calls by zealous 'kingdom publishers.' There was practically no permanent growth at all before 1928, and during the next decade the number of active publishers or preachers increased only 2.97 per cent per year to a total of 59,047.[101] In 1938 only 69,345 attended the annual Memorial of the Lord's Supper.[102] So, in terms of numbers, Jehovah's Witnesses could as yet hardly be said to have become a great success, and Rutherford's great proselytizing campaign had probably alienated far more members of the public than it had attracted.

A major factor inhibiting faster growth was that, while numerous new converts were being made, almost as many old-time Bible Students were severing association with the society.[103] Continual doctrinal changes and the struggle between Judge Rutherford and the elders caused many to drift away; and when in 1929 and 1930 a more active, traditional 'Russellite' movement, the Dawn Bible Students Association, began to come into being, many joined it.[104] Thereafter, when Jehovah's Witnesses sought more liberal and traditional Bible Student fellowship, they tended to gravitate to that group.

Yet, slowly, Jehovah's Witnesses began to expand and, in the last few years of the judge's life, thousands of new converts joined them. A number of factors, all of which deserve some analysis, were responsible for that growth. These included improved organization under theocratic government, the doctrine of the vindication of Jehovah's name, the new doctrine of the 'great multitude,' and serious world-wide conditions caused by the Depression, the rise of Fascism, and the outbreak of the Second World War. Finally, the steadfast faithfulness of the Witnesses during terrible persecution in the 1930s and 1940s gave them a prominence and sympathy which drew many to them.

Theocratic government changed the nature of the Witness community. Not only were company servants and their assistants appointed directly by the society, but local companies were organized into 'zones' under 'zone servants' who visited them regularly to encourage the preaching work and 'maintain unity of action.' About twenty congregations were formed together in a particular area to form a zone and from time to time zone conventions were held. The zones were in turn organized into regions under regional servants who visited the zones at convention times. On 1 October 1938, the United States was divided into eleven regions which were subdivided into 148 zones.[105] Thus, theocratic government entailed the creation of a full-fledged system of hierarchical governance with 'servants' who wielded every bit as much authority among Jehovah's Witnesses as did archbishops and bishops among Roman Catholics. And these servants emphasized, as had never been done to the same extent before, that if one wanted to be approved by the society, and therefore Jehovah, he must preach.

By 1938 few of the more independent-minded Bible Students were left in association with the Watch Tower Society. To oppose the theocracy in any way was to be branded a 'troublemaker' and shunned. With few exceptions this meant that most Jehovah's Witnesses were thoroughly supportive of door-to-door preaching and everything else published in *The Watchtower*. As one elderly California Witness woman put it: 'If *The Watchtower* said the moon was made of green cheese, I'd believe it.' Fortunately, *The Watchtower* did not go that far; yet when the society instructed the Witnesses to carry on a regular evangelizing campaign under any and all circumstances, they were ready to obey unto death itself. Small wonder that the Nazis considered them to be a dangerous, rival political movement.[106]

The Vindication of Jehovah's Name

An important factor behind such zeal was the doctrine of the vindication of Jehovah's name, a doctrine still taught by Jehovah's Witnesses today. Under Russell, the central doctrine of Bible Students had been that of the ransom atonement of Christ which was seen as the expression of God's love for mankind. Consequently, to Russell and the Bible Students of his day, the New Testament was regarded as more important than the Old. Although they sometimes stressed the importance of God's wrath, it was not a primary doctrine to them. Under Rutherford that all changed. Writing on page 320 of the book *Jehovah*, published in 1934, he stated boldly: 'God provided that the death of Christ Jesus, his beloved son, should furnish the ransom or redemptive price for man; but that goodness and loving-kindness toward mankind is secondary to the vindication of Jehovah's name.' The judge stressed how, by being faithful to their commission, God's witnesses throughout history had had a part in the vindication of the divine name. But the ultimate vindication of the Almighty would come at Armageddon when the wicked would be destroyed. Using allegorical interpretation, Rutherford argued that in bringing down vengeance upon the wicked in the days of ancient Israel, Jehovah was simply prefiguring what he would do in the last days of this wicked world. So it became of ultimate importance that men should choose: they would have to join with Jehovah, Christ, and the Theocracy, or go down with the Devil and his system at the battle of the great day of God the Almighty.

Significantly, the doctrine of the vindication of Jehovah's name was in many ways like John Calvin's doctrine of the majesty of God. Equally significantly, it was no doubt a major factor in developing a burning, almost fanatic zeal in the Witnesses of the twentieth century just as Calvin's teaching had done among his followers in the sixteenth. That meant that, like the Calvinists of that era, the Witnesses became ever more intolerant of everything and everyone not in harmony with God's new nation, the Theocracy, as they saw it.

The Attack on Religion

Linked with the doctrine of the vindication of Jehovah's name was a bitter campaign of invective against those whom the Witnesses regarded as God's enemies. Judge Rutherford and those in close association with him never forgot the trauma of 1918 and 1919. So, until his death in 1942, he poured forth a series of bitter attacks on commerce, politics, and religion – 'the three chief instruments of the Devil.' As far as capitalism was concerned, the judge hated it as had Russell before him, and it is somewhat understandable that the Bible Students and the Witnesses of the 1930s should have occasionally been accused of Marxist, or at least socialist, sympathies.[107] The judge, however, had no more use for leftist politicians than for any others; all, he asserted, would be destroyed at Armageddon. Yet neither commerce nor politics came in for the verbal abuse that Rutherford, Woodworth, and the Witnesses heaped upon the churches and, particularly, the clergy.

Rutherford quite rightly blamed members of the clergy for his imprisonment in 1918 and, although he was certainly negative towards Protestantism and Judaism, he saved his choicest epithets for the priests and hierarchy of the Church of Rome. For example, in typical fashion, in the book *Enemies,* the judge stated: 'All organizations on earth that are in opposition to God and his kingdom, therefore, necessarily take the name of "Babylon" and "harlot," and those names specifically apply to the leading religious organization, the Roman Catholic church, which claims to be the mother of the so-called "Christian religion." That mighty religious organization, foretold in the Scriptures, uses the method of harlots to induce politicians and commercial traffickers and others to fall into her arms and yield to her supposed charms.'[108]

Rutherford's attacks became more and more vitriolic, particularly as Witnesses came under terrible persecution in Nazi Germany, Italy, Great Britain, Canada, and the United States. Eventually he even came to use the term 'religion' to mean *false* religion which he publicly damned as 'a snare and a racket.'[109] And, as Rutherford's jeremiads grew more severe, the Witnesses took more delight in publishing them.

When, in the mid-1930s, the judge was forced off the airwaves as the result of pressure from both the business community and the churches in Canada and the United States,[110] the Watch Tower Society produced phonograph records of his booming denunciations which were played on portable phonographs carried from door to door by willing Jehovah's Witnesses. In other instances, those same Witnesses would play Rutherford's talks over loudspeakers to whole communities, often of irate Catholics. In one instance, in the province of Quebec, they even went so far as to build an armour-plated sound car – of which various pictures are extant – from which they could broadcast condemnation of the Church of Rome to hostile mobs in two languages.

In other instances, Witness publishers invaded hostile towns and cities in the hundreds, often in violation of local anti-peddling ordinances and in the face of threats of mass arrests.[111] Finally, in displays of both courage and their contempt for 'Satan's world,' great numbers of them, young and old, male and female, would march through cities and towns of the English-speaking world in what were called 'information marches.' Spread out in long lines, they would tramp through busy thoroughfares carrying signs and placards bearing slogans coined by Judge Rutherford such as 'Religion Is a Snare and a Racket' and 'Serve God and Christ the King.'[112]

Naturally, many found the Witnesses' behaviour offensive and bizarre. Yet their constant attacks on commerce, politics, and religion attracted many to them. During the 1920s and throughout the Depression, labour leaders frequently praised Judge Rutherford for his attacks on big business.[113] Labour, political liberals, and socialists admired his equally severe denunciations of Mussolini, Hitler, Franco, and right-wing movements throughout the world. Thousands of Protestants and anti-clericals agreed with everything the Witnesses had to say about the Roman Catholic hierarchy and admired their courage in saying it. Finally, as Jehovah's Witnesses often openly courted and met martyrdom with bravery, even their enemies began to develop a degree of respect for them.

The Great Multitude

Probably the most significant contributor, however, to the more rapid growth of the Witness community during the last years of Rutherford's life was the new doctrine of 'the great multitude.' Almost from the beginning of his ministry, Pastor Russell had taught that the Bible Students were members of the elect class of

144,000 mentioned in Revelation 7 and 14, who would rule as king-priests with Christ during the millennium. In addition, he stressed that the vast majority of mankind would inherit perfect life through the resurrection in a restored paradise – earth. But besides the 'elect' and the majority of saved humans, *The Watch Tower* had taught there was a third group, the 'great multitude' of Revelation 7:9, which would receive heavenly life on a secondary plane. *The Watch Tower* also explained in 1923 that there would be a 'sheep class' mentioned in Matthew 25:31– 46, which would be divided from the 'goats' in the time of the end. In 1932 Rutherford stated that those 'sheep' were pictured by the ancient Rechabite chieftain, Jonadab, who had joined King Jehu of Israel at the time of his destruction of Queen Jezebel's priests of Baal.[114]

Such concepts were complex and, more significantly, they meant that the Witnesses saw their preaching work as directed only to the gathering of the 144,000 elect of God. Jehovah himself would deal with the other classes of mankind in his own due time. That all changed dramatically when, in the spring of 1935, the Watch Tower Society's president delivered a speech at Washington, DC, in which he argued that the 'great multitude,' the 'sheep' of Matthew 25, and the 'Jonadabs' were all one class who would receive everlasting life on earth as a reward for faith and obedience to Christ's kingdom.[115] As a result, the Witnesses felt that they must gather great numbers of men to God's organization so they could be saved from the impending battle of Armageddon for life on a new earth. Instead of simply preaching to gather the elect and announce the world's coming end, they began to make a far more concentrated effort to gain converts.

Rutherford's Personal Life and Last Days

Sometime after becoming president of the Watch Tower Society, Judge Rutherford and his wife, Mary, were quietly separated. Although she is generally described by older Witnesses as 'a semi-invalid who could not render the judge his marital dues,' their separation was caused by more than her health or his work. They were alienated and apparently quite bitter towards one another, although just why is unclear. Perhaps, though, factors which may have caused strife between them were Rutherford's choleric and self-righteous temperament and what was quite evidently a serious case of alcoholism.

Although Jehovah's Witnesses have done everything possible to hide accounts of the judge's drinking habits, they are simply too notorious to be denied. Former workers at the Watch Tower's New York headquarters recount tales of his inebriation and drunken stupors. Others tell stories of how difficult it sometimes was to get him to the podium to give talks at conventions because of his drunkenness. In San Diego, California, where he spent his winters from 1930 until his death, an elderly lady still speaks of how she sold him great quantities of liquor when he came to purchase medicines in her husband's drugstore. But perhaps the most damning account of his drinking habits appears in an open letter to him from former Canadian Watch Tower branch overseer Walter Salter.

For years, Salter was a close friend and confidant of the judge, but in 1936 he broke with him over doctrinal issues and was excommunicated. So on 1 April 1937 he published the letter referred to above which was a stinging personal indictment of Rutherford and one that in its general outline, at least, is quite accurate. Accordingly, Salter claimed that he had purchased 'whiskey at $60.00 dollars a case' for the Watch Tower president 'and cases of brandy and other liquors, to say nothing of untold cases of beer,' all with the society's money. So that no one might think that what was bought was for others, the former Canadian branch overseer stated: 'A bottle of liquor or two would not do; it was for the PRESIDENT and nothing was too good for the PRESIDENT.' Then after describing Rutherford's ostentatious style of life, Salter said with bitter irony: 'And oh Lord he [Rutherford] is so courageous and his faith in Thee so great that he gets behind four walls, or surrounds himself literally with an armed bodyguard and bellows away his dreams ... and sends us out from door to door to face the enemy while he goes from "drink to drink" and tells us if we don't we are going to be destroyed.'

As far as personal accommodations and creature comforts were concerned, Salter relates that Rutherford lived like a prince or baron of industry. In New York he rented an apartment with luxurious furnishings which Salter estimated as easily worth $10,000 a year during the Depression. Besides that, the Watch Tower president had a 'palatial residence' on Staten Island, 'camouflaged' as essential to the Society's broadcasting station WBBR. Also on Staten Island he maintained a small, secluded residence in the woods where he could isolate himself from the world. Then, too, expensive quarters were kept for him in a number of other places including London and, prior to the Nazis' rise to power, in Magdeburg. And if that were not enough, because of his health, in 1929 he began building Beth Sarim, a San Diego mansion which was to become his winter home.

Strangely, Rutherford found a doctrinal excuse for building Beth Sarim which, in part at least, he may really have believed. According to the society's exegesis of Psalm 45:16 (King James Version) – 'Instead of thy fathers shall be thy children, whom thou mayest make princes in all the earth' – Christ would resurrect Abraham, Isaac, Jacob, David, and many other pre-Christian servants of Jehovah to rule mankind during the millennium. Furthermore, Daniel, also one of these 'ancient worthies,' had been told that he would stand in his lot 'at the end of the days' which the Watch Tower Society taught would be *before* Armageddon. Judge Rutherford and the society therefore concluded that those faithful, pre-Christian men could come back any time within the next few years or even months. In fact, many ordinary Jehovah's Witnesses would often expect the resurrected 'princes' to be present at the next major Watch Tower convention. Thus when the judge was supposedly donated the money to build Beth Sarim on a one-hundred-acre San Diego estate, he 'humbly' had the deed for it made out to himself in trust for David and the other 'princes' who would shortly need somewhere pleasant to reside.[116] That, however, did not stop him from living in it with a fairly large retinue of retainers and with one of his two sixteen-cylinder Cadillac cars that, according to popular Witness lore, had been given to him 'as the greatest man on earth' by a wealthy Iowa believer.

In spite of all this, in some strange way Judge Joseph Franklin Rutherford continued to take himself and the doctrines he proclaimed seriously. When the Second World War came, it therefore seemed to him to be a fulfilment of apocalyptic prophecy, and he became convinced that the war would lead directly to the destruction of both the demons and wicked mankind at Armageddon. So in the last year of his life, as he showed unmistakable signs of being a very sick man dying with cancer, from Beth Sarim he began to disassemble part of the theocratic organizational structure he had just recently put in place. In December 1941, he discontinued the offices of regional and zone servants and terminated the custom of holding zone conventions. At the time he wrote: '"The strange work" of the Lord [the public preaching work] is drawing to an end and requires haste, with watchfulness, sobriety and prayer.'[117] Yet he insisted that every Witness should continue with that work until God called a halt to it. 'With full determination to be obedient to the Lord,' he said, 'let these words of the apostle be a guiding slogan: "This one thing I do" that is to advertise THE THEOCRACY.'[118]

Rutherford's Death and Legacy

Rutherford died at Beth Sarim on 8 January 1942, after a long illness. Yet he died still active or, as his fellow Witnesses reported, 'fighting with his boots on.'[119] He had wanted to be buried on a canyonside about a hundred yards beneath the House of the Princes that he had long used and enjoyed while it awaited the return of the ancient pre-Christian 'worthies,'[120] but that was not to be. The area was not zoned for the creation of private cemeteries, and the neighbours complained that to bury the judge where he had requested would lower the value of their properties. Hence, local officials refused to issue a burial permit.[121] Watch Tower publications asserted bitterly that this was simply a last act of spite by the Devil's organization against Jehovah's faithful, departed spokesman,[122] and local Witnesses carried on a protracted, three-month battle to honour Rutherford's last wish.

Records of the case show that there was little substance to Watch Tower charges of religious prejudice,[123] and physical evidence at Beth Sarim suggests that the neighbours had some reason for concern. For instead of wanting to bury Rutherford's body in a simple canyonside grave, as they later asserted, his closest personal retainers – the Beth Sarim 'family' – wanted to place it in a large, rather imposing, cement crypt which they began building as he was dying. Thus, the neighbours no doubt feared that Rutherford's prospective tomb might well become a monument which would be visited by Jehovah's Witnesses from far and near.

Of course that did not happen. When San Diego County officials finally refused to allow Judge Rutherford to be interred at Beth Sarim, his remains were taken to Rossville, New York, laid to rest there,[124] and were quickly forgotten by all but a few close friends. The records of the attempt to have him buried at Beth Sarim show that neither high Watch Tower officials nor even his widow or son, Malcolm, seemed greatly concerned about his last resting place, for they were notable at public hearings on the matter by their absence. Furthermore, since the judge himself had taught the Witnesses to be loyal to Jehovah's organization, the theocracy, rather than to any man, they quickly gave their full allegiance to his successors at the Brooklyn Bethel. So today, only a handful of Witnesses who are in their late fifties or older know much about the man who reshaped their movement, and fewer still are aware that Beth Sarim and Rutherford's uncompleted cement crypt still stand as monuments to him – although the House of the Princes is no longer kept for all the righteous men from Abel to John the Baptist.

Judge Rutherford's real monument is not a cement crypt, however; it is the movement which, upon Pastor Russell's death, he shepherded through the dark days of the First World War and reshaped thereafter. In a real sense it was he, rather than the Pastor, who developed Jehovah's Witnesses into what they are today – a fact continually emphasized by anti–Watch Tower Bible Student groups. While he was doubtlessly a hard, ruthless, and frequently cantankerous person whose reasoning was dominated far more by casuistry than his fellow Witnesses would like to admit, it is probable that only someone like him could have created the basis for making Jehovah's Witnesses the important, world-wide sectarian movement that they are today. For under his severe exterior he seems to have believed, as had Russell before him, that he had a divinely appointed mission. In spite of Bible Student schisms, outside persecution, personal imprisonment, and the failure of the world to end either in 1918 or 1925, he was able to maintain control over a body of zealous men and women who continued to look forward to the near approach of Christ's revelation and the battle of Armageddon. And it was his hardness and organizational abilities, unpopular as they often were, which were to give Jehovah's Witnesses the iron-like character which they needed to pass through the persecution of the 1930s and 1940s.

As William Whallen has noted, Judge Joseph F. Rutherford was to Pastor

Charles T. Russell what Brigham Young was to the Mormon prophet Joseph Smith.[125] While both Smith and Russell were able religious leaders, to a great extent both were rather naïve visionaries who could – through the use of fertile imaginations – mislead themselves as much as others. Both Young and Rutherford were, however, hard-bitten pragmatists who gave a degree of permanency to the movements they dominated. While the judge had little time or interest in one wife, let alone a whole harem, he none the less resembled the stern Mormon Lion of the Lord in a great many ways – although neither Jehovah's Witnesses nor Mormons will likely appreciate the comparison.

CHAPTER THREE

The Era of
Global Expansion

When Judge Joseph F. Rutherford died, Jehovah's Witnesses were under total ban in many parts of the world. Many languished in prisons or in concentration camps. Even in the United States the Supreme Court held that their children must salute the flag when required by law to do so or face expulsion from public schools. Because they were regarded as unpatriotic slackers who would neither salute the flag nor fight for their country, they were subjected to mob violence unexperienced by any religion in America since the nineteenth-century persecution of the Mormons.

As already indicated, the judge had believed that the apocalypse was near in the early 1940s, and he saw in the persecution of the Witnesses the final attack of God's enemies, both spiritual and human, on the little flock of Christ's brethren and the great multitude. Yet the men closest to him evidently believed that the end would not come until they, personally, had directed a world-wide preaching work on a grander scale than either Russell or Rutherford.

Rutherford's Successors

The men who succeeded Rutherford to power in the Watch Tower Society hierarchy were a close-knit band whose most outstanding qualities were administrative ability, a total devotion to the judge's concept of the preaching work, and a sense of loyalty to the society as representative of God's organization. They were, above all, thoroughgoing organization men with all that that term implies.

Most outstanding among this group was Nathan Homer Knorr,[1] Rutherford's last vice-president and the man who was elected to replace him as president on 13 January 1942. Although young, regarded by many of his associates as little more than one of Rutherford's sycophants, and outwardly a much more mild-mannered man than his predecessor, Knorr was a man of iron will. Determined to expand the preaching activities of Jehovah's Witnesses until the Lord Jehovah himself should call a halt, he was to preside over the development of the Witnesses into a major religious force of millions in the period following the Second World War.

Born at Bethlehem, Pennsylvania, in 1905, Knorr was raised in the Reformed church of his Dutch ancestors. But at the age of sixteen, he became associated with the Bible Students. In 1923 he became a full-time colporteur and was invited to the Brooklyn Bethel which remained his home until just before his death. By 1932 he had become general manager of the New York Watchtower Society's publishing office and plant. Two years later, he became a director of that corporation and in 1940 became a member and vice-president of the Watch Tower Bible and Tract Society of Pennsylvania. He gained almost all of his experience as a loyal Jehovah's Witness at the society's central offices and carried on many of the programs initiated by Rutherford.

Knorr was a hard, business-like person. Only occasionally, especially when he was with close friends and Witness missionaries for whom he had real affection, would he demonstrate the ebullient good humour shown by Judge Rutherford when he was enjoying himself or the kindness so often manifested by Pastor Russell. But he could be stern and severe like Rutherford to any and all who, in his eyes, were *disloyal* or failed in their duties. Furthermore, he could sometimes be petulant, unkind, and thoroughly mean to those for whom he developed a dislike. Although he himself complained of being 'trimmed' or given a public tongue-lashing by Judge Rutherford before his fellow workers at Bethel,[2] when he assumed the judge's mantle, he also assumed the custom of 'trimming' others, in some cases scathingly.[3] As years went by, he became more and more of a paternalistic figure whose character was not unlike that of his stern Calvinistic forbears. Still, like Pastor Russell and Judge Rutherford before him, he enjoyed a comfortable lifestyle and a good table. Unlike either of them, he had a normal and healthy appreciation for the opposite sex.

Although possessing little if any ability as a writer, and certainly lacking the personal charisma of his predecessors, in many ways Knorr was a more able man than either. Under his administration, a policy of de-emphasizing the role and prestige of individuals, which Rutherford had begun, at least for others, was brought to a conclusion. In 1942 Knorr developed the policy of having all Watch Tower literature published anonymously – a policy which still is followed – and of even de-personalizing correspondence from the society. Instead of bearing the name of the writer, letters were simply to be stamped with the 'signature' Watchtower Bible and Tract Society, Inc. Thus, the Witness community was to be made to feel that it must be loyal to an organization, *the Lord's organization,* rather than to any man.

Of course, there may have been another reason why Knorr wanted to develop this cult of de-personalization. Since he was unable to research and write the society's major publications, he knew that he would not be able to gain the prestige that both Russell and Rutherford had obtained as authors. So Nathan Knorr may very well have wanted to hide his own inadequacy by having practically all Watch Tower literature published anonymously. More importantly, however, he sought to turn Jehovah's Witnesses into a far more sophisticated, moral, and effective band of preachers of Jehovah's kingdom than they had ever been in the past.

The man who became Knorr's vice-president in 1942 was the society's new legal counsel, Hayden Cooper Covington.[4] Born in 1911, in Hopkins County, Texas, Covington studied law at the San Antonio Bar Association School of Law and was admitted to the Texas bar in 1933. In the following year he was baptized as a Witness. In 1939, he was invited to the Brooklyn Bethel to help with the onerous task of fighting Witness cases at law.

Covington was tall, handsome, an effective speaker, and a very able lawyer. During the period between 1939 and 1955, he was to argue approximately fifty cases per year and was to appear before the u.s. Supreme Court in forty-one separate cases involving American Bill of Rights questions. But he was a rather proud, sometimes arrogant man who could combine libertarian arguments, which he characteristically used in courts of law, with the most completely authoritarian views imaginable when speaking of the spiritual and organizational authority of the board of directors of the Watch Tower Society.[5] Although he worked closely with Knorr, the two frequently clashed over various issues and developed a deep sense of resentment towards one another.[6] Ultimately, overwork and tension were to be Covington's undoing and in the early 1960s he was forced to leave New York with a severe drinking problem. Only after being excommunicated and reinstated was he to die in good standing as a Witness in 1979.[7] But in 1942 he was in the prime of his life and ready to make important contributions to his brethren.

A third figure, and also one of major importance among those who succeeded Rutherford to power, was Frederick William Franz.[8] Born on 12 September 1893 at Covington, Kentucky, Franz developed into a deeply religious youth who early set out to become a Presbyterian minister. While he was attending the University of Cincinnati in 1913, his brother sent him some Watch Tower publications. Shortly thereafter, he became convinced of Bible Student teachings. In the spring of 1914, he dropped classes before he had completed his junior year to become an active Bible Student colporteur. In 1920, he was invited to the Brooklyn Bethel and, in 1922, gave the discourse at Nathan Knorr's baptism. While at university Franz had been an honour student and, although not offered a Rhodes scholarship as A.H. Macmillan has claimed, his professors evidently considered recommending him for one.[9] By the time he left the University of Cincinnati he knew German and could read Latin and Greek. Later, he learned Spanish, Portuguese, and

French, and acquired a reading knowledge of Hebrew. So, over the years, he was to become a highly useful aide to Rutherford, and even before the judge's passing was to become the society's foremost biblical exegete and scholar. Although he was not immediately chosen as one of the society's officers, his close friendship with Knorr and his role as the primary source of Watch Tower doctrine gave him immense, if indirect, authority. He gradually became the society's 'oracle.'

Franz, who was to become Watch Tower vice-president in 1949 and president in 1977, is a small, spry, outwardly attractive person. Although a powerful, sometimes bombastic, speaker with a strange speaking cadence, he is a far more congenial person that either Rutherford or Knorr. In dealing with others, he has generally been approachable and kind, at least so long as not challenged. Yet in many ways he may rightly be described as eccentric, with some of the characteristics of a Paul Johnson or a Clayton Woodworth. His allegorical interpretations of prophetic 'types' have often been turbid, turgid, and un-necessarily involved. Also, his public talks have sometimes embarrassed straight-laced Witnesses. For example, in 1958, at an international convention attended by a quarter of a million persons, he compared teenaged girls to cows in heat. And, in spite of his usually pleasant demeanour, he is no less authoritarian than were Rutherford, Knorr, Covington, and many other high Watch Tower officials. In fact Franz, more than anyone except perhaps Rutherford, has created an aura of almost mystic authority around the offices of Watch Tower president and the Watch Tower Society's board of directors.

Along with Knorr, Covington, and Franz were a number of old Rutherford supporters who had been with the society since Russell's day and several younger men. Among the former were William Van Amburgh, Alexander H. Macmillan, and Hugo Reimer. Among the latter was Grant Suiter who was to become Watch Tower secretary-treasurer upon Van Amburgh's death in 1947. Thus when Judge Rutherford died, there was no power struggle as there had been in 1917. All were determined to see the judge's hand-picked successor, Knorr, elected to the presidency in the interests of the theocracy, and no Jehovah's Witness was to be allowed to question or even criticize its earthly activities.

The Olin Moyle Case

Just how thoroughly authoritarian the society and its directors had become is indicated by the Olin Moyle affair.[10] Accompanied by his wife and son, Peter, Moyle had come to the Brooklyn Bethel from his home in southern Wisconsin in 1935 to act as legal counsel for the Watch Tower Society and to fight the many freedom-of-worship cases which the Witnesses were to face during the next four years. Moyle proved to be a faithful and dedicated Witness who apparently had no serious doctrinal differences with Judge Rutherford. Nevertheless, as time went by he became critical of the judge's personal behaviour and what he regarded as improper conduct on the part of members of the Bethel family. Consequently, on 21 July 1939, he submitted an open letter of resignation to Rutherford as a protest over what he considered to be the low moral conditions at the Watch Tower headquarters. Therein he accused the judge of unkind treatment of the staff, outbursts of anger, discrimination, and vulgar language.

Even though a teetotaller, Moyle can hardly be charged with being overly critical of the drinking habits of his brethren at Bethel, and he was quite accurate in his assessment of the judge's self-righteous, choleric actions and breakfast-table tirades. Furthermore, he was simply eager to correct what to him were serious examples of unchristian conduct and to stress that Rutherford had an immediate responsibility to remedy the conditions which had caused his resignation and protest. But Rutherford, who sometimes had difficulty in distinguishing his own position from that of Jehovah or Christ Jesus, regarded Moyle's letter as nothing short of apostasy itself. The following account from *The Watchtower* of 15 October 1939 (pp. 316–17) indicates his attitude and that of the directors:

INFORMATION

Being reminded that this is the time when God is removing from his organization everything that can be shaken, 'that those things which cannot be shaken may remain' (Hebrews 12:26, 27), the members of the board of directors of the WATCH TOWER BIBLE AND TRACT SOCIETY, for the information and protection of those who are devoted to God's organization, request that the *Watchtower* publish what follows:

On the 21st of July, 1939, a paper written in the form of a letter, signed by O.R. Moyle, was left in the desk of the lobby of the Bethel Home addressed to the president of the Society. Because that paper involved the entire family at Bethel, it was properly brought before the board and before the family. The letter, being filled with false, slanderous and libelous statements, was vigorously condemned by the board, and by all the members of the Bethel family. The board unanimously adopted the following Resolution, which was also approved by the family:

'At a joint meeting of the boards of directors of the Pennsylvania corporation and the New York corporation of the Bible and Tract Society held at the office of the Society at Brooklyn, N.Y., this 8th day of August, 1939, at which other members of the family were present, there was read to said boards and in the presence of O.R. Moyle a letter dated July 21st, 1939, written by said Moyle and addressed to the president of the Society.

'For four years past the writer of that letter has been entrusted with the confidential matters of the Society. It now appears that the writer of that letter, without excuse, libels the family of God at Bethel, and identifies himself as one who speaks evil against the Lord's organization, and who is a murmurer and complainer, even as the Scriptures have foretold (Jude 4–16; 1 Cor. 4–3; Rom. 14:4).

'The members of the board of directors hereby resent the unjust criticism appearing in that letter, disapprove of the writer and his actions, and recommend that the president of the Society immediately terminate the relationship of O.R. Moyle to the Society as legal counsel and as member of the Bethel family.'

Aside from the introductory paragraph announcing the writer's purpose to leave Bethel at a fixed time, every paragraph of that letter is false, filled with lies, and is a wicked slander and libel not only against the president but against the entire family, and for that reason the letter has not been published by the Society. He requested *Consolation* to publish his letter, and Moyle, being refused, now causes his libelous paper to be published and circulated among certain companies of the consecrated, causing the same to be publicly read, and then by his own words which may be called 'fair speech', he pretends to be in harmony with the Society, and thus further deceives the unsuspecting ones. His only possible purpose in further publishing is to justify himself and to 'cause division among the brethren', both of which are condemned by the Word of God (Luke 16:15; Rom. 16:17, 18). For this reason the brethren should be warned. 'The afore-mentioned letter' being filled with lies leveled against the brethren, the same is hated by Jehovah: 'Six things doth the Lord hate; yea, seven are an abomination unto him ... a false witness that speaketh lies, and he that soweth discord among brethren.' – Prov. 6:16–19.

By inducing others to join with him in the circulation and publication of his slanderous letter among the consecrated he makes others party to his wrong. The slanderous paper, being in opposition and against the interest of the Theocratic government, is pleasing only to the Devil and his earthly agents.

For four years Moyle was entrusted with the confidential matters of the Society, and then, without excuse, he assaults and maligns those who trusted him. Judas was entrusted by Christ Jesus with confidential matters, and Judas proved his unfaithfulness by furnishing to the enemy that which they could use and did use against the Lord. He who maligns the brethren of the Lord maligns the Lord himself, and the end of such the Scriptures plainly point out. Having been warned, each one must choose to join the 'evil servant' and take the consequences (Matthew 24: 48–51) or remain faithful to Jesus and his government by Christ Jesus. Choose whom you will serve. [Signed]: Fred W. Franz, N.H. Knorr, Grant Suiter, T.J. Sullivan, W.P. Heath, W.H. Reimer, W.E. Van Amburgh, M. Goux, C.A. Wise, C.J. Woodworth. Approved for publication J.F. Rutherford, Pres.

Moyle sued Rutherford and the board of directors of both the Pennsylvania and New York societies for libel. After much litigation he was able to collect $15,000 plus court costs two years after the judge's death.[11] But neither Rutherford nor the directors were willing to attempt to make peace with one whom they believed to be a 'Judas' and an 'evil slave.' They seemed willing to accept the notoriety and bad reputations they gained over the matter in order to maintain the central principle of unquestioned authority to do as they saw fit.

In Wisconsin, Moyle's home state, Witness congregations divided over the issue with a few persons leaving the movement. Most supported Rutherford and the society, however, and showed open contempt for Moyle. The Jefferson Company of Jehovah's Witnesses wrote: 'We are in full accord with Jehovah's word the Bible which he is now revealing to us through the earthly channel, The Watchtower.[12] The Waupun Company stated: 'we absolutely refuse to consider the malicious letters which those of the "evil servant" class have been circulating among the brethren, seeking self-justification and sympathy.'[13] And most illustrative of general Witness attitudes was a letter from Granville and Grace Fiske who signed themselves as 'Your brethren and fellow locusts.'[14] In it they stated: 'We do not know of the contents of the letter written by Mr. Moyle, nor do we care to know. It is enough for us that our great God, JEHOVAH, is pleased to use you all in his service, and is showering you with blessings.'[15]

As extreme as they may seem to most persons, including some Jehovah's Witnesses, these were the sorts of professions of blind, mindless loyalty that Rutherford and those who succeeded him wanted from the 'locust army' of Witnesses. In 1954, many years after the Olin Moyle case, Frederick Franz and Hayden Covington went so far as to state that Jehovah's Witnesses must even *accept false teachings* from the Watch Tower Society in order to gain everlasting life. As Covington then stated, the society sought 'unity at all costs, because we believe and are sure that Jehovah God is using our organization, the governing body of our organization, to direct it, even though mistakes are made from time to time.'[16]

The Remoulding of the Witness Community

Knorr set out to improve the preaching work of Jehovah's Witnesses. Almost immediately he restored the system of zone and regional servants.[17] Eventually the zone servants came to be known as circuit servants or overseers and the regional servants as district servants or overseers. In 1946, Knorr provided for semi-annual circuit conventions[18] and in 1948 and 1949 for annual district conventions.[19] While local, national, and international conventions had been held since Russell's time, and had become very important publicity events under Rutherford, Knorr now placed them on a regular basis, more easily available to all Witnesses who wished to attend. Most important, however, was the fact that in 1943 he provided for the establishment of a 'theocratic ministry school' in each Witness congregation and the missionary training school of Gilead at South Lansing, New York.[20] All these events had a profound effect on the Witness community.

New organizational and educational developments began to bring about major changes. Knorr was slightly more conscious of public relations than Rutherford had been. In spite of events such as the Moyle case and the continued bitter criticism of 'politics, commerce and religion,' the Witnesses gradually began to adopt an outwardly more sophisticated appearance. In 1948 Beth Sarim was sold.[21] The journals which replaced *The Golden Age – Consolation* (1937 to 1946) and *Awake!* (1946 to the present) – quietly abandoned a number of positions which had made the society look foolish; gone were the tirades against vaccination and aluminum poisoning. Watch Tower literature assumed a more measured and subdued tone, at least in comparison with the one it had maintained under Judge Rutherford. The Witnesses as a people also gradually became more tactful and effective in their evangelizing. The congregational theocratic ministry schools taught many to improve their use of language and to become more able door-to-door preachers and better public speakers. Over the years, Gilead trained class after class of zealous missionaries which Knorr dispatched throughout much of the world 'to preach the good news of the kingdom and gather Christ's other sheep.' To those Gilead graduates much credit must go for the Witness growth in the period during the latter years of the second World War and thereafter.

The Growth of the Witness Community

Just how successful the Witnesses were to be during Knorr's presidency is hard to realize unless one sees some of the Watch Tower Society's rather conservative statistics on the matter. Table 1, taken from those statistics, gives the numbers of active Witnesses, that is those 'publishers' who engaged in attempting to convert others to their faith, rather than all who accepted Witness doctrines. 'Memorial Attenders' indicates how many met for the annual celebration of the Lord's Supper.

TABLE 1
World-wide growth of Jehovah's Witnesses, 1942–77

Year	Peak publishers	Memorial attenders
1942	115,240	98,076
1947	207,552	335,415
1952	456,265	667,099
1957	716,901	1,075,163
1962	989,192	1,639,681
1967	1,160,604	2,195,612
1972	1,658,990	3,662,407
1977	2,223,538	5,107,518

It would be wrong to infer that such growth occurred solely because of the efforts of Jehovah's Witnesses themselves through their almost unbelievably active proselytizing. Political and social events around the world aided them greatly. For example, when in 1945 German Witnesses came forth from Hitler's concentration camps or, in some cases, found themselves expelled from the Polish and Czech occupied territories of Silesia and the Sudetenland, they were in terrible straits. But they immediately began to reorganize into congregations and to preach to their neighbours. Undoubtedly their anti-Nazi record and their proclamation of a new world paradise sounded good to the many war-weary, starving Germans. Consequently, by 1946, some 500 additional publishers were being added to their ranks every month.[22] Thus they began once again to grow rapidly, and their numbers increased dramatically until the famous *Wirtschaftswunder* or economic miracle of the 1960s dulled the religious interest of the German people.

In 1946 the Watch Tower Society recorded a total of 11,415 German Witnesses;[23] by 1950 it reported a peak of 52,473.[24] In the latter year, the communist East German authorities banned them in what had been the Russian-occupied zone, and the society no longer gave statistics regarding Witnesses in the German Democratic Republic. Yet in 1955, West Germany alone reported 54,635 publishers[25] and in 1960 nearly 69,000.[26]

Much the same thing happened in Italy. There were only 138 publishers in that country in 1946.[27] But immediately the Witnesses began to grow in numbers even more dramatically than did their brethren in Germany. In 1950 alone they increased by an amazing 69 per cent to 1,211 publishers.[28] Ten years later there were nearly 6,000 of them.[29] Yet this was only the beginning. Unlike Germany, Italy never has experienced dramatic material prosperity. So, during the last two decades, the Italian Witness population has continued to wax in an amazing fashion. As of 1984 there were nearly 117,000 active Italian Witnesses.[30] The same story was to be repeated in many lands throughout the world. Almost everywhere the aftermath of the Second World War, the birth of the Atomic Age, hunger, poverty, the Cold War, the Korean War, and the nearly universal fear that mankind might be living close to the apocalypse caused many thousands to swell the ranks of Jehovah's Witnesses, even in communist lands.

For a time after the Second World War the Witnesses were relatively free in such eastern European countries as East Germany, Poland, Czechoslovakia, and Hungary. And their growth in those lands was as rapid as in West Germany and Italy. Hence, even when the communists placed them under ban after only five years of freedom, they were numerous and devout enough to continue to make converts.[31]

Amazingly, they did the same in the Soviet Union under terrible persecution. Although there were almost none of them in that country prior to the war, they appeared in it in a major way in 1945. Soviet troops who had been converted to Witness teachings in German prisoner-of-war camps brought their new-found faith back to their homeland. More importantly, whole communities of Witnesses were annexed to the USSR along with territories which had formerly been parts of Poland, Czechoslovakia, and Romania. Curiously, then, by his policies even Stalin, a man who hated religion, contributed to the growth and spread of Jehovah's Witnesses.[32]

New World Assemblies

Perhaps the most outstanding example of the Witnesses' success was the series of gigantic international conventions sponsored by the Watch Tower Society during the late 1940s and 1950s. The first held in North America was one at Cleveland, Ohio, in the summer of 1946, attended by more than 80,000 persons.[33] But the Cleveland convention was far less spectacular than three which were held in New York City in 1950, 1953, 1958.

In 1950 tens of thousands of Americans and Canadians streamed to Yankee Stadium to participate in the 'Theocracy's Increase Assembly.' Some 75,000 were lodged in New York homes, and on 8 August, 123,707 persons listened to N.H. Knorr deliver a talk entitled 'Can You Live Forever in Happiness on Earth?' Although the United States Immigration Department stopped the entry of hundreds of foreign Witnesses who attempted to come to the assembly because of their anti-war beliefs, ten thousand of them from seventy-seven lands were able to attend.[34] Besides being such a great gathering of persons, the 1950 convention was successful in many other ways. The Watch Tower Society released several new publications which were to be of great value to the Witnesses. In 1946 at Cleveland the society had first produced a major doctrinal study of the teachings of Jehovah's Witnesses entitled *'Let God Be True.'* Then at New York, President Knorr first presented the *New World Translation of the Christian Greek Scriptures,* the Witnesses' own version of the New Testament. During the same assembly, the society released *Defending and Legally Establishing the Good News* by Hayden Covington which could be used by publishers undergoing police harassment or arrest for door-to-door preaching. Finally, it published *Evolution Versus the New World,* the first of a series of Watch Tower publications printed to support the doctrine of direct, divine creation of plant and animal species.[35]

In 1953 the second great New York convention, called the 'New World Society Assembly,' was held. In terms of numbers it was even greater than that of 1950. On Sunday, 26 July, more than 165,000 persons, with nearly 50,000 of them at a trailer camp at New Market, New Jersey, listened to Knorr deliver another public discourse.[36]

Two years later the society staged a series of international conventions, the most outstanding of which was held at Nuremberg, Germany. On the final Sunday of that convention, 107,423 persons attended Knorr's public discourse, the largest audience to ever attend an assembly of Jehovah's Witnesses in Europe. The Nuremberg assembly was held at the Zeppelinwiese stadium where, less than two decades earlier, Adolf Hitler had spoken to Nazi rallies from the imposing *Steintribuene* (Stone Tribune). Naturally, the Witness faithful were overjoyed. In the early 1930s Hitler had promised to drive them out of Germany or destroy them; and he had tried to do so. But they had survived his concentration camps; and while he and his Third Reich had perished, they had triumphed. Consequently, they saw the Nuremberg assembly as outstanding evidence of divine providence and Jehovah's favour.[37]

The greatest of all Witness conventions was, however, to be held in New York City in 1958. In that year, the Watch Tower Society rented both Yankee Stadium and the soon-to-be-demolished Polo Grounds, for they realized that no single stadium would be able to hold the vast throngs of Witnesses who were to descend on America's largest city. And they were quite right. From 27 July to 3 August thousands upon thousands of delegates from 123 lands and islands of the seas attended sessions to hear speech after speech delivered by the society's leaders. Furthermore, on Wednesday, 30 July, a total of 7,123 men and women were baptized at the Ocean Beach swimming area in the cold waters of Long Island Sound. Some of the baptizers became numb with the cold and exhausted from baptizing their new brethren, but the society was able to boast that 4,136 more were immersed than at Pentecost. Then, on the Friday following, the society's vice-president, Frederick Franz, read a declaration which was adopted by 194,418 men, women, and children then present to the effect that the clergy of Christendom were the most reprehensible class on earth today. Finally, on Sunday, 3 August, Nathan Knorr addressed a gigantic crowd of 253,922 souls on the subject 'God's Kingdom Rules – Is the World's End Near?'[38]

The Witnesses were greatly impressed by this assembly and so, too, were the press, many businessmen, and the general public, especially in New York. New converts were often made among the many New York householders from whom Witness families rented rooms. Newspapers gave positive reports about their orderliness and politeness. New York policemen were pleased by the respect shown them by visiting delegates.[39] But clerks, restaurant workers, and others were often happy to see Jehovah's Witnesses leave. Their presence caused overwork and they were notoriously poor customers and tippers. Nor were the churches and religious press particularly gladdened by their diatribes against the clergy. Most significant, however, was the fact that New York's city fathers were concerned by the impact that the vast throngs of visitors had upon facilities within the city. They realized, as did the Watch Tower Society, that no similar convention could be held in the future. There were just too many Jehovah's Witnesses. Thus the 1958 convention was the last of the single, great international Witness assemblies to be held in one place. Thereafter, numerous smaller district and 'international' assemblies were to be held throughout the world.

Fighting for Freedom of Worship

Another important factor under Knorr's administration was the way in which Jehovah's Witnesses carried on legal battles in democratic societies. During the late 1930s and throughout the Second World War they were subjected to terrible persecution in the United States. Their refusal to salute the flag, to perform military service, and their insistence on carrying on a sometimes tactless campaign of door-to-door preaching caused them to get into serious trouble with both the public and law-enforcement agencies. In fact, between 1933 and 1951 there were 18,866 arrests of American Witnesses and about 1,500 cases of mob violence against them.[40] After the war their Canadian brethren in the province of Quebec experienced similar persecution. As a result the Watch Tower Society turned to the courts to obtain redress of grievances.

Although Judge Rutherford was the first to use the judicial process in defending the Bible Student–Witness community, and the Witnesses were already obtaining favourable decisions from the u.s. Supreme Court before his death, great Witness victories were won during Knorr's presidency, largely under the direction of Hayden Covington. As discussed more fully in Chapter 5, Covington led the Witnesses to one judicial victory after another before America's highest courts. Between 1938 and 1955 they were to fight a total of forty-five cases before the u.s. Supreme Court and were to win thirty-six.[41] But Covington does not alone deserve credit for having fought Witness judicial battles. Victor V. Blackwell, a Louisiana attorney and a stately southern gentleman, played a major role as their advocate.[41] So, too, did W. Glen How, an outstanding Canadian lawyer who was to duplicate later before the Supreme Court of Canada what Covington had done before the Supreme Court of the United States.[43]

Significantly, the Witnesses' fight for freedom of worship and the right to proselytize publicly served to create a real sense of *esprit de corps* among them. Especially was that so in Quebec. Consequently, the legal battles were perhaps more important to the Witness communities as morale builders than they were in gaining legal acceptance and a degree of good will, especially in the United States and Canada. Curiously, however, just as Jehovah's Witnesses were beginning to gain a very favourable reputation as champions of freedom of speech and worship, and were beginning to revel in it, the Watch Tower Society began to establish a system of 'theocratic law' which was illiberal in the extreme.

Congregation Committees and Disfellowshipping

Even after 1938 local congregations were left a 'scrap'of autonomy in that they could nominate a slate of capable men from whom the zone servant, as the society's representative, would choose one.[44] Knorr changed that, however, and replaced such nominations with 'congregation committees' of three men. These committees plus the circuit servant were to nominate prospective congregational 'servants' to the Watch Tower Society for appointment.[45]

More significant was the fact that such committees were now to act as church courts or 'judicial committees.' During Russell's day and even during much of Rutherford's presidency, Bible Students or Witnesses were tried before the whole 'church' or local congregation in an attempt to follow Jesus's command at Matthew 18:17. Under the new arrangement that custom was abolished. *The Watchtower* of 15 May 1944 stated: 'The offended one may tell the "church." According to theocratic order this would not mean a congregational meeting with all present, but telling it to those charged with the cares of the congregation and representing it in special service capacities.'[46] What this meant was that the Watch Tower Society had really established a clergy class, in spite of denials to the contrary, and church courts which were inquisitions in the dictionary and legal sense of the term. They were to fulfil 'the role of judge, jury and prosecutor of the accused.'

At first congregational judicial committees acted largely against persons who disagreed openly with the society's teachings and policies. Such were those who 'created divisions' or 'promoted sects' as described by Romans 16:17, 18 and Titus 30:10, 11. Although from 1952 forward for many years, this was not to be the case. What the society became primarily concerned with from that date until the late 1970s was 'keeping the organization clean.' Consequently, through congregational committees, it began to disfellowship fornicators, adulterers, drunkards, and persons guilty of other immoral practices.[47] As time went by, it broadened the number of offences for which one could be cast out of the Witness community. For example, associating with a disfellowshipped person was, for a dedicated Jehovah's Witness, declared a ground for disfellowshipment[48] as was the taking of a blood transfusion after 1961.[49]

Disfellowshipment became a terrible weapon. Witnesses in good standing were not to speak to disfellowshipped persons or even to greet them. In business dealings, they were to relate to them as little as possible. When they died, they were not to attend their funerals. To all intents and purposes they were regarded as eternally damned. Timothy White describes vividly the significance of all this:

When one becomes a Witness he cuts off from himself all former friends and builds an entirely new life completely wrapped up in his religion. He becomes separate from the world, renounces many of his hobbies, sports and other interests. Even his secular job becomes second in importance. If he is an extrovert, as all successful Witnesses must be, he gains happiness in his new role of spiritual salesman. His interest and energy become centered on the multifarious activities of the New World Society – preparing talks, conducting studies, teaching his children, attending assemblies and working at them and associating with his new found friends. A disfellowshipping cuts him suddenly and sweepingly off from all of this. His brothers avoid him for fear of becoming in like condition and he may no longer give talks at meetings. He cannot discuss religion at all with his wife and she takes over the teaching of the children for fear he may contaminate them with wrong ideas.[50]

A possibility of reinstatement to repentant excommunicants was held out. But often that entailed sitting silently in meetings without having anyone speak to the penitent for from one to three years; and when he was restored to fellowship, he would usually still be kept on 'probation' and denied certain congregational privileges.[51] For years, if one were disfellowshipped, he was told that never again would he hold an appointed position under the society's direction.[52]

Naturally, such severe discipline tended to mould Jehovah's Witnesses into an extremely moralistic, if not always moral, community. They became notable for strict styles of life which by their less devout neighbours were often seen as super-pietistic and sometimes rather foolish. Yet that fact had little or no impact on the Witnesses at all. Disfellowshipping had other effects, too. In African lands where polygamy was common, African males were told to give up all but their first wives or face exclusion from the Witness community. In other parts of the world where consensual marriages were common, Witnesses were also forced to legalize their unions. In places like Africa, Latin America, and the islands of the South Pacific, Jehovah's Witnesses forced upon their adherents traditional European and North American Protestant marriage values to a greater extent than had any important missionary movement in modern times.[53] Interestingly, although many were disfellowshipped when they refused to comply with these monogamous and legalistic standards then so strictly enforced by the Watch Tower Society, those who conformed were seemingly made more zealous. Like the society itself, they took great pride in being members of a 'morally clean' organization.

Of course disfellowshipping also increased greatly the control of both local congregational overseers and the society over the Witness faithful. There did not seem much objection to that, however, so long as most persons were excommunicated for moral infractions such as sexual immorality or drunkenness. There were amazingly few public complaints during the 1950s and 1960s over what, in other religious communities, might have created strong opposition to authority among many members.[54]

A Slowdown in Growth

An interesting factor relating to growth in the number of converts made by Jehovah's Witnesses since the First World War is that the greatest numbers of conversions have been made either 1 / during the periods when the Watch Tower Society pointed to a specific apocalyptic date near at hand, or 2 / when the world was in the midst of war or serious cold war. For example, growth was quite rapid between 1919 and 1925, but it was slow from 1926 through most of the 1930s. While some of the small increase in Witness numbers during the latter period was caused by the fact that many were leaving the movement in reaction to the creation of Judge Rutherford's 'theocratic arrangement,' not all of it was. As already noted, growth again became significant just prior to the Second World War and remained high throughout the 1940s and the early 1950s. Despite the creation and development of a highly efficient preaching organization under Knorr, in the latter years of the 1950s percentage increases in the number of converts began to taper off. During most of the 1960s growth was also relatively slow, certainly in comparison with what it had been in the earlier decades of the third Watch Tower president's administration.

The graphs which appear below give a fairly clear picture of the nature of Witness growth during the years from 1928 to 1982.

Stay Alive till '75

Growth in the number of publishers during the 1940s and 1950s had commonly been used by the Watch Tower Society as proof of divine favour. Watch Tower leaders revelled in the journalistic description of Jehovah's Witnesses as 'the world's fastest growing religion.' They also seemed to take a peculiarly American sense of satisfaction, not only from the dramatic increases in the numbers of baptisms and new Witness publishers, but also out of the construction of new printeries, branch headquarters, and the phenomenal amounts of literature which they published and distributed. Bigger always seemed better. Visiting speakers from the Brooklyn Bethel would often show slides or movies of the society's New York printing factory while they waxed eloquent to Witness audiences around the world on the amounts of paper used to print *The Watchtower* and *Awake!* magazines. So when the major increases of the early 1950s were replaced by the slow growth of the following ten or twelve years, this was somewhat disheartening to both Witness leaders and individual Jehovah's Witnesses throughout the world.

The result of such feelings on the part of some Witnesses was a belief that perhaps the preaching work was nearly finished: perhaps most of the other sheep had been gathered. Perhaps Armageddon was at hand. But in 1966 the society

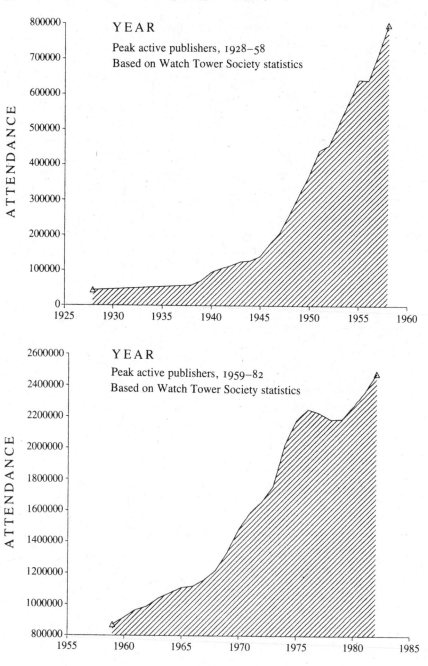

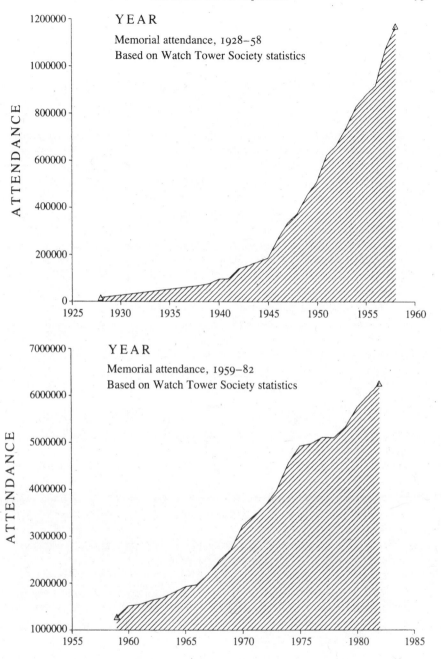

YEAR

Memorial attendance, 1928–58
Based on Watch Tower Society statistics

YEAR

Memorial attendance, 1959–82
Based on Watch Tower Society statistics

electrified the Witness community by pointing to the year 1975 as the end of six thousand years of human history and, therefore, *in all probability,* the beginning of the millennium. This it did in a new book entitled *Life Everlasting in Freedom of the Sons of God.*

On pages 28 and 29 of that book, its author, later to be revealed as Frederick Franz, states:

Since the time of Ussher intensive study of Bible chronology has been carried on. In this twentieth century an independent study has been carried on that does not blindly follow some traditional chronological calculations of Christendom, and the published timetable resulting from this independent study gives the date of man's creation as 4026 B.C.E. According to this trustworthy Bible chronology six thousand years from man's creation will end in 1975, and the seventh period of a thousand years of human history will begin in the fall of 1975 C.E.

So six thousand years of man's existence on earth will soon be up, yes, within this generation. Jehovah God is timeless, as it is written in Psalm 90:1, 2: 'O Jehovah, you yourself have proved to be a real dwelling for us during generation after generation. Before the mountains themselves were born, or you proceeded to bring forth as with labor pains the earth and the productive land, even from time indefinite to time indefinite you are God.' So from the standpoint of Jehovah God these passing six thousand years of man's existence are but as six days of twenty-four hours, for this same psalm (verses 3, 4) goes on to say: 'You make mortal man go back to crushed matter, and you say: "Go back, you sons of men." For a thousand years are in your eyes but as yesterday when it is past, and as a watch during the night.' So in not many years within our own generation we are reaching what Jehovah God could view as the seventh day of man's existence.

How appropriate it would be for Jehovah God to make of this coming seventh period of a thousand years a sabbath period of rest and release, a great Jubilee sabbath for the proclaiming of liberty throughout the earth to all its inhabitants! This would be most timely for mankind. It would also be most fitting on God's part, for, remember, mankind has yet ahead of it what the last book of the Holy Bible speaks of as the reign of Jesus Christ over earth for a thousand years, the millennial reign of Christ. Prophetically Jesus Christ, when on earth nineteen centuries ago, said concerning himself: 'For Lord of the sabbath is what the Son of man is.' (Matthew 12:8) It would not be by mere chance or accident but would be according to the loving purpose of Jehovah God for the reign of Jesus Christ, the 'Lord of the sabbath,' to run parallel with the seventh millennium of man's existence.

However, it was only in 1968 that the new date for the present world's end was really highlighted. In the district conventions of that year a small, new publication, *The Truth That Leads to Eternal Life,* was released to replace the old text *'Let God Be True'* as the primary study tool for making converts. More important, though, was the fact that the society suggested that home studies with interested persons in the new book ought to be limited to a period of no more than six months. By the end of that time prospective converts should already be Jehovah's Witnesses or at least be attending kingdom halls. The times were so limited, it was suggested, that if people did not want 'the Truth' within six months, others should be given a chance to learn it before it was too late. Needless to say, tremendous urging prompted many catechumens to get on the society's apocalyptic bandwagon. Furthermore, many lukewarm Witnesses also began to be reinvigorated spiritually. Then, in the autumn of 1968, the society began to publish a series of articles in the *Awake!* and *Watchtower* magazines which left no doubt that it expected the world to end in 1975.[55]

It is true that the society's literature never stated dogmatically that 1975 would definitely mark the end. Their leaders, particularly Frederick Franz, had undoubtedly learned *something* from the failure of 1925. None the less, the vast majority of Jehovah's Witnesses knew little or nothing about that or other, earlier, apocalyptic failures. Many, if not most, therefore accepted the new date quite uncritically. Especially was that so with the most active evangelists. Circuit overseers used the argument that the end was at hand to encourage proselytizing. Pioneer evangelists used it as a form of validation of their vocation and way of life.

It is also quite true that some older Witnesses and many with better educations questioned the society's speculation concerning 1975. Yet such doubters were often forced to remain silent. To many, to doubt the new date was to question the 'faithful and discreet slave' itself. Refusal to become outwardly excited or to openly deny the society's schedule for Armageddon was looked on as somewhat heretical and therefore spiritually dangerous within the highly disciplined community of Jehovah's Witnesses.

While doubters could say little, enthusiasts began preaching the coming of paradise immediately following 1975. Others, including Frederick Franz, suggested that tribulation for the world might begin even earlier. Thousands of Witness young people became pioneers as did many new converts. Businessmen sold prospering businesses. Professional men gave up their jobs. Families sold their homes and moved to serve 'where the need [for evangelists] was greater.' Young couples delayed their marriages or at least refrained from having children if they did marry. Old couples sometimes withdrew all their pension funds at once. Many, both young and old, male and female, delayed having surgery or proper medical attention. Often, as a theme for the times, young pioneers repeated the doggerel:

> Make do till '72
> Stay alive till '75

Growth in the number of converts soared, and so did literature placements. The Witness community therefore began to experience some of the euphoria of the early 1920s and the early 1950s. Spotty persecution in parts of the world, particularly in places like Greece and Malawi, only made the average Witness feel that Satan was about to make his final attack on God's Witnesses just before Christ cast him into an abyss of 'deathlike inactivity' at Armageddon.

Table 2 shows Witness growth during the years 1968 to 1975. Statistics are taken directly from the society's *Yearbook of Jehovah's Witnesses* for the years 1969 to 1976.

TABLE 2
World-wide growth of Jehovah's Witnesses, 1968–76

Year	Peak publishers	Memorial attenders
1968	1,221,504	2,493,519
1969	1,336,112	2,719,860
1970	1,483,430	3,226,168
1971	1,590,793	3,453,542
1972	1,658,909	3,662,407
1973	1,758,429	3,994,924
1974	2,021,432	4,550,457
1975	2,179,256	4,925,643
1976	2,248,390	4,972,571

Organizational and Congregational Liberalization

In 1971 the society took further major steps, but this time seemingly in the direction of brief but real liberalization. For the first time, a governing body, apart from the board of governors of the Watch Tower Bible and Tract Society of Pennsylvania, was created, theoretically on the model of the apostolic council of Jerusalem described in Acts 15. The new governing body did include the society's board of directors but added a number of faithful 'anointed' Witness men with a heavenly hope to their number. In all, the new governing body then included eleven members.[56] Of equal importance, however, the society announced that the old pre-1932 system of elders and deacons (now called ministerial servants) was to be restored. Although these congregational officers were to be appointed by the governing body through the society or its agents, at least the one-man rule under congregation servants that had been the case in Witness companies or congregations since 1938 was to be ended in September 1972. No longer would one individual dominate a congregation like a monarchical bishop.[57]

If the society was not democratizing Witness ecclesiastical governance, at least it was providing checks on the frequently dictatorial behaviour of local overseers, and also of district and circuit overseers. After the creation of the new system, the chairmanship of the governing body was to rotate on a yearly basis so that theoretically the president of the Watch Tower Society no longer would act as a supreme autocrat with more powers over Jehovah's Witnesses than the pope at Rome had over Catholics.[58] Rotation was to apply at the local congregational level and among district and circuit overseers as well. Every year the office of presiding overseer and chairman of the body of elders was to rotate to a different elder if at all possible. Other offices were also to be filled on a rotational basis.[59] District and circuit overseers were to exchange positions regularly and, more importantly, when they visited local congregations, their powers were to be largely persuasive rather than coercive. Although they were to participate on local bodies of elders as full members, they were given no more administrative rights than other elders.[60]

The plan for this arrangement was all carefully laid out in the book *Organization for Kingdom-Preaching and Disciple-Making* which set an entirely new tone for the Witness community. Besides the description of the now greatly modified system of organizational policy, it also recognized many needs that had long been ignored. In particular, it placed an emphasis on pastoral care of the 'shepherding work.'[61] Even Acts 20:20, which had long been a favourite Witness proof text for door-to-door evangelizing, was rightly recognized as applying to teaching within the Christian congregation rather than to converting non-believers. In that text the Apostle Paul is quoted as having stated that he had taught the Ephesian Christians 'publicly and from house to house' – hence the earlier confusion on the matter. But then, in 1972, the society indicated, albeit somewhat obliquely, in the pages of the *Organization* book that it understood that passage to refer to the apostle's teaching of Christians in their various homes.[62] Of course, by doing so, the society temporarily, at least, began to place more emphasis on ministering to the Witness community and less on external proselytizing.

The effects of this policy of liberalization on the Witness community were great. Individual elders often expressed their opinions in a way that they had not been able to do before, and some began to state openly that they believed that too much emphasis had been placed on the preaching work. Naturally, this brought a reaction from their more conservative fellows and from circuit overseers. Bodies of elders in many congregations began to split into liberal and conservative camps and, just as frequently, over a variety of personal issues. Being chosen an elder or ministerial servant also became a matter of social importance, and frequently one of congregational politics and in-fighting. Even more significantly, the new system undercut much of the authority of circuit and district overseers and made the offices of those men less attractive to persons who had long held great spiritual authority and with it great prestige.

More liberal-minded Witnesses hoped and believed that their community was going through a period which would lead to greater freedoms. But the primary reason behind liberalization, at least on the part of most Watch Tower leaders in Brooklyn, was no feeling that such change was fundamentally necessary and good. Rather, they believed that with 1975 approaching, great persecution might and no doubt would strike Jehovah's Witnesses on a world-wide scale. And if that should happen, direction from Brooklyn and the society's branch offices would cease. Hence it would be necessary for local elders and ministerial servants to act independently during the 'Great Tribulation' so near at hand, and that could only happen if they were given some independent pastoral authority prior to that time of troubles.[63]

Nevertheless, granting such increased authority to local elders was not always popular with local Witness publishers. If anything, some elders, now given more powers over their flock, acted with extreme severity over even the most inconsequential infractions of what *they* considered to be proper deportment. Consequently, individuals who chaffed under their rule and who generally idealized the society, looked back to the rule of congregation servants and circuit overseers as a more benevolent time. Also, publishers were sometimes shocked by the congregational politics which became almost ubiquitous in Witness congregations throughout the world. Yet local Jehovah's Witnesses were no doubt more satisfied with the new system and greater freedom than circuit and district overseers and many Watch Tower officials at the branch offices and Brooklyn. Like commissars and bureaucrats in a communist state, they disliked both their loss of power and prestige on one hand and the turmoil that resulted on the other. Furthermore, many were against the greater emphasis on shepherding. For time spent on internal pastoral work meant less time spent in 'field service' or door-to-door proselytizing. After all, the very basis of the prestige of members of the Witness hierarchy had long been based on the fact that they had practically all risen in the ranks as pioneers, as evangelists. Although most Witnesses high and low were unaware of it, the liberalization policy which was evident both in new organizational forms and the society's literature was as fragile as the brief period of democracy in Czechoslovakia in 1968. A powerful and entrenched bureaucratic hierarchy waited only to reassert spiritual control over a community which had been governed by the theocracy since 1938. But as long as Jehovah's Witnesses continued to grow at an unprecedented rate and to look forward to 1975 for their ultimate escape from 'this old world' with its sin, sickness, and corruption, the society continued to allow a high degree of freedom within local congregations – so long, at least, as such freedom did not conflict with traditional Watch Tower values.

CHAPTER FOUR

Prophetic Failure, Reaction, and Rebellion

When 1975 came and went with nothing spectacular having happened, many Jehovah's Witnesses were greatly disillusioned. Untold thousands left the movement. The *1976 Yearbook* reported that during 1975 there had been a 9.7 per cent growth in the number of Witness publishers over the previous year.[1] But in the following year there was only a 3.7 per cent increase,[2] and in 1977 there was somewhat more than a 1 per cent decrease![3] In some countries the decrease was far greater. In the Philippines, for example, in 1975 the average number of publishers was 76,662.[4] By 1979 it had dropped to 58,418 after four years of steady decreases.[5] So, in effect, more than 20 per cent of the entire active Witness population defected or at least became inactive. Similar, although less severe, temporary decreases also occurred in many other lands such as Germany, Nigeria, and Great Britain where there were large Witness populations.[6] In the few lands where there were still increases, they were far smaller than in the past. Only Japan seemed a real exception.[7]

Response to Prophetic Failure

The society's outward response to another prophetic failure of such significance was typical. Watch Tower leaders seemed stunned but refused to admit that they and they alone were responsible for the cognitive dissonance that was now so common among Jehovah's Witnesses world wide.[8] Some members of the governing body were concerned that Nathan Knorr and Frederick Franz had been so dogmatic about 1975 and were surprised that Franz, especially, had made so much of it in public discourses.[9] At the time Knorr was a very sick man whose mind was seriously affected by terminal brain cancer and could make little response. But Franz, who was to become the Watch Tower Society's fourth president two weeks after Knorr's death on 7 June 1977, had a novel explanation as to why Armegeddon had failed to happen in 1975. At Toronto, Ontario, in the spring of 1975, when speaking before a large Witness audience, he had stated that he and his associates were 'looking forward confidently' to what the autumn of the year would bring. But a year later, speaking before a similar audience in the same city, he asked rhetorically: 'Do you know why nothing happened in 1975?' Then, pointing at his audience, he shouted: 'It was because *you* expected something to happen.' In other words, since Jesus had predicted that no one would know the 'day or the hour' of his coming to judge mankind, the Witnesses should not have believed that they *could know* that it would occur in 1975. Incredibly, Franz placed the blame for the entire fiasco on the Witness community and acted virtually as though he had had no responsibility in the matter at all. Yet what about the prediction that 1975 had marked the end of 6,000 years of human history? Some explanation had to be given as to why the millennium had not begun then. So, Franz argued that God's seventh creative day or sabbath, a period of 7,000 years according to Pastor Russell's old reckoning, had not begun until after Eve had been created. Thus the society should have counted from Eve's creation rather than from Adam's; and, by Franz's latest reckoning, no one really knew when that had taken place.[10] Strangely, in making such an assertion, he blithely ignored the society's own recently published statements which held that Eve had been created *in the same year as Adam.*[11] Like Franz himself, most Witnesses either failed to note that fact or simply ignored it for the Watch Tower Society's latest 'new light.'

Throughout the Witness community circuit and district overseers – frequently the very men who had placed the greatest stress on 1975 as a year of prophetic significance – now often suddenly acted as though the fault for expecting the end in that year had lain with ordinary Jehovah's Witnesses. They held that the society had never said *definitely* that something would happen then, a fact which was quite true. But they completely ignored the additional fact that Knorr, Franz, and Watch Tower literature had implied over and over again that that year would see the end of the present dispensation of human history. Some circuit overseers and elders even stated that they 'couldn't understand why some people were so upset over the fact that Adam had had a birthday,' and Harley Miller, a senior official in the society's Service Department at Brooklyn, went much farther. Speaking sarcastically at a specially called meeting at the Del Mar Race Track in San Diego, California, sometime early in 1977, he remarked that those Witnesses who were 'disappointed' or 'upset' over 1975 should go out to sit under a large palm tree near the race track stadium and cry. Strangely, many Witnesses, particularly those in responsible positions, seemed to suffer from some sort of collective amnesia which caused them to act as though the year 1975 had never held any particular importance to them at all.

Ordinary Witnesses were sometimes somewhat more honest and began to deluge Brooklyn with letters.[12] Why had nothing happened in 1975? Equally importantly, why did not the society frankly admit that it had made a serious mistake? Ultimately, after a long period of trying to ignore the whole matter at Watch Tower headquarters, in 1979 an apology to the Witness faithful was finally given on behalf of the governing body at the district assemblies of that year.[13] In the meantime the society began to divert the attention of congregation publishers from the failure of 1975: The end was 'near at hand,' it again proclaimed, and therefore everyone *must* again be encouraged to preach. More must be converted before it was too late.

At district assemblies in 1978 it became fully obvious that the society was determined to set the clock back; the liberalization of the early 1970s was abandoned. The greatest emphasis was again placed on the preaching work, and Jesus was described as a 'pioneer.' In an assembly drama or 'morality play' on the Apostle Paul's companion Timothy, young persons fresh from high school were strongly discouraged from attending academies of higher learning, and an always latent Watch Tower animosity towards university education became more evident. At some assemblies, too, members of the governing body heaped scorn on the many former Witnesses 'who had left the truth.'

In the meantime, the society again began to tighten organizational reins over local congregations. During the early 1970s, the local presiding elder of each congregation had been requested to evaluate the effectiveness of his circuit overseer in a year-end report to the society; and quite evidently many had often been straightforward in their criticism of those circuit overseers who were too authoritarian. But in 1976 the society ended its policy of requiring reports on circuit overseers. Furthermore, it gradually restored pre-1972 powers to both circuit and district overseers and informed local elders, through meetings with branch representatives, that circuit and district overseers were the society's special representatives, its 'apostles.' Although circuit overseers had been regarded as 'fellow elders' during the period of liberalization, local elders were now told bluntly that 'the circuit overseer was not *just another elder.*'[14]

At the same time, the system of the rotation of elders was gradually abandoned to give more stability to local congregational governance.[15] In 1977, the society also created the office of congregational secretary[16] and thereby saw to it that it once again had a permanent anchorman in every congregation who could work with Brooklyn or the various branch offices and circuit overseers.

A tightening of control came in other ways as well. For a time during the early 1970s, elders were encouraged to spend time 'shepherding' their flocks by visiting members of their congregations on a personal, pastoral basis to aid them with any problems that they might have had. The reporting of time in public proselytizing or preaching, which for many years had been encouraged on a weekly basis, was de-emphasized. Rather than urging publishers to turn in a 'time report' once a week, they were by then allowed to report once a month only.[17] For several years elders were to report time spent in the 'shepherding work' as well as for that devoted to proselytizing or preaching to outsiders.[18] But with the drop in numbers of publishers in the late 1970s, the shepherding work was largely forgotten. Elders were now encouraged to do their 'shepherding work' at study centres and while they accompanied publishers in the door-to-door preaching work.[19] Great pressure was placed on them to get more time in 'the field service.' If a 'brother' or 'sister' had some serious personal problem, the elders would have to deal with it in their own time. No longer could they report time in pastoral or shepherding work; only proselytizing, preaching to the unconverted, now seemed to hold value to the society.

In Canada, this was demonstrated in another way. In the early 1970s a number of leading Canadian Witnesses (including Watch Tower officials at the Canadian branch) had organized 'hospital committees' to act as chaplains for Witnesses in hospitals, nursing homes, and senior citizens' homes. Among other things, they were interested in developing contacts with doctors and hospitals so that Witness patients would not have to face the possibility of being forced to accept blood transfusions, a procedure which the society had long taught to be scripturally unacceptable to Jehovah's Witnesses.[20] In a short time, the idea of establishing such committees spread from Toronto to a number of Canadian cities, and the 'hospital' or 'blood committees,' as they were often called, were generally very popular with local Witnesses. For the first time since the 1920s, certain Witness elders began to comfort the dying, encourage the convalescing, and show regular attention to their brothers except when pressing them to proselytize or disciplining them for some infraction of congregational law.[21]

The head offices of the society in Brooklyn soon put a stop to the hospital committees.[22] Some elders throughout Canada had complained about them for several reasons. For one thing, they had been developed by individual Witnesses in Toronto without express sanction from Brooklyn. Second, many of the elders involved on the committees began to become personally prominent with ordinary Witnesses, something which evoked both concern and some jealousy on the part of a number of their peers. And most important from the standpoint of those devoted primarily to the preaching work, if certain elders were spending so much time in hospital work, it was asked how they could take the lead in the field service.

Surprisingly, the governing body, in abolishing the Canadian hospital committees, argued that they tended to violate private and family medical rights and could come between the individual patient and his doctor. In addition, Brooklyn held that there should be no special committee chosen by local bodies of elders for special tasks *without the society's consent*. If shepherding or chaplaincy work was to be done, it would have to be carried on by all elders on an unorganized basis.[23]

The society's Canadian branch seemed somewhat embarrassed, and in a few places the hospital committees continued to operate in spite of the governing body's dictum.[24] But the whole matter caused some bad feelings, particularly among those elders who had given so much service to their brethren. The society's arguments over personal and family rights seemed facetious at best to many who were quite aware of the fact that a Witness could be and would be disfellowshipped for voluntarily accepting a blood transfusion. Also, it seemed equally evident that unless Brooklyn itself thought of something first, it was not willing to accept any new ideas. Then, finally, some of the elders affected negatively by the clampdown on the hospital committees began to feel that the governing body cared little about human health or welfare, only the preaching work.

Greater control over local congregations tended to bring with it a conservative reaction and a severe disciplining of anyone who had become too independent during the early 1970s. For some years there had been a great deal of bickering in many congregations, particularly in North America, over the dress and grooming of individual Witnesses, especially young persons. The length of teenaged boys' hair, the colour of shirts to be worn while giving talks at the kingdom hall, and the length of young women's skirts had frequently led to long and bitter debates at elders' meetings. Of course this had come, particularly in the United states, as a direct reaction to the anti-war youth movements of the late 1960s and the early 1970s which had frequently made slovenliness almost an outward badge of their social and political beliefs. Many working- and middle-class Witnesses were horrified by students' riots, the new morality, the prevalence of homosexuality, and a general lack of respect for authority. Consequently, Witness leaders often manifested attitudes in reference to dress, grooming, and deportment which were virtually identical to those of American fundamentalists, Mormons, and other religious conservatives.

The Attack on Intellectuals

With such negative attitudes towards 'rebellious youth,' popular dress, and grooming styles, Jehovah's Witnesses also took a dim view of anyone in their ranks who might tend to sympathize with more liberal cultural and spiritual views. Sometimes, too, they became frankly and rather shockingly anti-intellectual. In an article written by a Watch Tower missionary in Hong Kong, the 8 September 1968 *Awake!* had stated:

Those who belong to the professional classes may be said to be fair samples of the fruitage of 'higher education.' They form a sort of aristocracy of learning. Often they are proud, untouched by the needs of less fortunate people, opinionated, competitive, independent, and inconsiderate of others. They have deeply imbibed the godless theory of evolution. In their view educated men, college and university trained, are the sole hope for progress.

Who, for example, have substituted for the fine moral teaching of the Bible their human philosophies? Is it not the professional clergymen? And who are the ones today that are insistent upon having their own way and openly flaunting the authority of God's Word in the matter of the sacredness of blood? Is it not the professional doctors? Politicians, lawyers, educators, most of them without any real faith in the existence of God, are they not the end product of 'higher education'?[25]

In that same article other persons with higher education – clergymen, teachers, and university students – were blamed for the 'violent demonstrations, protests and other activities without legal restraint.' *Awake!* stated, 'Surely it is those men with all the advantages of their "higher education" who unscrupulously use their talents to put over their get-rich-quick schemes at the expense of the man in the street!'[26]

Naturally, with such 'spiritual food' coming from the 'faithful and discreet slave,' Witness university students were under tremendous social pressure to give up their studies, and young persons graduating from high school were faced with equally great pressure not to enter institutions of higher learning. Yet some did and could point to the fact the the society had placed no absolute ban on university or college studies. When the society began to tighten its control over the Witness community after the failure of 1975, however, it began to carry on a quiet, perhaps unintentional, campaign against many persons with higher education within its own ranks. University students were severely criticized for trying to build up careers in 'this dying old world,' and professional persons frequently found themselves in disfavour with circuit and district overseers.

Part of this resulted from a fear of the ideas and activities of more liberal-minded individuals who had some prominence in the Witness community because of their education and secular occupations. In spite of the society's hostile, or at best ambivalent, attitudes towards academe, many ordinary Witnesses tended to respect the handful of physicians, lawyers, dentists, professors, teachers, pharmacists, and scientists within their own congregations. After all, such persons often gave some prestige to their faith and could usually be counted on to aid less well-educated Witnesses with a variety of personal problems. But because many times they were the most outspoken critics of the religious conservatism which was sweeping over Jehovah's Witnesses everywhere, they were frequently the targets of severe personal criticism from intolerant elders and circuit overseers. In addition, they were sometimes the victims of the anti-intellectualism and personal jealousy of some prominent Watch Tower officials.

Just how far this went is shown by the fact that even apologists for the society and Jehovah's Witnesses came under attack for their efforts. For years the society had taken a very negative attitude towards almost anyone who wanted to study the Witnesses in depth. When, in 1943, Herbert Stroup sought assistance from N.H. Knorr to have individual Witnesses fill out questionnaires that he had prepared for a sociological study of the movement, Knorr replied: '[the] Society does not have the time, nor will it take the time, to assist you in your publication concerning Jehovah's Witnesses.'[27] As noted earlier, William Cumberland had much the same sort of experience in the 1950s. Over the years Watch Tower leaders did begin to see some value in quoting the works of scholars, so long as they had positive things to say about the Witnesses.[28] Yet they remained largely suspicious of students of the movement. Even Witness Marley Cole, who had published an 'approved' history, *Jehovah's Witnesses: The New World Society,* under the Watch Tower's all too close supervision,[29] became somewhat unpopular with some of the society's officials when he independently published a second and far better book on the Witnesses entitled *Triumphant Kingdom.*[30] Cole did not, however, come under the stern censure that Witness writers did in the late 1970s and early 1980s.

For example, when Victor Blackwell wrote *O'er the Ramparts They Watched,* an account of Witness court cases in the United States, he became quite popular with many of his brethren. This was not the case with the governing body. Although Blackwell had long defended fellow Witnesses in court at virtually no charge, had taught at Gilead, and had written for the society, he was accused of trying to 'exalt himself.' Brooklyn discouraged Witnesses from attending public meetings at which he was invited to speak; he was removed as an elder and came close to being disfellowshipped.[31]

Blackwell received better treatment than a Swedish Witness, Ditlieb Felderer. Felderer did extensive research and produced a manuscript history of Jehovah's Witnesses which, in particular, cast a very good light on Pastor Russell. When he presented it to Brooklyn, however, he was treated with what he regarded as utmost discourtesy and became alienated. Later he was disfellowshipped.[32]

All this fit in with the society's policy of discouraging individual Witnesses from publishing anything relating to their faith. The stated attitude of most high Watch Tower officials and the governing body in particular was that if something needed to be published, the society would do it. Witnesses who worked independently were therefore in grave danger of being accused of 'trying to exalt themselves,' trying to 'run ahead of God's organization,' or of trying 'to make money' on their brothers. Thus, for so large a religious community, Jehovah's Witnesses produced remarkably few persons to speak independently on their behalf during the 1960s and early 1970s. After 1976 it became virtually impossible to write as a Jehovah's Witness scholar without being in danger of being 'disciplined' by the Watch Tower Society or some of its agents.

Although the society's policy of discouraging independent research and publication was no doubt caused in part by an attitude of spiritual arrogance, there was far more to it than that. Over the years Watch Tower officials had created an idealized history of the Bible Student–Witness movement by distorting and suppressing many unflattering historical facts. Although Pastor Russell believed that 1914 would mark the end of the present world, today the Watch Tower Society makes it appear as though he had predicted that that year would usher in 'the last days.' During the late 1920s and early 1930s, the society failed to publish memorial attendance statistics, no doubt because those statistics would have demonstrated just how many were leaving the movement at that time. *Jehovah's Witnesses in the Divine Purpose* and Alexander H. Macmillan's *Faith on the March* presented false history, in particular with respect to the Watch Tower schism of 1917. As it had done for decades, the society continued to gloss over past prophetic disconfirmations as though they had never happened. Average Jehovah's Witnesses were, therefore, almost totally unaware of these facts, and the society had no desire to enlighten them. Thus it did what it could to prohibit independent Witness research. Nevertheless, during the 1970s a number of professionals, academics, and self-educated Witness scholars began to investigate Witness history, doctrines and practices with far-reaching negative consequences to the Watch Tower power structure.

In the first place, early in the 1970s Chris Christenson of Vancouver, British Columbia, began to question the authority of the governing body of Witness disfellowshipping practices. Consequently Christenson, who had contributed research material for the society's allegorical and typological study of Ezekiel, *'The Nations Shall Know that I Am Jehovah' – How?,* became engaged in a campaign to reform Jehovah's Witnesses from within. Over a period of time, he openly censured the governing body for many of its practices, produced a major essay on disfellowshipping, and, along with a number of anonymous Witnesses, circulated thousands of copies of a document known as 'The Pronouncements' which questioned many Witness teachings. As one might expect, these activities led to Christenson's disfellowshipment in 1972,[33] but his activities had some small but significant impact in both Canada and the United States.

In the mid-western United States, Dr Randy Wysong, a veterinarian, college instructor, and creationist scholar, sincerely raised a number of questions with fellow elders based on 'The Pronouncements' and found himself the victim of a whispering campaign among his fellow Witnesses. Eventually, Wysong was removed as an elder, and when he appealed to Brooklyn, the society refused to answer his letters. Sometime later, he and his family resigned from Jehovah's Witnesses with great bitterness.[34]

In another instance, Carl Olof Jonsson, a well-educated Swedish Witness, became concerned about the accuracy of the society's 'biblical chronology' which is used to 'prove' that the Gentile Times covered a period of 2,520 years from 607 BC to AD 1914. As a result, Jonsson began a careful study of ancient Middle-Eastern chronology dating back to the eighth century BC and discovered that the society's contention that Jerusalem had fallen to Nebuchadnezzar of Babylon in 607 BC was historically, archaeologically, and astronomically indefensible. He thereupon prepared a careful typescript of his findings in English entitled 'The Gentile Times Reconsidered' and, in 1977, loyally submitted it to Brooklyn for analysis and comment.

At first the society indicated it would examine the Jonsson typescript and evaluate it. But shortly thereafter it began a campaign of innuendo against him which was echoed in *The Watchtower*. As a result he felt constrained to resign as an elder and in July 1982 was disfellowshipped as disloyal to the society. Recently his story has been told in the Swedish press.[35]

Of course Jonsson was viewed by the society as most dangerous. If his manuscript became widely known among Jehovah's Witnesses not only would Watch Tower chronology have to be discarded or at least revised in a major way but, equally important, the very basis of the governing body's authority as the collective spiritual overseer of Jehovah's Witnesses would be destroyed.

This fact quickly became obvious. Although Jonsson had approached the society as a scholar rather than a reformer, he had circulated a few copies of 'The Gentile Times Reconsidered' to certain intellectually minded Witness friends. Unfortunately for the Watch Tower Society, some of these copies were photocopied and sent to such far-away places as South America, Australia, and Canada. And in the latter two places, Jonsson's findings were to have effect. In Australia, for example, a number of Witnesses who were questioning the society's chronology were strengthened in their doubts by reading 'The Gentile Times Reconsidered.' Eventually a number of them left Jehovah's Witnesses to become Seventh-Day Adventists.[36] In Canada, the results were not so immediate, but the Jonsson typescript was also to be a significant factor in outbreaks of dissidence throughout that country in the early 1980s.

Quite evidently, then, the society had good reason to fear the activities of Witness scholars. For its leaders were being made aware that many of their fundamental teachings could not bear close historical and scientific scrutiny. Yet in their zeal to suppress almost any questioning among the Witness faithful, the society no doubt went too far. By trying to stop questioning and independent study, Witness leaders often alienated able men and women to such an extent that they sometimes left the movement and began to oppose it openly or began to carry on underground activities against the society's authority from within the Witness community. The society's leaders seemed completely unaware of the seriousness of the situation, however, and in their desire to stop any type of outspokenness or independence of mind began to chastise some of their most loyal professional supporters. Even W. Glen How, who had been named a Queen's counsellor for his notable record of defending Jehovah's Witnesses before the Canadian courts, was for a time removed as an elder. He admitted that had he not moved from one congregation to another, he would have been disfellowshipped 'for no reason at all.'[38]

Naturally, this suppression of intellectuals tended to reduce the number of academics and highly trained professionals among Jehovah's Witnesses and, at the same time, made it more difficult for the Witnesses to convert new members from among the well educated. Commenting on this situation, Havor Montague remarks:

Very few intelligent or well-educated people join the Witnesses, and those few who do involve themselves with the Witnesses do not stay. It is difficult for an active, intelligent, aware person to remain a Witness – not because their beliefs are unfounded, but because the Wt. hierarchy tends to want to control the belief structure of its members in even minor areas. Even a Witness endeavoring to serve as an apologist is not tolerated. The authoritarian Wt. hierarchy prohibits religious publishing among members and even discourages most theological research and discussion. JW's are constantly encouraged not to 'run ahead of the Society' as though this was even possible according to the Society's own teachings. Many Witnesses, through their independent Bible research, have anticipated major changes that the Society later brought out. Until that time, those who have the audacity to mention the results of their own research have often been severely reprimanded, even if the Society may later on confirm the results of their research.[39]

One prominent Witness also stated: 'One of the things that bothers me most about the Society is the incredibly arrogant attitude of those at Bethel – refusing to listen to reason or give credit for the individual members having a mind ... Actually, virtually everyone I know that is fairly well educated has left them, even though there were a few bright members who were, at one time, in the movement.'[40]

Closing Heaven's Gates

Another group of persons who started to experience repression both locally and from the society itself in the late 1970s were those Witnesses who began to manifest a heavenly hope. As noted earlier, since 1935 the society had taught that all of the 144,000 members of the church – Christ's body – had been chosen and that only *replacements* for those of that class who had become unfaithful would be selected from the 'great crowd' of Revelation 7:14. Of course, as older 'anointed' Witnesses died off over the years, this meant that the number of persons looking forward to a heavenly reward within the movement declined. At least this happened until 1973 when, to the shock of some Witness leaders, the number proclaiming themselves to be of the body of Christ actually increased.[41] In the following year this happened again,[42] contrary to the society's belief that the *remnant* of the 144,000 would steadily decrease in numbers as Armageddon approached.[43] The increase in the number of those proclaiming themselves to have a heavenly hope in the early 1970s was probably inevitable. It is not surprising that of the hundreds of thousands who were becoming Witness converts prior to 1975, some should see themselves as having that hope. What is noteworthy is that more did not do so, especially during the organizationally and doctrinally more liberal period. For the one mystic, entirely individualistic rite of Witness religion which the society had allowed to remain after the 1930s was the right of each individual to determine whether he would participate in the Lord's Supper at the spring Memorial or not. As a result, each person could indicate to his congregation by partaking of the *emblems*, the bread and wine, that he considered himself to have received the spirit's call to become one of the *anointed*, a member of the 144,000; and in theory his brothers were to respect that calling.

Curiously, though, many Watch Tower officials, in particular circuit overseers, often looked on the 'new partakers' with the utmost suspicion. Congregation publishers and elders often questioned whether the new partakers had *really* received the heavenly call. And most strangely, in spite of the society's teaching of the need to show great respect for Christ's brothers, new partakers were often treated as 'individuals who were filled with pride' or 'persons who thought they knew more than the society.' Consequently, if one were much less than sixty-five years of age and began partaking of the Lord's Supper, he was under intense social and organizational pressure to stop. Sometimes he would be gossiped about, virtually shunned, and treated with the utmost disrespect. Thus some partakers were bullied into denying their heavenly calling by peer pressure, the elders, or the circuit overseers.

Doctrinal Vacillations

What all of this indicated was that the relative liberalism of the early 1970s was for tactical purposes only, although some Watch Tower leaders were, as Raymond Franz shows in his *Crisis of Conscience,* truly committed to it for a time. But even during that period of organizational euphoria, the society continued to demonstrate a streak of authoritarianism and extreme arbitrariness. As in Rutherford's day, doctrinal changes could be made to fit the whims of the leadership or what they considered to be the pragmatic interests of the organization as a whole. Hence, important teachings were sometimes changed almost by sleight of hand. When reaction to the failure of 1975 set in at Brooklyn, this tendency to such arbitrary behaviour became even more obvious. A few well-documented examples will demonstrate this clearly.

One area in which thoughtless religious pietism has affected Witness doctrine erratically over the last twelve years had been in the area of grounds for divorce. Traditionally the Watch Tower Society has argued since the nineteenth century that adultery constituted the only proper basis for divorce according to Jesus's words at Matthew 19:9: 'whoever divorces his wife, except on the ground of fornication, and marries another commits adultery.' Basically, then, although a man could divorce his wife for having intercourse with another man, or a woman could divorce her husband for having sexual relations with another woman, no Jehovah's Witness could divorce a marriage mate for homosexuality, lesbianism, or for bestiality. In fact, Witnesses who had homosexual mates were actually instructed to continue rendering the marriage due to them.

In accord with this position, *The Watchtower* of 1 Janaury 1972 stated: 'While both homosexuality and bestiality are disgusting perversions, in the case of neither one is the marriage tie broken. It is broken only by acts that make an individual "one flesh" with a person of the other sex other than his or her legal marriage mate.'[44] Consequently, should a Witness have divorced his or her mate on the grounds of homosexuality, lesbianism, or bestiality at the time and married another, the one divorcing would have been disfellowshipped.

That all changed within the same year. Without a word of apology for doing a complete *volte face, The Watchtower* of 15 December 1972 argued that when Jesus used the term 'fornication' *(porneia)* in his statement on divorce, he had intended to include *all* types of illicit sexual intercourse. The society's official journal went on to say:

What, then, is the significance of the Bible's use of these terms [fornication and adultery] and what does it reveal as to the valid Biblical grounds for divorce? It shows that any married person who goes outside the marriage bond and engages in immoral sexual relations, whether with someone of the opposite sex or someone of the same sex, whether natural or unnatural and perverted, is guilty of committing *porneia* or 'fornication' *in the Bible sense* ...

Taking Jesus' words for what they mean, therefore, when a mate is guilty of such serious sexual immorality the innocent mate may Scripturally divorce such a one, if he or she so desires.[45]

The new teaching was regarded by most Witnesses very positively since it seemed more reasonable and allowed some faithful Witnesses – particularly women – to dissolve emotionally abhorrent marriages both with good conscience and without fear of being brought before judicial committees under threat of disfellowshipment. But if any felt that the society might become more truly 'liberal' with respect to sexual matters, they soon had such thoughts dispelled.

Curiously, as a direct response to personal feelings on the matter within the governing body, the society began to develop an attitude common among some of the post-Nicene Church Fathers and numerous Protestants during the sixteenth and seventeenth centuries. Fornication or *porneia*, it held, could occur *within marriage* as well as outside the marriage union; if a husband should forcibly perform 'unnatural acts' on his wife, she would have the right to charge him with *porneia* before her congregational elders and divorce him with the Watch Tower's sanction.

From 1973 on for a number of years, some of the society's publications became very graphic with respect to what constituted *porneia*. Sodomy, oral intercourse, and masturbation were all condemned,[46] although masturbation was not listed as grounds for divorce. And doubtlessly because of its concern for the 'sacredness of blood,' Brooklyn, in effect, reimposed the Mosaic prohibition as stated at Leviticus 20:18 on coitus during menstruation.[47] The subject of *porneia* as then defined became almost a major theme. Talks on the subject were frequently given at large assemblies, and much to the obvious embarrassment of many, elders were required to give explicit hour sermons at Sunday meetings on the matter from detailed outlines published by the society.

As a result of all this, many witnesses became almost paranoid on the subject of sex. Often normal marital relations between husband and wife were affected adversely. Some began to regard sex with abhorrence. Witness wives sometimes complained that they feared that if they did anything unseemly during lovemaking with their husbands, they might be judged adversely by God. After all, were not the angels watching their actions? Witness elders at Kingdom Ministry schools (occasional retreats for training elders) often discussed in almost talmudic terms just what actions were permissible and what were not during marital loveplay. In addition, many elders who had been raised when sex was not such an open topic of conversation wondered how to give counsel to couples and particularly women who came to them for advice.

Undoubtedly, the society's new doctrine on *porneia* caused much harm. Such stress was placed on the evils of masturbation that great numbers of young Witnesses, who were encouraged to delay marriage, developed thoroughgoing sin complexes. More seriously, married couples sometimes felt constrained to describe the intimacies of their personal, marital relationship to elders who were often both pietistic and totally untrained in dealing with such matters. Sometimes elders and ministerial servants were removed from office and disfellowshipped for committing *porneia* within marriage. Sometimes, too, wives used marital *porneia* as a basis to divorce their husbands, whether validly or not.

Naturally this caused deep perplexity and equally great resentment among some Witnesses. Elders often did not know how to deal ethically with some situations with which they were faced; and even many among those who were Watch Tower loyalists complained privately that 'the Society had no business in bedrooms of married couples.'

Finally, then, because of growing concern among so many Witnesses, and no doubt because of the great numbers of letters that Brooklyn and the society's branch offices received to ask for clarification on certain points or to complain, the society, again without warning, reversed itself on the whole issue. *The Watchtower* of 15 February 1978, stated simply: 'It must be acknowledged that the Bible does not give any specific rules or limitations as regards the manner in which husband and wife engage in sexual relations.' But that was not all. After having been thoroughly dogmatic on the subject of marital *porneia* for six years, *The Watchtower* stated in the same article: 'This should not be taken as condoning of all the various sexual practices that people engage in, for that is by no means the case. It simply expresses a keen sense of responsibility to let the Scriptures rule and to refrain from taking a dogmatic stand where the evidence does not seem to provide sufficient basis ... It expresses a willingness to leave the judgement of such intimate matters in the hands of Jehovah God and his son.'[48] Henceforth, elders were not to concern themselves with marital relationships. If wives divorced their marriage mates for acts of 'a gross nature' or 'lewdness' within marriage, then *they and they alone* would have to take full responsibility before God for their actions.[49]

Although the society did acknowledge that it had reassessed the whole matter, and some who had been disfellowshipped for so-called marital *porneia* had their disfellowshipments annulled,[50] there was no general apology from Brooklyn for having taught admittedly false doctrines for six years. Although marriages had evidently been improperly dissolved and reputations ruined, the 'faithful and discreet slave' manifested little sorrow for having been so indiscreet as to have taught doctrines which had caused such havoc.

Another instance of an equally serious doctrinal vacillation during the 1970s involved the society's dicta with regard to organ transplants. For many years the Watch Tower leaders apparently saw no moral or ethical problem respecting the replacements of body parts with organs donated by other persons. For instance, in the 22 December 1949 issue of *Awake!* there appeared an article entitled 'Spare Parts for Your Body' which stressed positively the wonders of modern surgery in transplanting both human and artifical organs. Although blood transfusions were described as unscriptural, cornea, kidney, and bone transplants were not condemned. In 1961 *The Watchtower* stated in reply to a question from a reader:

The question of placing one's body or parts of one's body at the disposal of men of science or doctors at one's death for purposes of scientific experimentation or replacement in others is frowned upon by certain religious bodies. However, it does not seem that any Scriptural principle or law is involved. It therefore is something that each individual must decide for himself. If he is satisfied in his own mind and conscience that this is the proper thing to do, then he can make such provision, and no one else should criticize him for doing so. On the other hand, no one should be criticized for refusing to enter into any such an agreement.[51]

Yet in 1967 the society suddenly decided that what had been permissible no longer was. Organ transplants suddenly became a form of human cannibalism. *The Watchtower* issue of 15 November stated:

When there is a diseased or defective organ, the usual way health is restored is by taking in nutrients. The body uses the food eaten to repair or heal the organ, gradually replacing the cells. When men of science conclude that this normal process will no longer work and they suggest removing the organ and replacing it directly with an organ from another human, this is simply a shortcut. Those who submit to such operations are thus living off the flesh of another human. That is cannibalistic. However, in allowing man to eat animal flesh Jehovah God did not grant permission for humans to try to perpetuate their lives by cannibalistically taking into their bodies human flesh, whether chewed or in the form of whole organs or body parts taken from others.[52]

In addition to taking such a stance, *The Watchtower* came out four-square against the 'mutilation of the body' after death. To those in possible need of transplant surgery it stated: 'Christians who have been enlightened by God's word do not need to make these decisions [to donate organs or receive them from another person] simply on the basis of personal whim or emotions. They can consider the divine principles recorded in the Scriptures and use these in making personal decisions as they look to God for direction, trusting him and putting their confidence in the future that he has in store for those who love him.'[53]

Of course the 1967 ruling caused terrible hardships for many individual Witnesses. Persons needing cornea transplants to see were told by the society that that would have to wait until the 'new order which was so near at hand' to have their sight restored. Those needing kidney transplants to live were told that to accept them would bring everlasting destruction. Yet after many faithful Jehovah's Witnesses had suffered for their faith by giving up transplants which in some cases could have made their lives more pleasant and comfortable and by saving them from early death in others, the society again reversed itself.

In a rather curious response to a question on whether a congregation should take judicial action against one who accepted a cornea or kidney transplant, the 15 March 1980 *Watchtower* stated: 'Regarding the transplantation of human tissue or bone from one human to another, this is a matter for conscientious decision by each one of Jehovah's Witnesses. Some Christians might feel that taking into their bodies any tissue or body part from another human is cannibalistic. They might hold that the transplanted human material is intended to become part of the recipient's body to keep him alive and functioning. They might not see it as fundamentally different from consuming flesh through the mouth.'[54] Still, remarked the Witness journal, 'other sincere Christians today may feel that the Bible does not definitely rule out medical transplants of human organs.'[55] No doubt was to be left that the society was reverting to its pre-1967 stance: 'While the Bible specifically forbids consuming blood, there is no Biblical command pointedly forbidding the taking in of other human tissue. For this reason, each individual faced with making a decision on this matter should carefully and prayerfully weigh matters and then decide conscientiously what he or she could or could not do before God. It is a matter for personal decision. (Gal. 6:5) The congregational judicial committee would not take disciplinary action if someone accepted an organ transplant.'[56] Jehovah's Witnesses could now accept transplants; divine principles on the matter had changed again.

Even more drastic were changes respecting the preaching work and the Watch Tower concept of what a minister of religion was. As noted in Chapter 3, in 1972 the society finally recognized that Acts 20:20 did not apply to door-to-door proselytizing. Although it continued to defend the King James and New World translations of that verse in which the Apostle Paul states that he taught the Ephesian Christians 'publicly and from house to house,' it recognized that what the apostle was doing was holding services in the homes of various Christian converts rather than going from door to door. In a somewhat obscure footnote on page 56, the book *Organization for Kingdom-Preaching and Disciple-Making*, remarked:

A similar work 'from house to house' is referred to in Acts 5:42. Here some modern translators (RS; MO; NA) render the Greek expression here *(kat' oi kon)* as 'at home.' On this we refer to a comment made by Dr A.T. Robertson, the author of the 1454-page book *A Grammar of the Greek New Testament in the Light of Historical Research* (1934). Referring to such a rendering, he says in his book *Word Pictures in the New Testament,* Volume III on 'The Acts of the Apostles,' page 70, paragraph 3:

'In the temple and at home (en toi hieroi kai kat' oikon). This was a distinct triumph to go

back to the temple where they had been arrested (verse 25) and at home or from house to house, as it probably means (chapter 2:46). It was a great day for the disciples in Jerusalem.'

As regards the translation 'from house to house' (kat' oi kous) in Acts 20:20, which some modern translators would render as: 'at your houses' (AT) 'in your homes' (JE;NE) 'in private' (NA), Doctor Robertson has this to say on pages 349, 350, paragraph 1:

'and from house to house (kai kat' oikous). By (according to) houses. It is worth noting that this greatest of preachers preached from house to house and did not make his visits merely social calls. He was doing kingdom business all the while as in the house of Aquila and Priscilla (1 Cor. 16:19).'

Of course, by referring to 1 Corinthians 16:19, Professor Robertson indicated clearly that he understood *kat' oikous* or 'from house to house' to mean in the various houses of the Ephesian Christians. That text says: 'The congregations of Asia send YOU their greetings, Aquila and Priscilla *together with the congregation that is in their house* greet YOU heartily in the Lord' (italics mine). So by including the citation of that verse in Robertson's remarks as they appear above, Watch Tower leaders were admitting for the first time – perhaps unintentionally – that their earlier understanding of a favourite proof text had been wrong.

During the next seven years, Acts 20:20 virtually disappeared from Watch Tower publications, although some members of the governing body wanted to retain the society's traditional interpretation of it.[57] But in the post-1975 period the governing body decided that virtually everything possible had to be done to press the Witness faithful to more strenuous efforts in the preaching work; new converts had to be found to replace those who were leaving the organization in such ever-increasing numbers. Thus, for what amounted to purely pragmatic reasons, Acts 20:20 was again given its pre-1972 meaning.

In 'Zeal for Jehovah's House,' an article probably written by Watch Tower Vice-President Lloyd Barry and approved by the governing body after some discussion, *The Watchtower* of 15 July 1979 dredged up all the old pre-1972 arguments for asserting that the Apostle Paul has established a pattern for the modern house-to-house preaching work of Jehovah's Witnesses. Barry, or whoever the author of the article was, again used Robertson's quotation on *kat' oikous* as it appeared in *Organization for Kingdom-Preaching and Disciple-Making* but, with a completely cavalier disrespect for scholarly honesty, failed to include within it the latter's citation of 1 Corinthians 16:19. Paragraph seventeen of 'Zeal for Jehovah's House' reads:

This phrase 'from house to house' is translated from the Greek *kat oikous*. Though there are other renderings, many well-known versions of the Bible use this expression – 'from house to house.' This is because the Greek preposition *kata* is used in a 'distributive' sense.

(Compare the similar use of *kata* at Luke 8:1 – '*from* city *to* city,' '*from* village *to* village'; and at Acts 15:21 – '*in* city *after* city.') Thus it may be said that Paul's 'thorough witnessing' was *distributed* house after house. Bible scholar Dr A.T. Robertson comments as follows on Acts 20:20:

'By (according to) houses. It is worth noting that greatest of all preachers preached from house to house and did not make his visits mere social calls.'

As Paul 'thoroughly bore witness,' Christians today search for spiritually inclined householders, making return visits to those homes and studying with interested persons. Later, as necessary, shepherding calls are made by faithful overseers.[58]

Some few Jehovah's Witnesses were shocked at the society's behaviour in this case. The *Organization* book was then still the official authority for the governance of the organization as a whole, and some elders had studied it closely. None the less, the governing body was determined to enforce its resurrected doctrine as an article of faith; district and circuit overseers were instructed to teach that anyone questioning it was opposing the preaching work and was verging on apostasy. Hence, one district overseer declared publicly that a refusal to accept the society's 1979 doctrine on Acts 20:20 was equivalent to spiritual adultery.[59]

The most open and dramatic flip-flop on a doctrinal matter involved the old question of ministerial status. For decades the society claimed that all Jehovah's Witnesses – men, women, and children – were without exception ministers of religion. Judge Rutherford had declared of all those claiming to be of the 144,000: 'The anointed ones are God's ministers; therefore God's servants.'[60] Later, under N.H. Knorr the society asserted that the same was true with respect to the 'other sheep' class as well. In fact, during the Second World War and for many years thereafter, hundreds of young Jehovah's Witness men claimed exemption from military service in western democracies as ministers of religion, even though in many cases they did not hold any officially appointed position in their respective congregations.[61]

Suddenly, in the 1 December 1975 *Watchtower,* this was all changed. After an extended discussion of the term 'minister' in various languages, that magazine held that only elders and ministerial servants could be regarded as ordained ministers in Witness congregations,[62] although pioneers could continue to claim to be 'regular ministers.'

Quite evidently the society was making such a serious definitional change for a specific reason. In many cases when Witness men had claimed the right to exemption from military or civilian service under legislation in places such as the United States, Canada, and Great Britain, induction boards had simply ignored their claims because they did not constitute a ministerial or clergy class in the general sense of that term.[63] In fact, British courts held that while Jehovah's

Witnesses constituted a religion, they had no ministers.[64] So the December 1975 position no doubt resulted because the society recognized that the assertion that all Jehovah's Witnesses were ministers was rather meaningless from a legal standpoint and that there was little biblical support for it in any case. The 1 December 1975 *Watchtower* therefore stated:

In view of all this [discussion on the term 'minister'], what should one do if, as at times occurs, a governmental agency inquires into the profession or position of citizens? By them, the expression 'ordained minister' is understood to mean one who is appointed caretaker and server of spiritual things to a congregation, one who acts as a 'pastor' or shepherd of a congregation. Dictionaries, for example, give the generally understood ecclesiastical definition of a 'minister' as 'one authorized to conduct religious services.' By the term 'minister' such governmental agencies do not describe or mean the service that every individual Christian may perform in his or her personal efforts to share the good news with others. In answering inquiries, then, one would reasonably reply in harmony with what the official inquirers are seeking to know, rather than imposing one's own definition on such terms.[65]

Such a position was most reasonable even if it did serve a pragmatic purpose. Nevertheless, the needs of the Watch Tower Society changed again, and again it found no more difficulty in changing doctrine than the average man does in changing his shirt. The 15 March 1981 *Watchtower* published several articles on the subject of who might be classified as ministers, and in doing so reverted to the pre-1975 doctrine. Under the heading 'Female Minister' it stated: 'Yes, all dedicated and baptized Christians, regardless of sex or age, can be proclaimers, preachers, ministers, "servants" in an elevated or sacred sense – provided they give proof thereof by their conduct and their witnessing.'[66] No doubt *their witnessing* was to be regarded as the more important.

The Growth of Dissent

The failure of 1975 and the society's reaction to it ultimately caused small but significant revolts against Watch Tower authority. Although a few individuals such as Chris Christenson had protested certain of the society's policies during the early and mid-1970s, there had been no general reaction among Witnesses to its teachings.

By 1975 that was beginning to change. In that year and early in the next the *Billings Gazette* of Billings, Montana, reported the disfellowshipment of a number of local Witnesses for teaching that the resurrection of the saints had not begun in 1918. Ultimately eighteen were disfellowshipped or resigned in the Billings area.[67] Then, early in 1976, the *Tri-City Herald* of Pasco, Kennewick, and Richland, Washington, announced: 'Twenty-one Jehovah's Witnesses in the Tri-Cities and Prosser have been excommunicated because their beliefs about resurrection do not agree with the church's teachings.'[68] Again the issue was Watch Tower chronology, specifically the importance the society placed on the years 1914 and 1918.[69]

Shortly thereafter, the same sort of dissent developed in the Australian state of Victoria just outside Melbourne. On 6 April 1977, the *Franklin Peninsula News* published an article entitled 'Witness in a Wilderness' which told of the upcoming excommunication of a number of Jehovah's Witnesses in the communities of Frankston, Morningston, and Rosebud. A statement given by one of the dissidents read: 'Jehovah's Witnesses teach that the Kingdom of Christ began to rule in heaven in the year 1914 and that the first resurrection of the apostles began and took place in 1918. We as a group have found this belief to be in serious error and we have begun to stand up and question what we now know to be wrong.'[70]

But none of these incidents nor Chris Christenson's lawsuit against the society for improper disfellowshipment caused much more than local public interest.[71] The society made sure it did not advertise such events, and most Jehovah's Witnesses were not aware of them. Few, also, knew of the serious disenchantment with the organization that was growing among Witnesses in places such as the Philippines.

Yet by 1979 there were undercurrents in many parts of the world among Jehovah's Witnesses. In places as far apart as Stoke-on-Trent, England, New York City, and Phoenix, Arizona, unorganized groups of Witnesses began to question the teachings of the Watch Tower Society.[72] Some Witnesses also were leaving the organization to join Bible Student groups such as the Dawn Bible Students, the Layman's Home Missionary Society, and other Bible Student fellowships.[73] Others were joining various Evangelical movements and were organizing specific ministries to convert Jehovah's Witnesses.[74] But perhaps most ominous for the society was the fact that a small number of Watch Tower leaders and workers at the Brooklyn headquarters itself began independently to question what the society was teaching and as a result began, privately, to re-examine basic doctrines.

Among this small but significant unorganized group were Raymond Victor Franz, nephew of the Watch Tower Society president and a member of the governing body himself; Edward Dunlap, a former registrar of Gilead; and several Spanish-speaking ex-district overseers, ex-circuit overseers, and elders, all of whom had long been faithful Jehovah's Witnesses. So, in effect, re-examination of Watch Tower doctrines and the bases of dissent were beginning to develop within the highest ranks of the Witness hierarchy itself.

Through their personal studies and informal discussions, members of this small group began quietly to abandon one Watch Tower doctrine after another and to question many more. Through a close examination of a series of articles in the Catholic Journal *Verbum Domini* of the Pontifical Biblical Institute at Rome, some of them came to the conclusion that the so-called composite 'sign' of the last days in Jesus's Synoptic Apocalypse or Olivet Sermon was no sign of the end of the world at all. Second, some also began to feel that all Christians should have a heavenly hope. So, as a result of these and other assumptions, several began to question whether the governing body or Jehovah's Witnesses as a whole had any unique role to play in salvation history.[75]

These doctrines were of course destructive to the basic theology and organization of the whole Witness movement. But the small band of doubters at Brooklyn was not anxious to harm the society by creating any sort of open schism. If anything, its members rather naively wanted to remain within the Witness fold which they hoped would ultimately see the wisdom of their new understandings.[76] But that was not to be.

When word of what was taking place reached other members of the governing body, they took swift and brutal action. On 28 April 1980, the following memorandum was sent by the Chairman's Committee of the Governing Body to the full membership of the governing body:

RECENT EVIDENCES OF WRONG TEACHINGS BEING SPREAD ABOUT

Following are some of the wrong teachings being spread as eminating from Bethel. These have been brought to the attention of the Governing Body from the field from April 14 onward.

1. That Jehovah does not have an organization on earth today and its Governing Body is not directed by Jehovah.

2. Everyone baptized from Christ's time (C.E. 33) forward to the end should have the heavenly hope. All these should be partaking of the emblems at Memorial time and not just those who claim to be of the anointed remnant.

3. There is no proper arrangement as a 'faithful and discreet slave' class made up of the anointed ones and their Governing Body to direct affairs of Jehovah's people. At Matt. 24:45 Jesus used this expression only as an illustration of faithfulness of individuals. Rules are not needed; only follow the Bible.

4. There are not two classes today, the heavenly class and those of the earthly class also called 'other sheep' at John 10:16.

5. That the number of 144,000 mentioned at Rev. 7:4 is symbolic and not to be taken as literal. Those of the 'great crowd' mentioned at Rev. 7:9 also serve in heaven as indicated in vs. 15 where it is claimed that such crowd serves 'day and night in his temple (nao)' or as *K. Int.* (The Kingdom Interlinear Version) says: 'In the divine habitation of him.'

6. That we are not now living in a special period of 'last days' but that the 'last days' started 1900 years ago C.E. 33 as indicated by Peter at Acts 2:17 when he quoted from the Prophet Joel.

7. That 1914 is not an established date. Christ Jesus was not enthroned then but has been ruling in his kingdom since C.E. 33. That Christ's presence *(parousia)* is not yet but when the 'sign of the Son of man will appear in heaven' (Matt. 24:30) in the future.

8. That Abraham, David, and other faithful men of old will also have heavenly life basing such view on Heb. 11:16.

Notes: The above Biblical viewpoints have become accepted by some and being passed on to others as 'new understandings.' Such views are contrary to the basic Biblical *'framework'* of the Society's Christian beliefs. (Rom. 2:20, 3:2) They also are contrary to the 'pattern of healthful words' that have come to be Biblically accepted by Jehovah's people over the years. (2 Tim. 1:13) Such 'changes' are condemned at Prov. 24:21, 22. Hence the above are 'deviations from the truth that are subverting the faith of some.' (2 Tim. 2:18) All considered is this not APOSTASY and actionable for congregational discipline? See *ks* 77 [*Kingdom Ministry School Textbook 1977*], page 58.

Chairman's Committee 4/28/80

Randall Watters, who was then a worker at the Watch Tower printery in Brooklyn and a resident of the Brooklyn Bethel, describes vividly what then happened:

While one member of the Governing Body [Raymond Franz] was away on leave of absence, a special committee was established to extract confessions of all his close friends and acquaintances, in order to determine everything he had ever said in private that could be used against him. For two weeks these committees intimidated members of the Bethel family and recorded their confessions. Then the unfortunate fellow was suddenly called back to Bethel and made to listen to these tapes in the presence of the Governing Body. Then he was cast out and stripped of his privileges. He had served in responsible positions for decades and had traveled the world visiting branch offices, but this made no difference.[77]

As Watters indicates, Raymond Franz was forced to resign from the governing body and leave Bethel with his wife. Few Witnesses knew what had happened, but coming at the same time as an official announcement of apostasy at Bethel, rumours of all sorts began to circulate throughout the world-wide Witness community. In the meantime, a number of Bethelites and their wives had been disfellowshipped. Along with his wife, Elsie, Rene Vasquez, once the society's first district overseer in Spain and Portugal, was disfellowshipped for apostasy. According to his own account, when he pleaded not to be, one of the members of his judicial committee ridiculed him by sayiing that he 'was not even a good apostate.' Elsie Vasquez claims that she was accused of insulting the body of Christ for having celebrated the Lord's Supper at home. Cristobal Sanchez and his wife, Norma, were also excommunicated after he defended his beliefs boldly. Nestor Kuilan, a former missionary and circuit overseer, was disfellowshipped for 'covering an apostasy' and was even denied the usual appeal in such cases. Then, after Raymond Franz's dismissal, the governing body turned its attention to two Bethelites – Mark Nevejans, a young, electronic-media expert, and Edward Dunlap, the former registrar of the missionary college of Gilead who, along with Raymond Franz, was one of the society's foremost writers. After being summoned before judicial committees, these two were also disfellowshipped.[78] This was only the beginning, however. Vasquez had been working three days each week at Bethel while he acted as a Shaklee Products vitamin distributor during the rest of the week to provide for his wife and ten-year-old son. Elsie Vasquez had been operating a travel agency. But following their disfellowshipment, Witnesses boycotted their businesses so that they were almost ruined financially.[79] A Witness woman who found a job for Nestor Kuilan in Puerto Rico was disfellowshipped, as were Lucy Quiles and her family, including her sixteen-year-old daughter, for providing a home for Mark Nevejans after his expulsion from Bethel.

Perhaps, though, the most extreme event in connection with the society's New York apostasy hunt occurred at the Elmhurst-Queen's, New York, Spanish congregation in May 1980. One of the two elders in that congregation was a friend of Rene Vasquez and had accepted certain of his ideas. When this fact became known to the governing body at Bethel, they became frightened that he might have been teaching 'apostate doctrines' to the entire congregation, in particular the idea that all Christians should have a heavenly hope. As a result, Frederick Franz, accompanied by an estimated fifteen Bethel workers, 'visited' the Elmhurst congregation on a Friday night and announced that on the coming Sunday a Bethelite, Fabio Silva, would give a special talk to the congregation. After the delivery of that talk, in which Silva argued strongly that most Jehovah's Witnesses should expect their eternal reward on a paradise earth, Franz himself shouted at the congregation in heavily accented Spanish to insist that Bible study should be carried on at the kingdom hall and not in the privacy of their homes.[80]

Although the society tried not to fan the flames of 'apostasy' by publishing much information on events in New York or by disfellowshipping too many, it manifested its deep concern over the matter in other ways. On 30 April 1980, Karl Klein, a member of the governing body and a close personal friend of Frederick Franz, stated: 'If you have a tendency towards apostasy, get a hobby and keep yourself busy to keep your mind off it. Stay away from deep Bible Study to determine meanings of the Scriptures.'[81] Nearly a month later, on 29 May, Watch Tower Vice-President Lloyd Barry said: 'When we talk about law, we talk about organization. With all our hearts we need to search after that law. Jehovah doesn't give individuals interpretation [of the Scriptures]. We need a guide, and that is *the "faithful and discreet slave."* We should not be getting together in a clique to discuss views contrary to the faithful and discreet slave. We must recognize the source of our instruction. We must be like an ass, be humble, and stay in the manger; and we won't get any poison.'[82]

If this were not enough, members of the governing body carried on a campaign of the most bitter vilification of those whom they had now chosen to label as apostates. Although those driven from Bethel were not mentioned by name, they were called 'spiritual fornicators,' 'mentally diseased,' and 'insane.'[83] Randall Watters tells further:

In one committee meeting where a married couple who had served faithfully for decades was disfellowshiped, one MEMBER OF THE GOVERNING BODY called them 'suckers' and 'liars.' One poor fellow had his phone calls redirected through the 'service department' to check up on his outside connections. 'Spies' were everywhere, and many members of the family would turn in even their own friends for suspicion of 'apostasy.' It is important to know that few of the family members knew what was really going on; the Governing Body kept it well-concealed and responded by defaming the characters of those involved.[84]

More importantly, the society also began to publish a series of articles in *The Watchtower* which were written in an attempt to counter the ideas of the former Bethel 'dissidents' and their handful of New York associates.[85] Broadside attacks were also made against 'disloyal ones' at conventions and in Watch Tower literature as well. Jehovah's Witnesses were warned to guard against 'apostate wolves.'

At about the same time a small but significant schism occurred at Lethbridge, Alberta. An attempt to remove the author of this volume as an elder and later to 'discipline' him ultimately led to the defection of some fifty to sixty Witnesses in southern Alberta and a number of others in other places, in both Canada and the United States.[86] What was more significant about this particular breach in the Witness community was that it received nation-wide publicity throughout Canada and began to bring about the creation of a new, loose association of ex-Witnesses and others which speedily came to include many groups and individuals in Canada, the United States, Great Britain, and northern Europe.[87] Then, in the spring of 1981, a number of Witness dissidents picketed the Toronto offices of the Watch Tower Society wearing brown-paper bags over their heads to conceal their identities.[88] Although protesting in sympathy with the ex-Witnesses in Lethbridge who styled themselves 'Christian Bible Students,' the 'brown-paper-baggers,' as they came to be known, acted quite independently and began to set a pattern for similar protests at Witness conventions in the United States.[89]

Surprisingly, throughout the next several years the revolt against Watch Tower authority continued to grow and receive even more publicity. By the first six months of 1982, more than 250 North American newspapers and magazines – including *Newsweek*, *Time*, *Christianity Today*, and *Maclean's* – had reported the growing upheaval among Jehovah's Witnesses and ex-Witnesses. In addition, more than one hundred television and radio programs had aired the matter. The Canadian nation-wide television program 'Fifth Estate' dealt with it as a twenty-minute documentary news story. Most serious from the standpoint of the Watch Tower Society, however, was the fact that several leading ex-Witnesses, including Raymond Franz who was disfellowshipped in December 1981, went on radio and television throughout North America to tell their stories and condemn the society for the 'spiritual oppression' of those Jehovah's Witnesses who dared to differ with it. In this way, the Witnesses' libertarian reputation, deservedly gained through long years of fighting in the courts to preserve freedom of speech and worship, has been thoroughly tarnished.

Such events were not confined to North America either. Besides the disfellowshipment of Carl Olof Jonsson and the resulting publicity in Sweden, the Witnesses were also suddenly faced with an important schism in Dublin, Ireland. What had happened is that two respected Irish elders, John May and Martin Merriman, had travelled to the United States to ascertain why Raymond Franz had been disfellowshipped. After visiting him in Alabama, they called the Brooklyn Bethel to seek a meeting with the governing body to question the appropriateness of what had been done to Franz, but they were in effect told that the matter was none of their business. They then returned to Ireland where, after some months, they resigned as Jehovah's Witnesses to lead a major revolt involving a large segment of the Irish Witness community against the society over the injustice of disfellowshipment and the blood-transfusion issue.[90] As a result, they received much publicity in both the Irish and British press, and in October 1983 they and a number of ex-Witnesses from Ireland, Scotland, and America picketed the first annual meeting of the board of directors of the Watch Tower Society to be held in Great Britain – an event well publicized by the British Broadcasting Corporation.

Jehovah's Witnesses Today

It would be wrong to imply that the problems caused by the failure of 1975, organizational regimentation, doctrinal vacillation, and the revolt of small numbers of Witnesses, particularly in the western world, have as yet created major schisms among Jehovah's Witnesses. In 1979 the Witnesses began to grow slowly in numbers again,[91] and by 1980 they were experiencing a 3.7 per cent increase in the number of publishers world wide.[92] The *1981 Yearbook of Jehovah's Witnesses* therefore put the rosiest interpretation possible on what had been happening to the organization in late years and boasted dishonestly: 'Over the past seven years, from 1974 to 1980 inclusive, Jehovah's Witnesses have made steady progress.'[93] To demonstrate this 'steady progress' it published a series of graphs which do show some growth in the Witness community during that period.[94]

Yet neither the society nor Jehovah's Witnesses are as healthy as they would like others to believe. Their growth since 1975 has been anything but outstanding, certainly in comparison to the amount of time and effort they have spent in trying to convert others; and that is only part of the story. Even despite growth, it can be argued that Jehovah's Witnesses are members of a sick religion. They are wracked with internal problems which their leadership is unwilling to recognize, let alone deal with satisfactorily. And most serious for them, they continue to experience a tremendous turnover in membership – something that the society refuses to talk about and a fact largely unrecognized by most Witnesses. Furthermore, as Havor Montague indicates so clearly, Jehovah's Witnesses continually lose most of their best-educated and most intelligent people. Hence, after many years of organizational 'brain drain,' the upper echelons of the Watch Tower hierarchy are largely an intellectually arid group with few persons of any real ability to call on for assistance.

At ninety-one years of age, Frederick W. Franz remains the chief idealogue of the movement and continues to dominate it. Other members of the governing body regard him as a virtual fount of truth. As one stated: 'He has been our oracle for 67 years.'[95] Franz shows no desire to initiate change, however. Speaking on 25 May 1980 to the entire Bethel family in reference to date-setting and building expectations, he remarked that some 'expected me to ignore the influence of world events in the light of Bible prophecy for the last 67 years, and to start over where we began 67 years ago'[96] – something which neither he nor his associates show any indication of being willing to do. Thus, at present the governing body and higher echelons of the Watch Tower Society seem to be seriously affected by a kind of organizational arteriosclerosis, and a form of *hubris* or spiritual pride which could very well destroy the viability of the Witness community.

For one thing, Watch Tower leaders seem determined to reinforce their authority at almost any cost. They insist on obedience to all of the various and sundry rules which they establish – rules which are virtually talmudic in extent. Speaking to the Brooklyn Bethel workers shortly after the dismissal of Raymond Franz, Edward Dunlap, and the others, Albert Schroeder, one of the younger and most determined 'apostasy hunters' on the governing body, proclaimed:

We serve not only Jehovah God but we are under our 'mother' [the organization]. Our 'mother' has the right to make rules and regulations for us ... This book, entitled *Branch Organization Procedure*, contains 28 subjects; and its sub-sections involve regulations and administration. In it there are 1,177 policies and regulations ... this is an improved, fine-tuned organization and we are all expected to follow its policies. If there are some who feel that they cannot subject themselves to the rules and regulations now in operation, such ones ought to be leaving and not be involved here in the further progressive work.

Some have fallen away from the organization, *not from the Bible,* saying there is no need for coming under law ... This great program of organization procedure is gathering the things of heaven and earth.[97]

Since Schroeder's statement the society has stressed its spiritual authority more and more. *Watchtower* magazine after *Watchtower* magazine has presented arguments – some of which are so slipshod that they are foolish[98] – as to why Jehovah's Witnesses should remain loyal to the Watch Tower hierarchy in the face of everything. Furthermore, it has boasted that the 'anointed remnant' of the 144,000 heaven-bound Witnesses of Jehovah, acting as the 'faithful and wise servant' or 'steward' (through the governing body, of course), has expelled all those unfaithful to the organization. 'It shut the door on all the expelled apostates and those who tried to sneak in to corrupt Jehovah's Witnesses.'[99]

In addition, the society has hardened the rules respecting how ordinary Witnesses should treat disfellowshipped persons. As with so many doctrines and procedures, it has vacillated on this matter. From the 1950s through 1974, Witnesses were not even to say 'hello' to anyone who had been officially cast out of their community. But in *The Watchtower* of 1 August 1974, the society decided to take a much softer position. It even admitted that some disfellowshipped ones had been treated with unnecessary cruelty.[100] Yet in the issue of 15 September 1981, *The Watchtower* stressed a harder line than it had even before 1974. In that issue, it came to demand that Witnesses in good standing sever practically *all ties* with family members, even ignoring parents and adult children except in cases of grave emergency.[101]

As one might reasonably expect, all this has tended to weaken the faith of many individuals rather than to strengthen it. Increasing dissension within the organization plus the governing body's shrill name-calling and reprisals against 'apostates' has created a siege mentality among Watch Tower loyalists, but many others have reacted with disgust and revulsion. During the purge at the Brooklyn Bethel in the spring of 1980, it seems from various reports that well over fifty workers at the world-wide headquarters of Jehovah's Witnesses left the organization. Since then many thousands of Jehovah's Witnesses throughout the world have openly broken with the Watch Tower Society, often to form independent fellowships and study groups. No doubt in response to the draconian measures outlined in the 15 September 1981 *Watchtower,* many more have left or are leaving. In the statistical year 1983, as in the four years previous, the number of Witness publishers grew as a result of the society's unrelenting pressure to proselytize. Thus for that year – from September 1982 to August 1983 – the society claimed a world-wide 6.8 per cent increase in publishers.[102] But what has not been told to the world at large is that in the month of September 1981, at the very time the society announced its new rules on shunning all who had been expelled from or resigned from the organization, there was an 8 per cent decrease in the number of Jehovah's Witness publishers in the United States alone. In concrete numbers 47,318 fewer American Witnesses were actively engaged in preaching to their neighbours than in the previous month.[103] Thus even to the most optimistic Watch Tower loyalist, it must be obvious that there is something seriously wrong.

None the less, while some former Witnesses suggest that the society has 'pushed the self-destruct button,' there is still much life in a movement which has experienced many vicissitudes. Furthermore, if new leaders do finally come to the fore and come to grips with the major problems facing Jehovah's Witnesses, they may, as a community, evolve into something very different from what they are today.

CHAPTER FIVE

Relations with the World

Although Witness relations with the world are only one aspect of their history, they are so important that they deserve a separate chapter. Nothing besides their apocalypticism itself has helped forge the nature of their community so much as what has been their ongoing conflict with the world on one hand and their occasional accommodations with it on the other. Also, an examination of those relations tells much about the general attitudes of Jehovah's Witnesses.

Attitudes towards Other Religions

One of the more common criticisms of Jehovah's Witnesses over the years has dealt with their outspoken denunciations of other faiths, religious leaders and clergymen. It should be noted that Pastor Russell came only gradually to develop a negative attitude towards the churches, their pastors, and priests. His early works show that he often associated with clergymen of various denominations and borrowed from their teachings. Even after the establishment of Zion's Watch Tower and Tract Society, he evidently continued to regard persons in the 'Second Advent' tradition as brethren in Christ.[1] He was also thoroughly sympathetic to the Jews and to Zionism. Yet as time went by he became more and more critical of most religions which he, in the tradition of George Storrs and many early Adventists, regarded as Babylon the Great, the mother of harlots.[2] During the First World War, he became particularly caustic in his statements respecting those men of the cloth who supported the nations' war efforts. But he was mild in comparison with Judge Rutherford and other Bible Students during the latter years of the war or in the period following it.

When Rutherford and his fellow Watch Tower directors were released from prison in 1919, they began a campaign of condemnation of the world in which 'commerce,' 'politics,' and 'religion' were labelled as the Devil's chief

Bingo

Typical Watch Tower Society anti-Catholicism
(from *Consolation*, 19 April 1939, 25)

instruments. Although the judge excoriated businessmen and politicians, he reserved his sternest words for the clergy. Increasing persecution during the period between the two wars brought ever more bitter responses from the Witnesses. When in 1932 they abandoned Russell's old belief that the Jews had a special relationship with Jehovah, they came to feel that they and they alone were his *chosen*, his elect. Hence, they held that the clergy of all religions had ranged themselves on Satan's side in opposition to the Lord, his Christ, and his Christian Witnesses. Judge Rutherford made this clear in the strongest terms in the book *Enemies* published in 1938 with respect to the clergy of the Church of Rome: 'The kingdom of God under Christ, as proclaimed by Jehovah's witnesses, is the only thing the Roman Catholic Hierarchy now really fear. The old "harlot" is now very diligent to hide from the people her long and bloody record as inquisitionist and the many crimes she has committed, and when her activity and filthy record, as recorded in history, are mentioned and the truth of God's Word is told about her, she howls and with great crocodile tears says: "That speech is shocking to our religious susceptibilities."'[3]

Protestant and Jewish clergy were seen as little better. In the same book the judge remarked:

Today the so-called 'Protestants' and the Yiddish clergy openly co-operate with and play into the hands of the Roman Catholic Hierarchy like foolish simpletons and thereby aid the Hierarchy to carry on her commercial, religious traffic and increase her revenue. Commercial religion is the stock in trade of all such merchants. The Hierarchy takes the lead, and the simpletons follow. The Hierarchy is now taking the lead in compulsory flag-saluting, and in building images or monuments, such as what is now widely advertised to be built in Washington, D.C.; and the clergy of the so-called 'Protestant' and Yiddish organizations fall in line and do what they are told, and when the 'sackbut' sounds they fall down and worship. (Daniel 3:5) Poor simpletons.[4]

For some years the Watch Tower Society became so negative to all other faiths that it refused to classify Jehovah's Witnesses as a religion. In the late 1930s large parades were staged throughout the English-speaking world in which Witnesses carried placards bearing slogans such as 'Religion is a Snare and a Racket' and 'Serve God and Christ the King.' In one of those 'information marches' held at London, England, in 1938, a six-mile-long parade line marched through the busy sections of the city carrying placards and banners and passing out handbills,[5] undoubtedly to the great annoyance of many devout Protestants, Catholics, and Jews.

Since the Second World War Witness language for public consumption has generally moderated, and Jehovah's Witnesses have long regarded themselves as a

religion in the dictionary sense of the word. But they remain hostile both to
Christendom and the religions of the non-Christian world and refuse to have
anything to do with ecumenical activities. Occasionally, too, the Watch Tower
Society has produced books and articles which echo the sentiments expressed
above from *Enemies*. As was pointed out in Chapter 3, a resolution distributed
throughout the World in the late 1950s described the clergy, as a class, as the most
reprehensible of all God's enemies.[6] At about the same time, as Witnesses began
to develop new communities in non-Christian lands, they also began to censure
Buddhism, Hinduism, Islam, and other great religions of the East.[7]

Not surprisingly, Jehovah's Witnesses have been criticized for their harsh
attitudes towards both the clergy and other doctrinal systems; and no rational
person can deny that much of the language used and the things said or written by
Watch Tower spokesmen were extreme by almost anyone's standards. *The Golden
Age* not only attacked the clergy consistently but frequently engaged in
unwarranted personal vilification. Rutherford's radio broadcasts, booklets, and
even *The Watchtower* magazine were frequently filled with vitriolic language.
Naturally, all of this said much about the personalities of men such as Rutherford,
Van Amburgh, Woodworth, and, later, Knorr, Covington, and Frederick Franz.
Witness use of polemics must be put in context, however, and can partly be
understood as responses to attacks on Russell, Watch Tower officials, and the
Bible Student–Witnesses in general. What is seldom recognized by critics of
Witness polemicizing is the nature of religious antipathy towards them during the
last century. Ken Jubber states: 'The persecution of the Watch Tower Society and
its members by national governments and their officials has been a recurrent
experience of the Society since it was founded a century ago. Viewed globally, this
persecution has been so persistent and of such intensity that it would not be
inaccurate to regard Jehovah's Witnesses as the most persecuted group of
Christians in the twentieth century. According to *The Watchtower* (1 May
1976:281), some form of official persecution was experienced by Jehovah's
Witnesses in more than 40 of the 210 countries in which Jehovah's Witnesses were
active during 1975.'[8] While some of that persecution has not been stimulated by
religious hatred, much of it has.

Religious Persecution

The record is clear. If one looks at the nature of the attacks made on Pastor Russell,
it is evident that they went far beyond the type of controversy in which he wished to
engage personally. Over and over again he was charged with being an adulterer, a
charlatan, a perjurer, and that he had no right to the title 'Pastor.' One may still go
into Evangelical and Bible Society bookstores and find books and pamphlets

produced by fundamentalist clergymen which unashamedly continue to repeat those anti-Russell falsehoods uncritically and, often, quite dishonestly. It would be interesting to examine the general effect of such hate literature historically to discover just what impact it has had on the press and public officials. In Canada and the United States there is much evidence that it was responsible for the terrible persecution of the Bible Students during the First World War and of Jehovah's Witnesses during the Second.

Although Russell, Rutherford, and the Bible Students were regarded as unpatriotic for their open hostility to warfare during 1914–18, the evidence is that in Canada during 1918 bans on Watch Tower literature were imposed as a direct result of clerical representations to the Canadian government.[9] In the United States the situation was the same. Inspired by what had happened in Canada, the American government's prosecution of Rutherford and his co-defendants was also encouraged by both Protestant and Catholic clerics.[10]

In the period between the world wars, religious persecution of Jehovah's Witnesses became ever more evident. During the 1920s and 1930s officials in the province of Quebec had Bible Student–Witnesses arrested hundreds of times, largely at the behest of Catholic priests and prelates. Although they were most frequently charged with peddling without a licence, they were also indicted on charges of blasphemous libel and sedition.[11] Clerical pressure was also a major factor in prohibiting the International Bible Students Association from relicensing four radio stations in Canada in 1928.[12] In the United States, during the 1930s, mob violence against Witnesses was frequently stirred up directly by clergymen. Outstandingly, the followers of Detroit-based Father Charles E. Coughlin launched a mob attack on a Watch Tower convention held in New York City's Madison Square Garden in 1938.[13] Shortly before, a Catholic boycott campaign against Gimbel Brothers Department Store forced that company to stop its sponsorship of Judge Rutherford's radio broadcasts.[14] In Britain, Africa, and many other parts of the world, clergymen played similar roles in harassing Jehovah's Witnesses,[15] but the worst examples of such activities occurred in Nazi Germany.

Under the Weimar Republic the Bible Students, known in German as *Ernste Bibelforscher* (Earnest Bible Searchers), grew more rapidly than in other parts of the world. They did not do so without much opposition, however, and during the 1920s they were arrested time and again. When the Nazis came to power in 1933, the Witnesses were among the first groups to suffer suppression. Much of the Nazis' hostility towards them was purely political, rather than religious, but there can be no doubt that Catholic clerics once again encouraged their persecution. In many instances local parish priests acted on behalf of the Gestapo to have Witness families seized and sent to concentration camps where thousands of them perished.[16]

Today's heroes—who will honor them?

Witnesses' view of their persecution in Europe
(from *Consolation*, 8 February 1939, 13)

The Witnesses did not fare well in western democracies during the Second World War either. No doubt their refusal to support national war efforts was a major factor, but once again religious persecution was an important element. Frequently they were charged with fomenting communism, a very serious matter between the signing of the Molotov–Ribbentrop Pact in August 1939 and Hitler's invasion of Russia in June 1941. That charge made it appear that Jehovah's Witnesses were an unpatriotic fifth column. Some segments of the Catholic press therefore stressed the Witnesses' refusal to salute flags, sing anthems, or hail political leaders. As a result, the Canadian government imposed a total ban on them in July 1940 which was followed by hundreds of arrests, fines, and imprisonments.[17] Nothing similar happened in the United States or Great Britain, although it did in Australia, British Africa, and a number of other places. Although outright persecution was not severe, Jehovah's Witnesses were outlawed in those latter lands also. As in Canada, the clergy played a part in their suppression.[18]

Following the war, various governments waged what amounted to religious crusades against Jehovah's Witnesses in a number of lands. In Quebec a few hundred were mobbed, beaten, expelled from schools, driven from communities, and arrested nearly 1,800 times in the five years between 1945 and 1950.[19] Spain and the Dominican Republic subjected them to bitter persecution, again largely on religious grounds.[20] Probably the most serious religious attack over the years came from the Greek Orthodox church during the entire period from 1945 to 1973. Not only did Greek Witnesses suffer numerous acts of violence and their young men the threat of firing squads for refusal to do military service, but for a time all of their marriages were declared illegal and their children illegitimate.[21]

While persecution arising out of religious animosity towards the Witnesses has lessened in the Christian world, especially since the Second Vatican Ecumenical Council, it is far from dead. The Watch Tower Society believes that a ban which occurred in Argentina under the recent military government several years ago was, at least in part, religiously inspired.[22] More serious today, however, is anti-Witness feeling among non-Christians. Most Islamic nations have placed them under ban, and some have subjected them to severe persecution.[23] Some Jewish communities in Israel and New York have manifested a good deal of hostility towards Witness attempts to proselytize among them and have reacted with violence.[24]

The Nature of Anti-Witness Propaganda

Religious attacks on Jehovah's Witnesses have followed certain patterns. Although Protestants and Catholics have frequently criticized Witness beliefs from a doctrinal standpoint – a completely understandable phenomenon – they have taken two other tacks as well. As discussed above, the first has been to discredit Witness leaders, particularly Pastor Charles T. Russell, through what has sometimes been fair criticism but has often been unfair personal vilification and innuendo. The second has been the effort to prove, under many circumstances, that the Witnesses are socially dangerous and, frequently, the agents of some *foreign* ideology or movement.

Published attacks on Russell and, to a lesser extent, other Bible Student–Witness leaders have been important. For by describing them as 'evil' figures, it was easy to picture the Witnesses as members of a non-Christian or semi-Christian 'cult' which by its very nature is a direct threat to 'peace, order, and good government.' Not surprisingly, some of this polemic literature – produced by clergymen of various denominations – has been taken up and used as a basis for claiming that the Witnesses are seditious. The same themes have been repeated over and over again.

Note the following. During the First World War, the standard clerical criticism of Bible Student leaders in the United States and Canada was that they were pro-German.[25] After the war, they were labelled as sympathetic to communism.[26] In the 1930s, after the Nazis rose to power in Germany, Judge Rutherford and Jehovah's Witnesses were described as 'pioneers for a Jewish world kingdom and dupes of the Jew, Karl Marx.'[27] Then, in October 1939, the *Canadian Messenger of the Sacred Heart*, a Jesuit publication based in Toronto, Ontario, published an article entitled 'Doctrine and Practice of the Witnesses of Jehovah.' Following a detailed report of old attacks on Russell and Rutherford, and a denial that the Catholic Church was persecuting the Witnesses, it stated: 'Whatever may be the profession of Jehovah's Witnesses ... there is no room for doubt that the practical effect of the Watch Tower activities is to stimulate Communism, not to say anarchy, and to undermine all feeling of reverence for authority. It is not only the churches that are brought into disrepute but every existing form of civil government is decried and caricatured.'[28] Following the Second World War many Catholics and Protestants repeated the arguments stated above in the *Messenger of the Sacred Heart*. In 1947 Damien Jasmin, with the support of Rodrique Cardinal Villeneuve, archbishop of Quebec, and Bishop Joseph Charbonneau of Montreal, published *Les Témoins de Jéhovah: Fauteurs de séditions, ennemis acharnés de la religion*. In that work he asked rhetorically: Was the 'Jehovist doctrine' married to the anti-religious teachings of Bolshevik communism? And thereupon he answered his own question by stating that there was an actual rapprochement between atheistic communism and Jehovah's Witnesses.[29]

Strikingly, the sedition theme has been taken up by North American capitalists, Nazis, Marxists, religions outside Western Christendom, and by numerous governments in the so-called Third World. For example, in 1927 Hector Charlesworth, editor of the Canadian magazine *Saturday Night,* penned an editorial directed against Judge Rutherford for his suggestion that there was one law for the poor and another for the rich. Charlesworth not only accused the Bible Students of having 'sold out to Bernstoff' and of distributing pro-German propaganda in Canadian towns and cities during the First World War, but went on to say of Rutherford: 'When the "Judge" indulges in tirades against capital and capitalists as oppressors of the common people, he not only prompts curiosity as to his own bank account, but utters a dangerous falsehood.' Later Charlesworth, as chairman of the Canadian Radio Commission, was largely responsible for banning Rutherford's broadcasts in Canada.[30] Shortly thereafter the Nazis, who – according to Professor John S. Conway – feared Jehovah's Witnesses as a possible rival political movement,[31] began their persecution of them. After the Second World War the Greek Orthodox clergy took up the sedition theme,[32] as did their archenemies, the Moslem mullahs of Turkey,[33] and the Marxists of the Soviet Union. Rather paradoxically, the Witnesses, long labelled the friends of communism, have been described as agents provocateurs of western capitalism. Writing in *Sovremennyi Iegovizm* (Contemporary Jehovism) A.T. Mosalenko states:

Jehovism appears as one of the modernized varieties of contemporary Protestant religion, a product of bourgeois social relations of the epoch of imperialism. The distinguishing feature of this organization is that, not only does it preach a more precisely 'purified' religion, but also it uses the perverse religiosity of the masses to further the political goals of the reactionary circles of the imperialist bourgeoisie. The American sect of 'Jehovah's Witnesses' is a typically bourgeois organization, intended not only for internal but also for external aims, first and foremost for *subversive work* [italics mine] in socialist and other democratic and peace-loving countries of the world. In common with the official churches and political parties of the reactionary bourgeoisie, the 'Jehovah's Witnesses' work for the perpetuation of a capitalism which has outlived its usefulness.[34]

The Charge of Sedition

If there is so much smoke, is there no fire? In other words, if Jehovah's Witnesses have been accused of sedition by so many diverse groups, is it not reasonable to suppose that they may really be seditious? The answer to that question must be based on two things: the definition of sedition and the Witnesses' view of their relationship to the secular state.

Sedition is a secular crime. *Webster's New Collegiate Dictionary* (1977) defines it as 'incitement of resistance to or insurrection against lawful authority.'

But many societies have gone farther. Even British law, as applied not only in Great Britain but in her dominions overseas, long held that creating ill will between the sovereign's subjects was seditious.[35] Jehovah's Witnesses have argued consistently, however, they they are not and never have been guilty of that crime under any reasonable definition of the term; and they have many important outside authorities who support their contention.

After the first World War, Judge Rutherford and his fellow Watch Tower directors were exonerated by an American court which overturned their earlier conviction. The American government then recognized that there was no satisfactory basis to prosecute them under the Espionage Act. Then, during the dark days of the Second World War, Great Britain refused to outlaw them, the U.S. Supreme Court stated specifically that they were not seditious,[36] and the Supreme Court of Australia held that a ban against them in that country was illegal. Justice Williams, speaking on behalf of the latter court, referred to the 'perfectly innocent principles and doctrines' of the Witnesses and ruled: 'As the religion of Jehovah's Witnesses is a Christian religion, the declaration that the association is an unlawful body has the effect of making the advocacy of the principles and doctrines of the Christian religion unlawful and every church service held by believers in the birth of Christ an unlawful assembly.'[37] Shortly thereafter, the Canadian ban on the Witnesses was removed after a select all-party committee of the House of Commons had held unanimously that there was no valid reason to continue the suppression of them.[38] In 1950, the Supreme Court of Canada held that they were innocent of sedition in the famous case of *Boucher* v. *the King*.[39]

It must be recognized also that others besides the courts have spoken in the Witnesses' defence and have denied emphatically that they are in any way seditious. During a period of extreme mob violence against them in the United States just before American entry into the Second World War, many liberal-minded Americans came to their aid. As much of the violence directed against them was fomented by the U.S. Supreme Court's decision in *Minersville School District* v. *Gobitis*,[40] wherein it held that Witness children could be forced to salute the American flag or face expulsion from public schools, the questions of sedition and disloyalty seemed real. But the American Civil Liberties Union, much of the American press, much of the legal profession, and many outstanding clergymen held Jehovah's Witnesses to be a law-abiding group.

A very important point that needs to be stressed – one too frequently ignored by the Watch Tower Society and Witness authors – is that while much persecution was being heaped upon them by religious opponents, they had their Protestant, Catholic, and Jewish defenders as well. Many Catholic law schools were as shocked by the Supreme Court's *Gobitis* decision as anyone, and they said so.[41] So, too, did some segments of the religious press as best represented by the liberal

Will Madame have a facial to match her fancy bracelets?

Watch Tower view of Franklin Roosevelt and the New Deal
in the United States
(from *Consolation*, 8 March 1939, 25)

Protestant magazine *Christian Century*. Finally, ten Protestant, Catholic and Jewish clergymen, including Dr Harry Emerson Fosdick, Rabbi Edward L. Israel, Bishop Francis J. McConnell, and Dr Reinhold Niebuhr, produced an introductory statement to a pamphlet published by the American Civil Liberties Union entitled *The Persecution of Jehovah's Witnesses*. It stated in part: 'The undersigned believe that the issues raised by the attacks on Jehovah's Witnesses constitute a challenge to American democracy and religious tolerance. Nothing in the beliefs of Jehovah's Witnesses justifies the charges of a lack of patriotism leveled against them. Their refusal on religious grounds to salute the flag rests upon a Biblical injunction which they accept literally. In the conflict between loyalty to God and loyalty to the State, Jehovah's Witnesses stand on the tradition of putting loyalty to God first.'[42] Thus those tolerant religious leaders affirmed in that one brief statement the major doctrinal basis on which Bible Students and Jehovah's Witnesses have always claimed to act. Witness concepts of the Christian's proper relationship to the secular state nevertheless deserve some discussion, for they have gone through certain changes over the years.

Witness Concepts of Relations with the State

Pastor Russell believed that the present secular governments of this world were bound to be destroyed by Christ at Armageddon: they were unquestionably outside Jehovah's favour. They were, in fact, under the rule of Satan and were 'ferocious, destructive, beastly and selfish.' Hence Christians should look for the coming of Christ's kingdom and keep themselves 'separate from the world.' That meant specifically that Bible Students should avoid voting, holding public office, or enlisting in military service. Members of the New Creation (the church) should regard themselves as 'strangers and pilgrims here, and to some extent aliens and foreigners.'[43]

Russell did feel that 'the ostensible object of all governments organized among men has been to promote justice and the well-being of all the people.' So while awaiting the re-establishment of the kingdom of God on earth, like Christ, his followers ought to obey secular authority to a great extent. The reasoning behind such counsel was that the Pastor believed firmly that God had granted to the nations the temporary right to rule, and that the 'higher powers' of Romans 13:1 – to which Christians were to be subject as 'ordained of God' – were secular governments.[44]

This interpretation led to some ambivalence on Russell's part as far as the Christian's duties to the state were concerned. For example, although he felt that under most circumstances voting in democratic elections was wrong, he stated: 'A law has been proposed that would compel all men to vote. Whenever that law shall be passed, the New Creatures [Bible Students], becoming subject to it should render obedience, and that without murmur.' He even admonished his fellows to accept military conscription as non-combatants if necessary and to serve in the ranks and 'to fire our guns' if compelled. But under such circumstances he stated that Christians 'need not feel compelled to shoot a fellow creature'[45] – in practice, a rather difficult proposition.

Such teachings, formulated at a time when the United States and the British Empire were at peace, had no compulsory voting laws, and no military conscription, caused few problems for Bible Students. With the advent of the First World War, Russell took a firmer anti-war stance and Bible Students uniformly refused combatant military service. Nevertheless, the 'higher powers' doctrine caused a good many problems among them, particularly after Russell's death. Often Bible Students were divided on how far they should go in obeying secular authorities.

Under Judge Rutherford's presidency of the Watch Tower Society, the Bible Student–Witness's position hardened. More and more they came to stress the apostolic injunction that they ought to obey God rather than men. Yet Russell's higher powers' concept was a matter of some concern among them until 1929. Judge Rutherford then took a new doctrinal stance as outlined in the issues of 1 and 15 June of *The Watch Tower* that year. Therein he developed a new position entirely respecting the higher powers of Romans 13. According thereto, they were no longer to be understood as secular rulers, but rather as Jehovah God and Christ Jesus. The governments of the world were therefore classified as having no basis in divine authority and were to be seen as demonic. Christians should pay taxes for the services they received, but they need obey no other human law *unless it was in harmony with God's.*

This new doctrine was very valuable to Jehovah's Witnesses during the 1930s and the Second World War. It caused them to take an unyielding stand against Nazism and nationalism. There were no divisions among them over questions of loyalty as there had been during the First World War. Nevertheless, the 1929 doctrine created new difficulties.

Judge Rutherford and Jehovah's Witnesses were not consistent in their attitudes with respect to secular authority. The judge always professed a deep love for the American Bill of Rights and the libertarian tradition. Also, the Witnesses were counselled to obey human laws which were not openly in conflict with scriptural commands in order to remain at peace, if possible, with their neighbours.[46] Then, finally, they began to appeal case after case to worldly courts to obtain their civil liberties.

After a number of years, when they had won an outstanding number of court cases in the United States, Australia, and Canada, they came to feel that it was obvious that there was much good in human governments. Hence, it was unreasonable to hold strictly to their 1929 position.

As a result of the doctrinal problem posed by their own rather amazing successes before the courts of democratic lands, the Witnesses re-examined their thinking concerning the nature of secular authority and the Christian's relationship to it. So, in 1962, *The Watchtower* published a series of articles by which the society officially reverted to a doctrinal stance on the matter very similar to that expounded by C.T. Russell, although a somewhat more sophisticated one.[47]

Since 1962 Jehovah's Witnesses have been model citizens in some ways. Under the terms of the 1962 'superior authorities' doctrine, they believe that they should obey all human laws *not directly in conflict* with God's. Even during the period between 1929 and 1962, they were notably law-abiding except when human law came in conflict with their understanding of the divine will. The position taken by their clerical advocates in the 1940 American Civil Liberties Union pamphlet therefore represents a very reasonable analysis of their role in democratic societies.

Secular authorities in the twentieth century have quite often failed to be impressed by the reasoning of Jehovah's Witnesses or their libertarian supporters. In nations with established religions, Witness teachings have frequently been regarded as subversive to 'true faith' and, hence, an assault on duly established authority. Until recently this was generally the case in many officially Roman Catholic countries and in Greece. It still is in most of the Moslem world. In other lands where there have not been religious establishments which have demanded the loyalty of all or most citizens, the Witnesses have run into the more pervasive phenomenon of nationalism. In the twentieth century most nations – even western democracies in times of stress – tend to take up the theme displayed so prominently on Spanish military establishments: *'Todo por la Patria'* ('All for the Fatherland'). So when the Witnesses have refused, as they have on thousands of occasions, 'to render what belongs to God unto Caesar,' they have been damned as unpatriotic enemies of the state. In Marxist countries their faith is also looked upon as a particularly dangerous 'opium of the people.'

It is none the less quite true that the Witnesses could probably have escaped much of the persecution directed at them in spite of their refusal to co-operate with secular governments of all sorts. Although like some traditional Anabaptist groups such as the Mennonites and Hutterites, they would no doubt have undergone some oppression, they could have avoided much except for their preaching work, their constant witness to the world. Most societies can and will tolerate a small, uncooperative religious minority which submits to a ghetto-like existence. But when such a group refuses to be isolated and attempts to make converts by the millions, then in the eyes of many political leaders it becomes a socially disturbing force which should be curbed or outlawed. It is important to note the direct causes for Witness persecution, however, and to examine the most outstanding examples related to each of those causes.

Opposition to Preaching

First, the Witnesses have experienced much opposition to their preaching. Pastor Russell was early attacked for his religious message rather than his ideas with regard to the secular state. Also, although the Bible Students' opposition to war was used against them in 1918 and 1919, it was primarily their tract campaign against the clergy which got them into trouble at that time. Their use of radio, phonographs, the printed page, and, above all, their door-to-door proselytizing since then have infuriated other religious and secular authorities and, in some parts of the world, the general public.

Between the world wars, they were often charged with peddling without a licence or violating Sabbath-Day legislation for preaching from house to house on Sundays in the United States, Canada, and the German Weimar Republic. Quebec attempted to outlaw their preaching work immediately after the Second World War, and communist lands actually did. Spain continued to prohibit their activities until the late 1960s and Portugal into the last decade. Currently, well over forty nations have imposed total or partial bans on them. In Zambia, the nation with the largest per-capita Witness community in the world, publishers cannot legally preach from house to house or to anyone they do not know personally.[48]

Witness preaching has also excited violence against them. In many parts of the world, they have been assaulted, mobbed, beaten, tarred and feathered, castrated, raped, and murdered. While this has not always been for their public testimony, often it has. Few long-time Witnesses of Jehovah have escaped threats to their persons with clubs, knives, guns, or fists; and many have had boiling water, offal, or stones thrown at them. Others have had dogs turned on them, and almost all have been subjected to verbal abuse. Often, otherwise perfectly civilized householders will become surprisingly violent when called on by Witnesses; and while some of their reactions may be owing to Witness tactlessness, frequently they are not.

Why this happens is not difficult to understand. Undoubtedly, many resent the unspoken implication that unless they accept the Witnesses' message, they are doomed to everlasting destruction. Others find themselves at a disadvantage in discussing religion with persons who can find biblical proof texts so readily for virtually every argument they present, and a great many resent the continual persistence of Jehovah's Witnesses in calling again and again at their homes after they have been told that the householders have no interest in their message.

One point of interest is that Witnesses who have preached in different parts of the world frequently remark that they are received with far more kindness in Latin countries, sub-Saharan Africa, and Asia than in Anglo-Saxon or Nordic lands. The idea that a man's house is his castle, so prevalent among English-speaking peoples and Northern Europeans, may be a major cultural factor with which Witness evangelists must contend to their discomfiture. In contrast, the other societies mentioned above have strong traditions of hospitality which may cause them to treat missionaries as guests, even when there is no interest in their message.

Military Service

Witness men and women have suffered more than the members of any religion in this century for their refusal to perform military service or certain forms of compulsory civilian alternative service. During the First World War, they were brutalized in American, British, and Canadian army camps and prisons.[49] In Germany and Austria-Hungary they also suffered, with some even being executed. When Hitler began building his dread war machine in the 1930s, they again experienced persecution for their refusal to have any part of it. Professor John Conway comments:

The resistance of the Witnesses was centred chiefly against any form of collaboration with the Nazis and against service in the army. Basing their case on biblical commandment, they refused to take up arms even against the nation's enemies. In a society where the right of private conscience had long since been stamped out, such a breach of discipline could not go unpunished, and it was no surprise when a special law was passed in August 1938 laying down that refusal or incitement to refuse to serve in the armed forces was to be punishable by death, or in lesser cases by imprisonment or protective custody. Since such refusal was an article of belief for Jehovah's Witnesses, they were thus all practically brought under sentence of death. Many in fact paid the penalty; others were sentenced to enforced service with the troops, while others were consigned to lunatic asylums, and large numbers were transported to Dachau.[50]

Although Witnesses in the democracies did not undergo such severe treatment, their plight was also grave. From the adoption of military conscription in the United States to the end of the Second World War and again from the Korean War to the Vietnamese conflict, Jehovah's Witnesses consistently made up the largest number of Americans incarcerated for conscientious objection. Thousands of them spent many thousands of man-years in federal prisons. Public records also show that American judges regularly imposed longer sentences on them than on conscientious objectors of other faiths.[51]

Great Britain and some European nations were less severe in the post-Second World War period, but they long continued to imprison Witnesses for refusal to do military service. On the other hand, Witness men suffered greatly in lands such as Spain and Greece. In Franco Spain they were sentenced and resentenced for not serving in the army. Some spent up to twelve years in prisons or the Spanish Sahara, sometimes under most gruelling circumstances.[52] Much the same thing had happened in Greece. During that country's war with Italy in 1940, three Witnesses were sentenced to death for conscientous objection[53] as were two others as late as 1966.[54] Even today the present Greek Republic is harsh towards Witnesses of military age.

Other countries that have imposed stern punishment on Witness draft resisters have been Turkey, Korea, Egypt, Cuba, and the communist republics of Eastern Europe. Of these, the worst have been communist lands and right-wing South Korea where Witness men have been tortured, beaten, and on a few occasions brutally murdered. For Jehovah's Witnesses, East Germany, Czechoslovakia, the Soviet Union, and Cuba are hardly socialist paradises or South Korea part of the so-called free world.[55]

Patriotic Exercises and Political Neutrality

A third and very important factor behind secular attacks on the Witnesses has been and is their refusal to participate actively in various patriotic activities and exercises. Their first problems in this area arose in the 1930s, particularly in Hitler's Third Reich and in the United States. To give the Hitler salute or to *heil Hitler* was nothing short of idolatry to German *Bibelforscher*. Thus they adamantly refused to participate in Nazi or state functions where they would be required to perform such activities.[56] From 1935 onward, they also refused to salute the flags of other nations or to stand for national anthems. Consequently, they came into severe conflict with American school authorities throughout most of the United States. Finally, after years of litigation, the matter was taken before the U.S. Supreme Court in the *Gobitis* case. In an eight-to-one decision, that court ruled against Jehovah's Witnesses.[57] As a result, mob action against them increased dramatically. Hundreds of such incidents, generally promoted by the American Legion, the Veterans of Foreign Wars, and certain Catholic writers, occurred throughout the nation[58] until the Supreme Court reversed its ruling in the *Gobitis* case in *Barnette* v. *West Virginia State Board of Education* on 14 June 1943 – Flag Day in the United States.[59]

The Canadian government used the flag-salute issue and the fact that Jehovah's Witnesses would not 'hail any man' as an ostensible reason for imposing the 1940 ban on them.[60] In fact, that was not the reason at all.[61] Yet a number of Canadian

Only a man with a conscience can be a true patriot

A 'conspiracy' against Jehovah's Witnesses
over the flag-salute issue
(from *Consolation*, 17 May 1939, 4)

Witnesses suffered greatly when their children would not salute the flag or sing 'God Save the King.'[62] After the Second World War the flag-salute or, more accurately, the patriotic-exercises issue was to cause severe problems for Witness children trying to obtain educations in such diverse lands as the Philippines, Costa Rica, Zambia, India, Liberia, and occasionally, even the United States and Canada.[63]

Lately the party-card issue, particularly in Africa, and the refusal of Witnesses actively to support one-party dictatorships – whether on the left or the right – has led to virtual pogroms of large Witness communities in central and south-central Africa. Most notorious and terrible has been the persecution of Malawian Witnesses and those in Mozambique.

The Malawian government began an all-out drive against Witnesses in 1967 as a result of their refusal to buy membership cards in the Malawi Congress Party of Dr Kamuzu Banda. In 1972 at least fifty Witnesses were murdered by the Malawi Youth League and the Young Pioneers. As a result some 21,000 victims of persecution fled to Zambia. There, thousands of them were held at the Sinde Masale refugee camp where many died from malnutrition, lack of water, and ill treatment much to the shame of the Zambian authorities and the United Nations. South African and Rhodesian Witnesses claimed that the Zambian authorities stopped them from giving aid to their brethren. Thus in November and December 1972 up to nine Witnesses a day were dying – many of them small children – and by 18 December, nearly 350 refugees had perished at that camp.[64]

Shortly thereafter the Zambian government forcibly repatriated the Witnesses to Malawi with the connivance of UN officials. When the Malawian government would not relent in its policies towards them, they were again forced to flee, this time to Mozambique. By July 1973 some 35,000 Jehovah's Witnesses and Witness supporters were settled there by Portuguese authorities who gave them land and treated them kindly. But when Mozambique became independent in 1975, it too drove Malawian Witnesses back to their native country to undergo another round of assaults, beatings, murders, and imprisonment in concentration camps.[65] At the same time, some 7,000 Mozambiquean Witnesses were arrested *en masse* to be sent to communist re-education camps.[66]

Witnesses have experienced similar treatment in many other African lands including the Cameroons, Angola, Zaire, Ethiopia, Benin, and a number of other black African and Islamic nations.[67] The degree of persecution in all those lands has not been as great as in Malawi and Mozambique, however. Curiously, white Witnesses in South Africa are now also under some threat of restriction.[68]

Marxist Persecution

Although not so well known, the general persecution of Witnesses in the Soviet Union, East European communist states, China, and Cuba has been every bit as harsh as that directed against them in Africa. In those lands Witnesses have not only had to face the general charges of refusal to do military service and show proper loyalty to the regimes but, even more seriously, they have been regarded as a perverse *religious* fifth column by Marxists who in a sense are representatives of a pseudo-religion which will brook no rivals.

Of these communist lands, the Soviet Union, East Germany, and Romania have consistently been the worst persecutors. In the Soviet Union as early as 1946 Witnesses from the newly acquired Republic of Bessarabia were subjected to mass deportations to Siberia and simply left to fend for themselves. Since that time, great numbers of them have been sent to work camps. East Germany has been particularly efficient in its brutality towards them. Thousands have been arrested, with some originally sentenced to life imprisonment, and a number have been killed during imprisonment or died of ill treatment. Romania has not been much better.[69]

At times Poland, Czechoslovakia, and Hungary – all with large Witness communities – have also been brutal in their actions towards the Witnesses. In recent years, the more liberal governments of Poland and Hungary have shown more tolerance, though Jehovah's Witnesses are still banned in those lands legally. In Czechoslovakia they were given brief respite during the Dubček interval in 1968,[70] but since then they have once again been proscribed.

In Cuba the Witnesses have been very badly treated and have, for some unknown reason, gained the personal animosity of Fidel Castro.[71] This may be because Cubans continued to be as warm to Watch Tower teachings after the revolution as before and continued to grow in numbers under his regime. Certainly their refusal to support his military adventures has been an important factor. Recently many have been freed from Cuban prisons and allowed to go to the United States.[72]

Witness Compromises with the World

The picture given above seems to indicate that Jehovah's Witnesses have been amazingly faithful to their basic teaching, regardless of its doctrinal nature at any given time, that they should be neutral in the affairs of the world and should not compromise with secular authorities on matters of faith. Their almost constant persecution in one place after another seems to indicate that. Yet it would be wrong to assume that the Witnesses have always been true to their principles in dealing with secular governments in spite of their oft-made boast that they have been 'loyal to Jehovah' and have remained 'separate from the world.' In fact, there have been three major situations during which the Watch Tower Society's leadership and, at its direction, many individual Bible Students and Witnesses have compromised or attempted to compromise with governments of the world in ways which are contrary to Witness tenets.

The first of these occurred in the spring of 1918 when Watch Tower leaders were facing imprisonment under the terms of the American Espionage Act. Although formerly Judge Rutherford and his associates had been belligerently outspoken against any Bible Student support for the Allied war effort during the First World War, in the 1 and 15 June 1918 issues of *The Watch Tower* they manifested a far more compromising attitude. Bible Students were called on to join with other Americans in a national day of prayer for an Allied victory over German 'autocracy,'[73] and the society now proclaimed that the purchase of 'Liberty' or war bonds had nothing to do with religion.[74] Individual Bible Students were therefore to be free to purchase or not to purchase those bonds as they conscientiously saw fit. Almost immediately this caused conflict in the Bible Student community and really became the major cause of the Standfast schism in western Canada and the northwestern United States.[75] Later, after Rutherford and his seven companions were released from Atlanta Penitentiary in 1919, *The Watch Tower* repudiated its 1918 compromising statements,[76] and the society always attributed them thereafter to having been taken 'captive to Babylon' or false religion.[77] But no apology has ever been forthcoming for another and, in many ways, more serious attempt at compromise with 'Satan's agents' when the society's officers tried to ingratiate themselves with the Hitler government of Nazi Germany.

As has been noted frequently, Jehovah's Witnesses have a fine, even outstanding record for their defiance of Nazism and their willingness to accept martyrdom in the Third Reich's concentration camps rather than renounce their faith. But what is not generally known by historians or most Witnesses themselves is that, in the spring of 1933, Watch Tower leaders tried to placate the Nazis by enunciating their loyalty to the principles of Hitler's National Socialist government and by engaging in clearly anti-Jewish statements.

In April of that year the Watch Tower's branch offices at Magdeburg were seized by government order, and by then the Witnesses were under ban throughout most parts of the Reich. Hence Judge Rutherford and Nathan Knorr flew to Berlin and prepared a 'Declaration of Facts' which was to be presented a few days later to a hastily called Berlin convention of some 7,000 German Witnesses after Rutherford and Knorr had returned to New York. After the convention, the German Witnesses – loyal to instructions from Brooklyn – distributed 2.1 million copies of the 'Declaration' throughout Germany while Watch Tower branch officials sent copies of it to important government officials.[78] The 'Declaration' was not, however, a stirring rallying-call for Jehovah's Witnesses to oppose the oppression of the Hitler government as has been claimed by the Watch Tower Society[79] but, rather, was an attempt to mollify the Nazi Führer and his party officials.

The *1974 Yearbook of Jehovah's Witnesses* admits that many at the Berlin convention were disappointed with the 'Declaration,' implying that they wanted a stronger, anti-Nazi statement. Furthermore, it quotes a letter to Adolf Hitler from the society's branch, sent with a copy of the 'Declaration,' which included the following untruthful statement: 'The Brooklyn presidency of the Watch Tower Society is and always has been *exceedingly friendly to Germany.* In 1918 the president of the Society and seven members of the Board of Directors in America were sentenced to 80 years imprisonment for the reason that the president *refused to let two magazines* in America, which he edited, *be used in war propaganda against Germany.'* The *1974 Yearbook* claims, though, that the 'Declaration' was weakened, evidently in translation, by the society's German branch overseer, Paul Balzereit; and it implies that it was he, rather than Judge Rutherford, who was responsible for trying to compromise with Nazism.[80] But that account is, at best, only partially true.

Balzereit may very well have 'weakened' the 'Declaration'; he and German Witnesses – not Rutherford or Knorr – were faced with the prospects of Nazi persecution. Also, the *1974 Yearbook* is no doubt justified in implying that he, or at least some member of the society's German branch staff, wrote the above-quoted letter to Hitler. None the less, the 'Declaration' appears in the *1934 Yearbook of Jehovah's Witnesses* as an official statement of the society and the society's president; and from the standpoint of Jehovah's Witnesses and others today is a most compromising document which pandered to Nazi anti-semitism and antipathy towards Great Britain and the United States. Under a sub-section entitled 'Jews,' the 'Declaration' stated:

It is falsely charged by our enemies that we have received financial support for our work from the Jews. Nothing is farther from the truth. Up to this hour there never has been the slightest bit of money contributed to our work by Jews. We are the faithful followers of Christ Jesus and believe upon Him as the Savior of the world, whereas the Jews entirely reject Jesus Christ and emphatically deny that he is the Savior of the world sent of God for man's good. This of itself should be sufficient proof to show that we receive no support from Jews and that therefore the charges against us are maliciously false and could proceed only from Satan, our great enemy.

The greatest and the most oppressive empire on earth is the Anglo-American empire. By that is meant the British Empire, of which the United States of America forms a part. It has been the commercial Jews of the British – American empire that have built up and carried on Big Business as a means of exploiting and oppressing the peoples of many nations. This fact particularly applies to the cities of London and New York, the stronghold of Big Business. This fact is so manifest in America that there is a proverb concerning the city of New York which says: 'The Jews own it, the Irish Catholics rule it, and the Americans pay the bills.' We have no fight with any of these persons mentioned but, as the witnesses for Jehovah and in obedience to his commandment set forth in the Scriptures, we are compelled to call attention to the truth concerning the same in order that the people may be enlightened concerning God and his purpose.[81]

This was not all. Besides damning the League of Nations, the 'Declaration' said: 'The present government of Germany has declared against Big Business oppressors and in opposition to the wrongful religious influence in the political affairs of the nation. Such is exactly our position.' Then it proclaimed: 'Instead of being against the principles advocated by the government of Germany, we stand squarely for such principles, and point out that Jehovah God through Christ Jesus will bring about the full realization of these principles.'[82] Of course, as the Witnesses were soon to discover, the Nazis were not impressed, and perhaps angered by the general distribution of the 'Declaration of Facts,' unleashed a wave of persecution against them almost immediately.[83] But it was then, and only then, that Rutherford, the society, and German Witness leaders decided to oppose Nazi policies in an uncompromising fashion.

More recently, Raymond Franz has brought to light another obvious violation of the Witness principle of neutrality with regard to worldly affairs. In a thoroughly documented chapter called 'Double Standards' in his recently published book *Crisis of Conscience,* Franz contrasts the society's unbending rule against Jehovah's Witnesses' buying party cards in the single national political party of Malawi with Brooklyn's relaxed attitude towards Witness men's bribing of Mexican military officers to avoid Mexican universal-male-conscription law and their (the Witnesses) acceptance of membership in the nation's standing military reserves.[84] As Franz points out, a long-time Watch Tower policy holds that membership in a political party, the military, and even in alternative civilian service programs is wrong. Ordinarily, if any Jehovah's Witness agrees to participate in any of the three, he is automatically regarded as 'disassociated' from the Witness community and shunned.[85] Yet in Mexico since 1960, Nathan Knorr, Frederick Franz, and the present governing body of Jehovah's Witnesses have permitted Witness men, including circuit and district overseers and members of the Mexican Watch Tower staff or Bethel family, to purchase illegally *cartillas* or certificates which falsely state that they have completed one year of required military service and which automatically place them in the standing military reserves. Curiously,

in spite of ongoing concern over this matter from Watch Tower branch officials in
Mexico itself, to this day the society maintains one policy for most of the world and
another for Mexico.[86]

This is made clear by Raymond Franz. In discussing the 2 June 1960 Watch
Tower letter to La Torre del Vigía de México (the Watch Tower's Mexican
corporation) which initially laid out the society's Mexican policy, he states:

One reason why this information is so personally shocking to me is that, at the very time the
letter stating that the Society had 'no objection' if Witnesses in Mexico, faced with a call to
military training, chose to 'extricate themselves by a money payment,' there were scores of
young men in the Dominican Republic spending precious years of their life in prison –
because they refused the identical kind of training. Some, such as Leon Glass and his
brother Enrique, were sentenced two or three times for their refusal, passing as much as a
total of nine years of their young manhood in prison. The Society's president [N.H. Knorr]
and vice president [F.W. Franz] had visited the Dominican Republic during those years and
visits had even been made to the prison where many of these men were detained. How the
situation of these Dominican prisoners could be known and yet such a double standard be
applied is incomprehensible to me.

Four years after that counsel was given to Mexico the first eruption of violent attacks
against Jehovah's Witnesses in Malawi took place (1964) and the issue of paying for a party
card arose. The position taken by the Malawi Branch Office was that to do so would be a
violation of Christian neutrality, a compromise unworthy of a genuine Christian. The world
headquarters knew that this was the position taken. The violence subsided after a while and
then broke out again in 1967, so fiercely that thousands of Witnesses were driven into flight
from their homeland. The reports of horrible atrocities in increasing number came flooding
in to the world headquarters.

What effect did it have on them and on their consciences as regards the position taken in
Mexico? In Malawi Witnesses were being beaten and tortured, women were being raped,
homes and fields were being destroyed, and entire families were fleeing to other countries –
determined to hold to the organization's stand that to pay for a party card would be a morally
traitorous act. At the same time, in Mexico, Witness men were *bribing* military officials to
complete a certificate falsely stating that they had fulfilled their military service obligations,
and when they went to the Branch Office, the staff there followed the Society's counsel and
said nothing to indicate in any way that this practice was inconsistent with organizational
standard or the principles of God's Word.[87]

It seems surprising that Watch Tower officials have been responsible for
developing and maintaining such logically contradictory and ethically indefensible policies for Jehovah's Witnesses in different lands. Unlike their brethren in the
United States in 1918 and those in Germany in 1933, Mexican Witnesses have not

been faced with the threat of persecution during the last twenty-four years. What, then, explains the Watch Tower's position as presently maintained by the governing body of Jehovah's Witnesses? The answer may be property, as Raymond Franz seems to infer.[88] Under the Mexican Constitution of 1917, no church or religious organization may own real properties of any kind in the Republic. While they may have the usufruct or legal right to use buildings designated for purposes of worship, all churches, temples, and synagogues are the property of the nation. But the Watch Tower Society, acting through La Torre del Vigía, avoids this constitutional provision by being incorporated as a cultural organization. Hence all Mexican kingdom halls are called *salones culturales* or cultural halls, and Mexican Witnesses never open their meetings with prayers or 'kingdom songs.' Nor do Mexican Witnesses go from door to door with Bibles. To do so might cause them trouble with the civil authorities and bring about the nationalization of their properties. And so, too, might raising an issue over military service. Hence, it seems that as long as officers of the Mexican Army are willing to compromise their morality by selling *cartillas,* Jehovah's Witnesses will continue to compromise theirs by buying them.

General Social Attitudes

The story of the Witnesses' relations with secular states is clear. But what about other matters? How, for instance, do they stand on economic issues? The answer is that they are somewhat indifferent. They do not believe that the Bible teaches any form of socialism, communism, or that it is necessary to hold 'all things in common.' Thus there are numerous Jehovah's Witnesses in the western world who are wealthy businessmen, some even millionaires.

For years, however, the Watch Tower Society took a dim view of capitalism. In spite of his own business activities, Pastor Russell saw it as essentially greedy and exploitative with a tendency to ruin the earth. He sympathized with labour movements, sometimes defended them publicly, and saw the coming battle of Armageddon essentially as a struggle between capital and labour, almost in a Marxist sense.[89] Judge Rutherford, an old Populist, maintained Russell's tradition of sympathy for labour and was far more caustic in his comments with respect to the business world.[90] But since the 1940s, the society's attitudes have undergone a subtle but major change with regard to the capitalist system.

True, Witness teachings do occasionally stress the 'just price–just wage' concept idealized in Europe during the Middle Ages. When pressed to give opinions on business-labour relations, the Watch Tower Society expresses itself in terms which sound like an echo of Pope Leo XIII's famous encyclical, *Rerum Novarum.*[91] But far more counsel on ethical conduct is given to workers than to

employers or managers. Although Witnesses may be members of labour unions,
they are taught to refrain from holding elected offices therein, to avoid picketing,
and in general to be loyal to their employers. They are told to work hard, be honest,
and remain apart from anything like militant union activities. This means that the
society also advises them to refrain from strike breaking. It is therefore quite
evident that today Watch Tower leaders have far more sympathy for management
than labour.[92]

Why this change in attitude has come about is not difficult to comprehend.
Watch Tower organization now operates very much like a giant business
corporation, and it has had need for persons with a high degree of managerial skills
(and attitudes) since Russell's day. The society also benefits greatly from the
contributions of wealthy Witnesses, as it has done for some time; and finally, for
many years now it has been investing in the stock markets of the United States,
Canada, and perhaps some other countries.[93]

Quite reasonably the society tries to avoid anything like class conflict in the
ranks of Jehovah's Witnesses. Such, it believes, would be 'worldly' and would
divert attention from 'kingdom interests.' After all, according to Watch Tower
doctrine the present economic systems, along with the religious and political, are
passing away. Thus Jehovah's Witnesses are advised not to express strong feelings
on economic issues. While individuals may privately hold opinions on them, the
fact that they must often associate and work with persons of other socio-economic
classes in their own congregations has the definite effect of keeping them from
engaging in economic class struggles of any kind.

The society therefore now claims that both it and Jehovah's Witnesses are
completely 'neutral' on such matters. But in fact this is not entirely true. As
indicated, if anything, they are *less* neutral on the side of western capitalism, a fact
which has not escaped the notice of politicians in communist and Third World
countries. More will be said about this in Chapter 8.

With respect to certain moral questions which often become burning political
issues, particularly in democracies, they do have strong feelings. For example, the
Watch Tower Society teaches that the secular state is justified in imposing capital
punishment for murder.[94] It regards abortion, gambling, lotteries, legalized
prostitution, legalized homosexuality, pornography, and certain other matters as
socially evil.[95] But unlike many Protestants, Catholics, and Jews, Jehovah's
Witnesses refuse to support legislation to implement their moral views. They
openly censure the world, government, and politicians for permitting activities
which they regard as immoral. Yet they do not believe that they have a right to
impose their values on persons outside their community or to put new moral wine
into old political wineskins. Their answer is not the social gospel or the
moral-political reform of present-day societies through Christian democracy; it is

Christ's kingdom. Thus their only direct concern is with the morality of those in their congregations, for is not 'the whole world lying in the power of the wicked one'?

Nevertheless, when Witnesses feel that their own Christian freedom is impinged upon in any area which they believe to be vital, they will resist legally and, if necessary, illegally. Not surprisingly, they have therefore fallen afoul of much of the medical profession, the press, the general public, and law-making bodies for their refusal to accept blood transfusions.

Blood Transfusions

From the time of the organization of the first Bible Student congregations to the late 1930s, Jehovah's Witnesses seldom took any position with regard to medical treatment except on vaccination in spite of Clayton Woodworth's tirades against the germ theory of disease, and the American Medical Association. Generally, they went to physicians without any serious religious conflict. But by the Second World War that situation began to change.

Witnesses had always accepted the strict scriptural injunctions against the eating of blood as in blood sausages or blood puddings. The question of the morality of blood transfusions did not arise until 1937, however, after the establishment of the first large-scale blood bank at Cook County hospital in Chicago in that year. Even then there was little concern about the matter, which affected few civilians, until 1945. Nevertheless, before the Second World War ended, *The Watchtower* took a stand on the issue in its 1 July 1945 issue. Since that time, Jehovah's Witnesses have officially refused transfusions or blood particles (with some exceptions in the case of the latter) as contrary to biblical teachings, particularly according to such texts as Genesis 9:5, 6; Leviticus 17:10; and Acts 15:20, 28, 29.

Although they have consistently emphasized their religious objections to blood transfusions,[96] Witness lawyers and scholars have argued that the use of such transfusions has often been a medical fad, that in the great majority of cases they are not necessary – since alternative therapies exist – and that there are great risks involved in their use. Since the question of their acceptance or non-acceptance involves the Witnesses' own well-being and since, as admitted by a standard medical text, 'blood transfusions must be regarded as a form of therapy which carries a significant risk which is potentially lethal,'[97] Jehovah's Witnesses feel they should be free to reject them for themselves and their families.[98] Many thousands have died or suffered serious harm from transfusions, a fact not known by the general public or, apparently, by many physicians.[99]

The Witnesses' refusal has, however, not been accepted lightly by many members of the medical profession, hospitals, or the press. In liberal, democratic lands today one may challenge the churches, politicians, and even nationalism, but science, especially medical science, remains a sacred cow. Thus Jehovah's Witnesses children *and adults* have been subjected to forced transfusions in societies where the courts have otherwise admitted that individuals may refuse medical treatment and have the right to die.[100] The Witnesses reply that such forced therapy has as often as not been death-dealing rather than life-saving. In Canada alone some twelve infants have been given forced transfusions and returned to their parents dead.[101] Whether or not these children would have died in any case, had they not received transfusions, is impossible to ascertain. But, not surprisingly, the Witnesses have tried to argue that they died because they were given blood.

In late years, it is true, the Witnesses' arguments have received more attention. So, too, has the fact that they have served as medical guinea-pigs.[102] Yet both the medical profession and the courts often continue to ignore what the Witnesses consider to be their right to the sanctity of their and their children's bodies, while in some cases the Witnesses themselves often fan the flames of prejudice unnecessarily over the issue. In Canada in particular, W. Glen How and other Witnesses have often used rather abusive terminology towards certain members of the medical profession in court cases, and How has often referred to forced transfusions as a form of 'rape.'[103] Curiously, in spite of the importance of the controversy and the whole issue of medical-religious ethics coming to the fore, few scholars have taken much time to examine the serious implications of such enforced therapy from the standpoint of law, medicine, or ethics. And fewer still have examined the Witnesses' teachings on the matter from a doctrinal standpoint. Only now are several persons who have either left the Witness fold or are in secret disagreement with Brooklyn's stand on the issue giving it the careful examination it deserves.[104]

Separateness and Social Concern

In practically every account of Jehovah's Witnesses, whether written by Witnesses, objective scholars, or Witness adversaries, an emphasis on alienation and conflict with the world has been stressed, something understandable from the discussion above. Witness eschatology continues to teach that the present evil world is passing away and that its time is short. There is, therefore, little time to devote to the building of schools, hospitals, or charitable institutions of any kind; publishers of the kingdom must give what time and energy they have to the preaching work. Furthermore, individual Witnesses continue to feel a sense of religious exclusiveness which is quite remarkable. In a recent study of three samples of Witnesses, Mormons, and Catholics, wherein members of the three faiths were asked to state their perceptions of some sixteen religious groups well known to them, all demonstrated a highly developed sense of the belief that theirs was the only true faith. Although perhaps not statistically significant, the Witnesses emphasized that aspect to a greater degree than members of the other two groups, although all three samples studied were chosen for their religiosity.[105]

Such religious exclusiveness has often developed unattractive characteristics among many of the Witnesses. As is frequently the case among those who believe that theirs is the only true religion, they have tended to manifest a sense of spiritual pride which is irksome to their acquaintances. They are also often austere to the point of severity and seldom manifest the sense of joy demonstrated by charismatic Christians or even by other sectarians such as the Mormons or Seventh-Day Adventists. Jehovah's Witnesses are, if anything, twentieth-century sectarian Puritans with many of the same taboos and social attitudes as their seventeenth-century English and New England spiritual forbears,[106] along with more than a touch of Victorian pietism.

It is not surprising, then, that they are looked on unfavourably by many of their neighbours: they repudiate the world, and they consistently preach to others who do not believe in the possibility of a paradise to be regained on earth what seems like a message of doom and gloom. They refuse to contribute to many charities. They do not carry on ministries of public education or healing as do Catholics, Mennonites, or Seventh-Day Adventists, a fact which has occasioned some criticism of them.[107] The Witnesses therefore have defined their role in this life in much the same way that the pilgrim Christian did in John Bunyan's famous allegory, *Pilgrim's Progress:* they are aliens who, in a land about to be destroyed, must constantly press on to a city belonging to heaven.

Yet there is another side to Witness life and attitudes. As 'ambassadors substituting for Christ,' Jehovah's Witnesses believe that they must lead lives which will reflect well on their message and their God. Consequently, they have come to be known for their physical cleanliness, their good work habits, and their personal honesty. In practically all societies they manifest the very qualities which make them the best of solid and productive citizens, a fact noted by certain outsiders.[108] Interestingly, too, both the Watch Tower Society and individual Witnesses have taken pride in the very substantial contributions that they have made to the laws of many lands through their broadening of civil liberties.[109] More recently, many of them are pleased that they have made an important, though indirect contribution to medical science through their stand on blood transfusions.[110]

But because of the Watch Tower Society's insistent teaching that mankind is living close to the apocalypse, the Witnesses show few signs of accommodating to the twentieth century or even of demonstrating the intellectual and social vitality of which they should be capable. Only in a very few places such as the southwestern United States have they established private schools, and they certainly have made fewer contributions to academic life, the arts, or biblical studies than one might reasonably expect. Had the Watch Tower Society encouraged such, the highly disciplined community of Jehovah's Witnesses no doubt would have been capable of great things. The Witnesses could have stressed both higher education and the arts in the way that the Mormons, Adventists, Quakers, and even some independent Bible Students' groups have done without compromising their most basic beliefs and thereby have become a much more attractive and productive community than they now are. Furthermore, they would also have been able to deal with the many problems they now face in a much more positive fashion. But this has not happened. As Joseph Zygmunt states: 'While moderating its conflicts with the world, the group has not surrendered its sectarian identity but rather has changed its "sectarian style." It has become less of an "anti-worldly" conflict group and more of an "unworldly" contrast group. Quite clearly, it has maintained its polarity, vis-à-vis the world, actively striving, in fact, to cultivate new marks of distinctiveness, to put greater symbolic distance between itself and the world.'[111]

Only time will tell whether or not Jehovah's Witnesses will eventually make a greater accommodation with the world. At present that is not happening, nor can it. The Witnesses are taught by their leaders that they and they alone are members of a pure, godly organization which alone will pass through Armageddon into a 'new order.' They are made to feel that they have no real stake in a system which, with all its supporters, is very shortly to suffer destruction at the hands of a vengeful Jehovah represented by Christ and his angels. Nevertheless, if – as has happened so often in the past – time and the present Watch Tower leadership pass into history while the apocalypse is delayed yet again, it will become increasingly difficult for a new generation of Witnesses not to reassess their entire apocalyptic schema and with it their attitude towards the rest of the world. Currently the leadership will not make an open and reasonably objective study of Bible Student – Witness history or doctrine, nor will it allow others of the movement to do so. For to permit that to happen would be to undermine the unique claims of the leadership to spiritual authority. Consequently, as Joseph Zygmunt says, the Witnesses are now somewhat 'unworldly,' living in an intellectually and psychologically isolated society of their own.

Part Two

Concepts and Doctrine

CHAPTER SIX

Bases of Doctrinal Authority

Dealing with the doctrinal concepts of Jehovah's Witnesses is a most difficult matter, even for one thoroughly familiar with them. The Witnesses have no systematic theologians and no systematic theology. Thus they seem unaware of many of the logical contradictions in their very complex doctrinal system and are unable to come to grips with them intellectually. Furthermore, as demonstrated earlier, since their doctrines are constantly in flux, it is really impossible to discuss Witness theology in the same way that one can discuss the more stable doctrinal systems of the great churches. Nevertheless there are certain concepts which do serve as foundations of Witness thought, and it is to these, the very bases of doctrinal authority, that we must first turn in order to understand their secondary and tertiary doctrines as well as their social behaviour.

The Faithful and Discreet Slave

In theory Jehovah's Witnesses claim to teach Martin Luther's doctrine of *sola scriptura* – the Bible alone – which they emphasize loudly as the basis of their faith. In fact, they condemn other churches and religious organizations for deviating from what they consider to be the Word of God. 'The Holy Scriptures of the Bible are,' according to them, 'the standard by which to judge all religions.'[1] Thus the book *'Let God be True,'* published originally in 1946, states:

To let God be true means to let God have the say as to what is the truth that makes men free. It means to accept his Word, the Bible, as the truth. Hence, in this book, our appeal is to the Bible for truth. Our obligation is to back up what is said herein by quotations from the Bible for proof of truthfulness and reliability. That is the course the inspired writers and faithful characters of the Bible took and recommended ... Unless we seek direct to the law and testimony of God's written Word, we shall never attain to the light whose beams show that the morning of a new world of righteousness is at hand.[2]

The same book goes on at some length to condemn the *oral* traditions of Jews and Catholics as having no validity alongside the Scriptures.[3] Speaking of Jesus, it says: 'In no case did he appeal to the rabbinic schools of teaching with their traditions and precepts of men. He faithfully referred his disciples to God's Word, thereby to glorify God as true, though at the same time it proved the publicly respected religious leaders liars.'[4]

Another traditional Witness textbook for prospective converts, *The Truth That Leads to Eternal Life,* takes much the same position. On page 13 it emphasizes: 'If our worship is to be acceptable to God, it must be firmly rooted in God's Word of truth. Jesus reproved those persons who claimed to serve God but who relied heavily on the traditions of men in preference to God's Word.'

So on the surface the Watch Tower Society and Witness leaders take what amounts to an aggressively 'Protestant' attitude towards the Scriptures: they stress that the Bible and the Bible alone is the basis of their doctrine. In fact, it appears that there is a strong element in their thinking which is far more Roman Catholic than Protestant in nature.

The basis of this Catholic element is their concept of the 'faithful and discreet slave' or, as it was originally known, the 'faithful and wise servant' doctrine. That teaching, as originally developed by Maria Russell and later modified by Judge Rutherford, is undoubtedly the central dogma of Witness theology today. For as was shown in Chapter 1,[5] once Pastor Russell conceived of himself as 'that servant' and the Watch Tower Society as the 'channel of truth,' his Bible Student followers were well on the way towards adopting a doctrinal stance which was close to, if not identical with, the Catholic doctrine of the *magisterium* of the popes of Rome. Of equal significance, Russell's teachings quickly attained the status of *tradition* and became the medium by which the Scriptures were to be understood. And while such teachings were always said to be of secondary importance to the Bible, in fact the reverse soon became true. It was Russell's ideas which came to be regarded as 'new light,' 'meat in due season,' and 'the Truth,' not simply the Bible canon held by all members of the Christian community in common. In addition, although Watch Tower leaders deny flatly that they accept the doctrine of apostolic succession,[6] in many places their own statements indicate otherwise. Writing in 1923, Judge Rutherford held: 'In connection with his presence and the harvest work, the office of that "faithful and wise servant" is important, and is made so by the Lord himself. The one who fills the office is made *ruler* over all the Lord's goods during the time of his incumbency in office. The office of that "faithful and wise servant" therefore *is a part of the orderly manner* in which the Lord carried on his work during his second presence.'[7]

At the time Rutherford held that Pastor Russell had been the 'faithful and wise servant' and that his, Rutherford's, authority over the Bible Student community (*the Society,* as he defined it) came from the fact that the Watch Tower Society had been established by Russell:

In modest phrase Brother Russell here clearly indicated that it was his thought that *the Society,* as organized in an orderly manner, would carry on the work begun by him and finish that which had been committed to him personally. Often when asked by others, Who is that faithful and wise servant? – Brother Russell would reply: 'Some say I am; while others say the Society is.' Both statements were true; for Brother Russell was in fact the Society in a most absolute sense, in this, that he directed the policy and course of the Society without regard to any other person on earth. He sometimes sought advice of others connected with the Society, listened to their suggestions, and then did according to his own judgement, believing that the Lord would have him thus do.

Since Brother Russell's 'change' some who believe that he filled the office of 'that servant' have said that the Lord has cast off the Society. Is such a conclusion either reasonable or Scriptural? Brother Russell's own thought was that the Society would continue to do the Lord's work as above indicated. Besides, if the Lord was pleased to have the organization *started originally* for *his purposes,* why should he cast if off? Why not continue to direct the servants therein according to his own will or supply other servants? Such is the reasonable conclusion.[8]

Years later, even after he had abandoned the idea that Russell was the 'faithful and wise servant,' Rutherford claimed that he held a peculiar authority as president of the society and, hence, as Russell's heir: 'The Society is made up of all those who are anointed of the Lord and who are in harmony with his work; and since by the action of the Society its officers have been clothed with certain power and authority, *the duty devolves on such to define a policy of action* [italics mine].'[9]

And again, he stated: 'We believe that his anointed as a company constitute really the Society as we use that term. Somebody in that visible organization must formulate plans of operation. It seems to have pleased the Lord to have done this at the Society's headquarters and that from there regulations are sent out to the various ecclesias.'[10]

That Rutherford used a doctrine of spiritual succession from Russell cannot be denied. While he later supplemented that teaching with the idea that he held office at the behest of the 'Society,' the 'faithful and wise servant' class, or the Bible Student community, that concept was never stressed. For when elected elders or others defied the judge, he simply declared that they were not truly part of the church of Christ. Hence no 'true' Bible Student could be out of harmony with Rutherford any more than he would have been with Russell, or than any faithful Catholic could be out of communion with the pope.

The same has been true with Rutherford's successors. In spite of the fact that subsequent changes in Watch Tower teaching have completely undermined all bases for Russell's spiritual authority,[11] they continue to claim their authority as *successors* to Russell and a non-existent 'governing body' of which he was said to have been a member. Shortly after the creation of the present governing body, *The Watchtower* made that clear. In its 15 December 1971 issue, on page 760, it declared:

How did this governing body make its appearance in recent times? Evidently under the direction of Jehovah God and his Son Jesus Christ. According to the facts available, the governing body became associated with the Watch Tower Bible and Tract Society of Pennsylvania. C.T. Russell was patently of that governing body back there in the last quarter of the nineteenth century. Being fully dedicated to God through Christ, he set himself up to apply his time, energy, abilities, wealth and influence to defending God's inspired Word and spreading its message. To that end he began publishing *Zion's Watch Tower* back there in July of 1879, believing, as he said in its columns, that this had Jehovah's backing, and hence there would be no solicitation for money.

Equally impressive is the Catholic way in which Rutherford, Knorr, Franz, and the present governing body have all demanded spiritual obedience from Jehovah's Witnesses. In fact, in some ways, Watch Tower leaders have even claimed more authority, on a far less rational basis, than the papacy. According to the First Vatican Ecumenical Council, held in 1869 and 1870, when the pope speaks *ex cathedra* (from his throne on behalf of the entire church) on matters of faith and morals, he is infallible. Thus all Catholics must accept the doctrines he proclaims at those times as dogmatically true; to do otherwise is considered heretical. Of course Watch Tower leaders have never claimed infallibility as such; yet, curiously, they have claimed consistently to speak *ex cathedra* on behalf of the entire Witness community. And woe betide the person who questions any doctrine they should teach, even if they later admit that it is false. So while the Catholic church insists that it can define 'truth' dogmatically and all faithful Catholics must accept such 'truth' to obtain a proper standing with God, Watch Tower leaders have argued that Jehovah's Witnesses must accept (or at least not question openly) *even false doctrines* as taught by the society in order to gain salvation.[12]

Judge Rutherford would certainly not accept correction from anyone except Jehovah or Jesus and neither have his successors. Nathan Knorr was a complete autocrat. Testifying in the Walsh case in 1954 Frederick Franz replied to questions from the Crown Counsellor as follows:

QUESTION: In matters spiritual has each member of the Board of Directors [of the Watch Tower Society] an equally valid voice?

ANSWER: The President is the mouth-piece. He pronounces the speeches that show advancement of the understanding of the Scriptures. Then he may appoint other members of the headquarters temporarily to give other speeches which set forth any part of the Bible upon which further light has been thrown.

QUESTION: Tell me; are these advances as you put it, voted upon by the directors?

ANSWER: No.

QUESTION: How do they become pronouncements?

ANSWER: They go through the editorial committee [an ad hoc body], and I give my O.K. after Scriptural examination. Then I pass them on to President Knorr, and President Knorr has the final O.K.[13]

Franz indicated further that while the Watch Tower Society, operating through its *mouthpiece,* then President Nathan H. Knorr, had taught errors, every Jehovah's Witness was *bound* to accept its teachings as presented in its publications.[14] The following, from the testimony of Hayden Covington, is also taken from the Pursuer's Proof or the transcript of record of the Walsh trial:

QUESTION: A Witness has no alternative, has he, to accept as authoritative and to be obeyed instructions issued in the 'Watchtower' or the 'Informant' or 'Awake!'?

ANSWER: He must accept those.

QUESTION: Are those books in a different position from these magazines?

ANSWER: 'Watchtower' is the official magazine of the Society.

QUESTION: Then is it your view that the present organization of Jehovah's Witnesses, with the Watchtower Bible and Tract Society as its legal agency, is the means by which the Will of God is worked out on earth?

ANSWER: That is our firm belief.[15]

Since 1954 the society's officers have not changed their position on this matter and over the years have come closer and closer to admitting that it is the governing body and the society (theoretically acting for the remnant of the 144,000 or the 'faithful and discreet slave'), and not the Bible, which is the primary spiritual authority among Jehovah's Witnesses. In its issue of 1 October 1967 *The Watchtower* stated: 'As the canon of books of God's Word was expanded and the Christian Greek Scriptures were added to complete the Bible, each book was written directly to the Christian congregation or to a member of the Christian congregation on its behalf. Thus the Bible is an organizational book and belongs to the Christian congregation as an organization, not to individuals, regardless of how sincerely they may believe that they can interpret the Bible. For this reason the Bible cannot be properly understood without Jehovah's visible organization in mind.'[16]

Very recently, the society has even argued that it is dangerous for Jehovah's Witnesses to study the Bible alone. In the 15 August 1981 issue, *The Watchtower* shrilly proclaimed:

From time to time, there have arisen from among the ranks of Jehovah's people those who, like the original Satan, have adopted an independent, faultfinding attitude. They do not want to serve 'shoulder to shoulder' with the worldwide brotherhood. (Compare Ephesians 2:19–22.) Rather, they present a 'stubborn shoulder' to Jehovah's words. (Zech. 7:11, 12) Reviling the pattern of the 'pure language' that Jehovah has so graciously taught his people over the past century, these haughty ones try to draw the 'sheep' away from the one international 'flock' that Jesus has gathered in the earth. (John 10:7–10, 16) They try to sow doubts and to separate unsuspecting ones from the bounteous 'table' of spiritual food spread in the Kingdom Halls of Jehovah's Witnesses, where truly there is 'nothing lacking.' (Ps. 23:1–6) They say that it is sufficient to read the Bible exclusively, either alone or in small groups at home. But, strangely, through such 'Bible reading,' they have reverted right back to the apostate doctrines that commentaries by Christendom's clergy were teaching 100 years ago, and some have even returned to celebrating Christendom's festivals again, such as the Roman Saturnalia of December 25! Jesus and his apostles warned against such lawless ones. – Matt. 24:11–13; Acts 20:28–30; 12 Pet. 2:1, 21.[17]

This statement, evidently developed by the Watch Tower Society in direct response to the schisms now of growing importance among Jehovah's Witnesses, demonstrates just how far the society has moved from any *sola scriptura* doctrine. In fact, its position now seems more like that of the Catholic adversaries of Luther and his colleagues than it does of the reformers. No church historian, in reading the above statement from *The Watchtower,* can be anything but impressed by its similarity to the 'Decree Concerning the Edition, and the Use, of the Sacred Books' of the Council of Trent as promulgated at its fourth session on 8 April 1546. That decree states in part:

Furthermore, in order to restrain petulant spirits, it decrees, that no one, relying on his own skill, shall, – in matters of faith, and of morals pertaining to the edification of Christian doctrine, – wresting the sacred Scripture to his own senses, presume to interpret the said sacred Scripture contrary to that sense which holy mother Church, – whose it is to judge of the true sense and interpretation of the holy Scriptures, – hath held and doth hold; or even contrary to the unanimous consent of the Fathers; even though such interpretations were never intended to be at any time published. Contraveners shall be made known by their Ordinaries, and be punished with penalties by law established.[18]

How strange it seems that an organization which has for more than a hundred years attacked the Church of Rome for its attitude towards the Scriptures has taken a position virtually identical with that of that church in proclaiming its own *magisterium* or teaching power, its right to speak *ex cathedra* on behalf of the faithful, and its right to restrain 'petulant spirits' with 'independent, faultfinding attitudes.' But that, following a surprisingly common pattern in history which is discussed in Chapter 8 and subsequently, is exactly what has happened.

Progressive Revelation

What concept permits members of the governing body to take the position that they – or, in many instances, one man – have the right to define doctrine, dogma, and 'new truths' for the entire Witness community? The answer is *'progressive revelation,'* a particularly hazy doctrine which is never clearly defined and never carefully analysed. Based primarily on a misapplication of Proverbs 4:18 – 'But the path of the righteous ones is like the bright light that is getting lighter and lighter until the day is firmly established'[19] – it is usually understood to mean a progressive *organizational understanding* of the Bible through the application of reason, study, and the undefined guidance of the holy spirit. But at other times it takes on the character of a direct, latter-day revelation comparable to those supposedly given to Mormons through their Prophet, Seer, and Revelator – their church's president. For example, Judge Rutherford used to speak of spiritual 'lightning flashes in the temple,'[20] and the society claims that the doctrine that the 'great crowd' of Revelation 7:9 and the 'other sheep' of John 10:16 are the same class was 'revealed' to him in 1935.[21] More recently *The Watchtower* has dubbed the 'faithful and discreet slave' class a *'prophet organization.'*[22] Of course such lack of clarity concerning the doctrine of progressive revelation serves Watch Tower leaders' purposes in a very direct way, although it is difficult to believe that they have consciously understood the full significance of their manipulation of doctrine through their use of it. For when they have spoken dogmatically on some doctrine, for example with respect to some future eschatological date, they have frequently claimed that they have had proof or definite knowledge which was revealed to them, evidently by the holy spirit acting through them as God's channel. But when their predictions have proved wrong, as time and again they have, Watch Tower writers have fallen back on the idea that progressive revelation can simply mean enhanced knowledge which can, of course, be mistaken, usually about certain details. In effect, then, the concept of progressive revelation has often been used, whether consciously or not, as a sort of spiritual shell game on the Witness community. That this has been so can be demonstrated clearly by the way the society has in fact used the concept over the years, especially with regard to prophetic speculation.

Note that most if not all of the major events expected by Russell, Rutherford, and the Watch Tower Society since Rutherford's day have not happened. Russell first believed that the rapture of the church would take place in 1878 and then in 1881.[23] When that event did not occur as he had expected, he reinterpreted the significance of those years. He felt that a time of trouble would begin about 1910 and would end in 1914 or 1915: 'But bear in mind that the end for 1914 is not the *beginning,* but the end of the time of trouble.'[24] 'The culmination of the trouble in October 1914 is clearly marked in the Scriptures and we are bound therefore to expect a beginning of that *severe* trouble not later than 1910; – with severe spasms between now and then.'[25] As noted earlier, Rutherford was equally certain about 1925, and for nearly a decade prior to 1975, the society pointed to that year.

But all these prophecies have failed, and the society has been forced to reinterpret much of its eschatology. In a number of instances it has reinterpreted the significance of certain dates, while it no longer says anything about others. The year 1914 is now seen as having marked the beginning of the time of trouble rather than the end, while Jehovah's Witnesses no longer believe that dates which were important to Russell such as 1799, 1846, 1874, 1878, 1881, or 1910 have any special meaning. They have abandoned as wrong much of the system of prophetic calculation used by Russell and for a time by Rutherford.[26]

What permitted this to happen was the way that Pastor Russell sometimes looked on such matters and the similar approach which the society has sometimes taken since his death. For example, as early as 1891, Russell discussed his view of the Millerite movement of the early years of the nineteenth century in the United States and stated: 'While as the reader will have observed, we disagree with Mr Miller's interpretations and deductions, on almost every point – viewing the *object* as well as the *manner* and the *time,* of our Lord's coming in a very different light – yet we recognize that movement as being in God's order, and as doing a very important work in the separating, purifying, refining, and thus making ready, of a waiting people prepared for the Lord.'[27] In other words, although the Millerites had made many mistakes in their search for truth, that search was the right one. Had the time been right, they would have received more light, more divine guidance. But they could only walk in the light they then had, and they should not have been censured for that.

While Russell believed that he had more light than the Millerites, like Miller, he considered himself to be a student of prophecy, not a prophet. He believed that he could be wrong in his chronological computations. As Timothy White has remarked: 'However awe-inspiring the chronological structure was, it was just one of the many important doctrines.'[28] Russell regarded the plan of the ages as a harp with many strings. Even without that one string, the harp could continue to produce beautiful music. 'So the omission of the chronology would mean that we would not know where we are in time, but would leave almost unimpaired the perfection of the divine plan as a whole.'[28] On this theme Russell expressed himself in 1907:

But let us suppose a case far from our expectations: suppose that A.D. 1915 should pass with the world's affairs all serene and with evidence that the 'very elect' had not all been 'changed' and without the restoration of natural Israel to favor under the New Covenant. (Rom. 11:12, 15) What then? Would that not prove our chronology wrong? Yes, surely! And would not that prove a keen disappointment? Indeed it would! It would work irreparable wreck to parallel dispensations and Israel's double, and to the Jubilee calculations, and to the prophecy of 2,300 days of Daniel and to the epoch called 'Gentile Times,' and to 1,260, 1,290 and 1,335 days, the latter of which marking the beginning of the 'harvest' so well fulfilled its prediction. 'Oh the blessedness of him that waits unto the 1,335 days!' None of these would be available any longer. What a blow that would be! One of the strings of our 'harp' would be quite broken!

However, dear friends, our harp would still have all the other strings in tune and that is what no other aggregation of God's people on earth could boast.[30]

On a concluding note in the same article, he remarked: 'If, therefore, dearly beloved, it should turn out that our chronology is all wrong, we may conclude that with it we have had much advantage everywhere. If the attainment of our glorious hopes and present joys in the Lord should *cost* us such disappointment as our friends fear, we should rejoice and count it cheap!'[31]

When 1914 did not bring what Russell expected, he admitted that fact frankly. Writing on 1 October 1916, in an Author's Foreword to a new edition of *The Time Is at Hand,* Volume II of *Studies in the Scriptures,* he stated: 'The author acknowledges that in this book he presents the thought that the Lord's saints might expect to be with him in glory at the ending of the Gentile Times. This was a natural mistake to fall into, but the Lord overruled it for the blessing of his people.'[32] And again: 'Our mistake was evidently not in respect to the ending of the Times of the Gentiles; we drew a false conclusion, however, not authorized by the Word of the Lord.'[33]

A few years later *The Watch Tower* of 1 July 1919 spoke with similar honesty: 'Brother Russell was sole editor of THE WATCH TOWER of many years and made many mistakes, because he too was imperfect ... Since Brother Russell left us, a committee of imperfect men have tried to edit THE WATCH TOWER, men even more likely to make mistakes than was Brother Russell. That these have made mistakes is freely admitted.'[34]

As discussed earlier, too, Judge Rutherford apologized for the failure of his prophecies respecting 1925. Older Witnesses thus point with pride to the fact that he apologized for being 'too presumptuous' over the matter at the International Bible Student convention of that year.[35] And, of course, Rutherford was able to point to what he had written in the 15 February 1925 *Watch Tower:*

It seems a weakness of many Bible Students that if they locate a future date in the Bible, immediately they center as many prophecies on that date as possible ... Many can remember how 'absolutely sure' some were about 1914. No doubt the Lord was pleased with the zeal manifested by his servants; but did they have a Scriptural basis for all they expected to come to pass that year? Let us be cautious, therefore, about predicting particulars. The Lord will make them clear as fast as they become meat in due season. However, we feel sure that he will not chide us if we earnestly and reverently search for what may be revealed, watching also the facts about us.[36]

In 1929 Rutherford again expressed himself in a similar vein, although on quite a different subject.[37] More recently *The Watchtower* has followed in Russell's and Rutherford's footsteps in this regard. In the 15 December 1962 issue it stated emphatically: 'The care of God's organization today is not in the hands of men who are inspired by God. They can make mistakes as any imperfect man can.'[38] Hence, Jehovah's Witnesses are told that no one should expect that the 'faithful and discreet slave' class will not make mistakes with respect to prophetic interpretation as well as other matters. Yet according to that *Watchtower* they have a 'sincere desire to search out accurate understanding of the things in God's Words.'[39] So they believe that God's spirit operates upon his dedicated servants, not to inspire them, but 'to move them gently in the direction of increased understanding.'[40] *The Watchtower* also has attempted to demonstrate Jehovah's Witnesses' feelings regarding their past mistakes and how they sometimes believe that a gradual increase in spiritual knowledge takes place: 'This progress in Scriptural knowledge might be likened to an overcast sky that is gradually breaking up. As the openings between the clouds grow, more and more light comes through. Sometimes a truth is seen but then is obscured by a misunderstanding just as a passing cloud momentarily obscures some rays of the sun. Later this truth returns in greater clarity when the misunderstanding is removed. God's spirit is evident upon the organization from the progress it is making along the path of Scriptural truth.'[41]

The society therefore does not claim to be 'inspired.' Like Pastor Russell, Jehovah's Witnesses today do admit that they can and do make mistakes. But they do feel that Jehovah is directing them 'gently' because they believe that they have fulfilled their stewardship as no others have and are being used by God in a unique way. In the 1 March 1979 *Watchtower* (pp. 23–4) the society made the following confession, while still calling on individual Witnesses to be loyal to it:

Because of this hope [in the fulfilment of Matthew 6:10], the 'faithful and discreet slave' has alerted all of God's people to the sign of the times indicating the nearness of God's Kingdom rule. In this regard, however, it must be observed that this 'faithful and discreet slave' was never inspired, never perfect. Those writings by certain members of the 'slave' class that came to form the Christian part of God's Word were inspired and infallible, but that is not true of other writings since. Things published were not perfect in the days of Charles Taze Russell, first president of the Watch Tower Bible and Tract Society; nor were they perfect in the days of J.F. Rutherford, the succeeding president. The increasing light on God's Word as well as the facts of history have repeatedly required that adjustments of one kind or another be made down to the very present time. But let us never forget that the motives of this 'slave' were always pure, unselfish; at all times it has been well-meaning. Moreover, the words found at Romans 8:28 are fitting here also: 'God makes all his works cooperate together for the good of those who love God, those who are the ones called according to his purpose.' Actually, any adjustments that have been made in understanding have furnished an opportunity for those being served by this 'slave' to show loyalty and love, the kind of love that Jesus said would mark his followers.

But there is another side to the matter of Witness attitudes with respect to chronology and prophetic speculation. In fact, it would be either a serious mistake or quite dishonest to argue that the restrained and undogmatic position just outlined has been the dominant one of Jehovah's Witnesses or Witness leaders over the years. In general, what has been the case, especially since Pastor Russell's death, has been that the Watch Tower Society has been extremely doctrinaire whenever it has held to a particular position, whether relating to prophetic speculation or otherwise. Then, later, when it became obvious that the doctrine in question was untenable, it would retreat to the assertion that Watch Tower leaders are not infallible and must progress with the light. A few examples make this point clear.

In an article published in the 1 May 1922 *Watch Tower* entitled the 'Gentile Times,' the writer reaffirmed Pastor Russell's chronology and stated: 'If the contention of his opponents concerning chronology is right, then everything that transpired in 1914 since must be disregarded as evidence of the Messiah's kingdom. It is admitted by them that the tenure of office of Israel's kings must be changed in order to agree with some historians who were agents of Satan. Such a change would put out of joint all our chronology, and destroy the value of the dates 1874, 1878, 1881, 1910, 1914 and 1918. Such would be equivalent to saying, "Where is the proof of his presence?" "My Lord delayeth his coming." '[42]

At the time, the society was facing a number of major schisms among Bible

Students, some of whom had come to doubt the Barbour–Russell chronology. *The Herald of the Morning,* the journal of the Pastoral Bible Institute, had re-examined that chronology and had come to the conclusion that Russell had been wrong in assuming that the fall of Jerusalem to Babylon had occurred in 606 BC. It suggested, rather, that that event had taken place in 587 BC – the date accepted by most historians since Usher – and that the Gentile Times would end in 1934.[43] Thus to rebut an attack on the society's chronology and its authority, *The Watch Tower* published a number of articles in support of the chronological system which it had inherited from its first president. In the article 'Seventy Years' Desolation – Part II,' on page 187 of its 15 June 1922 issue, that journal gave a number of arguments in an attempt to 'prove' it beyond the shadow of a doubt. Among these were 'the law of probabilities' and deductions from studies of the Great Pyramid of Gizeh. Accordingly, it stated: 'The chronology of present truth might be a mere happening if it were not for the repetitions in the two great cycles of 1845 and 2520 years, which take it out of the realm of chance and into that of certainty. If there were only one or two corresponding dates in these cycles, they might possibly be mere coincidences, but where the agreements of dates and events come by the dozens, they cannot possibly be by chance, but must be by the design or plan of the only personal Being capable of such a plan – Jehovah himself; *and the chronology itself must be right.'* Two paragraphs farther on, the article continued: 'It is on the basis of such and so many correspondencies – in accordance with the soundest laws known to science – that we affirm that, *Scripturally, scientifically, and historically, present-truth chronology is correct beyond a doubt ...* Present-truth chronology is a secure basis on which the consecrated child of God may endeavor to search out things to come.' If this were not dogmatic enough, the article, in its concluding comments, on the same page, remarked: 'Present-truth chronology is correct beyond the possibility of a doubt. Present-truth chronology is based upon divine prophecy and its Biblical fulfillment, that the seventy years were years of desolation, not part desolation and part captivity. The chronology stands firm as a rock, based upon the Word of God.'

The 'rock' must have been made of particularly easily erodable sandstone: already the Barbour–Russell chronology was undergoing change,[44] and in 1923 *The Watch Tower* remarked: 'Chronology itself is not a vital doctrine, necessary to salvation; but it is closely related to the doctrines, and gives great aid to a proper understanding of God's Word at this time.'[45] Two years later Judge Rutherford published 'Birth of the Nation,' a *Watch Tower* article which began to change much of the old chronology out of any recognizable form.[46] Finally, in 1928, he publicly classified the Great Pyramid, which had served as such a buttress to many of Russell's chronological speculations, as having been built under the direction of Satan rather than Jehovah.[47]

Nevertheless, since the 1920s Rutherford and his successors have continued to follow much the same contradictory policy towards the new chronology that they did towards the old. On a number of occasions, both in print and in private correspondence, they have held chronology to be no more than an imperfect tool for understanding the Scriptures, one constantly undergoing re-evaluation, and not necessary for salvation.[48] However, as shown in Chapter 4, woe betide the individual Jehovah's Witness who publicly doubts any aspect of the chronological system maintained by Watch Tower publications at any given time. Futhermore, when the society changes a doctrine, it always does so, at least in theory, because it has received 'new light' or 'new truths' under the direction of the holy spirit. Of course it admits that it must make 'adjustments.'[49] Yet in looking at the many times in which the society has changed major doctrines only to revert to the old ones later, one is forced to wonder whether the holy spirit is using a dimmer switch or whether the whole concept of 'new light' based on progressive revelation is not complete nonsense. In fact, the number of doctrinal gyrations is so great that it is inconvenient to go into a detailed discussion of them here.

Natural Theology and the Bible

Dependent as they are on nineteenth-century traditions which grew out of the Enlightenment, both Protestant and Catholic Christianity, and Judaism, Jehovah's Witnesses hold that accurate knowledge of man's place in space and time may be gained through an investigation of the physical universe, through revelation, and through the study of history. With respect to the first means – the study of the natural world – the Witnesses argue that mankind, through scientific investigation, may learn much that is true. They also stress the Apostle Paul's famous statement on natural theology at Romans 1:20 which says that God's 'invisible [qualities] are clearly seen from the world's creation onward, because they are perceived by the things made, even his eternal power and Godship.' They argue that all rational men should be able to reckon that there is a Creator.[50]

This presupposes that the world that we perceive is the real one, an idea they are willing to accept whole-heartedly. They therefore reject any and all systems, such as those of Hinduism or Christian Science, which teach that only mind or spirit is real. Pastor Russell criticized Christian Science[51] and in 1951, in the book *What Has Religion Done for Mankind?*, the society censured Hinduism.[52] Thus Jehovah's Witnesses give short shrift to any form of religious or philosophic spiritualism and seem unaware of the spiritualism of either Hegel or Bishop Berkeley. Of course, with respect to their position on the material world, they are in the mainstream of Western thought. Like most Christians and Jews they appeal to scriptural passages which state: 'In the beginning God created the heavens and earth' (Genesis 1:1), and 'after that God saw everything that he had made [as recorded at Genesis 1] and it was good' (Genesis 1:31). So, they hold, matter as created by God is real in itself.

But Jehovah's Witnesses do not believe that truth which can be obtained from what they sometimes refer to as the Book of Nature is sufficient for salvation. They therefore reason that Jehovah revealed his will to man in the Bible which is seen as the 'Word of God.' According to them, the evidence for this is its historical and scientific accuracy, its inner consistency, its correct view of the nature of man, and the fulfilment of prophecies contained in it.[53] Thus they take many of the same steps of deductive logic which Protestant and Catholic theologians have taken before them, and they have arrived at many of the same conclusions. Too, like many fundamentalists in the nineteenth century, they pay little attention to any basis for belief in the Bible which is not founded on supposedly rational arguments or historic evidence.

Since Pastor Russell's day the Watch Tower Society has held, along with the Apostle Paul, that 'All Scripture is inspired of God and beneficial for teaching, for reproving, for setting things straight, for disciplining in righteousness, that the man of God may be fully competent, completely equipped for every good work.' With but one slight caveat on Russell's part,[54] this has meant that they regard the Bible as 'verbally' inspired throughout and *inerrant*. They do realize, however, that they must define what they mean by the Bible or the Scriptures, so they call on non-biblical, historical arguments to determine just what they are. In this sense they are entirely within the traditions of Protestantism, in particular those of the Reformed churches and the Elizabethan Church of England.[55] To Jehovah's Witnesses the Bible is the sixty-six books of standard Protestant versions. What this means is that they rely – as did Luther and Calvin – on the traditions of the Jews to determine both what should be included in and excluded from the Hebrew Scriptures or Old Testament and on the primitive Christian community to establish what should be part of the Christian Greek Scriptures or New Testament. Hence they are in complete harmony with practically all historic Protestant churches on the form and size of the biblical canon. Like them, they deny the divine inspiration of the 'apocryphal books' found in Roman Catholic versions.[56]

These facts seem on the surface to place Jehovah's Witnesses in the same camp with many old-fashioned Protestants and fundamentalists; and to a certain extent – but only to a certain extent – they do. Unlike some fundamentalists, however, they have never felt wedded to the King James Version of the Bible or to the Greek Byzantine manuscript tradition behind the New Testament translation of it. Rather, they have been impressed by eighteenth- and nineteenth-century biblical textual criticism. From Russell to the present they have generally accepted as valid the studies and recensions (critically edited texts of the Scriptures based on ancient manuscripts) of men such as Griesbach, Ginsburg, Kittel, Westcott and Hort, and Nestle.

Pastor Russell demonstrated this positive attitude towards biblical textual criticism – the examination and comparison of ancient manuscripts – almost from the beginning of his public career as a preacher.[57] The Watch Tower Society has maintained it ever since. Not only has the society constantly attempted to keep itself abreast of current textual studies, but it has often appealed to renderings of the Scriptures in the original languages on the basis of non-Witness scholarship.

It has also published and distributed a number of versions of the Bible based on the recensions of the men mentioned above and has thereby demonstrated its positive support for this particular type of modern scholarship. Although the Witnesses long used the King James Version, which they began publishing in 1942, they have continually demonstrated a preference for versions based on more ancient manuscripts. In 1896 the Watch Tower Society published Joseph B. Rotherham's New Testament, Twelfth Edition, Revised; in 1902 it had the Berean Bible, an edition of Wilson's Emphatic Diaglott, printed; in 1944 it began printing and distributing the American Standard Version of 1901; between 1950 and 1960 it issued the New World Translation in six volumes; in 1969 The Kingdom Interlinear Translation; and in 1972, Byngton's the Bible in Living English.

It should be remarked here, however, that much of the Witnesses' commitment to textual analysis and the publication and use of a great variety of translations is based on a desire to overturn many traditional Catholic and Protestant beliefs or to buttress their own doctrinal traditions. Sometimes they will go far afield indeed in finding and using some largely unknown translation to support or attack a specific point. Frequently, although certainly not always, Jehovah's Witnesses have used the tools of textual criticism more like lawyers trying to prove a case than scholars trying to determine facts objectively. But, then, they are not alone in doing that. Many of their most severe critics are equally guilty of such an approach to the Scriptures.

Witness attitudes towards the Bible are, of course, most clearly reflected in their own New World Translation. In an attempt to provide a version supposedly as close to the original as possible, the New World Translation Committee, a formerly anonymous group of Witness 'scholars,' produced a so-called 'literal translation' based largely on Rudolf Kittel's Biblia Hebraica and the Greek text of Westcott and Hort, supplemented by the texts of Nestle and the Jesuit scholars, Bover and Merk. An important version because of its widespread distribution (it has since been translated *from English* into Dutch, French, Italian, German, Japanese, Portuguese, and Spanish), it has received some praise and much criticism.

One thing which has brought much criticism of the New World Translation is that the New World Translation Committee has refused since 1950 to reveal the names and academic credentials of its members. Of course, this has very little to do with the quality of the translation itself which deserves to be examined on the basis of its own merits rather than on who and what its translators were or were not. It may be, however, that the anonymity of the committee reflects more than a spirit of humility among its members. For on page 50 of *Crisis of Conscience* Raymond Franz states that the members of it were his uncle, Frederick Franz, Nathan Knorr, Albert Schroeder, and George Gangas. Then he notes: 'Fred Franz, however, was the only one with sufficient knowledge of the Bible languages to attempt [a] translation of this kind. He had studied Greek for two years in the University of Cincinnati but was only self taught in Hebrew.' So to all intents and purposes the New World Translation is the work of one man – Frederick Franz.

Criticism of the New World Translation itself seems largely directed at a few passages and certain consistently used word translations. For example, trinitarians have been most upset at the New World rendering of John 1:1 where the Word is said to be 'a god' rather than 'God.' They argue, on the basis of what is known as Colwell's rule, that Greek grammar does not permit any such translation.[58] But there is more room for doubt on this question than they would like to admit. First, while the Watch Tower Society seems largely unaware of it, there is considerable ancient support for its translation in the works of Justin Martyr and Origen. Both, in fact, call the Word a *'deuteros theos'* or 'second god.'[59] Second, in an article published in the *Journal of Biblical Literature* in 1973, Philip Harner has disputed Colwell's earlier hypothesis that the proper rendering of the phrase in question in English is 'and the Word was God.'[60] It is none the less true that the translation 'a god' is generally regarded as highly unsatisfactory; it smacks too much of a bitheism which is rejected throughout the Scriptures. But the Greek *'theos'* does not always mean exactly what the English 'God' does, and Harner is undoubtedly right in suggesting that the anarthrous *'theos'* (the word *'theos'* without the definite article *'ho'* or 'the') has a qualitative nature rather than a quantitative one. Furthermore, the Catholic theologians Karl Rahner and Hans Küng demonstrate that biblically there is often a significant difference between the term *'ho theos,'* which (in undisputed passages in the nominative case) always signifies God the Father, and *'theos'* which in a few instances is applied to the Word or Christ as the Son of God.[61] As Küng states: 'Neither is there any mention anywhere in the New Testament of the incarnation of God himself. It is always a question of God's Son or Word who became man, whose identification with God the Father is admittedly increasingly stressed by the transference of divine attributes. In the New Testament, however, the term 'God' (*'ho theos'*) in practice always means the Father.'[62] Hence, as Goodspeed, Moffat, and a note in the British and Foreign Bible Society's The Translator's New Testament would have it, a satisfactory translation of the expression in question might well be 'and the Word was *divine.*' So while the New World translation 'a god' is inadequate, the concept behind it has more support grammatically and historically than is generally recognized.

The same cannot be said for the translation 'torture stake' for cross or the use of the divine name, Jehovah, in the New Testament. Although *'stauros'* does not necessarily mean an upright beam with a cross member, the New World translators are both inaccurate and dishonest in saying that there is no evidence that Jesus was crucified or hanged on a cross.[63] While *'stauros'* may properly be translated as 'stake,' there is simply no basis at all for modifying it with the adjective 'torture.'

As far as the use of the divine name in the New Testament is concerned, that is, as Bruce Metzger has rightly noted, a piece of 'special pleading.'[64] There is not one ancient Greek manuscript of any New Testament book which contains either the sacred tetragrammaton or four-letter name of God in Hebrew or any other independent form of the divine name as it appears in either the ancient Hebrew text of the Old Testament or a *few* manuscripts of the pre-Christian Greek Septuagint version of the Old Testament. So, on the basis of the evidence – not conjecture – that we have before us, the New World translators' vaunted 'restoration' of the name Jehovah to the text of the New Testament is nothing more than an interpolation.

These are not the worst features of the New World Translation which does have some very positive aspects to it. Far more serious than the outwardly Arian and anti-traditional nature of this Watch Tower version are: 1 / its biased translation of certain texts to buttress specific Witness practices or secondary doctrines and 2 / its unattractive, unidiomatic English. For example, while the word *'homologeo'* is frequently translated 'confess' in various passages of the Christian Greek Scriptures, at Romans 10:10 it is rendered 'publicly declare.' Now 'publicly declare' is a perfectly acceptable translation: many lexicons give it. But when one of Jehovah's Witnesses reads the text – 'For with the heart one exercizes faith for righteousness, but with the mouth one makes public declaration for salvation' – he does not think, ordinarily at least, of a simple confession of faith at baptism.[65] Rather, the Watch Tower Society encourages him to believe that he must carry on a house-to-house *preaching work.* In another instance the translators have 'adjusted' the text of John 17:3 for similar purposes. The New World Translation reads at that verse: 'This means everlasting life, their taking in knowledge of you, the only true God, and of the one you sent forth, Jesus Christ.' The words 'taking in knowledge' are quite incorrect. The Greek from which they are 'translated' is the word *'ginoskosi'* which means simply 'that they should or may know'; and since the subjunctive sense of the word is not necessary in English, most translators are quite correct in rendering it 'that they know you.' That, however, would not serve Watch Tower officials' purposes, for they do not seem to want the ordinary

Witness to have the experience of knowing God spiritually; rather they want him to believe that his salvation is dependent upon his taking in knowledge – 'spiritual food at the proper time' – from the society's publications.

What is perhaps worse than all of this, however, is the fact that in many ways the New World Translation is a literary monstrosity which is wooden, cold, and filled with a curious American jargon which often comes straight out of Madison Avenue. There are certainly other translations which are as doctrinally *skewed* as is the New World Translation, but there are few which read so badly. When one examines Psalm 23:5, for example, this becomes evident. There the King James Version's 'thou anointest my head with oil' is replaced with the thoroughly unattractive 'with oil you have greased my head.'

All of this indicates, in part at least, how Jehovah's Witnesses view the Bible. They believe that the original texts in the original languages were inspired, and they are willing to use textual criticism to attempt to discover what those texts were. They are honest in admitting that no translation is inspired, but they have long claimed that the New World is the best extant today.[66] Evidently, then, what they are saying by making such a boast is that the New World Translation conforms most closely to Witness doctrine. So in a real sense, then, the Bible, in its translated form, is used as an apologia for Witness beliefs as much as a basis for them.

Biblical Interpretation

At this point it is perhaps useful to look at the basic interpretive assumptions and methods of Pastor Russell, for in large measure they are still those of Jehovah's Witnesses today. In an interesting analysis, retired Episcopal Bishop Chandler Sterling has described with some insight the approach to Scripture taken by Russell. According to Sterling: 'He seems to have developed a practice of approaching each and every biblical problem as though he were solving a jigsaw puzzle. He would lay out each verse and text on a table, so to speak, as a person would lay out a puzzle for solution containing as many as a thousand pieces. Russell did something like this, although he soon restricted the texts.'[67]

Sterling also assumes, quite inaccurately, that Russell was 'blissfully unaware of the late nineteenth-century activity among biblical scholars who were working in the newly developing fields of Biblical Criticism, Higher Criticism, *Formgeschichte* [*sic*] and the new biblical archaeology.'[68] Yet Sterling, who manifests much admiration for Russell, also notes: 'Many of the biblical doctrines that distressed him also distressed the biblical scholars of that day. In a way, they were on his side, though neither realized it.'[69] The matter is far more complex than Sterling indicates, however.

Russell did not start out on his own with his own method; he was heir to particular approaches to the Bible which had been present in the western world for centuries. As one raised in a Protestant environment, he accepted many of the basic propositions of the Reformation. To him, the Bible was the sole source of information necessary for salvation. It explains God's dealings with man, the nature of law and grace, and the story of Christ the King who will ultimately redeem the race from sin and death. But he recognized that while large sections of the Scriptures are reasonably clear to any reader – those that are historical, legal, or didactic – other portions, notably those of a prophetic nature, are very difficult to understand. Nevertheless, he felt that under the right circumstances God himself would aid in revealing such 'dark' passages through the application to them of spirit-directed human reason. Writing as early as 1876 on the Gentile Times, he stated: 'Doubtless our Lord intended to communicate to His disciples some knowledge, and possibly it was addressed more to the disciples in our day, than to the early church. Let us then search what times the prophecy, which was in Christ, did signify. Of course, if it is one of the secret things of God, we cannot find out; but if a secret why should Jesus mention it? If, on the contrary, it is revealed it *belongs* to us. Shall we guess and suppose? No, let us go to God's treasurehouse; let us search the Scriptures for the key.'[70]

About eight years later, he stressed the same approach. He counselled his readers to divest themselves of prejudice, to reject religious creeds, ignore the writings of both modern theologians and early church fathers, and go directly to God's Word, the Bible. Then he indicated how he felt that it should be approached: 'While thorough and orderly study is necessary to the application of any of the sciences,' he wrote, 'it is specially so to Divine revelation.'[71] In his own work he claimed that he had 'endeavored to build upon that foundation the teachings of Scripture, in such a manner that, so far as possible, purely human judgment may try its squares and angles by the most exacting rules of justice which it can command.'[72]

In spite of such statements, Russell was hardly just a rationalist in his approach to the Scriptures. It is quite true that, largely without knowing it, he was heir to the conceptual world created by men such as Descartes, Newton, and Leibniz and was, therefore, fascinated by mathematical logic and human reason. But his system of biblical interpretation was only partially rationalistic in nature. It was, in fact, a curious hodge-podge of ideas borrowed from the Enlightenment on one hand and from early Christianity, Judaism, and paganism (by way of medieval Catholicism and Anglo-American Protestantism) on the other. For, like so many of his immediate Protestant forbears and contemporaries, Russell used allegories and typological interpretations of the Bible to make Old and New Testament accounts relevant to the nineteenth and twentieth centuries.

This is not surprising. New Testament writers used allegories, types, and antitypes, as did early church Fathers such as Justin Martyr, Irenaeus, and

Tertullian. The major impetus for the wholesale allegorical and typological interpretation of the Bible came, however, from outside the New Testament and the early, major, sub-apostolic Fathers. Both used allegories and types rather sparingly. But like the Gnostics, other Christians, particularly those from Alexandria in Egypt, were given to allegories and types of the most extreme nature. Hundreds of years prior to the birth of Christ, the Greeks had developed allegorical interpretations of Homer and various religious myths. Then in the time of Christ, Philo Judaeus used this method extensively to explain the Pentateuch. And Philo had a major impact on the Christian community. Consequently, we encounter much allegorization in the Epistle of Barnabas, the works of Clement of Alexandria, and, most importantly, Origen;[73] and from Origen forward until Luther, allegorical interpretation became one of the standard means of 'understanding' the Scriptures.[74]

Luther did stress the importance of curtailing much of the allegorical interpretation which had by his day become part and parcel of virtually every Christian exegete's approach to the Bible.[75] Yet popular Protestantism, as much as popular Catholicism, continued to use allegories and types with wild abandon to proclaim that the Scriptures had really foretold modern-day events in detail. Even learned theologians returning to England from exile in Geneva after the reign of Mary Tudor brought with them an assortment of allegorical and typological explanations to make the Bible relevant to sixteenth-century Europe. Among other things they popularized the idea that the harlot of Revelation, Babylon the Great, was a symbolic type of the Church of Rome.[76]

Thus it was only natural that Russell should have combined pre-Enlightenment methods of understanding Holy Writ with those developed from the seventeenth and eighteenth centuries onward. And this much must be said for his methodology: Once he created a system of types and allegories, he tried to maintain it in a rational and consistent manner.

Unfortunately Russell's system has become far less systematic and far less rational in the hands of his successors. Jehovah's Witnesses have continued to use rationalist arguments, but more often than not, men such as Rutherford, Knorr, and Frederick Franz have used types and allegories to explain historical events, doctrines, and Witness practices with little attempt to be logically consistent. Thus Watch Tower interpretations over the years have often become so bizarre that almost any portion of Scripture can be used to explain almost anything that Witness writers want it to.[77]

Note, as one example among many, the book *You May Survive Armageddon into God's New World,* published in 1955. In that curious explanation of the coming great battle of God Almighty against the forces of wickedness, the Witness writer (or writers) describes forty-two biblical types of the earthly heirs of the New

World (Jehovah's Witnesses) who are to go on living on this earth into the millennium after the rest of mankind has been destroyed. Amazingly, these include the twelve non-Levite tribes of Israel on the annual day of atonement; Ebed-melech, the Ethopian eunuch discussed in Jeremiah; the mariners with whom the prophet Jonah shipped; Rebekah's nurse, Deborah, and other lady attendants; Noah's sons and daughters-in-law; the Queen of Sheba; Rahab the Harlot; Lot and his incestuous daughters; and, believe it or not, a very great multitude of fish that come to life in the healed waters of the Salt Sea.[78] To put it mildly, this last example is, as Alan Rogerson remarks, the 'most bizarre of all.'[79]

If all of this were not enough, it must be noted that frequently the interpretations of Watch Tower types have changed whenever the society has found it useful or necessary to make such changes. For instance, Pastor Russell long used Elijah as a type of the remnant of the 144,000 members of the church which he believed would meet the Lord in the air as in a firey chariot in 1914. He held that Elijah's successor, Elisha, was a type of the great multitude of Revelation 7:9–14 which he considered to be a secondary spiritual or heavenly class.[80] Judge Rutherford abandoned Russell's interpretation, however, and held that Elijah had pictured the activities of the Bible Student community prior to September 1919 while Elisha prefigured its work after that date.[81] But as time went on, Rutherford's teaching became at least partially out of date. Consequently, in 1965 the society decided that the Elijah work had continued up till the judge's death in 1942 and that the Elisha work had really only begun under Nathan Knorr.[82]

At this point, then, it can hardly be said that Jehovah's Witnesses have anything that can be described as a systematic method of hermeneutics or biblical interpretation. If they have anything it is a tradition and nothing more. And that tradition allows them to be arbitrary in using the Scriptures to explain what is wanted in terms of Witness doctrine or the notions of the dominant figures on the governing body.

Philosophy of History

Jehovah's Witnesses have always believed in the traditional Christian concept of linear progression in history. Accordingly, they hold that history as we know it began with the fall of our first parents in Eden. Jehovah destroyed the first world of mankind and wicked angels at the time of the flood in Noah's day. He later showed kindness to the patriarchs Abraham, Isaac, and Jacob; and after the exodus from Egypt, he gave Jacob's (Israel's) descendents a divine law through Moses. But that law simply made the sinfulness of the nation of Israel manifest. In order to save both Israel and mankind in general, God sent forth his son, Jesus Christ, to die at Calvary to ransom them from sin and death. At that point, through Jesus, Jehovah revealed his will for men and the means through which they might get saved. In addition, Christ began to choose for himself a church class of 144,000 *spiritual* Israelites from among all sorts of men and women. This class, known also as the 'bride of Christ,' 'Christ's body,' 'the little flock,' and 'the holy ones,' eventually receive a heavenly resurrection to reign and rule with Jesus as king-priests for a thousand years.

What about the rest of humankind? The answer is that except for those who have been 'willfully wicked' the dead will be resurrected during the thousand years – the millennial reign of Christ – to learn God's will and accept or reject it. Those living at the end of this world will either go down to destruction before God's wrath or, if they put faith in Christ and his kingdom, they will pass through Armageddon into a new earth which will eventually become a paradise like Eden. It will be to that paradise that most of the dead, whether just or unjust, will be raised. The righteous men of old, from Abel to John the Baptist, will then be made 'princes in all the earth.' Finally, at the end of the thousand years, Satan, who will have been cast into an abyss of death-like inactivity at Armageddon, will be loosed with his demon hordes to deceive the nations. Then he, his spirit supporters, and all those of mankind who join him in rebellion will be destroyed by the fire of God's wrath. Those remaining alive at the time will be declared justified and granted the loving reward of everlasting life.

This basic sketch of the official Witness view of human history has been outlined over and over again in Watch Tower publications since Russell first produced the *Divine Plan of the Ages* in 1884 with a number of changes since with respect to details.[83] But another point needs to be mentioned here. That is that Jehovah's Witnesses have always viewed mankind's history as a great controversy. They believe that Satan's rebellion against Jehovah occurred essentially over the question of whether man, having originally been granted freedom of the will, would obey his God under both temptation and persecution. The story of Job gives a key to this understanding.[84] Thus it becomes the foremost duty of all righteous men and women to magnify God's name through faith and obedience to him – something done by his witnesses throughout the ages but pre-eminently by Jesus Christ.

These concepts of *Heilsgeschichte* or 'salvation history' serve as the foundation for the Witnesses' understanding of their own place in history. Basically they teach that the early Christian church was the true church, but before the end of the first century a great apostasy began. By the time of Constantine and the Council of Nicaea, that apostasy had become nearly complete. Hence neither the Church of Rome nor the various eastern churches were thereafter in any sense churches of God; in fact they often persecuted true Christians.[85] Later the Reformation restored the true faith to an extent. Russell believed that 'many faithful souls in the days of the Reformation walked in the light, so far as it was shining.'[86] Since then Protestantism has not advanced with that light. Therefore it has become necessary for God to raise up a new body of Christian witnesses in the last days to make known his will before the impending battle of Armageddon.[87]

Jehovah's Witnesses believe, then, that they are heirs to a long tradition of true Christianity. It is for that reason that *The Finished Mystery* and *The Watch Tower* of 1 April 1919 posited that there were seven messengers of the church throughout the ages – St Paul, St John, Arius, Waldo, Wycliffe, Luther, and Russell. All of these except the first two were, of course, opponents of the institutional church or churches of their day. So the Witnesses have regarded some of the very persons who have been labelled arch-heretics by the Church of Rome as their predecessors.

This concept has come under attack, especially by Professor Alan Rogerson, who comes from a Witness background. His understanding of the Witness view of history is based on Marley Cole's analysis [88] and the 1 April 1919 *Watch Tower* mentioned above from which Cole's discussion originated. Thus to underscore the weakness of the Witnesses' philosophy of history, Rogerson argues that there is little connection between the beliefs of men such as Waldo, Wycliffe, and Luther on the one hand, and Russell on the other. After discussing the Lollards' lack of similarity to Jehovah's Witnesses, he says: 'A similar comparison with Waldo, Wycliffe, Luther and so on, indicates that the established Protestant churches are their successors and not the Watchtower Society.'[89] In these remarks Rogerson may be somewhat unfair, however.

In the first place, the Watch Tower Society has always recognized the fact that the teachings of all the other post-biblical figures of the past, listed above, are very different from those of Russell. God granted only so much light to each true Christian, and *that was sufficient for the time.* If the followers of those teachers of this limited light of true understanding – or, for that matter, the teachers themselves – turned their doctrines into permanent creeds which would not allow them to advance with new light, then they would lose God's approval. It is exactly that, the Witnesses feel, that happened to the Waldensians, Lollards, Lutherans, and others.[90]

More important is the fact that Jehovah's Witnesses have for years taken a slightly more sophisticated position. They no longer feel that the true church had specific prophets, teachers, or messengers throughout the ages; and as noted, since 1927 Russell has been regarded as no more than an outstanding Christian brother who performed an important historic role. In consequence, the society does not try to determine in a set doctrinal fashion who was and who was not individually within God's favour from the first to the nineteenth century at least.

They do feel, though, that many have obviously been outside divine favour, as their works have not accorded with the principles of God's word. Jehovah's Witnesses believe that from Constantine's time to the present, the clergy of Christendom have been a composite 'man of lawlessness' and the 'son of destruction' mentioned by the Apostle Paul at 2 Thessalonians 2:3–9. The book *God's 'Eternal Purpose' Now Triumphing* states:

For the next sixteen centuries (from AD 325), down into this twentieth century, what kind of record has Christendom made for herself? A record of her clergymen involving themselves in politics, introducing more and more pagan teachings into their religious faith, accumulating wealth and power for themselves, oppressing their religious flocks, fomenting religious wars, cruel crusades and persecutions, establishing hundreds of confusing sects, blessing the armies of so-called 'Christian' nations that were at war with one another, corrupting the morals of their church members, hiding God's 'eternal purpose' and really working against it, just like the earthly visible 'seed' of the Great Serpent.[91]

Conversely, they believe that the true church of Christ can be identified. They feel that when Jesus spoke at Matthew 24:45 of 'the faithful and discreet slave whom his master appointed over his domestics to give them food at the proper time,' he was referring to the church, spiritual Israel, the 144,000 of Revelation 7:4–8 and 14:1–3. The church, which began at Pentecost, must therefore be composed of a class of elect and chosen Christians who have kept themselves 'separate from the world,' have provided pure spiritual food for Christ's servants, and have been expecting the second coming of Jesus, 'the son of man.' Hence, over the centuries a small number of individuals have continued to look forward to Christ's *parousia,* have continued to preach the truth as they understood it, and have thereby identified themselves as members of the 'faithful and discreet slave' class. Only in the late nineteenth century were they to come together in a restored, united Christian movement. At that time the slave class had to be prepared for Christ's return and inspection as described in Matthew 24:46, 47. Jehovah's Witnesses thus teach that shortly after Christ began his invisible presence in 1914, he inspected both true and false Christianity and found only a small faithful remnant of true Christians on earth. Again these were identified by their separateness from the world of false religion, corrupt commercialism, and the political movements. Again, also, they demonstrated true love for Jehovah, his Messiah, and the world of mankind through a world-wide preaching work as foretold at Matthew 24:14: 'And this good news of the kingdom will be preached in the entire inhabited earth for the purpose of a witness to all the nations, and then the accomplished end will come.' Accordingly, they believe that *they* and *they alone* have manifested the characteristics of the faithful and discreet slave and have been truly faithful to their stewardship.[92]

From this particular view of world history and their own role in it, Jehovah's Witnesses take an amazingly narrow stance with regard to the academic study of it. There are few trained historians among them, and the Watch Tower Society largely ignores any sophisticated study which does not agree with its predetermined concept of what 'really' happened in the past. True, Watch Tower writers do often cite various historical works, but as they do with the Bible itself, they tend to use them as a basis for prooftexts. Thus it is that they maintain a so-called biblical chronology which is demonstrably false, and they use a curiously outdated speculative 'history' such as Dr Alexander Hyslop's *The Two Babylons or Papal Worship* which is still quoted in many Watch Tower publications as though it were the Gospel itself. Interestingly, the society never bothers to tell the Witness community that *The Two Babylons,* one of their major sources of 'true history,' is a long-standing Plymouth Brethren publication.[93] So by Witness standards, the Watch Tower Society is borrowing a source from Babylon the Great (false religion) to study about the role of Babylon in world history. All of this leads, then, to the maintenance of what amounts to a kind of nineteenth-century, fundamentalist history which ignores the last hundred years of scholarship in the field.

Major Doctrines

With a general knowledge of bases of doctrinal authority, it now becomes important to look at the primary or major doctrines of Jehovah's Witnesses. Although, as with all of their teachings, these have undergone some changes, in the main they have been fairly constant. Thus, what is said here had been *generally* true during the last hundred years unless specified to the contrary.

Theology

In its narrow sense the term 'theology' means the study of God and his nature. It is in that sense that the term is used here. What, then, can be said about the theology of Jehovah's Witnesses? In the first place, the term is somewhat misleading from a Witness standpoint and is seldom used in Watch Tower publications. They note that the Bible does not always use the Hebrew world *'elohim'* or the Greek *'theos'* to mean the Almighty or Eternal God of the universe. *'Elohim'* does, of course, often apply to the Almighty. When it does, it appears as a plural of 'majesty' with adjectives and verbs in the singular. In this way it is also used to denote the Philistine god, Dagon, at 1 Samuel 5:7 and is even used for the goddess Ashtoreth at 1 Kings 11:5. In other instances, when used with verbs and modifying adjectives in the plural, it means simply *'gods'* – whether true or false – or mighty ones such as judges or angels as at Psalm 8:5 and Psalm 82:1. Similarly, the Greek *'theos'* may be used to mean a false god, Christ, or even the Devil. Although in a pre-eminent sense there is only one true God: the Almighty.

Other terms used in the Scriptures to denote the Almighty are also titles. Among others these include the Hebrew *'adonay'* and the Greek *'kyrios,'* both of which mean 'Lord.' But the Witnesses feel that the Almighty God must be distinguished by his name – Jehovah.[1]

That name appears in the King James Version, the American Standard Version of 1901, the New World Translation, and many others. It is the commonest modern representation of the Hebrew tetragrammaton or four-letter name of the Eternal which is יהוה or YHWH, and is therefore the form used by Jehovah's Witnesses today. They are well aware, though, that because of Jewish reverence that name was not pronounced for many centuries and was often replaced in late Hebrew manuscripts of the Scriptures with the terms *'elohim'* and *'adonay.'* Since Hebrew had no vowel signs until well into the Christian era, no one knows exactly how the divine name was pronounced. More likely it should be written and pronounced 'Yahweh.' But the Witnesses feel that it is no more necessary to pronounce it exactly as it was originally than it is necessary to pronounce the name Jesus as it was in Aramaic or Hebrew. What is important is to note who Jehovah is and what his name means.[2]

Since 1882 Bible Students and Jehovah's Witnesses have stressed the *oneness* of Jehovah who is in no sense the first person of the Trinity. He is God the Father, the One inhabiting eternity. He is Jehovah God and the Lord Jehovah. To them his name means what J.B. Rotherham and other scholars have suggested, that is, 'He who becometh.'[3] The statement at Exodus 3:14, *Ehyeh' asher' eyeh'* which explains the divine name, does not mean the 'I am that I am' of the King James Version. Rather, it signifies the 'I shall prove to be what I shall prove to be' of the New World Translation.[4] What, however, does all this indicate? Simply that Jehovah is not just a self-existing One like Aristotle's 'Unmoved Mover'; he is active in history, in the affairs of men. He is pre-eminently alive, a Father to those who love and obey him, and a person of war to those who hate or deny him. To his people he has proclaimed: '"You are my witnesses," says Jehovah, "that I am God."'

Christology and Soteriology

The term 'christology' relates specifically to the study of the nature and person of Christ; 'soteriology' deals generally with his role as Saviour. Who, then, is the Christ and how has he become Saviour?

Jehovah's Witnesses stress that the word 'Christ' is simply the Greek translation of the Hebrew word 'Messiah.' Literally that title means 'the Anointed,' the term which refers to the ancient Israelite custom of anointing priests and kings to demonstrate publicly that they were chosen for their respective offices by Jehovah himself. As Christians, the Witnesses believe that Jesus is the Christ. They also emphasize that his personal name is a Hellenized form of 'Joshua' which means 'Jehovah is the Saviour.' Hence 'Jesus' is 'Jehovah's Anointed Saviour.'[5]

They hold, too, that Jesus had a prehuman existence prior to his birth here on earth. Accordingly, he was 'the beginning of the creation by God' (Revelation

3:14), 'the image of the invisible God, the firstborn of all creation' (Colossians 1:15), *'Wisdom'* as personified in Proverbs 8, and the *'Word'* of John 1. Rather than the second person of the Trinity, he was *'deuteros theos,'* a 'second god.' Consequently he was Jehovah's spokesman, his Word, through whom all else was created.[6]

In the Hebrew Scriptures he is spoken of many times prophetically, beginning with Genesis 3:15.[7] He was represented by many types including Melchizedek, Moses, Aaron, David, and others.[8] His coming to earth was foretold by Isaiah, Daniel, and Micah. Thus it was necessary for him to give up his spirit existence to be born into the family of Abraham and the house of David. So in the year 2 BC he was born in Bethlehem of Judah of the Jewish virgin-girl, Mary.[9]

Jehovah's Witnesses insist that acceptance of the doctrine of the virgin birth is absolutely necessary. Had Jesus been the natural offspring of Joseph or some other man, he would have been born sinful. But because his fleshly mother conceived of the holy spirit, he was born sinless.[10]

Throughout his life Jesus obeyed the law of Moses to the last 'jot and tittle.' Further, he became the Second Adam discussed by the Apostle Paul at 1 Corinthians 15. Jesus therefore spent his earthly ministry preaching the kingdom of the heavens, and on 14 Nisan AD 33 he gave his life as a ransom sacrifice to purchase Adam's descendants from the power of sin, death, and the Devil.[11]

Jehovah's Witnesses believe that by dying an ignominious death on a torture stake at Calvary, Jesus sanctified his Father's name by remaining loyal to him, through a complete love, a love unto death. That sanctification and love would have been meaningless had Jesus been anything more or less than a perfect human being. Hence Jehovah's Witnesses deny the doctrine of the hypostatic union or incarnation as defined by the Creed of Chalcedon – the idea that Christ was both wholly God and wholly man. Also, they reason, it was necessary for Jesus to be like the first man, Adam, in every way so that he could give his life as a *corresponding ransom (antilytron).* In that way Christ could buy back from Jehovah through complete obedience what Adam had lost through disobedience: the opportunity for men to live eternally on a paradise earth.[12] How, then, do men get saved? Through faith in the shed blood of Jesus Christ and his sacrifice. By responding to God's love, men of all kinds, Jews, and Gentiles, may dedicate their lives to Jehovah through Christ, the second Adam. But what about those who have died without having heard of Christ? In general they will be resurrected during the millennium, given an opportunity (their first) to know of Jesus, and to gain life through obedience to Christ's millennial government. Only those who have been classed by Jehovah as unalterably opposed to his will will not be brought forth from their graves.[13]

Other aspects of Jehovah's Witnesses' teachings concerning the Christ must also be mentioned. Although he was the 'son of God' throughout his existence and has been the 'son of man' since his human birth, he became the Christ or Messiah only at his baptism when he was anointed by holy spirit. When he died as a man, his human nature perished. The Witnesses point to several Scriptures which show he was raised as a spirit, not a man. Among these they stress 1 Peter 3:18 which says of him: 'He being put to death in the flesh, but being made alive in the spirit.' Witnesses also place emphasis on the presentation of the 'merits' of Jesus' sacrifice before Jehovah in the holy of holies, heaven itself, as outlined in Hebrews; the fact that Christ has waited at his Father's right hand over the centuries (Psalm 110:1, 2); that he is now invisibly present, ruling in the midst of his enemies, and that he is preparing for Armageddon. Eventually he will cast Satan into the abyss of Revelation 20:3 and destroy all wicked demons and men. Then he and his church will serve as king-priests over mankind to bring them to perfection on a paradise earth during his thousand-year reign. Finally, when Satan is loosed for a brief time at the end of the thousand years, he will again attempt to deceive mankind. But at that time he and his hosts will suffer everlasting destruction. Christ, the victor in this final war, will then turn his kingdom back to Jehovah so that the Father may be 'all in all.'[14]

Convenantal Relationships

Pastor Russell believed all of mankind, or at least *all* the nations, would be blessed through God's covenant with Abraham. At Genesis 22:16–18 according to the Authorized Version, Jehovah stated: 'By myself have I sworn, saith the Lord; for because thou hast done this thing, and hast not withheld thy son, thine only *son:* that in blessing I will bless thee, and in multiplying I will multiply thy seed as the stars of the heaven, and as the sand which *is* upon the sea shore; and thy seed shall possess the gate of his enemies; and in thy seed shall all the nations of the earth be blessed: because thou hast obeyed my voice.' Consequently Russell taught, as had the Apostle Paul, that this text meant that Christ was the *seed* in a primary sense and that the members of the church class were Abraham's seed in a more extended sense. Thus mankind in general would ultimately be blessed by Abraham's seed – Christ plus the 144,000 members of the church – during the millennium.[15]

As indicated in Chapter 1, Russell changed his mind at least twice on the question of whether the church was under the New Covenant mentioned both in Jeremiah and the New Testament.[16] Ultimately he came to the conclusion that it was not: the New Covenant would apply to natural Jews only after all members of the church had been joined with Christ in heaven.[17]

The reason that he believed that the New Covenant could not apply until after the last member of the church had died and been taken to heaven was that he felt that the mediator for the New Covenant was 'the Christ, head and body.' That expression meant, of course, that the 144,000 actually participated in Christ's sacrifice for the world and were joined to him as his 'bride' or his 'body.'[18]

But if the New Covenant was to be only with the *natural* Jews during the millennium, how would the rest of mankind benefit? Russell explained:

The Scriptures distinctly show that Christ and his Church, spirit beings, must constitute the Kingdom class, but they also show that the Ancient Worthies (faithful men from Abel to John the Baptist), and through them the nation of Israel under the New Covenant, will become the representatives of the heavenly kingdom amongst men. It will be with these that the blessing of the Lord in the Millennial morning will begin ... Thus the Prophet represents the matter, saying 'Many nations shall go and say, Come and let us go up to the mountain (Kingdom) of the Lord, and to the house of the God of Jacob; and he will teach us of his ways, and we will walk in his paths; for the law will go forth from Mount Zion (the spiritual Kingdom) and the Word of the Lord from Jerusalem (the center of the earthly Kingdom).'[19]

Judge Rutherford maintained Russell's doctrines for some years as is demonstrated by a series of articles published in several issues of *The Watch Tower* in the spring of 1928. But a few years later, after denying that natural Israel had any current part in God's plan of salvation, the judge decided that the New Covenant did apply specifically to the church class of Jehovah's Witnesses. In the book *Jehovah,* published in 1934, Rutherford proclaimed: 'The purpose of the new covenant was not for the salvation of men, but for selecting a people for the name of Jehovah, which people so selected must be witnesses of the name of Jehovah.'[20] Furthermore he stated: 'The church of Christ does not form any part of the mediator, but Christ Jesus alone is the mediator of the new covenant. (Heb. 12:24) Christ Jesus is the mediator of the new covenant toward his own brethren, that is to say, spiritual Israel, during the period of time God is taking out from the nations a people for his name.'[21]

What this meant was that Rutherford had virtually accepted the position of the New Covenant Believers in 1909, and he knew it! He had done a 180-degree doctrinal change in course. But more was to follow. When the judge had his famous 1935 revelation with respect to the earthly class of 'Jonadabs' or 'other sheep,' these were at first not even classified as Jehovah's Witnesses and were held to be *outside* the New Covenant. Thus they were told that Jesus was not their mediator.[22] Finally, the New Covenant was to come to an end when the last member of the 144,000 had been resurrected to heavenly glory.[23]

For years the society did not make much of the fact that Christ was not held to be the mediator for those Jehovah's Witnesses who had an earthly hope rather than a heavenly one. In fact, the book *'Let God Be True,'* which was used as their primary text from 1946 to 1968, left the clear impression that all 'Christians' (Jehovah's Witnesses) were under it.[24] True, *The Watchtower* of 1 November 1955 was slightly more explicit, but the society did not indicate bluntly to the vast majority of Jehovah's Witnesses that they had no mediator until the late 1960s.[25]

Spirit Creatures

Since 1882 Pastor Russell and the Watch Tower Society have taught that the holy spirit is not a person; it is simply God's active force.[26] Jehovah did create, through his son, other spirit creatures, however. These are the cherubs, seraphs, and angels or heavenly messengers mentioned in the Scriptures.[27] The Witnesses note that only one of these spirits is referred to as an archangel, that is Michael. They feel that because of his unique role as described in the Bible and because his name means 'Who is like God?' that Michael was and is the Word, the resurrected Christ.[28]

From all that has been stated earlier, it is evident that Jehovah's Witnesses also believe in the existence of the Devil. They teach that he was a mighty spirit creature (perhaps as represented by the king of Tyre, the 'anointed covering cherub' of Ezekiel 28:11-19) who was the original angelic rebel.[29] He it was who fell through the sin of pride, told the first lie, and caused mankind to lose paradise. 'When Satan approached Eve (through the speech of the serpent) he actually challenged the rightfulness and righteousness of Jehovah's sovereignty. He intimated that God was unrightfully withholding something from the woman, also declaring that God was a liar in saying that she would die if eating of the forbidden fruit.'[30]

Since Eden, he has continued to act as the adversary of both God and mankind. He is known also as Satan, Serpent, Dragon, and, in both Ezekiel and the Revelation, Gog of the land of Magog. He is also spoken of as the 'god of this world' and 'the prince of the power of the air.' He has dominated all nations except ancient fleshly Israel and Christian spiritual Israel, and he has deceived mankind through false religion, spiritualism, magic, and the occult. Today he continues to go about like a roaring lion seeking to devour.[31]

His hosts of wicked angelic spirits, the demons, were once 'Sons of God.' But prior to the flood of Noah's day they materialized as men, married the daughters of men, and fathered the Nephilim of Genesis 6:1-4. At the time of the flood they dematerialized and were cast into prison or the outer darkness of God's restraint, where according to 2 Peter 2:4 and Jude 6 they await destruction with Satan.[32]

Like Satan, the demons have become adversaries of God and man. They are therefore involved in tempting mankind to sin and may actually *possess* willing human subjects who become their mediums. Christ himself exorcised such wicked spirits while on earth, and Christians today must shun them in every way. Jehovah's Witnesses therefore have a sixteenth-century fear or outright dread of the demons that is sometimes so extreme that it becomes quite superstitious. But, paradoxically, it is true that by avoiding what they regard as 'demonistic practices' they have broken the hold that fear of spirits has had over large numbers of persons, particularly in Africa and Latin America.[33]

The Nature of Man

As indicated in Chapter 1, Jehovah's Witnesses and their Bible Student predecessors have always taught the doctrine of conditionalism. The book *The Truth That Leads to Eternal Life* states this position clearly and succinctly:

Since the soul is the person himself, what happens to a soul at death? The Bible is very clear in stating that the soul is subject to death, saying: 'The soul that is sinning – it itself will die.' (Ezekiel 18:4, 20) The apostle Peter quoted from the writings of Moses concerning Jesus, saying: 'Indeed, any soul that does not listen to that Prophet will be completely destroyed from among the people.' (Acts 3:23) Consistent with the basic truth, not once in any of its verses does the Bible say that either human or animal souls are immortal, deathless, cannot be destroyed or cannot perish. There are, however, dozens of scriptures that show that the soul can die or be killed (Leviticus 23:30; James 5:20). Even of Jesus Christ the Bible says: 'He poured out his soul to the very death.' (Isaiah 43:12) We see, then, that the human soul is the person himself, and when the person dies, it is the human soul that dies.[34]

But what about the spirit of man, mentioned in a number of texts in the Bible? Witness publications, notably *The Truth That Leads to Eternal Life,* point out that the Hebrew words for 'spirit' *('ru ahh')* and 'breath' *('neshamah')* are closely related. Thus the spirit is simply the 'life force' which 'might be likened to the electric current of a car's battery.' It is present in both men and animals. Ecclesiastes 3:19, 20 says: 'There is an eventuality as respects the sons of mankind and an eventuality as respects the beast, and they have the same eventuality. As the one dies, so the other dies; and they all have but one spirit' *(ru ahh).* So when men die their spirits are in no sense conscious.[35]

This means that Jehovah's Witnesses do not believe in hellfire or purgatory. They stress that the biblical hell (Hebrew *'sheol'; Greek 'hades'*) is mankind's common grave from which individuals can be resurrected to either a heavenly or an earthly life. The terms *'gehenna'* and 'lake of fire' as used by Jesus and in Revelation do not indicate eternal torment; rather they mean the second death, *eternal annihilation.*[36]

Why, however, does man die? The answer is that when Adam and Eve sinned willfully in Eden, they lost perfection and ultimately died: 'The effect of sin upon them might be illustrated by what happens to a piece of fine machinery when it is not used properly, according to the maker's instructions. The machine will develop weaknesses and, in time, break down. Similarly, as a result of ignoring the instructions of their Maker, Adam and Eve lost perfection. Their minds and bodies began to break down, and finally ceased to function in death.'[37] Accordingly, Adam and Eve could not pass on perfect, sinless natures to their offspring and descendants. As Job tells us: 'Who can produce someone clean out of someone unclean? There is not one.' (Job 14:4) Also, as stated at Romans 5:12: 'Through one man sin entered into the world and death through sin, and thus death spread to all men.'[38]

As demonstrated by the quotations above, the Witnesses argue that Adam and Eve and their offspring since have been depraved in both body and mind by sin. Men are born into a sinful state, and they are bound to miss the mark of perfection. Their imperfect minds and bodies cause them to desire wrong things and to act in violation of Jehovah's will. This is shown biblically by James 1:14, 15. Yet man has not lost all of God's attributes or reason. While he is often in bondage to sin and his eyes are blinded to truth by Satan, he retains enough freedom of the will to choose between good and evil. Thus he is accountable to God and will be judged by Christ on the basis of his heartfelt attitudes and actions. Those who manifest faith in Christ *and his arrangement for salvation* and demonstrate that faith through an active love for God and man will be saved. Those who do not will suffer eternal cutting off from life itself.[39]

Baptism and the Lord's Supper

The Witnesses do not regard either baptism or the Lord's Supper as sacraments: they are not 'an outward and visible sign of an inward spiritual grace' as described in the Anglican *Book of Common Prayer*. Neither are they ordinarily referred to as Christian 'ordinances,' although that, technically, is what they are.

Baptism in water is by total immersion. 'Proper Christian baptism is accomplished by having a devoted servant of God – a male, as John the Baptist was – completely immerse the person in water and raise him up again.'[40] Almost always such services are held at conventions or assemblies but may be celebrated at any time. In past years if one felt he was ready for baptism, he simply went to an assembly and was baptized. But since 1972, the Watch Tower Society has instructed local congregational elders to study eighty questions in the book *Organization for Kingdom-Preaching and Disciple-Making* or, since the spring of 1983, a detailed four-part catechism-like appendix in *Organized to Accomplish Our Ministry,* with baptismal candidates. Only after a person has demonstrated a knowledge of the answers to those questions may he be immersed. The meaning of baptism is outlined in *The Truth That Leads to Eternal Life:* 'What, then does Christian baptism signify? It is not a washing away of one's sins, because cleansing from sin comes only through faith in Jesus Christ. (Ephesians 1:7) Rather, it is a public demonstration, testifying that one has made a solemn dedication to Jehovah God and is presenting himself to do His will. Thus, baptism is not to be viewed as of little importance. It is a requirement for all who obediently walk in the footsteps of Jesus Christ.'[41] There are also definite personal requirements which must be met before a candidate receives valid baptism. He must 'hear the word,' embrace it heartily, repent from sin, and recognize the need for salvation through Jesus Christ. Although the formula at Matthew 28:19 is not understood in a trinitarian sense, Witnesses are 'baptized in the name of the Father and of the Son and of the holy spirit.'

Water baptism is not, however, the only baptism recognized by Jehovah's Witnesses. There is also a baptism into Christ Jesus and into his death by the holy spirit. Those so baptized are consecrated by God to become joint heirs with Christ. They are those of 144,000 who will die and attain heavenly glory. Today only a small handful of Witnesses believe they have received such baptism.

The Lord's Supper,[42] more commonly called the Lord's Evening Meal, is also termed 'the Memorial.' It is held once yearly on the supposedly traditional date of the Old Testament Passover, 14 Nisan (Abib) according to the Watch Tower Society's understanding of the ancient Jewish calendar. Since, according to John's gospel, the Lord's Supper was instituted on that day, Witnesses feel that it should be memorialized yearly as was the Passover. It is always celebrated after sundown and is unquestionably the most important single event in the Witness year.

The occasion is marked by solemn prayer, song, a detailed recounting and explanation of the original Lord's Supper, and the 'passing of the emblems.' The latter expression means the offering of unleavened bread and red, unadulterated wine (not unfermented grape juice) to all persons present. The bread symbolizes Christ's body, the wine his blood. Transubstantiation and consubstantiation, or the doctrine of the 'real presence,' are denied. Therefore, the Lord's Supper is most emphatically a Memorial. Yet the Lord's Supper is also celebrated as a communion meal. Those who partake of the emblems bear testimony to the fact that they have received the baptism of the spirit and have become members of Christ's body, the church.

One additional point needs to be made here respecting this aspect of the Witness concept of the Lord's Supper, however. That relates to their interpretation of the meaning of the unleavened bread, something which changed during the 1950s. At Matthew 26:26 Jesus himself said that the bread which he broke at the Last Supper was his 'body' which Bible Students and Witnesses have always understood in a representative or symbolic sense. Thus, the New World Translation inaccurately translates him as having said: 'TAKE, eat. This [bread] means my body.' But besides teaching that the bread is simply an emblem, the Watch Tower Society traditionally interpreted Christ's reference to his 'body' as an allusion, not to his *physical* body but rather to his *mystic* body, the church. For example, the 1 March 1943 *Watchtower* stated explicitly: 'Consequently Jesus' words "my body" must mean the great spiritual body of which Christ Jesus is the Head, namely, "the body of Christ."'[43] If that were not clear enough, it went on to say: 'Those to be associated with him in the kingdom of heaven make up that body, and the Word of God limits the final number of the "body" members to 144,000 under Christ Jesus the capital member.'[44]

The society's leaders, evidently believing they had received new light on the matter, ultimately decided that the 'body' discerned and memorialized at the celebration of the Lord's Supper on 14 Nisan was the literal, physical body of Christ. Hence, in 1956, with virtually no discussion of the significance of this major change in doctrine, *The Watchtower* said: 'His body? Yes; his own body, his whole body, head and all, that he was to give for them. Jesus meant his own body, the body with which he next associates his own blood when speaking of the cup.'[45]

Most surprisingly and quite dishonestly, a few years later the society acted as though this change had never occurred and that the present doctrine of 'discerning the Lord's body' had existed among Bible Students and Jehovah's Witnesses since the 1870s. Said *The Watchtower* of 1 July 1959: 'In obedience to this arrangement and command of the Lord Jesus Christ, Jehovah's dedicated, spirit-begotten people, whom he has brought into his new covenant, have celebrated the Lord's evening meal yearly on the anniversary of when Jesus introduced it, on Nisan 14, since the 1870's according to published reports. In the unleavened bread and the wine used on that occasion they have discerned the perfect human body and the blood of the Lord Jesus, with heartfelt gratitude.'[46]

The Church

The church or, as it is usually designated today, the congregation of God, is often referred to by such biblical titles as the 'bride of Christ,' 'Christ's body,' 'the New Jerusalem,' 'the little flock,' and several other names as well. But to Jehovah's Witnesses it is primarily the 144,000 of Revelation 7 and 14. Of course, according to Watch Tower teaching, since the selection of the 'saints' or the 'anointed' began at Pentecost, most of the congregation have been selected, died, and from 1918 onward have been raised to heavenly life. Thus, only a remnant of 'kingdom heirs' – now just over 9,000 in number – are left on the earth today.[47]

The doctrine that the number 144,000 literally represents the totality of Christians who go to be with Christ in heaven is based primarily on one argument.

Essentially it runs as follows: The 144,000 are first described at Revelation 7:4–8. But in verse 9, John, the writer of Revelation, states that he saw 'a great crowd which no man was able to number, out of all nations and tribes and peoples and tongues.' Therefore, say Watch Tower exegetes, the number 144,000 must be literal, 'because it is being contrasted with the "great crowd" that no man was able to number.'[48] It must be remembered here, too, that in Witness eyes the great crowd is an earthly class, since nowhere does Revelation specifically say that they are standing on the heavenly Mount Zion or have been purchased from the earth as it does of the 144,000 at Revelation 14:1, 3.

Membership in the congregation of God is a matter of God's choice or selection, not the individual's. Thus, in theory any baptized Jehovah's Witness may feel the holy spirit's call, be 'sealed,' and proclaim his membership in the little flock by partaking of the emblems at Memorial time. In fact, however, since 1935 the society has taught that virtually all of the 144,000 were sealed by that date. The 1 December 1973 *Watchtower* stated: 'Nearly all these, if not all, were already sealed many years ago with the initial sealing. While it is true that some, before the sealing is permanent, may prove unfaithful and so others have to be sealed, there is no general ingathering of the disciples at this late date.'[49]

As pointed out in Chapter 4, this has recently made it difficult for new converts or younger persons to announce a heavenly calling and remain within the Witness fold at all. Many such recent 'spiritual Israelites' have been disfellowshipped or driven to deny their hope completely. Yet in spite of psychological and social pressures every year there are a few new members of the anointed remnant of Jehovah's Witnesses. In 1981, because of these new partakers, there were 37 more than in the previous year.[50] So, while today most of the remnant are self-described 'old timers,' there are some younger Witnesses in this group as well.

The Great Crowd

The great crowd or other sheep, who were for years called 'Jonadabs,' make up the vast majority of the more than two and a half million active Jehovah's Witnesses and their families. But in spite of their numerical importance, they are definitely held to be a secondary class in every sense. They are almost always described in a dependent, subservient role in relation to the anointed remnant of kingdom heirs,[51] and they cannot hold the highest positions in the Witness community. That means that they cannot now hope ever to become members of the governing body.

Equally significantly, their position with regard to Watch Tower soteriological doctrine is very different from that of the remnant. Not only does the society say that they are not in the New Covenant and have no mediator, but it also teaches that they are not justified by faith, and not sanctified, and will attain ultimate salvation only after a long probationary period of more than a thousand years during which they will be subjected to two major tests by Satan and his hosts.[52] Regarding their growing to perfection, the society teaches:

The 'great crowd' of survivors of the 'war of the great day of God the Almighty' will then be on their way to gaining absolute righteousness and perfection in the flesh [during the millennium]. They want to become perfect human sons of God through their Eternal Father Jesus Christ. (Isaiah 9:5,6). For this reason they will not be justified or declared righteous either now or then as the 144,000 heavenly joint heirs have been justified while still in the flesh. The 'great crowd ' will not undergo a change of nature from human to spiritual and so do not need the justification by faith and the inputed righteousness that the 144,000 'chosen ones' have required. Not imputed human perfection by faith in Christ's blood, but actual human perfection in the flesh by the uplifting, cleansing help of God's Messianic kingdom – this is what the 'great crowd' will need and what they will attain by Christ's kingdom of a thousand years.[53]

This means the 'great crowd' do not receive salvation by grace or 'undeserved kindness' – they must work for it. 'Finally, through faithful *molding of themselves* [italics mine] to righteousness they will get that "law of sin" nullified in themselves and become perfect human creatures, like the perfect Adam in the garden of Eden.'[54] As they *strive* for this perfection they will be healed physically and will be able to stand before God on their own: 'Accordingly, as those of the "great crowd" more and more cultivate actual persistent righteousness within themselves, physical healing and betterment will be given. Eventually, before the thousand years of his [Jesus] healing reign are over, uplift to human perfection will be imparted to the obedient "great crowd." '[55]

Even after they stand before God in righteousness at the end of the thousand-year reign of Christ, they do not automatically receive life everlasting. When the millennium has ended, Satan and his demonic hordes will be released again and will go forth to tempt the great crowd as well as all those who have been resurrected since those wicked spirits were cast into the 'bottomless pit' at Armageddon more than a thousand years earlier. Hence, only when they have surmounted this final devilish assault on their integrity will those Jehovah's Witnesses with the hope of gaining everlasting life on a paradise earth finally receive their ultimate reward.[56] Yet there is no assurance that they will necessarily pass this test. Some may become rebels against God, and 'these willful rebels will be summarily executed, in a destruction as complete and everlasting as by fire, because they failed to prove worthy of being justified by the great Judge, Jehovah God.'[57]

Of course, the great crowd are constantly encouraged to look forward to the joys of a paradise earth in which every man will sit under his own vine and fig tree. Witness children are taught to expect a time when they will be able to play with wild beasts in fulfilment of Isaiah 11, and persons of marriageable age are encouraged to look forward to perfect marriage relationships and the having of children in a paradise near at hand. All this, most Jehovah's Witnesses believe, will be possible for them *without having to die.*

Creation

The Witness doctrine of the way in which creation took place is a rather involved one to say the least. They give no date for the original creation of the heavens and the earth as mentioned at Genesis 1:1. They see no reason for not assuming that the scientific community may be right for inferring that the universe is many millions of years old. When they discuss the six creative days of Genesis, the matter is quite different, however. On the basis of a system of reverse logic they assume that each of the creative days was 7,000 years in length.[58]

The length of these 7,000-year days is calculated from the millennium which is held to be a literal thousand-year period. Since both the Psalmist and the Apostle Peter indicate that a day with the Lord is a thousand years and a thousand years as a day (Psalm, 90:4; 2 Peter 3:8), Watch Tower writers have concluded that the millennium is a thousand-year day of rest – a sabbath – for mankind during which the race will be free from suffering and 'Adamic' death. At the same time they teach that if the millennium is a sabbath, it must 'logically' be preceded by six 1,000-year days from the creation of Eve. Thus a 'week' in the history of mankind is a period of 7,000 years.

They hold that this week is all a part of God's rest or sabbath from the work of creation, at least in so far as the earth is concerned. Hence God's seventh day from the end of creation on earth is a grand period of 7,000 years. Then, again, say Watch Tower exegetes, if this is so, the preceding six creative days must have been periods of 7,000 years each. Consequently, from the beginning of the creative days to the creation of Eve was, in all, a period of 42,000 years.[59]

In order to support this theory, since Russell's day the society has gone to great lengths. In the 'Photo-Drama of Creation' and again in Judge Rutherford's book *Creation,* published in 1927, these ideas were put forth as they have been numerous times since. To reconcile them with 'true science' both Russell and Rutherford adopted Sir Isaac Vail's canopy theory of the development of the earth,[60] and the society continues to use that theory to this day.[61] In addition, it has attacked sharply the theory of evolution. Since it has had to call on Witnesses with scientific and technical knowledge to produce works relating to the subject, such works are among the best published by the Watch Tower Society. Most notable among them are *Did Man Get Here by Evolution or Creation?* (1967) and *Is the Bible Really the Word of God?* (1969). None the less, none of them really deals in any sophisticated fashion with the problems of logic that lie behind the Witnesses' whole doctrine of creation, especially with regard to the 42,000-year, six creation-day periods.

Bible Chronology and Eschatological Prophecy

The system of 'Bible Chronology' used by the Witnesses today is based, with certain important modifications, on the one used by Pastor Russell. The eschatological prophecies and time calculations are also, in part, based on those which he adopted from Dr Nelson Barbour and John H. Paton as outlined in his first three volumes of *Studies in the Scriptures*.

Russell's system and that of his predecessors is far too complex to describe in full in a work such as this, but it is useful to list the most important *specific* dates which he felt marked certain events connected with biblical prophecies relevant to his own day and thereafter. These include the following:

1813 BC   The beginning of the existence of the nation of Israel, dating from Jacob's death.

606 BC   The fall of Jerusalem to Nebuchadnezzar and the beginning of the times of the Gentiles.

454 BC   The order to rebuild the walls of Jerusalem plus the beginning of the 2,300 days of Daniel 8:14 and the 70 Weeks of Daniel 9:24.

AD 29   The baptism and anointing of Jesus the Christ.

AD 33   The death of Christ.

AD 36   The end of the 70 weeks of Daniel 9:24 and the beginning of the preaching of Christianity to the Gentiles.

AD 70   The destruction of Jerusalem by the Romans.

AD 539   The beginning of papal domination in Christendom, the 1,260 days (a time, times, and half a time) of Daniel 12:7, the 1,290 days of Daniel 12:11 and the 1,335 days of Daniel 12:13.

AD 1799   The end of the 1,260 days and the debasement of the papacy by Napoleon.

AD 1828   The end of the 1,290 days and the beginning of the Millerite or Second Adventist movement.

AD 1846   The end of the 2,300 days, and the 'cleansing of the Sanctuary' by the exposing of false doctrines such as the immortality of the soul by George Storrs, et al.

AD 1873   The end of 6,000 years of human existence.

AD 1874 The end of the 1,335 days, the beginning of Christ's invisible *parousia*, and the beginning of 'the Harvest.'

AD 1878 The 'coming of the king (Christ) in power' and the resurrection of the saints sleeping in death.

AD 1881 The end of the general call to the little flock of 144,000 saints and the fall of Babylon the Great (the end of false religious influence over the Church).

AD 1914 The end of the times of the Gentiles and of a 'Time of Troubles' leading to Armageddon, the cleansing of the earth and the restoration of the natural Jews to Palestine.

Because 1914 did not bring the end of the present world as Russell had expected but did see the outbreak of the First World War, he revised his expectations and suggested that the war would lead to Armageddon.[62] Shortly after his death, the society published *The Finished Mystery* which included some of Russell's latest theories of end times and added significantly to them.[63] The new dates which then became important to the late Pastor's followers were:

AD 1918 The outbreak of anarchy on a world-wide scale, the beginning of the destruction of Babylon the Great (Christendom) by socialistic and anarchistic elements, and the exultation of the remnant of the 144,000 to heavenly glory.

AD 1920 God's 'fire' from heaven to fall on Christendom.

AD 1921 The Great Company class (still seen as a secondary heavenly class) cut off and glorified, thereby ending the heavenly resurrection.

AD 1925 The end of the world-wide anarchy and the full restitution of natural Israel.

AD 1931 The time of the full establishment of the kingdom of God in power on earth.

AD 1980 The possible regathering of all fleshly Israel from death through an earthly resurrection.

AD 2875 The restitution of the earth completed.

AD 2914 Dominion of the earth restored to mankind.

Shortly after the publication of *The Finished Mystery*, Judge Rutherford began to focus attention on 1925 as the date for the return of the ancient worthies and the restoration of all things.[64] But in 1926 the society revised the text of *The Finished Mystery* to take out a number of definite pronouncements concerning certain date-centred phophecies which had already failed to occur. Shortly thereafter *The Finished Mystery* was discarded as a source of 'present truth.'[65] Although, curiously, many ideas and even drawings from it have continued to crop up in later Watch Tower publications.[66]

During the 1920s and 1930s Rutherford and the society were forced to abandon or revise much of Russell's prophetic chronology as well as that found in *The Finished Mystery*. They came to feel that most of the dates given above had no special significance, and the average Jehovah's Witness today is completely unaware that at one time the Society regarded them as of the greatest importance. Nevertheless, the society's leaders did retain certain aspects of the chronology taught by its first president. They continued to regard his interpretation of the seventy weeks of Daniel as accurate, and with certain small changes, even today they accept the explanation which he, Barbour, and Paton gave regarding the 'times of the Gentiles.' Hence, they still use the 'year for a day' concept in interpreting two of the prophecies of Daniel as they understand them. Yet the present Witness chronology is radically different from that accepted prior to 1935.

In a simplified sense the most important dates for Jehovah's Witnesses today are:

607 BC	The fall of Jerusalem to Nebuchadnezzar and the beginning of the 'times of the Gentiles.'
455 BC	The sending forth of the decree to rebuild the walls of Jerusalem and the beginning of the 70 weeks of Daniel 9:24.
AD 29	The baptism and anointing of Christ.
AD 33	The death of Christ.
AD 36	The end of the 70 weeks of Daniel.
AD 1914	The end of the 'times of the Gentiles' and the beginning of the times of the end.
AD 1918	Christ's coming to his temple for judgement.
AD 1919	The fall of Babylon the Great and the birth of the New Nation of Jehovah's Witnesses.
AD 1975	The end of 6,000 years of human existence.

Important prophetic day periods such as the 1,260 days (a time, times, and half a time), the 1,290 days, and the 1,335 days of Daniel 12 are no longer interpreted as being years. They are now regarded as *literal* periods of days and are thought to have occurred during the First World War and up to 1925.[67]

As seen from all of this, the society has never been dissuaded from prophetic date-setting nor has it been bothered by the fact that it has felt it necessary or useful to 'adjust' its chronology over and over again. Russell, for example, thought that the end of 6,000 years had occurred in 1872. In the book *'The Truth Shall Make You Free,'* published in 1943, it was scheduled to take place in 1972,[68] but since

The Bible shows that there will be a resurrection of many to life on earth

The earthly resurrection
(from *The Watchtower*, 1 April 1982, 23)

then has been shifted to 1975, then to 1976, and finally, back to 1975 again.[69]

The Resurrection

Few doctrines among Jehovah's Witnesses have been as subject to change as that of the resurrection of the dead. According to Pastor Russell's teachings the 144,000 would all take part in the first or heavenly resurrection to immortality just as the society teaches today. Their resurrection began in 1878, however, and not in 1918 as has been Watch Tower doctrine since Rutherford's day.[70] As for the great crowd or, as Russell usually called them, the 'great company,' he believed that they would also have a spiritual resurrection, although it would not be the first one.[71] Finally, all the rest of mankind, both the just and the unjust, would come forth to an earthly resurrection during the millennium.[72] The 'ancient worthies' – faithful men from Abel to John the Baptist – would be among the first to be resurrected and would set up the kingdom arrangement under Christ to provide blessings to natural Israel and all of mankind. Thus, Christ's forefathers would rule over both the Armageddon survivors and those brought forth in the resurrection.[73] Russell felt that eventually the 'ancient worthies' might be given a heavenly reward.[74]

As late as 1916 the Pastor still believed that the resurrection of the 'ancient worthies' would take place only after the saints had all obtained their heavenly reward.[75] But by the late 1920s, Rutherford was teaching that those men of faith might appear on earth before the church class had all died.[76] And more dramatic changes were to come later. In 1930 the judge was still teaching that all, including Adam, would have a resurrection.[77] Yet following the announcement of the teaching that the 'great crowd' was an earthly class in 1935, he came to insist that Adam and many others who had lived in the past and most of those who were dying daily would have no resurrection.[78]

After Rutherford's death the society left his latest teachings unaltered for a number of years. In the book, 'The Truth Shall Make You Free' published in 1943, it did stress that those members of the great crowd who had the misfortune to die prior to Armageddon would come forth to life and be able to marry and have children.[79] But this was only building on the society's teachings during the last years of the Rutherford era.

A major change came in 1950. In a return to Russell's teachings, Frederick Franz announced that the ancient worthies or 'princes' would *not* be resurrected until after Armageddon.[80] However, far more important were the changes in resurrection doctrine in the mid-1960s which were a further, *partial* return to the Pastor's doctrines. According to a number of articles on the resurrection which appeared in the various issues of *The Watchtower* during the winter of 1964–5, hopes for mankind were somewhat brighter than the society had held for many years. In the 1 March 1965 issue, in an article entitled 'Who Will Be Resurrected from the Dead?,' the society suddenly seemed to discover anew that the inhabitants of the ancient cities of Tyre, Sidon, Sodom, and Gomorrah would all be resurrected.[81] So, too, it decided, would the unbelieving marriage mates of Jehovah's Witnesses and most others if they should die before Armageddon.[82] None the less, the society continued to stress in the most outspoken terms that neither the clergy of Christendom – the 'man of lawlessness' class – nor apostate Jehovah's Witnesses would have any hope of coming forth to any kind of resurrection, even to one of damnation.[83] They remained classified with Judas Iscariot who, they believed, had gone to *gehenna,* the second death.[84]

A final point which deserves passing notice here is that according to the latest Watch Tower doctrine there will be no marrying or procreating among those brought forth in the earthly resurrection, even among faithful members of the great crowd. Consequently, it is now held that should an individual pass child-bearing age, lose his or her reproductive powers, or die prior to the millennium, that person will have permanently lost the hope of fulfilling what Jehovah's Witnesses have long referred to as the 'divine mandate' – the power to bring forth perfect children under paradise conditions.[85]

The Sacredness of Life and Blood

Jehovah's Witnesses emphasize strongly the sacredness of life. They therefore refuse to serve in military forces or to manufacture weapons of war. Curiously, however, their objections to such service often have more to do with their belief that the secular state is opposed to Christ's kingdom than to the fact that they are against the taking of life. They emphasize that they are not pacifists but, rather, conscientious objectors.[86] They teach that it is quite proper to execute murderers.[87] Furthermore, Watch Tower literature seems to take great pleasure, especially since Rutherford's day, in condemning those whom it considers to be God's enemies to everlasting destruction.[88]

But in some areas Witness doctrines do show a real sense of concern for life, both human and animal. They are staunchly opposed to abortion since they feel that human life begins at conception.[89] While they believe that birth control is a 'personal' matter, they condemn any form which would prohibit the development of a fertilized ovum in a woman's uterus. Thus they have suggested that Witness women not use intra-uterine devices which may cause abortions rather than inhibit conception.[90]

For many years the Watch Tower Society strongly opposed sterilizations except in cases of extreme medical necessity. More recently it has agreed that a woman may have a tubal ligation if her health or life is endangered. Too, it is now permissible for a Witness husband to have a vasectomy to protect his wife; since he is one flesh with her, he may choose to undergo sterilization out of love for her.[91]

A most interesting and attractive doctrine among Jehovah's Witnesses is their concern for lower animal life. Since Russell's day they have held that while it is perfectly proper to hunt, fish, or take animal life for a variety of purposes, that must not be done wantonly. The basis for such reasoning is, according to the society, that God entered into an everlasting covenant with mankind through Noah. Said *The Watchtower* of 1 December 1938:

In a previous issue of *The Watchtower* it has been stated that the wanton slaying of the beast constitutes a violation of the everlasting covenant and that such was one of the primary sins committed by Nimrod. Some readers of *The Watchtower* have taken issue with that conclusion, holding that the chase and slaughter of wild animals for mere sport of so doing is right and proper. Is it Scripturally correct to conclude that the everlasting covenant is violated only when human blood is shed? Such conclusion is entirely erroneous, and this is shown by the language in which the everlasting covenant is stated by Jehovah.[92]

Why does the society maintain its well-known ban on blood transfusions and *some* blood particles? Although this matter has been discussed briefly in Chapter 5, more needs to be said here. Perhaps the question can best be answered by simply quoting from a reply to a question from a reader found in *The Watchtower* of 1 July 1951 (p. 414):

Jehovah made a covenant with Noah following the Flood, and included therein was this command: 'Flesh with the life thereof, which is the blood thereof, shall ye not eat.' (Gen.9:4) The Law given through Moses contained these restrictions: 'Eat neither fat nor blood' 'Eat no manner of blood.' 'Whatsoever man there be of the house of Israel, or of the strangers that sojourn among you, that eateth any manner of blood; I will even set my face against that soul that eateth blood, and will cut him off from among his people. For the life of the flesh is in the blood: and I have given it to you upon the altar to make an atonement for your souls: for it is the blood that maketh an atonement for the soul. For it is the life of all flesh; the blood of it is for the life thereof: Therefore I said unto the children of Israel, Ye shall eat the blood of no manner of flesh.' (Lev. 3:17; 7:26; 17:10, 11, 14; 19:26) And in the Greek Scriptures the instruction to Christians is: 'The holy spirit and we ourselves have favored adding no further burden to you, except these necessary things, to keep yourselves free from things sacrificed to idols and from blood and from things killed without draining their blood and from fornication.' – Acts 15:19, 20, 28, 29; 21:25, NW.

In other replies to similar letters, the same issue of *The Watchtower* claimed that the prohibition against eating blood applied to human as well as animal blood, applied to Christians as well as to Israelites under the law of Moses, and that even if a donor did not die when giving blood for a transfusion, it would be wrong to accept blood from him. The society argued that accepting a transfusion was tantamount to eating blood.[93]

Since 1951 the society's general position has altered very little, and the same arguments against transfusions are used today. But as time went by the society imposed generally stricter rules against the use of blood. Medically, it took a stand against autotransfusions. In 1959 an American *Watchtower* reader asked: 'Would it be allowable for a dedicated Christian to have some of his own blood removed and then put back into his body during an operation?' In answer the society stated:

According to the method of handling blood prescribed by the Bible, blood when taken from a body was to be poured out on the ground as water and covered over with dust. (Lev. 17:13, 14; Deut. 12:16, 23, 24; 15:23; 1 Chron. 11:18, 19) This is because life is in the blood and such shed blood is held sacred before Jehovah God. The covenant regarding the sanctity of blood stated after the Flood is still binding today, and it covers both animal and human blood, whether one's own or anothers'. Consequently, the removal of one's blood, storing it and later putting it back into the same person would be a violation of the Scriptural principles that govern the handling of blood. – Gen. 9:4–6.

If, however, hemorrhaging should occur at the time of an operation and by some means the blood is immediately channeled back into the body, this would be allowable. The use of some device whereby the blood is diverted and a certain area or organ is temporarily bypassed during surgery would be permissible, for the blood would be flowing from one's body through the apparatus and right back into the body again. On the other hand, if the blood were stored, even for a brief period of time, this would be a violation of the Scriptures.

The use of another person's blood to 'prime' any device employed in surgery is objectionable. In this case the blood would circulate through the system of the patient, becoming mixed with his own. Again if one's own blood would have to be withdrawn at intervals and stored until a sufficient amount had accumulated to set a machine in operation, this too would fall under Scriptural prohibition. The ones involved in the matter are in the best position to ascertain just how the blood would be handled and must bear responsibility before Jehovah for seeing that it is not handled unscripturally.[94]

In the early 1960s the society also extended its prohibition against the use of products made from animal blood. Jehovah's Witnesses were told to ask bakers and candy-makers if lecithin used in their products was derived from plants or blood.[95] The use of blood taken from cows in the manufacture of cosmetics was condemned.[96] Witness farmers were told not to purchase crop fertilizers which contained blood.[97] Witness pet owners were told that it was wrong to allow veterinarians to give tranfusions to sick animals.[98] Witnesses were not to feed their dogs or cats food with blood in it.[99] At the same time, Witness patients were told that they could not accept *anything* derived from blood in medical treatment. 'It is not just blood,' said *The Watchtower* of 15 February 1963 (p. 124), 'but anything that is derived from blood and used to sustain life or strengthen one that comes under this principle.'

Most curiously, however, this did not necessarily mean *all* blood fractions. For nearly six years earlier, the following question from a reader and the answer thereto had *also* appeared in *The Watchtower:*

Are we to consider the injection of serums such as diphtheria toxin antitoxin and blood fractions such as gamma globulin into the blood stream, for the purpose of building up resistance to disease by means of antibodies, the same as the drinking of blood or the taking of blood or blood plasma by means of transfusion? – N.P., United States.

No, it does not seem necessary that we put the two in the same category, although we have done so in times past. Each time the prohibition of blood is mentioned in the Scriptures it is in connection with taking it as food, and so it is as a nutrient that we are concerned with its being forbidden. Thus when mankind for the first time was permitted to eat the flesh of animals, at the time of the restatement of the procreation mandate to the Deluge survivors, blood was specifically forbidden. (Gen. 9:3, 4) In the law of Moses blood was forbidden as food, and therefore we repeatedly find it linked with fat as things not to be eaten. (Lev. 3:17; 7:22 – 7) And so in the days of the apostles; it was in connection with meat sacrificed to idols that the eating of strangled animals and blood was forbidden – Acts 15:20, 29.

The injection of antibodies into the blood in a vehicle of blood serum or the use of blood fractions to create such antibodies is not the same as taking blood, either by mouth or by transfusion, as a nutrient to build up the body's vital forces. While God did not intend for any man to contaminate his blood stream by vaccines, serums or blood fractions, doing so does not seem to be included in God's expressed will forbidding blood as food. It would therefore be a matter of individual judgement whether one accepted such types of medication or not.[100]

Although this statement can be reconciled with that found in the 1963 *Watchtower* as quoted above only with the greatest legalistic casuistry, it remains in force among Jehovah's Witnesses today. Evidently vaccinations do not 'strengthen one' in the face of disease. Or at least so the Watch Tower Society would have it.

Not even the eating of blood is absolutely forbidden. The society does not require that fish be bled before they are consumed. In 1973 the society quoted

Leviticus 17:13 to show that only land animals and fowl must be bled before they are used for food. That text states 'As for any man who in hunting catches a wild beast or a fowl that may be eaten, he must in that case pour its blood out and cover it with dust.' Thus *The Watchtower* commented: 'Fish that were suitable for food according to the terms of the Mosaic law did not contain a quantity of blood sufficient to be poured out and covered with dust. Evidently for this reason the Law set forth no precise statement about bleeding fish.'[101]

The strangest aspect of the society's policy is its recent granting of permission to allow the use of blood particles in the treatment of haemophiliacs. As late as 1975, *Awake!* took the strongest exception to such therapy,[102] and Witnesses with the disease were told to refrain from accepting it. Shortly thereafter, however, the society decided to take the same position on it that it had on gamma globulin and toxin antitoxins. So when someone made an emergency telephone call to the Brooklyn Bethel or a Watch Tower branch office, he was told he could accept the treatment in question. Yet the society published no statement on the matter in its literature until it finally revoked its earlier ban in the 15 June 1978 *Watchtower* (p. 30), thus leaving many desperately ill haemophiliacs to believe for several years that they still remained under the 'faithful and discreet slave's' earlier dictum on the matter.[103]

The Preaching Work

Tied to the doctrine of the vindication of Jehovah's name, the preaching work of Jehovah's Witnesses is seen as the 'touchstone' of their lives, central to their very *raison d'être*. Respecting this the book *Organized to Accomplish Our Ministry* says: 'Under divine command, the work of these ministers (Jehovah's Witnesses) involves preaching the Kingdom good news in all the earth and making disciples of people of all the nations.'[104] Thus it is evident that the society really holds that this work is a 'sacred duty' and essentially the means by which Jehovah's Witnesses get saved. As the 15 July 1979 *Watchtower* stated: 'It is in our endurance in proclaiming "this good news of the kingdom" that we may attain to salvation.'[105]

So while the governing body claims to teach the doctrine of salvation by faith, at least for the anointed remnant and *sometimes* for the other sheep class of Jehovah's Witnesses, in fact it lays much greater stress on salvation through a work, *through preaching*. And the reason for this is evident. As has been the case for well over a hundred years, the Watch Tower Society still teaches that both the apolcalypse and the dawning of a new age are at hand. Hence it holds that the Witnesses are engaged in a 'separating work' along with Christ and the angels which determines who will ultimately be saved and who damned eternally. Published in 1983, *Organized to Accomplish Our Ministry* proclaims boldly:

The establishment of God's Kingdom in the invisible heavens in 1914 inevitably forced this present system of things into its foretold 'last days.' (2 Tim. 3:1-5; Rev. 11:15, 18) Shortly after World War I Jehovah's people were revitalized by God's spirit to put forth a special effort in proclaiming the good news. From that time forward a tremendous witness has been given, resulting in a dividing of the people. During this period Jesus Christ, along with his holy angels, has been separating lovers of righteousness from those who are indifferent to, or who actively oppose, the truth. This separating, or dividing, work was foretold in Jesus' illustration of the sheep and the goats.(Matt. 25:31–46) Consequently there is no question about the profound effect that the established Kingdom of God is having on the people and nations of this world.

We are now nearing the end of the present ungodly world. (2 Pet. 3:7, 11, 12) The ministry has become more urgent than ever before. (John 9:4) This calls for faithful Christians to be filled with zeal. They cannot loiter at their God-assigned work or be indifferent to its being fully accomplished. (Rom. 12:11) This is no time for independent

"Do the work of an evangelizer, fully accomplish your ministry."
—2 Timothy 4:5.

The *Watchtower*'s concept of a minister of the gospel
(from *The Watchtower*, 1 January 1982, 16)

**Well-arranged dress
and good grooming
befit
Christian ministers**

(from *The Watchtower*, 1 January 1982, 19)

thinking or conflicting actions on their part. More than ever before, the remnant of Kingdom heirs, along with the increasing number of 'other sheep,' are determined to work together as a united body. As one organized flock they follow Christ's lead so as to finish the global witness before the outbreak of the 'great tribulation.' – John 10:14–16; Matt. 24:14, 21[106]

Naturally, then, since the preaching work – connected as it is with Watch Tower apocalypticism – is so important, it touches directly the lives of all members of the Witness community. For this reason, more detailed discussions of it and its effects appear in the next two chapters.

Part Three

Organization and Community

CHAPTER EIGHT

Organizational Structure

The formal organizational structure by which Jehovah's Witnesses are governed is very important; to them it is the government of God on earth – the theocracy. As British sociologist James Beckford has recognized, what the Watch Tower Society calls 'theocractic government' as directed by the governing body in Brooklyn, New York, 'has welded the witnesses into a more self-consciously unified and more determinedly united religious group than any other sect, denomination or church.'[1] Yet before discussing that structure, two points need to be made. First, the term 'theocratic' really means hierarchical and, second, there are informal organizational relationships which are often more important than the formal.

The Witness Hierarchy

The chart below is *The Watchtower*'s idealized diagram of the theocratic organization of Jehovah's Witnesses. As will be noted, it gives significance to the supposed role of the 'faithful and discreet slave' class. This class, however, *as a class,* plays no part in the governance of the organization and most of its members are relatively powerless. It is true, of course, that all those who actually govern the organization must be a part of it, as has been noted earlier. But, in fact, their authority stems, ultimately, from other factors. Also, *The Watchtower*'s chart fails to include within it much of the structure that is basic to the administration of the Witness community.

Although the word 'hierarchy' is a pejorative term to Jehovah's Witnesses,[2] to understand their organizational structure, it is most useful to describe it from the top down and to show just how similar it is to the hierarchy of the Church of Rome. For example, a direct comparison can be made between the Catholic and Witness offices and institutions listed below *The Watchtower*'s diagram:

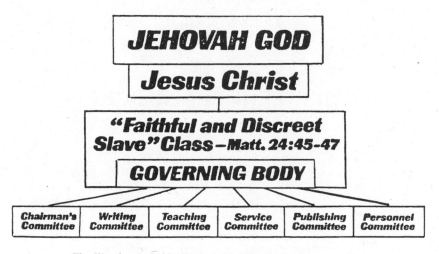

The *Watchtower*'s idealized view of the theocratic government
of Jehovah's Witnesses
(from *The Watchtower*, 1 January 1977, 16)

The Pope of Rome	The President of the Watch Tower Society
The College of Cardinals	The Governing Body of Jehovah's Witnesses
The Papal Curia	The Committee Structure of the Governing Body
The Vatican	The Brooklyn Bethel
Archbishops	District Overseers
Bishops	Circuit Overseers
Priests	Elders
Deacons	Ministerial Servants
Regular Orders	Pioneers
The Catholic laity	The Jehovah's Witness community

It would be wrong to push these comparisons too far, of course, and there are certain offices and institutions in the present Witness structure unlike anything in the Catholic church. Nonetheless, the above list serves a useful purpose in that in many ways it makes it possible for non-Witnesses to get a quick overview of the way in which, basically, Jehovah's Witnesses have been governed, particularly since 1972. But besides acting as a heuristic device, two additional things should be noted in connection with it. First, it no doubt represents what Max Weber recognized many years ago. Bureaucratic organizations – which is what both the Catholic and Witness hierarchies are – tend to approximate a 'pure' or 'ideal' type

THE ORGANIZATIONAL STRUCTURE
OF JEHOVAH'S WITNESSES

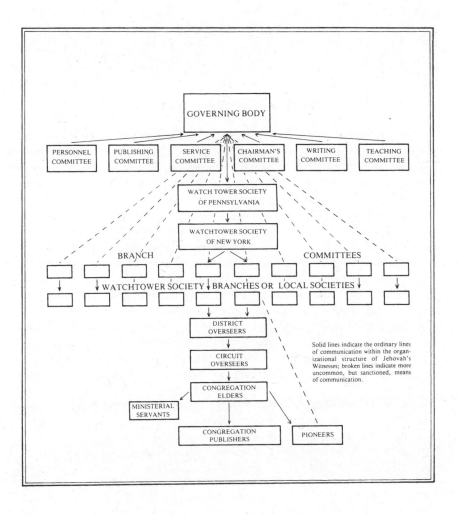

which with variations can be demonstrated to have been present historically in many business, charitable, political and religious organizations.[3] And second, since Jehovah's Witnesses have for so long and with such vehemence regarded the Church of Rome as their chief religious adversary, it is not surprising that their very fixation on it has caused them to copy unconsciously much from its organizational structure, its practices, and its traditional world-view. Simply stated, the Witness view of the Catholic hierarchy may accurately be subsumed under what the well-known American historian Richard Hofstadter calls the 'paranoid style,' and as he says: 'A fundamental paradox of the paranoid style is the imitation of the enemy.'[4]

The President of the Watch Tower Society

As president of the Watch Tower Society, Judge Joseph F. Rutherford became a complete spiritual autocrat, and his successor, Nathan H. Knorr, remained one until 1971. With the establishment of the formally created governing body in that year, an attempt was made to reduce his role, in theory at least, to that of *primus inter pares* – first among equals.

It is difficult to determine just how the governing body came into existence. The Watch Tower Society has never published the details, and even Raymond Franz's autobiographical account of what happened is rather incomplete.[5] Nevertheless, certain things can be ascertained. During the 1960s there was a good deal of unhappiness about the nature of the Witness organizational structure among Jehovah's Witnesses throughout the world; congregational and circuit overseers were often described as 'little dictators.' So over a period of time Brooklyn became more and more aware of restlessness within the larger Witness community.[6] Then, in 1965 Nathan Knorr called on a committee of five – the most prominent members of which were Raymond Franz, Edward Dunlap, and Reinhard Lengtat – to produce the society's Bible dictionary *Aid to Bible Understanding*. Although Knorr intended them to do no more than produce a small Scripture manual, he inadvertently gave them a green light to do sustained biblical research on non-Witness sources or commentaries. Hence, among many other things, they investigated the organizational structure of the early Christian church and came to the conclusion that the system of governance which had existed among Jehovah's Witnesses since 1938 was not in harmony with that model. So just at the time that the society at Brooklyn was becoming aware of the negative feelings among many Witnesses to the then-existing organizational hierarchy, Raymond Franz presented the idea to his superiors that local congregations should *properly* be superintended by bodies of elders and that the international community of Jehovah Witnesses should *properly* be ruled by a supreme council or governing body. The concept of that latter entity was, of course, not entirely new since the board of directors of the society had been designated by that title for some years. But Raymond Franz gave it more validity by suggesting that the Jerusalem council of apostles and elders described at Acts 15 had served as the first and model governing body of the Christian church.[7]

Both Nathan Knorr and Frederick Franz were at first opposed to the idea, but then the latter embraced it and proclaimed his support for it publicly in outspoken terms. In a speech commonly called the 'tail wagging the dog talk' which was later published in *The Watchtower* of 15 December 1975 (p. 760), he stated:

So the Society's voting members see that this governing body could most directly use the 'administrative agency' as an instrument in behalf of the work of the 'faithful and discreet slave' class by having members of the governing body on the Board of Directors of the Society. They recognize that the Society is not the administrative body, but is merely an agency for administering matters.

Hence the Society's voting members do not desire that there be any basis for conflict and division. They do not want to cause anything like a situation where 'the administrative agency' controls and directs the user of that agency, which user is the governing body as representing the 'faithful and discreet slave' class. No more so than to have the tail wag a dog instead of the dog's wagging its tail. A legal religious instrument according to Caesar's law should not attempt to direct and control its creator; rather, the creator of the legal religious instrument should control and direct it.

But the Watch Tower vice-president was playing church politics; neither he nor Nathan Knorr really had any intention of relinquishing power to the new governing body. Although they allowed the sweeping changes in congregational, circuit, and district governance recommended by Raymond Franz and his close associates to be implemented throughout the larger Witness community, nothing significant changed at Brooklyn for several years.[8] While the governing body came into being, in no sense did it truly govern. At best it served as a kind of presidential privy council or sanhedrin which spent most of its time discussing what should and what should not be considered as disfellowshipping offences. Often much of its time was spent discussing matters relating to sexual morality.[9]

Gradually a majority of the governing body became determined to take over the reigns of power from Knorr. What eventually occurred to bring about what amounted to an organizational coup of 1975 was a general feeling of revulsion against working conditions among a large segment of Bethelites and a belief shared by all of the members of the governing body (except the Watch Tower president and vice-president) that if it were to have *de jure* authority, it should have the *de facto* powers to go along with that authority.[10]

At the time, Frederick Franz resisted his fellow governing body members' move with bitterness. In a well-documented account, Raymond Franz relates how his uncle opposed his colleagues, arguing with insight that the Jerusalem council described at Acts 15 had never served as a general supervisory council for the early church. However, he did not bother to explain that there was no basis for the virtually papal monarchy of Watch Tower presidents either. Finally, when Knorr yielded, albeit reluctantly, to the recommendations of a five-man committee of the governing body whose prime spokesman was Raymond Franz, Frederick Franz submitted to the inevitable as well.[11]

When Knorr was succeeded by Frederick Franz as Watch Tower president in 1977, the office had been downgraded significantly. But Franz's personal influence remained so great that he was shortly able to regain some of the powers of his predecessors. He continues to be the primary ideologue on the governing body and has the prestige of having been the society's 'oracle' since the early years of Judge Rutherford's presidency. So today 'Freddy,' as he is often called by affectionate Witnesses and less affectionate ex-Witnesses alike, holds at least as much control over Jehovah's Witnesses as he did as vice-president of the society before 1975, However, it is quite true that his present authority springs more from his personal influence than from that of his office.[12]

The Governing Body

Since 1975 the governing body has been the supreme ruling council of Jehovah's Witnesses. But only a handful of its members probably exercise much real authority over the Watch Tower organization or the larger Witness community. The fact is that all of the present members were selected largely for their loyalty to the society rather than for any outstanding spiritual or intellectual abilities. Because they view the Witness organization as something much above and beyond themselves in practically the same way that Roman Catholics view their church, they are as much the servants of Witness tradition as its masters. Significantly, they refer to the organization as their 'mother.'[13] So, because of their own quite conservative mind sets and the bureaucratic routinization of Witness governance since the days of Judge Rutherford, they are incapable of making significant doctrinal or administrative changes which might solve many of the problems facing the Witness community today.

Between 1971 and 1974 the governing body was composed of eleven men. They were Frederick Franz, Raymond Franz, George Gangas, Leo Greenlees, John Groh, Milton Henschel, William Jackson, Nathan Knorr, Grant Suiter, Lyman Swingle, and Thomas Sullivan (who died on 30 July 1974 at the age of eighty-six).[14] Of these, seven were members of the board of directors of the Watch

Tower Society of Pennsylvania.[15] Knorr, Franz, Groh, Suiter, and Greenlees were also directors of the Watchtower Society of New York.[16] Consequently, the new governing body was little more than an expanded Watch Tower board of directors which had been promoted in name if not in fact.

In November 1974, the governing body was enlarged to eighteen members.[17] For the first time a majority were not Watch Tower directors. The new members – Lloyd Barry, John Booth, Ewart Chitty, Charles Fekel, Theodore Jaracz, Karl Klein, Albert Schroeder, and Daniel Sydlik – were committed organization men who had served as missionaries, circuit overseers, in the society's Brooklyn or branch Bethel homes, or on the society's kingdom farms. Since then three others – Carey Barber, John Barr, and Martin Poetzinger – have been appointed to the Witnesses' supreme council.[18] But the governing body is now composed of only fourteen members; five have died since January 1975,[19] Ewart Chitty has resigned under pressure,[20] and Raymond Franz has been forced out.

Besides their organizational loyalty, a few things stand out about the governing body. Most noticeably, they are *old men*. True, a few may be in their late fifties or sixties, but a majority are over seventy years of age. Hence some of them manifest a lack of vitality. However, it is not so much age which is the greatest liability from which they tend to suffer. It is, rather, that most of them have had little experience outside the Witness community in years, that few have much formal education or business experience, and that they have insulated themselves from intellectual stimuli for so long that they often have rather naive and jaundiced views of the rest of the world.

Of those who have served on the governing body since 1971, only a very few have had any university education. Watch Tower President Frederick Franz took almost three years of pre-seminary training at the University of Cincinnati, and both Albert Schroeder and Lloyd Barry are said to be university educated as well. But apart from these few, the rest of the governing body are notable for their lack of higher education, although some have had the society's intensive five-month missionary training course at Gilead.[21]

Besides Raymond Franz, whose primary experience was as a Watch Tower missionary in Puerto Rico and the Dominican Republic, a few other members of the governing body have been described as kindly and generally open-minded by Bethel workers. These have included Daniel Sydlik, Lyman Swingle, and John Booth, a former overseer of one of the society's kingdom farms for a number of years.

When the dramatic power shift described above occurred in late 1975, many Witnesses within Bethel believed for a time that the governing body would set the Witness community on a more open, less dogmatic course. Close friends of Daniel Sydlik assert that he went so far as to paraphrase Pope John XXIII in suggesting that it was time to open Watch Tower windows to let in a little fresh air.[22] According to Raymond Franz, he and Lyman Swingle pressed their colleagues on the governing body to abandon or at least examine the Society's Gentile Times chronology and its teachings concerning 1914.[23] But anyone who wanted a more open policy soon discovered that such was impossible: a majority of the governing body came within two years to favour, if anything, a return to the most rigid doctrines and practices of the Rutherford and Knorr eras.

What happened, evidently, was that the suggested reforms of those on the governing body who wanted to develop a new course frightened their more conservative confreres. The latter no doubt recognized that abandonment of the society's Gentile Times chronology would undercut the whole basis for the spiritual authority of the governing body.[24] If Christ had not come invisibly in 1914 and had not appointed the 'faithful and discreet slave' class as overseer of all his spiritual belongings in 1919, in what way could the governing body legitimately claim to govern Jehovah's Witnesses? Furthermore, a denial of the chronology would negate the significance of the preaching work – the very lynchpin and *raison d'être* of the Witness community.

Although deeply troubled by concern about the fact that Witnesses in general, Gilead students, and branch officials were questioning the society's 1914 doctrine,[25] Watch Tower traditionalists on the governing body were able to check any move to abandon it or make many other significant changes for that matter. From the time of its inception to April 1975, all decisions of the governing body had had to be unanimous. After that time, two-thirds of the full membership had to agree. So even when a majority favoured some of the proposals put forward by those who wanted a softening or change of policy, a minority could and usually did veto them.[26]

Then, in February 1980, three members of the governing body's Chairman's Committee, Albert Schroeder, Karl Klein, and Grant Suiter, brought forth a truly amazing proposal. Because the society had long taught that the generation which had witnessed the outbreak of the First World War in 1914 would live to see the end of this 'system of things,' and because that generation is fast dying off, they recommended that the governing body teach a new doctrine which would *adjust* but not invalidate Watch Tower chronology. Accordingly, they suggested that the society should teach that the generation which would see the end would not be that of 1914 but, rather, that which had only been old enough to have witnessed the beginning of the space age with the launching of the Russian space satellite Sputnik in 1957. While the governing body as a whole rejected this rather fantastic idea, the very fact that it was made shows that the members of the Chairman's Committee were more interested in shoring up the society's eschatology with Rutherford-like changes than in abandoning it.[27]

There were other factors which were causing the governing body to oppose changes, too. The failure of 1975 and the resultant defection of hundreds of thousands of Witnesses caused deep concern among them.[28] Second, they were gradually becoming more and more aware of the spirit of dissent which was coming to the fore among Jehovah's Witnesses in general and at Bethel in particular. By the summer of 1979 not only were many Witnesses at Watch Tower headquarters questioning the society's chronology, but some were coming to deny the doctrine that only a literal 144,000 would ultimately reign with Christ in heaven. And a great many, both inside and outside Bethel, were expressing serious doubts over the idea that Jesus was not 'the mediator' for the 'great crowd' or 'other sheep' class. Most serious, however, was the fact that the reactionary policies of the governing body from the summer of 1978 onward were causing a spirit of extreme bitterness among many Bethel workers high and low and a good deal of rather open rebellious talk.[29] Consequently, when some of this talk was reported to members of the governing body, they reacted with vehemence. On 14 November 1979 Watch Tower secretary-treasurer Grant Suiter stated in a full meeting of the body that there was considerable 'gossip' among Bethel workers, that there were reports that some of the Writing Committee and governing body had made public comments not in harmony with the society's teachings – an obvious reference to Raymond Franz and perhaps Lyman Swingle – and that some were saying that 'when King Saul [Frederick Franz?] dies then things will change.'[30]

By that time more and more members of the governing body were reacting against the ideas put forth by men such as Raymond Franz, Daniel Sydlik, Lyman Swingle, and perhaps one or two others. As Raymond Franz says concerning voting patterns in the body; 'If, for example, the hands of Milton Henschel, Fred Franz, Ted Jaracz and Lloyd Barry went up, one could *generally* be sure that the hands of Carey Barber, Martin Poetzinger, William Jackson, George Gangas, Grant Suiter and Jack Barr would go up as well. If the hands of the former stayed down, the latter would generally stay down also. Some others would *likely* vote with these but their vote was not as predictable. With rare exceptions, this pattern prevailed.'[31] Then, too, Raymond Franz and Edward Dunlap were becoming a focus of resentment for the majority of the body.[32]

Since Raymond Franz's dismissal from the governing body, the other members who also apparently favoured at least some major changes in Watch Tower policy have quite evidently acceded to the desires of the majority. While some of these latter such as Henschel, Barry, and Jaracz, the three whom Raymond Franz believes to be the most influential, may be able 'apparatchiks' or bureaucrats, not even that can be said for most of the rest.

Governing Body Committees

In December 1975, in order to take the administration of the world-wide affairs of
Jehovah's Witnesses out of the hands of Nathan Knorr,[33] the governing body
established a committee system which bears a remarkable resemblance to the
Papal Curia. Like the Vatican's 'congregations,' the committees are responsible
for various administrative functions within the Witness community. The *1977
Yearbook* describes their committees and their functions as follows:

CHAIRMAN'S COMMITTEE: This committee is composed of the current chairman of the
Governing Body, the previous chairman and the one next in line to be chairman. The current
chairman serves as coordinator and expedites matters for the Governing Body. Reports on
major emergencies, disasters or campaigns of persecution or any other matters affecting
Jehovah's Witnesses come immediately to the Chairman's Committee so that they can be
taken up with the Governing Body.

WRITING COMMITTEE: This committee supervises the putting of spiritual food into written
and recorded form of publication and distribution to Jehovah's Witnesses and the public in
general. Since it deals with the publications, it also supervises translation work done
throughout the earth.

TEACHING COMMITTEE: This committee's responsibility is to supervise school and
assemblies for the spiritual education of Jehovah's people, also Bethel family instruction.
Additionally, it supervises outlining the material to be used in teaching and takes oversight
of radio and television programs and assembly programs.

SERVICE COMMITTEE: This committee supervises all areas of the evangelizing work, and
has the responsibility of taking the lead in further developing these. The committee is
interested in the activities of the congregations, circuit and district overseers, missionaries,
Branch Committees and the periodic visits of the zone overseers.

PUBLISHING COMMITTEE: This committee supervises the printing, publishing and
shipping of literature throughout the world. Therefore, it has responsibility for oversight of
factories and properties owned and operated by the various corporations used by Jehovah's
Witnesses, as well as financial operations, legal and business matters connected with
publishing the good news of the Kingdom in all the earth.

PERSONNEL COMMITTEE: This committee has oversight of the arrangements made for
personal and spiritual assistance to members of the Bethel families, and it is responsible for
inviting new members to serve in the Bethel and Farm families around the world.[34]

How this structure has worked from a purely administrative standpoint is
difficult to say. But there can be little doubt that in so far as the development of
innovative organizational procedures or new doctrinal stances is concerned, it has
had a negative effect. The committee structure has become just another

bureaucratic level between the general Witness community and the governing body. Committees are incapable of making any significant independent decisions but can and often do slow down or inhibit decision-making by the governing body simply by not reporting certain matters to that council.[35]

What this often means today, then, is that many functions of the governing body are actually carried out on the basis of long-standing policies by lower echelons of the Watch Tower bureaucracy. This is particularly true of the Service Department which has long acted very much as did the Catholic Church's Congregation of the Inquisition before the reforms of the Second Vatican Ecumenical Council. The Service Department Committee has for decades handled all correspondence with Jehovah's Witnesses on moral and doctrinal matters, and it has also been the primary instrument through which 'judicial' and quasi-judicial actions have been taken. Significantly, many of the 'judicial hearings' carried out against the so-called 'apostates' at Bethel in the spring of 1980 were conducted through the Service Department Committee, and since then many of the directions to root out 'apostates' throughout the broader Witness community have come from that body.[36]

The World-Wide Headquarters

Watch Tower publishing houses or 'factories' in Brooklyn Heights are an impressive sight from across the East River in Manhattan. In fact, they are so noticeable that for years Manhattanites, working in New York's financial community, would even use changing slogans flashed on the main factory's neon sign as business omens. But when one visits the grand complex of buildings which serve as world headquarters for Jehovah's Witnesses, he is generally even more impressed. Besides two huge factory buildings, the complex includes several residence buildings for the many hundreds of workers who produce literature for Witnesses throughout much of the world and, additionally, for the administrative, clerical, and support staffs which are necessary for the governance of a highly centralized religious movement.

If the factory buildings and the residences – collectively called Bethel – are impressive, they are also austere. The factories, huge printeries, could be nothing more than giant, secular plants. Yet when one visits Watch Tower headquarters, he will be encouraged to 'tour the [main] factory' to see the huge presses pouring out 'spiritual food' for millions of Jehovah's Witnesses and prospective converts. Curiously, however, unless he is invited to stay at Bethel as a guest of a member of the 'family' he will find access to the Bethel and Gilead libraries, two very fine collections, restricted. As far as the residence buildings themselves are concerned, they bear that mark of American puritanical pragmatism which is so characteristic of Jehovah's Witnesses. There is nothing particularly attractive about any of them, and they also seem in a way to indicate that to Jehovah's Witness leaders a thing of beauty is more a snare and a delusion than a joy forever.

The rooms which serve as home for the officials and workers at Bethel are quite adequate but plain, although members of the governing body and older and more senior workers do have more attractive accommodations. It should be stated that no one lives in anything like sumptuous luxury, however, although both Rutherford and Knorr were criticized both covertly and overtly for providing attractive, comfortable apartments for themselves while ordinary Bethel and Kingdom Farm workers were sometimes forced to live in rooms which were unbearably hot or improperly heated.

Life at Bethel is highly regulated. A worker awakes at 6:30 am to the sound of bells, and from then on until the supper hour his working schedule will be determined by bells. He is summoned to meals by bells and, after prayer, characteristically begins to eat with gusto. When an outsider watches the Bethel family 'dine,' he may have the feeling that he is observing an old-fashioned American farm crew devouring their food to get back to harvesting rather than a community of Christian workers at the 'House of God.' For the time allotted to meals is very short by most standards, and if one does not eat his food quickly he will be interrupted by a prayer which formally concludes every breakfast, lunch, and supper. But then, Witness Bethel workers are not expected to waste time, even over the nutritious but rather plain food produced on Watch Tower farms and prepared in Bethel kitchens.

Meals serve another purpose. They are the only times during the day when the Bethel family gathers together in communal dining halls. It is at mealtimes that a daily Scripture text is read from the *Yearbook*, comments can be made, messages can be relayed to the family, and rare 'trimmings' or tongue lashings can be given to those who have committed some infraction or have fallen out of favour with members of the governing body. However, meals are seldom used today as occasions for giving 'trimmings' in the way that they were under Rutherford and Knorr.

Outward regimentation so evident from bell-ringing and at mealtimes only represents a small part of the control that is maintained over Bethel workers. As described by many who have lived and worked there, the headquarters staff is a highly disciplined community. Bethelites are assigned to local congregations in the New York City area to give them spiritual support. They must, therefore, spend much time travelling to and from meetings, are encouraged to engage in proselytizing activities in the evenings and on weekends with their congregations, and are asked to prepare themselves to participate in or conduct various congregational meetings. On Monday evenings, they are requested to attend a

Bethel 'family study.' Thus, if they fulfill these obligations, they have little time for anything but 'service to Jehovah and his organization.' It is true, though, that few can or do live up to this ideal schedule, even if they try.

When young Witness men come to Bethel as volunteer workers, they are instructed in the particularly strict set of rules regarding personal conduct. This is done in a series of eight lectures which in the past were popularly called 'new boy talks.' Therein they are told to keep their hair cut short and look properly groomed. For years only blacks and Hispanic Americans were allowed to wear mustaches, and while this is no longer the case, even today no one is permitted to wear a beard. Dress codes are strict as well. Although Bethelites often do very dirty work, they must not appear too casually dressed outside the factory buildings. In the past, even while going to and from the recreation area, they were strictly instructed not to wear bluejeans or tennis shoes. Significantly too, particularly when Nathan Knorr was alive, 'new boys' were warned against the evils of fornication and, above all, masturbation. Although few Witness leaders have as much concern over the matter as did Knorr, the sinfulness of masturbation still remains a subject which is brought to the attention of incoming Bethelites.

Women Bethel workers receive very similar discipline. As Barbara Grizzuti Harrison shows in her autobiographical account of life at Watch Tower headquarters, *Visions of Glory,* this has been the case for many years. In the main, though, they probably chafe under it less than do the men. Generally, they are employed in housekeeping and clerical work and accept their roles with equanimity. Unlike Maria Russell, they have no illusions; they know full well that they will never be given any positions of administrative authority and do not believe that they should be.

In the past, single women workers were in some demand as prospective marriage mates. During the Rutherford years marriage was discouraged at Bethel as it was everywhere else among Jehovah's Witnesses. After Knorr was married, he evidently felt it reasonable to allow other Bethel workers the freedom to marry also. Still, until 1976, a Bethelite could not wed anyone except another Bethelite and, then, only if both had spent a good many years at the Brooklyn headquarters. Hence single women usually had their pick of husbands from within a rather large male community and were treated with respect. In spite of that, many preferred to remain single.

Since 1976, things have changed rather dramatically. In that year Bethel workers who had been in residence for a year or more were allowed to marry within the larger Witness community and bring their mates to Bethel to live and work. So today a very large proportion of women at Watch Tower headquarters is married.

Although most of the work done by women at Bethel tends to be rather humdrum, in some ways men have more difficulty. Under both Rutherford and

Knorr the practice was developed and institutionalized that new workers could initially be placed in occupations for which they had no training and often no aptitude. Men with few mechanical skills would sometimes be assigned to learn highly technical jobs in printing while others with good educations and writing ability might very well be given the task of mopping floors and cleaning toilets. This was done to teach humility and make them realize that whatever they accomplished was done with the 'help of Jehovah' rather then on the basis of their own talents. Whether the society's leaders knew they were emulating the Jesuits with this practice is difficult to say; probably they did not.

The turnover of Bethel workers is great. Up until the mid-1970s, when men and women entered Bethel they agreed to stay for at least four years. If they left earlier, except for health or serious family reasons, they were treated as spiritual failures and temporarily denied any privileges in the congregations with which they later associated. In spite of this, many found institutional life at Brooklyn very difficult. According to public statements made by senior Watch Tower officials, the average staying time was less than two years per worker, not counting the fairly large, permanent core staff. Because this resulted in so many leaving with a spirit of bitterness, and often because morale was bad among those who stayed to complete their stint of service, the society decided to change the system.

Since 1976 workers coming to Bethel have had to agree to stay for only *one* year which is, essentially, probationary. Thereafter, if they maintain a good record, they may stay or go as they please. From various reports, few remain much longer than they did in the past,[37] but their leaving probably occurs with less resentment than it formerly did. Nevertheless, it is still evident that few can tolerate the highly regimented lifestyle for long. So, after a year or two at the society's headquarters, they generally leave to marry, settle down, and become integrated into the larger Witness community.

In spite of everything, Bethel workers undoubtedly accept the regimen of life at Brooklyn with less strain that the average non-Witness would. Many are the children of deeply devout families or are zealous converts. Also, many were pioneers before coming to headquarters. They are both ideologically committed and highly disciplined individuals who have been taught to accept authority, usually without question. But there is another equally important reason why the great majority conform to what their overseers demand. Jerry Bergman states quite correctly, at least for a large proportion of the Witness community: 'To Jehovah's Witnesses today the word Bethel means the headquarters of the organization – the place where their governing body is located and from which they believe God is directing them. Bethel is felt to be a holy place which imparts holiness both to its current and former residents. Even if a Witness swept Bethel's floors ten years ago, he is still a Bethelite and is seen as somehow more righteous, holy and knowledgeable of God's laws [than another Witness], no matter how many years of experience a non-Bethelite may have had as a Jehovah's Witness.'[38] So having successfully served a term at Bethel gives one a great deal of prestige with Witness friends, families, and most importantly, with the society and circuit overseers.

This does not mean that there are no serious problems brought about by the severity of lifestyle; there are. Although outright sexual promiscuity has not been common, it certainly is far from unknown. Prior to 1976, there were few cases of fornication or adultery, but since that date, with more women at Bethel, both have occurred more frequently. Heterosexual offences have never been the serious problem that homosexual ones have been, though. Over the years there have been a number of notorious cases of homosexuality caused, probably, by the society's long-standing near prohibition of the marriage of Bethelites and, also paradoxically, by the fact that Watch Tower officials, particularly Nathan Knorr, often preached about the evils of 'men lying with men.' In fact, Knorr, who seems to have had a fixation on sexual sins, kept the matters of homosexuality and masturbation so constantly before workers at the Watch Tower headquarters that one is forced to wonder if he did not have homosexual tendencies himself. On one occasion in the 1970s, when a male worker was disfellowshipped and expelled from Bethel for pederasty, the society's third president described his 'seductions' in such graphic terms at the Bethel meal table that many present were revolted.[39]

More serious is the constant use of alcohol. Pastor Russell, a man with few appetites, was both a vegetarian and a teetotaller. Judge Rutherford was neither and, as shown earlier, liked to drink. He regarded prohibition in the United States as a plot of both the Devil and the clergy and condemned it publicly.[40] Hence, after 1929,when he branded civil governments as having no authority from God, high Watch Tower officials at Brooklyn would often have officials at the society's Canadian branch headquarters at Toronto smuggle liquor across the border to them.[41] Drinking, then, almost became part of a cult of *machismo* into which new workers were usually quickly inducted. Old Bible Students such as Clayton Woodworth[42] and Olin Moyle[43] objected, and Nathan Knorr refused to go along with rum-running from Canada.[44] But the judge was not to be crossed in this matter any more than in any other.

Since Rutherford's death, drinking has continued to be common at Bethel and Watch Tower officials who can afford to do so will have cabinets well stocked with expensive liquors. Even the business-like, no-nonsense Nathan Knorr is still renowned among Bethelites, Watch Tower missionaries, and former personal friends for the twenty-year-old Bell Scotch whiskey which he would serve to favoured guests. The use of alcohol therefore holds great social value at Bethel and many workers, including high Watch Tower officials, drink regularly on a social basis. Also, it is well known that several prominent Bethelites, including the wife of a member of the governing body and the wife of a senior member of the society's Service Committee, have had problems with alcoholism.

Interestingly, *The Watchtower* has recently admitted the problem that many Jehovah's Witnesses have with the over-use of alcohol. It has threatened serious action against elders who drink more than 'a glass or two of wine' at a time. But, curiously, it still takes a less severe approach towards the excessive drinking of alcohol than to the use of tobacco;[45] and in its expressed concerns about drunkenness, never once does it admit that many Jehovah's Witnesses at the 'House of God' at Brooklyn appear to drink about as much if not more than other North American Witnesses.

Institutional strictness and poverty cause stress in other ways as well. Sometimes workers become disgruntled over the rules by which they must live and the lack of emotional warmth among members of the Bethel family. Those who speak out or show their feelings are frequently called 'BAs,' or workers with bad attitudes. Such ones must be careful in expressing themselves, however, lest they be reported to their superiors by extreme Watch Tower loyalists. These latter have been dubbed 'Bethel jacks' – a term, which like the sobriquet 'Jack Mormons,' carries an implicit note of contempt towards them. But whether regarded negatively or not, they serve a very important function in keeping malcontents or possible malcontents in line.

Certain workers are very short of money since they are paid only a pittance by the society.[46] However, some of their fellows state openly that they regularly receive a good deal of support from their families. As is well known, members of the governing body and other high officials are often given sizeable gifts when they travel and speak to the larger Witness community. Thus, there are significant income differences at Bethel. The rooms of poorer workers are often spartan in their furnishings with no air-conditioning units. Their more affluent brethren live in greater luxury and almost always have the air-conditioning, so important in hot New York summers.

Differences in accommodation cause some resentment. But more important is the fact that poorer workers have little money to spend on themselves or on any form of recreation. Thus a few have taken up what is called 'G-jobbing,' that is, working at some job outside Bethel in the evenings or at nights to make a few dollars for themselves. The society is not pleased with G-jobbers, though; in the past they were reprimanded seriously if discovered, and in late years the practice has been held to be a ground for dismissal from Bethel. Nevertheless, Bethelites report that some of it still persists.

None of the factors just described are the most stressful aspect of life at Bethel; institutional politics is. The climate of opinion described so vividly by William Schnell as a 'spy system'[47] is, according to Randall Watters,[48] very much alive today. As Raymond Franz and a great many others have discovered, anything perceived as dissent or disloyalty can bring the most severe repercussions. Equally significantly, there is a good deal of petty politics and personal rivalry among high Watch Tower officials and their wives. Sometimes jealousies and rivalries exist over small things such as who gets what room or apartment. In fact, there is much of the unhealthy personal rivalry at Watch Tower headquarters, and with it the animosity, that one might expect in any such authoritarian, quasi-monastic, bureaucratic atmosphere. Nevertheless, from the standpoint of the governing body of Jehovah's Witnesses, Bethel serves its purpose and does so well. It produces literature and aids the governing body in accomplishing its goals. Members of the governing body no doubt regard the stresses, strains, and politics discussed above as incidental to their major work of preaching the good news of Christ's kingdom. In spite of everything, most Bethelites no doubt agree.

The Legal Corporations

The legal entities through which the governing body carries on all its activities are the corporate societies of which the most important is the Watch Tower Bible and Tract Society of Pennsylvania. During Russell's day that body was simply a business corporation for carrying on publishing and evangelizing activities, but under Rutherford it became the legal agency by which Jehovah's Witnesses were governed. Its board of directors none the less continued to be subjected to periodic re-election by corporate shareholders whose voting shares were based on monetary contributions to the society. Knorr changed all that, however, by having the society's charter amended in major ways two years after becoming president.

Under that 1944 arrangement, membership in the society is to consist of no fewer than three hundred members and no more than five hundred, who according to the charter, are to be 'mature, active and faithful witnesses of Jehovah devoting full time to performance of one or more of its chartered purposes ..., or such men who are devoting part time as active presiding ministers or servants of Jehovah's witnesses.' Futhermore, these members all of whom are to be men, are to be chosen by the board of directors by majority vote. As was the case during the Rutherford era, there are to be seven directors on the board who are to be elected to three-year terms of office by the general membership.[49] Since 1944, general members have been most co-operative in electing or re-electing the directors as the directors have suggested. In fact, there is no case in which such elections have been anything but a rubber-stamping of the board's will. Commenting on the 1944 changes, Joseph Zygmunt remarks:

One of the immediate effects of these amendments was to reduce the membership of the Pennsylvania corporation from 4,428 to 438 ... A more important consequence was the reconstitution of the corporation's membership in a fashion that more closely reflected the operational structure of the movement at large without appreciable sacrifice of centralized authority. Another interesting feature of this reorganization was the manner in which it provided representation from the two symbolic classes of general group membership which had emerged by the middle thirties, viz., members of the 'anointed remnant' category and those in the 'Jonadab' or 'Great Multitude' [great crowd] category ... In 1945, the Pennsylvania corporation's membership included 332 of the former and 106 of the latter.[50]

Only two years after the charter was changed, it was decided that while persons whose hope was an earthly salvation could be members of the society, only members of the anointed remnant should serve on the board of directors. Interestingly, at the time the society taught that the governing body of Jehovah's Witnesses was Jehovah God, Christ Jesus and the 144,000 members of the church. Thus it was held that the administration of the earthly portion of the Theocracy ought to be entirely in the hands of members of the remnant of the church on earth, at least so long as possible. So, in effect, what was being said was that the *real* governing body *in practical rather than theoretical terms* was the board of directors.[51] Of course an important change was made in 1971 with the creation of the present governing body. As Joseph Zygmunt says: 'It soon became clear that this "Governing Body" no longer referred to the spiritual agency from which organizational authority derived, but rather to a group of men, all of the "anointed" class who occupied a special niche at the apex of the organizational hierarchy.'[52] Yet, while the society has tried to differentiate the governing body, 'both symbolically and structurally,' from the board since then, the actual separateness of the two has been 'far more "theoretical" than actual.'[53] Even today, because the governing body has no legal corporate existence, it must continue to operate through the society and its board of directors.

Next to the Pennsylvania corporation, the Watchtower Bible and Tract Society of New York, Incorporated, is the most important incorporated body of Jehovah's Witnesses. Although it is subservient to the Pennsylvania corporation and receives its funds from that society, it is the body which is the legal owner of the vast New York properties and directs the printing and publishing activities of Jehovah's Witnesses both in America and abroad.

In other lands it has sometimes been necessary or advisable to incorporate other organizations under the laws of those countries. Although all such entities are nothing but legal representatives of the American corporations, they do serve some practical purposes. The most venerable and important of such societies are the British International Bible Students Association and the International Bible

Students Association of Canada. Yet neither of these is as important from a legal standpoint as the Mexican corporation, *La Torre del Vigía de México,* which is registered as a cultural and educational organization rather than as a religious society for purposes described earlier.

Watch Tower Wealth

The governing body and the Watch Tower Society refuse to reveal publicly the full extent and nature of their resources. But there should be no assumption that in comparison with other religious organizations the society or its subsidiaries are very wealthy. Its monies and property are used almost entirely to promote evangelism, and neither the society nor Jehovah's Witnesses has established vast social-welfare or educational agencies which could become important financial empires in themselves. James Beckford has noted both these points. He shows that 'the Society seems to have no interest in amassing either fixed or movable assets in themselves but only insofar as they facilitate evangelism,' and 'most remarkably, the Society has resisted the pressures towards a proliferation of leisure and welfare agencies which were felt by most British and American religious groups in the twentieth century.' As a result, 'it has avoided the fragmentation of its followers into "endless class-specific, age-specific and sex-specific 'targets."'[54]

The physical properties now owned by the various Witness corporations are not particularly extensive. They include Bethel homes at Brooklyn and Watch Tower branches, large printing plants in New York State and at major branches, and kingdom farms in New York and New Jersey which produce food for volunteer Witnesses working at the Brooklyn Bethel, printeries, and literature depots. In the past, the various corporations also owned radio stations in the United States and Canada plus a campus in northwestern New York on which the missionary college of Gilead was located. Over the years all these properties have been sold, however, and Gilead is now located at the Brooklyn headquarters.

Where, then, does the society obtain the sums of money which it must have to operate? Remarkably, unlike many American religions such as the Mormons, Seventh-Day Adventists, and World-Wide Church of God, it has never levied tithes upon the faithful. Neither has it forced any direct contributions from Witness congregations. Therefore, most individual Jehovah's Witnesses take pride in believing that their organization 'is not just another money-grabbing religion.' But they are really not so free from monetary exactions as they would like to believe.

In the first place, the society certainly does make money on the sale of literature which must be paid for by individual Witnesses whether it is placed with the general public for fixed contributions or not. True, the society allows pioneer evangelists to obtain such literature at greatly reduced prices, but even then it probably does not do so at a loss. After all, while the Bibles, bound books, and booklets are much less expensive than similar publications produced by other publishing companies, the society's production costs are so low that it can still make a significant profit on them.

The sale of literature is only one source of Watch Tower income. The society receives numerous direct contributions, money left in wills, and regular contributions from circuit, district, and other conventions. In the case of the latter, seldom do conventions in North America and other industrialized Western nations fail to send a certain amount of money to the society after the assemblies themselves have been paid for. Besides contributions gathered from contribution boxes which are displayed prominently in the hallways of the convention buildings, convention overseers regularly see to it that there is a sizeable profit from the sale of cafeteria meals at most assemblies. While such meals are inexpensive by general standards, much of the food that is sold is often contributed, and meals are prepared entirely by volunteer labour. Hence, it is usually quite easy to make money for the society on convention meals and snacks sold at various snackbars or lunchstands which run almost constantly between sessions at every convention. Since assemblies are such a regular feature of Witness life, the society no doubt makes a significant income from them.

Finally, the society has regularly invested money in stocks for some years. In Rutherford's day stock markets were regarded negatively as part and parcel of greedy, industrial capitalism or big business. But since the judge's death his successors have become far more sympathetic to capitalism and see no reason why they should not invest savings in stock markets. Yet because most ordinary Witnesses still regard the stock markets as part of this 'doomed old world,' the society is very careful not to let the faithful know much about such financial activities. Only under sharp questioning from a few of their concerned brethren have Witness officials occasionally done so. It is easy to tell that this is happening, though, from statements in the society's literature which tactfully suggest that investing in stocks is perfectly moral[55] and by the society's angry retorts when an individual Witness asks directly whether playing the stock market is wrong or not.[56]

In late years, the Watch Tower Society has become more bold in asking for contributions than it was in the past, and it has increased the price of its literature somewhat faster than the general rate of inflation in North America. However, just how much it and its subsidiary organizations are worth today is impossible to say with any exactitude. It has never published any kind of financial statement, and there are no public tax records available from most countries which would indicate its wealth. Raymond Franz does state, though, that in 1979 it held some $332 million in monies and properties,[57] but undoubtedly its assets have grown since then. Perhaps the rumours circulating among ex-Bethel workers are not far wrong; they suggest that the society has some $500 million in tangible and intangible assets - not a great deal for a religious organization representing nearly 2.7 million active members.[58] But then it has virtually no ongoing charitable functions, and when money is needed for some special activity such as disaster relief for Witnesses in certain areas, the burden of providing it is generally assumed by the larger Witness community acting through local congregations.

Watch Tower Literature

Probably no religious organization has used or uses the printed page to such an extent as have Jehovah's Witnesses. In 1983 alone they distributed 53,517,808 Bibles, books, and booklets around the world, plus 460,072,255 copies of the *Awake!* and *Watchtower* magazines.[59] But why do they continue to do this? After all, as every Jehovah's Witness knows from making return visits to householders who have accepted the society's literature at their doors, much of this vast quantity of publications is never read by anyone. The answer, in part, seems to be that in spite of a good deal of evidence to the contrary,[60] Watch Tower leaders continue to believe that it is an effective means of spreading their message. Equally significant, however, is the fact that the literature is a major source of income for the society, it is considered most important in the door-to-door preaching work, and it is the basic means of inculcating ideas into the heads and hearts of ordinary Jehovah's Witnesses.

On this last point, former Witness elder David Reed has noted that each year every Jehovah's Witness is expected to read more than 3,000 pages of the society's publications according to its suggested program for personal study. In 1981 this would have included:

1,536 pages from *Awake!* and *The Watchtower*
+ 208 pages from *The Watchtower* for weekly studies
+   48 pages from *Our Kingdom Service*
+ 384 pages from a bound book for mid-week studies
+ 384 pages from the *1981 Yearbook*
+ 360 pages from material for the Theocratic Ministry School
+ 258 pages of Assembly releases

In all, according to Reed, Witnesses were expected to read 3,178 pages of Watch Tower literature but *only* 197 pages of the Bible during that year.[61]

The quality of this literature varies greatly. *The Watchtower* contains some reasonably well-written articles, especially when dealing with moral or social issues. Often, though, it doggedly repeats in tiresome fashion old doctrines or themes which, in one way or another, have been printed again and again since the First World War. Numerous Witnesses who have visited the Writing Department at Brooklyn report that very often they have seen *Watchtower* writers research material for new articles by going back through old volumes of the society's official journal published in the 1920s and 1930s.

Awake! is a rather low-grade version of *Reader's Digest.* Many of its articles are dated and pedestrian. It hammers hard on the themes of societal breakdown and moral decay. To a certain extent, it serves a useful function in alerting the broader Witness community to bans, persecution, and legal developments in many lands around the world, although this is less true today than it was in the past.

Our Kingdom Ministry or *Our Kingdom Service,* as it was known for a short time, is a dull, monthly bulletin which outlines weekly congregational service meetings and discusses various aspects of Witness proselytizing techniques with nearly constant repetitiveness. Yet it, like *The Watchtower,* is studied 'religiously' every week in local kingdom halls throughout the earth.

The various bound books which are released each year at district and international conventions are of greatly mixed quality. Some, like *Aid to Bible Understanding, 'All Scripture is Inspired of God and Beneficial,' Qualified to be Ministers,* and *Commentary on the Letter of James* are useful study aids. Basic study books such as *'Let God be True'* and *The Truth That Leads to Eternal Life* are simple and usually sensible presentations of important Witness doctrines. A few books on scientific themes such as *Did Man Get Here by Evolution or by Creation?* and *Is the Bible Really the Word of God?* are well written and provocative, although they quote from a veritable menagerie of sources. Books written for children and youth demonstrate that their authors frequently have little understanding of young minds and little, if any, experience in raising families. For example, while *From Paradise Lost to Paradise Regained* was published in 1958 as the society's first book for persons with little knowledge of Christianity, the uneducated, and *for children,* it has an almost horrifying fixation on the destruction of the wicked. Speaking of the Battle of Armageddon (pp. 208, 209) that publication proclaims:

Christ's angels will smite all the opposers of God's kingdom and his kingdom Witnesses with a terrible destruction. A flesh eating plague will destroy many. Says Jehovah: 'Their flesh shall rot while they are still on their feet, their eyes shall rot in their sockets, and their tongues shall rot in their mouths.' (Zekariah 14:12 R.S.) Eaten up will be the tongues of those who scoffed and laughed at the warning of Armageddon! Eaten up will be the eyes of those who refused to see the sign of 'the time of the end'! Eaten up will be the flesh of those who would not learn that the living God is named Jehovah! Eaten up while they stand on their feet.

Listening to the Great Teacher and *My Book of Bible Stories* are somewhat more sensitive to their audiences but tend to stress *obedience* at the expense of any independence of thought. So, too, does the very interesting little volume *Your Youth: Getting the Best Out of It*. Although it is bluntly frank about the subject of human sexuality, it is puritanical in the extreme as far as sexual behaviour and male-female relations are concerned.

Most books of a doctrinal nature are in one way or another allegorical interpretations of some biblical book of prophecy or are recapitulations of the old theme of the controversy between God and Satan from Adam until after the millennium. Often they are badly written, verbose, and fantastic in nature. For instance, *'Babylon the Great Has Fallen': God's Kingdom Rules,* published in 1963, is, as Alan Rogerson notes, a 'phantasmagoria of wild beasts' taken from Daniel and Revelation along with a detailed but often inaccurate Watch Tower history of the world since the seventh century BC. Interesting, too, is the way in which such books present some supposedly 'new truths' to the Witness community when these 'new truths' are often lifted, practically verbatim, from old *Watch Tower* articles of the 1920s.

District and Circuit Overseers

District overseers[62] are described by the society as 'visiting elders' whose primary duty is the visitation of the various circuits (about twenty in number) in their districts. Each district servant's duties include participation in the program at all circuit assemblies and working closely with the local circuit overseer during the week of the semi-annual circuit assembly. During the same week the district overseer organizes 'group witnessing' at one of the local congregations and spends some time in the public preaching work with local Witnesses. He will go from house to house and make return visits to interested persons. Or perhaps he will go with pioneers or congregation publishers to sit in on home studies with prospective converts. As the book *Organized to Accomplish Our Ministry* says: 'Primarily, during the week [of his visit to a congregation hosting a circuit convention] he will take the lead in group witnessing. He and his wife will have a full schedule for field service.'[63]

Circuit overseers[64] are appointed to oversee circuits of roughly twenty congregations. So they are able to spend most of two separate weeks with each congregation or isolated group every year. Additionally, they will see practically all active members of their circuits at the one district and two circuit conventions held every year.

For many years prior to 1972 no local congregational officer or 'servant' dared question the authority of the circuit overseer: he was to be obeyed in virtually everything he said. During the period of relative Watch Tower 'liberalism' from

1972 to 1977, he simply assisted the local elders in each congregation, and his powers were really more suasive than coercive. Beginning in the summer of 1977 the society gradually restored the old system through talks at district assemblies, articles in the organizational monthly bulletin, *The Kingdom Ministry,* and letters from the branches to local congregations. Today, circuit overseers are again as powerful as they were prior to 1972.

When a circuit overseer visits a congregation, on the Tuesday of the week of his visitation, he examines all local files to determine how well or how badly the congregation is doing. That night he will address it to encourage local publishers to join him during the next several days in the preaching work or field service. On another night he will meet with the congregational elders alone. At that latter meeting, one which is regarded as quite secret, he will discuss the health of the congregation, who should be recommended to the society for appointment as elders or ministerial servants, and who should be counselled, deleted, or disciplined. Then, on one evening of his visit, following another meeting, he will give a talk to the congregation after a brief quiz on the society's latest doctrines called 'New Things Learned.' During the talk he will discuss any points of commendation or censure that he feels like directing to the congregation, and occasionally he may administer a tongue-lashing to any whom he feels to be out of line. On Sunday, he will deliver a public talk and closing comments to the congregation.

The circuit overseer's powers arise largely from the fact that seldom if ever can one become an elder or ministerial servant without his approval. He also gives a written evaluation of each congregational officer to the society after every visit to each congregation. So he can destory the reputations of elders or ministerial servants with the branch or Brooklyn. Under extraordinary circumstances he can even bring about the dismissal of a whole body of elders. Finally, he has a small but significant system of patronage. He recommends the appointment of city overseers to act as anchormen for the society in each city. In certain political jurisdictions, he recommends that various elders be given the power to solemnize marriages. No one is given any part on circuit or district convention programs or position in convention administration without his approval. To rise within and beyond one's own congregation in authority, practically *every* Jehovah's Witness must work with and please his circuit overseer. His role is, then, virtually identical with that of an episcopal ordinary or bishop in the Roman Catholic church.

What sort of men are district and circuit overseers? Some few are formerly successful businessmen, professionals, farmers, or blue-collar workers who have given up their occupations to become pioneers and rise in the Watch Tower hierarchy. More often, they are persons who have never held any position of responsibility or regular occupation in secular society but, rather, have risen in the

Watch Tower ranks by beginning as young pioneers shortly after leaving school. Few, therefore, have much secular education above secondary- or high-school level, and their religious knowledge has been learned almost entirely in the kingdom halls which they have attended. In certain lands many are single, but in North America, Europe, and other industrialized countries, most are married. Some few have grown families, but younger couples in the district or circuit 'work' must forego having children or their positions. What this means is that practically all these men are zealous and are completely given to the society's policy of promoting the preaching work above everything. While some are gentle and kindly, district and circuit overseers very frequently manifest the authoritarian tendencies which characterize the Watch Tower hierarchy as a whole. Also, because of lack of both training and personal experience, they are very often insensitive to the needs and problems of families.

In underdeveloped countries the lot of district and circuit overseers can be hard. Like Bethel workers they receive only minimal support from the society and nothing like any kind of regular income from their districts or circuits. In travelling from place to place, sometimes under governmental bans, they must live by accepting the hospitality of local Witnesses. And that often means sleeping on hard beds and eating food of the poorest sort. Yet many carry on their work (with their wives if they are married) for many years out of a sense of real commitment.

In more affluent lands, district and circuit overseers are often just as zealous, but in such countries life is much easier. Although constant travelling from one congregation and one home to another must be somewhat difficult, the society's 'travelling representatives' and their wives are almost always treated with the greatest hospitality. In addition, they will frequently receive private gifts of a substantial nature from various Witnesses in the territories under their jurisdiction, and they will be provided with automobiles by their districts or circuits. Then, finally, after their visit to each congregation, they will receive a gift of money from the congregation itself. So while these men receive almost nothing in the way of regular salaries, and there are no income data on them, they live rather well.

The society has no system of pensions for 'retired' district or circuit overseers. Unlike elderly Bethelites who will at least receive board, room, and medical attention until they die, former district and circuit overseers are left entirely to their own devices or on the charity of local congregations. Frequently this leads to serious hardship for such persons, but the society obviously continues to believe that the New Order 'so near at hand' will take care of the needs of most. That it has failed to do so for many years seems to have little effect on the society's thinking.

Branches

The nearly one hundred branch offices of the Watch Tower Society around the world are small replicas of the Brooklyn Bethel, although many of them have only very small or no printeries. Prior to 1976 the branches were under the direct supervision of a branch overseer, more commonly called the branch servant. Such men were directly responsible to Brooklyn for virtually everything but were very powerful persons in so far as branch administration was concerned. Usually this meant they were in charge of all the affairs of Jehovah's Witnesses in an entire country or some major area thereof.[65] However, when the various committees of the governing body were set up, the governing body also made provision for branch committees which came into existence on 1 February 1976. Depending on the size of a branch, its committee was to have as few as three members or as many as seven. Although in the past the chairmanship of the committee was to rotate among all its members, *Organized to Accomplish Our Ministry*, the society's present manual for organization procedures, now makes no mention of such rotation.[66] The specific duties of such committees were 'to work with the governing body to administer the organizational arrangements, and to keep the governing body informed of the progress of the Kingdom work in the territory assigned to the branch.' According to that arrangement, branch committees were to have chairmen who served for a year at a time on a rotating basis.

To make certain that the branches never get out of line with policy established in Brooklyn, one member of the branch committee serves as a co-ordinator or liaison man with the governing body. In addition, the branches are often visited by zone overseers[67] who have regular oversight of them and by members of the governing body itself. Thus, there is little chance that branches may openly defy the centralized authority of the governing body except perhaps in lands where Jehovah's Witnesses are under ban by secular governments. Even in communist nations, the governing body is able to maintain a high degree of control over local branches and through them the various national Witness communities.

Like the Brooklyn Bethel, the branches operate under the regulations of *Branch Organization Procedure*, a formidable rulebook with 1,177 policies and regulations. They are often more relaxed, however, and more of a truly 'family' atmosphere may exist within them simply because they are far smaller with far fewer workers. Sometimes, too, as at Watch Tower House in London, the British branch, there is much more of a sedate air of gentility. Much of the sense of nearly constant bustle that pervades the American bethel is absent, and one may see an occasional old-fashioned Edwardian moustache of grand proportions on an older British Bethelite. Such, of course, would never be permitted at Brooklyn. Yet differences between Brooklyn and the branches are generally more cosmetic than real. In the final analysis the branch committees do what they are told. If they 'get out of line,' even in the most minute fashion, they will be disciplined severely. This is seldom observable to the outsider, though, who is generally treated with more warmth and attention than at the American headquarters.

In industralized lands, the branches are usually self-supporting and sometimes quite wealthy. For years the Canadian branch has had well over a $1.5 million in 'investment income'[68] alone. Yet many smaller branches are really dependent for monies on the American branch with its great resources, and for years even the important British branch could not support itself without such help.[69] This fact naturally increases Brooklyn's control over many of the branches.

Elders and Ministerial Servants

Each congregation is served by its body of elders.[70] As a collective unit this group has great powers. It is true that its members must abide by the instructions of the society and are under the supervision of the circuit overseer, but within the context of the authority delegated to them, the elders are almost totally responsible for the well-being of their home congregation. They are in charge of congregational meetings, selecting speakers and readers, directing the public preaching work, recommending the appointment of new elders and ministerial servants, creating local 'judicial committees' to act as church courts, taking rare actions to extend help to the needy, and overseeing the use of money and property. In effect, they maintain general responsibility for congregational governance. Although their authority is theoretically limited by the Scriptures and by the fact that they are to set meeting times in accord with the needs of their congregation as a whole, the only real checks on them are exerted by the circuit overseer and the society. For with respect to money matters and meeting times, their congregations will almost always follow their wishes.

Individuals become members of the body of elders through appointment by the society. If a male Witness is at least twenty-five years old, has been baptized for five years or more, has a record of zealous preaching, and supposedly fulfils the requirements laid out at 1 Timothy 3:1–6 and Titus 1:5–9, he will most likely be recommended to the society as a prospective elder by his local body of elders *if he has first served as a ministerial servant*. Once he has been appointed he will remain an elder on an equal basis with his fellows unless he moves to another congregation, is derelict in his duties, commits an act 'unbecoming to a Christian,' falls afoul of his fellow elders or the circuit overseer, or resigns. As an elder, overseer, and spiritual shepherd, he takes his place in the body of elders to help direct congregational affairs.

Individual elders have duties delegated to them by the society on the recommendation of the body of elders. There are six specific offices within the congregation, each held by an elder: presiding overseer, service overseer, *Watchtower* study overseer, theocratic ministry school overseer, congregational secretary, and book study overseer. Sometimes, in smaller congregations one or two men may assume all these offices, but in larger ones individuals will usually hold only one of the first five offices listed above and that of book study overseer.

The presiding elder has very important duties. He acts as chairman to the body of elders, assigns elders and ministerial servants parts in a weekly *service meeting,* and maintains general oversight of the ministerial servants. The service overseer directs evangelism, door-to-door preaching, the division of territory for such preaching, and the distribution of magazines and other Watch Tower publications. *The Watchtower* study conductor directs the weekly study of the *The Watchtower* magazine and, along with the theocratic ministry school overseer, is one of the two primary teachers within the congregation. The secretary is perhaps the busiest elder of all: he keeps virtually all files relating to evangelism, all accounts, and carries on most congregational correspondence with the society and its travelling representatives. Three elders – the presiding overseer, the secretary, and the field overseer – serve as a 'service committee' which handles forms, recommends publishers for the pioneer ministry, and carries on certain other occasional duties under the direction of the Watch Tower Society.

Each elder is usually expected to serve as a book-study overseer. In that capacity he meets with a small group of roughly fifteen to twenty publishers once a week, usually at a Witness home, to study an assigned Watch Tower publication. Then, on two or more occasions a week he or an assistant will meet with the group and lead them in 'field service' which usually means house-to-house preaching. He is therefore expected to 'take the lead in service.'

The average congregational elder is an extremely busy man. Not only does he spend five hours a week at congregational meetings, but he must devote much time to evangelizing and to personal study as well. He is often called on to visit the sick, conduct funeral and marriage services, and perform various duties at Witness conventions. If there are serious moral problems or divisions in the congregation, he may also spend many hours on an appointed judicial committee. Ordinary Witnesses will bring personal problems to him, and he may be called on at any time in case of emergencies. On top of this he is generally a man who will have to support and care for a family. He will usually hold a full-time secular job since he receives no money for any of his services. While some elders become slack in fulfilling their responsibilities, it is amazing that so few do. The average congregational body of elders is therefore composed of men who, although often quite ordinary in other respects, are notably zealous if not always particularly able.

Ministerial servants[71] must be zealous publishers and must fulfil the requirements stated at I Timothy 3:8–10. They are not required to teach within the congregation, and their duties are largely those of clerk and attendant. Able ministerial servants often do teach and conduct meetings, however, and if they continue to manifest zeal, demonstrate reasonable ability, and remain deferential, they are almost always eventually recommended as elders. There are quite a few who, because of a lack of natural gifts or the desire to 'reach out' for the position of elder, remain ministerial servants for many years.

Pioneers

Another very important group within many congregations and among Jehovah's Witnesses in general is the pioneers.[72] These evangelists, known until the 1930s as colporteurs, are usually among the most zealous of Witnesses. Among them are three sub-groups: auxiliary pioneers, regular pioneers, and special pioneers. Auxiliary pioneers are simply committed congregational publishers who agree to carry on public evangelism for a total of sixty hours in a certain month. Often elders, ministerial servants, housewives, or students will use a vacation period or some other time when they are not fully engaged in their ordinary affairs to auxiliary pioneer. After that month they will usually go back to their former status of publisher. Regular pioneers agree to evangelize for a total of ninety hours each month, generally under the superintendance of their home congregation, while they continue to be self-supporting. Special pioneers receive a small monthly stipend of twenty-five dollars or thereabouts to go into outlying areas to spread the gospel. Although they are sometimes sent to work with small congregations or isolated Witnesses, often they will be placed in communities where there are no Witnesses at all. In a real sense they truly become pioneers.

Although not necessarily congregational officers, the pioneers are extremely important. Not only do those men and women who work with local congregations contribute much to their growth, but in a way they serve as the right arm of the society. All circuit and district overseers, missionaries, and the great majority of senior overseers at the branches and Brooklyn Bethel served first as pioneers. So, too, have most of the workers at Watch Tower printing plants and kingdom farms. In addition, pioneers and those who act as circuit and district overseers are almost always given positions of prominence at conventions and on assembly programs. Seldom can one rise above the position of congregational elder, no matter how great his ability, unless he is a pioneer or, more rarely, a full-time Bethel worker. Undoubtedly this has a major effect on the nature and thinking of the society; it is a central organizational factor which has kept the society so consistent in stressing evangelism as the primary feature of Witness life.

ROUTES OF UPWARD
ORGANIZATIONAL MOBILITY
AMONG JEHOVAH'S WITNESSES

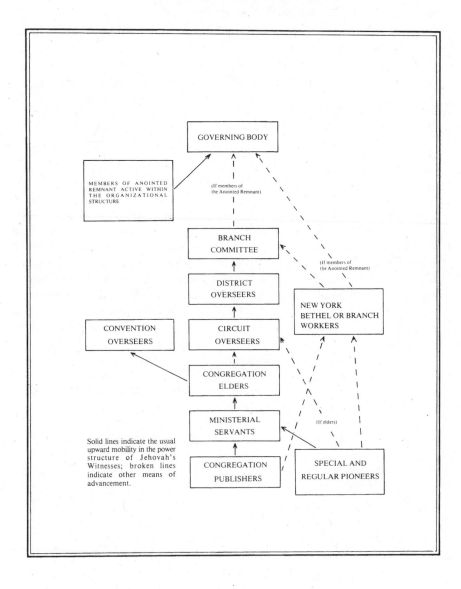

Congregational Meetings

Whether elders, ministerial servants, pioneers, or ordinary publishers, all Jehovah's Witnesses are continually fed a hardy diet of religious instruction.[73] They meet weekly – generally on Sundays – for two hours to hear a public talk or sermon delivered by an elder or, occasionally, by a ministerial servant, followed by a study of some doctrinal subject outlined in *The Watchtower*. On a weekday evening two other meetings are held. These are the theocratic ministry school and service meetings. The former is devoted to five short sermons or discussions by members of the congregation; and through the medium of the theocratic ministry school Witnesses of all ages and both sexes are taught how to use their Bibles, improve their reading and speaking, and to develop techniques of argumentation and evangelism. The service meeting is directed even more heavily towards teaching evangelism, but it may also include occasional information on Christian ethics and family life. The book study is the place where Witnesses engage in involved study of some doctrinal topic or theme. There they examine carefully, paragraph by paragraph, one of the society's publications.

Meetings are sometimes described by non-Witnesses as warm and friendly but rather stodgy. Characteristically, when the congregation meets as a whole, they will begin services with song and prayer. Then a discourse or study follows. Very important is the fact that during highly formalized and directed question-and-answer studies, all members of the congregation are encouraged to comment. Almost everyone has an opportunity to participate in the theocratic ministry school, and many are assigned portions of the service meeting program. Thus members of the congregation are made to feel a part of it; so Witness attendance at meetings is extremely high.

A May 1978 article in *McCall's* magazine, based on a survey of some 60,000 American women on the question of how religious beliefs affect their morality, noted: 'Denomination-by-denomination analysis reveals that those women who are most likely to attend church during the week as well as on weekends are Jehovah's Witnesses (91 percent), Mormons (52 percent) and Baptists (48 percent).'[74] Watch Tower Society statistics indicate that for the Witnesses this assessment is accurate, and not just for women.[75] Men, women, and children regularly attend most congregational meetings, and seldom will zealous publishers miss except for sickness or some other serious reason.

This fact is in some ways surprising in spite of the high level of congregational participation. Witness meetings are in no sense emotional activities with much praying, singing, and thunderous preaching. Rather, emphasis is placed on an informally programmed and styled 'reasonableness.' Often meetings in kingdom halls take on the atmosphere of a public-school class with the elders and ministerial servants acting as teachers. If these men are able, mildly charismatic, and warm, the meetings can become pleasant experiences during which the congregation may occasionally laugh or applaud. If the elders and ministerial servants lack imagination, meetings can and frequently do become dull affairs. Although this may affect attendance slightly, the average Witness is so disciplined and deeply devout that he will listen to uninspiring topics delivered in an uninspiring manner without murmuring, at least publicly.

Because much emphasis is placed on doctrine and a rationalistic (if not always rational) approach to it, there is a fear among many Witnesses of expressing emotion. They feel a deep sense of disdain for the type of worship that exists in Pentecostalism, for example, or the formalized liturgies of Anglicanism or Catholicism. As with old-fashioned Calvinists and Anabaptists, this has tended to make them book-oriented, with a knowledge of their faith that undoubtedly outstrips that of most members of other religions.[76] Still, it has to be recognized that as a result, Witnesses sacrifice much. As was pointed out in Chapter 5, no religious group in the twentieth century outside the Jews has had so many martyrs. Also, a few Jehovah's Witnesses have proved themselves to be able composers and musicians.[77] Yet in meetings one seldom hears of the more inspiring aspects of the history of the Bible Student–Witness community: and little stress is placed on musical expression or on the singing of 'kingdom songs.'

Evangelism

The main task to which every Jehovah's Witness is regularly directed is that of evangelism, something which grows out of the Witness movements' millenarian eschatology. If the end is soon to come upon this generation, Witnesses must warn their neighbours of the coming time of tribulation. They must 'exercise love' and 'be free from all blood guilt' – a term which means that they must not be responsible for the deaths of others either now or at Armageddon. Thus everyone is pressed to participate in the public preaching work which is held to be 'life saving.'

Witness evangelism takes many forms, but the most important is making house-to-house visits wherever possible. One day a week, usually Saturday in Christian lands, groups of publishers will engage in 'magazine work.' That means calling on households to offer the latest copies of *The Watchtower* and *Awake!* magazines. Customarily, publishers ask for a small contribution of thirty cents or its equivalent, but occasionally the magazines are given away. On other days attempts are made to spend more time preaching to people at their homes. If a Witness has experience in proselytizing, he meets the householder with a friendly greeting and then tries to direct him into a discussion of world conditions or some Bible topic. If the householder is courteous, the publisher will offer him Watch Tower literature.

Whenever someone shows interest, the Witness publisher will attempt to make a return visit with the hope that he may establish a so-called home Bible study. If he does, one of the society's publications such as *The Truth That Leads to Eternal Life* will serve as a textbook for a one-hour, weekly study. By that means it is hoped that the householder (and his or her family) will ultimately become Jehovah's Witnesses.

The Watch Tower Society feels that house-to-house preaching is the most effective means of evangelism, and it is true that many people have become Jehovah's Witnesses as a result of an initial knock on the door. Yet this method of prosyletizing is extremely inefficient as is demonstrated by the Society's own statistics. In 1983, for example, Jehovah's Witnesses world wide spent 436,720,991 hours in recorded preaching activities,[78] most of which were in door-to-door cold canvassing for prospective converts. But during that year there was an average yearly increase of only 159,008 publishers.[79] In other words it took 3,642.78 hours or the equivalent of nearly two normal working years to produce *each* new active Witness. And this is only part of the story. A great many persons – perhaps the majority around the world in recent years – have accepted baptism as a result of other types of contact. Many first learn of Witness teachings through relatives, schoolmates, workmates, and neighbours. Hence Witness growth probably owes more to 'informal witnessing' than to formal door-to-door evangelism.

James Beckford notes that in a large sample of British Witnesses he had studied, only 46 per cent had become converts through door-to-door preaching.[80] Quirinus J. Munters states that in the Netherlands 'more than 80 percent of Jehovah's Witnesses respondents had joined together with relatives or after relatives had done so.' He therefore reasons that 'the significance of door-to-door recruiting methods followed with zeal should not be overestimated.'[81] Bryan Wilson found that in Japan – where the number of pioneers is proportionately greater in terms of the Witness community than practically any country on earth – only 58.3 per cent had become converts through 'house calls.'[82] In North America in recent years probably far fewer have accepted baptism as a result of such activity. Several unpublished studies carried out by academics in the United States and Canada support that inference.[83]

Few Witnesses seem to have noted that door-to-door evangelism may also have a serious negative effect in alienating otherwise friendly persons who may come to look on Witness publishers as no more than peddlers of their religion. It should be stated, however that the society does not regard Witness preaching work as only directed towards making converts; it is also seen as a dividing and judgmental activity. If householders reject the message of Christ's kingdom preached by his Witnesses, they may be rejecting God's love and life itself. That is both their right and their responsibility. The society therefore feels that attempts should be made to contact *every individual personally* to the greatest extent possible.

Another form of evangelizing is 'street work.' Street work commonly means that individual Witnesses will stand on a busy corner unobtrusively offering *The Watchtower* and *Awake!* to passers-by. In decades past this was an important activity which gave the Witnesses a high public profile and excited persecution. Now, although some publishers continue to make many productive contacts in the street work, the majority do little more than stand as a silent, largely ignored testimony to their faith. In America Witnesses engaged in this form of preaching seldom encounter more hostility than does the Salvation Army. Wonder and irritation are now more frequently directed at groups like the Krishna Consciousness movement and the Moonies. Jehovah's Witnesses have become an accepted part of the social milieu and attract little attention. For that reason far less emphasis is put on street work, and many Witnesses never engage in it.

Jehovah's Witnesses do also use radio, television, and the newspapers rather indifferently to draw attention to their message. But since 1937, they have never purchased time or space from those media on any regular basis. Several years ago the Canadian branch of the Watch Tower Society began to develop a series of taped television programs to show on community cablevision channels throughout Canada which did not charge for program time. But this activity did not last long. In spite of some success in having programs aired, various former Bethelites state that Brooklyn ordered the Toronto branch to stop producing them since some of the more conservative members of the governing body felt that they might detract from the house-to-house preaching work.

The governing body has also taken a generally negative stance towards the production of movies which could be used to spread the Witness message. Although a few short film and slide-show programs have been developed by the Watch Tower Society within the last ten years or so, the governing body has rejected suggestions from Witnesses in California close to the secular movie industry to develop professional-quality short moving pictures on Witness teachings or on the Witness community. The governing body seems to feel that the production and showing of such movies might also take something away from the ordinary Witness's commitment to door-to-door proselytizing. So Brooklyn has recently refused to have much, if anything, to do with movie-making.

Because of large conventions, frequent persecution, the blood transfusion issue, and their severity towards anyone they consider to be a dissident within their ranks, Jehovah's Witnesses nevertheless receive some positive and much negative publicity through the public news media. Of course they are conscious of the importance of both the electronic news media and the press, and each circuit has its 'news' or 'public relations' overseer. Strangely, however, they seem to have little understanding of how to relate to newsmen and, consequently, have rather poor public relations.[84]

Formal Organizational Controls

Acting through the Watch Tower Society, the governing body demands almost absolute obedience from Jehovah's Witnesses. Ordinary Witnesses and even senior Watch Tower officials must not disagree with the society's policies or doctrines openly. Ex-Witness and former Bethelite William Cetnar makes the following observation: 'At headquarters the men of the Editorial Department often had differences of opinion. Each had to carefully "pad" his differences so as not to be considered a heretic. President Knorr made a significant and revealing statement in 1952 after some of the brothers in editorial had argued over a doctrinal matter. He stated, "Brothers, you can argue all you want about it, but when it gets off the sixth floor *it is the truth.*" What he was saying was that once it was in print (the presses were on the sixth floor), it is the truth and we had to stand unitedly by it.'[85]

Frederick Franz expressed the same view only two years later when he said regarding any Watch Tower teaching, 'If it is published it is accepted.'[86] More recently, *The Watchtower* has gone so far as to state:

The proper spirit after offering suggestions is to be content to leave the matter to the prayerful consideration of the mature brothers directing the work in Jehovah's organization. But if those making the suggestions are not content with that and continue to dispute the subject in the congregations with a view to getting others to support them, what then? That would create divisions, and could subvert the faith of some. So Paul counsels: 'Keep your eye on those who cause divisions and occasions for stumbling contrary to the teaching that you have learned, and avoid them.' Paul also counseled Titus to 'reprove those who contradict,' adding: 'It is necessary to shut the mouths of these, as these very men keep on subverting entire households by teaching things they ought not ... For this very cause keep on reproving them with severity.' – Romans 16:17, 18; Titus 1:9–13.[87]

To an amazing extent, in spite of a good deal of ongoing dissent over the years, the society has been able to exercise great control over the Witness community. How has it accomplished this? Primarily through two factors: the preaching work and the system of 'judicial committees.'

Not only is the preaching work doctrinally central to the Jehovah's Witnesses, it is organizationally central. For it is on the basis of individual commitment to that work that the society has created its hierarchy – its elite. As noted earlier, one can seldom rise significantly in position or prominence above the level of his own congregation unless he is a pioneer. Hence, the entire hierarchy or organizational elite of Jehovah's Witnesses is devoted to the preaching work as the primary aim of the Watch Tower leadership. Whether consciously or unconsciously, it knows full well that it owes its status and even its very existence to that work.

Local elders are not usually pioneers and have often been less than enthusiastic about pushing the preaching work. Thus it was that in the 1920s Judge Rutherford carried on a war with congregationally elected elders and ultimately succeeded in having their offices abolished. And in the 1970s, when history began to repeat itself in that many elders again began to question the doctrinal centrality of public proselytizing, the society found it necessary to force them into line by taking away what little independence they had. Consequently, elders must now support the preaching work fully or their days in positions of oversight (and often in the movement) are numbered.

Some elders find a variety of 'theocratic' activities to keep them from spending a great deal of their free time in the preaching work or at least in door-to-door proselytizing. Often they will create administrative duties, 'judicial' activities ('keeping the congregation clean!'), or secular concerns to keep from spending some portion of each of their weekends and holidays 'in the service.' They are pressed, none the less, to lead their Bible study groups in 'group witnessing' at certain specified times each week. So, in effect, the elders are forced to 'take the lead in service.' Too, unless they go from house to house with other publishers at least once a week – usually on a Saturday or Sunday in most western lands – they will be criticized by ordinary congregational publishers and may be counselled by fellow elders. More likely, if they malinger over a period of time, they will be reprimanded by the circuit overseer. If they do not 'improve' by his next visit, they may be removed from office.

Of course, elders are also required to promote tirelessly the public preaching work during all of the five official congregational meetings held each week. And this, it must be recognized, is an important fact not only for the congregation as a whole but for the elders personally. By encouraging others to engage in 'this life-saving work,' they are under great psychological and social pressure to practice what they preach from the kingdom hall platform. Then, also, they are constantly encouraged to praise pioneers and pioneering and to engage in that activity as auxiliary pioneers for at least two weeks out of every year.

Ministerial servants are watched closely by the elders to see how they fulfil their responsibilities in the congregation and how active they are in preaching. They too, if they want to maintain their positions or move up the ladder to become elders, must spend much time proselytizing.

A more important factor which buttresses the preaching work is the system of reporting that activity on a bi-monthly or monthly basis. Every publisher, that is every Jehovah's Witness who engages in preaching work, is encouraged in the strongest fashion to maintain a good, regular record and to report it to the congregational secretary. Twice during the month or at least once at the end thereof the publisher will fill out a report slip detailing the number of hours in which he or she engaged in 'the service,' the specific amounts of literature placed, the number of return visits made on interested persons, and the number of 'home Bible studies conducted.' If the publisher conducts one or more home Bible studies, he or she will fill out a separate slip for each such study.

At the beginning of the next month, the congregational secretary tabulates all publishers' reports and sends an over-all report of all congregational preaching activities during the previous month to the society's branch office. In addition, the secretary records each publisher's activities on his or her personal publisher's report card *which is held by the secretary*.

The society argues that this system is maintained merely to encourage preaching work in a positive way. But nothing could be farther from the truth. It provides both goals and goads! Not only is the publisher's report card used to measure one's 'spirituality' or lack thereof, but it allows elders, circuit overseers, district overseers, and the society itself to determine how well or how badly a certain individual, congregation, circuit, or even branch is doing in promoting the society's primary goal. If one becomes slack in maintaining a good and consistent preaching record, he or she will receive encouragement to improve. If the publisher is a man, he will receive no promotion to the position of ministerial servant or elder unless he does. If he already holds one of those positions, he will be removed from it unless he quickly shows that he is willing to give more time to that ministry. Furthermore, unless a man is an elder, ministerial servant, pioneer, or at least an *active publisher* in the congregation, he loses virtually all influence and prestige with his fellow Witnesses. No matter how able, intelligent, or responsible he is, unless he is a regular, *active publisher*, he will be regarded as spiritually sick. And if one should stop preaching altogether his fellow Witnesses will often say 'he has stopped serving Jehovah.'

In the past the society used to set specific preaching goals such as ten hours per month for each publisher. For years charts were kept on kingdom hall walls to allow everyone to see how the congregation was doing in the preaching work. But both disappeared many years ago. In recent years, however, informal quotas have been re-established, at least for elders and ministerial servants, by many circuit overseers. If, for instance, an elder or ministerial servant does not have more hours' preaching time over a six-month period than the congregation average, he may be in serious trouble.

More incidental props to the preaching work also serve as means to keep members of the Witness community in line. Territory cards are issued to individuals and study groups to make certain that Witnesses 'work' all their congregational territory in an organized and consistent fashion. House-to-house record forms are provided for pioneers and publishers to keep track of what happened at each house or apartment in a given area. Finally, elders are instructed to see that the territories are worked and that publishers follow up on the calls that they make. But these aspects of the preaching work are often complied with in a rather haphazard fashion. Even a highly disciplined community such as Jehovah's Witnesses is seldom capable of following *all* of the Watch Tower's elaborate rules.

Constant indoctrination plus constant activity serves well to keep most Jehovah's Witnesses in conformity with the society and its policies. Yet over the years many Witnesses, particularly more able and intelligent ones, have become highly critical of their superiors or the society itself. Many others have deviated 'morally' from biblical values or the society's own constantly changing set of rules. But when any have done so, the local congregation, acting through the elders or the circuit and district overseer, have been able to bring such ones before a judicial committee to discipline or expel them.

Although judicial committees are supposed to operate on the basis of certain minimal established procedures, these are frequently ignored by committee members, circuit oversers, and the society itself. In addition, when the society decides that someone is troublesome, it will actually conspire to have such a person cast out in flagrant violation of its own rules. When Walter Salter, former Canadian branch overseer, was disfellowshipped in 1937, his witnesses were shouted down and denied the right to speak at a congregational trial, even according to *The Watchtower's* own account.[88] Olin Moyle's disfellowshipment occurred as the result of a vendetta against him on the part of Judge Rutherford and his official lieutenants. More recently, Raymond Franz was excommunicated for the violation of one of the society's rules which was applied to him in a retroactive or *ex post facto* manner.[89]

Numerous others have experienced even more severe treatment. An Ottawa, Ontario, woman, Mrs Elana Bartlett, was verbally harrassed so severely by a judicial committee several years ago that she was rendered unconscious and had to be taken by ambulance to a local hospital and given oxygen.[90] In a more recent situation, John Higgins, a Port Moody, British Columbia, Witness who had not been attending meetings at the local kingdom hall, was spied on by elders who, in an attempt to determine whether he was attending the services of another religion, hid in bushes on a playground near his home with a camera and peered at him through binoculars. When he discovered what was going on, he slipped up behind them, took a picture of them, and asked what they were doing. Shortly thereafter they ordered him to appear before a judicial committee which excommunicated him, even though it had no witnesses or positive evidence against him.[91]

These cases and many others like them are too well documented to be denied. But the Witness community is told always that it must respect what judicial committees do. Even though hearings before them take place in secret and the average Witness knows little or nothing of what has transpired, he is told that he must accept the rulings of the committee without question. Interestingly, Watch Tower officials now state that such committees virtually have the apostolic power 'to bind and to loose.' More importantly, however, if a Witness should refuse to go along with a committee decision respecting another person (particularly if that one has been disfellowshipped), he too will suffer excommunication.

In this fashion the judicial committees of Jehovah's Witnesses act in a manner similar to the Holy Office of the Inquisition in the fifteenth, sixteenth, and seventeenth centuries when opposition to its decrees resulted in one's being tried for heresy or apostasy. Judicial committees cannot use physical torture nor can they have anyone 'relaxed' to the secular authorities for burning. But being cast out of 'God's organization,' to the average Jehovah's Witness, is tantamount to being condemned to everlasting destruction. So the system of judicial committees serves as the ultimate control mechanism among the Witness faithful, and a terrible one it is.

Informal Controls

Besides the formal controls that exist over members of the Witness community, there is an equally important set of informal ones. For one thing, it is very difficult for an ordinary Witness to challenge the authority of an elder, even when the elder in question is violating some of the written or unwritten canons of the community. Generally, elders tend to support or at least excuse their fellows, something the society encourages them to do. When faced with the combined spiritual powers of the body of elders, there is little that any individual or even group of publishers can do. Thus, they must submit, leave the Witness fold, or at least isolate themselves by becoming 'inactive' Jehovah's Witnesses. For even if they do not do anything which technically merits their open disfellowshipment, the elders can stigmatize them and cut them off from all normal congregational association by the device of 'marking disorderly ones.' In a relatively recent pronouncement spelled out on page 152 of the book *Organized to Accomplish Our Ministry*, all the elders have to do is discuss publicly the 'principle' which a certain person within the congregation is not following, and the congregation is required to 'mark' such a one: 'Even though no name has been mentioned, individual members of the congregation would then be obliged to "mark" a person, or persons, of that kind, just as Paul advised the brothers in Thessalonica.'

If it is difficult to take a stand against an elder or the local body, it is even more so with respect to a circuit overseer or some higher Watch Tower official. Even whole bodies of elders have discovered that it does little good to appeal to the society over the head of their circuit overseer. As with any hierarchical administrative system, be it political, commercial, academic, or religious, superior officials tend almost always to support those immediately under them. Senior officials know full well that their own positions and the smooth operation of the entire system within which they function is dependent on the maintenance of the chain of command. And so it is with the Watch Tower hierarchy, perhaps to a greater degree than is usually the case because of the outlook of the men in the governing body.

Although Jehovah's Witnesses claim that there are no clergy-laity distinctions among them, this is a myth. Watch Tower officials are an 'in group' or caste who will protect a member even when he has become extremely unpopular with a whole circuit or district. If several elders or even a whole body of elders bring charges against a circuit or district overseer, as happens rarely, the society will give every benefit of the doubt to its special representative. While it may name a committee to hear charges against him, it will characteristically predetermine the outcome of any such hearing by selecting committee members favourable to the circuit or district overseer in question. For example, if a circuit overseer is brought before a special committee, the committee will usually be composed of the district overseer and two other circuit overseers, ex-circuit overseers, ex-missionaries, or former Bethelites. And these men will almost always support the circuit overseer against the elders.

When in recent years elders have appealed to the society against the actions of their peers or circuit overseers in cases such as that of Elana Bartlett, mentioned above, often the society has made all correspondence available to the latter but has refused to do the same for the plaintiffs.[92] In other instances, the society has refused to answer its mail and has simply permitted local officials to carry out their (or its) wishes without any interference. But perhaps most execrable from the standpoint of Witness morality has been the fact that a number of district and circuit overseers have instructed local elders to solicit letters from various publishers in certain congregations to destroy the reputations of ones whom they have marked as troublesome. And only when all of the supposedly incriminating charges have been gathered have the ones targeted for 'discipline' been made aware of what was happening.[93] Thus the society and its representatives openly and flagrantly violate primary Watch Tower teachings on the way the Jehovah's Witnesses are to conduct themselves towards one another. But it must be admitted that through what amounts to informal police-state controls, the society is able to maintain dominance in the Witness community when its formal control measures prove ineffective.

Organizational Efficiency

How efficient is the organizational structure of Jehovah's Witnesses and the Watch Tower Society? Most Witnesses believe that it is very efficient. For example, they point to the massive publication of literature, the direction of the preaching work, the control over local congregations, and above all, the smooth functioning of their giant conventions. Outsiders have tended to agree. Writing in the late 1970s, Wilton Nelson and Richard Smith stated: 'The Jehovah's Witnesses is one of the most successful religious movements in the twentieth century – successful in terms of marshalling its members and their resources, ordering its priorities and arguments, and utilizing its opportunities for face-to-face and mass communication. Critics of the movement may have many misgivings when evaluating its precepts and propagation, but most of them will also have much to learn in the latter category.'[94] But it is evident from all that has been said earlier that this vaunted efficiency, at least for today, is more apparent than real.

No one would deny that the society was highly efficient during the earlier years of Knorr's administration in particular. Because of his personal administrative abilities and a degree of managerial sense which none of the other Watch Tower presidents have manifested, he streamlined the organization, developed Gilead, created the congregational theocratic ministry schools, and abandoned many of the more eccentric doctrinal aspects of the Rutherford era. Thus the Witness community grew and flourished.

The very growth of the community which the society hailed as a sign of Jehovah's favour has ultimately created problems for the Watch Tower Society. For while the strict controls of Rutherford and Knorr developed a dramatic sense of *esprit de corps* among the small band of Witnesses who were to pass through the persecution of the Third Reich and the Second World War, no such spirit could be passed on to the larger and much more amorphous community of the last two decades. During the Second World War and even during the decade thereafter, ordinary Witnesses often had a personal knowledge of and sometimes even a personal relationship with Watch Tower leaders. But as the organization grew, the sense of contact with them declined, at least for the vast majority of the community.

Up until after the war most Witnesses were English-speaking or at least northern Europeans. With Knorr's program of preaching the gospel on a world-wide basis, however, very rapidly the ethnic and linguistic nature of the community shifted. So, by the 1960s, while the largest group within the Witness fold were English-speaking, that group represented less than half of the total membership.

Without doubt this change in the nature of the community tended to make the Brooklyn leadership seem more distant and more aloof. When Witnesses saw

Knorr, Franz, and others from Brooklyn, it was often no more than as prophetic figures speaking to thousands or sometimes hundreds of thousands at conventions in what to many was a foriegn language.

But the gradual isolation of the leadership was not caused just by such natural developments which occurred from the growth of the community. The cult of anonymity which resulted in no one's personal name appearing on a Watch Tower letter and the practice that Knorr developed in shielding himself from contact with both ordinary Witnesses and the press exacerbated the situation. Often, he appeared at great conventions surrounded by retainers who acted as body guards for him, and when newspaper correspondents approached him he would frequently be peevish if not rude to them.[95] So, like Judge Rutherford before him, he created an aura of psychic distance from the Witness community.

More importantly, Knorr tended to narrow the base of the top echelons of the organizational elite by eliminating those who were independent-minded. As is well known, not only did he carry on an ongoing battle with Hayden Covington, but he virtually exiled Colin Quackenbush, the intelligent and able editor of *Awake!* from Bethel for a number of years. Thus, for a time at least, he eliminated virtually anyone who might have been able to generate new ideas to meet the increasing problems of the Witness community. Knorr, of course, did have the insight to accept some of the suggestions of men like Raymond Franz and Edward Dunlap in the early and mid-1970s. So during the last years of his active life, there was some real possibility of constructive change within the Watch Tower organization. Knorr, in spite of real human shortcomings, was both a sincere and generally practical man. Raymond Franz says: 'I doubt seriously [had he lived to 1980] that Nathan would have gone along with some of the harsh actions that were later to come from the collective body that inherited his presidential authority.'[96]

Since Knorr's death, all chance for immediate reform has ended, and his successors seem more isolated from both the world and the Witness community than was he. But they seem largely unconcerned. Except for the problems caused by 'dissidents and apostates,' they wait confidently for their heavenly reward and the great tribulation which has been delayed so long.

CHAPTER NINE

The Witness Community

Although there have been some good sociological and anthropological studies of Jehovah's Witnesses over the years, the number is surprisingly small. Groups such as the Hutterites and Unificationists (the Moonies) are much smaller in both North America and the world,[1] but there are far more studies of them. The following information, based on both published data and personal observation, may serve in a modest way, then, to increase the general knowledge of a community which is one of the largest Christian sects which has developed out of America to become a world-wide movement.

Membership, Recruitment, and Conversion

As Reginald Bibby and Merlin Brinkerhoff state so accurately, 'it has been a popular pastime in armchair and social scientific reflections upon religion to assert that the religious are drawn from the ranks of society's deprived,'[2] and this has certainly been said about Jehovah's Witnesses.[3] According to this deprivation theory, men and women become religious essentially because they are economically, psychologically, or socially disprivileged in some way or other. And since Karl Marx, Sigmund Freud, Max Weber, H. Richard Niebuhr, and many others have held it in one way or another, it has become a popular and social-scientific myth of major proportions.[4] But is it necessarily true?

Bibby and Brinkerhoff argue that while deprivation *is* a factor which explains religiosity in some instances, it is not always or even necessarily the most important one. Many people are religious for other reasons which, for convenience sake, the two Canadian sociologists describe under the three headings of 'socialization,' 'accommodation,' and 'cognition.' Respecting socialization they state what should be obvious: 'Clearly many of the new recruits to churches and sects are the children of members. For such offspring, church involvement is often likely to be an end in itself rather than a means to problem solving.' At the same time, they note that new recruits to religious groups may reflect a type of *accommodation* to social pressures, particularly from family members, close friends, and prospective marriage mates. Then, finally, in discussing cognition, they suggest that many become religious because to them a religious explanation of life and the universe 'makes sense.' In other words, an individual may choose to be religious because 'his decision is largely based on cognition or perception which he sees as essentially rational.'[5] Who, then, are Jehovah's Witnesses and why do people join them?

Loss of a large percentage of old members during the Rutherford era and rapid growth since the Second World War means that only a small proportion of Jehovah's Witnesses have anything like a family tradition in their faith. Although some few adult Witnesses in English-speaking lands, Scandinavia, and Germany can claim to have had Bible Student grandparents or great-grandparents, they are quite rare. Even today most congregational publishers are first- or second-generation Witnesses: and even in lands where they have existed throughout the twentieth century, in urban centres the majority are new Witnesses who have been converted in the last thirty-five to forty years. In rural areas and small towns throughout North America and in a few other parts of the world, this is not always so. There are small Witness communities with ethnic or family bases which have long had a definite local tradition and importance, but the numbers associated with such communities are very small. So, in evaluating Jehovah's Witnesses today, it becomes far more important to examine the backgrounds and statuses of the many persons who have become and remained such during the last forty years.

Although it is difficult to say with certainty who most early Bible Students and Jehovah's Witnesses were, several facts stand out. Up until 1950 the largest numbers were to be found in English-speaking or Northern European lands in which the majority of people were and are Protestants. It must be noted, however, that many Africans, in both British West Africa and British Central Africa, were attracted by Watch Tower teachings.[6] Hence up to 1950 most Witnesses in the world were from Protestant or non-Christian African backgrounds. Since then dramatic changes have occurred. Although Witness growth has continued to be significant in Protestant countries and the former colonies of Great Britain in Africa, recently it has been much more rapid in the Catholic nations of Europe, Latin America, Africa, and the Phillipines. While in 1950 nearly 75 per cent of all Jehovah's Witnesses lived in Protestant countries or what was then British Africa, by 1981 only about 50 per cent did so.[7] It is notable that today more than 40 per cent live in countries in which a majority of the people are Roman Catholics.[8] Today it is generally recognized among Jehovah's Witnesses that ex-Catholics make up the largest proportion of their numbers, perhaps 50 per cent. It should also be noted, though, that in places such as Japan and Korea sizable numbers of generally secularized ex-Buddhists and members of other Eastern religions have become Witnesses.[9] In effect, the only major religious communities which have not yet contributed in a large way to Witness growth are the Islamic and Hindu.

The social-class affiliation of Jehovah's Witnesses is more difficult to determine. Undoubtedly it varies somewhat from nation to nation and locality to locality. Nevertheless, on the basis of certain data it is possible to suggest that it is amazingly similar throughout much of the world.

Historical information gleaned from Watch Tower literature, newspaper articles, and discussions with older Witnesses indicates that in the nineteenth century the Bible Student community in the United States, Britain, and Canada was largely upper-working and lower-middle class. Among farmers, labourers, and small businessmen there was a considerable number of professionals – medical doctors, lawyers, dentists, teachers, ex-clergymen, and retired army officers.[10]

All evidence seems to indicate that during the period between the two world wars, most Bible Student–Witnesses were farmers and labourers. In both the United States and Canada large numbers of immigrants joined their ranks as did many American blacks in the United States.[11] Apparently many were responding to Judge Rutherford's attacks on capitalism and the exploitation of the poor. The same factor seems also to have been at work in Britain and Germany. For there, too, most were humble folk. In Britain many were skilled and unskilled labourers,[12] while in Germany many were peasants, foresters, household servants, and factory workers. In the latter country a rather clear picture of the nature of the Witness community between 1933 and 1945 has been obtained from the documents of the Nazi concentration camps.[13]

What this seems to indicate is that during Russell's time, while some may have become Bible Students out of a sense of deprivation, more were probably attracted by the rationalism so evident in the Pastor's writings and the whole idea of the 'divine plan.' In contrast, Rutherford's approach appealed far more to the emotions of the lower classes. He attacked 'politics, commerce, and religion' as exploiters of the masses in an almost Marxist fashion. It is, therefore, probable that far more of those who joined the Bible Student–Witnesses in his day did so from a perceived lack of socio-economic privilege. No doubt, too, many wanted the earthly paradise promised to the Witness faithful so repeatedly after 1935. As Max Weber has recognized, religion among the disprivileged often causes them to substitute in their minds what they are with what they wish to become.[14] But this should not be taken to mean that the Bible Student–Witnesses were the 'dregs of society.' In evaluating the analyses of Milton Czatt and Herbert Stroup on this matter, Alan Rogerson questions the reliability of their assessments that the

Witnesses of the 1930s and early 1940s were of 'very limited education' and were not even 'average.' He states: 'It seems that they were "pretty average" in most respects: that is, the Witnesses reflected the percentage norms for the whole population (for example, about one percent had had college education, which was about the national percentage at that time).'[15]

In recent decades several historians, sociologists, and anthropologists have asserted that, in many parts of the world, Jehovah's Witnesses tend to be drawn once again from among such groups as artisans, skilled workers, and members of the lower-middle class. For example, in an excellent chapter on social stratification and Jehovah's Witnesses in Great Britain, James Beckford relates that according to a statistical survey of occupational status among 180 persons which he conducted, 15 per cent were in junior-managerial and technical occupations, 24 per cent were in clerical and supervisory roles, 15 per cent were in skilled manual positions, 12 per cent were in semi-skilled manual jobs, and 11 per cent were employed in unskilled work. He then shows from a comparison with overall British social-class composition based on a number of studies 'that the Watch Tower movement contains a disproportionately small number of people from social classes at society's extremes.' There are, he holds, few rich and famous or few in the 'poorest strata.'[16] And what is true of British Witnesses seems generally true of their brethren in other developed countries.

Bryan Wilson's rather limited study of Jehovah's Witnesses in Japan suggests that Japanese Witnesses tend to belong to the same classes as do those in Great Britain[17] while Jesús Jiménez holds that Spanish Witnesses are most probably average as well. In comparing them with the Spanish population in general he says that they are 'citizens more or less like the rest,' except for their religiosity.[18] As for the Witnesses in Canada and the United States, although data on them are not entirely satisfactory, there is at least some solid evidence that they are very similar to their brethren in Britain, Japan, and Spain.[19] It is true that Quirinus Munters found that the majority of Witnesses he studied in the Netherlands were poorly paid, skilled or semi-skilled manual workers or petty clerks (*petits employés*) who had been born in large or medium-sized cities.[20] But Munter's study seems to present a picture of Jehovah's Witnesses which, while it cannot be disregarded, is somewhat atypical.

What about in underdeveloped lands or the so-called Third World? Are Jehovah's Witnesses there of the same classes? At least in south-central Africa the answer seems to be 'yes.' Sholto Cross shows that Watch Tower teachings have had the dramatic effect of promoting a 'cult of literacy' which has tended to create a community roughly analagous, *mutatis mutandis,* to the Witness communities in a majority of the developed nations described above. Says Cross: 'A high proportion of skilled and literate migrants joined the movement, many of whom of course had had some mission training. Surface rather than underground [mine] workers, clerks, hawkers and traders, "natives of the detribatized class," and those with some intellectual aspirations joined the movement.'[21] Similarly, in writing specifically about Witnesses in Luapula, Zambia, Karla Poewe says: 'Jehovah's Witnesses, whose teachings constitute a learning process designed to build mature servants [of God], have been more successful that other denominations in making people feel comfortable with notions of trust and its correlate, honesty ... In fact, they have earned the reputation among their countrymen of being scrupulously honest and thus are preferred for jobs in which money is handled.' In addition, she remarks: 'Politically, Witnesses are determined egalitarians. They practice economic self-reliance, and the gap between rich and poor is closed.'[22]

These data from Africa are important, for they show how potent Watch Tower doctrines have been and are in moulding Witness attitudes and, through these attitudes, styles of life. For it is evident that the society has, in large measure, been able to create more or less the same types of communities, at least from a social-class standpoint, in many lands where Witnesses are present in large numbers. This seems to suggest, then, that what is true of Jehovah's Witnesses in Britain is probably true of them in most other lands as well. For what James Beckford says about the British community is pretty well universally the case. Writing about what he calls 'the Watch Tower movement,' he says; 'It cannot emulate Moral Rearmament, Christian Science or Mormonism in deliberately attracting and retaining eminent people from the political, business or intellectual spheres, nor has it ever received patronage from anybody even loosely associated with the British "ruling class." Similarly, the poorest strata are underrepresented in the sect, and it may be significant in this respect that the Watch Tower ethos would seem to frown upon anything but the most unavoidable instances of prolonged unemployment.'[23]

What this means is that Jehovah's Witnesses have created their own sectarian society which they referred to for a time during the 1950s as the 'New World Society'; and their 'sectarian exclusiveness,' to use Beckford's phrase, has doubtlessly developed certain values among them which are ordinarily considered to be middle class or bourgeois. Jesús Jiménez says they may be described as 'on the right,'[24] for the Watch Tower Society has always placed great emphasis on self-discipline, the work ethic, and the development of the basic knowledge and skills which frequently contribute to the acquisition of the wealth necessary to a middle-class style of life. Yet conversely, there are values among them which inhibit the upward social mobility of most Witnesses beyond certain levels. They have traditionally been taught that materialism is a great spiritual and social danger, and since Rutherford's day at least, their leaders have deprecated worldly social prominence. Consequently, if a Witness sacrifices too much time either to business or to professional interests, he will be told quite directly that he is 'not putting the interest of God's kingdom first.' To be a zealous Witness and pursue a prominent business or professional career is difficult from another standpoint. The demands of both the congregation and one's secular activities are often most time consuming and frequently stressful. If one has a particular skill or profession, he will soon discover that fellow Witnesses will rely heavily on him for aid, counsel, and advice. Particularly is this true of Witness lawyers, medical doctors, dentists, chiropractors, nurses, teachers, and accountants. At the same time, somewhat paradoxically, the very able businessman or professional person may suffer a certain amount of disapproval from within his congregation because, by his very success or abilities, he is viewed as somewhat 'worldly.' Should he not, rather, be 'devoting more of his time to preaching the good news of the kingdom?' Hence, it often means great sacrifice for outside persons of wealth and prestige to become Witnesses. Their young people are constantly admonished not to consider a career in a world that will soon pass away, a factor which causes a great many of them not to enter university or to accept a type of employment which would cause them to experience upward social mobility. In fact, in some instances, most notably in Japan, so many Witness publishers give up full-time work to become pioneers that they experience downward social mobility.[25] It is not surprising, then, that there are not a great many rich or socially prominent Jehovah's Witnesses.

It may seem somewhat strange that Jehovah's Witnesses are subjected to two types of influences, both of which are so opposed to one another and both of which are taught by the Watch Tower Society. Yet in looking at the nature of the Witness community, both are absolutely necessary to its growth and maintenance. In the first place, it simply must have 'a sizeable group of people with managerial experience to occupy leadership positions'[26] within the Watch Tower hierarchy and Witness districts, circuits, and congregations as well. Second, in order to carry on proselytism among all or at least practially all classes, it must have persons who can relate to the many social types with whom the Witnesses come in contact. For evangelism is benefitted greatly by the 'wide range of class backgrounds' among Jehovah's Witnesses 'because it ensures that Witnesses of the appropriate social class can work among people of similar backgrounds.'[27] But by converting skilled workers, some professionals, and businessmen while also promoting certain typically Protestant middle-class values, Jehovah's Witnesses have created within their own ranks a sizeable group which would, under ordinary circumstances, rise socially and tend to become assimilated by the larger societies in which the Witnesses live.

Speaking of his own Methodist society as long ago as the eighteenth century, John Wesley noted this problem for every revivalistic religion. 'Wherever riches have increased,' he wrote, 'the essence of religion has decreased in the same proportion. Therefore I do not see how it is possible in the nature of things for any revival of religion to continue long. For religion must necessarily produce both industry and frugality, and these cannot but produce riches. But as riches increase so will pride, anger, and love of the world in all its branches.'[28] And in a way this has happened among the Witnesses. As Armageddon has been delayed, many have become less and less committed to the Watch Tower Society's preaching program, and where both the larger societies in which the Witnesses have lived and the Witnesses themselves have become more prosperous, the latter's growth and dynamism have tended to falter. Nothing shows this so dramatically as their experience in Germany since 1960.[29]

Still and all, what Wesley suggested regarding religious movements has not happened to Jehovah's Witnesses – and for a very good reason. The society has continued to maintain such an unremitting pressure on all members of the Witness community to preach that those members of it who have not done so on a regular basis have left the organization quietly or been forced out of it in a variety of ways. Thus, in spite of a great loss of publishers, tremendous tensions caused, and the bitterness engendered – particularly in recent times – by this policy, the society considers it necessary. For only by encouraging middle-class values and at the same time keeping a constant check on their logical development can the Watch Tower Society maintain its and the Witness community's commitment to preaching the 'good news of Christ's kingdom' and the impending destruction of 'Satan's system.' Not surprisingly, this has had the effect of creating a Witness society with small numbers of the very rich or very poor; it has tended to develop a body of believers who are *and must remain* 'average' – in everything except their religion.

There are many reasons why persons become Jehovah's Witnesses. While in the pre–Second World War period few did so because of socialization, that can no longer be said to be the case. Since 1945 the Witness community has grown so dramatically, and there has been a much more positive attitude towards the training of youth to accept their parents' faith, that today there are many second-generation Witnesses. Yet because the conversion rate of outsiders to their community has been so high for such sustained periods of time, they are still greatly outnumbered.

What about the converts? Why have they become Jehovah's Witnesses? Some undoubtedly have felt socially underprivileged and therefore look forward to the millennium as a time when they will experience material as well as spiritual blessings. In relation to this point, it is interesting to note that in Canada, Jehovah's Witnesses have long had the greatest success in making converts in the two provinces – British Columbia and Saskatchewan – in which socialist movements have been most consistently of major importance.[30] But a sense of personal deprivation does not seem to be one of the major reasons why people become Jehovah's Witnesses.

Alan Rogerson remarks: 'The Witnesses offer a variety of reasons for their conversion, the most common being that they were convinced that the doctrines were correct. How much of this is true and how much rationalization is difficult to say, but obviously there must be some rational co-operation on the part of the convert before he can embrace the doctrines of the Witnesses.'[31] So, as Rogerson recognizes, what Bibby and Brinkerhoff classify as 'cognition' plays a heavy part in the conversion of persons of many backgrounds to Jehovah's Witnesses; and when it is realized that such conversion takes place in the great majority of cases only after a long period of discussion and religious indoctrination, it is understandable why. Of course, the cognitive ground or grounds for conversion differ from individual to individual. Yet most of them fall within a few categories according to what many Witnesses themselves state. Broadly speaking, these are: 1 / disillusionment with chaotic political, social, and economic conditions throughout much of the world; 2 / strong feelings of disillusionment with the religious groups with which they were formerly associated in both the Christian and non-Christian worlds; 3 / admiration for both Witness moral values and behaviour; 4 / appreciation for a religion which claims ultimate answers for mankind's ultimate questions; and 5 / an equal appreciation for a social and organizational structure in which the life of the individual can become eternally meaningful.

Of course these reasons indicate that the recruitment of prospective Jehovah's Witnesses must take place among persons who are actually predisposed to Witness doctrines in one way or another, and this is certainly the case. For example, many Japanese are attracted to the Witnesses because 'Watch Tower ideology is capable of awakening the old attitude to consumer buying that is said to have prevailed in Japan before the war – namely, a distrust of the idea that satisfaction is to be derived from amassing commodities.'[32] In that country and in parts of Africa, too, many seem impressed by what seems to be the practical 'common sense' of Jehovah's Witnesses in comparison with more esoteric religions.[33] In a world heavily influenced, either directly or indirectly, by industrialization, pragmatism, secularism, and Marxism, Witness doctrines have certain definite advantages. As Bryan Wilson says in speaking of Japan: 'The Witnesses offer things not available through the indigenous movements.'[34] Furthermore, their organization is seen as 'western; apparently non-hierarchical; fraternal and egalitarian in spirit; and in the implications of the future world order that it promises, it is as radical as a thorough-going communist party in its proletarian, rational, anti-nationalist, and anti-racial emphases.'[35] Yet both in Japan and the western world it has the power to attract persons who long for the 'old-time virtues' that were once so commonly taught by other, more traditional religions.[36] So Witnesses can appeal to a broad spectrum of individuals from many social as well as ethnic and religious backgrounds as prospective recruits to their community. There are, however, many from among whom they have little chance of making converts. In spite of the Watch Tower Society's supposed commitment to a world-wide preaching and proselytizing work through which Jehovah's Witnesses should, theoretically at least, try to teach everyone, individual Witnesses spend far more time directing their message to persons whom they believe to be real prospective converts than to others.[37]

Although primarily rational in their approach to prospective converts, Jehovah's Witnesses do appeal to people's emotions as well. Often someone has just lost a loved one in war or perhaps is deeply concerned over the raising of children. And at the very time that he or she feels a need for spiritual solace or instruction, the Witnesses are often there to give it, whether through their door-to-door ministry or through association as family members or friends. Thus many find the Witnesses persons to 'lean on' who seem to have the answers.

Finally, many people become Jehovah's Witnesses through Bibby and Brinkerhoff's third category – 'socialization.' Often when one member of a family becomes a Jehovah's Witness, others will follow simply, at least in the first instance, out of respect for the initial convert or to keep a family together. Then, too, sexual attraction and conversions for marriage purposes are, in many places, major reasons why certain persons become Jehovah's Witnesses. Norman Lang, writing about Witness men in Zambia, has stated: 'Although Jehovah's Witnesses emphasize the importance of finding a wife from within the church, most in fact, marry outside. Thus proselytization provides a means by which one can meet and court one's future wife.[38] While this means of conversion is far less overt in the Americas, Australia, Europe, and much of the rest of the world, practically any Jehovah's Witness who has been with the movement for any length of time can recount various instances of successful conversions through courtship.

Sex, Marriage, and the Family

In describing Bible Student–Jehovah's Witness attitudes towards marriage and the family, it is quite possible to make them appear both unsatisfying emotionally and somewhat bizarre, at least prior to the 1950s. But in examining these subjects one must always keep certain factors in mind. First, as in practically every other aspect of Witness history and life, one must remember that Watch Tower teachings with respect to sex, marriage, and the family have been heavily coloured by apocalyptic concerns like those of the Apostle Paul as expressed in 1 Corinthians 7. Not only did he counsel celibacy, but at verse 29, he states: 'Moreover, this I say, brothers, the time left is reduced. Henceforth let those who have wives be as though they had none.' Second, as noted in Chapter 1 with respect to Charles and Maria Russell, they were also influenced by strict Victorian ideas which often held sexuality to be somewhat 'unspiritual.' But after having said this, it should be recognized that the personal feelings and views of all four Watch Tower presidents and, recently, those of members of the governing body of Jehovah's Witnesses as well have had much to do with forming Bible Student–Witness attitudes towards these subjects.

Although Pastor Russell seemed to understand the sexual needs of members of the Bible Student community, he personally had little interest in sex, regarded it as more animalistic than spiritual, and after his legal break with his wife became extremely sensitive about male-female relationships. Naturally, his attitudes had an important impact on the thinking of large numbers of early Bible Students. For example, according to reports from elderly Witnesses and Bible Students who remember the Russell era, couples emulated the Russells and lived together as husband and wife without engaging in sexual relations.

Russell's outlook on sex and marriage was quite temperate in comparison with Rutherford's. The judge obviously regarded women as inferiors 'who should keep their proper place.' His bias probably arose from resentment towards Maria Russell, whom he regarded as a rebel, his own non-relationship with his wife over many years, and, finally, his paternalistic view of the nature of 'true religion.' Respecting the last-named factor, he wrote: 'The father represents Jehovah, from whom comes every good thing, while the mother represents God's organization, used for His good purposes and His glory.'[39] Furthermore, the Watch Tower's second president believed that 'putting women to the fore in the affairs of religion and the councils of state has much to do with destroying the sacredness of the home and with turning men away from God.'[40]

Women were fine, according to Rutherford, so long as they took up the preaching work and remained subservient in the home and the congregation. If they remained single and became pioneers, so much the better. But they were not to be the objects of adulation or of romantic love. Such would only take them (and stalwart young men also) out of God's service and into the mundane business of home-making and the raising of families at best. At worst, it might turn them into proud 'Jezebels' who would attempt to disrupt proper theocratic order in Jehovah's organization.

Just how far the judge carried his view of these matters is shown by an article in the 27 January 1937 *Golden Age* which he endorsed fully in *The Watchtower*.[41] Talking specifically about romantic love, *The Golden Age* proclaimed: 'But what do we find stored up in the vast warehouse of Fact that lies back of this charming exterior? Innumerable murders perpetrated for "love." Hosts of suicides commit-

1. Satan, the wily foe of man, induced the clergy (they are induced so easily) to magnify human passion and give it precedence over love for God, and to tax it, deriving from it wealth, power, pomp and free advertising.

(from *The Golden Age*, 27 January 1937, 270)

ted because of unrequited or departed "love." Infidelities and divorces brought about because of "love" for some other man or woman. Note the multitude of petty tyrannies exercised by loved ones over their "lovers," the disappointments, the hatreds, the jealousies, and the unrest in absence. Last but not least, note the fact that "love" has even changed the course of nations.'[42]

In a curious sense of unreality, *The Golden Age* article just quoted – 'That Delusion Called Love' – suggested that the only proper way to have a marriage arranged was as it had been done in ancient Israel; by the parents of the bride and groom. Single persons were therefore not to touch a person of the opposite sex, not to exchange confidences, and to recognize that being in love is like the 'ecstacies'

FOR I'M FALLING
IN LUST WITH
SOMEONE

THE
TRUTHFUL
TROUBADOUR

**2. Modern song writers
soon discovered the potential wealth in giving voice
to the baser passions un-
der the label of "L-O-V-E",**

(from *The Golden Age*, 27 January 1937, 270)

of the opium addict or 'imbibing too freely in alcoholic beverages.' 'So then,' said
The Golden Age, 'stripped of all its glamour, what do we find instead of love? We
find "desire," in many cases so strong as to be properly termed "lust." ' Then, in
closing, the Witness magazine said that 'God's consecrated people do well to
refrain from marriage unless they find themselves continually tormented with
desire for sexual intercourse, in which case they should marry.' One wonders, of
course, how they could accomplish this without the courting so sternly condemned
by the society. Did the judge really expect Witness men who had no parents to
arrange their marriages to approach women with the candid statement that they
needed to have intercourse and then propose marriage? Evidently so: 'For those of
the younger or older who have need to marry *on this score,* let them dispose of the
matter in candor and honesty … shunning the blight, the delusions and illusions of

"love" so called and courtship, which bring reproach on the holy name of Jehovah.'[43]

This counsel had a dramatic effect on the family life of Jehovah's Witnesses, and during the late 1930s and 1940s, husband-wife relationships among them were often quite bad. Witness men frequently neglected their wives both spiritually and materially as was noted at the time by Herbert Stroup.[44] Since 'love-making' was condemned with such sternness by the society, their sexual relationships must often have been affected adversely as well.

The ones who frequently suffered the most were the faithful young Witnesses who were told over and over again that they should give up *everything*, including marriage, for the sake of the preaching work. Since Armageddon was near at hand, perhaps only a few months or at most a few years away, they should *if at all possible* wait to establish a home and family in the New World.[45] If they did show signs of wanting to marry, they were under intense social pressure not to do so. Sometimes, when a young pioneer, either male or female, did marry, his or her pioneer partners would show their contempt by spending the wedding day preaching Jehovah's kingdom from door to door rather than attending the ceremony.[46]

Young couples, who had shown themselves incapable of avoiding 'lust' until after Armageddon, often found themselves under equally strong pressure not to have children. Shortly after her marriage, many a young Witness woman would be taken aside by a number of older 'sisters' who would assure her that 'now is not the time to have children.' After all, did not Christ say: 'Woe to those who give suck in the last days.'

Rutherford had equally little concern for the family and family obligations. In 1938 an eighteen-year-old youth, Robert Whitney, wrote to the judge for advice. He had earlier made application to sail on the society's Australian missionary ship *Lightbearer* and had been told he could join its crew. But Whitney felt obligated to his parents. His father, who had suffered 'shell shock' during the First World War, wanted him to help work on the family's mortgaged farm. His mother was suffering with a leakage of the heart. His brothers, aged thirteen and four, were too young to do farm work. So he was desperately needed by his parents and sought Rutherford's counsel. Rutherford, however, saw no problem in the matter. Acting as though he had never read Jesus's comments about one's obligation to parents at Matthew 15:1–9, he stated bluntly: 'A covenant to do God's will takes precedence over all prior agreements, contracts, or obligations. That is to say, the agreement to do God's will must be performed and nothing permitted to interfere ... This applies to all persons, without regard to sex or family relationship.'[47] Of course, in so stating, he assumed that he, Joseph Franklin Rutherford, knew that the Lord's will was for every Witness *to pro-*

selytize under the society's direction, no matter what the consequences to family or person might be.

Nathan Knorr had a much different view of sex, marriage, and the family. Although he was affected – some would say scarred – psychologically by the ideology of the Rutherford era and was always preoccupied with sexual matters, he changed the society's attitudes towards marriage in a dramatic way. Early in the 1950s, Hayden Covington, then regarded by most Witnesses as a hero, began to establish a new trend by getting married. Shortly thereafter, Knorr followed suit and, thereby, ended the Watch Tower's anti-marriage stance. Thus weddings became popular among Jehovah's Witnesses in a way that they had not been for years.

Knorr and those around him went beyond setting a new and positive example. Under their leadership the society came to teach that the family was the basic unit of the theocratic society of Jehovah's Witnesses,[48] and much rather charming counsel was given to married couples.[49] Ultimately, too, it was suggested that it was perfectly all right for Witnesses to have children in 'these last days.'[50] In a major switch from what had occurred in Rutherford's day, the society came to insist that Witness marriages be *legally* recognized so far as possible. The old religiously recognized consensual unions of the Rutherford era – then considered quite proper by many[51] – become matters of shame. Hence, if a couple did not marry according to law during most of Knorr's administration, they would be disfellowshipped.[52]

Some of the old concepts of romantic love gradually appeared in the society's literature, too. For example, much attention came to be devoted to the Song of Solomon in public talks given both at conventions and in kingdom halls. While it continued to be allegorized in typical Witness fashion, none the less the society began to use it as a basis for instruction on the 'proper' mode of courtship and love between man and woman. So, under Nathan Knorr, romantic love was rehabilitated, albeit under the strictest of moralistic provisos.

In spite of these changes much has been retained from the past that affects the Witness community even today. Singleness is still encouraged 'if one can make room for it.' Young marriages are discouraged with vigour,[53] and birth control continues to be subtly promoted among childless couples. For if they have no children, they can continue to pioneer or fulfil some other full-time preaching assignment.[54] In addition, there are still strong overtones from the Rutherford era in the society's counsel on courting. When single couples start going together, they are advised to avoid petting and kissing.[55] In fact, for a time in the 1970s, they were even counselled to avoid touching one another or holding hands.[56] Nevertheless, the Knorr years saw the sanctification of marriage among Witnesses, and individuals who now feel the need to find a mate are encouraged to pray over the matter so that they may find one 'mature in faith.'

For these reasons marriages within the congregation are usually occasions of great joy. Furthermore, when persons who have been living together in consensual or common-law unions are officially married prior to being baptized – as they must be – their weddings are regarded in the most positive light by all Witnesses. Interestingly, couples who are to be married choose the form their weddings will take in co-operation with the local congregational elders. Hence Witness weddings usually follow the basic forms of those held in the non-Witness communities where the respective Witness couples live. If possible the marriage ceremony takes place in the kingdom hall; no confetti, rice, or flowers are ever thrown,[57] and the excessive drinking of alcoholic beverages and gluttony are strictly prohibited at wedding receptions. So, too, is the custom of toasting the bride. In some parts of the world such as western Canada, Witness wedding dances are common in spite of the Watch Tower Society's rather negative attitude towards most dancing.

After the marriage, the couple will take up residence, if possible, in a separate home. Thereafter the husband is expected to provide for his wife in both a physical and a spiritual sense. The wife is to care for the home and to obey her husband as 'unto the Lord.' When children come, both parents are expected to love them, care for them, and train them in the precepts of their faith. Witness homes are therefore ideally male-dominated but with the caveat that the husband-father must 'love his wife as the Christ does the congregation.' Thus the women's liberation movement receives little encouragement among Jehovah's Witnesses. Nevertheless, Witness families as such are generally reasonably happy. Wives, whether in white, European societies or the rest of the world, are ordinarily quite well treated.

Karla Poewe shows that in Luapula, Zambia, Witness women trust their husbands to an unusual degree for women in that society. But what is perhaps most important about Poewe's findings with respect to the Zambian Witness community is that she demonstrates that Watch Tower teachings have created a whole new set of familial relationships which make marriages much more stable and divorces far more rare.[58] And while such dramatic results have not occurred in most other parts of the world, the Watch Tower Society asserts, probably quite correctly, that its teachings often do make families happier and healthier. Of course, the society does not admit, at least directly, that it is sometimes responsible for family friction and breakup, a matter discussed below.

Children born into Witness homes typically receive a great deal of care and religious instruction. Their fathers are expected to have regular home Bible study with them weekly, to study a biblical text from the *Yearbook of Jehovah's Witnesses* daily, to offer prayer at the table and at bedtime, to discuss Bible stories with them, and to inculcate the principles of biblical Christianity. In addition, the children will be taken to regular congregational meetings, to Witness conventions, and, when they are old enough, in the door-to-door preaching work. As a result, most Witness children from zealous families grow up knowing literally dozens of scriptural texts by memory and the basic doctrines of their faith.

Since the family is treated as the basic unit of the congregation, the various members thereof are continuously helped and encouraged to fulfill their respective religious responsibilities. Husbands and fathers must 'take the lead,' and if they do not they will receive counsel. In the first place they are reminded of their duties by Scriptures read at meetings and by the society's literature, much of which does give fine advice with respect to family life. However, if a Witness husband and father fails to attend meetings, does not regularly report his preaching activities to the congregation, or does not provide for either the physical or spiritual welfare of his family, elders in the congregation may approach him and discuss these matters with him directly. If his wife creates congregational problems or his children are unruly or undisciplined, he may be refused certain congregational privileges and will receive stern admonition.

Wives are expected to be subject to their husbands, to keep the family home clean, to care for the children, to dress modestly – although in the common garb of the larger society in which they live – and to participate in the preaching work and those areas of responsibility open to them in the congregation. Although they may answer questions in meetings when called upon, they are never to teach directly in their congregations, nor are they ever appointed as elders or ministerial servants. Wives usually carry on most of the preaching work accomplished by congregation publishers and frequently visit the sick, care for the poor, and entertain. To Witnesses the good wife is described in Proverbs 31:10–31.

Children are taught obedience to parents, school authorities, the police, and, above all, elders within the congregation. They are instructed, however, that all such obedience is relative; they must respect God above all, and if parents or others order them to violate a Christian principle, they 'must obey God rather than men.' So while Witnesses are now raised with a deep respect for secular authority, they are also taught that their ultimate allegiance must be to Jehovah. They are, however, left in no doubt that such allegiance also means *complete obedience* to his organization, both heavenly and earthly.

In spite of what the Watch Tower Society regards as a 'positive picture,' there are many strains on the modern Witness family. Although neither the society nor most Jehovah's Witnesses would admit it, those strains are at bottom the result of the society's own ongoing policies. While Knorr sanctified marriage and incorporated it into the basic fabric of 'theocratic society' rather than regarding it as an obstacle to the preaching work, never has the society seen the needs of individuals within marriage nor the marriage relationship as of primary importance. Thus the family remains something to buttress the society's fundamental goals – 'theocratic order' and the preaching work – rather than as a proper end in itself. So while marriage may be sacred to Jehovah's Witnesses, it is certainly no sacrament which by its very nature confers grace upon believers. Hence, the society continues to give advice and pursue policies which are often frankly unhealthy to family relationships. A few examples will demonstrate this.

First, because of the extreme organizational and community pressures on young persons to begin pioneering immediately following their graduation from secondary schools in places like Canada and the United States, many will marry and have a child as soon as possible. Only by so doing can they find a socially acceptable means of avoiding those pressures within the Witness community. But this, of course, means that many of the couples who enter such early marriages are quite immature and frequently unable to provide for themselves and their children. Thus they must rely on the support of their own parents and sometimes become a real burden to them.

In addition, because of the stresses that occur from immaturity and young husbands' frequent inability to provide for their families because of lack of skills or education, many of these families suffer discord and become spiritually apathetic. Often young Witness marriages, in the United States in particular, end in divorce. While there are no statistical studies on this matter, both the society and Jehovah's Witnesses in general are well aware of the problem of young marriages and try to discourage them.[59] In fact the matter has received constant attention at conventions and kingdom halls for the last two decades. But Brooklyn does not seem to recognize that by its unremitting pressure to preach, it brings about many of these young marriages and their later disruption.

On this last point, Heather Botting, in a recently submitted doctoral dissertation in religious anthropology, relates a case study in which a young Ontario couple even engaged in pre-marital intercourse with the object of getting the girl pregnant and obtaining her parents' permission to marry. In that way, according to their own statements, they were able to avoid congregational requirements, such as the door-to-door preaching work, and were eventually able to isolate themselves from their congregation. Although they were sternly reproved by local elders, they avoided disfellowshipment when the young man claimed that they had had intercourse only once 'in a fit of passion.' In that way they were able to maintain family and other social contacts within the Witness community but were prohibited from public proselytizing – the very thing they wanted.[60]

While this is no doubt an extreme case of a type which does not often occur, it none the less demonstrates what effects the society's pressure to preach can have on Witness youth, sexual relationships, and marriage. It suggests, too, why many Witness parents who are well aware of the organizational stresses placed on their children are anxious to see them married off at early ages even despite Watch Tower recommendations and the more than occasional fulminations of elders and circuit overseers.

Sometimes the society's policy of male domination has other negative effects, too. Women are generally told to put up with their husbands even when they suffer beatings and other forms of abuse.[61] Thus there have been quite a number of cases of elders supporting husbands against their wives, even when the husbands have been guilty of abusing them. Certainly, the society is not directly at fault for this because it is anxious to promote family harmony if at all possible. Yet local elders are often so committed to Watch Tower policies of male domination that sometimes, like Judge Rutherford, they regard a woman as 'a hank of hair and a bag of bones' and demand that she submit to all kinds of mistreatment.

From the above it would be quite wrong to suggest that the typical Witness family has never developed into the warm, supportive unit that many Orthodox Jewish families, some pious Catholic families, and a great many Evangelical Christian families have become. Still, most Witness families appear to be more 'utilitarian' than affective in nature. Although there is now an emphasis on 'healthy relationships' in the Witness home, no great importance is placed on the family as such. Since Jehovah's Witnesses celebrate no holidays, family gatherings tend to be uncommon. Additionally, since few graduate from universities, become involved in the arts, or participate in sports activities, little sense of family pride is developed around the accomplishments of outstanding family members. Finally, not much attention is given to the extended family, for in most cases many near relatives will be non-believers.

Despite the reforms of the Knorr years, one of the Watch Tower Society's ongoing problems has been with respect to the Witness family. Instead of developing it in such a way that it could serve as a primary means whereby most young Witnesses would be spiritually nourished and supported to keep them within the community – as has been done so successfully by many Evangelicals – it has been used more as a squad of theocratic soldiers to promote the preaching work than anything else. Thus certain studies and observation indicate that there is a heavy loss of young men and women from the Witness community when they grow to adulthood.[62] Family ties seem to do little to stem this tide and neither does the intense childhood indoctrination that many who leave received when they were children.

Education

Witness attitudes towards education are somewhat ambiguous. Beginning with Pastor Russell, while the Bible Students greatly respected many aspects of scholarship and certain academic studies, they were also critical of what was taught in the universities of Europe and America in the late nineteenth and early twentieth centuries. Russell was very negative towards the religious seminaries of his day and to the teaching of evolution. To him and Jehovah's Witnesses since, Darwinism has been a particular *bête noire*. In addition Bible Students and Witnesses have never believed that higher education is necessary for the training of preachers and evangelists: were not the apostles 'unlettered and ordinary men'? Russell therefore counselled that Bible Students not send their children to universities, colleges, or even high school. In 1910 he stated: 'My advice is, then, give your children an education up to public school limit, not even attempting to take them through high school, for they get plenty of Higher Criticism [*sic*] in the high schools, and it will not be long before they have it in the common schools also.'[63]

Little changed among Jehovah's Witnesses during Rutherford's day. If anything the judge was more anti-intellectual than his predecessor. But under Knorr emphasis was placed on improving the knowledge and educational skills of the Witnesses. He felt that to be preachers and ministers, individual Witnesses must raise their educational levels. Hence, he oversaw the development of the theocratic ministry schools and the missionary college of Gilead. In lands where many Witnesses were illiterate, congregational reading classes were established. In Africa alone many thousands were taught to read and write.[64] Today the society continues to stress the importance of basic education.

Over the last decade some Witness parents began to remove their children from the 'worldly' environments of some North American high schools in fear of violence, the 'drug cult,' and 'low morals' among many high-school students. Although the Watch Tower Society indicated that the matter was ultimately one to be decided by the parents, it advised sternly that Witness children be kept in school until they graduated.[65]

Nevertheless the old Watch Tower anti-university spirit persists as has been demonstrated so vividly, and the society continues to stress the value of practical studies. Boys have consistently been encouraged to study carpentry, auto mechanics, or some other vocation in secondary or high school while girls have been impressed with the value of secretarial studies. These subjects, the society believes, permit young adults to enter the field of pioneer evangelism immediately upon graduating from high school and allow them also to provide for themselves and future families if they should later marry. Strangely, Witness leaders seem unwilling to recognize or simply fail to care that many young persons have little or no aptitude for the 'practical' subjects suggested by the society and in later years have often come to resent bitterly that they were not trained for professions more fitted to their interests and abilities.

Dotage.—Isaiah 29:14

A Watch Tower view of higher education
(from *Consolation*, 12 June 1940, 21)

It is true that the society has never placed an absolute ban on university attendance and numerous strong-willed Witnesses have gone on to obtain university educations. But the pressure to quit is sometimes very great. Circuit overseers and elders have frequently preached publicly against higher education while elders and fellow publishers have sometimes made life extremely unpleasant for Witness students attending university. In fact, as a result there have been many instances in which such students were forced either to drop their programs of study or leave the Witness community altogether. A post-doctoral fellow in microbiology and student at Harvard Divinity school states: 'I was a Jehovah's Witness for 5 1/2 years and served as a full-time pioneer for some of that time. I was too young to be considered for any elder type positions and was never completely trusted because I was a college student. As you are certainly aware, academic quality is not encouraged by *the Society*. I left in 1976 after being badly abused by the congregation in Ithica, N.Y., where I was a student.'[66] A married woman now living in California gives a similar account:

I was the first young woman of the Witnesses in Montreal to enter university (1965). The criticism that ensued was bitter. But when I told the Witnesses I intended to pursue my studies further since McGill [University] was financing five years of graduate work for me, Mother and I were automatically ostracized. Thereafter the persecution, the injustice, the wickedness, and psychological harassment, particularly on the part of the servants, grew so fierce [that] Mother and I had to leave to retain our sanity. To this day I have not heard of having been officially disfellowshiped. However, I did ask one of my congregation servants and a circuit servant to leave my home and kindly never return upon being told I was definitely manifesting Satan's spirit of independence![67]

In developing countries and perhaps even in some industralized lands, Witness educational levels seem to be somewhat above average, although this is probably not true in North America. That they are often craftsmen or middle class and that they place so much stress on the ability to read, write, speak, and study gives them advantages over many of their neighbours. Furthermore, since they must become aware of other people's ideologies through their preaching work, they often develop an awareness of certain aspects of the societies in which they live that members of less missionary-minded religions do not have. As a result, many intelligent Witnesses become very interested in education at all levels in spite of the society's fulminations against higher forms of it. James Beckford makes the following observation: 'Without wishing to make pretentions to unjustified precision, then, it seems reasonable to infer that Jehovah's Witnesses display an unusually high degree of interest in further education of a variety of forms.'[68]

There are also some psychological data which suggest that Witness children are highly creative. In a study of 'creativity' amongst twelve-year-olds in the March 1973 Australian *Journal of Personality,* Kathleen Dewing reported: 'In particular, a disproportionately large number of highly creative children were Jehovah's Witnesses. Four children from this total sample of 394 were members of this sect, and all four showed high creative ability. The girl who gained the highest total score on the Torrence tests, and the girl who was the only child, male or female, to be included in the top 20 percent of all five performance measures, were both Jehovah's Witnesses.'[69]

One could, of course, dismiss the sample as too small to be statistically significant, but personal studies of Jehovah's Witness children over the years lead me to believe that there is some validity to these findings. Perhaps Dewing was correct in suggesting that the conflict situations faced by Witness children in school over such matters as patriotic exercises make them more alert and discriminating than other children. Barbara Grizzuti Harrison suggests, however, that the creativity of Witness children may be caused by 'sexual repression.' 'Sexuality rigorously repressed in puberty conduces to a strongly colored fantasy life,' she states. Hence, 'the imagination of very young Witnesses is fueled and fired by the rich imagery of destruction and creation with which they live.' Accordingly, says Harrison: 'It is not surprising that the tension produced by the clash between force-fed dogmatic certainty and inner confusion, and the friction created by the rules of the socially isolated against the world, may be, for a time, *creative* tension.'[70] Harrison's argument seems more than a little strained, however; it is hard to believe that the creativity of Witness twelve-year-olds develops suddenly, full-grown, like Athena from the head of Zeus, at puberty. But she does no doubt have a point respecting the colourful ideological world in which Witness children grow up. Both Dewing and Harrison may miss another rather simple point, though. Witness children are highly disciplined and at least up until their teen years are strongly encouraged to succeed in school. Yet, significantly, it is often the very *creativity* and educational curiosity so evident in Witness children and young adults which causes many of them to leave the movement. Barbara Grizzuti Harrison says: 'The tragedy is that creative young Witnesses will not be permitted to explore or fulfill their potential – unless, for them the knot [of Witness faith] unravels.'[71] And for a good many it does just that.

Entertainment, the Arts, and Literature

Official Witness attitudes towards various forms of entertainment are quite negative. Especially is this so with respect to athletics and sports in general. In a small booklet entitled *School and Jehovah's Witnesses* which was published in 1983, the Watch Tower Society states: 'Jehovah's Witnesses appreciate the value of physical education courses during school hours.'[72] But then it makes it clear that Witness children and youths are to be discouraged from any involvement with organized sports:

At the same time, however, Witness parents feel that schools often overemphasize sports. Therefore in training their children, they try to moderate the emphasis on athletic achievement. They hope their young ones will want to pursue careers, not as athletes, but as ministers of God. So Witness parents encourage their children to use after-school hours principally to pursue spiritual interests, rather than to excel in some sport.

Participation in organized sports, we believe, would expose Witness youths to unwholesome associations. We also feel that the competitive spirit in modern sports – 'the winning isn't everything, it's the ONLY thing' ideology – has harmful effects. So if Witness youths feel the need for extra recreation, their parents encourage them to seek such recreation with fellow believers, yes, 'along with those who call upon the Lord out of a clean heart.'[73]

As far as becoming cheerleaders or homecoming queens, the society's booklet says: 'At athletic events it is the responsibility of cheerleaders to orchestrate the crowd in frenzied cheering for a school. They also encourage the people into hero worship and lead them in standing for the school song. Jehovah's Witnesses consider it inappropriate to do this. Similarly we feel that for a Witness youth to serve as a homecoming or beauty queen would be a violation of Bible principles that show the impropriety of glorifying humans. Romans 1:25; Acts 12:21–23.'[74]

Dances, school clubs, and school plays are all discouraged for the young, and dating is forbidden. *School and Jehovah's Witnesses* argues, in what must seem insulting terms to many teachers and school administrators who are given the booklet, that for Jehovah's Witness children or youths to participate in school dances, clubs, or plays might place them in environments with 'unwholesome associations.'[75]

Naturally, what these strictures do is dampen the interest of Jehovah's Witnesses, young and old, in sports, various social activities, dancing, and the theatre. While going to watch most sporting events or a play is not absolutely prohibited, attendance at such is frowned upon by many Witnesses as 'a waste of precious theocratic time' and therefore somewhat worldly. While dancing is also not outlawed entirely, it is circumscribed by so many Watch Tower regulations and caveats that many Witnesses never learn it or, if they do, seldom engage in it. Many forms of modern dance and 'close dancing' which involves bodily contact with anyone but one's marriage mate or an immediate family member are all said to be improper. They are frequently held to invoke Satan, sexual passion, or both.[76]

This means, too, that Jehovah's Witnesses are constantly bombarded by articles in Watch Tower literature and talks at kingdom halls and conventions on the evils of listening to various types of modern music on radio, television, or records;[77] about the morally low nature of most movies;[78] and about the importance of limiting television viewing.[79] Significantly, the last is held to be as much of a time-waster as a moral danger and is often referred to by strict Witness elders and circuit overseers as 'the Devil's eyeball.'

What all this means is that for many young Witnesses there is little opportunity to develop athletic, musical, or artistic talents. To do so would cause them to be marked officially or unofficially by their fellow believers as 'immature,' 'worldly,' or 'rebellious.' Should a Witness youth set out to become a professional athlete, he would find life in the Witness communiity almost impossible; and becoming a professional musician, actor, or artist would be almost as difficult. In the past it was possible to learn to play any of a variety of musical instruments with the expressed hope that one might become a member of one of the orchestras which were used to lead Witness throngs in singing 'kingdom songs' at circuit, district, and international conventions. However, six or seven years ago, the Watch Tower Society decided that members of such orchestras were spending too much time practising music at assemblies and not enough time listening to the society's speakers. Thus, the orchestras were replaced with tape-recorded music. So today, unless one wants to learn to play the piano (used in most kingdom halls), really or ostensibly wants to teach music as a part-time profession while pioneering, or takes up something like amateur guitar, there is little room within the Witness community for the development of musical aptitudes. In so far as professional or even polished amateur singing is concerned, it too is discouraged, although not so overtly. Choirs are simply not permitted in kingdom halls, and no one is ever expected to take voice lessons. To have either a group or an individual – especially a woman – stand before a congregation to lead it in singing would be regarded as giving too much prominence to individuals or, worse, a specific individual. Consequently, most Witnesses sing rather badly, a fact demonstrated over and over again both in kingdom halls and at Watch Tower conventions.

What about Witness converts who are professional athletes, musicians, or entertainers? These, it must be said, are generally given something like a popular Witness dispensation to continue practising their professions, and ordinary Witnesses take delight in stating that someone prominent in the world has become one of them. In fact, so great is the desire of many members of the Witness community to have famous or outstanding persons within their ranks that false rumours have often abounded· among them about the conversion of well-known entertainers. For example, it was long claimed inaccurately that American singing star Glen Campbell was a Witness, and some went so far as to state that they had seen him at district conventions. But the Watch Tower Society has not been anxious to exploit the genuine conversions of a very few prominent persons to Jehovah's Witnesses in the athletic or entertainment worlds except in one way: to have them publicly renounce or at least curtail their secular careers to become active publishers and pioneers. Thus, over the years, *The Watchtower* and *Awake!* have published a number of articles by athletes and musicians which have been used to demonstrate how 'success in the world' has been exchanged for the ministry of Jehovah's Witnesses.[80]

Ordinarily, athletes tend to give up their participation in sports shortly after becoming Jehovah's Witnesses, partly because athletic careers are generally of short duration in any case and partly because they are encouraged by fellow Witnesses to do so. The same is not true of entertainers and musicans, however, of whom there are a number. In the United States, for example, actress Eve Arden and jazz artist George Benson are known to be Witnesses, as are various members of popular orchestras and dancebands. But such persons seldom make much of their faith, at least to the press and electronic media; to do so would violate the important Watch Tower canon that one should never become too prominent within the Witness community except as a Watch Tower official. So, in the recent past, only one person, television actress Teresa Graves, has been used by the society to promote Witness interests. On a number of occasions she spoke publicly against the persecution of her brethren in Malawi. Yet during the last five or six years, the society has allowed her to sink into public anonymity after becoming a pioneer.

Michael Jackson, perhaps the most famous entertainer in modern times, has violated the society's anti-prominence canon and certainly caused both the society and many Witnesses much consternation by so doing. Although he is noted for personal asceticism, vegetarianism, sexual continence, and refusal to use drugs or alcohol, he has broken many written and unwritten Watch Tower rules. His costumes, birthday parties, sometime association with actress Brooke Shields, public appearance with u.s. President Ronald Reagan, and his strange fixation on the movie 'space creature' E.T. – all well publicized – have offended Watch Tower officials. But more serious from their perspective, if possible, is the fact that a personality cult has developed around Jackson and that he produced the video 'Thriller' in which he is transformed into a 'cat person' and spirits in a graveyard come to life. So, he is seen as having 'exalted himself' and having involved himself with 'demonism' in spite of a disclaimer which appears at the beginning of 'Thriller' stating that he does not believe in the occult.

No doubt in partial response to Jackson's activities and the youth cult that has developed around him, the society has taken a strong stand. The 15 October 1983 issue of *The Watchtower* (pp. 10–15) criticized contemporary music and making a cult of personalities. In addition, it called on all Witnesses to destroy albums and videos with verbal or visual references to witches, demons, or devils and discouraged them from imitating 'worldly musicians' in 'dress, grooming and speech by wearing T-shirts or jackets that advertise such performers.'

This was only the beginning of the society's actions with respect to Michael Jackson, however. On 2 January 1984, the society answered a letter from Michael Pagano of St Louis, Missouri, by stating: 'The society has been advised that Michael Jackson is a baptised member of the Christian congregation. However, his being one of Jehovah's Witnesses should not be construed by anyone to mean that either the Society or congregation with which he is associated approves or endorses the music that he sings or plays, or all the aspects of his life-style.' Then, in attempting to imply inaccurately that Jackson was a new convert rather than having been raised as a Witness in a Witness home, the society remarked: 'As you are well aware, some individuals who reach the point of dedication and baptism still have some worldly habits and ways which characterize the "old personality that must be stripped off." (Ephesians 4:22–4; Colossians 3:7–10) These adjustments must continue to be made after baptism, as an individual progresses toward maturity. Christianity should be a way of life and we should not use our Christian freedom as a "blind for badness." – I Peter 2:16.' In a final slap at Jackson's music and performances, the society then advised: 'As to the need to avoid music that debases, we refer you to the article that appeared on pages 10–15 of the October 15, 1983 issue of *The Watchtower*. The dangers of pursuing fads and idolizing humans are discussed in the December 8, 1964, issue of *Awake!*, pages 5–8, and the article on pages 309–13 of May 15, 1968, issue of *The Watchtower*.'

Since the writing of the above letter, press reports have appeared to the effect that Jackson has been 'publicly reproved' for his conduct by his home congregation in California. The tabloid *Globe* (of West Palm Beach, Florida), in its 20 March 1984 issue (p. 5), stated specifically 'GLOBE has learned that the religious group, to which Michael, his mother and three sisters belong, has chided him because it fears his reclusive lifestyle – which includes fasting, vegetarianism, herbal enemas and frantic dancing – paints the faith in a bizarre light.' Then it went on to quote Watch Tower spokesman William Van De Wall at Brooklyn and individual Witnesses in Ventura County, California, and Las Vegas, Nevada, all of whom were openly critical of the youthful entertainer. And to demonstrate that this is not just another baseless story published by the tabloid press, in May 1984 *Awake!* has published an apology by Jackson for making 'Thriller.'[81]

In spite of all this, the Watch Tower Society continues to face a dilemma with respect to Michael Jackson. He shows no overt willingness to abandon his career, and to discipline him too severely or disfellowship him would in all likelihood create a public uproar. Furthermore, there is good reason to believe that he has been making large monetary contributions to the society which it would not want to lose. Yet the society's officers must be under tremendous pressure to take action against him from within their own ranks and from conservative Witnesses in general who do not want Jackson to have too dramatic an influence on their children. So if Watch Tower conduct in the past is an indication, even Jackson faces the real threat of excommunication from 'God's theocratic arrangement.'

Literary tastes among Jehovah's Witnesses tend to be particularly narrow. The Watch Tower Society forbids the reading by Witnesses of anything overtly critical of the society or its teachings, especially if written by an ex-Witness, an 'evil slave.'[82] In addition, anything even slightly pornographic or risqué is regarded as highly improper. Thus, the society, like the Catholic church prior to the Second Vatican Ecumenical Council, has its *Index Librorum Prohibitorum* or list of forbidden books. But besides that, it openly discourages reading worldly publications which are not necessary for one's faith and may take too much time away from studying the Bible and Watch Tower publications. Often it is held quite naively by both the society's spokesmen and ordinary Witnesses that one can gain the equivalent of a college or university education solely by carefully reading *Awake!* and *The Watchtower*. So, many rigorous Witness loyalists limit their reading to what comes to them from the society and their local newspaper. A few of these may subscribe to magazines such as *Reader's Digest* and *The National Geographic Magazine*. But romantic novels, style and fashion journals, and even news magazines such as *Maclean's, Time, Newsweek,* and *U.S. News and World Report* are often regarded as 'not upbuilding.'

It would be wrong, however, to suggest that such attitudes are representative of all Witnesses. Many better educated and more urbane ones do, of course, have more liberal reading tastes and read what they choose in the privacy of their homes. But unless they are particularly independent-minded, even they will generally limit their appetites for reading to works of a 'practical' or scientific nature rather than to history, fiction, plays, or poetry. In effect, then, unless they have read the great literary classics of the societies in which they live before becoming Witnesses, have been required to do so in school, or are exceptional, most will probably never read them at all. To the average publisher or pioneer – if he is aware of them – Chaucer and Shakespeare are too 'smutty,' Dante too Catholic, Dostoevski and Goethe too involved with the occult, and most modern writers too decadent. To Jehovah's Witnesses in general 'life is real; life is earnest; and its goal is not the grave' – it is rather to praise Jehovah and vindicate his name by reading Watch Tower literature and placing it at the doors.

Moral Values and Social Relationships

Witness moral values are in certain ways liberal, in most others very strict. But it is the legalistic rules of the community which make Jehovah's Witnesses true sectarians as defined by Bryan Wilson. Since they have no prohibitions against any foods – except those containing blood – or any beverages such as tea, coffee, or alcoholic drinks, no peculiar dress styles, and no absolute prohibitions against most forms of entertainment, they are seldom immediately distinguishable from others in the places where they live. Yet every true Witness feels a constant sense of alienation from the world which is heightened by the fact that there are many things which he *must not* do and many others which he *should* not.

From the standpoint of occupation alone, theoretically no Witness may serve in the military, work in the direct employment of another religious organization, hold elective governmental office, work in a munitions factory, produce or sell tobacco, engage in certain violent sports such as boxing or wrestling, participate in gambling activities or those involving the commercial exploitation of sex. In addition, he must not join a political party, vote for public officials, perform jury duty, attend bull fights, fence, stand for the national anthem, salute the flag, offer toasts, smoke, chew tobacco, use hallucinogenic drugs, celebrate holidays, engage in improper sexual relations (as defined by the Watch Tower Society), accept a blood transfusion, or, as mentioned earlier, participate in certain types of dancing or listen to certain types of music.

These and numerous other restrictions plus the society's constant counsel to engage in the preaching work help to remind practically every Witness that he is separate, distinct, and apart from 'the world.' Consequently, most Witnesses tend to think of society outside their own community as decadent and corrupt. Every political, economic and military crisis is therefore seen as another sign that the world is fast coming to its end and is beyond repair. This in turn means to Jehovah's Witnesses that they must keep themselves apart from Satan's 'doomed system of things.' Thus most tend to socialize largely, although not totally, within the Witness community.

Of course, to the average Witness his community is first and foremost his local congregation. For life revolves around the kingdom hall. Although kingdom halls are generally rather plain, low structures (often adorned with watchtowers) which never serve as social centres in the way that other churches do, they none the less dominate the lives of those who attend them. True, only congregational meetings, funerals, and weddings are ever held in them. But because so much Witness activity revolves around the five regular meetings and regular rendezvous for preaching, what occurs at the local kingdom hall becomes fundamental to the establishment of most social relationships within the congregation. Hence individuals and families will plan both religious and non-religious activities with others when they meet for worship or for the preaching work.

This means that by developing relationships *inside* the congregation or at most with other Witnesses, individual Jehovah's Witnesses cut down their association with 'worldlings,' something the Watch Tower Society encourages. In fact the society has gone so far as to urge Witnesses to cut all social ties with outsiders except those involving business dealings and attempts to convert them. It has, however, never really been able to get full conformity from the Witness community on this matter. As a result *The Watchtower* of 15 February 1960 stated:

Still there are those who think they can allow themselves to seek association with worldly friends or relatives for entertainment. But how can a Christian 'put away the old personality which conforms to his former course of conduct' and 'put on the new personality which was created by God's will in true righteousness' by continuing to associate with those who still have deceptive desires? (Eph. 4:22–4) Rather 'do not become *partners* with them; for you were once darkness, but you are now light in connection with the Lord. Go on walking as children of light ... Keep on making sure of what is acceptable to the Lord; and *quit sharing* with them in the unfruitful works which belong to the darkness.' (Eph. 5:7–11) Peter also advised one to 'live the remainder of his time in the flesh, no more for the desires of men, but for God's will ... Because you do not continue *running* [or associating] with them in this course ... they are puzzled and go on speaking abusively of you.' We should be as aliens and temporary residents with respect to the conduct of this generation. – 1 Pet. 4:2–4; 2:11, 12.[83]

Still, many Witnesses have tried to obey the society's dicta on this matter and have reduced social contacts with non-Witnesses to a minimum. At the same time, many relatives and associates have cut their ties with their Witness family members or acquaintances because they often know that they are regarded as 'children of darkness' and resent ongoing attempts to convert them when they do not want to be converted. So, to a large degree, many members of the Witness community are, as Raymond Franz has noted, 'hermetically sealed' from the outside world – at least in so far as attitudes and thought processes are concerned.

It should be recognized that this is certainly *not* true of the entire community. Many refuse to break ties with old friends and relatives in spite of the society's wishes. Others quietly use the excuse of business relationships to develop close social ties with non-Witnesses. And as noted earlier, sometimes young persons of both sexes will date 'worldlings' with marriage as the end in view. In many cases, they will sincerely seek to convert such prospective marriage mates, but in others they will simply go through the motions of doing so while they themselves are in the process of leaving the Witness fold.

Naturally, social isolation is difficult for Jehovah's Witnesses to maintain, for except in a few areas in central Africa, they must constantly relate to non-Witnesses. On top of that, there are factors *within* their own congregations which often cause Witnesses to look for outside associations. Frequently local congregations will be dominated by authoritarian personalities or they will be beset by a good deal of 'theocratic politics' and infighting. Life on the inside is thus not the 'spiritual paradise' that the Watch Tower Society would like to make out that it is. Consequently, to achieve happier existence, certain Witnesses will turn their attention to 'the world' and 'friends in the world.'

Jehovah's Witness business relationships with other Witnesses are often unstable also. In the first place, it is difficult to work with someone on a daily basis, worship with him four or five times a week, join him in the preaching work, and relate to him socially without becoming aware of his faults. Simply stated, familiarity frequently breeds contempt. Not surprisingly, then, many Witnesses will not enter into business partnerships with co-believers.

This is only one aspect of the problem. During their years as pioneers and special pioneers many young Witnesses are forced to find ways of earning a living while continuing their evangelical activities. Thus many of them enter secular occupations which are highly competitive. For example, in the last two decades or so, literally thousands of North American pioneers and other Witnesses have gone into what is commonly called 'the cleaning business.' That simply means that they have taken out contracts to do janitorial work for stores, theatres, and other businesses at night, and therefore can have their days free for proselytizing. Because the number seeking such employment is great and the number of jobs limited, much competition – sometimes of a cutthroat nature – has occurred among Witness brethren. Too, the spirit of capitalism has often overtaken the thinking of many young pioneers. In a number of cities throughout Canada and the United States some have even become janitorial entrepreneurs who have built up cleaning 'empires' by subletting jobs to other pioneers. In a few such cases these evangelist entrepreneurs have gained sizeable income but, then, have become unpopular with many of their brethren for storing up treasures on earth rather than in heaven.

Others – again, in particular, pioneers, – have used their skills as evangelists to become successful salesmen. They frequently become involved in some part-time sales job while pioneering, then later gravitate to a full-time secular occupation or business. Naturally, this causes many of them to be heavily influenced by the competitive instincts of capitalism and frequently to treat fellow Witnesses as competitors rather than as Christian brothers. So tensions can and often do develop in business relationships between Jehovah's Witnesses.

In fact, what often happens in such cases is that the entrepreneurial instincts that have been developed willy-nilly among many of the most zealous Witnesses in order to survive as pioneer evangelists come into direct confrontation with other, equally important communitarian values. Even the most simple-minded Witness finds it difficult to understand how a 'brother' can worship beside him four or five times a week and yet engage in ruthless business competition with him in the work-a-day world where he must earn his living. So a good deal of resentment is engendered which sometimes disrupts personal congregational relationships.

Witness employer-employee relationships are often not good either. Both sides tend to expect better treatment or service than they would from outsiders. Often, too, they tend to confuse master-servant relationships with the fraternal religious ones of the kingdom hall.

However, bad employer-employee relationships do not often cause internal strife within Witness congregations. For although some large businessmen regularly employ fellow Witnesses, most small enterpreneurs probably do not. Furthermore, many workers do not like to work under their religious confrères. Often they are well aware of the possibilities for conflict and will state privately that they 'will not work with or under a brother.' In all probability, many also want to be away from those who will be constantly engaged in monitoring their personal behaviour to ascertain whether they are acting as good Jehovah's Witnesses or not. So, because Jehovah's Witnesses generally do not work well together in the secular world – at least in developed nations – they are forced and sometimes elect to lead much of their lives outside the close confines of 'theocratic society.'

Moral Behaviour

The strictness with which Jehovah's Witnesses are governed forces them to live lives which are generally highly moral. Since Nathan Knorr became president of the Watch Tower Society in 1942, the society has placed a heavy emphasis on personal honesty, business integrity, and since 1962, on obedience to secular as well as spiritual authority. Additionally, every Witness is constantly made aware that he should not 'bring reproach on Jehovah or his organization.'[84] Hence, over the years the Witnesses have gained a well-earned reputation for moral behaviour. For example, in the concentration camps of the Third Reich, the Nazis could trust them as personal servants when they could trust no others.[85] As Karla Poewe has stressed, they are noted for honesty in central Africa and, if press reports are to be believed, in North America as well.

Of course it is very difficult to measure honesty and moral behaviour, but from both reputation and observation, most ordinary Witnesses lead lives that are highly exemplary from the standpoint of their neighbours as well as their own community. If any criticisms can be made of them in these areas it is 1 / that their morality is one dictated largely by the whims of the Watch Tower Society and may, therefore, often shift, and 2 / they tend not only to be critical of outsiders but of fellow Witnesses as well. As psychologist Havor Montague says: 'Jehovah's Witnesses tend to be both highly critical of the world, which they clearly see does not follow their set of rules, and highly critical of fellow Witnesses, who also fail to live up to the ideal picture of a Witness painted by the Witness Society.'[86]

Then, too, there is another factor to Witness morality that bears mention. Both outsiders and insiders frequently point to the almost unbelievable pride and self-righteousness manifested by many persons in authority within their community. So Watch Tower officials and elders at all levels are frequently charged with Pharisaism of the worst sort. But while this criticism may properly be directed at many Witness leaders on the basis of the historical data presented in previous chapters, it should not be applied to the average Witness publisher who is usually a truly meek and decent individual.[87]

Finally, life among ordinary Witnesses seems far more morally and socially stable than it does among the higher echelons of the movement. The ongoing use of alcohol is probably far less common among congregational publishers, for instance, than it is at Bethel, branch homes, and even among district and circuit overseers.[88] Neither is life quite so thoroughly prescribed nor church politics so intense, at least in most cases.

Ethnic and Racial Attitudes

One of Jehovah's Witnesses' proudest boasts is that they are free of either ethnic or racial prejudice. Speaking of conditions in South Africa, the *Awake!* magazine of 8 May 1979 stated: 'racial unity is not mere "surface toleration" but is deeply rooted in the feeling of the Witnesses. For decades many white Witnesses have labored as missionaries with black local Witnesses. A bond of genuine love has been developed.'[89] And there seems much evidence to support this claim. For example, since Pastor Russell's day Bible Students and Jehovah's Witnesses have long appealed to the Jews, some of whom have joined their ranks and become prominent among them. Blacks, Orientals of many backgrounds, and American Indians have also become Witnesses in large numbers with the general belief that the Witness community was and is quite free from prejudice. In fact, the number of blacks among Witnesses in the United States is disproportionately large in comparison to the number of blacks in the total population.[90]

However, Jehovah's Witnesses have been charged with being hypocritical on matters of ethnic and racial tolerance. Ex-Witnesses especially have censured them regarding this matter. Barbara Grizzuti Harrison claims that the Watch Tower Society and its leaders have always been anti-semitic[91] while Bonnie Gaskill and Toni Jean Alquist Meneses go much farther. They state:

The Watchtower, like the Mormons, also stated that God had cursed the descendants of Canaan with black skin and destined them to be servants of others. We read that this servitude is a positive thing when they say: *'There is no servant in the world as good as a good colored servant, and the joy that he gets from rendering faithful service is one of the purest joys there is in the world.'* (THE GOLDEN AGE [now AWAKE!] July 24, 1929, pg. 207] Is it any wonder that the black African governments hate the white racist Watchtower Society. Their hatred for the Society is not based on religion, but politics and race. The tragedy is that the black African Witnesses are the ones who suffer, not the Watchtower Society. It's always the brothers who suffer so much.[92]

Ex–Jehovah's Witnesses are not the only ones to accuse the Watch Tower Society of ethnic and racial prejudice. Writing in 1945, Herbert Stroup stated boldly: 'The Jews are also hated by the Witnesses.' Stroup claimed: 'Prevalent among the Witnesses is the notion that all Jews are rich. Even refugees who have escaped to this country from persecution abroad are believed to have brought scads of money with them.' Nevertheless, he admitted: 'In spite of this generally unfavorable attitude, which is, indeed, sometimes shared by Jewish Witnesses themselves, the movement is able to satisfy its Jewish members who find its theology the natural, developed expression of essential Judaism.'[93] Respecting blacks, Stroup asserted: 'More often the Negroes are accepted and tolerated, but not taken into intimate confidence, and there are no Negroes in influential positions in the organizational set-up.'[94]

In 1955 Werner Cohn made even harsher comments about Witness racial attitudes. In a book review of Marley Cole's *Jehovah's Witnesses: The New World Society* published in *The New Leader* of 17 October 1955, Cohn wrote:

Until recent years, Negroes were not allowed to attend regular conventions of the organization but were furnished, instead, with separate Jim Crow assemblies. To this day, there are separate 'companies' (local groups) for Negro members in all southern and border states; even as far north as Asbury Park, N.J., Negro Witnesses are segregated. When I visited the Brooklyn headquarters of the organization about two years ago, only two out of more than 400 of the headquarters staff were Negro. The top national leadership of the organization is completely white; and in one of its rare direct references to Negroes, the organization has declared itself against racial intermarriage.[95]

What, then, are the facts behind these claims and counterclaims? In the first place, Barbara Grizzuti Harrison's attempt to paint Charles T. Russell as an anti-semite completely ignores the times in which he lived. By the same token, Abraham Lincoln could be described as anti-black. If anything, Russell was a philo-semite of the first order and heavily influenced by Paul S.L. Johnson, a man raised a Jew.[96] Second, although he was affected to an extent by then-current, late-nineteenth- and early-twentieth-century attitudes which held Caucasians to be intellectually superior to members of other races, so were most white persons in his time. If anything, Russell was ahead of most of his contemporaries on this issue.[97] The case is less clear with Rutherford and Knorr. Both seem to have had a love-hate attitude towards the Jews,[98] and while they sympathized with blacks, neither had a particularly high regard for them, at least intellectually.[99] It is hard to say how Frederick Franz feels on such matters but, in general, he seems to be more openly tolerant of persons of other ethnic and racial backgrounds. He has always liked to travel, has mixed well with persons of other cultures, and, of course, is often able to speak to other language groups in their own tongues – something no other Watch Tower president could do.

What about the community as a whole? In general, Jehovah's Witnesses are amazingly tolerant ethnically and racially. As far as the Jews are concerned, there is still probably a stronger sense of identity with them among Witnesses than with any other single group.[100] After all, the 'chosen people tradition,' which comes directly from Judaism, is as much a part of their heritage as it is that of the Mormons and many American fundamentalist Protestants. And today there is virtually no instance of the racial segregation that Stroup and Cohn wrote about several decades ago.

But what about scholarly criticisms of the Witnesses' ethnic and racial attitudes, and the very harsh ones of Gaskill and Alquist Meneses? Do they have no foundation? Probably very little, for all seem to have overlooked several factors. First, it would be very surprising indeed if Jehovah's Witnesses – even today a community largely composed of converts – did not carry with them many of the values and attitudes of the larger societies out of which they have come. Hence one often finds among ordinary Witnesses a certain degree of rather covert prejudice towards persons of other nationalities or races. Occasionally one may hear Witnesses, high and low, make racial slurs. Yet if the Watch Tower Society deserves general credit for anything, it is that it has emphasized the value of ethnic and racial tolerance among its adherents to a greater degree than is the case with most other religious organizations – the Baha'is and Unification church excepted. Seldom, therefore, do divisions or troubles among Witnesses at the congregational level or other levels of community life come about as a result of questions of language, ethnicity, or race.

Also, Witness segregation practised in the United States until the late 1950s and in South Africa up to the present must be put into perspective. True, Jehovah's Witnesses have sanctioned segregation wherever it is legal or socially sanctioned, but this is not because they have approved of it or, in general, wanted it. Rather, they have looked on it as a temporary evil to be ignored in order to preach the gospel of Christ's kingdom. Like the Apostle Paul who recognized and accepted the institution of Roman slavery, the Witnesses argue that in order to carry on their primary work of preaching the good news, they must not get embroiled in civil-rights questions. For if the present world is ending and a new, completely integrated world is near at hand, why should they worry about those evils of segregation which really do not affect their worship? As far as inter-racial marriage is concerned, the society has held that it is in no way wrong, but it has argued realistically that persons who enter into such marriages may find severe hardships ahead of them. Nevertheless, Cohn may have a point when he infers that there is some degree of prejudice in Watch Tower counsel against inter-racial marriage.

Peter Gregerson is probably quite right in his evaluation of Witness ethnic and racial attitudes, then, when he states that while there is very little significant prejudice at 'lower levels' there is some 'at the top.'[101] Werner Cohn's assessment of the fact that in the past there were few blacks at the Brooklyn Bethel and *none* in the leadership of the Witness movement was quite accurate and while there are now many black and Latin American workers there, the leadership is still almost totally white. Some black and Latin American Bethel workers and ex-workers complain that racism exists at the world-wide headquarters of Jehovah's Witnesses. In addition, there are complaints that sometimes Jehovah's Witnesses of certain ethnic groups dominate Witnesses of other ethnic or racial communities among whom they settle. For example, English-Canadian Witnesses in positions of authority have often claimed that their French-speaking brethren in Quebec have lacked leadership qualities and have sometimes been quite patronizing towards them. Americans, Australians, Britons, Canadians, Germans, and other Witnesses of northern European origin have sometimes shown the same attitude of condescension to their African, Asian, and Latin American brethren as well.

It may be asked, if the society teaches ethnic and racial tolerance, why is it that the leadership itself and many of the most zealous Witnesses practice a certain amount of intolerance? The answers seem to be: the most senior Witness leaders are older men whose attitudes were formed in an age when ethnic and racial tolerance was regarded as less important than it is today, and the Watch Tower hierarchy is an 'in-group' which operates as a power elite which restricts its membership socially, and therefore, ethnically and racially. Like the Papal Curia at Rome which has been dominated by Italians for centuries, the Watch Tower Society is dominated by white Americans. Then, too, because of cultural and educational factors, northern Europeans, North Americans, and Australians are often more efficient administrators and organizers than the members of many other nationalities. And since the Watch Tower Society places so much emphasis on *organization*, it is not surprising that those Witnesses with organizational skills and educations should look down on those other ethnic or racial communities who, in general, have fewer of either. Still, after recognizing that some intolerance exists, it must be stressed that the degree of ethnic and racial tolerance among Jehovah's Witnesses is remarkable.

Witness Mental Health

The subject of mental health among Jehovah's Witnesses deserves far more study than it has received. For on the one hand, the Watch Tower Society asserts that Jehovah's Witnesses are among the healthiest of persons from a psychological standpoint while, on the other, some psychologists and psychiatrists claim that they suffer from a disproportionately high degree of mental illness.

On the society's side of this issue there are some amazing instances of psychological toughness. For example, in his book *The Theory and Practice of Hell*, Eugen Kogon remarks that in the concentration camps of the Third Reich 'one cannot escape the impression that psychologically speaking, the ss was never quite equal to the challenge offered them by Jehovah's Witnesses.'[102] And German Witnesses have not been alone in manifesting such dramatic pluckiness. Both their Japanese and Canadian brethren showed the same spirit at the same time,[103] and since then numerous Witness communities have stood before persecution with amazing fortitude. In particular this has been true of the Malawian community. Then, in addition to such data, there seems little reason to doubt the society's claims that by becoming Jehovah's Witnesses many persons have achieved greater solace and better mental health.[104]

It would be wrong, though, to suggest that Jehovah's Witnesses do not have certain serious problems with mental health. After all, as with many missionary-minded religions, they openly boast that they attract individuals who have suffered severe social and psychological deprivation and those who have been alcoholics and drug addicts. So it is not surprising that some of those persons bring the effects of their old problems into the Witness community when they are baptized. But besides that fact, there can be little doubt that to live as one of Jehovah's Witnesses, with feelings of alienation from the world, causes a high degree of unhealthy stress. To argue, as do some, that this is just the reflection of a 'martyr complex' is unfair. Although some Witnesses may sometimes feel that they are persecuted when they are not, they do suffer real persecution and discrimination in much the same way that the Jewish community outside Israel does; and that certainly may cause a good deal of psychological damage, particularly to children.[105]

In addition, there are factors characteristic of Witness life itself which undoubtedly bring about a degree of mental illness. Zealous pioneers have on many occasions sacrificed both their physical and mental health out of a spirit of devotion.[106] Some elders and publishers also give of themselves to the point of exhaustion. The Christian doctrine of self-sacrifice, admirable as it no doubt may be, causes some serious mental stress among the most devout Witnesses of Jehovah. At the same time, attitudes of super-pietism also have a detrimental effect on some of the persons manifesting them or, additionally, on a number of those who are objects of their 'over-righteousness.'

All of this is well known to the governing body of Jehovah's Witnesses. Over the last decade a number of Witness lawyers, physicians, and other professionals have held annual closed meetings with representatives of the governing body to discuss legal and medical questions relating to their faith and to make suggestions to the Witnessses' supreme governing council. At one of those meetings, Dr Lawrence Onda, a California psychologist, delivered an unpublished paper on 'Selection of Mental Health Care' in which he drew attention to a number of psychiatric studies of Witness mental health and stated the following:

I would like to consider another reason why Jehovah's people have mental problems, but I want to be cautious that some do not misunderstand the following statements. I have tremendous love, respect, and devotion for Jehovah's true organization, but it can contribute to or accelerate an existing problem rather than making it better. What Biblical teaching contributes to making a problem worse? It is guilt. Jehovah's people are confronted with a higher standard and thus have greater psychological pressure. The 'world' says, if it makes you feel guilty, get rid of it. But we have to maintain the high level of Christian conduct in our families, daily lives and personalities. We cannot think a wrong thought without feeling guilty. If the Witness becomes unbalanced, he/she may become overly despondent and feel like a failure because perfection cannot be attained in mind, body and thought. In essence, some of the 'Friends' try so hard to please Jehovah that they become mentally ill.

In spite of the significance of such remarks, which suggest very strongly that the Watch Tower Society's oft-trumpeted statement that 'Jehovah's Witnesses are the happiest of people' is far from being totally accurate, the governing body seems content to ignore the problems of Witness mental health. Although it has softened its stand against psychiatric medicine, which it formerly described as 'demonic,'[107] in general it remains hostile to all aspects of that therapy.[108] In particular, it damns the use of hypnotism.[109] At the same time, it goes on proclaiming that the best way to find happiness is to become one of Jehovah's Witnesses in spite of the fact that many Witnesses are really not very happy or mentally sound people.

The governing body's attitudes are, of course, predictable in this matter given the fact that the members of that council believe that they are carrying out a divine mission. They tend to feel that those Witnesses who have psychological problems in response to Watch Tower teachings and practices, or even to other matters, must ordinarily be suffering either from their own sins or from attacks by the demons – a concept which is constantly promoted at every level of the Witness community. So when an individual Witness is deeply depressed – sometimes because of a physical ailment – and goes to his elders for aid and counsel, frequently they will question him to determine whether he has been practising some secret sin (such as masturbation or the reading of pornographic magazines), has been failing in his personal Bible study, his meeting attendance, his door-to-door ministry or, very often, if he is suffering from some demonic hex.

Actions such as these repeated many, many times by Witness elders throughout the world no doubt bring a good deal of increased strain to those who are depressed. Witnesses who have already begun to question certain inconsistencies in Watch Tower teachings are especially affected. It is not surprising, then, that Havor Montague states: 'In my clinical work with Witnesses I have noticed a tendency for the better educated, more intelligent, more conscientious Witnesses to have emotional problems.' Furthermore, Montague claims that 'a number of very prominent Witness officials have become severely mentally ill, including several branch servants, many members of the Society's former legal staff, and even several members of the board of directors [of the Watch Tower Society].'[110]

However, it is certainly not just the more intelligent among Jehovah's Witnesses who suffer a good deal of mental illness. The belief in 'demonism' and 'demon influence' that is so common among them has a powerful negative effect on many less sophisticated ones. Montague states that he 'has worked with many cases where the suggestion of "demon influence" has been the factor that has caused a neurotic witness to become completely psychotic';[111] and there is little reason to doubt him. The Watch Tower Society teaches that any object used in 'false worship' such as a crucifix, rosary, religious picture, or book may be 'demonized.' But this is not all. The society also claims that such objects as clothing, blankets – almost anything – can, if formerly owned by someone who is in league with Satan, be used by the demons to bedevil Jehovah's Witnesses. So, when approached by emotionally or sometimes physically troubled Witnesses, their elders will urge them to find some 'demonized' possession and dispose of it. It is therefore not uncommon for such disturbed persons to burn their clothing, get rid of valuable paintings, ornaments, or furniture, and destroy whole libraries of books. Sometimes precious heirlooms are disposed of in this way.

With this background in mind, it is not surprising to discover that the professional studies of Witness mental health hold that Jehovah's Witnesses have a severe mental health problem. In his article 'The Pessimistic Sect's Influence on Mental Health: The Case of Jehovah's Witnesses,' Havor Montague states: 'The exact rate of mental illness among Jehovah's Witnesses is difficult to determine, but it is clear that it is significantly higher than the rate for the population as a whole.'[112] Later in the same article, he 'estimates that the mental illness rate of Jehovah's Witnesses is approximately 10 to 16 times higher than the rate for the general, non-Witness population.'[113] While these statements are rather damning, they need careful analysis.

Montague's study is based upon both his own data and that of several psychiatrists. Two studies which he reviews deal with young American and Swiss Witness men who were imprisoned as conscientious objectors. The first of these, written by the American M.H. Pescor, asserts that '8% of the total number of Witnesses imprisoned [in the United States] were classified as psychotic.'[114] The second, by Swiss psychiatrist J. von Janner, claims that many of the Witnesses whom he studied were experiencing 'a high level of fear, anxiety, were severely introverted, were loners, or severely neurotic.'[115] Yet such data do not necessarily imply that mental illness is more rampant among Jehovah's Witnesses than others. Some of the statements in their analyses of Witness men are so extreme that they raise questions regarding their objectivity. Furthermore, imprisonment is generally such an emotionally disturbing experience that it is difficult to understand why these studies are used to determine the mental health of an entire religious community.

Seemingly more significant, however, is another article cited by Montague which was written by John Spencer and published in the *British Journal of Psychiatry*. Spencer claims to have examined the records of all in-patient admissions to all West Australian psychiatric hospitals during a thirty-six-month period in the early 1970s. Among 7,546 mental patients he discovered fifty whom he classifies as 'active members of the Jehovah's Witness movement.' As a result, he deduces that there were 2.54 psychiatric in-patients for every 1,000 West Australians but that there were 4.17 for every 1,000 Witnesses in West Australia. Hence mental illness among Jehovah's Witnesses was much higher than it was among the general population.[116]

But it would not be going too far to describe the methodology used by Spencer as thoroughly unsatisfactory. In the first place, he gives no definition of what he means by an 'active' Witness, and it would be remarkable if West Australian hospital records differentiated between *publishers* and other persons who regard themselves as Jehovah's Witnesses. Then, too, he determined the total number of West Australian Witnesses by using the society's statistics for publishers in that state, not realizing that the number of persons in almost any Witness community is usually twice or more as large as the number of publishers. So in reality, Spencer's study probably does not indicate what both he and Montague think that it does.

Montague himself makes a number of assertions which are questionable. His strongly held belief that Witnesses are 'lower class' and that their rate of criminality is very high is based almost entirely on personal intuition rather than on any statistical evidence.[117] Furthermore, his statements often do not agree with sober analyses by sociologists, anthropologists, and historians, or more sig-

nificantly, with certain important census data. Still, Montague's study is
particularly important because it does give much direct evidence respecting
Witness mental-health problems.

In summation, then, it is quite true that Jehovah's Witnesses, particularly active
ones, are under great psychological pressure. Also, it seems evident that arising
from that pressure in its various forms and from certain beliefs (such as those
relating to demonism) many Witnesses do suffer from mental illness, but that such
sickness is as common as seen by Pescor, Von Janner, Spencer, and Montague is
highly questionable.

Decreasing Zeal

It is an outstanding phenomenon that a religious organization now well over one
hundred years old can still maintain the fervour of such a large community after
having suffered so many crises of prophetic disconfirmation. Nevertheless, as
James Beckford in particular has noted, over the years the zeal of a majority of
Witnesses has cooled somewhat.[118] True, the percentage of zealots at the centre of
the movement seems to have increased. The ratio of pioneers to congregation
publishers has grown rather substantially over the years as table 3 indicates.

TABLE 3

Ratio of pioneers to congregation publishers, 1950–80

Year	Total publishers including pioneers	Pioneers	Ratio of pioneers to congregation publishers
1950	373,430	14,093	1 to 26.5
1955	642,929	17,011	1 to 37.8
1960	916,332	30,584	1 to 29.9
1965	1,109,806	47,853	1 to 23.2
1970	1,483,430	88,871	1 to 16.7
1975	2,179,256	130,255	1 to 16.7
1980	2,272,278	137,861	1 to 16.5

While this has occurred there is evidence that particularly since 1975 the hours
preached per publisher per month have dropped rather consistently if one does not
include the pioneers. To illustrate: in 1950 all Jehovah's Witnesses – both pioneers
and congregation publishers – devoted an average of 12.2 hours per month to their
public preaching ministry, while in 1980 they devoted 12.45 hours per month to
that work. But since the ratio of pioneers (who are supposed to preach 140 hours
per month as special pioneers and 90 hours per month as regulars) to publishers
was much greater in 1980 than in 1950, it is clear that they are doing *more* in

preaching work than formerly while congregational publishers are doing significantly less.[119] Speaking of this factor and the growing number of inactive Jehovah's Witnesses, James Beckford remarks: 'The waning of some Jehovah's Witnesses' enthusiasm for service work presents as many problems for the Watch Tower Society as does their high turn-over rate, since they both have deleterious effects on the movement's evangelistic efficiency.'[120]

Regarding this fact Beckford makes another point which is evident both by observation and the society's own statistics. He says: 'Concomitant with the high drop-out rate among Jehovah's Witnesses, the declining rates of service-work practice have produced a novel effect on the social structure of Watch Tower congregations – they have swollen the size of the peripheral group of lapsed and inactive publishers who make only occasional appearances at Kingdom Hall.'[121] If one examines the primary Watch Tower statistics on this matter – the number of memorial attenders in contrast with the peak number of publishers from 1950 to 1980 – this becomes dramatically clear.

TABLE 4
Peak publishers and Memorial attenders, 1950–80

Year	Peak publishers	Memorial attenders
1950	373,430	511,203
1955	642,929	878,303
1960	916,332	1,519,821
1965	1,109,806	1,933,089
1970	1,483,430	3,226,168
1975	2,179,256	4,925,643
1980	2,272,278	5,726,656

Of course, in examining the statistics in table 4, it is possible to say, as the society regularly does, that they represent a greatly *increasing* interest in the teachings and activities of Jehovah's Witnesses. Even the society must admit, however, that among memorial attenders there are many inactive, ex-publishers who may simply put in an appearance at spring celebrations of the Lord's Supper to please family members or to indicate that they still have vague, if illusive, ties with the Witness community. It also seems evident that an increasing proportion of persons who show some initial interest in Jehovah's Witnesses fail to reach the point of becoming publishers. Consequently, the Watch Tower Society now sees a large, relatively uncommitted population outside the core Witness community which no longer actively supports the society's goals.

Paradoxically, this may in part be the society's own fault. Beckford states: 'Despite, therefore, the operation of mechanisms to ensure that the Society's allegedly divine mandate is indissolubly equated in Jehovah's Witnesses' minds with the obligation to pursue its objectives, there are signs that loyalty to "the *objectives* of the organization" is being partially eclipsed by loyalty to the *organization* itself.'[122] And this may have occurred simply because the society has placed such great emphasis on the idea that it, in effect, is God's channel of communication with his people, his organization. So, many simply feel that if they keep *some* connection, however vague, with the organization their chances of salvation are at least greater than the rest of mankind.

What about the loss of publishers as such? Just how many people who should *by the Society's own criteria* be 'publishers of the good news' today are not? It is difficult to say with great exactitude, but if one uses the society's statistics judiciously, a rather clear picture emerges. For example, if one takes the world-wide number of publishers for 1966, the year in which the book *Everlasting Life in Freedom of the Sons of God* heralded 1975 as a 'marked year,' then adds to it the world-wide number of baptisms up to the end of 1983, he will arrive at the number 3,674,315. Of course that figure must be reduced to take into consideration deaths which would have occurred during the years 1967 through 1983. So, taking a death rate of 1 per cent per year (roughly the world mortality rate), one arrives at a total of 3,385,176 – the minimum number of persons who, according to Witness teachings, should have been publishers in 1983. In fact, though there were only 2,652,323 throughout the world in that year.

It can be demonstrated, then, that at *the very least* Jehovah's Witnesses have lost 732,853 publishers in seventeen years or roughly 20 per cent of their active community. But in reality that figure is far too low. For it must be recognized that many publishers are unbaptized children or interested adults who may or may not ever become baptized Witness. So if one estimates conservatively that 20 per cent of all Witness publishers are unbaptized, he must subtract that number from the total to determine how many more than the 732,853 noted above have become inactive. If this is done, at least another 530,465 persons must be added, making a grand total of 1,263,318 – most of whom have been lost between 1971 and 1983.

Does it not seem that at least at the core of the community there is more zeal than formerly, however? Does not the increase in the ratio of pioneers to publishers clearly indicate that? Perhaps so, but even that is not clear. As indicated earlier, there is tremendous pressure on youth to begin pioneering immediately upon graduation from school. So in response to this pressure and the society's greatly increased emphasis on the preaching work since 1975, many young persons will join the pioneer ranks for a few months or even a few years before returning to the ranks of the congregation publishers. Thus there is a large turn-over in pioneers today to an extent that was unknown a generation ago. *Unofficially*, what is happening among Jehovah's Witnesses is very much like what takes place *officially* among the Mormons: young men and women do their stint of full-time evangelizing and then turn to marriage, a secular job, and sometimes even to leave the Witness community. So instead of being a life-time vocation as the society would like most Witnesses to regard it, pioneering is more and more becoming a temporary service which is to be finished and done before one settles into a more sedentary lifestyle.

Dissonance and Dissent

That many people who stop being active publishers still remain Jehovah's Witnesses emotionally and intellectually is quite true, but as was brought out in Chapter 4, there is increasing dissonance within the community. Furthermore, there is at present more open rebellion against Watch Tower authority than has been the case at any time since the 1920s. So what, then, are the factors behind such dissonance and dissent?

Until recently it has not generally been doctrine as such, at least in the first instance, or even the prophetic failure of 1975 which has caused disaffection. Certainly one may point to exceptions to this statement. Yet as long as most dissenters believed that there was hope for satisfactory reform within the community, they continued to regard themselves as sincere Jehovah's Witnesses who wanted to remain such. Over the years there had always been a few who were attracted by other religions or found themselves so seriously in disagreement with the society over some specific doctrine or doctrines that they had had to resign from the Witness community for conscientious reasons. But such persons were a small minority of those who left or were forced out.

What generally seemed to be more important factors were a sense of a lack of intellectual freedom and a strong feeling of revulsion against Watch Tower authoritarianism. In a yet unpublished preliminary study of over forty outstandingly successful professional and academic persons who have either left Jehovah's Witnesses or are now on the periphery of the movement, Jerry Bergman has discovered that practically *all* objected strongly to the lack of freedom to pursue and express ideas independently within the Witness community. Few stated that they had any significant objections to most aspects of Witness home life with which they had grown up and felt comfortable. They had had no particular desire to engage in non-Witness social activities, celebrate birthdays or holidays, or engage in political activities outside the community. But they had bitterly resented the frequent interference of elders in their personal and family lives and, above all, were very negative about the fact that they had not dared to question or criticize in even the most constructive manner virtually anything taught or practised by the society or its representatives and overseers.

It would be wrong to suggest that Witness dissonance has not been affected by the doctrinal factors however, although that is just what James Beckford does. He says:

'Coherence' in a doctrinal system is a measure of its overall truth as perceived by the believers, whereas 'consistency' is a measure of the logical fit between separate components of the system ... Thus, to argue, as do some opponents of the Watch Tower movement, that its system of doctrine is riddled with logical inconsistencies is to miss the point as far as sociology is concerned. What is sociologically interesting about Jehovah's Witnesses is that they derive psychological satisfaction from perceiving a coherent pattern in their beliefs regardless of possible inner inconsistencies, and that, even if they do notice inconsistencies, they can abrogate personal responsibility for their own beliefs in the safe conviction that *someone, somewhere* in the Watch Tower Society must be able to solve the problem.[123]

This is an oversimplification of the facts. What Beckford did not seem to realize when he made that statement in 1975 was that many Jehovah's Witnesses were feeling deep misgivings over many Watch Tower teachings and were questioning the 'consistency' of them. Yet so long as they believed that changes could come and that the society *might* candidly admit its faults, they were unwilling to wash their dirty linen in public. Second, to attribute to a whole community the monolithic belief system that Beckford does to Jehovah's Witnesses is unrealistic, as events have demonstrated.

Central to the misgivings of many was a rather simple fact. In *The Truth That Leads to Eternal Life,* a book long studied by virtually every Jehovah's Witness, the Watch Tower Society states: 'The Bible tells us that "God is love." In harmony with this, Jesus showed that the most outstanding mark of those who follow his example in worshipping God is that *they should have love among themselves*.'[124] Many Witnesses have felt, however, that there is little love or compassion in the society's iron-fisted disciplining of anyone who violates its rules, and many others complain bitterly over the fact that Witnesses in dire financial straits or the victims of individual tragedies seldom receive much assistance from their brethren. Consequently, many Witnesses in prominent positions have faulted both the society and fellow Witnesses for not manifesting the Christian love ethic.

The case of Peter Gregerson, now a well-known Watch Tower critic and the man who offered a home and work to Raymond Franz after he was forced to leave Brooklyn, is in many ways typical. After having served as a pioneer, elder, and convention overseer in the mid-western and southern United States, in 1975 Gregerson was invited to a special meeting of prominent elders who were asked to tell the society's officers and the governing body why the organization was facing so many problems. But instead of giving him enhanced confidence in Jehovah's Witnesses, that meeting served to undermine his faith.

According to Gregerson's account, when Watch Tower officials asked why the Witness community was facing serious problems, many of the elders present openly censured the society's harsh system of judicial committees and lack of justice. Yet the society's officers were either unwilling or unable to respond to such criticism, and Gregerson returned home greatly disillusioned.

Because of this experience, Gregerson decided to examine the bases of the society's claim to having been chosen as God's channel or 'slave' organization in 1919 and determined to read Watch Tower publications from that time. As a result, he came to the conclusion that 'there was not one chance in a thousand' that Jehovah would have selected the Watch Tower as his means of dispensing truth to mankind during the last seven decades and, thereupon, with the support of nearly his entire family, resigned from Jehovah's Witnesses. Since then, like hundreds of others, he has been active exposing what he considers to be the Watch Tower's false teachings.

More to the point is the fact that over the last few years literally dozens of small, secret Bible study groups have developed independently among Jehovah's Witnesses throughout the western world like the separatist conventicles that grew up in England in the days of Elizabeth I, James I, and Charles I. And these study groups have spread from one place to another among Witnesses. What is most interesting about them from the standpoint of Beckford's comments is that they *do* notice inconsistencies in Watch Tower doctrine and, more often than has been the case for many years, are breaking with the Witness community over them. Many of them even publish newsletters and journals which are circulated far and wide.

Response to Dissent

The Watch Tower Society has used a number of tactics to deal with dissent. In the first place, as early as 1978 it brought great pressures on those within the organization who were re-examining basic Witness doctrines not to make any of their data known to the Witness community. Then it began a not-so-quiet attack on those who were restudying the Gentile Times chronology.

By the summer of 1979 the society gave official approval to open and harsh criticism of a group of persons who still considered themselves to be loyal Jehovah's Witnesses. *The Watchtower* of 15 July 1979 stated on page 13: '*Lawless persons* have even tried to penetrate the true Christian congregation, arguing that the "promised presence" of the Lord is not in this day ... Persons of this kind are included in Jesus' warning recorded at Matthew 7:15–23: "Be on the watch for *false prophets* that come to you in sheep's covering, but inside are ravenous wolves ... [In that day] I will confess to them: I never knew you! Get away from me, you workers of lawlessness.'"

Then, following the purge of the Watch Tower's Brooklyn Bethel in the spring of 1980, the society unleashed a series of attacks against any and all of the so-called 'apostate ideas' proposed by Raymond Franz, Edward Dunlap, and the small band of men and women who had been driven from the world-wide headquarters of Jehovah's Witnesses.[125]

Interestingly, the society's attack on both privately held dissonance and open dissent within Witness ranks followed a pattern described by Robert Carroll. Carroll states: 'In religious contexts one of the standard methods of treating the dissonance caused by encountering people with different belief structures, whose morality appears to be so impeccable that they qualify as "righteous", is to call them "self-righteous", or even "righteous in their own eyes."'[126] And that is what the Watch Tower Society has done recently to anyone who has dissented in even the slightest degree from Witness teachings. The very expressions 'self-righteous' and 'righteous in their own eyes' have become standard Witness phrases applied to anyone who is independent-minded. Furthermore, in its 1 August 1980 issue, *The Watchtower* listed 'lack of faith,' a 'spirit of independence,' 'ingratitude,' and 'presumption' as causes of a 'loss of joy,' 'rebelliousness,' a 'lack of spiritual nourishment,' and 'works of the flesh.'[127] It stated further:

Thus the one who doubts to the point of becoming an apostate sets himself up as a judge. He thinks he knows better than his fellow Christians, better also than the 'faithful and discreet slave,' through whom he has learned the best part, if not all that he knows about Jehovah God and his purposes. He develops a *spirit* of *independence,* and becomes proud in heart ... something detestable to Jehovah.' (Prov. 16:15) Some apostates even think they know better than God, as regards his ordering of events in the outworking of his purposes. Two other causes of apostasy are therefore *ingratitude* and *presumption.* – 2 Pet. 2:10B–13A.[128]

The society has used other familiar tactics. 'One of the major ways in which dissonance may be reduced is for a group committed to a certain set of cognitive beliefs to engage in proselytizing activities,'[129] something which Witness leaders have evidently recognized since Russell's day and recently have stressed once again, very much as they did during Rutherford's presidency. As noted by sociologists Festinger, Riecken, and Schachter in 1956 and Robert Carroll twenty years later: 'As more and more believers join the group the strength of the dissonance producing event is steadily eroded and becomes less and less a source of significant cognitive dissonance.'[130] This is, however, only one way in which proselytizing may be important. By encouraging believers to engage in it, the society knows that they will have less time and energy to concern themselves with 'heretical' thoughts. Hence, Witness leaders have recently placed strong emphasis on the preaching work and have urged ordinary Witnesses to 'keep busy in the work of the Lord.'

With respect to proselytizing, it is interesting to note just how subtly the Watch Tower Society has pushed this matter. For example, in 1976 *The Watchtower* proclaimed that the Greek word *'latreia'* ('sacred service') could be used to describe any proper Christian good work.[131] But more recently it has stated that it means partaking of the bread and wine of the Lord's Supper for the anointed remnant and the preaching work for *all* Jehovah's Witnesses. Caring for widows and orphans, feeding the poor, and showing love to one's family or fellow believers is no longer regarded as 'sacred service,' but calling at a neighbour's door with *The Watchtower* and *Awake!* magazines on a Saturday morning is. [132] Significantly, although the 1976 *Watchtower* articles were main study articles entitled 'Appreciating the Treasure of Sacred Service' and 'Rendering Sacred Service Night and Day,' there is no reference to them in the *Watch Tower Publications Index 1976–1980* under 'sacred service.'

The most extreme Watch Tower response has not been its program to discredit dissidents or divert the attention of the larger Witness community away from them through the preaching or proselytizing work. Rather, it has been its attempt to isolate them. In the 1950s when disfellowshipment became common, Witnesses were to have nothing to do with disfellowshipped persons. Family members were always permitted some exemption from this rule, however, so long as they did not discuss spiritual matters.[133] Furthermore, in 1974 *The Watchtower* admitted that as a result of the strict shunning of disfellowshipped persons 'needlessly unkind and inhumane' situations had developed. So it suggested that while Witnesses were not to fraternize with disfellowshipped ones, they could greet most of them and treat them with ordinary courtesy and compassion. Only those described at 2 John 9–11 as antichrists were to be avoided completely. In so far as relatives were concerned *The Watchtower* stated:

As to disfellowshipped family members (not minor sons or daughters) living outside the home, each family must decide to what extent they will have association with such ones. This is not something that the congregational elders can decide for them. What the elders are concerned with is that 'leaven' is not introduced into the congregation through spiritual fellowshipping with those who had to be removed as such 'leaven'. Thus if a disfellowshipped parent goes to visit a son or daughter or to see grandchildren and is allowed to enter the Christian home, that is not the concern of the elders. Such a one has a natural right to visit his blood relatives and his offspring. Similary, when sons or daughters render honor to a parent, though disfellowshipped, by calling to see how such a one's physical health is or what he or she may have, this act in itself is not a spiritual fellowshipping.[134]

But in the 15 September 1981 issue of *The Watchtower* this position was reversed. Suddenly, Witnesses were to stop greeting practically *all* disfellowshipped persons, not even saying 'hello' to them, and for the first time family members were to cut *any and all* unnecessary ties with relatives. Although husbands and wives had to continue rendering marriage dues to disfellowshipped mates and parents were to provide for minor children, except in cases of extreme illness or emergency, disfellowshipped family members were to be shunned. As for disfellowshipped relatives not living in Witness homes, they were to be treated in virtually the same way that any other excommunicated ones would be. Witnesses were told: 'We should keep clearly in mind the Bible's inspired direction: "Quit mixing in company with *anyone* called a brother that is a fornicator or a greedy person ..., not even eating with such a man."' Then, to make absolutely certain that *no* dissenter might continue to have ongoing association with Jehovah's Witnesses in good standing, *The Watchtower* proclaimed that the rules relating to disfellowshipped persons were to be applied also to those who had resigned from the organization voluntarily.[135]

The Effects of Watch Tower Policy

Perhaps to the surprise of many, the society's policies have caused a major backlash from many of those who have left Jehovah's Witnesses or been expelled. Many dissenters have organized fellowships, study groups, congregations, and even missions to Jehovah's Witnesses. More significantly for the Witness community, particularly in North America, numerous disfellowshipped and dissociated persons have taken criticisms of Watch Tower authoritarianism and complaints of cruelty to the press, radio, and television

Just what effect such publicity is having on Jehovah's Witnesses in general is difficult to say, but there is some evidence to suggest that it has created a 'siege mentality' among North American, Irish, and British Witnesses at least. Many have met hostile questioners in their door-to-door preaching work and, when asked about the charges of the dissidents, have simply walked away.

At a higher level, in spite of Brooklyn's official recommendation to ignore apostates and the public news media, Watch Tower spokesmen have manifested anger at their critics. Curiously, they have gone so far as to deny that the Watch Tower Society takes any action against people who leave the movement,[136] denying that the society has changed its policy respecting disfellowshipped persons since the 1950s[137] and claiming that the dissidents are persecuting them.[138]

In May 1982 the society evidently became so alarmed about 'apostasy' in western Canada that the then eighty-eight-year old Frederick Franz flew to Calgary, Alberta, to deliver two public talks, each of several hours in length, to Witness faithful gathered at the Calgary Jubilee Auditorium. Prior to his arrival in Canada, newsmen had asked local Jehovah's Witness spokesmen if Franz would discuss the matter of dissent and schism in their midst. In reply, they were told that he would not; the dissidents were too unimportant to notice. Yet during the first moments of his talks, he stated: 'Right now among God's people there are going to be those who will rise up against the fulfilled ones. They will hate us. By their actions they will show they hate us.' Then he added that Jehovah's Witnesses should not be surprised that some 'are dissociated from us or have to be cast out.' Accordingly, such dissenters would 'be put to shame' by God, Franz said.[139]

Other Witness spokesmen have continued to play down dissonance and dissent, asserting that the whole matter is inconsequential. For example, Glen How, speaking as legal counsel for the Watch Tower Society in Canada, has said, 'stories about apostates involve only about 25 to 30 people out of 2,000,000 members.'[140]

Most indicative of the society's concern about dissent is the way its spokesmen have reacted to the news media. When asked to appear on television or to speak on radio to defend their position, Watch Tower representatives have either refused or, often, have demanded the right to determine what subjects interviewers would discuss before appearing on their programs.[141] In dealing with some elements of the press, Witness public-relations officers have often been abrupt. In one instance, Walter Graham, press secretary for the Watch Tower Society in Canada, stated that documented comments by several ex-Witness families in Ottawa were 'nonsense' and went on to claim that the Ottawa *Citizen* was being 'manipulated' by a 'few malcontents' who had conspired to make up a story against their brethren. He then suggested that the Watch Tower might not hold future conventions in Ottawa in order to withhold money from that city because of its English-language newspaper's willingness to publish unflattering remarks about the Witness community. 'That's a lot of money for the capital,' he stated.[142] And if Graham was peevish, American Watch Tower public-relations men have proved to be openly irascible. Newspaper magazine reporters state that, over and over again, when calling the Watch Tower's news service in Brooklyn to ask questions about the society's attitude towards 'apostates' or Michael Jackson, its officers have been unpleasant, have occasionally denied that they knew whether Jackson was a Witness or not, and have sometimes even slammed the telephone receiver in reporters' ears.

Witness Instability and Conservatism

Although Witness leaders rightly claim that their community is growing – an important psychological factor from their standpoint – and therefore healthy, in fact it is highly unstable. The great turn-over in membership, the loss of intellectuals, and, recently, the defection of many of its formerly most loyal and able members are unquestionably having an adverse affect on it. As Raymond Franz has stated: 'What I find notable is the kind of people now being disfellowshipped on charges of apostasy are people of long standing, of 30–40 years with the association, people who were very active members.'[143] Thus the community is undergoing very fundamental changes in its nature – at least in Western countries. But the organizational structure remains basically the same, and because of its fundamental conservation, the general Witness population is becoming more 'world denying,' more ghettoized, as it waits impatiently for God's day of wrath on the nations.

Conclusion

No religion in the modern world demonstrates the tremendous potency of millenarian ideas more obviously than do Jehovah's Witnesses, even in what has been often dubbed a 'secular age.' It shows the willingness of millions to trust in the prophetic authority of certain individuals or a group even despite the fact that time and again their prophecies have proven false. Then, too, it indicates how, by using a date-setting eschatology which has long promised great rewards – both spiritual and material – to the Bible Student–Witness community, men such as Charles Taze Russell, Joseph Franklin Rutherford, and their successors have come to wield an almost 'Orwellian' influence over it.

But the question must still be asked, how can this be? Unlike Tertullian, Jehovah's Witnesses do not proclaim a faith based upon the absurd; they are rationalists *par excellence*. Of course it is evident that many ordinary Witnesses are simply unaware of the failure of apocalyptic prophecies made by the Watch Tower Society in the past and the many logical contradictions that have always been present in the society's teachings. Few are either old enough or have been associated with the Witnesses long enough to be aware of their early history, and they are not encouraged to delve into it. As for doctrines, unless one makes a concentrated study of them, it is difficult to become aware of even a small number of the incongruities, paradoxes, and outright distortions of historical truth that have been and are present within them. Yet ignorance is not the only factor which keeps Jehovah's Witnesses loyal to the Watch Tower Society. Like many Christian sects, the Witnesses have long seen themselves *alone* as 'spiritual Israel,' successors to natural Israel. Thus while the more sophisticated and knowledgeable among them often are aware of many of the serious doctrinal and organizational problems created, in the last analysis, by their organization's date-setting eschatology, they will frequently argue that while their leaders may be 'wicked' as were many of the kings of ancient Israel and Judah, in *some* way God is guiding and directing their community, their 'nation,' for an especial divine purpose. In the end, they hold, Jehovah will cleanse his organization and remove those who have ruled them with harshness and injustice. Like some of the workers at the Brooklyn Bethel in the autumn of 1979, they wait for 'King Saul to die.' In this regard, it is instructive to note that while some of those who have been branded 'apostates' by the Watch Tower society left Jehovah's Witnesses voluntarily, by far the greater number were driven out either through harassment or by excommunication.

However, there are other factors which cause most Witnesses to remain loyal to their leadership and the society. They are, as Joseph Zygmunt has indicated, a world-denying 'contrast group' which is amazingly isolated psychologically from the larger societies in which it exists. Hence the average Witness is so preoccupied with the evils of this 'dying old world' and his involvement in proselytizing his neighbours that he usually has little time or desire to examine his faith or community objectively. Even should he wish to do so, he would be in danger of being disciplined, 'marked,' or disfellowshipped and driven from the community as an apostate. So, as the *Watchtower* of 1 January 1984 puts it, 'loyal Witnesses do not so much as "touch" such apostasy.'[1]

Undoubtedly, too, outside persecution, a sense of general alienation from the world, and the ongoing criticisms of so-called apostates have created a siege mentality among them. In consequence, they are now afflicted, as they have not previously been since the Second World War, with a high degree of that type of millenarian paranoia described so well by Norman Cohn[2] and discussed so thoroughly by Richard Hofstadter in what has now almost become a classical historical interpretation – his *The Paranoid Style in American Politics*. Like the political right in both Great Britain and the United States and the present Muslim fundamentalist regime in Iran, Witness leaders have reduced all issues 'to a battle between Good and Evil influence,' they manifest 'qualities of heated exaggeration, suspiciousness and conspiritorial fantasy,' and they emulate the past or present conduct of organizations such as the Church of Rome and the Communist party in following inquisitorial practices and carrying out purges.[3] While their attitudes and actions have caused a good deal of turbulence within the Witness community and alienation from it, they have been able to rally the support of the majority of their followers who now 'press on in kingdom service.'

This does not mean that they do not continue to lose a large portion of their membership both to 'apostasy' and 'moral uncleanness.' They do, and they are deeply concerned about it.[4] Still, so long as they convert more than they lose and continue to grow in overall numbers, their leaders seem determined to maintain the course that, in general, they have followed since Judge Rutherford created 'the Theocracy' in the 1920s and 1930s.[5]

Where, then, are Jehovah's Witnesses going today? Their movement is suffering from significant internal problems. As early as the 1960s they began to experience 'an unbearable strain on [Watch Tower] management structures,'[6] and there have been no satisfactory developments since then to ameliorate what continues to be a growing problem. Their leadership is aging and seems quite incapable of developing new ideas. In fact, since 1978 it has attempted, rather successfully, to turn the clock back to conditions like those of the 1960s and in some cases even to those of the Rutherford era. Then, too, continual attacks on dissidents and those who violate Watch Tower moral strictures cause ongoing strains at congregational level and a good deal of bad publicity which could have serious, long-run negative consequences for the movement. Disfellowshipped persons are turning more and more to the secular courts with suits against local elders, the Watch Tower Society, and the governing body of Jehovah's Witnesses;[7] and should the movement begin to lose such suits, the effects might prove costly both in monetary terms and prestige. At the same time, some secular governments are becoming more and more concerned by what many perceive as the extreme actions of various religious sects and cults (including Jehovah's Witnesses), and in Canada the federal government recently proposed legislation which would, if it had been passed, have limited their power to excommunicate.[8]

Conversely, the movement seems to be scoring some notable successes. Concern over the failure of 1975 now seems largely forgotten or, among recent converts, unknown. Thus in 1984, Jehovah's Witnesses had a world-wide growth rate of 7.1 per cent in the number of regular (monthly) publishers over 1983 and counted a total of 7,416,974 persons at their annual spring celebration of the Memorial of the Lord's Supper. Although much of that growth occurred in places like Mexico, Japan, Brazil, and Italy, even in Australia, Britain, Canada, and the United States there were impressive gains in the numbers of new converts.[9]

Not surprisingly, these successes are used by the Watch Tower Society to assert that Jehovah is still blessing his Witnesses, and all is essentially well with his organization. Consequently, even some ex-Witnesses such as Raymond Franz expect few changes or reforms in the movement. Franz believes that those who will succeed the current Watch Tower leadership are as committed to present policies as are the latter; and he feels that they will be able to come up with some new doctrine to explain away their teaching that the world must end before the generation which was old enough to witness the events of 1914 passes away in death.[10]

In the short term, Franz is probably correct. But any shift away from 1914 anchor date will certainly have major repercussions, especially now that ex-Witnesses are holding Watch Tower date-setting up to devastating analyses.

More significant, however, is the fact that if Witness growth continues even as it has within the last year or two, the present hierarchical Watch Tower organization will become less and less satisfactory in a managerial sense. James Beckford recognized in 1977 that 'the sheer influx of new Witnesses has created organizational difficulties which call for a more flexible and less remote structure of authority relations,'[11] and that is more true today than it was then. So eventually, whether they like it or not, Witness leaders may have to abandon some of their tight control over the Witness community. When and if that happens, changes of an important nature will follow willy-nilly, much as they have in the Church of Rome since the Second Vatican Ecumenical Council.

It is also highly unlikely that the Watch Tower Society will be able to maintain the high level of commitment among the Witness faithful for any length of time without setting some other near-at-hand apocalyptic date as a goal to strive towards. Yet doing that could prove very dangerous indeed. Then, finally, it is difficult to believe that the society will be able to continue its present system of 'judicial' coercion, with all its serious personal, familial, organizational, and societal effects without incurring costs that are too high to make it worthwhile. In other words, if it should find itself the object of too much litigation or direct governmental interference, it will have to soften or abolish its coercive tactics or face serious legal consequences of a type which it cannot afford.

In effect, then, while it is always dangerous to predict the future, it is reasonable to believe that while in the short term Jehovah's Witnesses will maintain their 'unworldly' sectarian style, eventually they will be forced to come to terms with the world which today they would so much like to see destroyed. That is, unless mankind as a whole is overtaken by that great apocalypse or battle of Armageddon which not only Jehovah's Witnesses but many others as well see as a real possibility during the last years of the twentieth century.

Jehovah's Witnesses since 1985: An Afterword

During the years since *Apocalypse Delayed* was first published in 1985, the number of Jehovah's Witnesses has grown significantly. The trauma caused by the disappointment of 1975 seems nearly forgotten within the community today; while in 1986 there was a peak of 3,229,022 Witness publishers, and 8,160,597 attendees at the Memorial celebration, in 1995 those figures had increased to 5,199,895 publishers, and 13,147,201 Memorial attendees.[1]

The graphs below show the average and peak Witness publishers, the number of persons baptized as Jehovah's Witnesses, and the number of Memorial attendees for each year from 1986 to 1995.

Taken alone, these data indicate that Jehovah's Witnesses remain a dynamic religious movement with a bright future. The Watch Tower Society asserts that Jehovah has blessed the Witnesses' world-wide preaching work and points to growth as 'proof' of that blessing. It rejoices that the Witnesses have been able to thrive dramatically in the formerly communist nations of eastern Europe and in most of the republics that used to form the Soviet Union. Additionally, the society expresses satisfaction over the major increase in the Witness community in countries such as Brazil, Japan, and, above all, Mexico. In 1995 Brazil had 416,638 publishers, or a ratio of 1 to 380 Brazilians. A total of 1,144,271 persons attended the Witnesses' annual spring Memorial in Brazil during the same year.[2] As for Japan, Jehovah's Witnesses seem to be one of the few, if not the only, Western Christian religions experiencing significant growth in that largely Buddhist/Shintoist country. As of 1995 there was 1 Witness publisher for every 603 Japanese – a ratio far higher than those in most non-Christian nations. Outstanding, too, are certain facts about the Japanese Witness movement: more than 40 per cent of all Japanese Witness publishers are pioneer evangelists, Witness growth rates in Japan remain higher than in most industrialized countries, and Japanese Witnesses tend to be extremely loyal to their faith and to Watch Tower Society instructions emanating from Brooklyn.[3] It is in Mexico, however, that the Witnesses have made their most spectacular gains in recent years. In 1986 there

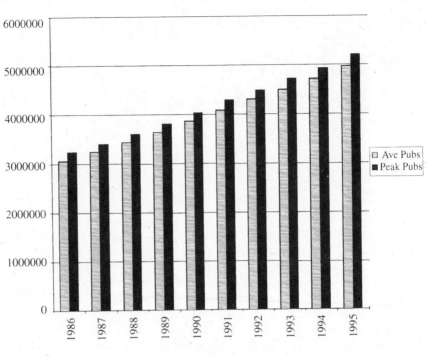

Figure 1
Average and peak publishers, 1986–95

were 198,003 publishers in the republic, and 838,467 attended the Memorial celebration, but in 1995 there were 443,640 publishers, and 1,492,500 were present at the Memorial. Such growth has made the ratio of Witness publishers to total population appreciably higher in Mexico than in the United States. As of 1995 it was 1 to 206 in Mexico, compared with 1 to 274 in the United States.[4]

The expanding size of the Witness community has brought about an increase in the numbers of congregations, branch offices, and Watch Tower facilities. In addition, the governing body has provided for the further instruction of Witness elders and ministerial servants at Kingdom Ministry Schools. Perhaps the most important result, though, has been the establishment of Hospital Information Services (HIS) on the model of the hospital-committees system that was first developed in Canada in the 1970s. From 1988 on, HIS began to train Witness elders in the United States and other countries to become members of Hospital Liaison Committees, whose purpose was to support Witnesses in their opposition to cer-

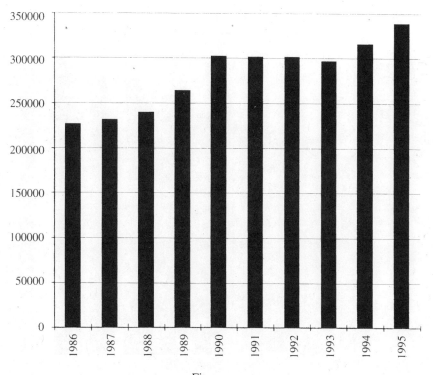

Figure 2
Numbers baptized, 1986–95

tain types of blood therapy, notably transfusions, and to encourage physicians and hospitals to respect individual Witnesses' wishes in this matter.[5]

Hospital Liaison Committees have undoubtedly been a major influence in decreasing opposition to the Witness stand on blood therapy. However, public concern about the transference of AIDS, hepatitis C, and Creutzfeldt-Jakob disease through blood serum and blood particles, plus a number of scandals involving the Red Cross and blood banks in several countries, has probably had a greater effect. Although Witnesses continue to face serious objections from the medical and legal professions when they reject transfusions for minor children and, in particular, newborn infants, the 'blood issue' no longer seems to be a major problem for Jehovah's Witnesses in the English-speaking world or in many third-world countries.

Jehovah's Witnesses also tend to suffer far less persecution than they did in the past. Although they are still banned in the few remaining communist countries of the world, many Islamic states, and Singapore, it is only in the last named nation

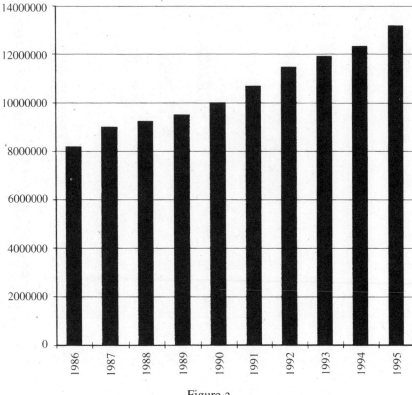

Figure 3
Memorial attendance, 1986–95

that they have recently been subjected to much direct persecution. There they have been outlawed for refusing military service and for a general lack of patriotism, and they have been arrested, jailed, and fined for holding illegal meetings. Canadian Witness lawyer Glen How recently acted on their behalf in appealing their cases to Singapore's highest court; however, the presiding judge ridiculed him openly in these efforts and upheld the original sentences against How's Singaporean brethren.[6] It must be emphasized, though, that in comparison with the levels of persecution that the Witnesses have experienced in the past, their difficulties in Singapore and the rest of the world are rather mild.

There is, however, another side to the picture, which the Watch Tower Society does not advertise. First, suffice it to say here that, while Jehovah's Witnesses' numerical increases in the republics of the former Soviet Union, in Japan, and in much of the non-Muslim third world are quite high, their rates of growth in the industrialized countries of Europe, North America, and the Antipodes have slowed appreciably.[7] Second, there are still great numbers of individuals being forced out of the movement or leaving voluntarily. According to the society's own statistics, roughly 40,000 per year have been disfellowshipped from the world-wide Witness community,[8] and many thousands more have either dissociated themselves formally from the Jehovah's Witnesses or simply isolated themselves from their congregations.[9] Third, and perhaps more significant, the society is now under attack from former members to an extent not seen previously, and both Watch Tower doctrine and the Witness movement are being studied, evaluated, and criticized as never before. Thus, Watch Tower leaders and the Witness community as a whole manifest a growing sense of paranoia and open hatred of 'apostates' and 'opposers.' These factors are discussed in more detail below.

Table 5 shows the growth of Jehovah's Witnesses from 1986 to 1995 for the largely industrialized, or 'first world,' countries of western and Mediterranean Europe, Australia, Canada, Japan, South Korea, New Zealand, and the United States. It should be noted that the figures for Germany are not complete for 1985 since they do not include statistics for what was then the German Democratic Republic (GDR, or East Germany). On the basis of what was reported in the *1991 Yearbook of Jehovah's Witnesses* (p. 40), there were 20,874 publishers in the GDR in 1990. Thus, much of the apparent growth in Germany during the decade 1986–95 is attributable to German reunification rather than to an actual increase in numbers. The graph below compares the growth of the Witnesses in the same countries and that recorded on a world-wide basis.

Changes in Watch Tower Practice and Doctrine

Despite the fact that the Witness community is expanding rapidly and is currently experiencing less antagonism from secular authorities, other religions, and the medical profession than it has since before the First World War, it is obvious to careful observers that the governing body and its legal societies are not responding adequately to the problems facing the movement. It is true that the governing body has made a few organizational and doctrinal changes since the mid-1980s, but these have largely been responses to outside factors over which they have little control. An inability to change in ways that, in the long run, will be necessary for the community's healthy development demonstrates the intellectual aridity of the Witness leadership.

A change that currently seems to be of minor significance occurred in 1992, when the governing body appointed a number of trusted lieutenants of the 'great crowd' class to assist them in carrying on the governance of Jehovah's Witnesses, including sitting on formerly exclusive governing-body administrative commit-

TABLE 5

Percentage increase in publishers in developed countries, 1986–95

Countries or branches	Average pubs. – 1986	Average pubs. – 1995	Percentage increase
Alaska	1,868	2,146	15
Andorra	98	137	40
Australia	42,998	59,474	38
Austria	16,185	20,598	27
Belgium	21,343	26,853	26
Britain	101,863	125,138	23
Canada	84,343	109,168	29
Cyprus	1,096	1,627	48
Denmark	14,796	15,604	5
Finland	15,533	18,906	22
France	89,785	123,408	37
Germany	116,152	165,746	43
Gibraltar	124	234	89
Greece	22,815	25,764	13
Iceland	173	302	75
Ireland	2,472	4,372	77
Italy	134,677	210,012	56
Japan	108,702	201,266	85
Korea, Republic of	41,751	78,782	89
Liechtenstein	43	60	40
Luxembourg	1,246	1,796	44
Netherlands	28,367	31,142	10
New Zealand	9,165	12,573	37
Norway	7,929	9,687	22
Portugal	29,617	43,633	47
Spain	63,453	97,674	54
Sweden	20,350	23,792	17
Switzerland	13,373	18,196	36
U.S.A.	710,344	912,002	28
Total	1,700,661	2,340,092	38

tees.[10] Known by the esoteric names 'Nethinim,' 'sons of the servants of Solomon,' or 'Given Ones,' this body of individuals was no doubt created because those who act as the governing body are gradually dying off or, with the exception of one fairly recently appointed member, are of advanced age. The Nethinim may eventually take over primary leadership roles, which could lead to reforms within the Witness movement. At present, however, the governing body refuses to surrender any of its authority. As well, another barrier to increased Nethinim authority currently exists – namely, that in order for the Nethinim to take greater control of the Watch Tower Society and Jehovah's Witnesses, doctrinal changes must be made. This barrier should prove surmountable: if Witness

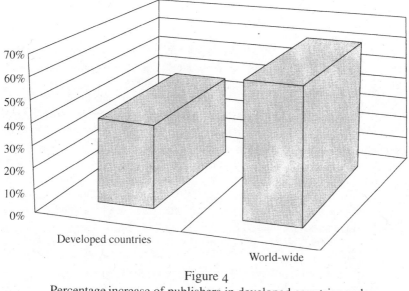

Figure 4
Percentage increase of publishers in developed countries and
world-wide, 1986–95

history teaches anything, it is that major doctrinal changes come in response to the pragmatic needs of the people controlling the organization. As the current governing body dies out, members of the Nethinim class may replace members of the so-called anointed remnant in the highest offices of the Witness movement.

Another factor that may have long-range importance is the governing body's softening of its position towards higher or advanced education. As indicated earlier, the Watch Tower movement has historically opposed higher education, except in rare cases. Although there was never any outright prohibition against enrolling in college or university, ongoing negative statements in Watch Tower publications and psychological pressure from elders, circuit overseers, and family members kept many young Witnesses from attending institutions of higher learning. None the less, some young persons left the Witness movement over the years rather than give up the opportunity to pursue college or university studies, with the result that the Jehovah's Witnesses lost a number of their brightest members. So, in recent years, the Watch Tower Society slowly came to recognize that: (1) it needed highly trained individuals, particularly in fields such as accounting, computing science, and law, to carry on its own activities; and (2) in many countries of the industrialized world, college or university education was becoming an essential prerequisite for jobs that would provide incomes adequate to support young men and women and their families. The society also came to recognize that many pioneers were quitting their ministries because they could not obtain decent jobs. *The Watchtower* of 1 November 1992 stated: 'What is often the situation today? It has been reported that in some countries many well-intentioned youngsters have left school after completing the minimum required schooling in order to become pioneers. They have had no trade or secular qualifications. If they were not helped by their parents, they had to find part-time work. Some have had to accept jobs that required them to work very long hours to make ends meet. Becoming physically exhausted, they gave up the pioneer ministry. What can such ones do to support themselves and get back into the pioneer service?' Rather reluctantly, the society's official magazine stated further: '... when parents and young Christians today, after carefully and prayerfully weighing the pros and cons, decide for or against post secondary studies, others in the congregation should not criticize them.'[11]

This did not mean that *The Watchtower* was abandoning its open distaste for higher education; its change of position was clearly pragmatic and is covered by a curious statement: 'If additional [postsecondary-school] courses are taken, certainly the purpose should not be to shine scholastically or to carve out a prestigious worldly career. Courses should be chosen with care. This magazine has placed emphasis on the dangers of higher learning, and justifiably so, for much higher education opposes the "healthful teaching" of the Bible. (Titus 2:1; 1 Timothy 6:20, 21) Further, since the 1960's, many schools of advanced learning have become hotbeds of lawlessness and immorality. "The faithful and discreet slave" has strongly discouraged entering that kind of environment. (Matthew 24:12, 45) It must be admitted, however, that nowadays youngsters meet up with these same dangers in high schools and even in the workplace. – 1 John 5:19'[12]

Whatever its thinking, the governing body of Jehovah's Witnesses, speaking through *The Watchtower*, has opened the world of higher education to Jehovah's Witness youth, and many are now entering it. Eventually this may lead to a more open-minded Witness community and to more questioning of the Witness authority structure. But it would be wrong to be too sanguine about the likelihood of this outcome. The Watch Tower Society still emphasizes that higher education should be pursued only to obtain a reasonable living; it never makes any suggestion that college or university courses should be taken to broaden students' general knowledge of the universe in which they live. In fact, it seems as though Witness leaders – like large segments of the conservative religious and business communities in the industrialized world – have never heard of the concept of liberal education. The likelihood is that, as is the case in certain other sectarian groups, in particular, the Mormons, there will be a tendency for young Jehovah's

Witnesses to take courses in 'practical fields' such as computing, accounting, and business management that tend not to threaten their belief system. Few are likely to take studies in such areas as the humanities, the social sciences, or the biological sciences, disciplines that are most threatening to the Witness world-view.

More recently the Watch Tower Society has also taken a more positive attitude towards elementary and secondary education and educators – again for obviously pragmatic reasons. For years the Watch Tower Society's brochure *School and Jehovah's Witnesses* had carried an extreme message to teachers and school administrators regarding the things that Witness children could *not* do in school. In fact, *School and Jehovah's Witnesses* was virtually insulting about many extracurricular school programs, and about non-Witness students, who were labelled 'unwholesome associations.'[13] Perhaps more significant, though, was the fact that non-Witness and ex-Witness parents began using the brochure in child-custody cases to prove that, if their children were left with their Witness parents, they would be deprived of normal education and psychologically healthy lives.[14] So, in 1995 the Watch Tower Society produced a much less inflammatory brochure entitled *Jehovah's Witnesses and Education*. This publication, to be placed with teachers and administrators, concluded with the following statement: 'The Witnesses endeavor to be realistic about life, so they attach great importance to education. It is, therefore, their wish to work along with you [the teacher or administrator] to the best of their abilities. For their part, in their homes and in their places of worship around the world, they will continue to encourage their children to play their part in this fruitful collaboration.'[15]

Frederick W. Franz, the Watch Tower Society's fourth president, died on 22 December 1992,[16] and his passing has seemed to open the door to at least one doctrinal change of major importance. Franz was in many ways the last authority link with the Russell and Rutherford eras, and the last person to have had any charismatic impact on the Witness community as a whole.[17] As he had guided and developed Watch Tower doctrine from Judge Rutherford's day until shortly before his death, it seems evident that Franz's confrères on the governing body were reluctant, before his passing, to make any changes that were not in harmony with his ideas. His nephew, Raymond Franz, had attempted to do so in the mildest manner possible and had been driven from the governing body and Jehovah's Witnesses as a result. But, with the fourth Watch Tower president's death, it no doubt became easier to make doctrinal changes.

Eight days after his death, Franz was succeeded as president of the Watch Tower Bible and Tract Society and other Jehovah's Witness societies by Milton G. Henschel,[18] an equally conservative member of the governing body, but one without any of the public panache so characteristic of Russell, Rutherford, and Franz. Although he is one of the more important members of the governing body, his position as president of the society is far more honorary than was the case with past Watch Tower presidents.[19] Thus, it has been possible for the governing body to deal with a doctrinal matter that was becoming a serious embarrassment to Jehovah's Witnesses.

For years the Watch Tower Society had proclaimed that Christ had returned invisibly in 1914 and the generation who had witnessed that year would see the 'final end' of the system of things. Following the débâcle of 1975, this doctrine began to become more and more of an embarrassment. Carl Olof Jonsson's *The Gentile Times Reconsidered* raised seriously damaging questions about the society's so-called biblical chronology that is used to support the 1914 date. The society has largely been able to discount that work, however, by disfellowshipping Jonsson and ignoring the most damning aspects of his work in an area which is far too complex for the average Jehovah's Witness to understand. Still, as year followed year and the generation of 1914 began to die off, it became obvious that, if Armageddon was again delayed, something would have to be done to avert another impending crisis in Witness date-setting. Consequently, beginning with the 15 February 1994 issue of *The Watchtower*, the society began to revise its eschatology.

Raymond Franz notes: 'For about a half a century the *Watchtower* taught and argued that Jesus' statement regarding the "signs in the sun and moon and stars, and on earth the anguish of nations" applied from 1914 onward. (See as but one of numerous examples, the *Watchtower* of July 15, 1946, page 217.) Now, these are moved up to the future, after the start of the "great tribulation" to come, and these articles assign an *extended period* to this tribulation.' Basing further comments on an upcoming study entitled 'This Generation Shall Not Pass Away' by Ray Mattera of Wheaton, Illinois, Franz points to the fact that 'the sealing of the chosen ones,' or the remnant of the 144,000, is now held to occur in future and will take place during the great tribulation.[20]

Although typically difficult to understand, even for loyal Jehovah's Witnesses, this new teaching served as a small harbinger of events to come and showed that the Watch Tower Society was giving greater emphasis to futurist interpretations of eschatological prophecies found in the 'little apocalypse' of Matthew 24, Mark 13, Luke 21, and in Revelation. In the 15 October 1995 issue of *The Watchtower*, the society decided that the separation of the sheep and goats mentioned by Jesus at Matthew 25 had not been taking place since Christ had come invisibly in 1914, but, would also take place during the future great tribulation. Of course, in typical fashion, *The Watchtower* stressed that the great tribulation was soon to take place, and the sheep and the goats (humankind in general) would then be judged on how they had treated the anointed remnant of Jehovah's Witnesses.[21] Once again, this was a change of rather minor significance.

On 1 November 1995, the society came to grips with its greatest immediate eschatological problem by reinterpreting the meaning of the term 'this generation' as used by Jesus at Matthew 24: 34. As indicated above, the Watch Tower Society had long continued to teach that those who were alive in 1914 would see the end of the present world or system of things. Accordingly, 'this generation' was understood to mean people living contemporaneously, in this case with the grand event of Christ's invisible presence and enthronement in 1914. Until a week after the society changed its 'this generation doctrine,' *Awake!* was still making this proclamation about itself on its masthead: 'Most important, this magazine builds confidence in the Creator's promise of a peaceful and secure new world before the generation that saw the events of 1914 passes away.' Thus, because of this long-standing doctrine, Jehovah's Witnesses had speculated time and again over the years about the length of a biblical generation. In the 1 November 1995 *Watchtower*, however, the society decided that it was wrong to hold that the term 'this generation' could be linked to a specific date. It quoted with approval history professor Robert Wohl's statement in *The Generation of 1914*: '"A historical generation is not defined by its chronological limits ... It is not a zone of dates."' Then it asserted that 'in the final fulfillment of Jesus' prophecy [at Matthew 24 and 25] today, "this generation" apparently refers to the peoples of the earth who see the sign of Christ's presence but fail to mend their ways.'[22]

What this means is that the Watch Tower Society, acting for the governing body of Jehovah's Witnesses, has created a situation whereby it can go on arguing that Christ came invisibly in 1914 and that the 'final end' is near at hand, but the society can say, with some equivocation, as is noted below, that it no longer preaches even an approximate date for the apocalyptic events of the great tribulation. So now Jehovah's Witnesses are not so likely to be disappointed if the old system of things is not finally destroyed or the millennium does not begin by the year 2000.

A less doctrinally but practically important change came in the 1 May 1996 issue of *The Watchtower*. For decades the society had held that Jehovah's Witnesses must not perform alternative civilian service in lieu of being drafted into the armed forces of many nations where conscription still exists. As a result, many thousands of ordinary Witness men and a few women had suffered incarceration for their beliefs, in some cases for many years. On the other hand, when some individual Witnesses did accept alternative civilian service assignments, they were treated as spiritually weak and were denied many privileges in their congregations. But in the article 'Paying Back Caesar's Things to Caesar,' *The Watchtower* of 1 May 1996 stated that, if a Jehovah's Witness should decide to perform national civilian service, it is a matter of 'personal conscience.' It stressed further: 'That is his decision before Jehovah. Appointed elders and others should fully respect the conscience of the brother and continue to regard him as a Christian in good standing.'[23]

The Effects of Watch Tower Doctrinal Changes on the
Witness Community

To a great extent the broad Witness community has responded to the new doctrinal changes with apathy. Some of *The Watchtower*'s new teachings are simply
too complex to be understood by most Jehovah's Witnesses, and many simply
pass over them as 'new light' from the faithful and discreet slave. As James
Beckford has remarked: 'What is sociologically interesting about Jehovah's witnesses is that they derive psychological satisfaction from perceiving a coherent
pattern in their beliefs regardless of possible inner inconsistencies, and that, even
if they do notice inconsistencies, they can then abrogate personal responsibility
for their own beliefs in the safe conviction that *someone*, *somewhere* in the
Watch Tower Society must be able to solve the problem. An implicit premise in
the argument is usually that, if the perceived inconsistencies were real, then the
beliefs would not have gained widespread popularity.'[24]

It would be wrong to assume that all Jehovah's Witnesses feel this way. Every
time the Watch Tower Society makes major, and sometimes even minor, doctrinal shifts, it loses numerous adherents, among whom are often the most intelligent and sometimes the most active Witnesses. It is becoming more and more
apparent to such persons that even the society's millenarian eschatology – the
driving force behind community élan and growth – is geared to maintaining the
Witness organization under the domination of the governing body. As Ray Mattera has commented privately: 'Jehovah's Witnesses have little truly systematic
theology, christology, or pneumatology. In fact, they have almost no consistent
doctrinal system at all except for one thing: they do have an ecclesiology that
stresses loyalty to the Watch Tower organization above everything else.' So
when the society announced its new 'this generation' doctrine in November
1995, various ex-Witness ministries to Jehovah's Witnesses received many calls
asking for spiritual help from ordinary Witness publishers, and even from numerous elders.[25] More recently there has been some backlash over the change made
respecting national civilian service. Many individuals who were forced to go to
jail rather that to perform alternative civilian service because of Watch Tower
legislation wonder why they had to suffer imprisonment if there is now nothing
wrong with such alternative service.

Governing Body Attitudes and Policies

In the appendix to the latest edition of *Crisis of Conscience*, Raymond Franz
points out that in many ways the governing body and the Watch Tower Society
have become more rather than less conservative since he was expelled from the

society's Brooklyn headquarters in 1980.[26] Besides developing a much harder line concerning the shunning of disfellowshipped persons and a new dictum that persons who voluntarily resigned from Jehovah's Witnesses were to be treated as though they were disfellowshipped, in 1983 the governing body went back to its earlier stand that Witnesses could be disfellowshipped for practising oral or anal intercourse with their marriage mates.[27] Then, in order to deal with the assertion of many individuals who were leaving the Witness community that they had made their dedication and baptism to Jehovah God and Christ Jesus rather than to an organization, the society changed the nature of the questions asked of baptismal candidates. According to *The Watchtower* of 1 August 1970 (p. 465), the two questions asked were: (1) 'Have you recognized yourself as a sinner and needing salvation from Jehovah God? And have you acknowledged that this salvation proceeds from him, and through his ransomer Jesus Christ?'; and (2) 'On the basis of this faith in God and in his provision for redemption, have you dedicated yourself unreservedly to Jehovah God to do his will henceforth as that is revealed to you through Jesus Christ and through God's Word as his holy spirit makes plain?' However, in *The Watchtower* of 1 June 1985 (p. 30), the new questions were printed in bold, as follows: (1) 'On the basis of the sacrifice of Jesus Christ, have you repented of your sins and dedicated yourself to Jehovah to do his will?'; and (2) 'Do you understand that your dedication and baptism identify you as one of Jehovah's Witnesses in association with God's spirit-directed organization?' Finally, after vacillating numerous times on the matter, the society again decided that the inhabitants of the ancient cities of Sodom and Gomorrah will not have a resurrection.[28] Curiously, the society is not prepared to leave this decision to Jehovah.

The reason behind the governing body's conservatism lies largely in the attitudes of the persons on it, many of whom were chosen for their 'long service and organizational dependability' rather than because they have any particular ability or outstanding spirituality. They are like many of the old party bureaucrats who came to power in the Soviet Union after the death of Stalin: loyal to the past, they have little or no desire to change the nature of basic Witness doctrine or governance. They seem content to wait for their 'heavenly reward,' which they must feel is very close. Based on what Raymond Franz says, as of July 1996 the ages of governing body members are as follows: Gerrit Loesch, who is the single member to have been added to the governing body in more than a decade and a half, is now 55; Ted Jaracz, 71; Milton Henschel, 76; Dan Sydlik, 77; Lloyd Barry, 80; Jack Barr, 83; Albert Schroeder, 85; Lyman Swingle, 86; and Carey Barber and Karl Klein, 91.[29] What this means is that, even counting Loesch, the average age of governing body members is 79.5 years. So, with the exception of Loesch, members of the governing body are the 'old guard' in every sense of that term. In addition, the three most influential members of the Witness Sanhedrin are Jaracz, Henschel, and Barry, all of whom are noted for their extreme conservatism and desire to push the Witnesses' door-to-door preaching work.

The governing body's conservatism is expressed in ways that may be described as more than a little devious. For example, for many years Jehovah's Witnesses and Bible Student colporteurs before them had 'placed' or 'sold' Watch Tower literature at the doors of prospective converts for fixed money 'contributions,' including subscription rates for *The Watchtower* and its companion magazines – *The Golden Age, Consolation,* and *Awake!* During the late 1980s, however, Jimmy Swaggart Ministries went to court to try to have its religious publications, for which it charged, exempted from California sales tax.[30] Despite its antagonism to all other religions, the Watch Tower Society supported Jimmy Swaggart Ministries with an *amicus curiae* brief before the U.S. Supreme Court. But when the Court decided that religious literature could be taxed, the Watch Tower changed its policy in the United States almost immediately, and in other countries somewhat later. As *Comments from the Friends*, an ex–Jehovah's Witness publication out of Stoughton, Massachusetts, noted: 'On February 25th [1990] a letter from Brooklyn headquarters was read at Kingdom Halls throughout the United States, announcing a major switch in Watchtower policy. Reversing a practice of 110 years, prices would no longer be set for books, magazines or subscriptions. In a subsequent letter dated February 21st, the Society explained the new policy this way: "By adopting a method of literature distribution based completely on donation, Jehovah's people are able to greatly simplify our Bible education work and separate from those who commercialize religion."'[31] What this meant was that, before leaving kingdom halls, Witnesses would be expected to 'contribute what they wanted' for literature that they would give away in their door-to-door ministry. Of course, suggestions were made by the society through local elders as to what Witness publishers should 'want to contribute.' Thus the Watch Tower Society passed on the responsibility of paying for its publications to Jehovah's Witnesses rather than to the general public.

As the *Brooklyn Heights Press* recognized, the society had a less spiritually elevated reason for its new policy: by offering its literature gratis to the public, it avoided paying sales taxes that could have amounted to many millions of dollars.[32] *Comments from the Friends* remarked that Jimmy Swaggart Ministries had been required to pay $183,000 in sales taxes on $2 million in literature sales. So, had the Watch Tower Society had to pay a proportionate amount on its books, booklets, brochures, and magazines placed with the public in the United States in 1989 alone, it would have been required to pay $6.5 million in sales tax.[33]

A similar example of organizational cynicism relates to the society's changed status in Mexico. Despite the fact that, for many years, Jehovah's Witnesses had

full religious freedom in that country under the constitution of 1917, as noted earlier the society had chosen to be registered as a cultural society. This meant that
the society could own property outright rather than just having the ongoing use of
it while it was owned by the republic. Nevertheless, Mexican Jehovah's Witnesses were forced to pay a high price for the society's stratagem. Their kingdom
halls were called 'cultural halls,' and neither could Witnesses pray in them nor
open their meetings with 'kingdom songs.' They could not go from door to door
with the Bible, as they did in most other democratic lands. After Mexico moved
to change its constitution in the late 1980s, on 1 April 1989 the Witnesses suddenly became a religion according to Mexican law.[34] Commenting on this development, Raymond Franz says:

After nearly a half century of holding the status of a 'cultural' organization in Mexico, the
Watch Tower organization finally changed to that of a religious organization. The *Watchtower* magazine of January 1, 1990 (page 7) announced that 'change of the status' of Jehovah's Witnesses had taken place in 1989. It describes the Mexican Witnesses as *for the
first time* being able to use the Bible when going from house to house, and *for the first time*
being able to open meetings with prayer.

The magazine describes how 'thrilling' this change was to Mexican Witnesses and that
it brought 'tears of joy' to them. It attributes an immediate jump in 'publishers' by over
17,000 to this change.

The article tells the reader absolutely nothing as to what the *previous* status had been,
why it prevailed, or how the change in status came about. Anyone reading the article would
assume that the change in status, with the benefits described, was something the organization had wanted all along. From reading the article one would assume that it was the government of Mexico or its laws that had till now prevented the Witnesses from praying at
meetings or using the Bible in their door-to-door activity. It never tells the reader that the
reason the Mexican Witnesses were deprived of these things – for at least a half century –
was because *their own headquarters organization chose to have it so*, voluntarily opted in
favor of another status. It does not tell the reader that these 'thrilling' changes that brought
'tears of joy' had been available all along, for many decades, requiring only an organizational decision to abandon its pretense that the Witness organization in Mexico was not a
religious organization but a 'cultural' one. The only reason the Mexican Witnesses had not
engaged in these things before was because the headquarters organization *instructed* them
not to do so, in order to protect the status chosen of a 'cultural' organization. These are facts
known by those in responsible positions in the Mexican Witness organization. They are not
known by the vast majority of Witnesses outside that country and the January 1, 1990
Watchtower let them remain in the dark on the subject. It presented a 'sanitized' picture of
the occurrence, one that was as misleading as the pre-1989 practice of pretending to be
something other than a religious organization while knowing full well that they were.

As a more recent July 22, 1994 *Awake!* article shows, the Watch Tower organization's willingness to abandon its decades-long pretense was connected with the amendments to the Mexican constitution that have been progressively adopted by the legislative bodies there. Under the new amendments, churches are once again allowed to own buildings and property. This is true not only of the Catholic Church but of all denominations.[35]

The Continued Promotion of False History

Such behaviour on the part of the governing body demonstrates that it is primarily interested in maintaining the authority of the Watch Tower organization by any means, including devious ones, even as it criticizes other religious movements for lacking moral integrity. So, too, does the incredibly distorted history, so called, that it continues to publish for the Witness faithful. In 1993 the Watchtower Society of New York and the International Bible Students Association published a 750-page book entitled *Jehovah's Witnesses: Proclaimers of God's Kingdom*. According to the foreword, 'The editors of this volume have endeavored to be objective and present a candid history.' But if they have 'endeavored to be objective' – which is more than doubtful – they have failed, and what has come to be known as the *Proclaimers* book is far from 'candid.'

In the first place, it is written in a style that makes it difficult to tie various events together chronologically or in context. Certain occurrences are discussed in different places in the book rather than in chronological order, and in this way many embarrassing facts are glossed over. Second, it sanitizes various events that it long ignored until they were brought to light in *Apocalypse Delayed* and other non–Watch Tower publications. Third, a number of historically important persons and events are omitted completely. For example, there is no mention of former Watch Tower attorney Olin Moyle or his successful suit for defamation against the boards of directors of the Watch Tower Society of Pennsylvania and the Watchtower Society of New York, despite the fact that the *Moyle* case was central to the establishment of Watch Tower disfellowshipping or judicial committees. It is even more curious that Raymond Franz is never mentioned in the book when it is widely known that he played a central role in the development of the current governing body and sat as a member of that group for some years. Perhaps not surprisingly, the *Proclaimers* book never mentions that two governing-body members – Ewart Chitty and Leo Greenlees – were forced off that council for ongoing homosexual practices but were never disfellowshipped.[36] Fourth, the *Proclaimers* book repeats a number of outright falsehoods that have become part of Watch Tower mythology. It argues, as have many Watch Tower publications in the past, that the reason Judge J.F. Rutherford drove four Watch Tower Society directors from office in July 1917 is that they opposed the publication of the book *The Finished Mystery*, which he had personally authorized. In fact, this is an outright lie, as is clearly shown by Rutherford's own statements made in court under oath in 1918.[37] Equally mendacious is a statement on page 78 of the *Proclaimers book*. The remark is made there that, after the society's prophecy that Jesus' faithful forefathers would be resurrected and that the world would end in 1925 had failed, '... the majority of Bible Students remained faithful' to the Watch Tower.[38] Most shocking, however, is that the *Proclaimers* book still ignores the fact that the society's second president attempted to ingratiate the Witness movement with Adolf Hitler and the Nazis in June 1933.[39]

It is not only in the *Proclaimers* book that the governing body and the society have been less than honest. The 22 August 1995 *Awake!* had emblazoned on its cover 'The Holocaust: Who Spoke Out?' above the notation that that issue of the magazine was being published on the '50th Anniversary of Liberating the Camps.' Within the magazine itself are several short articles claiming that Jehovah's Witnesses were 'one voice' that spoke out amidst Nazi oppression. Yet not a word is said about the anti-Semitic nature of the society's 1933 Declaration of Facts or its fawning letter to Hitler sent at the same time.[40] On the other hand, the 22 August 1995 *Awake!* continued the long-standing policy of attacking other churches for their collaboration with Hitler's government, and even reprinted a number of luridly anti-Catholic pictures taken from Watch Tower publications issued during the period of the Third Reich. In this matter Watch Tower leaders behave like Lord Frollo in the Disney cartoon-movie *The Hunchback of Notre Dame*, who, according to the film's narrator, 'saw evil everywhere but within.'

The Watchtower of 1 May 1996 gives similar bogus history. In order to argue that the society has developed a continually more progressive understanding of who the 'superior authorities' of Romans 13 are, that magazine makes a number of statements. On page 13 it says the following: 'In 1904 the book *The New Creation* stated that true Christians "should be amongst the most law-abiding of the present time – not agitators, not quarrelsome, not faultfinders." This was understood by some to mean a total submission to the powers that be, even to the point of accepting service in the armed forces during World War I.' It then goes on to describe briefly Judge Rutherford's 1929 doctrine that Jehovah God and Christ Jesus were the 'superior authorities' or 'higher powers' of Romans 13 rather than secular governments – a doctrine which described all of this world's secular institutions as 'of the devil.' Finally, it discusses the society's 1962 teaching on relations with secular governments, which it refers to as a doctrine of 'relative subjection.'[41]

There are many things wrong with the article in question. First, there is no evidence that, during the First World War, Bible Students believed in total submission to 'the powers that be.' There was a question about how far they should be obedient to secular authority, but all believed in the principle of 'relative submission.' Second, Rutherford's 1929 doctrine is described as being something positive. There is no admission that it was wrong exegesis, regardless of its effects, or that in many ways the society itself ignored it. *The Watchtower* states: 'Looking back, it must be said that this view of things, exalting as it did the supremacy of Jehovah and his Christ, helped God's people to maintain an uncompromising neutral stand throughout this difficult period.'[42] Third, *The Watchtower* asserts that its most recent 'superior authorities' doctrine came about after the completion of the New World Translation of the Holy Scriptures in 1961. Accordingly, 'its preparation had required an in-depth study of the textual language of the Scriptures. The precise translation of the words used not only in Romans chapter 13 but also in such passages as Titus 3:2 and 1 Peter 2:13, 17 made it evident that the term "*superior* authorities" referred, not to the *Supreme* Authority, Jehovah, and to his Son, Jesus, but to human governmental authorities.'[43] But this account is thoroughly misleading. The New World Translation of the Christian Greek Scriptures had been published in 1950, and that edition contained all of the relevant passages discussed above. So, if the society's exegetes had carried on 'an in-depth study of the textual language of the Scriptures' regarding this matter, they were painfully slow in doing so. Furthermore, the Watch Tower Bible and Tract Society, the Watchtower Bible and Tract Society Incorporated of New York, the International Bible Students Association, and other Witness societies remained legally incorporated bodies under 'satanic' governments. Jehovah's Witnesses had also been appealing to 'satanic' court systems throughout the democratic world for years. So Witness leaders and lawyers would have been exceptionally obtuse had they not come to realize that, if legislative bodies and the courts were totally dominated by the devil, they would not have been giving legal shelter to the various Witness societies or deciding law case after law case in Jehovah's Witnesses' favour. It is therefore quite apparent that doctrinal change came more in response to outside circumstances than through abstract study, but as the human governing council of the 'Lord's organization,' it is difficult for the governing body of Jehovah's Witnesses to admit that. Then, though the current 'superior authorities' doctrine is spelled out more concretely than in Russell's day, it is essentially the same one that he enunciated during the First World War. For the governing body to say so, however, would endanger the basic teaching that its members use to impose doctrinal change on the Witness community – *the concept of progressive revelation through God's channel organization.*

The Growing Critical Study of Jehovah's Witnesses

Almost from the beginning, the Bible Student–Jehovah's Witness movement has had its severe critics. In the past, criticism of the movement was ordinarily directed at it largely for doctrinal reasons, because of its attitude towards civic responsibilities, or because of the blood-transfusion issue. While it is true that some dissidents who broke with the society also censured the Watch Tower authority structure and inconsistencies in Watch Tower theology, few of them attempted to take their concerns to the general public. Beginning in about 1980, all of that changed.

Over the years the Watch Tower Society had been able to drive many persons from the movement with little or no harm to itself. The one major exception was Olin Moyle. After his case against the society's directors was concluded in 1944, Watch Tower lawyers were able to create a situation in which it was nearly impossible to win a suit against the society or its officers for defamation, improper disfellowshipment, or the disciplining of persons considered to be dissidents or troublemakers. When the society and its lieutenants began to take harsh actions against a number of able persons within the Witness fold in the late 1970s and early 1980s, an entirely new situation developed. Instead of trying to gain redress of grievances primarily through the legal system, many of these individuals, whom the society branded 'apostates,' began to take their cases to the public press and news media. Several began to write and publish books about their experiences and about Jehovah's Witness practices and doctrines. Some formed a variety of ministries to persons leaving the movement. Various ex-Witness conferences and conventions were held throughout North America and Europe, and in other parts of the world. Some of the ex-Witness ministries began to produce journals and magazines. As the Internet became popular, a number of ex-Witness discussion groups were formed, and several web sites were established to evaluate critically every aspect of Jehovah's Witnesses' doctrines and practices. Commenting on these facts, Ray Mattera states: 'In the past, Witness leaders encouraged face-to-face confrontation with opponents. However, the devastating criticism unleashed against the Society, especially since 1980, has been directed not at its denial of such doctrines as the Trinity and hellfire, but to the heart of the movement: its ecclesiology. The Watch Tower history of date-setting speculation, shifting and changing doctrines, and concealment-of-errors strategies [has] been exposed by recourse to Watch Tower literature itself. The effect is to undermine the authority of the leaders which, as I have argued, is the central tenet of the Witness religion. The criticism is such that Witness leaders have not been able to respond adequately. Therefore, Watch Tower officials now have declared that the Bible prohibits the reading of "apostate," that is, anti-Witness, materials.'[44]

Although those who have left the Witnesses voluntarily or have been forced to do so through disfellowshipment are a diverse lot and range from individuals who are now atheists to those who still hold many Witness beliefs or have joined other religions, many of them do feel extreme bitterness towards the governing body, the society, and to those within the Witness fold. As a result, some of the attacks on Jehovah's Witnesses by such persons are ill conceived, and sometimes quite unfair. However, much of the recent published material that has been produced by former Witnesses is well documented and meets the canons of sound scholarship. This is particularly true of the works of Raymond Franz, Carl Olof Jonnson, Rud Persson, and Achille Aveta. Franz's book *Crisis of Conscience* has now been translated into a number of languages and has been updated recently. Franz has also produced *In Search of Christian Freedom* (Atlanta: Commentary Press 1991), an important and revealing work. A chapter from this book on the subject of the Jehovah's Witnesses' stand on blood therapy has been translated into Spanish. Jonsson has continued to work on ancient Middle Eastern chronology with regard to the Witnesses' eschatological schema, has produced a supplement to his *The Gentile Times Reconsidered*, and is at present updating that work. In 1987 he and Rud Persson, then writing under the pseudonym Wolfgang Herbst, published *The Sign of the Last Days – When?* (Atlanta: Commentary Press 1987), which is a historical critique of the Witnesses' and various fundamentalists' insupportable position that times have been worse during the current century than at any time in the past. Aveta's most important work in his native Italian is *I Testimoni di Geova: un'ideologia che logora* or *The Witnesses of Jehovah: An Ideology that Consumes* (Rome: Edizioni Dehoniane 1989). In conjunction with Sergio Pollina he has also published *I Testimoni di Geova e la Politica: martiri o oppertunisti?* or *Jehovah's Witnesses and Politics: Martyrs or Opportunists?* (Rome: Edizioni Dehoniane 1990).

Another book by a former Witness, just published by Lutterworth Press of Cambridge, England, that should certainly be classified as a scholarly study is Robert Crompton's *Counting the Days to Armageddon: The History of Jehovah's Witnesses Doctrine of the Second Presence of Christ and the Kingdom of God*. It outlines the influence of William Miller and John Nelson Darby on Charles Taze Russell, demonstrates the consistency of Russell's date-setting eschatology despite its failure, and shows how post-Russell Watch Tower eschatological doctrine is thoroughly inconsistent and filled with inner contradictions.

While a number of ex-Witness authors, such as Jerry Bergman, Duane Magnani, David Reed, and Randy Watters, have generally been more polemical in their critiques of the Bible Student–Jehovah's Witnesses, and in the case of the last three assert that Jehovah's Witnesses are a mind-controlling cult, their research has added greatly to both the historical and the contemporary understanding of the nature of the Witness movement. Bergman's bibliography, *Jehovah's Witnesses and Kindred Groups*, remains a valuable work, and his recently published article, 'Dealing with Jehovah's Witness Custody Cases,' is a major contribution to the study of the Witnesses' currently most important legal struggles.[45] Several of Reed's publications are also important reference and historical sources.[46] Magnani's most important work has been to collect, copy, and reproduce many early Watch Tower publications and also to place some of those publications on compact disks for computers – a major contribution to students of the Watch Tower movement.[47] Watters publishes *The Free Minds Journal* and has produced a number of works that are useful to an understanding of the contemporary Witness movement. The most important of these is his *Thus Saith the Governing Body* (Manhattan Beach, CA: Printed privately 1996).[48]

Gary Botting's *Fundamental Freedoms and Jehovah's Witnesses* (Calgary: University of Calgary Press 1993) is a work of a different sort. It is a fair-minded examination of the Witnesses' contributions to civil liberties in Canada that demonstrates clearly that an ex–Jehovah's Witness can write positive things about his former brethren, contrary to Watch Tower propaganda.

Scholars who have never been associated with Jehovah's Witnesses have also produced many studies of the movement during the last decade, some of which have been of major significance. Although a majority of these studies have been in the area of church–state relations, not all have been. Among those written in English are James A. Beverley's *Crisis of Allegiance: A Study of Dissent among Jehovah's Witnesses* (Burlington, ON: Welsh 1986), Melvin D. Curry's *Jehovah's Witnesses: The Millenarian World of the Watch Tower* (New York and London: Garland 1992), William Kaplan's *State and Salvation: The Jehovah's Witnesses and Their Fight for Civil Rights* (Toronto: University of Toronto Press 1989), and Merlin Owen Newton's *Armed with the Constitution: Jehovah's Witnesses in Alabama and the u.s. Supreme Court, 1939–1946* (Tuscaloosa and London: University of Alabama Press 1995). Beverley's *Crisis of Allegiance* details the separation of more than eighty persons in Lethbridge, Alberta, from Jehovah's Witnesses in 1980 and 1981. It outlines fairly how the Watch Tower Society acts in such a situation, and how the Alberta ex-Witnesses fought back. Curry develops an interesting sociological thesis in opposition to James Beckford and Rosabeth Moss Kanter, in which he holds that millenarianism rather than organizational maintenance is central to Witness organizational structure. Kaplan's study gives a detailed assessment of the persecution of Jehovah's Witnesses in Canada and is particularly strong in its account of the flag salute issue. Newton's *Armed with the Constitution* is a sympathetic look at the background of two major Witness u.s. Supreme Court cases that originated in Alabama.

Works written in other languages of importance to the study of the Witnesses include Bernard Blandre's *Les Témoins de Jéhovah: Un Siècle d'histoire* or *Jehovah's Witnesses: A Century of History* (Paris: Desclée de Brouwer 1987),

Pauline Côté's *Les Transactions politiques des croyants: Charismatiques et Témoins de Jéhovah dans le Québec des années 1970 et 1980* or *The Political Relations of Believers: Charismatics and Jehovah's Witnesses during the Years 1970 to 1980* (Ottawa: Les Presses de Université d'Ottawa 1993), Detlef Garbe's *Zwischen Widerstand und Martyrium: Die Zeugen Jehovas im 'Dritten Reich'* or *Between Resistance and Martyrdom: The Jehovah's Witnesses in the 'Third Reich'* (Munich: R. Oldenbourg Verlag 1993), and Rolf Nobel's *Falschspieler Gottes: Die Wahrheit über Jehovas Zeugen* or *God's Double Dealers: The Truth about Jehovah's Witnesses* (Hamburg and Zurich: Rasch und Röhring Verlag 1985). Blandre's study is a review of Witness history over the last century. Côté's work is an interesting sociological study of Jehovah's Witnesses and Charismatic Christians in Quebec. It contrasts the group conformity of the Witnesses with the individualism of the Charismatics. Detlef Garbe's book is a revision of his University of Hamburg doctoral thesis and may well give the best account to date of Jehovah's Witnesses under the Third Reich. Garbe presents a careful analysis of the number of Witnesses who died of all causes at the hands of the Nazi state. He feels, on the basis of solidly presented evidence, that instead of 2,000, the figure traditionally given, only about 1,100 or 1,200 perished.[49] Nobel's study is extremely important because of the many data in it. Although the book is quite polemical, as the title indicates, and Nobel, as an undercover journalist, represented himself falsely as a person interested in becoming a Witness when he studied them, *Falschspieler Gottes* reveals certain important facts about Jehovah's Witnesses in the Europe of the Second World War. Among other information not known generally in the English-speaking world that Nobel discloses is the fact that Erich Frost – long Watch Tower branch overseer in West Germany after the Second World War – betrayed a number of his brethren to the Gestapo during the Nazi period[50] and that the Society of Jehovah's Witnesses in Switzerland published a declaration in the German edition of the *Consolation* magazine that the Witnesses saw nothing wrong in performing military service and many had done so.[51]

One thing that is striking about all of these 'non-apostate' works and many others is that they repeatedly quote and cite the works of ex-Witness scholars. As was not the case in the past, even Evangelical authors have begun to pay far more attention to various ex-Witness works, regardless of their authors' religious orientations, and are gradually gaining a more sophisticated understanding of the Witness movement. This is particularly true of someone like Ruth A. Tucker, whose chapter on Jehovah's Witnesses in her *Another Gospel: Cults, Alternative Religions and the New Age Movement* (Grand Rapids: Zondervan 1989) is far superior to most older books and articles produced by Catholic and Protestant critics of the Watch Tower movement. So it is now almost impossible for Jehovah's Witnesses to read a non–Watch Tower publication, or even encyclopedia articles about themselves, without being faced with the names and works of persons whom the Watch Tower Society calls 'apostates.'

The Watch Tower's Response to 'Apostates'

The Watch Tower Society has become shrill in its attacks on 'apostates.' In the latest version of the society's Watchtower Library CD-ROM, which includes many of the movement's publications from 1950 to the present, there are 575 references to 'apostates,' most of which are to be found in publications printed since 1980. It is quite evident that Witness leaders are extremely fearful of the effect that critical ex-Witnesses may have, and actually are having, on the Witness community. As a result, the society has done everything possible to isolate Jehovah's Witnesses from 'apostates.' Rather than attempt to refute ex-Witness allegations made against the Watch Tower doctrines and practices, the society has unleashed a hate campaign against them.

Quotations from *The Watchtower* illustrate this clearly. In an article entitled '"Search Through Me, Oh God,"' *The Watchtower* of 1 October 1993 (p. 19) says:

Regarding them [people who hate Jehovah], the psalmist said: '*Do I not hate those who are intensely hating you, O Jehovah, and do I not feel a loathing for those revolting against you? With a complete hatred I do hate them. They have become to me real enemies.*' (Psalm 139: 21, 22) It was because they intensely hated Jehovah that David looked on them with abhorrence. Apostates are included among those who show their hatred of Jehovah by revolting against him. Apostasy is, in reality, a rebellion against Jehovah. Some apostates profess to know and serve God, but they reject teachings or requirements set out in his Word. Others claim to believe the Bible, but they reject Jehovah's organization and actively try to hinder its work. When they deliberately choose such badness after knowing what is right, when the bad becomes so ingrained that it is an inseparable part of their makeup, then a Christian must hate (in the Biblical sense of the word) those who inseparably attached themselves to badness. True Christians share Jehovah's feelings towards such apostates; they are not curious about apostate ideas. On the contrary, they 'feel a loathing' toward those who have made themselves God's enemies, but they leave it to Jehovah to execute vengeance – Job 13: 16; Romans 12: 19; 2 John 9, 10

In the article 'At Which Table Are You Feeding,' *The Watchtower* of 1 July 1994 (pp. 11 and 12) states: 'Food on the table of demons is poisonous. Consider, for example, the food dispensed by the evil slave class and the apostates. It does not nourish or build up; it is not wholesome. It cannot be, for the apostates have

stopped feeding at Jehovah's table. As a result, whatever they had developed of
the new personality is gone. What motivates them is, not the holy spirit, but vitriolic bitterness. They are obsessed with only one aim – beating their former fellow
slaves as Jesus foretold. – Matthew 24: 48, 49.' Then, after quoting C.T. Russell
to the effect that those who had broken with him and the Watch Tower Society as
a result of the New Covenant schism seemed to be 'inoculated with madness,
with Satanic hydrophobia,' it proclaimed:

Yes, apostates publish literature that resorts to distortions, half-truths, and outright falsehood. They even picket Witness conventions, trying to trap the unwary. Hence, it would
be a dangerous thing to allow our curiosity to move us to feed on such writings or listen to
their abusive speech! While we might not think it a risk for us personally, the hazard
remains. Why? For one thing, some of the apostate literature presents falsehoods by means
of 'smooth talk' and 'counterfeit words.' (Romans 16: 17, 18; 2 Peter 2: 3) What would
you expect from the table of demons? And while the apostates may also present certain
facts, these are usually taken out of context with the goal of drawing others away from the
table of Jehovah. All their writings simply criticize and tear down! Nothing is upbuilding.

Jesus said: 'By their fruits you will recognize them.' (Matthew 7: 16) What, now, are
the fruits of the apostates and their publications? Four things mark their propaganda. (1)
Cleverness. Ephesians 4: 14 says they are 'cunning in contriving error.' (2) Prideful intel-
ligence. (3) Lack of love. (4) Dishonesty in various forms. These are the very ingredients
of the food that is on the table of demons, all of which is designed to undermine the faith
of Jehovah's people.

Such diatribe is never supported by concrete examples, nor does the society
ever try to counter 'apostate' assertions with direct argumentation. In years past,
the Watch Tower Society called on non-Witnesses and, by extension, Jehovah's
Witnesses to examine their religion freely. For example, in 1968 the society's
primer for prospective converts, *The Truth that Leads to Eternal Life*, stated on
(p. 13): 'We need to examine, not only what we personally believe, but also what
is taught by any religious organization with which we may be associated. Are its
teachings in full harmony with God's Word, or are they based on the traditions of
men? If we are lovers of the truth, there is nothing to fear from such an examination.' Evidently this is no longer true: Jehovah's Witnesses now need to fear what
'apostates' say and write.

In order to keep Witnesses away from 'apostates' and 'apostate teachings,' the
society continues to take other measures. It has not relented in its campaign to
disfellowship anyone showing signs of dissidence, and when individuals are
brought before Witness judicial committees they are almost invariably asked,
'Do you accept the Watch Tower Society as God's channel of communication

with faithful Christians?' or words to that effect. Unless a person answers that question without qualification, he or she will almost automatically suffer excommunication and shunning, which sometimes results in severe personal trauma, family alienation, divorce, emotional breakdown, loss of employment, and even suicide. Knowing the possible legal results from such disfellowshipments, the society has tried to distance itself from any possible suits, leaving local congregational elders to face them if they arise. Writing to me personally in June 1996, one former elder who wishes to remain anonymous to avoid being cut off from the Witness community states:

The Society only makes the rules that the elders must follow and keeps the records. They have been very careful not to become too involved in individual cases. Several times while I was an elder, we contacted the Society on judicial cases. We never once received what I would consider a straight answer. They would point out a couple of scriptures that vaguely applied and then tell us to make the decision.

This was emphasized at the last Kingdom Ministry School for elders that was held a year ago ... This was given to the elders to write in their 'Pay Attention' Book. It was repeated twice to make sure that everyone got it word for word. S77 and S79 forms are the forms that the elders use to report a disfellowshipping to the Society.

'Six expressions that should not be used on S77 and S79 forms: (1) Anything alluding to or naming one of the Society's attorneys, (2) any mention of the Legal Department, (3) any comments referring to direction from the Society, (4) any comments mentioning anyone other than the committee itself as a possible influence in the decision reached, (5) any comments that might suggest to someone with a critical eye that the committee did not reach its decision on its own but, instead, somehow yielded to the influence of an outside party, and (6) any comments indicating that the elders mishandled the case or committed any error in the investigation or the judicial committee process.'

Since family contacts are often the most important means by which Jehovah's Witnesses pick up what the society considers to be apostate ideas, the ban against disfellowshipped or 'disassociated' relatives has been left in place, at least publicly. The society still states that there should be no spiritual fellowshipping with such persons, and most Witnesses are still led to believe that they should shun their relatives, including parents and adult children. Although the Watch Tower Society's Kingdom Ministry School textbook for appointed elders, '*Pay Attention to Yourselves and to All the Flock*,' which was published in 1991, indicates that a Jehovah's Witness is not ordinarily to be disfellowshipped for associating with a disfellowshipped relative unless he or she has spiritual fellowship with that relative or justifies or excuses his or her course of action,[52] most Jehovah's Witnesses do not know this. The *Flock* book, which devotes more than seventy pages to what amounts to the society's canon law and warns that apostates can contaminate the congregation like gangrene, has a stern warning printed on its inside front cover to the effect that it belongs to the congregation and must be returned to the congregational service committee when one ceases to serve as an elder. No copies are to be made of any portion of it. So Jehovah's Witnesses are largely ignorant of the fact that they can associate with relatives, at least on a regular familial basis, not being privy to 'elder business.'

Other actions have been taken to combat the constant evaluation and criticism of the Watch Tower record and practices. The society has counselled Witnesses to refuse invitations to go on radio or television when any controversial issue involving their faith arises.[53] It has reduced publicity about conventions and other activities.[54] It has warned Witnesses not to read publications written by 'apostates,'[55] and it has called on them to ignore web sites and chat groups on the Internet that are negative towards the Watch Tower message.[56] The society has also shown itself willing to make *ad hominem* attacks on its critics[57] and to interfere with the scholarly work of ex-Witnesses.[58]

Unfortunately for the Watch Tower Society, its anti-apostate activities often have the reverse effect from what it intends. Jehovah's Witnesses and the society itself face a growing incidence of litigation. In the United States, Canada, and a number of other countries, the number of child-custody cases involving Jehovah's Witness and non- or ex-Witness parents has increased greatly,[59] often with negative results for the Witnesses. More serious has been legal action taken against the society by a number of individuals who formerly worked at the Watch Tower's German offices and printery. For years the society failed to pay its Witness workers any kind of pension, based on the argument that they would not need one after Armageddon. As the result of its former employees' suit, the German Watch Tower branch must now pay pensions for past services, and pay into pension funds for its present workers as well, at considerable expense.[60] In addition, certain democratic governments have begun to look into the society's activities with respect to its treatment of former members, frequently with a somewhat jaundiced eye. This has been particularly true in Canada[61] and Denmark.[62]

The labelling of Jehovah's Witnesses as a cult by various 'ministries' is also having an impact. Although the Witnesses are too well established to be affected greatly by such propaganda in North America, Europe, or Australia and New Zealand, this is not the case in a country like Japan. Recently there have been reports on the Internet of the forcible deprogramming of Witness converts there, generally at the behest of family members.

Finally, as the Witnesses expand in the so-called developing world at a much faster rate than they do in industrialized nations, the Watch Tower may well begin to experience financial problems. Most of the money it uses to finance its publishing empire comes from the developed world, and if growth in Europe and North America continues to slow, as it has in recent years, the society will have to press harder to obtain the funding necessary to carry on its activities. It has already begun to act more and more like other religions in soliciting funds from its adherents despite the fact that, by so doing, it is violating a long-standing Bible Student–Jehovah's Witness tradition.

The Future of Jehovah's Witnesses

What does all this mean for Jehovah's Witnesses, and what does the future seem to hold for them? It is difficult to believe that they will change dramatically in the short term, although stranger things have happened. In many ways they are like the Catholic Church before the Second Vatican Ecumenical Council, or the Soviet Union before the Gorbachev era. Like both of those entities, the Witnesses are governed by a centrally dominated hierarchy which is committed to the traditional policies of the movement. Speaking of the Witness leadership, Raymond Franz says:

If the past is any indication, the direction taken by those leading members will follow a conservative line, resisting any course or recommendation that does not uphold and promote the traditional teachings, methods and policies now in force. What has been published and done in the past few years gives no basis whatsoever for expecting the kind of 'reform' some feel must come. It is true that only one Governing Body member (recently appointed member Gerrit Loesch) is under 70, and the ages of the others range from the 70s up through the 90s. New replacements however, must meet the approval of the remaining members and particularly those with dominant influence. There is no question but that it is becoming more and more difficult to find 'suitable' candidates for membership on the Body in view of the dwindling number of 'anointed' men. This may some day oblige the Governing Body to back away from the fundamental requirement that its membership is open only to those of such class. That would be difficult to harmonize with their doctrine about the privileged status of the 'faithful and discreet slave class,' and may be avoided as long as possible. They may be helped by the fact that periodically younger members of the organization decide that they are 'of the anointed' and thus become possible candidates for membership in the Body.[63]

Franz is also pessimistic about the possibility of major 'reforms' within the Witness community as a result of changes at the top. He states: 'A major mistake in looking for reform from the direction of personnel changes is, I believe, in thinking that the situation owes to the men in charge. Only in a secondary sense is that the case. Primarily, it is not the men. It is the *concept* that controls, the *premise* on which the whole movement is founded.'[64] This is a debatable point. The primary concept, 'the concept that controls,' is the need to maintain the Watch Tower organization intact, and if it becomes necessary to reform in order to save that organization, such reform will no doubt occur. The leadership of the Catholic Church and the Soviet Union were every bit as ideologically committed to the past and to institutional maintenance as is the leadership of Jehovah's Witnesses. Yet no one can deny that Pope John XXIII and Mikhail Gorbachev – two men who had been nurtured by their respective systems – were responsible for bringing sweeping changes to the institutions and communities that they came to govern. An American religious movement that was certainly as doctrinally and organizationally hide-bound as the Witnesses, that is, the Worldwide Church of God, has also recently gone through sweeping and dramatic reforms as the result of a change in its leadership.[65] It is therefore wrong to discount the *possibility* of change from the top within Jehovah's Witnesses. But the *probability* is that, when it comes, it will come gradually, as the result of pressures from 'the world,' from 'apostate' critics of the governing body and the society, and from the larger Witness community itself.

One Watch Tower teaching could shortly cause the Witnesses a serious problem and could bring about major change. Although the great tribulation and Armageddon have been put off to the indefinite future, the governing body continues to have a serious problem with its eschatology. If the tribulation fails to occur reasonably soon, the Watch Tower Society's doctrine concerning the earthly hope for the vast majority of Jehovah's Witnesses will have proven to have been false. The 'great multitude,' or the 'great crowd' as the New World Translation renders it, are, according to Revelation 7:14, those who will have come out of the great tribulation. And according to Watch Tower teachings, those persons began to be identified as present in association with Jehovah's Witnesses as early as 1932. So the youngest members of that small group of persons who were identified at a Watch Tower convention in Washington, D.C., on 31 May 1935 will be persons who are now in their seventies or eighties.[66] The time line is running out for those Jehovah's Witnesses, and it has the potential of adversely affecting hundreds of thousands of other Witnesses within the next ten to twenty years. Perhaps doctrinal 'reinterpretation,' or, better stated, *doctrinal legerdemain*, will be used to solve this problem, as was the case with the long-standing 'this generation' doctrine. But it is difficult to see how this can be done if the apocalypse is delayed too long.

As the Witnesses see time passing without the fulfilment of their hopes for new heavens and a new earth, no doubt they will begin to settle in as a more stable, less unworldly community, just as the early church did when Christ's second coming was delayed. That will mean that the society will no longer be able to enforce its strictures so severely on Jehovah's Witnesses, any more than the Vatican can now impose its rules on the vast majority of Catholics. In fact, there are already signs that this is happening, especially in cultures where the Watch Tower's American-style dicta are regarded as too severe.

The society's spiritual iron curtain is beginning to break down. It cannot keep many Witnesses from reading books and other publications put out both by ex–Jehovah's Witnesses and others attacking the society root and branch. Nor can it keep Witnesses in the industrial world from reading similar information on the Internet. Further, it is being undermined by a growing underground movement within the Witness community which cooperates with so-called apostates in obtaining information, sometimes from the society's headquarters itself, to aid in exposing its doctrines and activities. The future for Jehovah's Witnesses as they now exist – despite continued growth – does not seem bright. In the long run they will have to change and moderate to survive, and that will probably mean that they will settle down to becoming just another denomination among denominations.

Notes

For reasons of economy, certain titles of Watch Tower publications are abbreviated as stated below. Except when first listed among the notes for the Introduction, individual chapters, or the Conclusion, they appear under their shortened titles. Specifically, they are *Jehovah's Witnesses in the Divine Purpose* (1959), which appears as *Divine Purpose; Aid to Bible Understanding* (1972), which is designated *Aid;* and *Organized to Accomplish Our Ministry* (1983), which is listed as *Organized*. As the magazine known since March 1939 as *The Watchtower Announcing Jehovah's Kingdom* was originally *Zion's Watch Tower and Herald of Christ's Presence* (1879–1908), then *The Watch Tower and Herald of Christ's Presence* (1909–31), *The Watchtower and Herald of Christ's Presence* (1931–8), *The Watchtower and Herald of Christ's Kingdom* (1938–9), it is cited simply as WT in all instances. *Yearbooks of Jehovah's Witnesses* are usually listed by specific year and the word *Yearbook*.

When reference is made to 'WT reprints,' that designation indicates that the citation in question is to *Zion's Watch Tower and Herald of Christ's Presence* or *The Watch Tower and Herald of Christ's Presence* (July 1879 through June 1919) as edited and published in volume form in 1919. Since the pagination is sequential in volumes or 'reprints,' as they are commonly called, page numbers are, of course, quite different from those which appeared in the original issues of the magazine.

Introduction

1 H. Richard Niebuhr, *The Social Sources of Denominationalism* (New York: Henry Holt and Co. 1929)
2 Thomas F. O'Dae, *The Sociology of Religion* (Englewood Cliffs, NJ: Prentice-Hall, Inc. 1966), 66–9; Bryan R. Wilson, *Sects and Society* (Berkeley: University of California Press 1961)
3 Melvin Dotson Curry, Jr, 'Jehovah's Witnesses: The Effects of Millenarianism

on the Maintenance of a Religious Sect' (doctoral dissertation, Florida State
University, Gainsville 1980), 243

4 See pages 44–5.

5 Curry, 183

6 See page 32.

7 Trotsky called Lenin's scheme of government an 'orthodox theocracy' and stated:
'Lenin's methods lead to this: the Party organization [the caucus] at first substi-
tutes itself for the party as a whole, then the Central Committee substitutes
itself for the organization; and finally a single "dictator" substitutes himself for the
Central Committee.' Isaac Deutscher, *The Prophet Armed, Trotsky: 1879–1921*
(London: Oxford University Press 1954), 90

8 Werner Cohn, 'Jehovah's Witnesses as a Proletarian Movement,' in *The
American Scholar,* 24: 3 (summer 1955), 288

9 Ibid, 292

10 See 'Millennium, Millenarianism' in *The New Schaff-Herzog Encyclopedia of Religious Knowledge* (Grand Rapids, Michigan: Baker Book House 1977), 7: 374–8.

11 For a discussion of millenarianism over the centuries, see Norman Cohn, *The Pursuit
of the Millennium* (New York: Oxford University Press 1961), and Edwin Leroy
Froom, *The Prophetic Faith of Our Fathers* (Washington, DC: Review and Herald
Publishing Association 1954), vols 1–4.

12 On this matter, see especially Jesús Jiménez, *La Objeción de conciencia in España*
(Madrid: Editorial Cuadernos para el Diálogo, SA. 1973).

13 See pages 99–100.

14 See page 218.

15 See page 305.

Chapter One

1 Unless otherwise noted, information on Russell is taken from *Zion's Watch Tower*,
1906, reprints 3820–8; *The Watch Tower*, 1916, reprints 5997–6013; *The Laodicean Messenger* (Chicago: The Bible Students Book Store 1923); *Jehovah's Witnesses in the Divine Purpose* (Brooklyn, NY: Watchtower Bible and Tract Society
1959); Timothy White, *A People for His Name* (New York: Vantage Press 1967).

2 According to Richard Rawe, of Soap Lake, Washington, who has investigated
Russell's business activities closely, many of the claims regarding his great business talents are somewhat exaggerated. For example, In *The Laodicean Messenger* his biographer says on page 6 that the store business 'soon enriched him, and
before he was well past the year of his majority, he was well worth a quarter
million dollars.' Rawe argues that Russell's wealth came somewhat later after he
had inherited $6,000 (which he used for capital investment) from an uncle.

Nevertheless, Russell was an extremely able enterpreneur who used his early, rather modest wealth to accumulate a significant fortune.

Russell admitted in 1907 that he had a 'cash valuation of $60,000 in 1879 which included two clothing stores in Alleghany and three in Pittsburgh.' In fact, he was probably worth much more. In a letter to a Mr J.H. Brown, sent about 1898, he had written: 'You knew me in a business way over 20 years ago, when you sold me merchandise. You probably knew at that time that I had a rating in commercial agencies of about $150,000 – that I had the largest gents furnishing store in Pittsburgh, besides several smaller branches.' Transcript of record in the case of *Russell* v. *Russell* on appeal in the Pennsylvania Superior Court (April 1907), 23, 42, 43

3 *Pastor Russell's Sermons* (Brooklyn, NY: International Bible Students Association 1917), 517

4 Notice of correspondence from J.L. Russell appears in the Life and Advent Union's *Herald of Life and the Coming Kingdom*.

5 See the author's foreword to the *Laodicean Messenger* and *The Finished Mystery* (Brooklyn, NY: International Bible Students Association 1917), 45–7.

6 WT, 1906, reprints 3821

7 Stetson preached for some time in Pittsburgh but moved later to Edinboro, Pennsylvania, where he served as pastor of a large congregation. Notice of his death may be found in WT, 1879, reprints 46. His dying wish was that Russell should conduct his funeral service.

8 Most of the information presented here on Storrs is taken from *Herald of Life and the Coming Kingdom*, 7 January 1880; *Bible Examiner*, March 1880; Frank S. Mead, *Handbook of Denominations in the United States* (New York: Abingdon-Cokesbury Press 1951), 19; and LeRoy Edwin Froom, *The Conditionalist Faith of Our Fathers* (Washington, DC: The Review and Herald Publishing Association 1967), 2: 305–15.

9 Froom, 2: 300–5

10 Froom's two-volume history of conditionalism is the only complete history of the subject in English. For a shorter treatment, see 'Annihilationism' in *The New Schaff-Herzog Encyclopedia of Religious Knowledge*, 1: 236, 237.

11 See 'Annihilationists' in *McClintock and Strong's Cyclopaedia of Biblical, Theological and Ecclesiastical Literature* (Grand Rapids, Michigan: Baker Book House 1980) 1: 236, 237.

12 *Bible Examiner*, March 1880, 404

13 Dr John Thomas, the founder of the Christadelphians, associated briefly with the Millerites. Like so many who did, he came to accept conditionalism.

14 'Synopsis of Our Faith' in *Bible Examiner*, January 1877, 104. Storrs's

last ideas on the ransom and restitution were worked out in 1870 and
1871.

15 The custom of celebrating the Lord's Supper on 14 Nisan began among members
of the Life and Advent Union in the 1860s. Storrs continued the practice until his
death. See, for example, *Bible Examiner*, February 1877, 131.

16 Jonathan M. Butler, 'Adventism and the American Experience,' in Edwin Scott
Gaustad, ed., *The Rise of Adventism* (New York: Harper and Row 1974), 177

17 It is true that Storrs had second thoughts on the matter after the American Civil War.

18 In *The Last Times and Great Consumation* (1863), Seiss teaches on pages 218–20
that after their resurrections Christ and the saints have 'glorified spiritual bodies.'

19 There is real question as to the exact date of the first publication of *The Object
and Manner of Our Lord's Return*. Although the Watch Tower Society gives the
date 1873, there do not seem to be any extant copies which bear a date prior to
1877 when an edition was published by *The Herald of the Morning*, edited by
Nelson H. Barbour. Furthermore, according to Paul S.L. Johnson, Russell
himself stated that he came to accept the doctrine of Christ's invisible presence in
October 1874. Paul S.L. Johnson, *The Parousia Messenger* (Philadelphia:
Paul S.L. Johnson 1938), 368, 369, 437

20 C.T. Russell, *The Object and Manner of Our Lord's Return* (Rochester, NY: *The
Herald of the Morning* 1877), 45

21 There are three traditional interpretations of the Revelation: the *preterist*, which
claims that its prophecies were fulfilled at the end of the first century; the *historicist*, which argues that it gives a symbolic, prophetic history from the first
century through to beyond the end of the millennium; and the *futurist*, which
holds that it deals only with eschatological events which begin just prior to
Christ's second advent. In adopting a historicist position, Russell was in accord
with most of traditional British and American Protestantism.

22 Jonsson's article, entitled the 'Theory of Christ's *Parousia* as an "Invisible Presence,"' appears in the November-December 1982 and January-February 1983 issues
of *The Bible Examiner* published by Christian Koinonia International of Lethbridge,
Alberta.

23 Carl Olof Jonsson, *The Bible Examiner* (January-February 1983), 3: 12. For an
excellent survey of the history of millenarianism in Great Britain and the United
States during the nineteenth century, see Ernest R. Sandeen, *The Roots of Fundamentalism: British and American Millenarianism 1800–1930* (Chicago: University
of Chicago Press 1970).

24 Alan Rogerson, *Millions Now Living Will Never Die* (London: Constable and Co.
Ltd. 1969), 8, 9. During the years 1879 to 1882 Keith wrote several articles for
Zion's Watch Tower on the doctrines of the ransom, the church, Christ's invisible
presence, and the restitution of all things.

25 WT, 1906, reprints 3822

26 *Herald of the Morning*, May 1879, 88. Russell also repeatedly refers to Barbour
    as 'the author' of *Three Worlds* in early issues of *Zion's Watch Tower*.

27 The idea, taken from Numbers 14:33,34 and Ezekiel 4:1–8, that prophetic days
    such as those mentioned in Daniel and in Revelation in particular should be
    understood to represent *years* was one commonly accepted by many Catholic
    and Protestant apocalypticists and millenarians from the time of Joachim of Flora
    to Russell's day, including Wycliffe and many of the major reformers.

    Interestingly, Russell's mentor, George Storrs, regarded the year-day theory as
    nonsense. In an article in *Herald of Life and the Coming Kingdom* of 2 October 1867
    on page 2, he congratulates his old adversary Dr Josiah Litch for abandoning the
    theory.

28 The 360-day 'prophetic year' is often called a lunar year. In fact a lunar year is a
    fraction more than 354 days, and there is no evidence that a 360-day calendar was
    used by the ancient Israelites at all, unless they used it in relation to other ancient
    peoples such as the Egyptians. The prophetic year as such is based upon a seven-
    teenth-century Protestant extrapolation from Revelation 12:6, 14, in which 1,260
    days are equated with 'a time, times, and half a time.' On the basis of these verses
    and, also, Revelation 13:5, it came to be held by many 'prophetic students' that a
    'time' was a 'year' of 360 days.

29 N.H. Barbour and C.T. Russell, *The Three Worlds and the Harvest of This World*
    (Rochester, NY: *The Herald of the Morning* 1877), 42

30 Ibid, 63, 67–77, 93–103

31 Ibid, 85–93

32 Ibid, 68

33 Ibid, 93–103

34 Ibid, 158

35 Virtually nothing is known about Brown.

36 Pages 27, 28

37 John A. Brown, *The Even-Tide: or Last Triumph of the Blessed and Only Poten-
    tate, the King of Kings, and the Lord of Lords; Being a Development of the Myster-
    ies of Daniel and St. John* (London: J. Offor and other publishers 1823), 2:
    130–52. Brown did not refer to the 2,520 years as the Gentile Times of Luke 21:24;
    that was done by a number of persons including William Miller who followed his
    interpretation of Daniel 4.

38 Barbour and Russell, 77–85. Evidently John Brown had recognized that if one
    started the 'seven times' in the autumn of the year 604 BC, the 2,520 years would
    end in AD 1917, not 1916.

    Karl Burganger says, respecting Russell and the 1914 terminus: 'Gradually,
    Russell and his associates had begun to realize that the arithmetic [used by

Barbour] employed in reckoning the 2,520 years from 606 BC to AD 1914 (2520–606 = 1914) was not so simple as it had seemed at first. It was pointed out that from October 606 BC to the beginning of the Christian era was not 606 whole years, but 605 years and 3 months. This would move the termination date for the "Gentile times" from October 1914 to October 1915.' Karl Burganger, *The Watch Tower Society and Absolute Chronology: A Critique* (Lethbridge: Christian Fellowships International 1981), 9. See also WT, 1912, reprints 5141, 5142.

39 Barbour and Russell, 19–22

40 Ibid, 84

41 *Bible Examiner* (July 1877), 317

42 White, 80, 81

43 See for example *Jehovah's Witnesses in the Divine Purpose* (Brooklyn, NY: Watchtower Bible and Tract Society 1959), 17–21.

44 Ibid. Barbour continued to publish his ideas in the *Herald* and in 1907 published a book entitled *Washed in His Blood* which gives a clear picture of his thinking in his later years.

45 WT, 1906, reprints 3823. Actually the picture given by Russell and by Jehovah's Witnesses today is a somewhat biased one to say the least, and Russell certainly quoted Barbour out of context. What Barbour did deny was the doctrine of *substitutionary* atonement and the significance of Christ's death. To the end of his life Barbour continued to use the terms 'ransom' and 'atonement.'

His position is fully outlined in *The Herald of the Morning* (August 1877), pages 26–8 and in reply to criticisms from Russell and Paton on pages 40–3 of the September issue and pages 56–8 of the November issue. Russell's first statement on the matter appears in the September issue on pages 39 and 40; Paton's more irenic one appears on page 56 of the October issue.

It is difficult to believe that either Barbour or Russell understood the ramifications of the issues over which they were arguing. Although Barbour believed in the doctrine of the incarnation, his 1877 stance respecting the atonement was far more Socinian (Unitarian) in nature than orthodox. However, Russell, who did not believe in the incarnation in any orthodox sense, held to substitutionary atonement. If one analyses his ideas on this matter, they were virtually Arminian. For a brief historical overview of the doctrine of the atonement, see Louis Berkhof, *The History of Christian Doctrine* (Grand Rapids, Michigan: Baker Book House 1975), 165–99.

46 WT, 1906, reprints 3822, 3823. In his description of Barbour's attack on him, Russell was certainly not exaggerating. For example, see *The Herald of the Morning*, May 1879, 87, 88.

47 WT, 1906, reprints 3822, 3823

48 Ibid

49 Ibid

50 Ibid, 1881, reprints 224. See also WT, 1880, reprints 172.

51 Melvin Dotson Curry, Jr, 'Jehovah's Witnesses: The Effects of Millenarianism on the Maintenance of a Religious Sect' (doctoral dissertation, Florida State University 1980), 147

52 WT, 1881, reprints 224, 288, 289

53 See Curry, 150, and Joseph F. Zygmunt, 'Prophetic Failure and Chiliastic Identity: The Case of Jehovah's Witnesses' in Patrick H. McNamara, ed., *Religion American Style* (New York: Harper and Row, Publishers 1974), 148. Russell's comment in *Zion's Watch Tower* is found on reprints 152 in the November 1880 issue.

54 WT, 1880, reprints 167

55 Ibid, 224

56 Russell's commitment to Barbour's chronology was so complete that he was certain that something important *must* happen in the autumn of 1881. Nevertheless, he had been forced to spiritualize the failure of 1878 and seemed uncertain in his own mind as to how the 'change' would take place in 1881. Thus he made new suggestions to fit fact to theory on an almost monthly basis and, in his zeal to do so, contradicted himself in an extraordinary fashion.

57 James Parkinson, *The Bible Student Movement in the Days of Pastor Russell* (Los Angeles: printed privately 1975), A-2

58 WT, 1881, reprints 214

59 *The Laodicean Messenger*, 62, 63. 105, 106; *Divine Purpose*, 62, 63.

60 WT, 1916, reprints 5998

61 WT, 1906, reprints 3745, 3746

62 Ibid, 1884, reprints 584, 585; 1887, reprints 918; 1887, reprints 1071; 1906, reprints 3746

63 Ibid, 1882, reprints 369–77

64 Barbour and Paton were trinitarians. On pages 57 and 58 of *Three Worlds* the former attacked the Christadelphians for denying the personality of the Holy Spirit. For George Storrs's position on the matter, see *Bible Examiner* (May 1878), 231.

   Although Henry Grew and George Stetson – two others who had influenced him – were non-trinitarians, Russell did not take a stand on the matter, at least publicly, until after his split with Paton. His earlier statements on christology really forced him to take an Arian stance.

65 Since according to Russell the Church of Christ was limited to 144,000 members, most persons either would gain salvation as members of the 'Great Company' – a secondary heavenly class – or would survive into a new Edenic paradise on earth. The natural Jews were to be restored to Palestine. See Russell, *Thy Kingdom Come*, chapters VI and VIII.

66 WT, 1907, reprints 3942, 3943; 1916, reprints 5998

67 Ibid

68 For a full account of the development of the Bible Student–Witness movement in Great Britain, see the *1973 Yearbook*, 88–141.

69 M. James Penton, *Jehovah's Witnesses in Canada* (Toronto: Macmillan of Canada 1976), 35, 36. See also the *1979 Yearbook*, 78–80.

70 These debates have recently been reprinted by the Chicago Bible Students in *Harvest Siftings*, vol I (Chicago: Chicago Bible Students undated).

71 *The Laodicean Messenger*, 99

72 WT, 1915, reprints 5730

73 C.T. Russell, *The New Creation* (Brooklyn, NY: International Bible Students Association 1924), 280

74 All classes were held to be completely independent. Leslie W. Jones, MD, ed., *What Pastor Russell Said* (Chicago: printed privately 1917), 346. See also WT, 1915, reprints 5743; and 1916, reprints 5981, 5982.

75 Jones, 479, 480

76 Ibid, 100–2, 232, 233; Russell, *The New Creation*, 263, 264, 326–8

77 Russell, *The New Creation*, 289–93

78 Ibid. For an excellent discussion of this whole matter, see White, 115–17.

79 Russell, *The New Creation*, 326–8. See also WT, 1913, reprints 5284.

80 Russell, *The New Creation*, 449, 450

81 Ibid, 263, 264

82 For Russell's general attitude on this matter, see the extra edition of WT, April 1894, 16, 17.

83 For a discussion of Russell's control over the society, see White, 122, 123. Although Russell was generally most careful *not* to attempt to control the 'church' or local ecclesias through his office as president of the society, within the society he maintained firm control. A schism in 1894 resulted largely from that fact. See the extra edition of WT, April 1894.

84 WT, 1894, reprints 1320. Timothy White says: 'There was only one point, so far as I know, where Russell used the corporation carelessly, and this was appointing his pilgrims as representatives of the corporation rather than himself or a congregation' (White, 123).

85 WT, 1895, reprints 1868

86 Ibid, 1905, reprints 3517, 3518

87 WT 1910, reprints 4684–6

88 See White, 135–7; and Walter R. Martin, *Jehovah of the Watchtower* (Chicago: Moody Press 1974), 24, 25.

89 Timothy White accuses Russell of relying on a 'tyranny of the majority' in forcing his will on his brethren. See White, 129–37. Nevertheless, Russell *was willing* to

rely on his influence, *not administrative authority* to obtain his *will* with his brethren. While he was sometimes caustic towards critical Bible Students, never did he
condemn them to eternal damnation as does the Watch Tower Society today.

90 Reprints 5156

91 White, 137

92 WT, 1881, reprints 291

93 Ibid, 1906, reprints 3811

94 Ibid

95 Ibid. See also WT, 1895, reprints 1796, 1797; and 1896, reprints 1946.

96 Ibid, 1895, reprints 1797

97 *The Watch Tower* of 15 February 1927, page 56, stated that Russell had never
claimed to be the faithful and wise servant. It said in so many words: 'He never
made that claim himself.'

More recently the society has made the same assertion. The book *God's Kingdom of a Thousand Years Has Approached* quotes Russell's statement from the 1881
Watch Tower (reprints 291) on pages 345 and 346 and then remarks: 'From this it
is clearly seen that the editor and publisher of *Zion's Watch Tower* publicly dis-
avowed any claim to being individually, in his person, that faithful and wise servant. He never did claim to be such.'

In a footnote on this statement, the author of the *God's Kingdom* book rather
strangely refers the reader to Russell's *The Battle of Armageddon*, 613. On that page
Russell indicates fully that he considers that the 'faithful and wise servant' is *a
person*, not the Christian church. Evidently, then, the author of the *God's Kingdom*
book completely misunderstood Russell's remarks or is guilty of attempting to
distort the facts.

98 Reprints 5998

99 Barbour and Russell, 96–9. The idea was *and is* a common one among Protestant
Dispensationalists.

100 WT, 1918, reprints 6212

101 *The Laodicean Messenger*, 150

102 WT, 1918, reprints 6212; *The Laodicean Messenger*, 150

103 For Russell's discussion of his tribulations with his wife, see WT, 1906, reprints
3808–20. Further information may be found in the transcripts of record in the
trials of *Russell* v. *Russell* in the court of Common Pleas of Allegheny,
Pennsylvania (June 1906), and on appeal before the Pennsylvania Superior Court
(April 1907); the opinion of Justice Orlady on behalf of the Superior Court in
37 Pennsylvania Superior Court 348, *Russell* v. *Russell* (1908); and J.F. Rutherford, *A Great Battle in the Ecclesiastical Heavens* (Brooklyn, NY: printed
privately 1915), 17–19.

104 WT, 1906, reprints 3815

105 Ibid

106 Ibid. No statement to this effect appears in the transcript of record of *Russell* v. *Russell* (1906). Russell, however, undoubtedly refers to a conference which occurred between Maria's attorney and his own before the judge on a 'delicate matter'. It seems that the judge would not allow the Russell's failure to cohabit to be discussed in open court.

107 See the transcript of record in *Russell* v. *Russell* (1906), 10–17.

108 See the transcript of record in *Russell* v. *Russell* (1907 on appeal), 117–27.

109 Ibid. See also WT, 1906, reprints 3816.

110 WT, 1906, 3810

111 Ibid

112 Ibid

113 Transcript of record in *Russell* v. *Russell* (1907 on appeal), 130

114 Justice Orlady, in speaking for the Superior Court of Pennsylvania, was particularly critical of Russell's conduct towards Maria. Said Orlady in a decision in which he evaluated Russell's own remarks: 'His [Russell's] course of conduct towards his wife evidenced such insistent egotism and extravagant self praise that it would be manifest to the jury that his conduct towards her was one of continual arrogant domination, that would necessarily render the life of any Christian woman a burden and make her condition intolerable.' 37 Pennsylvania Superior Court 348, *Russell* v. *Russell* (1908)

115 WT, 1906, reprints 3812

116 Ibid, reprints 3811

117 Page 99

118 WT, 1906, reprints 3812

119 Ibid

120 Ibid

121 Ibid, reprints 3813

122 Ibid

123 Ibid, reprints 3814, 3815. See also the transcript of record in *Russell* v. *Russell* (1907 on appeal), 210, 211, 225–8.

124 The 'Jellyfish Story' is still repeated as though there was real substance to it by many of Russell's critics. In fact the 'Jellyfish Story' reflects more negatively on Maria Russell than on Charles. It seems, from all the evidence, that she was excessively bitter towards him – perhaps with some justification – and simply wanted to strike at him in any way she could.

125 White, 39

126 As Timothy White rightly notes, the two views of the Russell divorce that have become popular are both 'extreme.' The truth probably lies somewhere in between. White, 33–9

127 WT, 1906, reprints 3824, 3825; Russell, *Tabernacle Shadows of the Better Sacri-*

fices, passim

128 The Catholic doctrine of indulgences is based upon this concept. See the *Catholic Encyclopedia*, 8: 784, 785.

129 WT, 1909, reprints 4370, 4371

130 Ibid, 1881, reprints 283

131 White, 109, 110

132 Ibid, 110

133 WT, 1909, reprints 4310

134 WT, reprints 4191, 4192

135 Ibid

136 See 'What the Vow Signifies' in WT, reprints 4263–6.

137 Ibid

138 Ibid

139 White, 111; Parkinson, P-3, P-4

140 White, 111

141 Ibid

142 Parkinson, P-3, P-4

143 White, 111

144 Ibid

145 Ibid; Parkinson, P-3, P-4

146 Parkinson, P-4

147 Rutherford, 10

148 Ibid, 19

149 Ibid, 22–30. A copy of the transcript of record of Russell's suit against the *Brooklyn Eagle* is in the Watch Tower Society's Bethel Library at Brooklyn, NY.

150 For a full discussion of this case, see Penton, Appendix A.

151 C.T. Russell, *The Time Is at Hand* (Brooklyn, NY: International Bible Students Association 1908), 77

152 Curry, 157, 158

153 Macmillan, 47

154 Ibid, 48–63. Macmillan refers to the outbreak of the First World War as 'the wrong thing at the right time,' an idea held by Jehovah's Witnesses to this day.

155 Penton, 42–7

156 Ibid, 4

157 For details of his death, see WT, 1916, reprints 5997–6016.

158 WT, 1916, reprints 5950–1

Chapter Two

1 Most of the information on Rutherford comes from Marley Cole, *Jehovah's Witnesses: The New World Society* (New York: Vantage Press 1955); Timothy White, *A People for His Name* (New York: Vantage Press 1967); A.H. Macmillan, *Faith on*

the March (Englewood Cliffs, NJ: Prentice Hall 1957); *Jehovah's Witnesses in the Divine Purpose* (Brooklyn, NY: Watchtower Bible and Tract Society 1959); and Justice Department files respecting the case of *United States* v. *Rutherford et al.* in the U.S. National Archives at Washington, DC.

2 Rutherford actually campaigned for Bryan in 1896.

3 Page 68

4 On 27 April 1926 George H. Fisher wrote a letter to W. Nieman of Magdeburg, Germany, accusing Rutherford of attending Al Jolson's Winter Garden Theater to see the Paris Edition of the then notorious show 'Artists and Models.' Fisher wanted to bring Rutherford, as an ex-officio elder of every Bible Student ecclesia, before the individual churches for discipline. Fisher claimed that he had the necessary witnesses to do so. But in July of the same year Fisher died and the matter never got any further. Nieman did, however, publish Fisher's letter and an analysis of his charges in a German leaflet entitled 'Bruder George H. Fisher.' Rutherford's lame answer to Fisher's charge was that he was too busy in the Lord's work to be bothered with replying to such criticism and, anyway, had never seen Al Jolson in his life and did not know what he looked like. See *The Golden Age* (4 May 1927), 505, 506.

5 WT, 1916, reprints 5999, 6000

6 Ibid

7 Ibid, 1917, reprints 6035

8 For further details, see page 51.

9 Macmillan, 75, 76; *1973 Yearbook of Jehovah's Witnesses*, 101–6

10 *1973 Yearbook*, 101

11 Ibid, 101, 102

12 Ibid, 102, 103

13 Ibid, 103–5

14 Ibid, 106; *1975 Yearbook*, 90

15 Macmillan, 76, 77; *Divine Purpose*, 70; *1975 Yearbook*, 87

16 Pages 91,92

17 J.F. Rutherford, *Harvest Siftings – Part I* (Brooklyn, NY: International Bible Students Association 1917), 17

18 *1975 Yearbook*, 90

19 WT, 1906, 3825

20 *Divine Purpose*, 70, 71

21 Rutherford, *Harvest Siftings – Part* II, 30. For other accounts of this event, see A.N. Pierson, J.D. Wright, A.I. Ritchie, I.F. Hoskins, and R.H. Hirsh, *Light after Darkness* (Brooklyn, NY: printed privately 1917), 9; Paul S.L. Johnson, *Merarism* (Philadelphia: Paul S.L. Johnson 1938), 73-84.

22 Macmillan, 81

23 See Johnson's own comments in *Harvest Siftings Reviewed* (Brooklyn, NY: printed privately 1917), 8, where he states: 'It seemed to me that my experiences in Britain were pictured by those of Nehemiah, Ezra, and Mordecai (Brother Hemery believed that he antityped Eliashib and Hanani in Nehemiah): that my credentials were in Ezra 7:11–26 and symbolized in Esther 8:2, 15. I concluded that I was privileged to become the steward and Brother Russell's successor.'

Others besides Rutherford thought that Johnson was mentally ill. Francis H. McGee, a Bible Student attorney at law who supported the four dismissed directors, certainly thought so. In an open letter written to the four on 15 August 1917 which was published in *Light after Darkness*, he made that abundantly clear. See page 18.

24 Johnson, *Harvest Siftings Reviewed*, 83, 84; Pierson *et al.* 5, 6; Rutherford, *Harvest Siftings – Part I*, 10; Alan Rogerson, *Millions Now Living Will Never Die* (London: Constable and Co, Ltd. 1969), 33, 34

25 Johnson, *Harvest Siftings Reviewed* 82, 83. Pierson *et al.*, 3,4

26 Rutherford, *Harvest Siftings – Part I*, 20

27 Ibid, 16

28 See 'Vice-President's Statement against the Management in August' in A.I. Ritchie, J.D. Wright, I.F. Hoskins, and R.H. Hirsh, *Facts for Shareholders of the Watch Tower Bible and Tract Society* (Brooklyn, NY: printed privately 1917), 5.

29 Russell's will as published shortly after his death may be found in WT, in 1916, reprints 5999 and 6000.

30 Barbara Grizzuti Harrison, *Visions of Glory: A History and a Memory of Jehovah's Witnesses* (New York: Simon and Schuster 1978), 118–20

31 William H. Cumberland, 'A History of Jehovah's Witnesses' (doctoral dissertation, University of Iowa 1958), 131

32 Pierson *et al.*, 4

33 Harrison, 118–20

34 Cumberland, 131

35 Rutherford, *Harvest Siftings – Part I*, 19, 20

36 Ritchie *et al.*, 5

37 Ibid

38 Rutherford, *Harvest Siftings – Part I*, 20; Johnson, *Harvest Siftings Reviewed*, 19

39 Pierson *et al.*, 8

40 Ibid, 6; Macmillan, 78–80. The accounts given by the ousted directors and A.H. Macmillan as to what happened on this occasion are in agreement except that the ousted directors claim that the policeman *did not* force them to leave while Macmillan claims he did. The account from *Light after Darkness* is as follows: '"Officer, put these men out!" said the President's representative. "Move on, Gentlemen!" said the policeman to the Directors. "You have no right to put us

out, Officer," replied one of the Directors; "we are employed by this Society
and are not disturbing anybody or anything." "Of course I have no right to put you
out!" responded the policeman. "It is I who should go out instead"; and away
he went.'

Macmillan's account reads: 'I said "Officer, these men have no business
here. Their place is up at 124 Columbia Heights, and they are disturbing our work
here. They refused to leave when we ordered them to. Now we just thought we
would call on the law."

'They jumped up and began to argue. The policeman twirled his stick and
said: "Gentlemen, it's after being serious for you now. Faith, and I know these
two, Macmillan and Martin, but you fellows I don't know. Now you better be
after going, for fear there'll be trouble."

'They grabbed their hats and went down the steps two at a time and hurried
up to Borough Hall to get in touch with a lawyer.'

Whatever the facts of the case, Macmillan admits he did not want the
directors to get a quorum to transact business and was determined to stop them
from holding a business meeting while Rutherford was away. Macmillan was
therefore lying when he said that the directors were disturbing the work of those at
the Hicks street offices. Furthermore, he fails to mention that the four were in
the Hicks St Chapel when he called the police to have them ejected.

41 Pierson *et al.*, 10
42 'An Open Letter to the People of the Lord throughout the World' and 'A Petition to
Brother Rutherford and the Four Deposed Directors of the W.T.B. and Tract
Society.' Both undated, 1917
43 WT, 1918, reprints 6197, 6198
44 Cumberland, 118
45 Ritchie *et al.*, 3
46 WT, 1917, reprints 6184, 6185
47 Rogerson, 39
48 For a discussion of these movements since 1918, see Alan Rogerson, 'Oui est schismatique?' in *Social Compass*, 24:1 (1977), 33–43; and J. Gordon Melton, *The
Encyclopedia of American Religion* (Wilmington, NC: McGrath Publishing Co.
1978), 487–91.
49 The Standfasters also believed that the preaching work was over and that the door to
the 'higher calling' (to sainthood among the 144,000) was ended. The 'Preamble
and Resolutions of the Stand Fast Bible Students Association' of 1 December 1918
began with the words: 'WHEREAS, Now that Passover 1918 is passed, and
therefore the "Harvest" has ended, the "Gospel Age" closed, the "Wheat" garnered,
the "Saints" sealed and the "Door" shut...' For further details on the standfast
movement, and groups that grew out of it, see Johnson, *Merarism*, 731–49.

50 *The Golden Age* (British and Canadian edition) 29 September 1920, *passim*; J.F. Rutherford, *Millions Now Living Will Never Die* (Brooklyn, NY: International Bible Students Association 1920), 83; M. James Penton, *Jehovah's Witnesses in Canada* (Toronto: Macmillan of Canada 1976), 56–62

51 *Divine Purpose*, 74–8

52 Penton, 69–80

53 *Divine Purpose*, 81–3; *The Golden Age* (29 September 1920), passim

54 *Divine Purpose*, 83

55 Macmillan, 105, 106

56 Ibid, 107–9

57 Ibid, 112, 113

58 WT, 1919, 280; *Divine Purpose*, 89, 90

59 Russell had stated specifically: 'As the Society is already pledged to me that it will publish no other periodicals, it shall also be required that the Editorial Committee shall write for or be connected with no other publications in any manner or degree. My object in these requirements is to safeguard the committee and the journal from any spirit of ambition or pride or headship, and that the truth may be recognized and appreciated for its own worth, and that the Lord may more particularly be recognized as the Head of the church and the Fountain of truth.' WT, 1916, reprints 5999

60 *Divine Purpose*, 95

61 Ibid, 96

62 Penton, 84

63 *Divine Purpose*, 96, 97

64 Ibid

65 Ibid

66 Rutherford, *Millions Now Living Will Never Die*, 88

67 Rutherford, *The Harp of God* (Brooklyn, NY: International Bible Students Association 1921), 230, 231

68 Pages 214–36

69 Page 57

70 William J. Whalen, *Armageddon around the Corner* (New York: The John Day Company 1962), 66

71 *'Then Is Finished the Mystery of God'* (Brooklyn, NY: Watchtower Bible and Tract Society 1969), 209–47, 283–96

72 Ibid. See also *Divine Purpose*, 101–11; and the *1975 Yearbook*, 135–9

73 *1975 Yearbook*, 192

74 WT, 1925, 67–74

75 WT, 1938, 185. See also White, 186–8. The other members of the editorial committee – W.E. Van Amburgh, J. Hemery, R.H. Barber, and C.E. Stewart –

were all Rutherford loyalists. But when they opposed the judge's ideas, he felt
they were acting contrary to the Lord's will. Writing in 1938 in the issue of *The
Watchtower* cited above, he stated: *'The Watchtower* of 1 March 1925, published the article "Birth of the Nation", meaning the kingdom had begun to
function. An editorial committee, humanly provided for, then was supposed to
control the publication of *The Watchtower*, and the majority of the committee
strenuously objected to the publication of the article "The Birth of the Nation", but
by the Lord's grace, it was published, and that really marked the beginning of the end
of the editorial committee, indicating the Lord himself is running the organization.'

76 White, 181, 182

77 Page 7

78 WT, 1927, 51–7

79 WT, 1921, 329; White, 181, 182

80 *Consolation*, 4 September 1940, 25

81 WT, 1931, 278, 279

82 White, 260

83 See the chart on page 61.

84 No doubt much of the chagrin caused by this article was linked with the failure of
Watch Tower prophecy concerning 1925 and the gradual repudiation of Russell's
teachings.

85 To realize how completely Rutherford and the society's officers detested the elected
elders, note a list of articles attacking them under such headings as 'exposed and
unclean' and 'rebellious' in the *Watch Tower Publications Index: 1930–1960*,
91.

86 *1975 Yearbook*, 165. See also William J. Schnell, *Thirty Years a Watchtower
Slave* (Grand Rapids, Michigan: Baker Book House 1956), 56, 57, 59.

87 This was begun as early as 1923. *Divine Purpose*, 104

88 See for example WT, 1938, 87, 233.

89 Werner Cohn, 'Jehovah's Witnesses as a Proletarian Movement' in *The American
Scholar*, 24 (1955), 281, 282

90 WT, 1923, 310–13

91 WT, 1930, 275–81

92 *Consolation*, 6 May 1936, 508; WT, 1938, 133, 313, 314, 326, 376, 377; 1939, 170;
J.F. Rutherford, *Salvation* (Brooklyn NY: Watch Tower Bible and Tract Society
1939), 43

93 J.F. Rutherford, *Vindication – Book* II (Brooklyn, NY: Watch Tower Bible and
Tract Society 1932), 257, 258

94 *Divine Purpose*, 143, 144

95 Based on an account by my father, Levis B. Penton, who was present at the time

96 Rutherford, *Vindication – Book I*, 155–7, 188, 189; *The Golden Age* (20 June

1934), 594. Rutherford's quotation of Kipling was made at the St Louis, Missouri, Watch Tower convention in 1941 before thousands of Jehovah's Witnesses. It causes some offense.

97 *1975 Yearbook*, 147–9

98 It was not restored until over two years after Rutherford's death. *Divine Purpose*, 215

99 *1974 Yearbook*, 97, 98

100 White, 173. A clear picture of Woodworth's ideas can only be seen by examining *The Golden Age* itself. Although White describes Woodworth as 'intelligent,' one must question his emotional stability in publishing the many things which he did.

101 *Divine Purpose*, 312

102 Ibid, 313

103 It is impossible to say just how many who were Bible Students during C.T. Russell's day eventually broke their association with the society, but Rutherford himself admitted that many had done so. WT, 1930, 342. See also White, 251–8.

104 *When Pastor Russell Died*, 24–30; Melton, 491

105 *Divine Purpose*, 190

106 John S. Conway, *The Nazi Persecution of the Churches 1933–1945* (Toronto: Ryerson Press 1968), 195–200

107 Penton, 128

108 Page 198

109 This was the title of another of Rutherford's phonograph records.

110 *Divine Purpose*, 134–40; Penton, 94–110

111 *Divine Purpose*, 133

112 Ibid, 145

113 Penton, 98, 106

114 *Divine Purpose*, 140

115 Ibid

116 *The Golden Age* (19 March 1930), 404–7; Herbert H. Stroup, *The Jehovah's Witnesses* (New York: Columbia University Press 1945), 42

117 *Divine Purpose*, 191, 192

118 Ibid

119 Ibid, 194

120 *The San Diego Union* (12 January 1942), 2A

121 *The Tribune-Sun* (San Diego), 21 January 1942, 12; *The San Diego Union*, 21 January 1942, 3A

122 WT, 1945, 45; *Consolation*, 4 February, 17 and 27 May, 3–16

123 Minutes of Regular Meeting of the County Planning Commission (San Diego, California), 24 January 1942, 229–35. Meeting of the Board of Supervisors (San Diego, California), 26 January 1942, no 63. Minutes of the Meeting of the

County Planning Commission, 28 February 1942, 240–3. Minutes of the Meeting
of the County Planning Commission, 14 March 1942, 247

124 Whalen, 67

125 Ibid

Chapter Three

1 Most of the bibliographical data presented here on Knorr are taken from *Jehovah's Witnesses in the Divine Purpose* (Brooklyn, NY: Watchtower Bible and Tract Society 1959); the *1975 Yearbook of Jehovah's Witnesses;* Marley Cole, *Jehovah's Witnesses: The New World Society* (New York: Vantage Press 1955); Timothy White, *A People for His Name* (New York: Vantage Press 1968); and Alan Rogerson, *Millions Now Living Will Never Die* (London: Constable and Co., Ltd. 1969).

2 Transcript of Record in the case of *Moyle* v. *Franz, et al.,* 568

3 Many report cases of Knorr's 'trimmings' of Bethel workers and others. His remarks have been described as 'cruel,' 'vicious,' and 'vulgar' by many who have heard them as neutral listeners.

4 Most of the data on Covington are taken from Rogerson, A.H. Macmillan, *Faith on the March* (Englewood Cliffs, NJ: Prentice-Hall, Inc. 1957), and various court records and personal interviews.

5 See pages 83 and 163.

6 The conflict between Knorr and Covington is public knowledge among Jehovah's Witnesses who knew both at the Brooklyn Bethel, although there is, of course, no public documentation of it.

7 Colin Quackenbush, one-time editor of *Awake!,* friend of Covington, and a man who had gained Knorr's bitter animosity, preached at Covington's funeral in the spring of 1980. In his address Quackenbush claimed that Covington was 'a workaholic rather than an alcoholic.' To buttress this assertion there is some evidence that Covington may have suffered from an inner-ear disease which was affected dramatically by any ingestion of alcohol.

8 Data on Franz are taken largely from Macmillan, various court records, and personal interviews.

9 Macmillan, 181. Macmillan evidently embroidered the account. The most Franz has ever claimed is that he would have been *recommended* for a Rhodes scholarship had he remained at the University of Cincinnati.

10 Information on this case is taken largely from the transcript of record of *Moyle* v. *Franz et al.*

11 *Moyle* v. *Rutherford et al.,* 261 App. Div. 968; 26 N.Y.S. 2d 860; *Moyle* v. *Franz et al.,* 267 App. Div. 423; 46 N.Y.S. 2d 667; *Moyle* v. *Franz et al.,* 47 N.Y.S. 484

12 WT, 1940, 207

13 Ibid

14 Ibid. This strange complimentary close referred to the *The Watchtower*'s allegorical interpretation of an account from the book of Joel which describes a locust plague on the nation of Israel. According to *The Watchtower,* Jehovah's Witnesses were plaguing antitypical Israel (Christendom) with messages of doom.

15 WT, 1940, 207

16 Pursuer's Proof in the case of *Walsh* v. *Clyde,* 340–3

17 Zone servants were then called 'servants to the brethren.' *Divine Purpose* 198

18 Ibid, 216

19 Ibid, 237, 238

20 Ibid, 201–5, 213, 214

21 Rogerson, 48

22 *1947 Yearbook,* 137–49

23 Ibid, 149

24 *1951 Yearbook,* 24

25 *1956 Yearbook,* 32

26 *1961 Yearbook,* 38

27 *1947 Yearbook,* 174

28 *1951 Yearbook,* 26

29 *1961 Yearbook,* 38

30 WT, 1 January 1985, 21

31 *Divine Purpose,* 277–9

32 *1947 Yearbook,* 215–18; *Divine Purpose,* 169, 171, 172, 279–81

33 *1947 Yearbook,* 215–18; *Divine Purpose,* 279–81

34 *Divine Purpose,* 251

35 Ibid

36 Ibid, 264–8

37 Ibid, 274; WT, 1956, 152–6; *1974 Yearbook,* 237, 238

38 *Awake!,* 22 September 1958, 13–18; WT, 1959, 114–23; *Divine Purpose,* 283–92

39 For example of such favourable responses, see the *1959 Yearbook,* 73–8.

40 *Qualified to Be Ministers* (Brooklyn, NY: Watchtower Bible and Tract Society 1955 ed), 330

41 Actually twenty-three favourable decisions were given in thirty-seven cases and ten unfavourable decisions in thirteen cases. WT, 1955, 618

42 See Victor V. Blackwell, *O'er the Ramparts They Watched* (New York: Carlton Press, Inc. 1976).

43 See M. James Penton, *Jehovah's Witnesses in Canada* (Toronto: Macmillan of Canada 1976), passim.

44 White, 368

45 Ibid
46 Page 151
47 WT, 1951, 239, 240; 1952, 113–15; 1954, 590–6
48 WT, 1955, 607
49 WT, 1961, 63, 64
50 White, 372
51 WT, 1956, 597, 598; *'Your Word Is a Lamp unto My Foot'* (Brooklyn, NY: Watchtower Bible and Tract Society 1967), 182–6
52 This stricture was abolished in 1972. See *Organization for Kingdom-Preaching and Disciple-Making* (Brooklyn, NY: Watchtower Bible and Tract Society 1972), 177, 178
53 Many *Watchtower* articles dealt directly with marriage customs in countries where polygamy and consensual marriages are common. See for example WT, 1956, 567–74.
54 To my knowledge, there was only one court case over the matter during the entire period and very few complaints even among those disfellowshipped.
55 See 'Why are You Looking Forward to 1975?,' WT, 1968, 494 - 501; and 'What Will the 1970's Bring?,' *Awake!* (8 October 1968), 13–16
56 WT, 1971, 755–62
57 Ibid, 695–701
58 Ibid, 755–62
59 Ibid, 695–701
60 *Organization for Kingdom-Preaching and Disciple-Making,* 82–9
61 Ibid, 53–90
62 Ibid, 56
63 For an excellent discussion of this matter and another opinion as to why the new system came into existence, see Joseph F. Zygmunt, 'Jehovah's Witnesses in the USA.: 1940–1975,' in *Social Compass,* 24:1 (1977), 52, 53.

Chapter Four

1 Page 30
2 *1977 Yearbook,* 30
3 *1978 Yearbook,* 30
4 *1976 Yearbook,* 28
5 *1980 Yearbook,* 28
6 According to the 1976 and 1980 *Yearbooks,* there were 17,546 fewer Jehovah's Witnesses in Nigeria in 1979 than in 1975. In Germany there were 2,722 fewer, and in Great Britain, there was a loss of 1,102 over the same period of time.
7 During the same period (1975–9) the Japanese Witness community grew by

16,990 publishers. So in effect, the Witness population of Japan grew by about a third.

8 The society tended to blame 'materialism,' 'nationalism,' and 'various factors' for the major decrease in publishers in 1977. See the *1977 Yearbook*, 8–13, 32.

9 In January 1975 Franz gave a public talk in Australia in which he indicated that he believed that 1975 was a *marked* year. Although he recounted how the Bible Students had been disappointed that Russell's prediction regarding 1914 had failed, and he quoted Judge Rutherford to the effect that he 'had made an ass of himself' with respect to 1925, Franz hinted over and over again that 1975 would see the beginning of the millennium.

Governing body member Karl Klein discussed this matter for over an hour at a meeting with the Convention News Service Department at a Vancouver, British Columbia, district convention in 1977. Klein stated openly that 'we cautioned Nathan [Knorr] and Fred [Franz] not to be so dogmatic.'

10 Franz delivered several public talks which emphasized this theme. The same arguments appeared in WT, 1975, 579–84.

11 Some two decades earlier the Watch Tower Society had taken the same position on this matter that Franz enunciated after nothing eschatologically significant happened during 1975. See WT, 1955, 93–5. In 1963 the book *'All Scripture Is Inspired of God and Beneficial'* again took the same position. After calculating that Adam had been created in 4026 BC, it stated on page 286: 'Of what significance is this today? It means that by the fall of 1963 mankind has dwelt upon this earth 5,988 years. Does this mean, then, that we have progressed 5,988 years into the "day" on which Jehovah "has" been resting from all work? (Gen. 2:3) No, for the creation of Adam does not correspond with the beginning of Jehovah's rest day. Following Adam's creation, and still within the sixth creative day, Jehovah appears to have been forming further animal and bird creations. Also he had Adam name the animals, which would take some time, and he proceeded to create Eve ... Whatever time elapsed between Adam's creation and the end of the "sixth day" must be subtracted from the 5,988 years in order to give the actual length of time from the beginning of the "seventh day" until now. It does no good to use the Bible chronology for speculating on dates that are still future in the stream of time. Matt. 24:36.' By 1968, however, both *The Watchtower* and *Awake!* proclaimed that Eve was created in the same year as Adam. *The Watchtower* of 1 May 1968 stated on page 271: 'To calculate where man is in the stream of time relative to God's seventh day of 7,000 years, we need to determine how long a time has elapsed from the year of Adam and Eve's creation in 4026 BC.' The 8 October 1968 *Awake!* stated emphatically on page 14: 'According to reliable Bible chronology Adam and Eve were created in 4026 B.C.'

12 Various Witnesses in administrative positions at the Brooklyn Bethel admitted this to me in the summer of 1979.

13 See the *1980 Yearbook*, 30, 31.

14 In Canada representatives from the society's branch headquarters were sent out throughout the country to speak to special meetings with elders from various localities. Such statements – in sharp contrast to what was published in *Organization for Kingdom-Preaching and Disciple-Making* – were made by the Bethel representatives in the strongest and bluntest terms. Elders were being told to get in line; hierarchical control was being reimposed.

15 At first only a few positions were isolated from the rotational system. Eventually, all were. For information relating to these changes, see the Canadian edition of *Our Kingdom Service*, August 1975, 3–6; September 1977, 3–6; August 1978, 3; and *Organized to Accomplish Our Ministry* (Brooklyn, NY: Watchtower Bible and Tract Society 1983), 41.

16 Since they control practically all correspondence to and from the society and relate most closely with circuit and district overseers, congregational secretaries have most of the powers wielded by the pre-1972 congregation servants. Also, since many secretaries are persons who hold management positions in their secular occupations, they often tend to be quite conservative in outlook. Many treat the congregations as 'small businesses.' That seems exactly what the society wants. For a description of the secretaries' duties, see *Our Kingdom Service* (Canadian edition), September 1977, 3, 4; and *Organized to Accomplish Our Ministry*, 42.

17 *Organization for Kingdom-Preaching and Disciple-Making*, 126, 127

18 They were to note the time they spent in the 'shepherding work' on their field-service report slips.

19 This idea was stressed particularly at circuit assemblies but also in various articles in *Our Kingdom Ministry*. See for example *Our Kingdom Service* (Canadian edition), August 1979, 1, 3, and September 1979, 1, 3.

20 At the time of the establishment of the hospital committees, a number of large meetings were held in Toronto at which numerous prominent Canadian Witnesses were present. As a result of the 'hospital work,' three books containing photocopied articles from medical journals and the popular press were produced and bound at the society's Toronto branch. These were: *Jehovah's Witnesses – Alternatives to Blood Transfusions in Adults, Jehovah's Witnesses – Alternatives to Blood Transfusions in Minors*, and *Jehovah's Witnesses – Alternatives to Blood Transfusions*. Most of the material in them was compiled by Alex Trost, a former Watch Tower missionary and chemist from Hamilton, Ontario.

21 Committees were established in a number of communities in both eastern and western Canada. I was personally involved in helping organize one of these 'hospital committees' which for a time was very active and effective.

22 A letter from the Watch Tower Bible and Tract Society, Canadian Branch, 150 Bridgeland Ave., Toronto, Ontario, to William D. Johnson, 2726–25 Ave., Vancouver BC, dated 4 October 1974 quotes extensively from a letter sent to the Canadian branch from the society's Brooklyn office. One quotation from that letter states: 'We have not encouraged the elders in general or any committee of elders in a particular city to visit all the hospitals as if they are the representatives and spokesmen for all of Jehovah's Witnesses in that city. When it comes to medical treatment, they definitely are not.'

23 Letter from the Watch Tower Bible and Tract Society, Canadian Branch, 150 Bridgeland Ave., Toronto, Ontario, to the Bodies of Elders of the Galt Park, Lakeview, and Westminister Congregations of Jehovah's Witnesses, Lethbridge, Alberta, dated 30 May 1975

24 This was particularly so in the Toronto area.

25 Page 10

26 Ibid

27 Herbert H. Stroup, *The Jehovah's Witnesses* (New York: Russell and Russell 1967), *vi*

28 Curiously, the society virtually refused to quote directly from the works of Witness scholars. My own *Jehovah's Witnesses in Canada* received comment in *The Watchtower* by way of a review in the *Toronto Daily Star* and, eventually, in the historical report on Jehovah's Witnesses in Canada in the *1979 Yearbook*. In general, however, the society – particularly at Brooklyn – was cool to it and refused to allow any general notice of it to appear in its publications or at conventions. As a result, some Witnesses manifested direct hostility towards it. On occasions, I was openly criticized by particularly narrow Witnesses with 'trying to make money on the brothers' or trying 'to make a big fellow out of myself.'

29 Cole has admitted that the society insisted that he redraft his first manuscript of *Jehovah's Witnesses: The New World Society* because *it was not positive enough.*

30 Before his death several years ago, Percy Chapman, a former Canadian Watch Tower Society branch overseer, stated to me personally that Cole's second book 'didn't do very well because he didn't have the society or Brother Knorr's approval.' 'He was,' said Chapman, 'running ahead of the society.'

31 Although part of my information on the Blackwell case is based on correspondence with Blackwell himself, much of it was obtained from statements from a number of Witnesses throughout Canada and the United States and from a conversation with Karl Klein of the governing body. Klein remarked to me that 'Blackwell wanted the Society to publish his book.' Blackwell has stated this to be 'absolutely false.' In fact Blackwell published *O'er the Ramparts* at great personal cost to himself. It should be said, however, that some of Blackwell's problems arose from troubles in his home congregation and from the fact that he wrote long and

rather sharp letters to the governing body. Nevertheless, there can be no doubt
that he suffered directly from the publication of his book.

32 Letter from Ditlieb Felderer of Taby, Sweden, to M. James Penton, 21 October
1976. For a time Felderer published a magazine entitled *Bible Researcher* which
contains much information on the history of Mormons and Jehovah's Witnesses. The *Bible Researcher* is an excellent source for information on Witness
dissent during the early 1970s.

33 Details of the Christenson case may be found in the transcript of record of *Christen-
sen* v. *Bodner et al*, Manitoba Court of Queen's Bench, Winnipeg, Manitoba
(September 1977).

34 Letters from R.L. Wysong of East Lansing, Michigan, to the Watchtower Bible
and Tract Society Brooklyn, NY, dated 23 September 1975, 7 October 1975, 17
October 1975, 28 October 1975, 7 November 1975, 23 January 1976, and 13 February 1976. Letters from R.L. Wysong to the Governing Body of Jehovah's Witnesses, 9 October 1975 and 28 October 1975. Letters from Watchtower Bible and Tract
Society, Brooklyn, NY, to R.W. Wysong, 29 September 1975, 13 October 1975,
and 17 October 1975.

35 See, for example, the *Göteborgs-Tidningen,* 30 September 1980, 14, 15.

36 For further details, see *Witness,* the Official Organ and Communication Department
of the Victorian Conference of Seventh-Day Adventists, 3: 4 (September-December
1977).

37 Many of Jonsson's findings were published in 1981 by Christian Fellowship
International of Lethbridge, Alberta, in a booklet entitled *The Watch Tower
Society and Absolute Chronology* by Karl Burganger. Prior to this, Jonsson's
typescript had had a major impact on persons leaving Jehovah's Witnesses
throughout western Canada between 1979 and 1982.

38 Based on a tape-recorded statement which was reproduced in part in the *Toronto
Star* (21 February 1981), G6.

39 Havor Montague, 'The Pessimistic Sect's Influence on the Mental Health of Its
Members: The Case of Jehovah's Witnesses,' in *Social Compass,* 24: 1 (1977)
141

40 Ibid

41 According to the *1974 Yearbook,* 31, there was an actual increase of 173 Witnesses who claimed a heavenly hope in the year 1973.

42 In 1974 there was a further increase of 200 'Memorial partakers.' *1975 Yearbook,*
31. In two years the *remnant of anointed Jehovah's Witnesses* had grown by 373
persons.

43 See the *1981 Yearbook,* 31.

44 Page 32

45 Pages 767, 768

46 The society produced several outlines for public talks which are very explicit on these matters. For further information, see WT, 1974, 160, 484–6, 703, 704. The 15 November 1974 *Watchtower* stated on page 704: 'That *por nei'a* can rightly be considered as including perversions within the marriage arrangement is seen in that the man who forces his wife to have unnatural sex relations with him in effect "prostitutes" or "debauches" her. This makes him guilty of *por nei'a,* for the related Greek verb *por neu'o* means to prostitute, debauch.'

47 WT, 1972, 575, 576. When the society originally enunciated its position on this matter, it counselled elders that they should not inquire about whether married couples were violating this *Levitical* 'Christian principle' or not.

48 Page 31

49 Ibid, 32

50 This was announced quietly at elders meetings and in the congregations where persons had been disfellowshipped for marital *porneia*. To my knowledge, never did any of the persons who were disfellowshipped receive any kind of a personal apology in spite of what the society, acting through congregational judicial committees, had done to them.

51 Page 480

52 Page 702

53 Page 704

54 Page 31

55 Ibid

56 Ibid

57 According to Raymond Franz, this was the case.

58 Page 12

59 Stated during a public discourse delivered by Canadian District Overseer Larry Gray on 1 December 1979 at Lethbridge, Alberta

60 WT, 1935, 254

61 See *Divine Purpose* (Brooklyn, NY: Watchtower Bible Tract Society 1959), 222–31.

62 Pages 728–34

63 *Divine Purpose*, 222–31

64 For a brief overview of this issue, see the *1973 Yearbook*, 133–5, which discusses quite fairly the famous *Walsh* case in Great Britain. According to the British courts, while Jehovah's Witnesses are a 'religion,' they had no 'ministers' in the sense that parliament had intended that term to be understood.

65 Page 733

66 Page 18

67 The *Billing's Gazette*, 23 October 1975; 26 January 1976; 22 May 1976, 14-B; 5 July 1976, 8-A

68 The *Tri-City Herald*, 27 February 1976, 13

69 Ibid

70 The *Franklin-Peninsula News*, 6 April 1977. More information on this schism appeared in the Dandenong *Journal* in the issues of 7 and 14 April 1977.

71 For press reports of the Christenson case, see the 16 and 17 September 1977 issues of the Winnipeg *Tribune*.

72 Details of these developments are only now beginning to be known widely. For obvious reasons the Watch Tower Society has not published information on them and most Jehovah's Witnesses are still unaware of them.

73 Although the numbers have not been large, they have certainly strengthened traditional Bible Student movements. Bible Students have been most active in helping ex-Jehovah's Witnesses. See *The Bible Examiner* (Lethbridge, Alberta), September 1981, 1.

74 These movements are very active and are having much success in converting ex-Jehovah's Witnesses. Some of those who left the Brooklyn Bethel in the spring of 1980 have become Evangelical Protestants.

75 Based on interviews with Rene Vasquez, Mark Nevejans, Cristobal Sanchez, Nestor Kuilan, and Edward Dunlap during the early months of 1981.

76 All of those active in independent study seem to have considered themselves completely loyal Witnesses. Since the society had often changed doctrines in the past, they saw no reason why it could not do so again. Thus there is no reason at all to imply, as the governing body has since done, that these 'dissidents' were 'apostate wolves' with evil motives.

77 Randall Watters, *What Happened at the World Headquarters of Jehovah's Witnesses in the Spring of 1980?* (A pamphlet printed and published privately by Randall Watters, Drawer CP-258 Manhattan Beach, California). Watters served at the Brooklyn Bethel for six years up until July 1980. He left in 'good standing' and later resigned as one of Jehovah's Witnesses because he felt the society was teaching false doctrine. His account is therefore one of a concerned onlooker rather than that of a person directly involved in the events he describes.

78 Although much of the information given here is based on personal interviews, much also has been published or electronically reproduced concerning these events. A good deal of what happened to Rene and Elsie Vasquez is described in the *St. Paul Dispatch* (31 July 1982), 5D and 6D. Sanchez's and his wife's accounts may be obtained from an audio tape recording now distributed by Bethel Ministries, Drawer CP-258 Manhattan Beach, California. Information on Kuilan's case is taken from a letter of appeal from Nestor Kuilan to Lyman Swingle of the governing body, 6 June 1980. However, the best overall account of what happened at Watch Tower headquarters in the spring of 1980 is found in Raymond Franz, *Crisis of Conscience* (Atlanta: Commentary Press 1983), 223–88. Although the disfellowshippings and events surrounding them are public knowledge, there is, of course, no

way of verifying statements about remarks made during hearings before the judicial committees as all such are always held in camera.

79 The *St. Paul Dispatch* (31 July 1982), 5D, 6D

80 Franz's remarks were recorded electronically.

81 Watters, 5

82 Ibid

83 Ibid, 4

84 Ibid

85 See for example WT, 15 July 1980, 22–28; 1 August 1980, 17–22; 15 August 1980, 14–20.

86 The *Toronto Star*, 19 February 1981, G-6

87 The Lethbridge community, other ex-Witnesses, Bible Students, and others have formed what is known as Christian Koinonia International and publish literature, including *The Bible Examiner*.

88 The *Toronto Star*, 1 April 1981

89 Ex-Witnesses picketed numerous conventions throughout the United States in the summer of 1981. Press reports appeared throughout the country. See for example, *The Seattle Times*, 19 July 1981.

90 The Dublin *Evening Herald*, 22 November 1982, 18

91 In that year they experienced a 0.5 per cent world-wide increase. *1980 Yearbook*, *30*

92 *1981 Yearbook*, 30

93 Ibid, 31

94 Ibid, 32

95 Watters, 3

96 Ibid

97 Ibid

98 See for example the article 'The "Steward" as He Faces Har-Mageddon' in the 1 October 1981 *Watchtower*, 25–31: In that article the society's writer gives an allegorical interpretation of Isaiah 22:15–25. Elaikim, the son of Hilkiah, is described as 'a peg in a lasting place' who pictures the 'anointed remnant' or the 'faithful and discreet steward' class. Curiously, however, the society's Writing Committee has chosen not to comment on Isaiah 22:25 although the 1 October *Watchtower* quotes it in 'The "Steward" as He Faces Har-Mageddon.' That verse says: '"In that day", is the utterance of Jehovah of armies, "the peg that is driven in a lasting place will be removed, and it must be hewn off and fall."' Evidently, then, if their allegorical interpretation is to be extended, by their own logic Watch Tower writers expect the 'anointed remnant' to be 'hewn off' and 'to fall.' Of course, they do not intend this, but the article in question is so badly written that it is extremely difficult to make much sense of it at all.

99 WT, 1 October 1981, 28

100 WT, 1974, 467

101 See 'If a Relative Is Disfellowshipped,' 26–31

102 WT, 1 January 1983, 21

103 According to statistics published in *Our Kingdom Service* (American edition) for November and December, there were 588,503 American publishers in August, but in September there were only 541,185.

Chapter Five

1 This was especially so of Storrs, Stetson and a number of other such people. Russell always felt that Adventism was closer to the truth than other denominations. For his ideas on 'the church', see C.T. Russell, *The New Creation* (Brooklyn NY: International Bible Students Association 1924), 80–4.

2 C.T. Russell, *The Divine Plan of the Ages* (Brooklyn, NY: International Bible Students Association 1924), 15–18

3 Pages 282, 283

4 Pages 222, 223

5 *Jehovah's Witnesses in the Divine Purpose* (Brooklyn, NY: Watch Tower Bible and Tract Society 1959), 145

6 WT, 1959, 658

7 *What Has Religion Done for Mankind?* (Brooklyn, NY: Watch Tower Bible and Tract Society 1951), passim

8 Ken Jubber, 'The Persecution of Jehovah's Witnesses in Central Africa' in *Social Compass*, 24: 1 (1977), 121

9 M. James Penton, *Jehovah's Witnesses in Canada: Champions of Freedom of Speech and Worship* (Toronto: Macmillan of Canada 1976), 52–5, 262–5

10 A.H. Macmillan, *Faith on the March* (Englewood Cliffs, NJ: Prentice Hall, Inc. 1957), 84–90

11 Penton, 91–3, 120–8

12 Ibid, 94–102

13 *Divine Purpose*, 150–2

14 Ibid, 134–40

15 Jubber, 222–4

16 Guenter Lewy, *The Catholic Church and Nazi Germany* (New York: McGraw-Hill Book Company 1965), 43

17 Penton, 129–55

18 Jubber, 122–4; *1942 Yearbook*, 125–34

19 Penton, 182–223

20 *Awake!*, 8 June 1968, 17–20; Jesús Jiménez, *La objeción de conciencia en España* (Madrid: Cuadernos para el Diálogo 1973), 95–126, 215–52; *1972 Yearbook*, 150–71

21 *Time*, 9 September 1966, 72

22 Although the refusal of Witness children to participate in patriotic exercises was the issue which seems to have unleashed governmental displeasure, there is little doubt that Catholic hostility towards Jehovah's Witnesses at governmental level was an important factor behind the ban. See *Awake!*, 22 September 1978, 3–16

23 Persecution was severe in Egypt and, more recently, in Indonesia.

24 Within the last several years Witnesses have been attacked physically in the Hasidic area of Brooklyn, New York, while in Tel Aviv, Israel, the local kingdom hall was vandalized.

25 Penton, 69; Macmillan 88, 89

26 Penton, 90; *1979 Yearbook*, 114

27 Hans Jonak von Freyenwald, *Die Zeugen Jehovas: Pioniere für ein Judisches Weltreich die politichen Zeile der internationalen Vereinegung Ernster Bibelforscher* (Berlin: Buchverlag Germania Aktien-Gesellschaft 1936)

28 Page 653

29 Pages 114–16, 178–82

30 *Saturday Night*, 6 August 1927, as quoted in the *Debates of the House of Commons of Canada*, 1932–33, 5: 4672. See also Penton, 102–10

31 John S. Conway, *The Nazi Persecution of the Churches: 1932–1945* (Toronto: Ryerson Press 1968), 196–7

32 Theodoros Chr. Lanaras, *Hoi Chiliastic* (Athens: no publisher given 1949)

33 Ali Arslan Aydin and Huseyin Atay, *Yehova Şahidleri' nin iç Yüzü* (Ankara: Diyanet İşleri Baskanliği Yayinlari 1973)

34 For this comment and further details see A.T. Mosalenko, *Sovremennyi Iegovism*, 220–6, and, also, the *Sovietskaia istoricheskaia entsiklopediia* (1969), 12: 196, 197. A brief but excellent overview of Jehovah's Witnesses in the Soviet Union is given in Christel Lane, *Christian Religion in the Soviet Union: A Sociological Study* (London: Allen and Unwin 1978), 185–91.

35 This principle, the classical common-law definition of sedition, is stated in Sir James Stephen's *A Digest of Criminal Law*. See D.A. Schmeiser, *Civil Liberties in Canada* (London: Oxford University Press 1964), 206, 207

36 *Taylor v. Mississippi*, 319 U.S. 583, 589, 590; 63 S.Ct. 1200, 1204; 87 L. Ed. 1600 (1943)

37 *Adelaide Company of Jehovah's Witnesses Inc. v. The Commonwealth* (1943) 67 C.L.R. 116, 124

38 Penton 147–55

39 9 C.R. 127; 96 C.C.C. 48; [1950] 1 D.L.R. 657; reversing 8 C.R. 97; 95 C.C.C. 119

40 310 U.S. 586; 60 S. Ct. 1010; 87 L.Ed. 1375

41 David R. Manwaring, *Render unto Caesar: The Flag Salute Controversy* (Chicago: University of Chicago Press 1962), 155, 156.

366   Notes to pp. 138–45

42 Published in January 1941, this statement showed the genuine concern of these clergymen for religious freedom.

43 Russell, *The New Creation*, 594. For an overview of Witness concepts of relations with the secular state, see M. James Penton, 'Jehovah's Witnesses and the Secular State: A Historical Analysis of Doctrine,' in *Journal of Church and State*, 21: 1 (1979), 262, 263.

44 Russell, *The Divine Plan of the Ages*, 262, 263

45 Russell, *The New Creation*, 594, 595

46 Penton, 'JWs and the Secular State,' 66

47 Ibid, 67–72

48 For a short analysis of this persecution, see James Beckford, 'Jehovah's Witnesses World Wide,' in *Social Compass*, 24: 1 (1977), 25–9; Jubber, 121–34; and Tony Hodges, *Jehovah's Witnesses in Central Africa* (London: Minority Rights Group 1976).

49 *The Golden Age* (Special edition for Great Britian and Canada), 29 September 1920, passim; Penton, 56–62

50 Conway, 198

51 *Federal Prisons, 1946: A Report of the Work of the Federal Bureau of Prisons.* See also Joseph F. Zygmunt, 'Jehovah's Witnesses in the U.S.A. – 1942–76,' in *Social Compass*, 24: 1 (1977), 47.

52 Jiménez, 95–126, 218–52

53 *1941 Yearbook*, 140, 141. Actually their sentences were commuted.

54 *Time*, 9 September 1966, 72. In this instance an international outcry over the matter also forced the Greek government to commute the sentences of the men involved.

55 Marley Cole, *Jehovah's Witnesses: The New World Society* (New York: Vantage Press 1955), 186–8; *Divine Purpose*, 279–82; *Newsweek*, 25 March 1963, 72. Information on Korea is based largely on oral reports.

56 Conway, 197

57 310 U.S. 586, 605. Ct. 1178, 87 L. Ed. 1375

58 See Manwaring, 163–76. Manwaring claims that the Catholic church was in no way involved in promoting anti-Witness sentiment at the time. The same cannot be said for various Catholic spokesmen.

59 319 U.S. 624, 634, 642; 63 S. Ct. 1178, 1183, 1187; 87 L. Ed. 1628 (1943)

60 *Debates of the House of Commons of Canada*, 1940, 2: 1646

61 Penton, *JWs in Canada*, 129–36

62 Ibid, 137–42

63 *1964 Yearbook*, 235, 236; *1963 Yearbook*, 113, 114; *1972 Yearbook*, 249–53; *1977 Yearbook*, 121, 122; *Awake!*, 8 August 1963, 5–15; 22 August 1965, 10, 11; Penton, *JWs in Canada*, 225

64 Hodges, 5–7; *Awake!*, 8 March 1973, 19–21

65 Hodges, 6, 8

66 Ibid

67 WT, 1973, 529, 530; *1976 Yearbook*, 176, 177; *Awake!*, 8 September 1976, 3–12. Letter from the Governing Body of Jehovah's Witnesses to 'Our Dear Brethren Around the World,' 1 May 1978.

68 Jubber, 127

69 Cole, 186, 187; *Divine Purpose*, 227–81

70 *Divine Purpose*, 227–81; *Awake!*, 8 September 1968, 23–6

71 *Newsweek*, 25 March 1963, 72

72 WT, 15 October 1980, 30

73 WT, 1918, reprints 6271

74 WT, 1918, reprints 6257, 6268

75 WT, 1919, reprints 6439

76 Ibid

77 *Divine Purpose*, 83–90

78 *1974 Yearbook*, 110, 111

79 *Divine Purpose*, 130

80 *1974 Yearbook*, 111

81 *1934 Yearbook*, 134

82 Ibid, 135, 136, 138–9

83 *1974 Yearbook*, 111, 112

84 Raymond Franz, *Crisis of Conscience* (Atlanta: Commentary Press 1983), 110–35

85 For comments by members of the governing body of Jehovah's Witnesses on these matters, see Franz, 116, 117.

86 Franz, 129

87 Ibid, 123

88 Ibid, 131–2

89 'We need not detail the coming trouble. Everybody sees it. It will be a battle between giants – on one side financial giants, trusts, etc.; on the other side gigantic labor organizations. Both parties are preparing. Both parties expect to fight to the finish. Both parties expect to win.' C.T. Russell, *Scenario of the Photo Drama of Creation* (Brooklyn, NY: International Bible Students Association 1914), 92. For a more complete overview of Russell's ideas on this matter, see his *The Battle of Armageddon* (Brooklyn, NY: International Bible Students Association 1924), studies VII-XI.

90 On page 34 of the book *Enemies*, Rutherford stated: 'The earthly or visible primary elements that are employed by Satan to carry forward his fraudulent, deceptive work are these, to wit: religion and politics and commerce.' Such a remark was typical.

91 See *Choosing the Best Way of Life* (Brooklyn, NY: Watchtower Bible and Tract Society 1979), 72–7.

92 WT, 1961, 128, 285. Interestingly, while one may find much admonition to
   employees – whose role is often compared to that of Roman slaves – in the pages
   of the society's literature, there is very little which stresses the moral obligations of employers to their workers. It is evident that in their attitude toward
   labour, Watch Tower leaders are thoroughly bourgeois.

93 See pages 230, 231.

94 *Awake!*, 22 November 1975, 26–9

95 WT, 1975, 191, 192; 1974, 581–3; 1972, 591–600; 1974, 483–6; *Awake!*, 22
   November 1973, 27, 28

96 W. Glen How, 'Religion, Medicine and Law' in *The Canadian Bar Journal*,
   October 1960, 367–74; *Jehovah's Witnesses and the Question of Blood* (Brooklyn, NY: Watchtower Bible and Tract Society 1977), 4–24

97 F. Foerster and M.M. Wintrobe, 'Blood Groups and Blood Transfusions,' in Max-
   well M. Wintrobe et al., eds, *Harrison's Principles of Internal Medicine*, 7th ed.
   (New York: McGraw-Hill, Inc. 1974), 1636

98 *Jehovah's Witnesses and the Question of Blood*, 24–43.

99 How, 374–85; Richard M. Titmuss, *The Gift Relationship: From Human Blood to
   Social Policy* (Harmondsworth, Middlesex: Penguin Books, Ltd. 1973), 160–78

100 The right to die has been recognized under American law in a number of instances,
    most notably in the Karen Quinlan case. The right has seldom been accorded
    Jehovah's Witnesses, however. Penton, 243, 244.

101 *1979 Yearbook*, 157

102 'Without Transfusions' in *Inside Baylor Medicine*, no 2 (1968), 1–4; 'Babies "Iced"
    for Heart Operations,' in *Medical World News*, 13 December 1968, 28, 30

103 How has repeatedly made this assertion which has often been picked up by other
    Jehovah's Witnesses. Many better educated Witnesses, especially professionals,
    have been very critical of his 'analogy' in this matter, however, believing that it often
    offends the public and medical professional unnecessarily.

104 Several ex-Witnesses in Europe, America, and Australia are now doing careful
    biblical-exegetical studies on the matter.

105 Gordon W. Russell, Arthur M. Goddard, and M. James Penton, 'The Perception of
    Judeo-Christian Religions' in *Canadian Journal of Behavioural Science*, 2: 2
    (1979), 22–8

106 It is quite interesting to note that many of the taboos still retained by Jehovah's
    Witnesses, such as refusing to drink toasts, are those which were taken up by the
    Puritans in reaction to both Catholic and pagan customs in existence in Eng-
    land at the time of the Reformation. For an interesting discussion of the subject,
    see Keith Thomas, *Religion and the Decline of Magic* (New York: Charles
    Scribner's Sons 1971), 51–77

107 Jubber, 132, 133

108 For an example of this view of Jehovah's Witnesses, see p. 000
109 *Divine Purpose*, 175–85
110 'Patients' Beliefs Aid Surgery,' in *The San Diego Union*, 27 December 1970, 3;
    'Terry and the Parents' in *Newsweek*, 18 January 1972, 43; 'Bloodless Surgery
    Reduces Hazards of Transfusion' in *The Expositor* (Brantford, Ontario), 27 June
    1972, 17
111 Zygmunt, 54

Chapter Six

1 *What Has Religion Done for Mankind?* (Brooklyn, NY: Watchtower Bible and
   Tract Society 1951), 32
2 Revised edition of 1952, 9, 10
3 Ibid, 12–19
4 Ibid, 15
5 See pages 32–5.
6 *'Make Sure of All Things'* (Brooklyn, NY: Watchtower Bible And Tract Society
   1953), 20–5
7 WT, 1923, 68
8 Ibid
9 WT, 1928, 187
10 WT, 1928, 332
11 As Karl Burganger rightly points out, Russell's position of spiritual authority was
   entirely dependent on the accuracy of the Barbour–Russell chronology. Karl
   Burganger, *The Watch Tower Society and Absolute Chronology* (Lethbridge, Alberta: Christian Fellowships International 1981), 4, 5
12 See page 83.
13 Pursuer's Proof in the case of *Walsh* v. *Clyde*, 100
14 Ibid, 105–14. When Franz was asked explicitly: 'So that what is published as truth
   today by the Society may have to be admitted as wrong in a few years?' he
   answered: 'We will have to wait and see.' He was then asked: 'And in the meantime
   the body of Jehovah's Witnesses have been following error?' At first he replied:
   'No. They have been following misconstructions of Scripture.' But when the crown
   counselor asked again: 'Error?' Franz replied reluctantly: 'Well, error.'
15 Ibid, 124
16 Page 587
17 Pages 28, 29
18 Published in Philip Schaff, *The Creeds of Christendom* (Grand Rapids, Michigan:
   Baker Book House 1977), 2: 83
19 If one examines the context of this verse, he will see that the writer of the

Proverbs is making a simple contrast between what happens to the wicked on one hand and the righteous on the other. The passage has nothing to do with a 'revealing of new truths' either to individuals, a community, or an organization.

20 WT, 1933, 53, 62
21 *Life Everlasting in Freedom of the Sons of God* (Brooklyn, NY: Watchtower Bible and Tract Society 1966), 149
22 'He had a "prophet" to warn them [the people of Christendom]. This "prophet" was not one man, but a body of men and women. It was the small group of footstep followers of Jesus Christ, known at that time as International Bible Students. Today they are known as Jehovah's Christian Witnesses.' WT, 1972, 197
23 See Joseph Zygmunt, 'Prophetic Failure and Chiliastic Identity,' in Patrick H. McNamara, ed., *Religion American Style* (New York: Harper and Row Publishers 1975) 148.
24 WT, 1894, reprints 1677
25 WT, 1901, reprints 2876
26 The old Barbour-Russell chronological system was definitely abandoned by the society through the presentation of a *new* or *thoroughly revised* chronology in *The Golden Age* of 13 April 1935. Timothy White notes that the new chronology 'eliminated all the symmetry of the old.' Timothy White, *A People for His Name* (New York: Vantage Press 1968), 82
27 C.T. Russell, *Thy Kingdom Come* (Brooklyn, NY: International Bible Students Association 1924), 86
28 White, 89
29 Ibid
30 WT, 1907, reprints 4067
31 Ibid, reprints 4068
32 Page IV
33 Ibid. As this statement shows, Russell still believed that the 'Gentile Times' had actually ended in 1914. The outbreak of the First World War seemed a *verification* to him of most of his system! See page 45.
34 Page 198
35 Frederick Franz has stated that Rutherford also apologized to the Bethel staff over the matter. See the Pursuer's Proof in *Walsh* v. *Clyde*, 120, 121.
36 WT, 1925, 57
37 WT, 1929, 166, 167
38 Page 762
39 Ibid
40 Ibid
41 Ibid
42 Page 139

43 *The Herald of Christ's Kingdom*, 15 April 1921, 120

44 See White, 163, 164, 175.

45 Page 195

46 WT, 1925, 67–74

47 WT, 1928, 339–45, 355–62

48 See for example the WT, 1974, 378, 379

49 Most recently, in order to try to make some sense out of its rapid doctrinal shifts, it has used the example of a sailing ship which zigzags on its course by 'tacking to the wind.' WT, 1 December 1981, 26–31

50 *What Has Religion Done for Mankind?*, 24

51 C.T. Russell, 'New Danger in Christian Science,' *The Bible Students Monthly*, 8: 7 (15 January 1911)

52 Page 191–202

53 See the book *'All Scripture Is Inspired of God and Beneficial'* (Brooklyn, NY: Watchtower Bible and Tract Society 1963), 331–49

54 Russell did not feel that the historic books of the Bible, especially Kings and Chronicles, were inerrant. L.W. Jones, MD, ed., *What Pastor Russell Said* (Chicago: printed privately 1917), 42

55 See the *Confessio Fidei Gallicana*, articles III and IV in Schaff, 3: 360–2; and *The Thirty-Nine Articles of the Church of England*, articles VI and VII as also found in Schaff, 3: 489–92. The *Confessio Fidei Gallicana* or *French Confession of Faith* was drafted by John Calvin himself.

56 *'Equipped for Every Good Work'* (Brooklyn, NY: Watchtower Bible and Tract Society 1946), 85–96

57 WT, 1881, reprints 248, 249

58 See, for example, Bruce M. Metzger, 'On the Translation of John 1:1,' in *The Expository Times* January 1952; Walter R. Martin and Norman Klann, *Jehovah of the Watchtower* (Chicago: Moody Press, 1974), 48–52; and Edward C. Gruss, *Apostles of Denial* (Nutley, NJ: Presbyterian and Reformed Publishing Company, 1975) 115–9.

59 For a full discussion of Justin Martyr's thinking, see Edwin R. Goodenough, *The Theology of Justin Martyr* (Amsterdam: Philo Press 1968), 141–7. For Origen's views, see Philip Schaff, *History of the Christian Church* (Grand Rapids, Michigan: W.B. Eerdman's Publishing Co. 1971), 2: 551–3. Schaff states: 'But on the other hand he [Origen] distinguishes the essense of the Son from the Father; speaks of a difference of substance; and makes the Son decidedly inferior to the Father, calling him with reference to John 1:1, merely *theos* without the article, that is, God in a relative or secondary sense (*Deus de Deo*), also *deuteros theos*, but the Father God in the absolute sense, *ho Theos* (Deus per se), or *autotheos*, also the fountain and root of divinity.' See also Hans Leitzman, *A History of the Early Church* (London: Lutterworth Press 1967) 3:180, 181, 192, 209, 210.

60 Philip Harner, 'Qualitative Anarthrous Predicate Nouns: Mark 15:39 and John
    1:1' in *Journal of Biblical Literature* 92 (March 1973), 75–87
61 Karl Rahner, 'Theos in the New Testament,' in *Theological Investigations* (New
    York: Crossroads Publishing Company 1982) 1: 125–48; and Hans Küng, *Does
    God Exist?* (New York: Vintage Books 1975) 680–702
62 Küng, 685
63 See Appendix 5C of the New World Translation of the Holy Scriptures with
    References (1984) under 'Torture Stake,' 1577–8. The society has, of course,
    pointed out something useful by noting that *stauros* does not necessarily mean
    'cross' but simply a pale or timber. But nothing demonstrates so clearly how
    much their scholarship is affected by dogmatism than does this issue. There is
    a great deal of evidence from early church fathers such as Justin Martyr that
    Christians in his day believed that Christ was put to death on a cross, Roman
    writers such as Cicero state that Roman criminals were often executed on a cross,
    and modern archaeology supports the theory that Jews in Jesus' day were
    crucified on a cross. (See *Time*, 18 January 1971, 64, 65.) Finally, by showing
    but one illustration from Justus Lipsius' *De cruce libri tres* – a picture of a man
    impaled on a *crux simplex* or upright pale – on page 1578 of The New World
    Translation of the Holy Scriptures with References, Watch Tower scholars
    falsely leave the impression that Lipsius thought that Jesus was put to death in that
    way. In fact, Lipsius gives sixteen illustrations of impalement, thirteen of
    which show stakes with some sort of cross member. Although there is no conclu-
    sive proof, *there is* evidence that Christ died on a cross.
64 See Bruce Metzger's book review of the New World Translation of the Christian
    Greek Scriptures in *The Bible Translator,* July 1964.
65 In *The Watch Tower* of 1 November 1978, on page 15, the society finally admitted
    that this text did apply to a baptismal confession. Later, they went back to apply-
    ing it to the house-to-house preaching work.
66 *'All Scripture Is Inspired and Beneficial,'* study 8, 326–30; WT, 1963, 760–3
67 Chandler W. Sterling, *The Witnesses* (Chicago: Henry Regnery Company 1975), 24
68 Ibid, 23, 24
69 Ibid
70 *Bible Examiner,* October 1876, 27
71 C.T. Russell, *The Divine Plan of the Ages* (Brooklyn, NY: International Bible Stu-
    dents Association 1924), 12, 13
72 Ibid, 10, 11
73 For a discussion of these matters within the early church, see R.P.C. Hanson
    'Biblical Exegesis in the Early Church,' P.R. Ackroyd and C.F. Evans, eds., *The
    Cambridge History of the Bible* (Cambridge: Cambridge University Press
    1970), 1: 426–38.

74 In a 'General Introduction' to *Luther's Lectures on Romans,* Wilhelm Pauck gives an excellent, short historical analysis of biblical hermeneutics from Origen to Luther. See especially xxiv–xxxiv.

75 Luther learned his *new* approach largely from the French humanist, Faber Stapulensis. See Pauck, xxx, xxxi.

76 Paul Christianson, *Reformers and Babylon* (Toronto: University of Toronto Press 1978), 13–46

77 Alan Rogerson, *Millions Now Living Will Never Die* (London: Constable and Company, Ltd. 1969), 22

78 Pages 367, 368

79 Rogerson, 112

80 For an overview of Russell's teachings on these types, see White, 141–3

81 WT, 1919, 292; WT, 1937, 126

82 WT, 1965, 492–9

83 For examples of the society's interpretation of salvation history in more recent times, see *'The Truth Shall Make You Free'* published in 1943 and *God's 'Eternal Purpose' Now Triumphing* published in 1974.

84 This is outlined in *The New World,* the first Watch Tower bound book produced after J.F. Rutherford's death in 1942.

85 *Babylon the Great Has Fallen* (Brooklyn, NY: Watchtower Bible and Tract Society 1963), 483–505

86 Russell, *The Divine Plan of the Ages,* 23

87 *Divine Purpose,* 7–27

88 Rogerson, 79–80

89 Ibid

90 C.T. Russell, *Scenario of the Photo-Drama of Creation* (Brooklyn, NY: International Bible Students Association 1914), 82, 86; *The Finished Mystery* (Brooklyn, NY: International Bible Students Association 1917), 155, 156

91 Page 170

92 WT, 1927, 51–7; *God's 'Eternal Purpose' Now Triumphing,* 171, 172

93 Originally published in 1853 and greatly expanded in 1858, *The Two Babylons* is published today by Loizeaux Brothers of Neptune, NJ. Plymouth Brethren have stated to me that Jehovah's Witnesses are their 'best customers' for *The Two Babylons.*

Chapter Seven

1 For a full discussion of this matter, see the Foreword to the New World Translation of Hebrew Scriptures I (1953), 20–4 and 'Elohim' in *Aid to Bible Understanding* (Brooklyn, NY: Watchtower Bible and Tract Society 1969), 513, 514.

2 *The Truth That Leads to Eternal Life* (Brooklyn, NY: Watchtower Bible and Tract Society 1968), 17–19

3 J.B. Rotherham, 'The Incommunicable Name' in 'An Expository Introduction' to the Emphasised Bible (1897), 22–9.

4 *'Let Your Name Be Sanctified'* (Brooklyn, NY: Watchtower Bible and Tract Society 1961), 88, 89

5 *'Let God Be True'* (Brooklyn, NY: Watchtower Bible and Tract Society 1954), 31–41

6 *'The Word – Who Is He According to John?* (Brooklyn, NY: Watchtower Bible and Tract Society 1962), passim

7 *God's 'Eternal Purpose' Now Triumphing (Brooklyn,* NY: Watchtower Bible and Tract Society 1974) 60, 61

8 Psalm 110:1, 4; and Hebrews 5:1, 4–6. See also 'Christ' in *Aid,* 315, 316

9 Ibid

10 Ibid

11 *The Truth That Leads to Eternal Life,* 50–3; 'Ransom' in *Aid,* 1371–4

12 'Adam' in *Aid,* 33

13 'Resurrection' in *Aid,* 1393–1400

14 'Jesus Christ' in *Aid,* 917–33; *The Truth That Leads to Eternal Life,* 46–54, 102–13

15 L.W. Jones, MD, ed., *What Pastor Russell Taught* (Chicago: printed privately 1919), 27, 28

16 See pages 40–2.

17 Jones, *What Pastor Russell Taught,* 28, 29, 31

18 Ibid, 31–50

19 Ibid, 28

20 Page 135

21 Page 153

22 In fact, in speaking of the 'great multitude' class of Revelation 7:9–17, Rutherford made that point even before 1935. Rutherford, *Jehovah,* 159, 160. However, the society made it clear after the judge's famous revelation that the New Covenant applied only to the 144,000 who alone had Christ as their mediator. WT, 1938, 70–2; 1949, 72, 73

23 WT, 1949, 75

24 See the chapter 'Not under the Law, but under Grace' in *'Let God Be True'* (1946 ed), 180–4

25 'Mediator' in *Aid,* 1130

26 WT, 1982, reprints 370, 371

27 *God's 'Eternal Purpose' Now Triumphing,* 29–33

28 'Michael' in *Aid,* 1152

29 'Satan' in *Aid,* 1450

30 Ibid
31 *The Truth That Leads to Eternal Life,* 55–64
32 Ibid
33 See, for example, *Awake!,* 22 February 1964, 26; and WT, 1973, 698
34 Page 37
35 *The Truth That Leads to Eternal Life,* 38–40
36 Ibid, 40–2
37 Ibid, 31
38 Ibid, 32–4
39 Ibid, 46–54, 94–101
40 Information on baptism given here is from *The Truth That Leads to Eternal Life,* 182–4. For further details on the subject, see the article 'Baptism' in *Aid,* 185–9.
41 Pages 183, 184
42 For further information on this topic, see 'Lord's Evening Meal' in *Aid,* 1075–8.
43 Page 71
44 Ibid
45 WT, 1756, 49
46 Page 410. A footnote on this statement refers the reader to *Zion's Watch Tower* of April 1880, under the title 'Christ Our Passover,' paragraph 3. If one examines that paragraph, he will note that Pastor Russell regarded 'discerning the body' as discerning the church or mystic body of Christ.
   One may also wonder how for years Bible Students and Jehovah's Witnesses could have been in the New Covenant when they denied that they were. See pages 187–9.
47 WT, 1 January 1984, 23
48 WT, 1960, 384
49 Page 730
50 According to the society's statistics there were 9,564 partakers in 1980 and 9,601 in 1981. See the 1981 and 1982 *Yearbooks,* page 31 in each.
51 The Old Testament types used to picture them are often quite degrading. For example, they have been held to be like the Gibeonites, 'the hewers of wood or drawers of water' who became servants to the Israelites when they conquered Canaan under Joshua. *You May Survive Armaggedon into God's New World* (Brooklyn, NY: Watchtower Bible and Tract Society 1955), 241–4, 300, 301
52 *Life Everlasting in Freedom of the Sons of God* (Brooklyn, NY: Watchtower Bible and Tract Society 1966), 369, 370, 398–400
53 Ibid, 391
54 Ibid
55 Ibid, 392
56 Ibid, 399, 400

57 Ibid
58 The idea of 7,000-year-long creative days originated with Pastor Russell's early
    associate W.I. Mann, of Braddock, Pennsylvania. John H. Paton, *Day Dawn*
    (Almont, Michigan: printed privately 1882), 63
59 For the first full-blown explanation of this teaching in the society's literature, see
    WT, 1913, reprints 5139.
60 C.T. Russell, *Scenario of the Photo-Drama of Creation* (Brooklyn, NY: International
    Bible Students Association 1914), 1–9; J.F. Rutherford, *Creation* (Brooklyn NY:
    International Bible Students Association 1927), 29–51
61 *'Let God Be True'* (1952), 177–9; *New Heavens and a New Earth* (1953), 41–3;
    From Paradise Lost to Paradise Regained (1958), 9–17; *Is the Bible Really the
    Word of God?* (1969), 17–20. All of the foregoing are Watchtower publications.
62 In 1916 Russell wrote: 'We could not, of course, know in 1889, whether the date
    1914, so clearly marked in the Bible as the end of the Gentile lease of power or
    permission to rule the world, would mean that they would be fully out of power at
    that time, or whether, their leasing expiring, their eviction would begin. The
    latter we perceive to be the Lord's program; and promptly in August, 1914, the
    Gentile kingdoms referred to in the prophecy began the present great struggle,
    which according to the Bible, will culminate in the complete overthrow of all human
    government, opening the way for the full establishment of the Kingdom of God's
    dear Son.' C.T. Russell, 'The Author's Foreword' in *The Time Is At Hand*
    (Brooklyn, NY: International Bible Students Association 1924), iii
63 See in particular 58–62, 128, 484, 513, 515, and the chart on 594 and 595.
64 See pages 57, 58.
65 On page 7 of the Dawn Bible Students Association booklet *When Pastor Russell
    Died*, the following accurate observation appears: 'The story of the "Seventh
    Volume" would not be complete should we fail to mention that in a remarka-
    bly short time after it was published it was virtually rejected by the publishers. It
    is well neigh impossible to believe, yet true, that whereas when this book was
    first published those who did not accept it were condemned and disfellowshipped,
    within a few years those who did accept it were disfellowshipped.'
66 Compare, for example, the 'prophetic' map on page 572 of *The Finished Mystery*
    with a virtually identical one on the inside back cover of the book *'The Nations
    Shall Know That I Am Jehovah' – How?* published in 1971.
67 *Our Incoming World Government – God's Kingdom*, 121–47
68 Page 152
69 See WT 1955, 94, 95; and *Life Everlasting in Freedom of the Sons of God*, 31–5.
70 C.T. Russell, *Thy Kingdom Come* (Brooklyn, NY: International Bible Students Asso-
    ciation 1924), 233, 234

71 L.W. Jones, MD, ed., *What Pastor Russell Said* (Chicago: printed privately 1917), 297, 308, 309

72 C.T. Russell, *The Divine Plan of the Ages* (Brooklyn, NY: International Bible Students Association 1924), 149–72

73 Jones, *What Pastor Russell Taught,* 28

74 Jones, *What Pastor Russell Said,* 11, 14

75 Ibid, 14, 15

76 In 1937 Rutherford claimed that the 15 December 1928 *Watch Tower* had first proclaimed this doctrine (see WT, 1937, 86). There is, however, no discussion of the subejct in that magazine although there is an oblique one in the 1 December 1928 issue on pages 366, 367.

77 WT, 1930, 332

78 WT, 1938, 314, 326, 376, 377

79 Pages 362–6

80 *Divine Purpose,* 252, 253

81 Pages 137–42

82 Ibid, 146–8

83 Ibid, 143, 149

84 Ibid, 142, 143

85 WT, 1959, 415; 1961, 703, 704

86 WT, 1951, 67–73

87 *Awake!,* 22 November 1975, 10, 26–8

88 See for example WT, 15 November 1981, 10–15

89 'Abortion,' in *Aid,* 22; WT, 1969, 767, 768

90 WT,1969, 766, 767

91 WT, 1975, 158–60

92 Page 356

93 Pages 414, 415

94 WT, 1959, 640

95 WT, 1963, 123

96 *Awake!,* 8 May 1964, 30

97 WT, 1964, 128

98 Ibid, 127

99 Ibid

100 WT, 1958, 575

101 WT, 1973, 224

102 *Awake!* 22 February 1975, 30

103 According to Edward Dunlap who was present at the Brooklyn Bethel at the time, this situation caused some resentment among those Bethel workers who knew

what was happening. For an account of a similar happening, see William and Joan Cetnar, 'An Inside View of the Watchtower Society,' in Edmund C. Gruss, ed., *We Left Jehovah's Witnesses – A Non Prophet Organization* (Phillipsburg, NJ: Presbyterian and Reformed Publishing Company 1978).

104 Page 6
105 Page 14
106 Pages 7, 8

Chapter Eight

1 James A. Beckford, *The Trumpet of Prophecy* (New York: John Wiley and Sons 1975), 96
2 *Everlasting Life in Freedom of the Sons of God* (Brooklyn, NY: Watchtower Bible and Tract Society 1966), 167–72
3 Max Weber, *Theory of Social and Economic Organization* (New York: Beacon Press 1957), 334
4 Richard Hofstadter, *The Paranoid Style in American Politics and Other Essays* (New York: Alfred A. Knopf 1965), 33–9
5 While he gives the details of what happened at the society's headquarters, he does not discuss the various outside pressures on Brooklyn from the larger Witness community. See Raymond Franz, *Crisis of Conscience* (Atlanta: Commentary Press 1983), 20–5
6 Based on statements made to me by a Watch Tower official at Brooklyn in the summer of 1979.
7 Franz, 20–5
8 Ibid, 40, 51, 64–6
9 Ibid, 41–50
10 Ibid, 69–74, 88–91
11 This in spite of the fact that, as he has suggested and his nephew points out, he believes that he should be Knorr's successor with Knorr's powers and that Lloyd Barry should succeed him on his death. See *Let Your Name Be Sanctified* (Brooklyn, NY: Watchtower Bible and Tract Society 1961), 335, 336; and Franz, 83–7, 91, 92.
12 Franz, 91–3
13 Although the term 'mother' is used specifically for 'God's woman,' that is his heavenly or universal organization, the theocratic arrangement of Jehovah's Witnesses is seen as an extension of that 'mother' organization. See for example *From Paradise Lost to Paradise Regained* (Brooklyn, NY: Watch Tower Bible and Tract Society 1958), 158; and WT, 1957, 274–6
14 *1973 Yearbook,* 257, WT, 1974, 554

15 *1973 Yearbook,* 258, 259

16 Ibid, 259

17 WT, 1975, 60

18 *1978 Yearbook,* 259

19 These have been Fekel, Groh, Knorr, Jackson and suiter.

20 Chitty was asked to resign for moral reasons.

21 WT, 1976, 672

22 Although Raymond Franz mentions this statement, he does not attribute it to Sidlik. See Franz, 92. When I visited the Brooklyn Bethel in the summer of 1979, I was told that Sidlik had said it by a number of responsible persons.

23 Franz, 214–18. As Raymond Franz notes, discussions on the subject of 1914 by the governing body were occasioned in part by the data submitted to it by Carl Olof Jonsson.

24 For a discussion of this matter, see the author's foreword to Carl Olof Jonsson, *The Gentile Times Reconsidered* (Lethbridge, Alta. and La Jolla, Cal.: Good News Defenders and Hart Publishers 1984).

25 Franz, 214–18

26 Ibid, 72, 217

27 Ibid, 218–20

28 Ibid, 209–12

29 When visiting the Brooklyn Bethel in 1979, I was amazed at the extreme outspokenness of many Bethel workers and the attitudes of open contempt manifested by them for the governing body. See also Franz, 234–5.

30 Although Raymond Franz indicates that he was unaware of much of this, Grant Suiter's assessment of the situation was essentially accurate. There is no indication, however, that there was anything like an organized movement in opposition to the governing body's authority as was later stated by Watch Tower officials.

31 Franz, 228–9

32 Ibid, 228–33, 236–40, 248

33 Ibid, 88–91

34 Pages 258–9

35 Although these facts need little verification since they demonstrate what is so commonly true of similar organizational structures, they are recognized by many at Bethel. With the present collective nature of governance at Brooklyn, it would be virtually impossible to replace the present committee structure even if it were deemed advisable to do so.

36 Much of the action taken against 'apostates' at Bethel in the spring of 1980 was taken through the Service Department Committee, and the society's general policy on 'apostasy' since that time was enunciated in a letter sent out by that body on 1 September 1980. See Franz, 292–5.

37 According to one internal reckoning, in the service year from 1 September 1977 through 31 August 1978 some 500 out of 1,800 workers left the Brooklyn Bethel. This rate is probably quite typical of the year-to-year turnover.

38 Jerry Bergman, 'What Is Bethel?' in *The Bible Examiner,* October 1981, 12

39 It is because of the customs of trimming and publicly announcing the sins of those expelled from Bethel that these cases are so well known. The case in question has been reported to me by many Bethelites and ex-Bethelites.

40 In 1930 Rutherford gave a radio broadcast attacking prohibition which was published in the booklet *Prohibition; the League of Nations: Of God or the Devil – Which?*

41 Based on comments by Frank Wainwright, former secretary treasurer of the International Bible Students Association of Canada during an interview with him, July 1971.

42 Woodworth, like Russell, was a teetottaler and resented some of the illegal activities of his brethren.

43 Moyle's letter to Rutherford may be found in the transcript of *Moyle* v. *Franz et al.*

44 Like many others, Frank Wainwright has claimed that Knorr had a great respect for the law and quietly refused to break it. He did not dare oppose Judge Rutherford on the matter, at least openly.

45 WT, 1 May 1983, 8–11

46 For years they received only $14 per month, but they now receive $25. In addition they can get $30 per month for subway transportation and a $100 per year clothing allowance.

47 William J. Schnell, *Thirty Years a Watchtower Slave* (Grand Rapids, Michigan: Baker Book House, 1956), 124–6

48 Randall Watters, *What Happened at the World Headquarters of Jehovah's Witnesses in the Spring of 1980?* (Manhattan Beach, Calif.: printed privately 1981), 4, 5

49 Joseph F. Zygmunt, 'Jehovah's Witnesses in the U.S.A.: 1942–1976,' in *Social Compass,* 24:1 (1977), 49, 50

50 Ibid

51 *1946 Yearbook,* 221–4. See also Zygmunt, 50.

52 Zygmunt, 51

53 Ibid

54 Beckford, 93

55 See for example *Awake!,* 22 October 1961, 21, 22; and 8 February 1962, 21–3.

56 On 21 April 1981, R.H. Armfelt of Fort McMurray, Alberta, wrote the Watchtower Society at Brooklyn to ask if investing in stocks constituted gambling. He wrote: 'I am raising a question that was put to me. Is playing the stock market a form of gambling? I looked up as much information as I could but could not find very

concrete answers.' Thereafter he simply gave the dictionary definition of gambling and criticized no one. The society replied to this letter with real pique. After stating, 'The fact that there is some risk involved does not put stocks in the same category as gambling at a casino,' it went on to say: 'We see no justifiable reason why you should be critical of those brothers and sisters who invest in the stockmarket. It is a personal decision and it would be entirely inappropriate for a Christian to "judge his brother" in this regard.' Letter from the Watchtower Bible and Tract Society, Brooklyn, NY, to R.H. Armfelt, 21 May 1981

57 Franz, 28

58 Much of its wealth has been put into the building of numerous branch offices and facilities around the world since 1975. So its liquid assets are probably no greater than in the past. In fact its recent building program evidently forced the society to sell many of its stocks about 1978. For a discussion of the building program, see the *1982 Yearbook*, 6–9.

59 *1984 Yearbook*, 8

60 In a study conducted in Japan, one of the most literate nations in the world and one in which the Witnesses are very active in placing literature, Bryan Wilson was able to ascertain that only 9 or 2.6 per cent of 377 converts in the greater Tokyo area had become Jehovah's Witnesses through reading the society's literature. In most other lands the percentage is probably even smaller. This suggests that from the standpoint of proselytizing the literature serves little purpose. Bryan Wilson, 'Aspects of Kinship and the Rise of Jehovah's Witnesses in Japan,' in *Social Compass*, 24: 1 (1977), 109

61 David Reed, *Comments from the Friends*, February 1982, 4

62 For discussions of the role of district overseers, see *Organized to Accomplish Our Ministry* (Brooklyn, NY: Watchtower Bible and Tract Society, 1983), 51–3; and WT, 1977, 601.

63 *Organized*, 52

64 For discussions concerning the role of circuit overseers, see ibid, 47–50; and WT, 1977, 601.

65 *Organization for Kingdom-Preaching and Disciple-Making*, 89, 90

66 *1977 Yearbook*, 259; *Organized*, 52, 53

67 *Organized*, 53, 54

68 This statement is based on 'Public Information Returns' of the Watchtower Bible and Tract Society, Inc. (Toronto branch) for the years 1977 through 1983 as made to Revenue Canada, Ottawa, Ontario.

69 Beckford, 67–9

70 *Organized*, 28–46

71 Ibid, 55–9

72 Ibid, 113–15

73 A formal description of Witness meetings may be found in *Organized,* 64–76.

74 Page 129

75 Attendance statistics for all meetings are kept by all congregations and reported to the Watch Tower Society. If attendance falls much below 100 per cent of the number of local publishers for any length of time, that is seen as cause for concern by circuiit overseers and local elders.

76 As long ago as 1949 Charles Braden stated: 'No modern Christians make a more constant use of scripture or memorize in greater quantities than the Witnesses.' Charles S. Braden, *These Also Believe* (New York: The Macmillan Company 1949), 380.

77 Their most recent songbook, *Sing Praises to Jehovah,* contains no hymns taken from traditional church music. Such church music is regarded as 'Babylonish.'

78 *1984 Yearbook,* 31

79 See the *1983 Yearbook,* 30, and the *1984 Yearbook,* 30, for comparative statistics on the peak numbers of publishers for 1982 and 1983 respectively.

80 Beckford, 160, 161

81 Ibid

82 Wilson, 109

83 Jerry Bergman claims that from surveys he made in Ohio, in his samples only about 5 per cent of all Witnesses had become such through door-to-door proselytizing. However, this statistic is probably unrepresentatively low. In western Canada several unpublished studies that I and my students have conducted show that about 20 per cent were attracted initially in that way. Most of those who were 'house-call converts' were persons who had been Jehovah's Witnesses for more than fifteen years. So such data suggest that in North America the door-to-door work has been declining in success for some years.

84 William Willoughby, former religion editor for the *Washington Star* of Washington, DC, states concerning Jehovah's Witnesses: 'they have never been accepted. They probably never will be. They are not visible in the sense that they are doing projects that commend themselves to people. They do not have a good public relations sense about putting on something like the Mormon Tabernacle Choir.' From an interview with William Willoughly entitled 'Religious Journalism and New Religions,' in *Religious Liberty in Canada,* M. Darrol Bryant, ed. (Toronto: Canadians for the Protection of Religious Liberty 1979), 52

85 William Cetnar, 'An Inside View of the Watchtower Society,' in Edmond C. Gruss, ed., *We Left Jehovah's Witnesses – A Non-Prophet Organization* (Phillipsburg, NJ: Presbyterian and Reformed Publishing Co. 1978), 77

86 Pursuer's Proof in *Walsh* v. *Latham,* 92

87 WT, 1 June 1982, 20

88 WT, 1937, 141, 159, 160

89 *The Los Angeles Times,* January 30, 1982, Part II, 4, 5

90 *The Ottawa Citizen,* July 5, 1982, 1, 3

91 Most of the information presented here is taken from a first-hand account by Catherine Clark of the *Vancouver Sun* in the *Sun* of 17 September 1982, on pages A1 and A2, although some few details are based on Higgins's personal account. Clark accompanied Higgins to his 'trial' before the judicial committee as one of his two witnesses. The members of the judicial committee did not want to allow Higgins to have any witnesses but grudgingly allowed them to remain present when Higgins produced a *Sun* article which quoted Eugene Rosam of the Canadian branch office of the Watch Tower Society as having stated that persons who were brought before judicial committees had a right to have their own witnesses present. Of course, Clark did not reveal the fact that she was a correspondent for the *Vancouver Sun.*

92 *The Ottawa Citizen,* July 5, 1982, 1, 3

93 There have been quite a number of such cases. I know from first-hand experience what happens to a person who has been so targeted. For further details, see *Maclean's* magazine, 16 March 1981, 46–9.

94 Wilton M. Nelson and Richard K. Smith, *Jehovah's Witnesses – Part II:* "Their Mission" in David J. Hesselgrave, ed., *Dynamic Religious Movements* (Grand Rapids, Michigan: Baker Book House, 1978), 199

95 For a first-hand description of Knorr's behaviour, see Heather and Gary Botting, *The Orwellian World of Jehovah's Witnesses* (Toronto: University of Toronto Press 1984), XI, XII.

96 Franz, 75

Chapter Nine

1 This in itself is an amazing fact. Although the Hutterites date from the sixteenth century, there are fewer than 30,000 of them found in only three Canadian provinces and four American states. Members of the Unification church have been present in America in the last several decades, and although it is difficult to ascertain just how many there are in the United States, Korea, and Japan together, that is, the places where they are most numerous, they are still a much smaller community than the Witnesses. It is rather certain that in North America, for example, there are fewer than 7,000 Unificationists while there are roughly 750,000 North American Witness publishers alone. However, part of the reason that Witnesses may not have received wider scholarly examination is that they are harder to study. Unlike the Hutterites and even the Unificationists, they are found in practically every community of size throughout western and Third World nations. And, also, they have often been hostile to scholars as is shown above.

2 Reginald W. Bibby and Merlin B. Brinkerhoff, 'Sources of Religious Involvement: Issues for Future Empirical Investigation,' in *Review of Religious Research* 15: 2 (Winter 1974), 71

3 See Alan Rogerson, *Millions Now Living Will Never Die* (London: Constable and Co. Ltd. 1969), 174, 175

4 Bibby and Brinkerhoff, 71, 72

5 Ibid, 74, 75

6 Sholto Cross, 'Social History and Millennial Movements: The Watch Tower in South Central Africa,' in *Social Compass* 24: 1 (1977), 83–95. The *1950 Year-book,* 24, 163–5, 203–12

7 *1951 Yearbook,* 30, 31; *1979 Yearbook,* 24–31

8 *1982 Yearbook,* 24–31

9 For discussions of Jehovah's Witnesses' missionary activities in Japan, see the *1973 Yearbook,* 209–55, and Bryan Wilson, 'Aspects of Kinship and the Rise of Jehovah's Witnesses in Japan,' in *Social Compass,* 24: 1 (1977), 83–95. For their Korean activities see *Awake!* 22 May 1973, 17, 18, and WT, 1975, 264–6. In the latter country many Buddhists accept some other form of Christianity before becoming Jehovah's Witnesses.

10 M. James Penton, *Jehovah's Witnesses in Canada* (Toronto: Macmillan of Canada, 1976), 22–7. James A. Beckford, *The Trumpet of Prophecy* (New York: John Wiley and Sons 1975), 13, 14, 135, 136

11 Penton, 24. Herbert H. Stroup, *The Jehovah's Witnesses* (New York: Russell and Russell 1945) 34, 79

12 Beckford, 13, 14, 136

13 Penton, 22–7. Beckford, 133–6. Both Bruno Bettelheim and Rudolph Hoess give a description of Jehovah's Witnesses in the Nazi concentration camps. Hoess categorizes them as 'working class and peasants.' Bruno Bettelheim, *The Informed Heart* (New York: The Free Press of Glenco 1961) 122, 123. Rudolph Hoess, *Commandant at Auschwitz* (Cleveland: World Publishing Co. 1951), 95–9, 149–50. In private conversations Professor John S. Conway assured me that in examining concentration camp records for his outstanding study, *The Nazi Persecution of the Churches: 1933–45,* he was clearly able to determine that the overwhelming majority of German Witnesses during the period were in fact workers and peasants.

14 Max Weber, *Sociology of Religion* (Boston: Beacon Press 1964), 106

15 Rogerson, 174, 175

16 Beckford, 136–41

17 Wilson, 113

18 Jesús Jiménez; *La objeción de conciencia en España* (Madrid: Editorial Cuadernos para el Diálogo, SA 1973) 79

19 Rogerson, 174, 175. Penton, 24

20 Quirinus Munters, 'Recruitement et candidats en puissance' in *Social Compass* 24: 1 (1977), 61
21 Cross, 88
22 Karla O. Poewe, 'Religion, Matriliny and Change: Jehovah's Witnesses and Seventh-Day Adventists in Luapula, Zambia,' in *American Ethnologist*, 5: 2, 391–3
23 Beckford, 140
24 Jimenez, 79
25 Wilson, 106, 107. This factor has often been commented on by western Witnesses who have visited Japan.
26 Beckford, 137
27 Ibid
28 As quoted in H. Richard Niebuhr, *The Social Sources of Denominationalism* (New York: World Publishing Company 1971), 70
29 See page 85.
30 This is clearly demonstrated by Canadian decennial censuses since the 1930s.
31 Rogerson, 176
32 Wilson, 101
33 Wilson, 102–4; Cross, 88; Poewe, 391–3. See also Norman Long, *Social Change and the Individual: A Study of the Social and Religious Responses to Innovation in a Zambian Rural Community* (Manchester: Manchester University Press 1968), 20–3, 215, 216, 218–33, 237–44.
34 Wilson, 101
35 Ibid
36 Many former Catholics have been attracted to the Witnesses since the reforms of Vatican II. They often state openly that their faith was shaken by changes in traditional Catholic practices and indicate that they were seeking a religion with 'definite commitments' to moral values and a firm authority structure.
37 See Munters's article 'Recruitement et candidats en puissance' for a discussion of this matter.
38 Long, 233, fn 1
39 *The Golden Age*, 9 May 1934, 489
40 Ibid
41 See 'Endorsement' in WT, 1937, 77
42 Page 268
43 Pages 269, 272
44 Herbert H. Stroup, *The Jehovah's Witnesses* (New York: Russell and Russell 1967), 117
45 J.F. Rutherford, *Children* (Brooklyn, NY: Watchtower Bible and Tract Society 1941), 364–8
46 I know of this from personal experience. At the time my wife and I were married

in 1951, she was a pioneer. Her pioneer partners did the very thing I have described.

47 WT, 1938, 255
48 *Qualified to Be Ministers* (Brooklyn, NY: Watchtower Bible and Tract Society 1955), 251
49 See, for example, WT, 1956, 585–8
50 WT, 1963, 639, 640
51 Stroup, 113–16. Rutherford felt that no third party was necessary to a marriage contract. Since he detested both the civil authorities and the clergy as agents of Satan, he was consistent in not wanting Jehovah's Witnesses to be married by them. Nevertheless, he never banned legal marriages outright and many Witnesses continued to insist on them. As Stroup notes, while a few couples were willing to be married at a service that was not legally recognized, 'Not many of these marriages have been entered upon, and they generally take place among those who are strong in faith.'
52 WT, 1956, 569, 572
53 WT, 1961, 181–5; 1974, 9
54 WT, 1956, 586
55 WT, 1961, 181–3. *Your Youth – Getting the Best Out of It*, 145, 146
56 WT, 1974, 12
57 The throwing of confetti and rice are regarded as 'pagan fertility rites.' The idea that the woman who catches a bride's bouquet will be the next to be married is held to be 'superstitious' or a 'false omen.'
58 Poewe, 392, 393
59 WT, 1974, 703. *Awake!*, 8 December 1972, 3–5. *Your Youth – Getting the Best Out of It*, 147, 148
60 Heather D. Botting, 'The Power and the Glory: The Symbolic Vision and Social Dynamic of Jehovah's Witnesses' (unpublished doctoral dissertation, University of Alberta 1982), 97–108
61 For a full overview of the society's thinking on this matter, see WT, 1975, 286–8.
62 This is clearly demonstrated in Heather Botting's generational study of a Jehovah's Witness congregation in a smaller city in southern Ontario. From my own surveys over a period of years, I estimate that between 50 and 60 per cent of the children raised in Witness homes leave the movement by the time they become adults. Significantly, however, many are often replaced by youthful converts to the movement.
63 Leslie W. Jones, MD, ed., *What Pastor Russell Said* (Chicago: printed privately, 1917), 57, 58
64 For an evaluation of the importance of the society's literacy program in Africa, see Cross, 92–4.

65 WT, 1975, 542–4

66 A letter sent to me, 8 July 1981. The author's name is withheld for personal reasons.

67 A letter from Theresa Parkinson to James and Marilyn Penton, 28 December 1980

68 Beckford, 142

69 This statement is quoted in WT, 1975, 217, 218. The citation for the original study is Kathleen Dewing, 'Some Characteristics of Parents of Creative Twelve Year Olds,' in *Journal of Personality*, 41: 1 (March 1973), 71–85

70 Barbara Grizzuti Harrison, *Visions of Glory: A History and a Memory of Jehovah's Witnesses* (New York: Simon and Schuster 1978), 97

71 Ibid

72 Page 25

73 Ibid

74 Ibid, 23–4

75 Ibid, 24–5

76 *Your Youth – Getting the Best Out of It* (Brooklyn, NY: Watch Tower Bible and Tract Society 1976), 124–9, *Awake!* 22 January 1979, 7–8; 22 December 1979, 20–4

77 The Watch Tower Society's attitude towards these matters may be found in a large number of articles which are listed in *Watch Tower Publications Indexes* for 1976–1980, 1981, 1982, and 1983 under the titles 'Music,' 'Radio,' and 'Television.' See also *Your Youth – Getting the Best Out of It*, 119–2

78 *Your Youth – Getting the Best Out of It*, 119–22. See also WT, 1 June 1979, 3, 4, 8, 13 and 15 June 1980, 23.

79 *Your Youth – Getting the Best Out of It*, 119–22. WT, 15 October 1983, 22–3 and 1 November 1983, 25

80 See, for example, *Awake!*, 8 October 1980, 25–8 and 22 October 1983, 24–7.

81 *Awake!*, 22 May 1984, 19–20. See also the *New York Times*, 29 August 1984, 15.

82 WT, 1 May 1984, 31

83 Pages 112, 113

84 Harrison, 346, 347, and Havor Montague, 'The Pessimistic Sect's Influence on the Mental Health of Its Members: The Case of Jehovah's Witnesses,' in *Social Compass*, 24: I (1977), 139

85 Bettelheim, 122–3. Hoess, 95–9, 149–50

86 Montague, 144

87 For a psychological profile of Jehovah's Witnesses, see S. Mellor and J. Andre, 'Religious Group Value Patterns and Motive Orientations,' in the *Journal of Psychology and Theology*, 8: 2 (Summer 1980), 129–39.

88 Watch Tower officials are generally involved in a constant round of socializing as they visit Witness congregations; and so since such socializing usually involves

the serving of alcoholic beverages, most of these men imbibe rather constantly. It has therefore not been unknown for circuit and district overseers to have to be removed from their positions for alcoholism, although the society quite naturally tends to hide this fact to the extent possible.

89 Page 26.

90 According to statements made at district conventions a few years ago, about 18 per cent of all Jehovah's Witnesses in the United States are black. Only about 12 per cent of the total American population is black.

91 Harrison, 159–61

92 Bonnie Gaskill and Toni Jean Alquist Meneses, *We Left the Watchtower for Jehovah* (Seattle: Trinity Printing 1982), 22

93 Stroup, 154

94 Ibid

95 Pages 24, 25

96 Certainly neither Jewish Bible Students nor the Jewish community in general seemed to think Russell anti-semitic. An anti-semite would hardly lead a Jewish audience in the singing of 'Hatikva.' *The Laodicean Messenger* (Chicago: The Bible Students Book Store 1923), 113–18. Furthermore, to criticize certain members of a community does not mean that one is opposed to that community as a whole.

97 See, for example, C.T. Russell, 'The Negro Question,' in *The Bible Student Monthly*, 3:14 (1914).

98 See pages 65, 147–8, and Harrison, 159–61.

99 Neither made overtly anti-black comments but showed their contempt for blacks by never placing any of them in major positions of responsibility. Although Herbert Stroup gives a rather damning 'quotation' on the Watch Tower Society's attitude to Negroes on page 155 of his book *The Jehovah's Witnesses,* which he cites as being taken from the August 1928 *Watch Tower,* no such statement appears in either the 1 August or 15 August *Watch Towers* of that year.

100 Gordon W. Russell, Arthur M. Goddard, and M. James Penton, 'The Perception of Judeo-Christian Religions,' in the *Canadian Journal of Behavioural Science,* 2:2 (1979), 149

101 Made on the 'Jack Webster Show,' BCTV Vancouver, BC, August 1981

102 Page 4. Bruno Bettelheim states of Jehovah's Witnesses in Nazi concentration camps: 'Members of this group were generally narrow ..., wanting to make converts, but on the other hand exemplary comrades, helpful, correct, dependable.' Bettelheim, 122, 123. See also John S. Conway, *The Nazi Persecution of the Churches: 1933–45* (Toronto: Ryerson Press 1968), 195–8

103 *1973 Yearbook,* 214–22. Penton, 156–81

104 For an example of such claims, see *Awake!,* 22 December 1976, 8–12.

105 Witness children often find the fact that they are not permitted to participate in patriotic exercises and other school activities quite stressful although practically all of them seem convinced that their conduct with respect to these matters is morally correct and necessary.

106 As examples of such conduct, see Raymond Franz, *Crisis of Conscience* (Atlanta: Commentary Press 1983), 8–38.

107 WT, 1975, 225

108 *Awake!*, 22 August 1975, 25, 26

109 *Awake!*, 8 September 1974, 4–7

110 Ibid, 143

111 Ibid, 144

112 Ibid, 138

113 Ibid, 139

114 Ibid, 140

115 Ibid

116 Ibid, 138, 139

117 Ibid, 140, 145

118 Beckford, 88, 89

119 Ibid

120 Ibid

121 Ibid

122 Ibid

123 Ibid

124 Page 123

125 See, for example, WT, 1 August 1980, 17–20.

126 Robert P. Carroll, *When Prophecy Failed: Cognitive Dissonance in the Prophetic Tradition of the Old Testament* (New York: The Seabury Press 1979), 96

127 Page 19

128 Pages 19, 20

129 Carroll, 95

130 Ibid, 96

131 WT, 1976, 592–602

132 WT, 15 August 1980, 14–26, 30, 31

133 See 'Family Responsibilities in Keeping Jehovah's Worship Pure' in WT, 1963, 443–6

134 Pages 467, 471, 472

135 Pages 27–31

136 The Toronto *Globe and Mail*, 1 April 1981, 1A; The *Toronto Star*, 1 April 1981, 1A

137 The Ottawa *Citizen*, 6 July 1982, 3

138 The *Calgary Herald*, 17 April 1982, 3

139 Ibid

140 The Toronto *Globe and Mail*, 3 July 1982, 1

141 Various television and radio program hosts have made this observation publicly.

142 The Ottawa *Citizen*, 6 July 1982, 3

143 The Toronto *Globe and Mail*, 3 July 1982, 1

Conclusion

1 Page 30

2 Norman Cohn, *The Pursuit of the Millennium* (London: Oxford University Press 1957), 309–10; see also 58–74.

3 Richard Hofstadter, *The Paranoid Style in American Politics and Other Essays* (New York: Alfred A. Knopf 1965), xii, 3, 5, 21, 22

4 WT, 1984, 30

5 Ibid, 8–13

6 James Beckford, 'Jehovah's Witnesses World-Wide,' in *Social Compass* 24:1 (1977), 14

7 See, for example, the *Calgary Herald*, 13 December 1983, B1. In the United States various ex-Witnesses have launched a series of suits against Witness elders, the Watch Tower Society, and the governing body of Jehovah's Witnesses.

8 The legislation as originally proposed would have made it illegal for any voluntary organization to expel members for anything not considered illegal under Canadian law. Although the bill in question has been modified at the behest of the churches and various religious organizations on the grounds that it involves the state in matters usually considered outside its jurisdiction, some modified version of it may ultimately be presented to Parliament.

9 WT, 1 January 1985, 20–3

10 Raymond Franz, *Crisis of Conscience* (Atlanta: Commentary Press 1983), 336–55

11 Page 17

Afterword

1 WT, 1 January 1987, 13; 1 January 1996, 15

2 WT, 1 January 1996, 12

3 With roughly the same number of publishers, Japanese Witnesses have more than twice the number of home Bible studies with prospective converts than do Italian Witnesses. Ibid, 13

4 Ibid, 14, 15

5 *1991 Yearbook*, 35–7. See also pages 102–3, 328 n20.

6 An Amnesty International News Service release (229/95) posted on the Internet and

dated 22 November 1995 gives the details of the arrests, fines, and jailings of Singaporean Witnesses. The release stated in part: "'The Jehovah's Witnesses should be allowed to meet and practise their religion peacefully without threat of arrest or imprisonment. Freedom of religion is a fundamental right which is guaranteed by the Constitution of Singapore," Amnesty International said today.'

The *u.s. News and World Report* of 2 May 1996 reported the dismissal of the Singaporean Witnesses' appeals and noted that Chief Justice Yong Pung How 'repeatedly criticized arguments of defense lawyer W. Glen How of Canada.' *u.s. News and World Report* also stated: 'Showing increasing irritation, Yong snapped twice at How with the comment: "You're out of your mind!" He later asked the Canadian: "Are you medically all right, Mr. How? You're rambling."'

7 Growth in most of these countries has recently been between 2 and 3 per cent per year. For example, in 1994 the Witness increases were down dramatically in most of the G-7 countries, the seven most industrialized nations in the world. France and Germany had increases of 1 per cent. Britain and Canada, 2 per cent; and Italy and the United States, 3 per cent. Japan had by far the greatest growth, with a 6 per cent increase. In effect, Jehovah's Witnesses are generally keeping only slightly ahead of normal population growth through births and immigration in most industrialized lands. In Western developed countries many new Witness converts come from among recent immigrant groups. So native-born populations in those lands are rejecting the Witness message to a greater extent than in the past.

8 WT, 1 April 1994, 16–17. It is true that some of those disfellowshipped are later reinstated.

9 If one takes the number of those who are disfellowshipped plus those who voluntarily dissociate themselves from the movement either formally or informally, the loss to Jehovah's Witnesses membership is quite probably more than 1 per cent per year.

10 For full details of this development, see the article 'Jehovah's Provision, the "Given Ones,"' in *The Watchtower*, 15 April 1992, 12–17. The terminology is taken from the book of Ezra.

11 Pages 18, 19–20

12 Ibid

13 See page 275 above.

14 There have been many custody cases involving Jehovah's Witness and non– or ex–Jehovah's Witness parents in the United States and Canada alone. In the former, ex-Witnesses such as Duane Magnani and Jerry Bergman have been active as expert witnesses in support of non– and ex–Witness parents. Magnani and Bergman have attempted to show that Witness parents are coached by Watch Tower lawyers to deny statements that were made in *School and Jehovah's Witnesses*. For further details regarding these custody cases, see note 59 below.

15 Page 31

16 WT, 15 March 1993, 32

17 Raymond Franz, *Crisis of Conscience* (Atlanta: Commentary Press 1992, 1994), 392. Although the second edition of *Crisis of Conscience* was published in 1992, Raymond Franz has since updated it for its second printing.

18 No biography of Henschel seems to exist in Watch Tower literature or anywhere else. What is known about him is that he served as N.H. Knorr's private secretary and that he has been a frequent speaker at the Watch Tower missionary school of Gilead and at foreign branch offices.

19 Franz, *Crisis of Conscience*, 394

20 Ibid, 389–90

21 WT, 15 October 1995, 24–7

22 WT, 1 November 1995, 18, 19

23 Page 20

24 James A. Beckford, *The Trumpet of Prophecy: A Sociological Study of Jehovah's Witnesses* (New York: John Wiley and Sons 1975), 170

25 This has been particularly true of Bible Research and Commentary International which has a help-line telephone number for Jehovah's Witnesses that can be reached in both the United States and Canada by calling 1-800-WHY-1914. However, other ministries have also indicated many contacts with disillusioned Jehovah's Witnesses over changed Watch Tower doctrine. For further information, see *BRCI Quarterly*, winter, spring, and summer 1996 issues. Copies of this publication may be obtained by writing Biblical Research and Commentary International, Inc., 1207 Marston Avenue, Gadsden, AL, 35904-1403 U.S.A.

26 Raymond Franz believes that changes in administration will not bring major reforms to the Watch Tower Society or Jehovah's Witnesses. See his comments on this matter on page 333–4 below.

27 WT, 15 March 1983, 30–1. It should be noted that one change from the society's earlier position on marital *porneia* (fornication) is that married women can no longer divorce their mates for engaging in oral or anal intercourse with them. This probably explains why the issue has not been as important as it was in the past.

28 The number of see-saw shifts the Watch Tower Society has made on this issue is rather amusing. In *Zion's Watch Tower*, July 1879, (p. 8), C.T. Russell held that the men of Sodom and Gomorrah would be resurrected. This view continued to be held until 1952, when the 1 June issue of *The Watchower* held that they would not be. Thirteen years later, *The Watchtower* of 1 August 1965 asserted that they would be. First published in 1982, early editions of the book *You Can Live Forever in Paradise on Earth* affirmed this position (p. 179), as did volume 2 of the society's Bible dictionary, *Insight on the Scriptures* (p. 985). In 1988, *The Watchtower* of 1 June again decided that they would not be. Consequently, the book *Revelation – Its Grand Climax at Hand* took the same position, and *Our Kingdom Ministry* (U.S. edition) for December

1989 stated: 'Some adjustments will be made in future printings of the *Live Forever* book. The only significant change is with regard to the Sodomites, on pages 178 and 179. This change appeared in the *Revelation* book, page 273, and in *The Watchtower* of June 1, 1988, pages 30, 31. You may wish to note it in earlier printings that you have on hand.' I am indebted to David Reed, Steve Huntoon, and John Cornell for having indexed these changes in David A. Reed, ed., *Index of Watch Tower Errors* (Grand Rapids: Baker Book House 1990), 116.

Does the society's hard line towards the long-dead Sodomites and their neighbours in Gomorrah not have something to do with the fact that two 'Sodomites' have been expelled from the governing body in recent decades?

29 Franz, *Crisis of Conscience*, 397. Two members of the governing body have died since the death of Frederick Franz. They were George Gangas, who died at age ninety-eight on 28 July 1994, and John Booth, who died at age ninety-three on 8 January 1996.

30 *Jimmy Swaggart Ministries* v. *Board of Equalization of California* 110 S. Ct. 688

31 *Comments from the Friends* 9:3 (Summer 1990), 3–4

32 22 February 1990, 1

33 *Comments from the Friends* 9:3 (Summer 1990), 4

34 WT, 1 January 1990, 7; *1990 Yearbook,* 10

35 Franz, *Crisis of Conscience*, 365–6

36 The *1980 Yearbook of Jehovah's Witnesses* (p. 258) tersely reported that 'in the past year Ewart C. Chitty resigned, so that at present there are 17 members of this [governing] body.' When Leo Greenlees was ousted from office, no statement appeared in the society's publications. Greenlees' name simply disappeared from Watch Tower publications after 1984. The only Watch Tower statement that may even be considered to hint at homosexuality on the part of governing body members is a brief comment that appears in the 1 January 1986 *Watchtower* (p. 13), which states: 'Shocking as it is, even some who have been prominent in Jehovah's organization have succumbed to immoral practices, including homosexuality, wife swapping and child molesting.' Nevertheless, the facts surrounding the expulsion of both Chitty and Greenlees are well known among former Watch Tower headquarters Bethel workers and many others. Greenlees contacted some ex-Jehovah's Witnesses personally after he was exiled from Booklyn.

The society's lack of candour regarding Chitty and Greenlees has led many Jehovah's Witnesses to infer and imply wrongly that the comment in *The Watchtower* of 1 January 1986 refers to Raymond Franz and other 'apostates.' To his credit, Franz has never wanted to expose either Chitty or Greenlees for their 'sins,' but since he and his ex-Witness associates are now the targets of Jehovah's Witness innuendo concerning homosexuality, the facts need to be known.

37 *Rutherford et al.* v. *The United States*, Transcript of Record, 1: 981–2 at 2943–5

38 The society's own statistics show this to be false. See the graph of Memorial attendance during the 1920s on page 61.

39 See pages 147–9.

40 Following the publication of the 22 August 1995 *Awake!*, I placed copies of the 1933 Declaration of Facts in both English and German and a copy of the Hitler letter with English translation with the Holocaust Museum in Washington, D.C., where these documents may be seen and read by the public.

41 For an overview of Watch Tower doctrines with respect to secular authorities, see M. James Penton, 'Jehovah's Witnesses and the Secular State: A Historical Analysis of Doctrine,' *Journal of Church and State* 21:1 (1979), 55–72.

42 WT, 1 May 1996, 14

43 Ibid

44 Quoted with the permission of the author from an article now in preparation for publication titled 'Theology and Art in a Sectarian Community'

45 *Creighton Law Review*, 29:4 (June 1996), 1483–1516. Bergman has also recently published an important article, 'The Jehovah's Witnesses' Experience in the Nazi Concentration Camps: A History of their Conflict with the Nazi State,' in *Journal of Church and State*, 38:1 (1996), 87–113.

46 These include David A. Reed, ed., *Index of Watch Tower Errors* and *Jehovah's Witness Literature: A Critical Guide to Watchtower Publications* (Grand Rapids: Baker Book House 1993). As of this time, I have not been able to examine Reed's most recent work, *Blood on the Altar* (Amherst, NY: Prometheus, 1996).

47 Magnani's work has been done through Witnesses Incorporated.

48 This book and Watters's other publications may be obtained from Box 3818, Manhattan Beach, CA 90266 U.S.A.

49 Pages 479–88

50 Nobel produces this information and photocopies of Gestapo records signed by Frost on pages 195–200 of *Falschspieler Gottes*. This information was uncovered earlier by the German news magazine *Der Spiegel* in its issue of 19 July 1961 under the heading 'Väterchen Frost' (Daddy Frost).

51 Under the date of 15 September 1943, the declaration, translated into English, reads as follows: 'Every war brings countless misfortunes upon mankind. Every war brings difficult moral dilemmas to thousands, yes, millions of people. This applies especially to this war, which has spared no corner of the earth and has been spread through the air, water and land. It is therefore inevitable that in such times, not only individuals, but also communities of every sort, unintentionally or deliberately, are falsely suspected.

'Even Jehovah's Witnesses have not been spared this fate. We have been made out to be an association, the object or activity of which is described as, "to undermine military discipline, especially to force or mislead conscripts into insubordination against military orders, neglect or refusal of duty, or becoming fugitives."'

'Such an opinion can only be put forward by someone who completely misunderstands the spirit and activity of our Society or who, despite his better knowledge, malevolently distorts it.

'We expressly state that our association neither commands nor recommends, nor in any other way suggests, acting against military orders. Questions of that sort are dealt with neither by our congregations nor in the Society's published literature. We do not at all concern ourselves with such questions. We view our business to be solely that of rendering a witness to Jehovah God and to proclaim Bible truth to all peoples. Hundreds of our members and fellow believers have performed their military duty and continue to do so.

'We have at no time presumed and at no time shall do so, to view the performance of military duty, as laid down by your statutes, as an offence against the principles and aspirations of the association of Jehovah's Witnesses. We beseech all our members and fellow believers, in the proclamation of the message of God's Kingdom (Matthew 24: 14), to confine themselves strictly to the proclamation of Bible truth, and always to avoid giving grounds for misunderstanding, and certainly never to be able to be misunderstood as offering any incitement to insubordination against military orders.'

52 Page 103
53 *Our Kingdom Ministry* (u.s. edition), June 1982
54 Prior to 1980, the society sought publicity for its conventions and the construction of kingdom halls. During the last decade, it has been far less active in seeking such publicity because it has given critics of the Witnesses a chance to make their views known by means of the press and electronic media.
55 wt, 15 March 1986, 12, 13
56 *Our Kindom Ministry* (u.s. edition), September 1995
57 This is evident from an affidavit of attorney James M. McCabe, the director of the Watch Tower Society's American Legal Department. In that affidavit, written in part in response to concerns expressed by the society's Norwegian branch office, McCabe claims that there is a network of ex–Jehovah's Witnesses who have attempted to serve as expert witnesses in custody cases against Witness parents. He names Jerry Bergman, Dwane Magnani, Raymond Franz, and Paul Blizard – all well-known ex-Witnesses. However, the only persons he discusses in his sworn statement are Bergman and Magnani, whom he attempts to discredit by attacking their personal backgrounds.
58 I know this from personal experience. While I was preparing an article on Jehovah's Witnesses for the second edition of *The Canadian Encyclopedia*, the editor of that work received a letter from Eugene Rosam of the society's Canadian branch offices in Georgetown, Ontario, complaining about the article that I had written for the first edition of the encyclopedia, and asserting that, since I was no longer associated with Jehovah's Witnesses, the editor should find a Witness in good standing to write the

article on the Witnesses. Rosam went on to cite the example of *The Encyclopedia Americana*, which had requested Frederick Franz to compose the article on Jehovah's Witnesses for its then current edition. Since then, the *Americana* has contacted me to replace Franz's article with one of my own. The current edition of the *Americana* contains my article, as does the third edition of *The Canadian Encyclopedia*.

59 As Jerry Bergman notes, 'Jeff Atkinson, former Chair of the American Bar Association's Child Custody Committee, concluded in 1990 that Jehovah's Witnesses were probably responsible for half of the contested custody cases that are in courts around the country.' Bergman, *Creighton Law Review*, 1488

60 E-mail newsletter from Stephan E. Wolf, November 1995, concerning the status of Jehovah's Witnesses in Germany

61 Susan Alter of the Research Branch of the Library of Parliament in Ottawa produced an unpublished paper in 1992 for members of Parliament entitled 'Jehovah's Witnesses, Disfellowshipping and Shunning,' the first two sentences of which read: 'The shunning or harassment of former Jehovah's Witnesses (JWS) by active members of the sect is behaviour that is mandated by the governing body of the Jehovah's Witness' church (officially titled the Watch Tower Bible and Tract Society). Shunning has been known to cause severe emotional distress to estranged Witnesses, occasionally even leading to their suicides.' While Alter ultimately decided, after reviewing the evidence, that for disfellowshipped ex-Witnesses 'a self-help approach may be more effective, at the end of the day, than pursuing legal avenues,' in her paper she indicates that Canadian law is changing in ways that may allow ex-Witnesses to take successful court action against Witness elders and the Watch Tower Society in future.

Since the production of Alter's paper, a number of members of Parliament, belonging both to the government and to the opposition, have shown concern over Witness disfellowshipping. In one recent case in Vancouver, British Columbia, one MP was so concerned that he actually offered to be present at a disfellowshipping hearing.

62 Some years ago, Støttegruppen for tidligere Jehovas Vidner (a Danish association concerned with the support of former Witnesses) contacted the Registertilsynets, the Danish Data Surveillance Authority, to complain that they believed that the Watch Tower Society was keeping files containing illegal information on disfellowshipped Jehovah's Witnesses. In 1991 a disgruntled Witness stole a number of files from the Watch Tower Society's branch offices at Holbaek. When he eventually turned these files over to the police in 1995, the Støttegruppen requested that the Registertilsynets examine those files to make certain that the society was not keeping illegal data on disfellowshipped Witnesses, including the reasons for their having been disfellowshipped. Although the Registertilsynets allowed representatives of the Støttegruppen to meet with the society's representatives, and insisted that the society take steps in conformity with Danish law to remove any information on the reasons for having disciplined or disfellowshipped anyone, it did return the files to the Danish Watch

Tower branch without taking further action. Because of press reports, the matter created serious embarrassment for Jehovah's Witnesses throughout Denmark and Norway.

63 Franz, *Crisis of Conscience*, 343

64 Ibid

65 For a discussion of this matter, see Ruth A. Tucker, 'From the Fringe to the Fold,' *Christianity Today*, 15 July 1996, 26–32.

66 *Jehovah's Witnesses: Proclaimers of God's Kingdom* (Brooklyn, NY: Watchtower Bible and Tract Society and International Bible Students Association 1993), 83–4

Bibliography

Major Scholarly Works

As the number of scholarly, or supposedly scholarly, studies of Jehovah's Witnesses is rather limited, brief descriptions of the major ones in English are given here.

Beckford, James A. *The Trumpet of Prophecy: A Sociological Study of Jehovah's Witnesses*. New York: John Wiley and Sons 1975
A trained sociologist at the University of Durham, Beckford has produced an important, though uneven, study of Jehovah's witnesses in Great Britain. His discussion of social stratification, conversion, induction, and integration among British Witnesses is excellent. Where he has strayed from his own field into historical and doctrinal topics, he is rather weak. His work is somewhat marred by errors, guesses, and a misunderstanding of certain basic Witness doctrines. For example, it is somewhat difficult for members of a community who teach that the soul perishes at death to believe in ghosts (p. 106). Finally, *The Trumpet of Prophecy* is poorly written and often difficult to follow, especially for those not thoroughly familiar with social-science jargon.

Beverley, James A. *Crisis of Allegiance: A Study of Dissent among Jehovah's Witnesses*. Burlington, ON: Welsh 1986
This is a sensitive, well-written account of the break of more than eighty persons in Lethbridge, Alberta, from Jehovah's Witnesses. It documents the totalitarian methods of the Watch Tower Society, the hatred of any form of dissent among Jehovah's Witnesses, and the way in which the dissidents were able to publicize what was happening to them. Beverley also attempts to give the Witnesses' side of the story, but, because they refused to cooperate with him, his sources are mainly the dissidents, court records, and the press. Unfortunately, the publishers did a poor job of editing and typesetting this book.

Blackwell, Victor V. *O'er the Ramparts They Watched*. New York: A Hearthstone Book 1976
A Jehovah's Witness lawyer who was involved in many Witness court cases in the United

States, Blackwell has written an interesting account. He gives a fine picture of the travails
suffered by the Witnesses duing some three decades and discusses their victories in state
and lower federal courts. Not only does he stress the Witnesses' important contributions
to constitutional law, he also gives credit to the u.s. judicial system. He is obviously both
a dedicated civil libertarian and a man with deep respect for American legal tradition.
Scholars interested in the Witnesses' role in u.s. history should consult this book.

Botting, Gary. *Fundamental Freedoms and Jehovah's Witnesses*. Calgary: University of
Calgary Press 1993
Botting's work is a valuable study of the role that Jehovah's Witnesses played in developing constitutional law in Canada. It gives insights into how the Witnesses were able
to influence no less a person than Pierre Trudeau and, through him as prime minister of
Canada, to see their dream of an entrenched Charter of Rights and Freedoms become
part of the Canadian Constitution. What is also useful about this book is that Botting
gives an excellent review of books that relate to Jehovah's Witnesses in Canada.

Botting, Heather, and Gary Botting. *The Orwellian World of Jehovah's Witnesses*.
Toronto, Buffalo, and London: University of Toronto Press 1984
The work of a wife–husband team who were raised as Jehovah's Witnesses, *The
Orwellian World* is a devastating critique of Watch Tower totalitarianism. Based in part
on Heather's doctoral dissertation in anthropology at the University of Alberta, this useful, well-written book is filled with both abundant factual data and outstanding illustra-
tions taken from Watch Tower publications. If the book has any major weakness, it is
that it focuses rather artificially on the year 1984 as another supposed Watch Tower
apocalyptic date. None the less, its major theme is well documented and sound.

Cole, Marley. *Jehovah's Witnesses: The New World Society*. New York: Vantage 1955
A semi-official history of Jehovah's Witnesses, Cole's book was sponsored by the
Watch Tower Society and became a best-seller. Easy to read, and written in the rather
racy style of journalism, it contains a great deal of useful information, particularly in the
appendix. Its major weakness is that it lacks footnotes and a bibliography, and that it
often makes unsupported assertions from a Witness standpoint that are contentious to
say the least. Had Cole not been 'supervised' in his writing of it by Watch Tower officials, it would be a better book than it is.

– *Trimphant Kingdom*. New York: Criterion 1957
Unlike *Jehovah's Witnesses: The New World Society*, this book was not sponsored by
the Watch Tower Society and did not obtain wide circulation. However, from the standpoint of the social scientist and historian, it is a much more useful study, for it gives a
clear picture of the nature of Witness society in the 1950s. As a chronicle of how the
ordinary Witness has viewed life in his congregation, his faith, and the world, *Triumphant Kingdom* is an important, if dated, work.

Curry, Melvin D. *Jehovah's Witnesses: The Millenarian World of the Watch Tower*. New
York and London: Garland 1992

Written originally as a dissertation under the direction of Professor Richard Rubenstein, this interesting and useful work contains a good deal of historical data on Jehovah's Witnesses. Curry develops a thesis, in opposition to James Beckford and Rosabeth Moss Kanter, that holds that millenarianism has been a primary factor in the structural development of Watch Tower organization. Although most non-Witness writers tend to agree with Beckford and Moss Kanter rather than Curry in this matter, it is a useful issue that deserves further academic attention. Unfortunately, Curry makes some serious factual errors in his analyses of the Witnesses.

Franz, Raymond. *Crisis of Conscience*. Atlanta: Commentary 1992
This book remains the major study of the internal workings of the Watch Tower Society during the 1960s and 1970s. A remarkably informative work, it provides the first inside picture of the Watch Tower Society and the governing body of Jehovah's Witnesses by a former governing-body member. Although it is an exposé of the first order, it is written more in a tone of sadness than of anger. Well documented and thoroughly revealing, it was updated in 1992, and again in its most recent printing in 1994. A new appendix is most informative on Watch Tower developments since 1983.

– *In Search of Christian Freedom*. Atlanta: Commentary 1993
Franz's second major work, this 732-page volume expands on much of the information in *Crisis of Conscience* and gives Franz's own non-dogmatic view of what Christian freedom is all about. As Professor Stephen Cox has written: '*In Search of Christian Freedom* is of unique importance as a study of the Watchtower movement, and a commentary on its current condition, but the relevance of the book is not limited to that movement. It is helpful in understanding a wide variety of social and psychological forces that shape people's interpretations of the Bible and religious life, often without their knowing it. Raymond Franz provides fresh illumination on the issue of freedom, as it arises in Scripture, in religious history, and in the decisions of today's men and women.' No better evaluation could be given.

Gruss, Edmond Charles. *The Jehovah's Witnesses and Prophetic Speculation*. Phillipsburg, NJ: Presbyterian and Reformed Publishing Co. 1972.
Although Gruss is known as an anti-Witness polemicist, he is also a well-trained and generally careful scholar. Thus, *Jehovah's Witnesses and Prophetic Speculation* is an excellent critique of the Witnesses' date-setting eschatology and demonstrates simply and straightforwardly why it lacks historical credibility. For anyone interested in the Witnesses' prophecies and their failures, this book is a must.

Harrison, Barbara Grizutti. *Visions of Glory: A History and a Memory of Jehovah's Witnesses*. New York: Simon and Schuster 1978
Harrison's autobiographical account of life as a young woman worker at Bethel during the 1950s is an extremely perceptive work. The book conveys some of the feeling of personal repression and emotional coldness that more sensitive individuals often experience as members of the Witness community. Unfortunately, while producing an

exceptionally important work, Harrison is at times somewhat unfair in her description of certain individuals, such as the Watch Tower's first president. None the less, this book gives a clearer picture of Watch Tower attitudes and bureaucracy than anything published, except Raymond Franz's works.

Hodges, Tony. *Jehovah's Witnesses in Central Africa.* London: Minority Rights Group 1976

Hodge's brief account is a fact-filled and highly accurate report of the persecution of Jehovah's Witnesses in Malawi, Zambia, and Mozambique. It explains the reasons behind anti-Witness hostility; shows the terrible nature of the attacks on African Witnesses, particularly in Malawi; and calls for a halt to government intolerance and barbarism. Finally, it argues forcefully that 'the suppression of the Jehovah's Witnesses has been part and parcel of the attempts of various African rulers to consolidate one-party dictatorial regimes.'

Jehovah's Witnesses in the Divine Purpose. Brooklyn, NY: Watchtower Bible and Tract Society 1959

As the first official Watch Tower history of the Bible Student–Witness community published in one volume, this is a valuable work. Its author had full access to the society's files in a way that no independent scholar has had, and it therefore gives some useful information. Nevertheless, it has several failings: it is far too brief; fails to discuss a number of important matters; and is written in the form of an unattractive, ongoing dialogue between a Witness couple and a family interested in the history and teachings of Jehovah's Witnesses. Although it makes extensive use of court reports, it generally ignores other public records. While it contains some useful information, the worst aspect of it is that it also contains many distortions, half-truths, and outright falsehoods. How anyone could have written such a book with a clear conscience is difficult to say.

Jehovah's Witnesses: Proclaimers of God's Kingdom. Brooklyn, NY: Watchtower Bible and Tract Society and International Bible Students Association 1993

Obviously written and published to counter books written by ex-Witnesses, the *Proclaimers* book, as it is commonly known, does contain more information than *Jehovah's Witnesses in the Divine Purpose*. Still, it is only a slight improvement over that work. It is far more hagiographic propaganda than history, and, like *Jehovah's Witnesses in the Divine Purpose*, it contains far too many sanitized accounts, omissions, half-truths, and outright falsehoods. In addition, it is written in a way which makes it hard to bring information together on many important issues. Anyone using it for scholarly purposes should recognize that it is little more than a bad piece of sectarian self-glorification.

Jonsson, Carol Olof. *The Gentile Times Reconsidered.* Atlanta: Commentary 1986

This book is the first complete study of the Watch Tower Society's Gentile Times doctrine and its origin. Interestingly, Jonsson traces the history of the doctrine to the early nineteenth century and certain ideas behind it (such as the so-called year–day principle) back to Medieval and Roman Jewry by way of Puritan England, the Reformers, John

Wycliffe, and Joachim of Flora. He also demonstrates through archaeological, historical, and astronomical evidence that Watch Tower chronology is wrong in asserting that Jerusalem fell to Nebuchadnezzar of Babylon in 607 BCE. Thus he shows clearly that Jehovah's Witnesses' whole eschatological calendar is based on demonstrably false assumptions. This extremely important work, in typescript form, helped cause the schism at Watch Tower headquarters in the spring of 1980.

Jonsson, Carl Olof, and Wolfgang Herbst. *The Sign of the Last Days – When?* Atlanta: Commentary 1987
Jonsson and Herbst have produced an important work which deserves much wider circulation than it has obtained. In it, the two Swedes – the name Wolfgang Herbst is a pseudonym – demonstrate from reputable historical sources that the twentieth century has not been the worst of all times. They show that Jehovah's Witnesses and various Evangelical fundamentalists who attempt to use current events as proof that we are living in 'the last days' do not know, or wish to know, the facts. One of the reasons for the book's limited circulation may well be that Evangelicals, who often purchase books by ex-Witnesses, are nearly as unhappy with Jonsson and Herbst's conclusions as is the Watch Tower Society.

Kaplan, William. *State and Salvation: The Jehovah's Witnesses and Their Fight for Civil Rights.* Toronto, Buffalo, and London: University of Toronto Press 1989
Although Kaplan retraces much of what I have covered in my *Jehovah's Witnesses in Canada* and writes almost entirely on the Witnesses during the Second World War, he has brought a good deal of new information to light. The most outstanding aspect of *State and Salvation* is his excellent account of the mistreatment of Jehovah's Witness children over the twin issues of the flag salute and patriotic exercises. He makes one serious mistake, however: he fails to understand that many Witness men were unjustly sent to alternative-service work camps when they were not subject to military conscription.

King, Christine Elizabeth. *The Nazi State and the New Religions: Five Case Studies in Non-conformity.* New York and Toronto: Edwin Mellon Press 1982
In her book, King studies five 'new religions' in Germany during the Nazi period: the Christian Scientists, the Mormons, the Seventh-Day Adventists, the New Apostolic Church, and Jehovah's Witnesses. Of these five, only the Witnesses opposed the Nazis to the death, whereas the other movements generally became more pro-Nazi than the Nazis themselves. The Witnesses' fortitude has earned King's admiration, but she also reveals the fact that the Watch Tower leadership tried to ingratiate itself with Hitler and the Nazi state in June 1933. Only after the Nazis rejected this attempt did Judge Rutherford call on the Witnesses to stand firm against the demands of the Third Reich.

Macmillan, A.H. *Faith on the March.* Englewood Cliffs, NJ: Prentice-Hall 1957
Macmillan was, until his death, a long-time Jehovah's Witness who served at the Brooklyn Bethel as a confidant of three Watch Tower presidents, and therefore played

an important, albeit somewhat Machiavellian, role in the history of the Witnesses. His book, an autobiography, therefore gives a pro-Rutherford, pro-society viewpoint. Although much of what he has written is in the form of an apology, and his picture of events in 1917 is a thoroughgoing distortion, he is none the less sometimes refreshingly candid. *Faith on the March* is therefore a far better book than *Jehovah's Witnesses in the Divine Purpose* or *Jehovah's Witnesses: Proclaimers of God's Kingdom*.

Manwaring, David R. *Render unto Caesar: The Flag Salute Controversy*. Chicago: University of Chicago Press 1962
Begun as a doctoral dissertation at the University of Wisconsin, Manwaring's book is excellent. It gives a useful history of the background to the flag-salute controversy, and discusses the nature, doctrine, and resources of Jehovah's Witnesses in the 1930s and 1940s and the history of flag-salute litigation through the u.s. courts. It is a balanced, fair, and thoroughly researched work which places the entire issue in the context of American history.

Newton, Merlin Owen. *Armed with the Constitution: Jehovah's Witnesses in Alabama and the u.s. Supreme Court, 1939–1946*. Tuscaloosa and London: University of Alabama Press 1995
In this book, Newton has produced a first-rate account of the travails of Jehovah's Witnesses in Alabama during the period of the Second World War and their success in two major cases that reached the u.s. Supreme Court. Newton was fortunate in being able to hold interviews with one of the litigants in those cases and with the other litigant's widow. She explains the various attitudes present in Alabama and the United States during the period and has come to understand clearly the importance of the litigious-gadfly role then played by Jehovah's Witnesses in extending civil liberties under the u.s. Constitution.

Penton, M. James. *Jehovah's Witnesses in Canada: Champions of Freedom of Speech and Worship*. Toronto: Macmillan of Canada 1976
Written as a narrative account of the relations of Jehovah's Witnesses with Canadian society and Canadian government, this book makes no claim to being an overall history of Witness organization or doctrine. It is, however, the first general historical account of Jehovah's Witnesses in a particular country, and also the first based to a large extent on materials found in public archives. Its quality must be determined by others.

Rogerson, Alan. *Millions Now Living Will Never Die: A Study of Jehovah's Witnesses*. London: Constable 1969
Raised as a Witness and a trained sociologist, Rogerson has written a useful, if short, book, based largely on original sources. Although it contains statements with which many Jehovah's Witnesses would take issue, it is quite accurate in its historical overview, and is one of the best works on the Witnesses in English. If it has any weakness, it is that Rogerson lacks a clear grasp of the nature of society and of religion in the United States.

Sterling, Chandler W. *The Witnesses: One God, One Victory*. Chicago: Henry Regnery 1975

Retired Episcopal bishop Sterling has produced a strange book. Sympathetic to Pastor Russell and Jehovah's Witnesses, it contains a few brilliant flashes of insight. At the same time, it is filled with errors of fact and tends to be superficial. For those reasons it cannot be considered an important work.

Stevens, Leonard A. *Salute! The Case of the Bible vs. The Flag*. New York: Coward, McCann and Geoghegan 1973

As the book's dust-jacket blurb states: '*Salute!* is an engrossing, suspenseful courtroom drama that clarifies the vital role of the Supreme Court in interpreting and defining the freedoms guaranteed by the [U.S.] Constitution.' Though narrower in scope than Manwaring's work, it is more accessible for the general reader, and demonstrates clearly the importance of the two major flag-salute cases – *Minersville School District* v. *Gobitis* and *West Virginia Board of Education* v. *Barnette* heard by the U.S. Supreme Court on the basis of the First Amendment.

Stevenson, W.C. *The Inside Story of Jehovah's Witnesses*. New York: Hart 1967

Published originally in Great Britain as *Year of Doom, 1975*, this is an interesting evaluation of the Witness community by an ex-Witness who was associated with the movement for fourteen years. In many ways it covers the same general history as other, similar studies and adds little that is significantly new. Stevenson's last chapter, 'Whither the Witnesses,' is most significant. In it he conjectures that, because the Witnesses' existence is based on 'false prophecy' concerning the nearness of the end of the world, the organization cannot continue to last long into the future. Evidently he expected that the failure of 1975 would have an even more catastrophic effect than was the case.

Stroup, Herbert Hewitt. *The Jehovah's Witnesses*. New York: Columbia University Press 1945

This is a dated book and suffers from the fact that it is a pioneer work in the field. Occasionally, too, it demonstrates its author's carelessness. For example, Stroup fails to give appropriate citations for paraphrases and quotations. In one instance, too, he gives a quotation from an August 1928 *Watch Tower* (155 n29) which does not exist. Yet there is a good deal of useful historical information here, and the book describes clearly the Witness community as it existed in the late 1930s and early 1940s.

Whalen, William J. *Armageddon around the Corner: A Report on Jehovah's Witnesses*. New York: John Day 1962

Produced by a professor of English who is also a Roman Catholic layman interested in religion in the United States, this book should be of better quality than it is. It is a superficial, breezily written work filled with errors. It also lacks critical apparatus. Nevertheless, it does contain much valuable information not easily available from other sources. The chapter on Witness schisms and heresies is most informative. Whalen is, however, quite inaccurate in suggesting that the Witnesses grew out of Seventh-Day Adventism.

White. Timothy. *A People for His Name: A History of Jehovah's Witnesses and an Evaluation*. New York: Vantage Press 1968

White's was long by far the most complete history of Jehovah's Witnesses extant, and in many ways it was the best. An examination of *A People for His Name* shows that its author has done an amazing amount of research and understands both the history and the doctrines of the Bible Students and Jehovah's Witnesses in a way that very few do. Although many Witnesses may disagree with some of his statements, what he says cannot be dismissed out of hand. At the same time, professional critics of Jehovah's Witnesses should note how he disproves many traditional anti-Witness arguments based on little more than gossip and slander.

Other Important Works about Jehovah's Witnesses

Alfs, Matthew. *The Evocative Religion of Jehovah's Witnesses*. Minneapolis: Old Theology Book House 1991

American Civil Liberties Union. *Jehovah's Witnesses and the War*. Pamphlet. New York: ACLU 1943

– *The Persecution of Jehovah's Witnesses*. Pamphlet. New York: ACLU 1941

Arellano, Angel. *Why You Should Believe in the Trinity*. Pasadena, CA: Browser's Book Store 1995

Assimeng, J. Max. 'Sectarian Allegiance and Political Authority: The Watch Tower Society in Zambia.' *The Journal of Modern African Studies* 8 (1970), 97–112

Aveta, Achille. *I Testimoni di Geova: un' ideologia che logora*. Rome: Edizioni Dehoniane 1990

Aveta, Achille, Fortunato Grottola, and Sergio Pollina. *I Testimoni di Geova tra mito e realita: vittime o artefici dell' intolleranz religiosa?* Foggia: Printed privately 1991

Aveta, Achille, and Sergio Pollina. *I Testimoni di Geova e la politica: martiri o opportunisti?* Rome: Edizioni Dehoniane 1990

Bach, Marcus. *Faith and My Friends*. New York: Bobbs-Merrill 1951

– 'The Startling Witnesses.' *Christian Century* 74 (1957), 197–9

– *They Have Found a Faith*. New York: Bobbs-Merrill 1946

Barber, H.W. 'Religious Liberty vs. Police Power: Jehovah's Witnesses.' *American Political Science Review* 41 (1947), 266–47

Beckford, James A. 'The Embryonic Stage of a Religious Sect's Development: The Jehovah's Witnesses.' *A Sociological Yearbook of Religion in Britain*, ed. Michael Hill, vol. 5: 11–32. London: SCM Press 1972

– 'Organization, Recruitment and Ideology: The Structure of the Watch Tower Movement.' *Sociological Review* 23 (1975), 893–909

– 'Structural Dependence in Religious Organization: From "Skid-road" to Watch Tower.' *Journal for the Scientific Study of Religion* 15 (1976), 169–75

- 'Two Contrasting Types of Sectarian Organization.' In *Sectarianism*, ed. Roy Wallis, 70–85. A Halstead Press Book. New York: John Wiley and Sons 1975
- 'The Watchtower Movement Worldwide.' *Social Compass* 24 (1977), 5–31

Bergman, Jerry. 'Dealing with Jehovah's Witness Custody Cases.' *Creighton Law Review*, 29:4 (June 1996), 1483–1516
- 'The Jehovah's Witnesses Experience in the Nazi Concentration Camps: A History of their Conflicts with the Nazi State.' *Journal of Church and State* 38 (Winter 1996), 87–113
- 'Modern Religious Objections to the Mandatory Flag Salute and Pledge of Allegiance in the United States.' *The Christian Quest* 2:1 (Summer 1989), 19–46

Blandre, Bernard. *Les Témoins de Jéhovah: Un Siècle d'histoire*. Paris: Desclée de Brouwer 1987

Bowman, Robert M., Jr. *Jehovah's Witnesses, Jesus Christ, and the Gospel of John*. Grand Rapids: Baker Book House 1989
- *Why You Should Believe in the Trinity: An Answer to Jehovah's Witnesses*. Grand Rapids: Baker Book House 1989

Chretien, Leonard, and Marjorie Chretien. *Witnesses of Jehovah: A Shocking Exposé of What Jehovah's Witnesses Really Believe*. Eugene, OR: Harvest House 1988

Cooper, Lee R. '"Publish" or Perish: Negro Jehovah's Witnesses Adaptation in the Ghetto.' In *Religious Movements in Contemporary America*, ed. Irving I. Zeretsky and Mark P. Leone, 700–21. Princeton: Princeton University Press 1974

Côté, Pauline, *Les Transactions politiques des croyants: Charismatiques et Témoins de Jéhovah dans le Québec des années 1970 et 1980*. Ottawa: Les Presses de l'Universite d'Ottawa 1993

Countess, Robert H. *The Jehovah's Witnesses New Testament: A Critical Analysis of the New World Translation of the Christian Greek Scriptures*. Phillipsburg, NG: Presbyterian and Reformed Publishing Co. 1982

Cross, Sholto. 'Social History and Millennial Movements: The Watch Tower in South Central Africa.' *Social Compass* 24:1 (1977), 83–95

Deriequebourg, Régis. 'Les Témoins de Jéhovah dans le Nord de la France: Implantation et expansion.' *Social Compass* 24:1 (1977), 71–82

Estes, T. 'Jehovah's Witnesses Won't Tell Who Translated Their Bible.' *Gospel Defender* 3:7 (1962), 4

Finnerty, Robert U. *Jehovah's Witnesses on Trial: The Testimony of the Early Church Fathers*. Phillipsburg, NJ: Presbyterian and Reformed Publishing Co. 1993

Garbe, Detlef. *Zwischen Widerstand und Martyrium: Die Zeugen Jehovas im 'Dritten Reich'*. Munich: R. Oldenbourg Verlag 1993

Gebhard, Manfred. *Die Zeugen Jehovas; eine Dokumentation über das Wachturmgesellschaft*. Leipzig: Urania-Verlag 1970

Greenshields, Malcolm, and Thomas A. Robinson. 'Authority among Jehovah's Witnesses: An Interview with a Former Member – M. James Penton and the NAR Editors.' *North American Religion, A Publication of the Centre for the Study of North American Religion at the University of Lethbridge* 4 (1995), 114–26

Gruss, Edmond Charles. *Apostles of Denial*. Revised ed. Nutley, NJ: Presbyterian and Reformed Publishing Co. 1975

– *We Left Jehovah's Witnesses – A Non-Prophet Organization*. Nutley, NJ: Presbyterian and Reformed Publishing Co. 1974

Henschel, Milton G. 'Who Are Jehovah's Witnesses?' *Religion in America*, Ed. Leo Rosten, New York: Simon and Schuster 1963, 95–102

Hérbert, Gérard, SJ. *Les Témoins de Jéhovah*. Montreal: Les Éditions Bellarmin 1960

Jonsson, Carol Olof. 'Charles Taze Russell and the Secret Rapture.' *The Christian Quest* 2:1 (Summer 1989), 47–58

Kater, M. 'Die Ernsten Bibelforscher im Dritten Reich.'*Vierteljahrshefte für Zeitgeschichte*, 17:2 (April 1969), 181–218

Knorr, Nathan H. 'The Jehovah's Witnesses.' In *Religion in the Twentieth Century*, ed. Vergilius Ferm, 381–92. New York: Philosophical Library 1948

Kogan, Eugen. *The Theory and Practice of Hell*. London: Secker and Warburg 1950

MacLeod, James M. 'The Sources and Structures of Authority among Jehovah's Witnesses: A Contemporary Survey.' *North American Religion, A Publication of the Centre for the Study of North American Religion at the University of Lethbridge* 4 (1995), 84–113

McCarty, William. *1914 and Christ's Second Coming* Washington, DC: Review and Herald Publishing Co. 1975

Magnani, Duane. *Bible Students? – Do Jehovah's Witnesses Really Study the Bible? – An Analysis*. Clayton, CA: Witness, Inc. 1983

– *The Watch Tower Files: Dialogue with a Jehovah's Witness*. Minneapolis: Bethany House 1985

– *The Watch Tower under Oath: The Trial of Olin R. Moyle*. Clayton, CA: Witness, Inc. 1984

– *Who Is the Faithful and Wise Servant? – A Study of Authority over Jehovah's Witnesses*. Clayton, CA: Witness, Inc. 1979

Martin, Walter R. *Jehovah's Witnesses*. Grand Rapids: Zondervan 1974

– *The Kingdom of the Cults*. Grand Rapids: Zondervan 1965

– *The Rise of the Cults*. Revised and enlarged ed. Grand Rapids: Zondervan 1957

Martin, Walter R., and Norman H. Klann. *Jehovah of the Watchtower*. Revised ed. Grand Rapids: Zondervan 1974

Mead, Frank S. *Handbook of Denominations in the United States*. New York: Abingdon-Cokesbury 1951

Metzger, Bruce H. 'The Jehovah's Witnesses and Jesus Christ.' *Theology Today* 10 (1953), 65–85

Montague, Havor. 'The Pessimistic Sect's Influence on the Mental Health of Its Members: The Case of Jehovah's Witnesses.' *Social Compass* 24:1 (1977), 135–7

Munters, Q.T. 'Recruitment as a Vocation: The Case of Jehovah's Witnesses.' *Sociologica Neerlandica* 7 (1971), 88–100

'The New World Translation of the Holy Scriptures.' *Biblical Research Monthly*, May 1975, 3–5; June/July 1975, 15–17

'The New World Translation of the Holy Scriptures.' *The Bible Collector* 7 (July/December 1971), 3–8

Nobel, Rolf. *Falschspieler Gottes: Die Wahrheit über Jehovas Zeugen.* Hamburg and Zurich: Rasch und Rohring Verlag 1985.

Pape, Gunther. *Die Wahrheit über Jehovas Zeugen.* Rottweil/Necker: Verlag Aktuelle Texte 1972

Penton, David J., and M. James Penton. 'Pyramidology in the Adventist/Bible Student Tradition: Science, Pseudo-Science and Religion.' *North American Religion, A Publication of the Centre for the Study of North American Religion at the University of Lethbridge* 4 (1995), 66–83

Penton, M. James. 'Jehovah's Witnesses and the Secular State: A Historical Analysis of Doctrine.' *Journal of Church and State* 21 (1979), 55–72

– 'The Jehovah's Witnesses: A Bibliographical Essay of Recent Books in English.' *North American Religion, A Publication of the Centre for the Study of North American Religion at the University of Lethbridge* 2 (1993), 95–133

– 'A Reprint of a Foundational Document of the Jehovah's Witnesses (1877) – *The Object and Manner of Our Lord's Return* by C.T. Russell.' *North American Religion, A Publication of the Centre for the Study of North American Religion at the University of Lethbridge* 1 (1992), 76–126

Pike, Edgar Royston. *Jehovah's Witnesses: Who They Are, What They Teach, What They Do.* New York: Philosophical Library 1954

Reed, David A. *Behind the Watchtower Curtain: The Secret Society of Jehovah's Witnesses.* Southbridge, MA: Crowne 1989

– *How to Rescue Your Loved One from the Watch Tower.* Grand Rapids: Baker Book House 1989

– *Jehovah's Witnesses Literature: A Critical Guide to Watchtower Publications.* Grand Rapids: Baker Book House 1993

Reed, David A., ed. *Index of Watch Tower Errors: 1879 to 1989.* Grand Rapids: Baker Book House 1990

Regehr, Ernie. 'Jehovah's Witnesses in Africa.' *Christian Century* 90 (1976), 17–18

Rogerson, Alan. 'Témoins de Jéhovah et Etudiants de la Bible. Qui est schismatique?' *Social Compass* 24:1 (1977), 33–43

Schnell, William J. *Thirty Years a Watch Tower Slave.* Grand Rapids: Baker Book House 1956

Seguy, Jean. 'Messianisme et echec social: Les Témoins de Jéhovah.' *Archives de Sociologie des Religions* 21 (1966): 89–99

– *Les Sectes protestantes dans la France contemporaine*. Paris: Beauchesne 1956

Stockdale, William. *Jehovah's Witnesses in American Prisons*. Putnam, CT: Wilda 1946

Van Buskirk, Michael. *The Scholastic Dishonesty of the Watchtower*. Santa Ana, CA: Caris 1976

von Suskind, Eckhard. *Zeugen Jehovas: Anspruch und Wirklichkeit der Wachtturm-Gesellschaft*. Neuhausen-Stuttgart: Hanssler 1987

Watters, Randy. *Letters to the Editor – Book I*. Manhattan Beach, CA: Free Minds, Inc. 1994

– *Letters to the Editor – Book II*. Manhattan Beach, CA: Free Minds, Inc. 1995

– *Thus Saith the Governing Body*. Manhattan Beach, CA: Free Minds, Inc. 1996

– *The Truth Will Set You Free*. Manhattan Beach, CA: Free Minds, Inc. 1988

– *Understanding Mind Control among Jehovah's Witnesses*. Manhattan Beach, CA: Free Minds, Inc. 1996

Wilson, Bryan R. 'Aspects of Kinship and the Rise of Jehovah's Witnesses in Japan.' *Social Compass* 24 (1977), 97–120

– 'Jehovah's Witnesses in Africa.' *New Society* 25 (12 July 1973), 73–5

– 'Jehovah's Witnesses in Kenya.' *Journal of Religion in Africa* 5 (1973), 128–49

– 'When Prophecy Failed.' *New Society* 43 (26 January 1978): 18–34

Zygmunt, Joseph F. 'Jehovah's Witnesses in the U.S.A. – 1942–1976.' *Social Compass* 24:1 (1977), 44–57

For an examination of background sources behind the thinking of Charles Taze Russell and Jehovah's Witnesses, the following works are useful:

Ahlstrom, Sydney E. *A Religious History of the American People*. New Haven: Yale University Press 1972

Ball, Bryan W. *A Great Expectation: Eschatological Thought in English Protestantism to 1660*. Leiden: E.J. Brill 1975

Froom, LeRoy Edwin. *The Conditionalist Faith of Our Fathers*, 2 vols. Washington, DC: Review and Herald Publishing Association 1954

– *The Prophetic Faith of Our Fathers*, 4 vols. Washington, DC: Review and Herald Publishing Association 1950

Harrison, J.F.C. *The Second Coming: Popular Millenarianism, 1780–1850*. London: Routledge 1979

Hill, John Edward Christopher. *The World Turned Upside Down: Radical Ideas during the English Revolution*. London: Temple Smith 1972

Persons, Stow. *American Minds: A History of Ideas*. New York: Holt, Rinehart and Winston 1958

Sandeen, Ernest R. *The Roots of Fundamentalism: British and American Millenarianism,*
　　1800–1930. Grand Rapids: Baker Book House 1970
Williams, George H. *The Radical Reformation.* Philadelphia: Westminster 1962

To understand direct influences on Russell, the following works should be consulted:

Books and Pamphlets

Barbour, Nelson H. *Washed in His Blood.* Rochester, NY: Unique 1907
Barbour, Nelson H., and C.T. Russell. *Three Worlds and the Harvest of This World.*
　　Rochester NY: Office of the Herald of the Morning 1877
Brown, John Aquinas. *The Even-Tide: or Last Triumph of the Blessed and Only Potentate,*
　　the King of Kings, and Lord of Lords: Being a Development of the Mysteries of Daniel
　　and St. John, 2 vols. London: J. Oppor and other publishers 1823
Gausted, Edwin Scott, ed. *The Rise of Adventism.* New York: Harper and Row 1974
Grew, Henry. *Future Punishment, Not Eternal Life in Misery but Destruction.* Philadel-
　　phia: Stereotyped at Moorbridge's Foundry 1850
Loughborough, J.N. *The Great Second Advent Movement,* repr. New York: Arno 1972
Paton, J.H. *The Day Dawn, or the Gospel in Type and Prophecy.* Pittsburgh: A.D. Jones
　　1880
Storrs, George. *An Inquiry: Are the Souls of the Wicked Immortal? In Six Sermons.*
　　Philadelphia: Published by the author 1847
– *An Inquiry: Are the Souls of the Wicked Immortal? In Three Letters.* Montpelier, VT:
　　Printed privately 1841
– *A Vindication of the Government of God over the Children of Men: or 'The Promise*
　　and Oath of God to Abraham.' New York: Published by the author 1871
– *The Wicked Dead: or Statements, Explanations, Queries Answered, and Exposition of*
　　Texts Relating to the Destiny of Wicked Men. New York: The Herald of Life 1870
Tompkins, Peter. *The Secrets of the Great Pyramid.* New York: Harper and Row 1971
Wellcome, Isaac C. *History of the Second Advent Message and Mission, Doctrine and*
　　People. Yarmouth, ME: I.C. Wellcome 1874

Journals

Bible Examiner, 1843–80
The Bible Examiner, 1981–4
Herald of Life and the Coming Kingdom, 1863–80
The Herald of the Morning, 1874–90

Many other journals and sources of value are listed in *The Millerites and Early Adventists:*

An Index to the Microfilm Collection of Rare Books and Manuscripts published by University Microfilms International.

Non–Watch Tower/Bible Student publications are also of some significance. These include:

Edgar, John, MD. *The Preservation of Identity in the Resurrection.* Glasgow: Hay Nisbet and Co. n.d.
– *Socialism and the Bible.* Glasgow: Hay Nisbet and Co. n.d.
– *Where Are the Dead?* Glasgow: Hay Nisbet and Co. 1908
– *A Tree Planted by the Rivers of Water.* Glasgow: Hay Nisbet and Co. n.d.
Edgar, John, and Morton Edgar. *Great Pyramid Passages,* 2 vols. Glasgow: Morton Edgar 1912
Edgar, Minna. *Memoirs of Dr. John Edgar.* Glasgow: Hay Nisbet and Co. n.d.
Edgar, Morton. *Abraham's Life-History an Allegory.* Glasgow: Hay Nisbet and Co. n.d.
– *'Faith's Foundations' and 'Waiting on God.'* Glasgow: Hay Nisbet and Co. n.d.
– *The Great Pyramid and the Bible.* Glasgow: Hay Nisbet and Co. n.d.
– *The Great Pyramid – Its Scientific Features.* Glasgow: Hay Nisbet and Co. n.d.
– *The Great Pyramid: Its Spiritual Symbolism.* Glasgow: Bone and Hulley 1924
– *The Great Pyramid: Its Time Features.* Glasgow: Bone and Hulley 1924
– *Mythology and the Bible.* Glasgow: Hay Nisbet and Co. n.d.
– *1914 AD and the Great Pyramid.* Glasgow: Hay Nisbet and Co. n.d.
– *Prayer and the Bible.* Glasgow: Hay Nisbet and Co. n.d.
Jehovah's Witnesses: Alternatives to Blood Transfusions. Toronto: Photocopied by Jehovah's Witnesses of Canada 1973
Jones, Leslie W., MD. *What Pastor Russell Said.* Chicago: The Bible Students Book Store 1917
– *What Pastor Russell Taught.* Chicago: Printed privately n.d.
– *What Pastor Russell Taught on the Covenants, Mediator Ransom, Sin Offering, Atonement.* Chicago: Printed privately 1919
Memoirs of Pastor Russell: The Laodicean Messenger: His Life, Works and Character. Chicago: The Bible Students Book Store 1923
Paton, J.H. *The Day Dawn: or The Gospel in Type and Prophecy.* Pittsburg, PA: A.D. Jones 1880
Russell, Charles T. *Object and Manner of Our Lord's Return.* Rochester, NY: Herald of the Morning 1877
Rutherford, Joseph F. *A Great Battle in the Ecclesiastical Heavens.* New York: Printed privately 1915

A number of publications by or about Pastor Russell and the Bible Students during his era have been reprinted by the Chicago Bible Students, P.O. Box 6016, Chicago, IL 60680

U.S.A. These include volumes entitled *Harvest Gleanings* I, II, and III, plus *Convention Reports* from the Russell era.

The following is a fairly complete list of works published by The Watch Tower Bible and Tract Society and associated organizations. Such publications are listed by type, chronologically.

Bibles

Rotherham, Joseph B. New Testament, twelfth ed. rev. 1896
Holman Linear Bible 1901
Wilson, Benjamin. The Emphatic Diaglot 1902
The Bible Students Edition of the Authorized Version 1907
The Authorized Version 1942
The American Standard Version of 1901 1944
The New World Translation of the Christian Greek Scriptures 1950
New World Translation of the Hebrew Scriptures, vols. 1–5 1953–60
New World Translation of the Holy Scriptures 1961
New World Translation of the Christian Greek Scriptures, Dutch, French, German, Italian, Spanish, and Portuguese eds. 1963
New World Translation of the Holy Scriptures, large-print ed. 1963
New World Translation of the Holy Scriptures, Spanish ed. 1967
The Kingdom Interlinear Translation of the Christian Greek Scriptures 1969
New World Translation of the Holy Scriptures, rev. 1970
New World Translation of the Holy Scriptures, rev. large-print ed. 1972
New World Translation of the Holy Scriptures, rev. 1971
Byington, Stephen T. The Bible in Living English 1972
New World Translation of the Christian Greek Scriptures Japanese ed. 1974
New World Translation of the Holy Scriptures, French ed. 1974
New World Translation of the Holy Scriptures, rev. 1981
New World Translation of the Holy Scriptures with References 1984
Kingdom Interlinear Translation of the Greek Scriptures (rev.) 1985

Books

Russell, Charles T. *Studies in the Scriptures*, 7 vols. 1886–1917. Numerous eds.
– Vol. 1: *The Divine Plan of the Ages*, 1886
– Vol. 2: *The Time Is at Hand*, 1889
– Vol. 3: *Thy Kingdom Come*, 1891
– Vol. 4: *The Battle of Armageddon*, 1897
– Vol. 5: *The Atonement between God and Man*, 1899

– Vol. 6: *The New Creation*, 1904
– Vol. 7: *The Finished Mystery*, 1917. *The Finished Mystery* was styled as the posthumous work of Russell since it was based largely on his notes and writings. It was prepared by George Fisher and Clayton Woodworth shortly after Russell's death.
Seibert, G.W. *Daily Heavenly Manna for the Household of Faith* 1907
Woodworth, Clayton J. *Bible Student's Manual* 1909
Russell, Charles T. *Tabernacle Shadows* 1911
Poems of Dawn 1912
Russell, Charles T. *Scenario of the Photo-Drama of Creation* 1914
– *Pastor Russell's Sermons* 1917
Rutherford, Joseph F. *The Harp of God* 1921
Van Amburgh, W.E. *The Way to Paradise* 1924
Rutherford, Joseph F. *Comfort for the Jews* 1925
– *Deliverance* 1926
– *Creation* 1927
– *Government* 1928
– *Reconciliation* 1928
– *Life* 1929
– *Prophecy* 1929
– *Light*, two books 1930
– *Vindication* (book one) 1931
– *Vindication* (books two and three) 1932
– *Preservation* 1932
– *Preparation* 1933
– *Jehovah* 1934
– *Riches* 1936
– *Enemies* 1937
– *Salvation* 1939
– *Religion* 1940
– *Children* 1941
The New World 1942
'*The Truth Shall Make You Free*' 1943
'*The Kingdom Is at Hand*' 1944
Theocratic Aid to Kingdom Publishers 1945
'*Equipped for Every Good Work*' 1946
'*Let God Be True*' 1946
'*This Means Everlasting Life*' 1950
'*What Has Religion Done for Mankind?*' 1951
'*Let God Be True*' (rev.) 1952
'*Make Sure of All Things*' 1953
'*New Heavens and a New Earth*' 1953

Qualified to Be Ministers 1955
You May Survive Armageddon into God's New World 1955
Branch Office Procedure of the Watch Tower Bible and Tract Society of Pa. 1958
From Paradise Lost to Paradise Regained 1958
'Your Will Be Done on Earth' 1958
Jehovah's Witnesses in the Divine Purpose 1959
Kingdom Ministry School Course 1960
'Let Your Name Be Sanctified' 1961
Watch Tower Publications Index (1930–60) 1961
'All Scripture Is Inspired of God and Beneficial' 1963
'Babylon the Great Has Fallen!' God's Kingdom Rules! 1963
'Make Sure of All Things: Hold Fast to What Is Fine' 1965
'Things in Which It Is Impossible for God to Lie' 1965
Life Everlasting – in Freedom of the Sons of God 1966
Watch Tower Publications Index (1961–5) 1966
Did Man Get Here by Evolution or by Creation? 1967
Qualified to Be Ministers (rev.) 1967
'Your Word Is a Lamp to My Foot' 1967
The Truth That Leads to Eternal Life 1968
Is the Bible Really the Word of God? 1969
'Then Is Finished the Mystery of God' 1969
Aid to Bible Understanding 1971
Listening to the Great Teacher 1971
'The Nations Shall Know That I Am Jehovah' – How? 1971
Theocratic Ministry School Guidebook 1971
Watch Tower Publications Index (1966–70) 1971
Organization for Kingdom-Preaching and Disciple-Making 1972
Paradise Restored to Mankind – By Theocracy! 1972
Comprehensive Concordance of the New World Translation of the Holy Scriptures 1973
God's Kingdom of a Thousand Years Has Approached 1973
True Peace and Security – From What Source? 1973
God's 'Eternal Purpose' Now Triumphing for Man's Good 1974
Is This Life All There Is? 1974
Man's Salvation out of World Distress at Hand 1975
Good News – To Make You Happy 1976
Holy Spirit – The Force Behind the Coming New Order! 1976
Watch Tower Publications Index (1971–5) 1976
Your Youth – Getting the Best Out of It 1976
Making Your Family Life Happy 1978
My Book of Bible Stories 1978
Choosing the Best Way of Life 1979

Commentary on the Letter of James 1979

Watch Tower Publications Index (1976–80) 1981

You Can Live Forever in Paradise on Earth 1982

Organized to Accomplish Our Ministry 1983

United in Worship of the Only True God 1983

Survival into a New Earth 1984

Life – How Did It Get Here? By Evolution or by Creation 1985

Reasoning from the Scriptures 1985

1986 Yearbook (without daily texts) 1985. All subsequent editions of the *Yearbook* have
    been without daily texts.

True Peace and Security – How Can You Find It? 1986

Worldwide Security under the 'Prince of Peace' 1986

Watch Tower Publications Index (1930–85) 1986

Insight on the Scriptures 1988

Revelation – Its Grand Climax at Hand 1988

The Bible – God's Word or Man's 1989

Questions That Young People Ask: Answers That Work 1989

Mankind's Search for God 1990

'All Scripture Is Inspired of God and Beneficial' 1990

The Greatest Man Who Ever Lived 1991

'Pay Attention to Yourselves and All the Flock' 1991

Watch Tower Publications Index (1986–90) 1992

Jehovah's Witnesses: Proclaimers of God's Kingdom 1993

Knowledge That Leads to Everlasting Life 1995

Booklets

Russell, Charles T. *Food for Thinking Christians* 1881

– *Tabernacle Teachings* 1882

– *'Thy Word Is Truth'* 1893

– *Harvest Siftings* 1894

– *What Say the Scriptures about Hell?* 1896

– *What Say the Scriptures about Spiritism?* 1897

– *The Bible vs. Evolution* 1898

– *What Say the Scriptures about Our Lord's Return?* 1898

– *Berean Studies on the At-one-ment between God and Man* 1910

– *Jewish Hopes* 1910

– *Berean Studies on the Divine Plan of the Ages* 1912

– *Berean Studies on Thy Kingdom Come* 1912

– *Berean Studies on the Battle of Armageddon* 1915

– *Berean Studies on the New Creation* 1915
– *Berean Studies on the Time Is at Hand* 1915
Outlines on the Divine Plan of the Ages 1917
Berean Studies on the Finished Mystery 1917
Berean Studies on Tabernacle Shadows of Better Sacrifices 1917
Rutherford, Joseph F. *Can the Living Talk with the Dead? (Talking with the Dead)* 1920
– *Millions Now Living Will Never Die* 1920
– *World Distress – Why? The Remedy* 1923
– *A Desirable Government* 1924
– *Hell* 1924
– *Comfort for the People* 1925
– *Our Lord's Return* 1925
– *The Standard for the People* 1926
– *Freedom for the Peoples* 1927
– *Questions on Deliverance* 1927
– *Restoration* 1927
– *Where Are the Dead?* 1927
– *Prosperity Sure* 1928
– *The Last Days* 1928
– *The People's Friend* 1928
– *Judgment* 1929
– *Oppression, When Will It End?* 1929
– *Crimes and Calamities, The Cause, The Remedy* 1930
– *Prohibition and the League of Nations* 1930
– *War or Peace, Which?* 1931
– *Heaven and Purgatory* 1931
– *The Kingdom, the Hope of the World* 1931
– *Cause of Death* 1932
– *Good News* 1932
– *Health and Life* 1932
– *Hereafter* 1932
– *Home and Happiness* 1932
– *Keys of Heaven* 1932
– *Liberty* 1932
– *The Final War* 1932
– *What Is Truth?* 1932
– *What You Need* 1932
– *Who Is God?* 1932
– *Dividing the People* 1933
– *Escape to the Kingdom* 1933

– *Intolerance* 1933
– *The Crisis* 1933
– *Angels* 1934
– *Beyond the Grave* 1934
– *Favored People* 1934
– *His Vengeance* 1934
– *His Works* 1934
– *Righteous Ruler* 1934
– *Supremacy* 1934
– *Truth – Shall It Be Suppressed?* 1934
– *Why Pray for Prosperity* 1934
– *World Recovery* 1934
– *Government – Hiding the Truth, Why?* 1935
– *Loyalty* 1935
– *Universal War Near* 1935
– *Who Shall Rule the World?* 1935
– *Choosing, Riches or Ruin?* 1935
– *Protection* 1936
– *Armageddon* 1937
– *Model Study No. 1* 1937
– *Safety* 1937
– *Uncovered* 1937
– *Care* 1937
– *Face the Facts* 1938
– *Warning* 1938
– *Advice for Kingdom Publishers* 1939
– *Fascism or Freedom* 1939
– *Government and Peace* 1939
– *Liberty to Preach* 1939
– *Model Study No. 2* 1939
– *Neutrality* 1939
– *Conspiracy against Democracy* 1940
– *End of Nazism* 1940
– *Judge Rutherford Uncovers Fifth Column* 1940
– *Refugees* 1940
– *Satisfied* 1940
– *Comfort All That Mourn* 1940
– *God and the State* 1941
– *Jehovah's Servants Defended* 1941
– *Model Study No. 3* 1941

– *Theocracy* 1941
Children Study Questions 1942
Organization Instructions 1942
Peace – Can It Last? 1942
Hope 1942
'The New World' Study Questions 1942
Course in Theocratic Ministry 1943
Fighting for Liberty on the Home Front 1943
Freedom in the New World 1943
Freedom of Worship 1943
'The Truth Shall Make You Free' Study Questions 1943
One World, One Government 1944
Religion Reaps the Whirlwind 1944
The Coming World Regeneration 1944
'The Kingdom Is at Hand' Study Questions 1944
'The Kingdom of God Is Nigh' 1944
The 'Commander to the Peoples' 1945
The Meek Inherit the Earth 1945
'Be Glad Ye Nations' 1946
The Prince of Peace 1946
The Joy of All the People 1947
The Permanent Governor of All Nations 1948
Counsel on Theocratic Organization for Jehovah's Witnesses 1949
Can You Live Forever in Happiness on Earth? 1950
Defending and Legally Establishing the Good News 1950
Evolution versus the New World 1950
Will Religion Meet the World Crisis? 1951
Dwelling Together in Unity 1952
God's Way Is Love 1952
After Armageddon – God's New World 1953
Basis for Belief in a New World 1953
Preach the Word 1953
Counsel to Watch Tower Missionaries 1954
'This Good News of the Kingdom' 1954
Christendom or Christianity – Which One Is 'the Light of the World'? 1955
Preaching Together in Unity 1955
What Do the Scriptures Say about 'Survival after Death' 1955
World Conquest Soon – By God's Kingdom 1955
Healing of the Nations Has Drawn Near 1957
God's Kingdom Rules – Is the World's End Near? 1958

'Look! I Am Making All Things New' 1959
When God Speaks Peace to All Nations 1959
Preaching and Teaching in Peace and Unity 1960
Security during 'War of the Great Day of God the Almighty' 1960
Blood, Medicine and the Law of God 1961
Sermon Outlines 1961
Watch Tower Publications Index 1961
When All Nations Unite under God's Kingdom 1961
Take Courage – God's Kingdom Is at Hand! 1962
'The Word' – Who Is He? According to John 1962
Living in Hope of A Righteous New World 1963
Report on 'Everlasting Good News' Assembly of Jehovah's Witnesses 1963
When God Is King over All the Earth 1963
'Peace among Men of Good Will' or Armageddon – Which? 1964
'This Good News of the Kingdom' 1965
'World Government on the Shoulder of the Prince of Peace' 1965
What Has God's Kingdom Been Doing since 1914? 1965
Rescuing a Great Crowd of Mankind out of Armageddon 1967
Man's Rule about to Give Way to God's Rule 1968
When All Nations Collide Head on with God 1971
A Secure Future – How You Can Find It 1975
Is There a God Who Cares? 1975
There Is Much More to Life 1975
Jehovah's Witnesses and the Question of Blood 1977
Topics for Discussion 1977
Unseen Spirits 1978
Enjoy Life on Earth Forever 1982
From Kurukshetra to Armageddon 1983
In Search of a Father 1983
Good News for All Nations 1983
The Time for True Submission to God 1983
The Divine Name That Will Endure 1984
The Government That Will Bring Paradise 1985
Examining the Scriptures Daily 1986 and subsequent years

Brochures

Jehovah's Witnesses in the Twentieth Century 1978
What Is the Purpose of Life? How Can You Find It? 1982

School and Jehovah's Witnesses 1983
Centennial of the Watch Tower Bible and Tract Society of Pennsylvania 1984
The Government that Will Bring Paradise 1985
Jehovah's Witnesses – Unitedly Doing God's Will World-wide 1986
Look! I Am Making All Things New rev. 1986
Should You Believe in The Trinity? 1989
How Can Blood Save Your Life? 1990
Spirits of the Dead – Can they Help You or Harm You? Do They Really Exist? 1991
Does God Really Care about Us? 1992
Jehovah's Witnesses and Education 1995
Jehovas Zeugen – Menchen aus der Nachbarschaft. Wer sind sie? 1995

Convention Reports

Souvenir (Notes from) Watch Tower Bible and Tract Society's Convention 1905
Souvenir Report from the Convention of the Watch Tower Bible and Tract Society 1906
Souvenir (Notes from) the Watch Tower Bible and Tract Society's Conventions (Pans I and
   II) 1907
Souvenir Notes of the Watch Tower Convention at Cincinnati, Ohio 1908
Souvenir Notes Bible Students' Conventions 1909
Souvenir Notes Bible Students' Conventions 1910
Souvenir Notes Bible Students' Conventions 1911
Souvenir Notes Bible Students' Conventions 1912
Souvenir Notes Bible Students' Conventions 1913
Souvenir Notes Bible Students' Conventions 1914
Souvenir Notes Bible Students' Conventions 1915
Souvenir Notes Bible Students' Conventions 1916
The Messenger 1927
The Messenger 1928
The Messenger 1931
The Messenger 1938
The Messenger 1939
The Messenger 1940
Report of the Jehovah's Witnesses Assembly 1941

Congregational Instruction Leaflets

Director 1935–6
Informant 1936–57

Kingdom Ministry 1957–77
Our Kingdom Service 1977–81
Our Kingdom Ministry 1981 to the present

Petitions and Letters

'A Petition to Bro. Rutherford and the Four Deposed Directors of the W.T.B. & T.
   Society.' From 156 members of the New York City Ecclesia of Bible Students 1917
'An Open Letter to People of the Lord Throughout the World.' From the New York City
   Ecclesia of Bible Students, undated but published in the autumn of 1917

Songbooks

Songs of the Bride 1879
Poems and Hymns of Millennial Dawn 1890
Zion's Glad Songs 1900
Hymns of the Millennial Dawn 1905
Kingdom Hymns 1925
Songs of Praise to Jehovah 1928
Kingdom Service Songbook 1944
Songs to Jehovah's Praise 1950
'Singing and Accompanying Yourselves with Music in Your Hearts' 1966
Sing Praises to Jehovah 1984

Tracts

Bible Students Tracts, known more commonly as *Old Theology Quarterly*, 1880–1908
The Bible Students Monthly, known at first as *People's Pulpit* and then *Everybody's
   Paper*, 1909–18
Morning Messenger 1918. Canadian publication
Kingdom News, 1918 to the present. Published sporadically
The Case of the International Bible Students Association 1919
Proclamation – A Challenge to World Leaders 1922
Proclamation – A Warning to All Christians 1923
Ecclesiastics Indicted 1924
Message of Hope 1925
Testimony to the Rulers of the World 1926
'It Must be Stopped' 1940
Quebec's Burning Hate for God and Christ and Freedom Is the Shame of All Canada 1946
Quebec You Have Failed Your People! 1946

Awake from Sleep! 1951

Hell-Fire – Bible Truth or Pagan Scare? 1951

Jehovah's Witnesses, Communists or Christians? 1951

What Do Jehovah's Witnesses Believe? 1951

Hope for the Dead 1952

How Valuable Is the Bible? 1952

Life in a New World 1952

The Trinity, Divine Mystery or Pagan Myth? 1952

Do You Believe in Evolution or the Bible? 1953

Man's Only Hope for Peace 1953

The Sign of Christ's Presence 1953

Which Is the Right Religion? 1953

How Has Christendom Failed All Mankind? 1958

Has Religion Betrayed God and Man 1973

Your Future – Shaky? or Secure? 1975

How Crime and Violence Will Be Stopped 1976

Why So Much Suffering – If God Cares? 1976

Blood Transfusion – Why Not for Jehovah's Witnesses 1977

The Family – Can It Survive? 1977

Relief from Pressure – Is It Possible? 1978

Why Are We Here? 1978

What Has Happened to Love? 1979

Hope for Ending Inflation, Crime, Sickness, War? 1980

Is a Happy Life Really Possible? 1981

Is Planet Earth Near the Brink? 1982

A United Happy Family – What Is the Key? 1983

Life – How Did It Get Here? By Evolution or Creation? 1985

How to Find the Road to Paradise 1990

A Peaceful World – Will It Come? 1991

Does God Really Care about Us? Will the World Survive? 1992

Comfort for the Depressed 1992

Enjoy Family Life 1992

Who Really Rules the World? 1992

Schismatic Sources

Heard, C.E. 'The Ship.' A stenographic report of an address delivered to the Standfast
    Bible Students Convention at Seattle, WA, 12 January 1919

Johnson, Paul S.L. *Another Harvest Siftings Reviewed.* Philadelphia, PA: Printed privately
    1918

– *Harvest Siftings Reviewed*. Brooklyn, NY: Printed privately 1917

'A Letter to International Bible Students' from I.F. Hoskins, Secretary to the Bible Students Committee chosen at Pittsburgh, PA, in January 1918. 1 March 1918. A statement from the committee is appended, as are other documents.

'A Letter to International Bible Students' from J.D. Wright, I. Margeson, F.H. McGee, R.G. Jolly, P.S.L. Johnson, I.F. Hoskins, and R.H. Hirsh. 1 March 1918

Pierson, A.N., J.D. Wright, A.I. Ritchie, I.F. Hoskins, and R.H. Hirsh. *Light after Darkness: A Message to the Watchers, Being a Refutation of Harvest Siftings*. Brooklyn, NY: Printed privately 1917

Ritchie, A.I., J.D. Wright, I.F. Hoskins, and R.H. Hirsh. *Facts for Shareholders of the Watch Tower Bible and Tract Society*. Brooklyn, NY: Printed privately 1917

Russell, Maria Frances. *This Gospel of the Kingdom*. Pittsburgh, PA: Printed privately 1906

– 'A Timely Letter of Importance to All Brethren' from Francis H. McGee. 10 September 1918

– *The Twain One*. Pittsburgh, PA: Printed privately 1906

Wright, J.D. *A Brief Review of Brother Johnson's Charges*. Bayonne, NJ: Printed privately 1918

Further Bibliographical Materials on Jehovah's Witnesses

Although now more than a decade old, Jerry Bergman's *Jehovah's Witnesses and Kindred Groups: A Historical Compendium in Bibliography* (New York: Garland 1984) and Duane Magnani's *The Collector's Handbook of Watch Tower Publications* (Clayton, CA: Printed privately 1984) remain excellent bibliographical sources on Jehovah's Witnesses. The latter may be obtained by writing to Witness Incorporated, P.O. Box 597, Clayton, CA 94517 U.S.A.

Index